MODELS OF BOUNDED RATIONAL...

Y0-BTA-548

Jeff MacKie-Mason
Dept- of Economics
MIT

Models of Bounded Rationality

Volume 1
Economic Analysis and Public Policy

Volume 2
Behavioral Economics and Business Organization

MODELS OF BOUNDED RATIONALITY

Volume 2

BEHAVIORAL ECONOMICS AND BUSINESS ORGANIZATION

Herbert A. Simon

The MIT Press
Cambridge, Massachusetts
London, England

See pages xi–xiv for acknowledgments to publishers.

Second printing, 1983

Printed and bound in the United States of America.

Library of Congress Cataloging in Publication Data
Simon, Herbert Alexander, 1916–
    Models of bounded rationality.

    Includes bibliographies and index.
    Contents: v. 1. Economic analysis and public policy — v. 2. Behavioral economics and business organization.
    1. Economics—Addresses, essays, lectures. 2. Social choice—Addresses, essays, lectures. 3. Decision-making—Addresses, essays, lectures. 4. Economics—Psychological aspects—Addresses, essays, lectures. 5. Industrial organization—Addresses, essays, lectures. I. Title.
HB171.S5633   330   81-18620
ISBN 0-262-19205-5 (v. 1)   AACR2
ISBN 0-262-19206-3 (v. 2)

To

GEORGE LELAND BACH

and

RICHARD M. CYERT

Economists, administrators, and warm friends

who, as Deans of Carnegie-Mellon University's
Graduate School of Industrial Administration,
created an exciting environment
in which behavioral economics flourished.

CONTENTS

ACKNOWLEDGMENTS

The preparation of these papers for publication brought back to me vividly the many pleasant and stimulating days spent with colleagues in the research that led up to them. The collaboration of these colleagues is acknowledged specifically on the title pages of the chapters that they authored jointly with me. I want to thank them for permission to reprint these chapters here, and even more for their contributions to my education in economics.

I am grateful to The MIT Press for proposing that I assemble my economics papers, and for agreeing to publish them. It has been a pleasure to work with the staff of the Press in completing this project.

Camera-ready copy of those pages of the text that could not be reproduced directly from the original publications were prepared on the word-processing and printing system of Carnegie-Mellon University's Computer Science Department. I owe a special debt to my assistant, Janet New, who penetrated the mysteries of this system in order to format, prepare, and edit these portions of the text.

The author and The MIT Press wish to thank the publishers of the following essays for permission to reprint them here. The selections are arranged chronologically, with chapter numbers in brackets.

"The Analysis of Promotional Opportunities," *Personnel* 27 (1951): 282-285. Copyright 1951 by the American Management Association. [5.1]

"A Formal Theory of the Employment Relationship," *Econometrica* 19 (1951): 293-305. Copyright 1951 by the Econometric Society. [5.2]

"A Formal Theory of Interaction in Social Groups," *American Sociological Review* 17 (1952): 202-211. Copyright 1952 by the American Sociological Association. [5.4]

"A Comparison of Organisation Theories," *Review of Economic Studies* 20, no. 1 (1952-53): 40-48. Copyright 1952-53 by the University of Birmingham, England. [5.3]

"Some Strategic Considerations in the Construction of Social Science Models," *Mathematical Thinking in the Social Sciences*, edited by P. Lazarsfeld, pp. 388-415. Copyright 1954 by the Macmillan Publishing Co., Inc. [7.1]

"Economic Expectations and Plans of Firms in Relation to Short-Term Forecasting: Comment," *Studies in Income and Wealth* 17 (1955): 352-359. Copyright 1955 by the National Bureau of Economic Research. [7.10]

"Organizing for Controllership: Centralization and Decentralization," (with G. Kozmetsky, H. Guetzkow, and G. Tyndall), *The Controller* 33 (1955): 11-13. Copyright 1955 by the Financial Executives Institute. [6.1]

"A Behavioral Model of Rational Choice," *Quarterly Journal of Economics* 69 (1955): 99-118. Copyright 1955 by John Wiley and Sons, Inc. [7.2]

"Framework of a Theory of the Firm: Comments," *The Business Enterprise as a Subject for Research*, edited by H. R. Bowen, Pamphlet No. 11, pp. 43-46. Copyright 1955 by the Social Science Research Council. [5.5]

"Rational Choice and the Structure of the Environment," *Psychological Review* 63, no. 2 (1956): 129-138. Copyright 1956 by the American Psychological Association. [7.3]

"A Comparison of Game Theory and Learning Theory," *Psychometrika* 21 (1956): 267-272. Copyright by the Psychometric Society. [7.4]

"Observation of a Business Decision" (with R. M. Cyert, and D. B. Trow), *Journal of Business* 29 (1956): 237-248. Copyright 1956 by The University of Chicago Press. [7.5]

"The Compensation of Executives," *Sociometry* 20 (1957): 32-35. Copyright 1957 by the American Sociological Association. [5.6]

"The Role of Expectations in an Adaptive or Behavioristic Model," *Expectations, Uncertainty, and Business Behavior*, edited by M. J. Bowman, pp. 49-58. Copyright 1958 by the Social Science Research Council. [7.11]

"Theories of Decision-Making in Economics and Behavioral Science," *American Economic Review* 49, no. 3 (1959): 253-283. Copyright 1959 by the American Economic Association. [7.6]

"Simulation of Individual and Group Behavior" (with G. P. E. Clarkson), *American Economic Review* 50, no. 5 (1960): 920-932. Copyright 1960 by the American Economic Association. [7.8]

"Decision Making and Planning," *Planning and the Urban Community*,

INTRODUCTION

This second volume of my collected papers in economics ranges over a narrower span of subjects than does the first volume. Running through the essays of all four sections is a central theme: that organization theory, economics (especially the theory of the firm), and cognitive psychology are all basically concerned with the same phenomena. All three are theories of human decision making and problem solving processes; yet each of the three domains has developed in relative isolation from the other two. These essays are concerned with both the causes for this isolation and its remedies.

Administrative Behavior, which was written in 1941 and 1942 and published in 1947, represented my initial effort to understand decision making in its most general sense and, in particular, to show what economics and psychology could contribute to illuminating organizational decision-making processes. Many of the essays of this volume take up where *Administrative Behavior* left off, develop themes that were first introduced in that book, or seek to answer questions that were asked there.

In particular, most of the essays of section V, *The Business Firm as an Organization*, are concerned with bringing organization theory closer to the classical theory of the firm by providing an economic rationale for important characteristics of organizations that have been observed empirically but not explained in theoretical terms. In a couple of instances, however (see especially chapters 5.4 and 5.6), the theoretical rationale is sociological rather than economic in character.

In section VII, *Economics and Psychology*, the order of analysis is somewhat reversed. Here we are concerned mainly with the possible contributions of psychology to the economic theory of decision. Most of these essays explore the implications of taking into account the boundedness of human rationality in formulating theories of decision making for economics.

Section VIII, *Substantive and Procedural Rationality*, treats matters somewhat more symmetrically. These essays are concerned with explaining why there has been so little mutual influence of economics and psychology upon each other, why a broader and deeper dialogue needs to be developed between these sciences, and what the subject matter of their discourse could be.

Section VI, *The Economics of Information Processing*, is concerned with the peculiarities of information as an economic resource and with the social and economic impact of the new information-processing technology introduced by computers and telecommunications. The economics of information provides a relatively new topic in the theory of organization, which accounts for the location of these essays in the volume, just after section V. Since it is a new topic, I think readers will sense a greater degree of tentativeness in these essays than in most of the others. Certainly they were written in an exploratory spirit and with the feeling that the topic still eludes a definitive formulation.

I will not attempt a further summing up in this introduction because such a summing up can be found at the very end of the volume, in my Nobel Lecture reprinted here as chapter 8.6. That chapter describes the personal odyssey that produced most of the essays I have collected here.

REFERENCES

Simon, H. A. *Administrative behavior.* New York: Macmillan Publishing Company, 1947 (3rd ed., 1976).

MODELS OF BOUNDED RATIONALITY

V

THE BUSINESS FIRM AS AN ORGANIZATION

The business firm of classical economic theory is little more than an entrepreneur to whom is attached a cost curve or a production function. Since profit maximization and internal efficiency are assumed, there is little or no room in the theory for the familiar institutional characteristics of real firms; for example, for the facts that one of their principal inputs is labor, a "commodity" that is contracted for on quite a different basis from other commodities, and that decisions are reached within a hierarchy of authority relations among the employees.

Most of the essays in this section are addressed to fleshing out the theory of the firm by providing formal explanations for some of the phenomena observed in real-world business organizations. Some of the explanations (see especially chapters 5.2 and 5.3) are economic, in a more or less classical sense. Others (for example, chapters 5.1, 5.4, and 5.6) are demographic or sociological. The remaining essays (chapters 5.5, 5.7, 5.8) contain less formal observations on various aspects of the theory of the firm.

My book with Yuji Ijiri, *Skew Distributions and Business Firm Sizes*, deals with another set of empirical phenomena — those relating to firm growth and size — in the same general spirit of mathematical modeling as is exhibited in the essays of this section.

THE "NEW INSTITUTIONAL ECONOMICS"

One of the first theoretical inquiries I undertook after the publication of *Administrative Behavior* was to try to give formal accounts of some of the important institutional features of business firms. This is a kind of inquiry that had, I believe, relatively few precedents at that time, although it has become rather popular in the past few years. Some current examples are the work of Williamson, Kornai, and such Carnegie-Mellon colleagues as Townsend and Raviv. I have even heard

1

this sort of analysis referred to as "the new institutional economics." Whether John R. Commons would have approved we will never know.

Chapter 5.2 provides an explanation within the framework of classical economics of the peculiar features of the employment contract. The theory set forth here has been developed extensively and improved over the years by a number of economists, especially Oliver Willliamson, but I think that the essential kernel of the contemporary theory can be found in this chapter. As I indicate in the final pages of the chapter, the theory of the employment contract is closely related to Jacob Marschak's (1949) views on the role of liquidity under uncertainty.

Chapter 5.3 is also classical in its analysis. It undertakes to map the Barnard-Simon theory of organizational equilibrium onto the theory of the firm in equilibrium. It shows that the two bodies of theory are fully compatible, except that the Barnard-Simon theory does not assume that, under imperfect competition, the "surplus" goes entirely to the owners of capital. Instead, it may be shared among owners, employees, and customers in proportions that are not fully determined by the theory. To explain this distribution, the theory of organizational equilibrium would have to be supplemented by an oligopolistic bargaining theory (game theoretical or otherwise). Since none of the hypotheses that have been put forth to handle these oligopolistic phenomena seem to me to have strong empirical grounding, I am at a loss to know which is the "right" one among the many competing alternatives. Nor do I have faith that more mathematical modeling, however ingenious, will solve the problem. The question will be answered only by painstaking empirical study at the level of the business firm of actual decision-making behavior in oligopolistic settings. Moreover, there may be no history-free explanation. The bargaining process and its outcomes may change significantly from one era to another.

SOME SOCIOLOGICAL MODELS

Chapters 5.1, 5.4, and 5.6 look outside economic theory in order to explain other important organizational phenomena. Chapter 5.1 is a primitive attempt to look at the flow of people through an organizational hierarchy. By simple algebraic means, and without the benefit of Markov processes, it shows how the age structure of management and the opportunities for promotion in an organization are influenced by the rate of growth of the organization and by the relative emphasis placed on seniority and merit, respectively, in promotions. Of course the simple tools employed in chapter 5.1 permit only a steady-state analysis of the system, ignoring important short-run dynamic phenomena; but if much more can be done on these questions with powerful tools, it is remarkable how much can be done with simple ones.

Since promotion is one of the important economic and psychological rewards business firms can offer their employees, hence an important element in competition in the labor market (and especially the market for managerial and technical personnel), it would be interesting to try to apply this kind of analysis to the theory of firm size and growth. To the best of my knowledge, this has never been done formally, although the association between "stagnation" in an industry (for example, railroads, steel) and lowered quality of managerial personnel has certainly been noted.

Chapter 5.4 uses the formal machinery of the dynamic theory of markets ("cobweb" theory), but with the economic variables replaced by psychological variables, to explain some of the patterns of personal interaction that have been observed in social systems, including business firms. This chapter, which applies the tools of mathematical economics (but not the substance of economic theory) to sociological subject matter, received a great deal of attention in sociology for a decade or two after its publication. It played a considerable role in the birth of the then-nascent mathematical sociology and laid some foundations for the "social exchange" theories made popular a little later by Homans and others.

There are no maximization processes in this model (any more than there are in a market theory that starts with supply and demand curves). Instead, adaptive feedback mechanisms bring about equilibrium. The analysis is carried out mostly by the familiar methods of comparative statics. Care is taken to draw only such conclusions as are compatible with the ordinal scaling of the observed variables. Hence all conclusions are invariant under monotonic transformations of the variables.

One important lesson we can draw from models like these (and the comparable models of economic markets) is that only weak assumptions of rationality (like those implicit in the adaptive feedback mechanisms) are essential for most analysis using the methods of comparative statics. Few of the conclusions reached depend on an assumption of optimality or would be altered if optimizing were replaced by satisficing.

With Harold Guetzkow I have published two other papers applying this same methodology to modeling some social psychological phenomena studied by Festinger and his associates. Because these papers have little direct relevance to the theory of the firm, I have not included them here.

Chapter 5.6 provides a sociological explanation for a well-known

3

empirical phenomenon that has never been explained in terms of classical theory. Executive salaries have been observed to grow as a power function of firm size. Deriving this result from standard economic analysis requires strong ad hoc assumptions about the distribution of managerial abilities (for example, Lucas, 1978). With the help of a plausible psychological hypothesis (related to the idea that in all psychophysical scales the psychological "distance" between two stimuli depends on the ratios of physical intensities), the observed facts can be given a simple interpretation — without assumptions about the distribution of abilities. This model of executive salaries has been used by Robin Marris (1964) in his theories of entrepreneurial capitalism, but has received little attention in classical economic treatments of the business firm.

RESEARCH ON THE BUSINESS FIRM

The remaining three chapters of this section, chapters 5.5, 5.7, and 5.8, do not fit under any single rubric. I will say a word about the origins and intent of each.

In 1955, the Social Science Research Council's Committee on Business Enterprise Research, of which Howard R. Bowen was chairman and I a member, issued a report on *The Business Enterprise as a Subject for Research*. The second chapter of that report was titled "Framework of a Theory of the Firm." Chapter 5.5 of this volume is a set of comments I appended to that chapter in the published committee report. In these comments, I sketch out a very general view of the main topics that belong to a comprehensive theory of the firm and express some attitudes about the interest of this area of human behavior for research. The "alternative framework" described in this note is very close to the one that guided James March and me, a few years later, in organizing our book *Organizations*.

Chapter 5.7, Decision Making and Planning, is an edited transcript of a talk I gave to a symposium of planners. It raises some issues about social planning processes that seem to me to be of considerable importance, but I have never had an opportunity to develop them in detail. Perhaps the most important of these issues, barely touched on in my talk, is whether social planning begins with goals or ends with them. By the latter possibility I mean that the execution of plans may bring about important changes in the utility functions of the planners and their clients. They may not know what they want until they see and live with a realized plan. James March (1978) has had some subtle and profound things to say on this topic. I have also returned to it recently in one of my Gaither Lectures, delivered in 1980 at the University of California, Berkeley, and published as chapter 6 of the revised edition (1981) of *The Sciences of the Artificial.*

Chapter 5.8, an invited lecture at the annual meetings of the American Economic Association, was the first of a number of attempts I have made to talk about the behavioral theory of the firm to economists in a way I hoped would make the theory appear relevant to their interests. The papers in section VIII of this volume can be regarded as further efforts in this direction or, alternatively, as attempts to view from a more detached and philosophical standpoint the reasons why this first attempt, and others like it, have thus far been less than fully successful. One of the consolations of the vocation of science is that in the long run (though we may all be dead) such issues as the relevance of the behavioral theory of the firm to economics will be settled by empirical facts rather than by the eloquence of protagonists of one view or another. In this instance, I am a little less sanguine than I was a quarter-century ago that the facts will render their verdict in my lifetime.

REFERENCES

Bowen, H. R. *The business enterprise as a subject for research.* New York: Social Science Research Council, 1955.

Cyert, R. M., and March, J. G. *A behavioral theory of the firm.* Englewood Cliffs: Prentice-Hall, 1963.

Harris, M., and Raviv, A. Optimal incentive contracts with imperfect information. *Journal of Economic Theory* 20 (1979): 231-259.

Kornai, J. *Anti-Equilibrium.* Amsterdam: North-Holland, 1971.

Lucas, R. E., Jr. On the size distribution of business firms. *Bell Journal of Economics* 9 (1978): 508-523.

March, J. G. Bounded rationality, ambiguity, and the engineering of choice. *Bell Journal of Economics* 9 (1978): 587-608.

March, J. G., and Simon, H. A. *Organizations.* New York: Wiley, 1958.

Marris, R. *The economic theory of "managerial" capitalism.* Glencoe: The Free Press, 1964.

Marschak, J. The role of liquidity under complete and incomplete information. *American Economic Review, Proceedings* 39 (1949): 182-195.

Simon, H. A. *Models of man.* New York: Wiley, 1957.

Simon, H. A. *The sciences of the artificial.* Cambridge, MA: MIT Press, 1969 (2nd ed., 1981).

Simon, H. A., and Guetzkow, H. A model of short- and long-term mechanisms involved in pressures toward uniformity in groups. *Psychological Review* 62

(1955): 56-68.

Simon, H. A., and Guetzkow, H. Mechanisms involved in group pressures on deviate members. *British Journal of Statistical Psychology* 8 (1955): 93-102.

Townsend, R. M. Optimal contracts and competitive markets with costly state verification. *Journal of Economic Theory* 21 (1979): 265-293.

Williamson, O. *Markets and hierarchies.* New York: Macmillan, 1975.

5.1
The Analysis of
Promotional Opportunities*

HERBERT A. SIMON

Carnegie Institute of Technology

Much has been said of the desirability of maintaining an adequate reservoir of potential executives and other key personnel for upgrading within the organization. But what is an "adequate" supply? How can management make a realistic estimate of its long-range demand for replacements at upper levels and determine now whether it may be "caught short" at some time in the future or is grooming some men on false hopes? The method outlined here for analyzing promotional opportunities is both simple and practical.

PERSONNEL ADMINISTRATORS and business executives are becoming increasingly aware of the value of long-range planning for the development and replacement of executives and other key personnel. In general, the principal technique that has been used in such planning has been a position-by-position study of the potential replacements available to fill the higher executive levels. Some attention has also been given to the establishment of "training" positions where promising juniors could understudy and prepare themselves for larger responsibilities.

These techniques have considerable value in providing potential executive material for a period of three or five years ahead. For longer time-spans it seems hardly useful to talk in terms of specific replacements for specific positions. Still, organizations are long-lived creatures (at least this is true of successful organizations), and there would appear to be considerable value in having techniques that could be used to analyze in a rough way not merely the availability of immediate replacements for executives, but the general adequacy of the job structure and promotional system in providing an adequate pool of potential high-level and middle-level talent. It is the purpose of this discussion to suggest some specific, simple techniques for making such studies. Application of these techniques to a particular organization might reveal, for example, that opportunities for promotion were so inadequate as to cause excessive turnover rates for the abler young employees. On the other hand, analysis might reveal that the number of employees with particular qualifications being brought into the organization were so few as to require too rapid promotions with too little experience, or promotion of too many mediocre men.

Identifying the Career Groups

Let us consider a group of jobs in an organization (a) that are arranged by level (in terms of authority relations, rank, or salary), and (b) such

* The methods for analyzing promotion policies presented here were first described in *Public Administration*, by Herbert A. Simon, Donald W. Smithburg, and Victor A. Thompson, Alfred A. Knopf, Inc., New York, 1950.

282

that openings at each level are normally filled by promotion from the next lower level, and jobs at the lowest level from outside. For example, we might consider the professional jobs in the engineering department of a firm. If it were normal practice to bring in junior engineers at the lowest level, and to fill the higher jobs in the department by promotion, then these jobs would form a group of the kind we are considering. In order to have a name for such a group of jobs, we will call it a "career group."

Normally, the employees of an entire firm or plant will form not one, but many career groups. There may be one career group, for example, consisting of women in assembly work at the operative and first supervisory levels; another consisting of accounting department employees; another of semi-skilled and skilled machine operators; and so forth. Each of these groups will have its lowest level—although the lowest level for, say, the engineering group may be above (in salary and rank) even the highest level of the assembly group. This lowest level in each group will be the point at which employees are normally recruited from outside—the "point of entry," so to speak.

Of course the separation between the different career groups will not always be watertight. For example, the lowest positions in the engineering group may in some cases be filled by young graduate engineers, in other cases by promotion of experienced draftsmen. In practice, it will not usually be difficult to separate, on a common-sense basis, the principal career groups in the organization by studying the normal recruitment and promotion practices. Where a particular class of positions may be filled through two or more distinct channels (as in the case of junior engineering positions mentioned above) it will usually be best to consider this class the lowest level in a separate career group.

Each career group will ordinarily form a pyramid. That is, there will be a relatively large number of jobs at each of the lower levels, and fewer at each of the succeeding upper levels. Let us consider, for example, the simplest case of a "line" organization, with a span of control of four, and with a policy of promotion from the ranks. In such an organization our career group might consist of 800 operatives, 200 first-line supervisors, 50 second-line supervisors, 12 third-line supervisors, three fourth-line supervisors, and one fifth-line supervisor.

However, the lowest level in a career group will not always be the most numerous. In a research department of a chemical firm, for example, there may be a relatively small number of junior chemists, a larger number of research workers at each of several intermediate levels, and then a tapering of the pyramid as the supervisory and executive levels are reached. Table I shows some typical forms of career groups. The first has a broad base with a span of control of about four; the second is similar, but with a span of control of two; the third has the "inverted beet" shape of a typical professional career group.

Table I

SOME TYPICAL CAREER GROUPS

Level	Number of Positions		
	(1)	(2)	(3)
V	3	32	14
IV	12	64	80
III	47	129	240
II	188	257	480
I	750	518	186
TOTAL	1000	1000	1000

Factors Affecting
Promotional Opportunities

The promotional opportunities of the employees in any career group depend principally upon: (1) the rate of growth (or decline) of the organization, (2) the shape of the career pyramid (in particular, how rapidly the number of jobs at each level decreases toward the top), (3) the number of appointments that are made from outside the group, rather than by promotion from within, and (4) the average length of time that employees serve in positions at any given level. The fourth variable depends, in turn, on (a) the average age at which appointments are made to each level and (b) the average age at which employees at and above a given level are separated from the organization by retirement, resignation (including promotions to jobs outside the group), death, or dismissal.

When these facts are known for any organization, it is possible to estimate what percentage of the employees appointed at the lowest level in a career ladder will reach any given higher level before they are separated from the organization. The method of carrying out the calculations can best be described by working through some actual illustrations.

How the Calculations Are Made

Let us consider the first career group in Table I, and calculate, under certain assumptions, the chances of an employee who enters at the lowest level reaching the third level. We suppose that employees on the average enter the group at age 25; that the average age at which we wish to promote employees to level III is 35; and that the average age at separation is 55. We assume also that the group is expected to remain about the same size.

Since the average length of service in the organization is 30 years, 1/30 of the 1,000 employees, or 33 employees must be brought into the group at the bottom each year. Since there are 62 jobs at level III and above, and since the average length of service above this level is 20 years, 1/20 of the 62 employees or about 3 employees, must be promoted to this level each year. Hence the chance of any new employee at the bottom reaching the third level or above before separation is about 3/33 or one chance in eleven.

In Table II there are assembled the results of similar calculations for various assumptions about the career groups shown in Table I. By comparing assumptions A and B, for example, for the first career group, we see that by increasing from 35 to 40 the "normal" or average age at promotion to level III, we will increase by one-third the number of employees who can in time expect to reach that level.

Application to Policy Questions

Such comparisons permit us to face up to the basic policy issues in promotion. Are 10 per cent or more of our new employees potentially promotable to the third level? If not, we have to accept either the alternative of promoting men by the time they reach age 35, or, if we feel they will not be sufficiently experienced, of promoting some men whom we do not feel are fully competent.

Comparison of assumptions A and C shows how we can assess the effect of a change in retirement policy upon promotional opportunities. If the average age at separation is reduced, we have to accept the alternative of promoting at earlier ages, being less selective in our promotions, or some combination of these. The analysis not only gives us these qualitative answers, but also tells us *how much.*

Table II

CALCULATION OF PROMOTIONAL OPPORTUNITIES

Assumptions			Career Group	Number of Positions at Level III and Above	Per Cent Promoted to Level III
Av. Age at Initial Appointment	Av. Age at Promotion to Level III	Av. Age at Separation			
A 25	35	55	1 2 3	62 225 335	9.3 33.9 50.0
B 25	40	55	1 2 3	62 225 335	12.5 45.3 66.7
C 25	35	50	1 2 3	62 225 335	10.3 37.5 56.0

As a final illustration, let us examine an "up-or-out" promotion policy, such as is sometimes applied in the armed forces, in some universities, and in a few business organizations. A university, for example, may follow the policy that after a man has served six years as an assistant professor, he must either be promoted or dismissed. Let us suppose that it is desired to have the following distribution of faculty by rank: professors, 40 per cent; associate professors, 30 per cent; assistant professors, 30 per cent. We assume further that persons at the rank of associate professor and above serve, on the average, 20 years before separation. In a faculty of 100 members, five assistant professors (1/6 of 30) will have to be replaced each year, since service at this rank is limited to six years. An average of 3.5 promotions will be made each year to the rank of associate professor (1/20 of 70). Hence, seventy per cent of the assistant professors can look forward to promotion—the rest had better be on the watch for other jobs. (This example has been obviously oversimplified by omitting consideration of resignations at the assistant rank, and appointments from outside at higher ranks.)

Perhaps enough examples have been given to indicate the possible applications of the technique, and its use in analyzing questions of personnel policy. Some further observations will be found in the reference cited in the footnote. The author is not aware of actual applications that have been made of these methods, except in connection with the "up-or-out" policy for senior officers in the Army and Navy. He would welcome information about applications, if any have been made, in industrial organizations.

5.2
A FORMAL THEORY OF THE EMPLOYMENT RELATIONSHIP

BY HERBERT A. SIMON[1]

A distinction is drawn between a sales contract and an employment contract, and a formal model is constructed exhibiting this distinction. By introducing a definition of rational behavior, a method is obtained for determining under what conditions an employment contract will rationally be preferred to a sales contract, and what limits will rationally be placed on the authority of an employer in an employment contract. The relationship of this model to certain other theories of planning under uncertainty is discussed.

IN TRADITIONAL economic theory employees (persons who contract to exchange their services for a wage) enter into the system in two sharply distinct roles. Initially, they are owners of a factor of production (their own labor) which they sell for a definite price. Having done so, they become completely passive factors of production employed by the entrepreneur in such a way as to maximize his profit.

This way of viewing the employment contract and the management of labor involves a very high order of abstraction—such a high order, in fact, as to leave out of account the most striking empirical facts of the situation as we observe it in the real world. In particular, it abstracts away the most obvious peculiarities of the employment contract, those which distinguish it from other kinds of contracts; and it ignores the most significant features of the administrative process, i.e., the process of actually managing the factors of production, including labor. It is the aim of this paper to set forth a theory of the employment relationship that reintroduces some of the more important of these empirical realities into the economic model. Perhaps in this way a bridge can be constructed between the economist, with his theories of the firm and of factor allocation, and the administrator, with his theories of organization—a bridge wide enough to permit some free trade in ideas between two intellectual domains that have hitherto been quite effectively isolated from each other.

1. THE CONCEPT OF AUTHORITY

The authority relationship that exists between an employer and an employee, a relationship created by the employment contract, will play a central role in our theory. What is the nature of this relationship?

[1] In preparing this I have been greatly assisted by comments on an earlier version by a number of persons, including Messrs. L. Hurwicz, R. Radner, D. Rosenblatt, and J. Templeton. The research was undertaken in my capacity as a consultant to the Cowles Commission for Research in Economics under its contract with The RAND Corporation. This paper will be reprinted as Cowles Commission Paper, New Series, No. 47.

293

We will call our employer B (for "boss"), and our employee W (for "worker"). The collection of specific actions that W performs on the job (typing and filing certain letters, laying bricks, or what not) we will call his *behavior*. We will consider the set of all possible behavior patterns of W and we will let x designate an element of this set. A particular x might then represent a given set of tasks, performed at a particular rate of working, a particular level of accuracy, and so forth.[2]

We will say that B exercises *authority* over W if W permits B to select x. That is, W accepts authority when his behavior is determined by B's decision. In general, W will accept authority only if x_0, the x chosen by B, is restricted to some given subset (W's "area of acceptance") of all the possible values. This is the definition of authority that is most generally employed in modern administrative theory.[3]

2. THE EMPLOYMENT CONTRACT

We will say that W enters into an employment contract with B when the former agrees to accept the authority of the latter and the latter agrees to pay the former a stated wage (w). This contract differs fundamentally from a sales contract—the kind of contract that is assumed in ordinary formulations of price theory. In the sales contract each party promises a specific consideration in return for the consideration promised by the other. The buyer (like B) promises to pay a stated sum of money; but the seller (unlike W) promises in return a specified quantity of a completely specified commodity. Moreover, the seller is not interested in the way in which his commodity is used once it is sold, while the worker *is* interested in what the entrepreneur will want him to do (what x will be chosen by B).[4]

We notice that certain services are obtained by buyers in our society sometimes by a sales contract, sometimes by an employment contract. For example, if I want a new concrete sidewalk, I may contract for the sidewalk or I may employ a worker to construct it for me. However, there are certain classes of services that are typically secured by purchase and others that are typically secured by employing someone to perform them. Most labor today is performed by persons who are in an employment relation with their immediate contractors.

[2] Our theory is closely related to the theory of a two-person nonzero-sum game, in the sense of von Neumann and Morgenstern. The various x's (the elements of the set of possible behavior patterns) correspond to the several strategies available to W.

[3] See Simon [4, p. 125] and Barnard [1, p. 163].

[4] A contract to rent durable property is intermediate between the sales contract and the employment contract insofar as the lessor is interested in the effect that the use of the property will have upon its condition when it is returned to him.

We may now attempt to answer two related questions about the employment contract. Why is W willing to sign a blank check, so to speak, by giving B authority over his behavior? If both parties are behaving rationally—in some sense—under what circumstances will they enter into a sales contract and under what circumstances an employment contract?

The following two conjectures, which, if correct, provide a possible answer to these questions, will be examined in the framework of a formal model:

1. W will be willing to enter an employment contract with B only if it does not matter to him "very much" which x (within the agreed-upon area of acceptance) B will choose or if W is compensated in some way for the possibility that B will choose an x that is not desired by W (i.e., that B will ask W to perform an unpleasant task).

2. It will be advantageous to B to offer W added compensation for entering into an employment contract if B is unable to predict with certainty, at the time the contract is made, which x will be the optimum one, from his standpoint. That is, B will pay for the privilege of postponing, until some time after the contract is made, the selection of x.

3. THE SATISFACTION FUNCTIONS

Let us suppose that W and B are each trying to maximize their respective *satisfaction functions*. Let the satisfaction of each depend on:

(a) the particular x that is chosen. (For W this affects, for example, the pleasantness of his work; for B this determines the product that will be produced by W's labor.)

(b) the particular wage (w) that is received or paid.

We assume further that these two components of the satisfaction function enter additively into it as follows:

$$(3.1) \qquad S_1 = F_1(x) - a_1 w,$$

$$(3.2) \qquad S_2 = F_2(x) + a_2 w,$$

where S_1 and S_2 are the satisfactions of B and W, respectively, and $w > 0$ is the wage paid by B to W. The opportunity cost to each participant of entering into the contract may be used to define the zero point of his satisfaction function. That is, if W does not contract with B, then $S_1 = 0$, $S_2 = 0$. Further, for the situations with which we wish to deal it seems reasonable to assume that $F_1(x) \geqslant 0$, $F_2(x) \leqslant 0$, $a_1 > 0$, $a_2 > 0$ for the relevant range of x.

Since $S_1 = 0$, $S_2 = 0$ if B and W fail to reach an agreement, we may assume that, for any agreement they do reach, $S_1 \geqslant 0$, $S_2 \geqslant 0$. When an x and a w exist satisfying these conditions, we say the system is *viable*. The condition may be stated thus:

(3.3) $$F_1(x) \geqslant a_1 w,$$

(3.4) $$-F_2(x) \leqslant a_2 w.$$

Equations (3.3) and (3.4) imply

(3.5) $$a_2 F_1 \geqslant a_2 a_1 w \geqslant -a_1 F_2.$$

Conversely, if for some x, $a_2 F_1(x) \geqslant -a_1 F_2(x)$, we can always find a $w \geqslant 0$ such that (3.5) holds. Hence (3.5) is a necessary and sufficient condition that the system be viable.

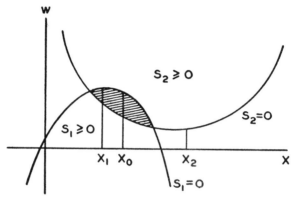

FIGURE 1

4. PREFERRED SOLUTIONS

Thus far we have imposed on the agreement between B and W the condition of viability—that the agreement be advantageous to both. In general, if an agreement is possible at all, it will not be unique. That is, if a viable solution exists, there will be a whole region in the (x, w)-space satisfying the inequalities (3.5), and only in exceptional cases will this region degenerate to a single point. (See Figure 1, where the set of x's is represented by a scalar variable; F_1 and F_2 are continuous in x, and reach extrema at $x = x_1$, $x = x_2$, respectively. The ruled area is then the region of viability.)

A stronger rationality condition[5] is the requirement that, when one agreement (i.e., a point $\{x, w\}$) yields the satisfactions (S_1, S_2) and a second agreement the satisfactions (S_1', S_2') to B and W, the first

---

[5] This stronger rationality requirement is also imposed by von Neumann and Morgenstern in their treatment of the nonzero-sum game.

will be preferred to the second if $S_1 \geqq S_1'$, $S_2 \geqq S_2'$, where at least one of the two inequalities is a proper one. Then we will speak of the second solution as an "inferior" one. The subset of solutions that are not inferior to any solutions we will call the set of *preferred* solutions.

We now define a function $T(x, w)$:

(4.1) $T(x, w) = a_2 S_1(x, w) + a_1 S_2(x, w) = a_2 F_1(x) + a_1 F_2(x) = T(x)$.

THEOREM: *The set of preferred solutions is the set $\{x, w\}$ for which $T(x)$ assumes its greatest value.*

PROOF: Let T_m be this greatest value. Then we will prove that: (1) if $T(x) = T_m$ for (x, w), then there is no point that is preferred to (x, w); while (2) if $T(x') < T_m$ for (x', w'), then there is a point (x, w), with $T(x) = T_m$, that is preferred to (x', w'). This will complete the proof.

(1) Suppose $T(x, w) = T_m$. Consider any other point (x', w') with $T(x', w') \leqq T_m$. Then $a_2 S_1 + a_1 S_2 \geqq a_2 S_1' + a_1 S_2'$; or, $a_2(S_1 - S_1') - a_1(S_2' - S_2) \geqq 0$. Hence (since $a_1 > 0$, $a_2 > 0$), we cannot have both $(S_1 - S_1') \leqq 0$ and $(S_2' - S_2) \geqq 0$ unless the equality holds in both cases (i.e., unless $S_1 = S_1'$ and $S_2 = S_2'$). Therefore, (x', w') is not preferred to (x, w).

(2) Suppose $T(x', w') < T_m$. Let x be such that $T(x) = T_m$. Let $w = (1/T)(x')\{F_1(x)S_2(x', w') - F_2(x)S_1(x', w')\}$. Then

$$S_1(x, w) = F_1(x) - a_1 w$$
$$= [1/T(x')]\{F_1(x)T(x') - a_1 F_1(x)S_2(x', w') + a_1 F_2(x)S_1(x', w')\}$$
$$= [1/T(x')]\{a_2 F_1(x)S_1(x', w') + a_1 F_1(x)S_2(x', w')$$
$$- a_1 F_1(x)S_2(x', w') + a_1 F_2(x)S_1(x', w')\}$$
$$= [1/T(x')]\{a_2 F_1(x) + a_1 F_2(x)\}S_1(x', w'),$$
$$S_1(x, w) = \frac{T(x)}{T(x')} S_1(x', w') = \frac{T_m}{T(x')} S_1(x', w') > S_1(x', w').$$

Similarly, it can be shown that $S_2(x, w) > S_2(x', w')$. Hence (x, w) is preferred to (x', w').

5. EFFECT OF UNCERTAINTY

The argument thus far suggests that the rational procedure for B and W would be first to determine a preferred x, and then to proceed to bargain about w so as to fix S_1 and S_2.[6] If they follow this procedure they will arrive at a sales contract of the ordinary kind in which W agrees to

[6] Of course, $T(x)$ may assume its greatest value for several elements, x, but this complication is inessential.

perform a specific, determinate act (x_0) in return for an agreed-upon price (w_0).

Let us suppose now that $F_1(x)$ and $F_2(x)$, the satisfactions associated with x for B and W, respectively, are not known with certainty at the time B and W must reach agreement. W is to perform some future acts for B, but it is not known at the time they make their agreement what future acts would be most advantageous. Under these circumstances there are two basically different ways in which the parties could proceed.

1. From a knowledge of the probability distribution functions of $F_1(x)$ and $F_2(x)$, for each x, they could estimate what x would be optimal in the sense of maximizing the expected value of, say, $T(x)$. They could then contract for W to perform this specified x for a specified wage, w. This is essentially the sales contract procedure with mathematical expectations substituted for certain outcomes.[7]

2. B and W could agree upon a specified wage, w, to be paid by the former to the latter, and upon a specified procedure that will be followed, *at a later time when the actual values for all x of $F_1(x)$ and $F_2(x)$ are known*, for selecting a specific x. There are any number of conceivable procedures that B and W could employ for the subsequent selection of x. One of the simplest is for W to permit B to select x from some specified set, X (i.e., for W to accept B's authority). Then B would presumably select that x in X which would be optimal for him (i.e., the x that maximizes $F_1(x)$, since w is already fixed). But this arrangement is precisely what we have previously defined as an employment contract.

At the time of contract negotiations F_1 and F_2 have a known joint probability density function for each element x: $p(F_1 , F_2 ; x) \, dF_1 \, dF_2$. Defining the expectation operator, $\mathcal{E}$, in the usual way, we have, for fixed x,

$$(5.1) \quad \mathcal{E}[T(x)] = \mathcal{E}[a_2 F_1(x) + a_1 F_2(x)] = a_2 \mathcal{E}[F_1(x)] + a_1 \mathcal{E}[F_2(x)].$$

ALTERNATIVE 1: *Sales Contract.* We suppose that at the time of contract negotiations B and W agree upon a particular x that will maximize $\mathcal{E}[T(x)]$ and agree on a w that divides the total satisfaction between them. We can measure the advantage of this procedure by the quantity $\max_x \mathcal{E}[T(x)]$.

---

[7] Von Neumann and Morgenstern have shown that introduction of mathematical expectations is equivalent to the definition of a cardinal utility function. We have already cardinalized our satisfaction functions by the simplifying assumptions leading up to equations (3.1) and (3.2).

ALTERNATIVE 2: *Employment Contract*. We suppose that at the time of contract negotiations B and W agree upon a set X from which x will subsequently be chosen by B and agree on a w that divides the total satisfaction between them. Subsequently [when $F_1(x)$ and $F_2(x)$ become known with certainty], B chooses x so as to maximize $F_1(x)$, i.e., he chooses $\max_{x \text{ in } x} F_1(x)$. We can measure the advantage of this procedure by the quantity

$$(5.2) \qquad T_x = \mathcal{E}[a_2 F_1(x_m) + a_1 F_2(x_m)],$$

where x_m is the x in X which maximizes $F_1(x)$.

Generalizing our concept of preferred solutions, we can define a *preferred* set, X, as a set for which T_x assumes its maximum value. Our previous theorem can also be extended to show that, if B and W agree upon an X which is not preferred, the expected satisfactions of both could be increased by substituting a preferred X and adjusting w appropriately.

Our notion of a preferred set provides us with a rational theory for determining the range of authority of B over W (W's area of acceptance). Moreover, the sales contract is subsumed as a special case in which X contains a single element. Hence, the difference between $\max T_x$ for all sets and $\max T_x$ for single-element sets provides us with a measure of the advantage of an employment contract over a sales contract for specified distribution functions of $F_1(x)$, $F_2(x)$.

6. THE AREA OF ACCEPTANCE

As an illustration of the meaning of our theory, we consider the case where W's behavior choice is restricted to two elements, x_a and x_b. If, for example, W's behavior pattern is x_a, B and W will receive the satisfactions $S_1(x_a, w)$ and $S_2(x_a, w)$, respectively, where

$$(6.1) \qquad S_1 = F_1(x_a) - a_1 w,$$

$$(6.2) \qquad S_2 = F_2(x_a) + a_2 w.$$

Let us assume that, at the time of contracting, $F_1(x_a)$ and $F_1(x_b)$ have a joint probability density function given by

$$(6.3) \qquad p(F_a, F_b) \, dF_a \, dF_b,$$

where $F_a = F_1(x_a)$ and $F_b = F_1(x_b)$.

Let us assume further that $F_2(x_a)$ and $F_2(x_b)$ have known fixed values:

$$(6.4) \qquad F_2(x_a) = \alpha, \qquad F_2(x_b) = \beta.$$

17

If B and W enter into a sales contract, they will need to choose between x_a and x_b. On our previous assumptions of rationality, they will choose x_a if and only if

(6.5)
$$\mathcal{E}[T(x_a)] = a_2 \int_{-\infty}^{\infty} \int_{-\infty}^{\infty} F_a\, p(F_a, F_b)\, dF_a\, dF_b + a_1\alpha$$
$$\geqslant a_2 \int_{-\infty}^{\infty} \int_{-\infty}^{\infty} F_b\, p(F_a, F_b)\, dF_a\, dF_b + a_1\beta = \mathcal{E}[T(x_b)].$$

Suppose that, in fact, inequality (6.5) holds. Will the parties gain anything further by entering into an employment contract instead of a sales contract, that is, by giving B the right to choose between x_a or x_b when F_a and F_b become known with certainty? To answer this question we must compare the $\mathcal{E}[T(x_a)]$ of (6.5) with T_X of (5.2), where X consists of the set x_a and x_b.

We have

(6.6)
$$\mathcal{E}\{\max_{x \text{ in } X} F_1(x)\} = \int_{F_a = -\infty}^{\infty} \int_{F_b = F_a}^{\infty} F_b\, p(F_a, F_b)\, dF_b\, dF_a$$
$$+ \int_{F_b = -\infty}^{\infty} \int_{F_a = F_b}^{\infty} F_a\, p(F_a, F_b)\, dF_a\, dF_b,$$

where $p(F_a, F_b)$ is the joint probability density of F_a and F_b. Hence,

(6.7)
$$T_X = \int_{F_a = -\infty}^{\infty} \int_{F_b = F_a}^{\infty} (a_2 F_b + a_1\beta) p(F_a, F_b)\, dF_b\, dF_a$$
$$+ \int_{F_b = -\infty}^{\infty} \int_{F_a = F_b}^{\infty} (a_2 F_a + a_1\alpha) p(F_a, F_b)\, dF_a\, dF_b,$$

and to choose between the employment contract and the sales contract we must determine the sign of

(6.8)
$$T_X - \mathcal{E}[T(x_a)] = \int_{F_a = -\infty}^{\infty} \int_{F_b = F_a}^{\infty} [a_2(F_b - F_a)$$
$$+ a_1(\beta - \alpha)] p(F_a, F_b)\, dF_b\, dF_a.$$

Since $(F_b - F_a) \geqslant 0$ in the region of integration, the employment contract will certainly be preferable to the sales contract (in which $x = x_a$) if $\beta \geqslant \alpha$ (if W prefers x_b to x_a), and even if $(\alpha - \beta)$ is positive but not too large.

To gain further insight into the meaning of (6.8) we may consider the special case in which $\alpha = \beta$ (W is indifferent as between x_a and x_b)[8] and F_a and F_b are independently normally distributed:

(6.9) $$p(F_a, F_b) = \frac{1}{2\pi\sigma_a \sigma_b} \exp\left\{-\frac{1}{2}\left[\left(\frac{F_a - A}{\sigma_a}\right)^2 + \left(\frac{F_b - B}{\sigma_b}\right)^2\right]\right\},$$

---

[8] This restriction is not essential. We could, instead, work with $F_a' = F_a + (a_1/a_2)\,\alpha$ and $F_b' = F_b + (a_1/a_2)\,\beta$. Then in (6.9) we would simply replace $(F_b - F_a)$ with $(F_b' - F_a')$.

where A and B are the means and σ_a and σ_b the standard deviations of F_a and F_b, respectively. Equation (6.8) then becomes

(6.10)
$$T_x - \mathcal{E}[T(x_a)] = \frac{a_2}{2\pi\sigma_a\sigma_b} \int_{F_a=-\infty}^{\infty} \int_{F_b=F_a}^{\infty} (F_b - F_a)$$
$$\cdot \exp\left\{ -\frac{1}{2}\left[\left(\frac{F_a - A}{\sigma_a}\right)^2 + \left(\frac{F_b - B}{\sigma_b}\right)^2 \right]\right\} dF_b\, dF_a.$$

The situation described by equation (6.10) is shown in Figure 2, where we take $A = 0$, $B < 0$. The ellipses about the center $(0, B)$ are contours of the probability function, and the region of integration is the region to the left of the 45° line, $F_a = F_b$.

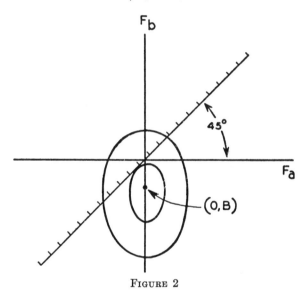

FIGURE 2

It is geometrically obvious from the figure, and can be shown analytically, that $T_x - \mathcal{E}[T(x_a)]$ will increase with an increase in σ_a or in σ_b, and with a decrease in the absolute value of B. Hence, an increase in the uncertainty of either F_a or F_b when the contract is made will increase the advantage of the employment contract over the sales contract, while a decrease in the average disadvantage of x_b as compared to x_a will have the same result.

It is also obvious that these results will hold, qualitatively, even when F_a and F_b are not independently distributed, or when the distribution is not exactly normal. In our model, then, both the conjectures set forth at the end of Section 2 prove to be correct.

One objection to the analysis needs to be raised and disposed of. We have assumed, in the employment contract, that B, when F_a and

F_b become known, will choose the larger. Why will he not choose, instead, the larger of $(a_1F_a + a_2\alpha)$ or $(a_1F_b + a_2\beta)$? If he did, the employment contract would always be preferred to the sales contract, and, indeed, it would be advantageous to the parties not to limit X at all.

The difficulty lies in the fact that, once agreement has been reached on w, there is no way for W to enforce the understanding that B will employ the magnitude of $(a_1F_1 + a_2F_2)$ rather than of F_1 as his criterion for choosing x. Moreover, it is to B's short-run advantage to maximize F_1 rather than $(a_1F_1 + a_2F_2)$ after w has been determined. Translated into everyday language, the worker has no assurance that the employer will consider anything but his own profit in deciding what he will ask the worker to do.[9]

If the worker had confidence that the employer would take account of his satisfactions, the former would presumably be willing to work for a smaller wage than if he thought these satisfactions were going to be ignored in the employer's exercise of authority and only profitability to the employer taken into account. On the other hand, unless the worker is thereby induced to work for a lower wage, the employer has no incentive to use his authority in any other way than to maximize F_1. Hence, we might expect the employer to maximize $(a_1F_1 + a_2F_2)$ only if he thought that by so doing he could persuade the worker, in subsequent renewals of the employment contract, to accept a wage sufficiently smaller to compensate him for this. Otherwise, the employer would rationally maximize F_1. We might say that the latter behavior represents "short-run" rationality, whereas the former represents "long-run" rationality when a relationship of confidence between employer and worker can be attained. The fact that the former rule leads to solutions that are preferable to those of the latter shows that it "pays" the employer to establish this relationship.

7. EXTENSION OF THE MODEL

It should hardly be necessary to state again that the model presented here, while it appears to be substantially more realistic in its treatment of the employment relationship than is the traditional theory of the firm, is still highly abstract and oversimplified, and leaves out of account numerous important aspects of the real situation. It is a model of hypothetically rational behavior in an area where institutional history and other nonrational elements are notoriously important.

In Section 6 we limited ourselves to a situation in which only two

[9] It must be remembered that our model does not take account of morale effects (e.g., that the worker may actually perform *better* if the employer makes allowance for his satisfactions). Our omission of this point does not imply that it it unimportant.

behavior alternatives were open to W—x_a and x_b. The foregoing analysis can be reinterpreted to answer the following question:

Suppose that B and W have already agreed to enter into an employment contract, with B to choose x from some subset, X_a, that does not include x_b. Is it now advantageous to the parties to enlarge W's area of acceptance to include x_b ?

We interpret x_a to mean the element of X_a that maximizes $F_1(x)$ for x in X_a. If, now, we know the joint probability distribution $p[F_1(x_1), F_1(x_2), \cdots]$ for x_1, x_2, $\cdots$ in X_a, we can calculate the probability distribution of $F_a = F_1(x_a)$. It is, in fact, the distribution of the maximum of a sample where each element of the sample is drawn from a different population. Placing this interpretation on the F_a that enters into (6.8), we see that it will be advantageous to enlarge X_a to include x_b if and only if

$$(7.1) \qquad\qquad T_{(x_a+x_b)} \geqslant T_{x_a}.$$

In another important respect the model can be brought into closer conformity with reality without serious difficulty. Any actual employment contract, unlike the hypothetical arrangements we have thus far discussed, specifies much more than the wage to be paid and the authority relationship. The kinds of matters over which the employer will not exercise his authority are often spelled out in considerable detail; e.g., hours of work, nature of duties (in general or specifically), and so forth. If the employment relationship endures for an extended period, all sorts of informal understandings grow up in addition to formal agreements that are made when the contract is periodically renewed. Under modern conditions when a labor union is involved, many of these contract terms are spelled out specifically and in detail in the union agreement. Our model has taken care of this fact in recognizing that authority is accepted within limits, but such limits can be introduced in another way.

In order to extend the model in this direction, let us suppose that the behavior of the worker (or a whole group of workers) is specified, not by a single element x, but by a sequence of such elements $(x, y, z, \cdots)$, where the elements in the sequence can be varied independently. Let us suppose that each of these determines a separate component in the satisfaction functions and that these components enter additively:

$$(7.2) \qquad\qquad S_1 = f_{1x}(x) + f_{1y}(y) + \cdots - aw,$$

and similarly for S_2.

Then the parties may enter into a contract in which certain of the elements, say, $x, \cdots$, are specified as terms in the contract (as in the sales contract); a second set of elements, say, $y, \cdots$, is to be subject to the authority of the employer; and a third set of elements, say, z , $\cdots$, is to be left to the discretion of the worker or workers. Analogously to our previous assumptions, we may assume that if the element y is subject to the authority of B, he will fix it so as to maximize $f_{1y}(y)$ while, if z is left to the discretion of W, he will fix it so as to maximize $f_{2z}(z)$. We can now derive inequalities analogous to (6.8) that will indicate which elements should, on rational grounds, fall in each of these three categories.

Reviewing the results we have already obtained, we can see that the conditions making it advantageous (1) to stipulate the value of a particular variable in the contract are

(a) sharp conflict of interest with respect to the optimum value of the element (f_1 high when f_2 low and vice versa);

(b) little uncertainty as to the optimum values of the element (σ_{f_1} and σ_{f_2} small).

The conditions making it advantageous (2) to give B authority over an element or (3) to leave it to the discretion of W are, of course, just the opposite of those listed above. Moreover, (2) will be preferable to (3) if B's sensitivity to departures from optimality is greater than W's.

8. APPLICATION TO PLANNING UNDER UNCERTAINTY

The model proposed here deals with a particular problem of planning under uncertainty. It analyzes a situation in which it may be advantageous to postpone decision (selection of x) in order to gain from information obtained subsequently. The postponement of choice may be regarded as a kind of "liquidity preference" where the liquid resource is the employee's time instead of money.

The same general approach can be applied to the problem of choosing among more or less liquid forms for holding assets. The function $F_1(x)$ would then represent the gain derived from using assets in the pursuit of strategy x. The function $F_2(x)$ would need to be replaced by some measure of the cost of holding assets in liquid form (e.g., interest costs). Then, the advantage of postponement, given by an expression like (6.8), with $\beta = \alpha$, would have to be compared with the cost of holding assets.

Indeed, comparison of the methods of this paper with Marschak's theory of liquidity under the assumption of complete information but uncertainty (particularly pp. 182–195 of [2]) reveals a close similarity of approach. In both problems the central question is to determine the optimum degree of postponement of commitment. In Marschak's case this is measured by the amount of assets not invested in the first period; in our case, by the range of elements included in the set X (area of acceptance).

9. CONCLUSION

We have constructed a model that incorporates rational grounds for the choice by two individuals between an employment contract and a contract of the ordinary kind (which we have called a sales contract). By a generalization of this model we are able to account for the fact that in an employment contract certain aspects of the worker's behavior are stipulated in the contract terms, certain other aspects are placed within the authority of the employer, and still other aspects are left to the worker's choice. Since administrative theory has been interested in explaining behavior within the framework of employment relations, and economic theory in explaining behavior within the area of market relations, the model suggests one possible way of relating these two bodies of theory. The most serious limitations of the model lie in the assumptions of rational utility-maximizing behavior incorporated in it.

Carnegie Institute of Technology and Cowles Commission for Research in Economics

REFERENCES

[1] BARNARD, CHESTER I., *The Functions of the Executive*, Cambridge, Mass.: Harvard University Press, 1938, 334 pp.

[2] MARSCHAK, JACOB, "Role of Liquidity under Complete and Incomplete Information," *Papers and Proceedings, American Economic Review*, Vol. 39 May, 1949, pp. 182–195, with discussion by F. Modigliani and J. Tobin. (Abstracts in ECONOMETRICA, Vol. 17, April, 1949, pp. 180–184.)

[3] NEUMANN, JOHN VON, AND OSKAR MORGENSTERN, *Theory of Games and Economic Behavior*, Princeton: Princeton University Press, 1944, 641 pp.

[4] SIMON, HERBERT A., *Administrative Behavior*, New York: The Macmillan Co., 1947, 259 pp.

5.3
A Comparison of Organisation Theories[1]

It is the purpose of this paper to suggest a framework that permits a comparison of certain theories of organisation that appear in the literature of economics with those in the literature of administration. The relations between the economist's theory of the firm and what is usually called in administrative writings the " theory of organisational equilibrium " have never been made explicit, and writers in the one field often appear unaware of the possible implications for their work of the investigations that have been carried on in the other.

Part I of this paper will set forth verbal descriptions and comparisons of the theories in question. In Part II a mathematical framework will be proposed capable of encompassing both theories as special cases.

I

The theory of the firm (F-theory) and the theory of organisation (O-theory) are both concerned with the behaviour of a person, or people, trying to gain certain ends by the manipulation of variables at their disposal (strategic variables). The problem of " optimal," " rational," or " efficient " behaviour with respect to these ends can be formulated as a problem of finding the maximum (with respect to the strategic variables) of some function that is taken as a measure of success in attaining these ends (e.g., in the theory of the firm, finding the output that maximises profit). Theories of organisation, perhaps to a greater extent than the theory of the firm, have been concerned not only with optimal solutions, but with the whole set of *viable* solutions— that is, solutions that permit the survival of the organisation (e.g., in the theory of the firm, outputs that yield a positive profit).

Theory of the Firm

In this paper, the term " theory of the firm " (F-theory) will refer to the classical form of that theory in which the entrepreneur is confronted with a production function, supply functions for the factors of production, and demand functions for the products ; and in which perfect divisibility is assumed for both factors and products so that bargaining takes place in terms of marginal units. Hence we include perfect competition and imperfect competition with product differentiation, but exclude from F-theory oligopoly theory and game-theoretical approaches. We do this in order to contrast the F-theory as sharply as possible with organisation theory (O-theory). As we shall see in the course of the exposition, newer directions in the theory of the firm (e.g., theories of monopoly-monopsony—including wage theory under collective bargaining—and oligopoly, in which the entrepreneur is confronted with " active " rather than " passive" opponents) point precisely toward the formulations of organisation theory.

In its usual form, the problem of optimality in the theory of the firm is to maximise profit—the difference between value of product and cost of production. The firm may produce a number of different products, and employ a number of different factors of production. The product prices may be given, or, more generally, may be functions of the quantities produced. Similarly, the factor prices may be given or may be functions of the quantities of factors employed.

[1] This paper represents work done as a consultant to the Cowles Commission for Research in Economics under contract with the RAND Corporation ; it will be included in the Commission New Series, No. 47. I am indebted to Mr. Leo Hurwicz and other members of the Cowles Commission staff, and to Mr. W. W. Cooper and other colleagues at the Carnegie Institute of Technology for valuable comments and suggestions on earlier drafts.

I

The problem of optimality may be divided into a problem of *technological optimality* (in the terminology of Koopmans : *efficiency*[1]) and a problem of *economic optimality*. Optimality in the latter sense implies optimality in the former. Outputs of product are connected with inputs of factors by certain relations or constraints, so that, for example, if all the inputs are given and all but one of the outputs, the remaining output will have a definite upper bound. These constraints define the " possibilities of production." A set of product outputs and factor inputs may be regarded as technologically optimal if no single output can be increased or input decreased without decreasing at least one other output or increasing at least one input. The set of technologically optimal outputs and inputs corresponds to the economist's usual notion of the production function. If there are n outputs and m inputs, the set of technologically optimal output-input combinations may have as many as $(n + m - 1)$ degrees of freedom.

By introducing fixed prices for outputs and inputs, or by introducing equations of demand and supply, respectively, for them, the point can be found on the production function which corresponds to economic optimality—i.e., to profit maximisation. (As noted above, we include here both the cases of perfect and imperfect competition, but not the case of oligopoly, where these prices are regarded as functions also of the quantities produced and consumed by other firms.)

Let us consider further the case where the output of the firm is a single product. In this case we may first find all technologically optimal input combinations for each output, and then determine which of these input combinations is economically optimal in terms of given prices or supply curves for the factors—i.e., which gives the lowest cost of product. In this way we derive the familiar cost curve which, when combined with the demand curve, permits us to determine the output that will maximise profits.

Theory of Organisation

In the F-theory, a single participant, the entrepreneur, is explicitly treated as a rational individual. The other participants—employees, customers, suppliers—enter into the theory only implicitly and only as passive " conditions " to which the entrepreneur adjusts in finding the solution that is optimal to him.[2] One such condition is the price of the factor " labour," another is the demand schedule, or the total revenue schedule, which describes the behaviours of customers.

In the O-theory the participants are generally treated in a more symmetrical fashion.[3] Each participant is offered an *inducement* for his participation in the organisation. Through his participation, he makes a *contribution* to the organisation. The participant's contributions may be regarded as " factors," the inducements offered to him as " products." Thus the organisation transforms its members' contributions into inducements which it, in turn, distributes to these members.

As a simple example, consider an organisation with an entrepreneur, one employee,

---

[1] See T. C. Koopmans, " Production as an efficient combination of activities," Chapter III of *Activity Analysis of Production and Allocation*, Cowles Commission Monograph No. 13, New York, 1951.

[2] It is on this point that oligopoly theory departs fundamentally from the older theories of the firm.

[3] The theory we are describing here is essentially that proposed by Chester I. Barnard in *The Functions of the Executive* (Cambridge : Harvard University Press, 1936). See also Herbert A. Simon, *Administrative Behavior* (New York : Macmillan, 1947), ch. 6 ; H. A. Simon, D. W. Smithburg, and V. A. Thompson, *Public Administration* (New York : Knopf, 1950), ch. 18, 23.

and one customer. The system of inducements and contributions may then be represented thus[1] :

Participant	Inducements	Contributions
Entrepreneur	Revenue from Sales	Costs of Production
Employee	Wage	Labour
Customer	Goods	Purchase Price

The customer's contribution of the purchase price is used to provide inducements to the entrepreneur in the form of revenue. The entrepreneur's contribution provides the employee's wages. The employee's contribution is transformed into goods that provide the customer's inducement. This last transformation corresponds to the usual production function. However, we also have another " production function " that constrains the money flows—these flows must obey the basic accounting equation.

We might now proceed, as is usually done in the F-theory, to prescribe criteria of optimality (in addition to the technological criteria we have already incorporated in the system) and to derive optimum values for the inducements and contributions. However, O-theory has generally been concerned not so much with optimality as with the conditions necessary for organisational survival, that is, the conditions under which the participants will continue to participate.

It may be postulated that each participant will remain in the organisation if the satisfaction (or utility) he derives from the net balance of inducements over contributions (measured in terms of their utility to *him*) is greater than the satisfaction he could obtain if he withdrew. The zero point in such a " satisfaction function " is defined, therefore, in terms of the opportunity cost of participation. In general, the survival criterion will not yield a unique solution to the values of inducements and contributions. The solutions that are compatible with survival we have previously referred to as viable solutions.

To restrict further the set of viable solutions, a weak optimality condition can be imposed that does not involve any assumption of interpersonal comparison of satisfactions or utilities.[2] A viable solution is regarded as optimal if no further increase could be made in the net satisfaction of any one participant without decreasing the satisfaction of at least one other participant. Imposition of this condition still leaves us, in general, without a unique solution—a unique set of values of the inducements and contributions.

To see this more clearly, we suppose that we have a solution in which each participant is receiving more than the minimum satisfaction required to retain him in the system—each has a satisfaction greater than zero. We suppose further that the satisfaction of all participants cannot be simultaneously increased—e.g., if the quantity of production is held constant, wages cannot be increased without increasing prices or reducing net profits. Then we could still maintain the system if we reduced wages to a point where the satisfaction of the employee was just above zero, and increased the satisfaction of the entrepreneur, or increased the customer's satisfaction by reducing prices.

To obtain a unique solution we may impose a stronger optimality condition. We may select, for example, that particular one of the optimal solutions for which the satisfactions of the entrepreneur and the customer are each equal to zero, and the

---

[1] In order to simplify this example as far as possible, the table includes only the obvious tangible inducements and contributions. In the general development of the theory this restriction is neither essential nor desirable. In particular, we are omitting the entrepreneur's contribution of managerial skill, and regarding him as a sort of " cash register " for monetary transactions.

[2] This condition is the weak optimality condition used in modern theories of welfare economics and in the theory of non-zero-sum games.

satisfaction of the employee therefore attains the maximum value that is consistent with viability. The employee, in this case, captures the entire " surplus " of satisfactions. Alternatively, we may select the solution in which the entrepreneur captures this " surplus ", and the satisfactions of customer and employee are held at zero. It is in fact this latter solution that is most closely analogous to the solution provided by the F-theory.

Comparison of the Theories

Comparison of the theories presented in the preceding two sections reveals the following differences between them :

1. The O-theory is concerned primarily with the conditions under which an organisation will survive ; since survival does not in general determine uniquely the distribution of satisfactions among the participants, it provides no answer to the question of distribution.

The traditional F-theory selects out of all the viable solutions that one which maximises in a certain sense the satisfaction of the entrepreneur. It assumes that he alone will seek to capture the " surplus " of satisfactions, and that the other participants will be persuaded to remain in the system by (marginal) inducements that just equal the (marginal) opportunity costs of their respective contributions.

2. In the O-theory it is assumed that the participants will make the all-or-none choice of participation or non-participation. In the F-theory it is usually assumed (remembering that we exclude theories of oligopoly and monopoly-monopsony) that there will be bargaining for the marginal unit of inducement and contribution. In fact, it will appear from the more rigorous mathematical treatment of Part II, that this bargaining in terms of small marginal units permits the customer and the employee to retain a part of the " surplus " (consumers' surplus and labour's surplus) in spite of their passivity. When the elasticity of the demand for product or the supply of labour become infinite (as in perfect competition in the market for the product and the labour market) these respective surpluses disappear.[1] In these cases, the F-theory requires that the inducement offered to customer and employer be just equal to the opportunity costs of their contributions.

If we consider the solution that is optimal to the entrepreneur in the O-theory and the F-theory, respectively, we find that in the O-theory the wage is equal to the *average* disutility of labour and the product price to the *average* utility of the product ; while in the F-theory it is the *marginal* utilities that come into question.

Comparison of the two theories leads us, then, to certain empirical differences in the behaviour they predict. To determine which is correct, we must seek answers to such questions as the following :

a. Are the participants other than the entrepreneur to be regarded as passive ? That is, are we to restrict ourselves to the solution that is optimal to the entrepreneur (as in F-theory) ; or to consider the wider classis of optimal, or even viable, solutions (as in O-theory) ? Many of the recent attempts at the reformulation of wage theory may be interpreted as essays in the latter direction.

b. Do the participants bargain in terms of increments of contribution and inducement, or is the bargaining an all-or-none question of participation or non-participation ? Traditional F-theory assumes the former alternative ; our formulation of the O-theory, the latter. Again, it would seem that any attempt to incorporate in the theory of the

---

[1] It should be noted that our surpluses are analogous to, but not identical with, the Marshallian surpluses for the industry, since we take as the zero point of utility the point at which the customer or employee would participate in a different firm, not necessarily in a different industry.

firm such elements as customer goodwill, or the social satisfactions derived by the employee from his employment would have to take the latter direction.

In any event, these are questions to be answered by empirical observation of the actual institutional processes. Institutional economists, and theorists of organisation who have perhaps been in closer contact than traditional economic theorists with the empirical phenomena, have been by no means satisfied that the F-theory coincides with the observed facts of organisational behaviour. Lest I be accused of being a " casual empiricist " I will let the matter rest with the observation that careful empirical investigation will be required to choose between the theories.

Whatever the empirical evidence may show, the theory of the firm has already been developing beyond the limitations of F-theory. First, enlargement of the F-theory to include oligopoly and bilateral monopoly has already begun to suggest a theory of organisation similar to that developed here. Second, the optimal solutions of the O-theory bear an obvious resemblance to the solutions of a non-zero sum game in the sense of von Neumann and Morgenstern.

II

We proceed now to a more rigorous formulation of the theory. It will be convenient to adopt a number of notational conventions. By $\mathbf{x}$ is meant the vector with components $(x_1, x_2, \ldots, x_n)$.

By $\mathbf{x} \geqq \mathbf{u}$ we mean that $x_i \geq u_i$ for all i, and $x_i > u_i$ for at least one i. By $\mathbf{x} \geqq \mathbf{u}$, we mean that $\mathbf{x} \geqq \mathbf{u}$ or $\mathbf{x} = \mathbf{u}$. All the functions that appear will be assumed to satisfy appropriate conditions of continuity and differentiability.

We postulate a set of satisfaction functions, S_i, where :

$$S_i = S_i (x_1, \ldots, x_n, y_1, \ldots y_m) = S_i (\mathbf{x}, \mathbf{y}), (i = 1, \ldots, p) \ldots\ldots\ldots(1)$$

and a set of constraints :

$$H_j (\mathbf{x}, \mathbf{y}) = 0 \qquad (j = 1, \ldots, k) \ldots\ldots\ldots\ldots\ldots\ldots(2)$$

In equations (1) and (2) the components of $\mathbf{x}$ are the various contributions made by participants in an organisation, the components of $\mathbf{y}$ are inducements received by the participants.

The pairs of vectors, $\mathbf{x}, \mathbf{y}$, that satisfy (2) we call *achievable*. We may also speak of achievable vectors $\mathbf{S}$, i.e., the $\mathbf{S}$ that satisfy (1) for some achievable $(\mathbf{x}, \mathbf{y})$. We assume that $\mathbf{S} \leqq \mathbf{K}$ for all achievable $\mathbf{S}$ and for some finite $\mathbf{K} \geqq 0$.

If (2) can be solved for k of the variables in terms of the remaining $r = m + n - k$, and the values are substituted in (1) we get :

$$S_i = S_i (Z_1, \ldots, Z_r) \qquad (i = 1, \ldots, p) \ldots\ldots\ldots\ldots\ldots(3)$$

where the Z_j are the remaining independent variables. Alternatively we may consider the Z_j to be parameters such that :

$$x_h = x_h (\mathbf{Z}) \ldots\ldots\ldots\ldots\ldots\ldots\ldots\ldots\ldots\ldots\ldots\ldots\ldots\ldots\ldots\ldots\ldots(4)$$

$$y_l = y_l (\mathbf{Z}) \qquad (h = 1, \ldots, n, l = 1, \ldots m) \ldots\ldots\ldots(5)$$

If there is at least one achievable $\mathbf{S}$ such that :

$$\mathbf{S} \geqq 0. \ldots\ldots\ldots\ldots\ldots\ldots\ldots\ldots\ldots\ldots\ldots\ldots\ldots\ldots\ldots\ldots\ldots\ldots\ldots\ldots\ldots(6)$$

we say that the system (1)–(2) is *viable*. Any such value of $\mathbf{S}$ is called a viable solution.

In order further to limit the set of solutions to be considered, additional restrictions, beyond those of achievability and viability, must be imposed. To obtain a unique solution, r independent additional restrictions will in general be needed.

These additional restrictions may be derived from assumptions that the participants in the system will, separately or severally, seek to make their respective S's as large as possible. Restrictions of this kind we will call *optimality* conditions.

The two theories we are considering, O-theory and F-theory, may be distinguished in terms of the kind of optimality conditions commonly introduced in them. We will consider the two theories in turn.

O-theory. It was pointed out in Part I that O-theory has generally been more concerned with viability than optimality. However, two criteria of optimality suggest themselves. The first is the weak welfare criterion, the second, the criterion that would be imposed by the ith participant if he could choose the solution he preferred from the whole set of viable solutions.

First, we define the weak criterion of optimality. A solution, **S**, of (4) is optimal in the weak sense if there does not exist another solution, **S'**, such that $S' \geq S$.

If our functions satisfy appropriate conditions of differentiability and convexity, the optimal solutions can be found by the use of Lagrangian multipliers. We consider :

$$T \equiv \sum_{i=1}^{p} \lambda_i S_i \dots\dots\dots\dots\dots\dots\dots\dots\dots\dots\dots\dots\dots\dots (7)$$

where the λ_i are non-negative constants to be chosen. The optimal solutions are then the solutions that maximise T, with respect to variation of **Z**.[1]

Necessary conditions for a maximum of T are :

$$\sum_{i=1}^{p} \lambda_i \frac{\partial S_i}{\partial Z_j} = 0 \qquad (j = 1, \dots, r) \dots\dots\dots\dots\dots\dots\dots (8)$$

These equations give r conditions to determine **Z** as a function of λ. Since the equations (8) are homogeneous of the first degree in the λ_i, λ is determined only up to multiplication by an arbitrary scalar, hence has $p - 1$ degrees of freedom.

Thus we can generally determine Z uniquely by imposing $(p - 1)$ auxiliary conditions, for example, the conditions :

$$S_i = L_i, \text{ a constant } (i \neq m) \dots\dots\dots\dots\dots\dots\dots\dots\dots\dots\dots\dots (9)$$

where the components of L_i are chosen so as to preserve the achievability of **S**—that is, so that (9) does not contradict (1) and (2). The solution that corresponds to $L_i = 0$ $(i \neq m)$, we will call the solution *optimal to the mth participant.*

It will not always be possible to solve (8) for **Z** as a function of λ. (In particular cases (8) may determine certain of the λ_i, and of the Z uniquely, and leave completely indeterminate others of the Z_i. We shall examine such a special case later.)

F-theory. In F-theory, we designate one of our participants, say the first, as the *entrepreneur.* We assume further that the variables, $x_1, \dots, x_n, y_1, \dots, y_m$ that enter into S_i can be divided into two sets : (1) those that the ith participant *controls,* and (2) those that the ith participant regards as *fixed.* (The ith participant may regard certain functions of variables fixed, rather than individual variables.) We may designate the variables controlled by the ith participant $(i \neq 1)$:

$$w_{ij} (j = 1, \dots, \rho_i)$$

and we assume that all the w_{ij} are distinct, for all (i, j). The variable w_{ij}, then, is identical with one of the x's or y's that appear in S_i.

---

[1] For a more explicit justification of this procedure, see Koopmans, op. cit., pp. 85–97.

Each of the participants, other than the entrepreneur, adopts the following behaviour rule : to maximise his S_i with respect to the variables w_{ij} $(_4 = 1, \ldots, \rho_i)$, regarding the other variables as fixed. This gives us :

$$\frac{\partial S_i}{\partial w_{ij}} = 0 \qquad (i = 2, \ldots, p \; ; \; j = 1, \ldots, \rho_i) \quad \ldots \ldots \ldots \ldots (10)$$

This process of maximisation yields a set of equations expressing the variables controlled by the participants (other than the entrepreneur) in terms of the remaining variables. These equations are the "supply" and "demand" functions for the entrepreneur's factors and product.

Finally, the entrepreneur maximises S_1, regarded as a function of **x** and **y**, subject to the technological constraints expressed in equations (2) and the constraints imposed, in equations (10), by the behaviour rules of other participants. Let $Z_1, \ldots, Z_r$ be the variables remaining in S_1 after the remainder have been eliminated by use of the k equations (2) and the $\rho = \sum_{i \neq 1} \rho_i$ equations (10). Then we have :

$$S_1 = S_1 (Z_1, \ldots, Z_r) \quad \ldots \ldots \ldots \ldots \ldots \ldots \ldots \ldots \ldots \ldots \ldots \ldots (11)$$

and the r equations :

$$\frac{\partial S_1}{\partial Z_i} = 0 \qquad (i = 1, \ldots, r) \quad \ldots \ldots \ldots \ldots \ldots \ldots \ldots \ldots \ldots \ldots (12)$$

Because the entrepreneur plays a very special role in this solution, it may be regarded as optimal with respect to him. Yet it involves optimising behaviour on the part of the other participants as well, and we should not be surprised when we discover, in the special case to be treated next, that it is not in general identical with the solution optimal to the first participant in the O-theory.

Further Analysis of a Special Case. The discussion of the previous two sections may be given concrete illustration by considering a special case of the model embodied in equations (1)–(6).

We assume that **S** takes the special form :

$$S_i = \phi_i(y_i) - \psi_i(x_i) \qquad (i = 1, 2, 3) \quad \ldots \ldots \ldots \ldots \ldots \ldots (13)$$

where S_i is the net satisfaction of the ith participant, y_i his inducement and x_i his contribution, and where $\phi'_i = d\phi_i/dy > 0$, $\psi'_i > 0$. The x's and y's are subject to one or more relations of the form (2).

In terms of our earlier example, involving three participants, the variables may be interpreted as follows : S_1 is profit, y_1 the entrepreneur's revenue, x_1 his payroll ; S_2 is the employee's satisfaction, y_2 his total earnings, and x_2 the quantity of labour he supplies ; S_3 is the customer's satisfaction, y_3 the quantity of goods he buys, and x_3 the amount he pays for them. In this example the production relations, (2) become :

$$y_1 = x_3 \quad \ldots \ldots \ldots \ldots \ldots \ldots \ldots \ldots \ldots \ldots \ldots \ldots \ldots \ldots \ldots \ldots \ldots \ldots \ldots (14a)$$
$$y_2 = x_1 \quad \ldots \ldots \ldots \ldots \ldots \ldots \ldots \ldots \ldots \ldots \ldots \ldots \ldots \ldots \ldots \ldots \ldots \ldots \ldots (14b)$$
$$y_3 = \xi (x_2) \quad \ldots \ldots \ldots \ldots \ldots \ldots \ldots \ldots \ldots \ldots \ldots \ldots \ldots \ldots \ldots \ldots \ldots (14c)$$

Equation (14c) is the ordinary production function, assumed already to incorporate the conditions of technological optimality. The first equation in (13) takes the special form :

$$S_1 = y_1 - x_1 = x_3 - y_2 \quad \ldots \ldots \ldots \ldots \ldots \ldots \ldots \ldots \ldots \ldots \ldots \ldots \ldots (15)$$

The right-hand equality in (15) may be regarded as the accounting equation, or in the form $(y_1 + y_2) = (x_1 + x_3)$ as a sort of "production function" for cash.

Substituting (14) in (13) we get relations of the form :

$$S_i = S_i (x_1, x_2, x_3) \quad \dots\dots\dots\dots\dots\dots\dots\dots\dots\dots\dots\dots\dots\dots\dots\dots (16)$$

(cf. equation (3)). For the system to be viable we require $S_i \geqq 0$ $(i = 1, 2, 3)$. Optimal solutions in the O-theory (with the weak criterion) then correspond to the maximum of :

$$T = \lambda_1 S_1 + \lambda_2 S_2 + \lambda_3 S_3 \quad \dots\dots\dots\dots\dots\dots\dots\dots\dots\dots\dots\dots\dots\dots\dots (17)$$

Where S_1 has the special form (15) our equations (8) become :

$$\frac{\partial T}{\partial x_i} = - \lambda_1 + \lambda_2 \phi'_2 = 0 \quad \dots\dots\dots\dots\dots\dots\dots\dots\dots\dots\dots\dots\dots\dots (18a)$$

$$\frac{\partial T}{\partial x_2} = - \lambda_2 \psi'_2 + \lambda_3 \phi'_3 \zeta' = 0 \quad \dots\dots\dots\dots\dots\dots\dots\dots\dots\dots\dots (18b)$$

$$\frac{\partial T}{\partial x_3} = \lambda_1 - \lambda_3 \psi'_3 = 0 \quad \dots\dots\dots\dots\dots\dots\dots\dots\dots\dots\dots\dots\dots (18c)$$

From this system we obtain x_1, x_2, and x_3 as functions of λ_1/λ_2 and λ_1/λ_3. Hence we have a two-parameter family of optimal solutions in the O-theory.

By setting $S_2 = 0$, $S_3 = 0$, we get the particular solution in the O-theory that maximises S_1 subject to the condition that the system be viable. This solution is closely analogous to the ordinary solution in the F-theory. For, using the relations (14) and (15), we may write :

$$S_1 = x_3 - x_1 \quad \dots\dots\dots\dots\dots\dots\dots\dots\dots\dots\dots\dots\dots\dots\dots\dots (19a)$$

$$S_2 = S_2 (y_2, x_2) = S_2 (x_1, \zeta (y_3)) = 0 \quad \dots\dots\dots\dots\dots\dots\dots\dots\dots (19b)$$

$$S_3 = S_3 (y_3, x_3) = 0 \quad \dots\dots\dots\dots\dots\dots\dots\dots\dots\dots\dots\dots\dots\dots (19c)$$

where ζ is the function inverse to ξ. Solving (19b) for x_1 and (19c) for x_3 we get :

$$S_1 = x_3 (y_3) - x_1 (y_3) \quad \dots\dots\dots\dots\dots\dots\dots\dots\dots\dots\dots\dots\dots\dots (20)$$

Maximising (20) with respect to y_3, we find the solution that maximises the entrepreneur's profit. Equation (19b) takes the place of the usual production cost curve ; (19c) defines the total revenue curve—both on the assumption that the employee and the customer each receive an inducement just sufficient to keep them in the system.

Before we accept the analogy with the F-theory as complete, we must look more closely at the " cost curve " and " revenue curve " that we have derived. To examine this question, we may carry through the usual derivation of the solution for the F-theory. We do this first for the case of imperfect competition, using a special form of the relations (19).

Consider the system :

$$S_1 = y_1 - x_1 \quad \dots\dots\dots\dots\dots\dots\dots\dots\dots\dots\dots\dots\dots\dots\dots\dots (20a)$$

$$S_2 = y_2 - \psi_2 (x_2) \quad \dots\dots\dots\dots\dots\dots\dots\dots\dots\dots\dots\dots\dots\dots (20b)$$

$$S_3 = \phi_3 (y_3) - x_3 \dots\dots\dots\dots\dots\dots\dots\dots\dots\dots\dots\dots\dots\dots\dots (20c)$$

We define the wage rate (w) and the product price (p) by the identities :

$$w = y_2/x_2 ; \quad p = x_3/y_3 \quad \dots\dots\dots\dots\dots\dots\dots\dots\dots\dots\dots\dots\dots (21)$$

We assume that the entrepreneur fixes p, w, and x_2 so as to maximise his profit for a given demand curve for the product, and supply curve for labour.

To derive the demand curve we assume that the customer maximises S_3 with respect to y_3 for fixed p :

$$S_3 = \phi (y_3) - y_3 p \quad \dots\dots\dots\dots\dots\dots\dots\dots\dots\dots\dots\dots\dots\dots (22)$$

$$\frac{\partial S_3}{\partial y_3} = \phi'_3 - p = 0 \quad \dots\dots\dots\dots\dots\dots\dots\dots\dots\dots\dots\dots\dots\dots (23)$$

Similarly, to derive the supply curve we assume the employee maximises S_2 with respect to x_2 for fixed w :

$$S_2 = x_2 w - \psi_2(x_2) \dots \dots (24)$$

$$\frac{\partial S_2}{\partial x_2} = w - \psi'_2 = 0 \dots \dots (25)$$

Substituting (25) and (23) in (20a) we get a function of x_2 :

$$S_1 = \xi(x_2)\, \phi'_3 - x_2 \psi'_2 \dots \dots (26)$$

Maximising this with respect to x_2, we find :

$$\psi'_2 = \xi' \phi'_3 + \xi \phi''_3 \xi' - x_2 \psi''_2 \dots \dots (27)$$

Since, from the second order conditions for a maximum in (23) and (25), $\phi''_3 \leqslant 0, \psi''_2 \geqslant 0$, it follows that :

$$\psi'_2 \leqslant \xi' \phi'_3 \dots \dots (28)$$

On the other hand, if we follow the procedure of equations (16)–(18) to find the optimal solutions for the O-theory, we get :

$$\psi'_2 = \xi' \phi'_3 \dots \dots (29)$$

We conclude that the solution of the F-theory is an optimal solution in the sense of the O-theory only in case $\phi''_3 = 0, \psi''_2 = 0$. But in this case, ϕ'_3 and ψ'_2 are constants, say p^* and w^*, respectively, so that $\phi_3(y_3) = p^* y_3$ and $\psi_2(x_2) = w^* x_2$. Then equations (23) and (25) reduce to :

$$p = p^* \qquad \qquad w = w^* \dots \dots (30)$$

This is the case where at a given price the entrepreneur can sell any quantity of his product, and at a given wage employ any quantity of labour. It is the case, in short, of perfect competition.

We may summarise the results of the foregoing paragraphs in two propositions :

1. The F-theory solution, in the case of perfect competition, is identical with the particular O-theory solution that is optimal to the entrepreneur.

2. In the case of imperfect competition, the solution of the F-theory is not an optimal solution of the O-theory.

Let (S^*_1, S^*_2, S^*_3) be the satisfactions corresponding to the solution S^*, of the F-theory under imperfect competition ; and $(S^\dagger_1, S^\dagger_2, S^\dagger_3)$ the satisfactions corresponding to the solution $S^\dagger$, that is optimal to the entrepreneur in the O-theory. Then, since $S^\dagger_2 = S^\dagger_3 = 0$, either $S^*_1 < S^\dagger_1$, or one of the components S^*_2, S^*_3 must be negative. Hence if the solution S^* is viable, it yields the entrepreneur a smaller profit than the solution $S^\dagger$.

We see also that equations (19b) and (19c) are not identical with the cost curve of the F-theory. From (20) we have for the former :

$$y_2 = \psi_2(x_2) ; \; x_3 = \phi_3(y_3) \dots \dots (31)$$

while from (23) and (25), we have for the latter :

$$y_2 = x_2 \psi'_2(x_2) ; \; x_3 = y_3 \phi'_3(y_3) \dots \dots (32)$$

If we define $w^\dagger$ as y_2/x_2 where y_2 is given by (31), we have $w^\dagger = \psi_2/x_2$ while $w = \psi'_2$. Similarly $p^\dagger = \phi_3/y_3$, while $p = \phi'_3$. For this particular solution in the O-theory, wages and prices are proportional to the *average* utilities of labour to the employee and of the product to the customer, respectively ; while in the theory of the firm, wages and prices are proportional to *marginal* utilities.

Pittsburgh, Pennsylvania.   H. A. SIMON.

5.4

A FORMAL THEORY OF INTERACTION IN SOCIAL GROUPS

Herbert A. Simon *

Carnegie Institute of Technology

To a person addicted to applied mathematics, any statement in a non-mathematical work that contains words like "increase," "greater than," "tends to," constitutes a challenge. For such terms betray the linguistic disguise and reveal that underneath the words lie mathematical objects—quantities, orderings, sets—and hence the possibility of a restatement of the proposition in mathematical language. But what purpose, other than an aesthetic one, does such a restatement serve? In this paper I shall attempt to show, by means of a concrete example, how mathematization of a body of theory can help in the clarification of concepts, in the examination of the independence or non-independence of postulates, and in the derivation of new propositions that suggest additional ways of subjecting the theory to empirical testing.

The example we shall use is a set of propositions that constitutes a part of the theoretical system employed by Professor George C. Homans, in *The Human Group*,[1] to explain some of the phenomena that have been observed of group behavior. This particular example was selected for a number of reasons: first, although non-mathematical, it shows great sophistication in the handling of systems of interdependent variables; second, Professor Homans takes care with the operational definition of his concepts, and these concepts appear to be largely of a kind that can be measured in terms of cardinal and ordinal numbers; third, Professor Homans' model systematizes a substantial number of the important empirical relationships that have been observed in the behavior of human groups. Whether his theory, in whole or part, turns out to be correct or incorrect (and this is a question we shall not raise in the present paper), it will certainly receive careful attention in subsequent research on the human group.

THE SYSTEM: CONCEPTS AND POSTULATES

The system will be described in my own language. After I have defined the variables and set forth the postulates, I will discuss what I believe to be the relationship between the system and the language that Homans employs in his book.

The Variables. We consider a social group (a group of persons) whose behavior can be characterized by four variables, all functions of time:

* I am indebted, for stimulation, assistance, and suggestions in the formulation of this theory, to my colleagues in a research project on administrative centralization and decentralization sponsored at Carnegie Institute of Technology by the Controllership Foundation, and particularly to Professor Harold Guetzkow, who has worked closely with me at every stage of the theory formulation. Valuable help has also been received from Professor George C. Homans of Harvard University, and from seminars at Columbia University and the University of Chicago, and a session at the 1951 annual meetings of the American Sociological Society, where various portions of the paper were read and discussed.

[1] New York: Harpers, 1950.

I(t)—the intensity of *interaction* among the members;

F(t)—the level of *friendliness* among the members;

A(t)—the amount of *activity* carried on by members within the group;

E(t)—the amount of activity imposed on the group by the external environment (the "*external system*")

This particular set of variables includes most of those employed by Homans in the first part of his book (he adds others in his later chapters), and the underlined terms are the ones he uses. In this paper we will assume that operational definitions (Homans' or others) have been assigned to the variables, such that the behavior of a group at any moment in time can be measured in terms of the four real numbers I, F, A, and E. For our purposes, we need to make only two points clear about these operational definitions.

First, since the units in which such variables can be measured are somewhat arbitrary, we shall try to make use only of the ordinal properties of the measuring scales—the relations of greater or less—and, perhaps, of certain "natural" zero points.

Second, since the variables refer to the behavior of a plurality of human beings, they clearly represent averages or aggregates. For the interaction variable, I, let I_{ij} represent the number of interactions per day (or the time, per day, spent in interaction), of the ith member of the group with the jth member. Then we could define I as the average rate of interaction per member—i.e., as $1/n$ times the sum of I_{ij} over the whole group, where n is the number of members. Similarly, we could define F as the average friendliness between pairs of members; and A might be defined as the average amount of time spent per member per day in activity within the group.[2] Finally, E might be defined as the average

amount of time that would be spent per member per day in activity within the group if group members were motivated only by external pressures.[3]

The Postulates. We postulate three sets of dynamic relations among the variables, treating I(t), F(t) and A(t) as endogenous (dependent) variables whose values are determined within the system: while E(t) is an exogenous (independent) variable.

(1) The intensity of interaction depends upon, and increases with, the level of friendliness and the amount of activity carried on within the group. Stated otherwise, we postulate that interaction is produced, on the one hand, by friendliness, on the other, by the requirements of the activity pattern; and that these two causes of communication are additive in their effect. We will postulate, further, that the level of interaction adjusts itself rapidly—almost instantaneously—to the two variables on which it depends.

(2) The level of group friendliness will increase if the actual level of interaction is higher than that "appropriate" to the existing level of friendliness. That is, if a group of persons with little friendliness are induced to interact a great deal, the friendliness will grow; while, if a group with a great deal of friendliness interact seldom, the friendliness will weaken. We will postulate that the adjustment of friendliness to the level of interaction requires time to be consummated.

(3) The amount of activity carried on by the group will tend to increase if the actual level of friendliness is higher than that "appropriate" to the existing amount of activity, and if the amount of activity imposed externally on the group is higher than the existing amount of activity. We will postulate that the adjustment of the activity level to the "imposed" activity level and to the actual level of friendliness both require time for their consummation.

These three relations can be represented

---

[2] The concept of "activity within the group" might require rather sophisticated treatment. For example, time spent by a worker in daydreaming about his family or outside social relations might, ideally, be excluded from his activity within the group. For some purposes, we might wish to regard as "activity within the group" *uniformities* of behavior among group members—that is, the degree to which activity lies within the group might be measured by similarity of behavior. On this point, see Homans, *op. cit.*, pp. 119–121.

[3] This formulation reveals that the direct measurement of E might pose greater problems than the direct measurement of the other variables. In most cases, we would attempt to measure E indirectly in terms of the magnitude of the force producing E—in somewhat the same manner as the force of the magnetic field is sometimes measured by the strength of the current producing it. The problem is by no means insoluble, but we do not wish to deal with it in detail here.

by the following equations, where $\frac{dx}{dt}$ represents the derivatives of x with respect to time.

(1.1) $I(t) = a_1F(t) + a_2A(t)$

(1.2) $\frac{dF(t)}{dt} = b[I(t) - \beta F(t)]$

(1.3) $\frac{dA(t)}{dt} = c_1[F(t) - \gamma A(t)] + c_2[E(t) - A(t)]$

All constants in these equations are assumed to be positive.

If we look at equation (1.2), we see that βF may be regarded as the amount of interaction "appropriate" to the level, F, of friendliness. For if $I = \beta F$, then F will have no tendency either to increase or decrease. The reciprocal of the coefficient β, that is, $1/\beta$, might be called the "congeniality coefficient" since it measures the amount of friendliness that will be generated per unit of interaction.

Similarly, from equation (1.1) we see that a_1F may be regarded as the amount of interaction generated by the· level, F, of friendliness in the absence of any group activity. That is, if $A = 0$, then $I = a_1F$. Further, the coefficient a_2 measures the amount of interaction generated per unit of group activity in the absence of friendliness. Hence, a_1 and a_2 might be called "coefficients of interdependence."

Finally, from equation (1.3) we see that the reciprocal of the coefficient γ measures the amount of activity that is generated per unit of friendliness, in the absence of external pressure. We may call $1/\gamma$ a coefficient of "spontaneity." The remaining coefficients, b, c_1 and c_2, determine how rapidly the system will adjust itself if it starts out from a position of disequilibrium.

Relation to Homans' System. These equations, and their verbal interpretations, appear to represent with reasonable accuracy the larger part of the generalizations about the interrelations of these four variables which Professor Homans sets forth in Chapters 4 and 5 of his book.[4]

---

[4] See especially the italicized statements in *op. cit.*, pp. 102, 111, 112, 118, 120. The reader can perhaps best test the translation himself by reference to Professor Homans' text. In doing so, he should take due note of footnotes 2 and 3, above. Professor Homans has been kind enough to go over the equations (1.1)-(1.3) with me. He concludes that the mathematical treatment does not do violence to the meanings of his verbal statements, but

The next section of this paper will be devoted to an analysis of the system represented by equations (1)-(3). It should be emphasized again that this system is only a partial representation of the complete system of hypotheses proposed by Homans, and, of course, an even sketchier representation of reality. Furthermore, the assumption of linear relations in the equations is a serious oversimplification, which will be remedied in a later section of the paper. Nevertheless, the system incorporates several of the important relationships that might be hypothesized as holding among the four variables and which Homans found did, in fact, hold in the situations he investigated.

THE SYSTEM: DERIVATIONS FROM THE
POSTULATES

A number of well-known techniques may be applied to derive consequences from the system of postulates that could be tested by comparison with empirical data.

(1) The equations might be solved explicitly to give the time path the system would follow from any particular initial position. This presents no mathematical difficulties, since systems of linear differential equations with constant coefficients can be solved completely and explicitly. On the other hand, the solutions would be useful for prediction only if the constants of the equations were known or could be estimated. For this reason, the explicit solutions would seem to be of interest at a later stage in the development of measurement instruments and testing of the theory, and we will not dwell on them here.

(2) The equilibrium positions, if any, of the system might be obtained, and their properties examined. This would permit us to make certain predictions about the behavior of the system when it was in or near equilibrium.

(3) The conditions for stability of the equilibrium might be examined. Since a system that is in equilibrium will not generally remain there unless the equilibrium is stable, we will ordinarily be justified in using the conditions of stability in predicting the behavior of any system that is observed to remain in or near equilibrium.

that the equations do not capture all of the interrelations he postulates—that they tell the truth, but not the whole truth. With this later qualification I would concur.

(4) Starting with the assumptions of equilibrium and stability, we may be interested in predicting what will happen if the independent variables or the constants of the system are altered in magnitude—that is, what will be the new equilibrium position to which the system will move. This method, the method of "comparative statics," is one of the most powerful for deriving properties of a gross qualitative character that might be testable even with relatively crude data.

Our method, therefore, will be to derive first the conditions of equilibrium, next the conditions of stability, and finally the relations that can be obtained by applying the method of comparative statics.

Equilibrium. An equilibrium position is one in which the variables remain stationary. Hence the conditions of equilibrium can be found by setting dF/dt and dA/dt equal to zero in equations (1.2) and (1.3), respectively, and solving the three equations for I, F, and A in terms of E. Designating by I_o, F_o and A_o the equilibrium values corresponding to E_o, we find:

(1.4) $I_o = a_1 F_o + a_2 A_o$

(1.5) $0 = b(I_o - \beta F_o)$

(1.6) $0 = c_1(F_o - \gamma A_o) + c_2(E_o - A_o)$

Eliminating I_o from (1.5) by using (1.4), we get:

(1.7) $F_o = \dfrac{a_2}{\beta - a_1} A_o$

Substituting this value of F_o in (1.6) and solving for A_o, we get:

(1.8) $A_o = \left[\dfrac{c_2(\beta - a_1)}{(c_1\gamma + c_2)(\beta - a_1) - (c_1 a_2)} \right] E_o = \left[\dfrac{c_2(\beta - a_1)}{c_2(\beta - a_1) + c_1 \{ \gamma(\beta - a_1) - a_2 \}} \right] E_o$

whence:

(1.9) $F_o = \left[\dfrac{c_2 a_2}{(c_1\gamma + c_2)(\beta - a_1) - (c_1 a_2)} \right] E_o$

Stability of Equilibrium

To determine whether the equilibrium is stable, we consider the so-called "characteristic equation" associated with equations (1.2) and (1.3) after I has been eliminated by substitution from (1.1): [5]

(1.10) $\begin{vmatrix} -b(\beta - a_1) - \lambda & ba_2 \\ c_1 & -(c_1\gamma + c_2) - \lambda \end{vmatrix} = 0$

When expanded, this becomes:

(1.11) $\lambda^2 + \{ c_1\gamma + c_2 + b(\beta - a_1) \} \lambda + b \{ (\beta - a_1)(c_1\gamma + c_2) - a_2 c_1 \} = 0$

It is a well-known property of such dynamical systems that for stability the real parts of the roots of λ must be negative, and conversely, that if the real parts of the roots are negative, the system will be stable. By solving (1.11) for λ, this can be shown to imply:

(1.12) $c_1\gamma + c_2 + b(\beta - a_1) > 0$, and

(1.13) $(\beta - a_1)(c_1\gamma + c_2) - a_2 c_1 > 0$.

Since all constants are assumed positive, we obtain from (1.13) the requirement that:

(1.14) $\beta > a_1$

If (1.14) holds, (1.12) will, in turn, be automatically satisfied.

Hence (1.13) and (1.14) together give us necessary and sufficient conditions for stability. We proceed now to an interpretation of these conditions.

Stability condition (1.14) may be written:

(1.15) $\beta F_o > a_1 F_o$

That is, we require for stability that the amount of interaction (βF_o) *required to generate* the equilibrium level of friendliness be greater than the amount of communication ($a_1 F_o$) that would be *generated* by the equilibrium level of friendliness in the absence of any group activity. For if this were not so, (i.e., if $a_1 > \beta$) an initial level of friendliness, F_1, would produce interaction, $I_1 = a_1 F_1$, which would further increase the friendliness to $F_2 = I_1/\beta = \dfrac{a_1 F_1}{\beta} > F_1$, and we would get an ascending spiral such that the amount of friendliness and the amount of interaction would increase without limit:

$F_1 < F_2 < F_3 < \ldots < F_n$, and
$I_1 < I_2 < I_3 < \ldots < I_n$

We can show that the other stability condition (1.13), is required to prevent a similar ascending spiral between A and F.

Behavior of the System: Comparative Statics. The equalities and inequalities we have derived as conditions for equilibrium and stability of equilibrium enable us to deduce çertain propositions about how the

---

[5] The mathematical theory involved here is discussed in Paul A. Samuelson, *Foundations of Economic Analysis*, Cambridge: Harvard University Press, 1947, p. 271.

system will behave when its equilibrium is disturbed, assuming the equilibrium to be stable.

Equilibrium may be disturbed by a change in E, the task imposed on the group, or by changes in one or more of the coefficients of the system (e.g., an increase or decrease in a_2). We wish to predict how the variables of the system will respond to such a shift.

The change in the equilibrium value of A with a change of E can be determined from (1.8). Stability requires (by (1.14)) that the numerator of the right-hand side of (1.8) be positive, and (by (1.13)) that the denominator be positive. Hence:

$$(1.16) \quad \frac{dA_o}{dE_o} > 0$$

From (1.7), remembering (1.14), we get similarly:

$$(1.17) \quad \frac{dF_o}{dA_o} > 0, \text{ hence } \frac{dF_o}{dE_o} > 0$$

Finally, from (1.4), we get:

$$(1.18) \quad \frac{dI_o}{dE_o} = a_1 \frac{dF_o}{dE_o} + a_2 \frac{dA_o}{dE_o} > 0$$

We conclude that an increase in the activities required of the group by the external environment will increase (when equilibrium has been re-established) the amount of group activity, the amount of friendliness, and the amount of interaction. As E decreases toward zero, A, F and I will decrease toward zero. But this is precisely the hypothesis that Homans employs to explain social disintegration in Hilltown,[6] and to explain the difference in extension between the primitive and modern family.[7]

We ask next how large A_o will be in relation to E_o. From (1.8), in its second form, we see that the numerator on the right-hand side will be larger than the denominator if and only if:

$$(1.19) \quad \gamma(\beta - a_1) < a_2$$

If (1.19) holds, then, we will have $A_o > E_o$, otherwise $A_o \leqq E_o$. We will refer to a group satisfying condition (1.19) as one having *positive morale*. If the condition is not satisfied, we will say the group has *negative morale*.

What relations among the coefficients are conducive to positive morale? From (1.19),

[6] *Op. cit.*, pp. 356–362.
[7] *Op. cit.*, pp. 263–265.

we see that a_2 should be large, relative to the product of γ and $(\beta - a_1)$. But large a_2 means high interdependence, i.e., the group tasks are highly interrelated. From our previous interpretation of γ (i.e., that $1/\gamma$ measures spontaneity), we see that a high degree of spontaneity is conducive to positive morale—with large $1/\gamma$, or small γ, friendliness will tend to produce a relatively large amount of activity in addition to that required by the external environment.

As mentioned above, another condition conducive to positive morale is that $(\beta - a_1)$ be small: that there be a strong feedback from friendliness to more interaction to more friendliness. But we have seen that an approach to zero of $(\beta - a_1)$ means an approach to an unstable condition of the system (see equation (1.13)).

Now, from the stability condition (1.13), we know that a large value of $(\gamma c_1 + c_2)$ aids stability, but if we want γ small relative to a_2 for positive morale, we must depend on the ratio c_2/c_1 for stability. That is, under conditions of positive morale we require that the activity level, A, be more strongly influenced by the external demands than by the level of friendliness.

While we must be careful not to expect too much from a theory as highly simplified as this one, it may be interesting to note that the phenomenon of negative morale appears to be not unrelated to Durkheim's concept of *anomie*. In particular, a division of labor within a group that would result in little interrelationship of tasks (a_2 small) would, in our theory, be conducive to negative morale. This is a prediction that has received a considerable amount of substantiation from the Hawthorne studies and other empirical observations in industrial sociology.

We may inquire finally as to the time path whereby the system readjusts itself when it is disturbed from an initial equilibrium by a change in E_o. It can be shown that the roots of λ in (1.11) are real. This implies that the system will not oscillate, but will start out toward the new equilibrium at a rapid rate, approaching it asymptotically.

GENERALIZATION TO A NON-LINEAR SYSTEM

It is time now to relax the assumption of equations (1.1)—(1.3) that the relations among the variables of the system are linear. The reason for dwelling at length on the linear equations is that they can be regarded as an approximation to the more general equations of the non-linear system in the neighborhood of points of equilibrium.

Since we really do not have much empirical data as to the exact forms of the functions relating our variables, we shall strive in our treatment of the non-linear system to make as few assumptions as possible about these functions. The price we shall have to pay is to restrict ourselves largely to a graphical treatment and to the derivation of gross qualitative results. Nevertheless, in view of the roughness of the empirical observations we might hope to make, this restriction cannot be regarded as unduly serious at the present stage of development of the theory.

We will now assume our equations to be:

(2.1) $I = f(A, F)$

(2.2) $\dfrac{dF}{dt} = g(I, F)$

(2.3) $\dfrac{dA}{dt} = \psi(A, F ; E)$

where f, g, ψ are functions whose properties remain to be specified. If we replace I in (2.2) by its value as given by (2.1) we obtain, in place of (2.1)−(2.2) a new equation:

(2.4) $\dfrac{dF}{dt} = g(f(A,F),\ F) = \phi(A,F)$

where ϕ is again a function of unspecified form. Henceforth, we will work with the system comprised of equations (2.3)−(2.4) —two differential equations for the determination of F and A.

Our method will be graphical, based on the "phase diagram" of F and A.[8] Let us regard E, for the present, as a constant—a given parameter. Equation (2.3) gives us the time rate of change of A, and (2.4) the time rate of change of F, both as functions of F and A. Dividing the second by the first we get

$$df/dA = \dfrac{dF/dt}{dA/dt} = \phi(A,F)/\psi(A,F;E)$$

the rate of change of F relative to A for each pair of values of F and A. Now consider a graph (Figure 1) whose x-axis measures A, and whose y-axis measures F.

[8] On the method employed, see Alfred J. Lotka, *Elements of Physical Biology*, Baltimore: Williams and Wilkins, 1925, pp. 77–97, 143–151.

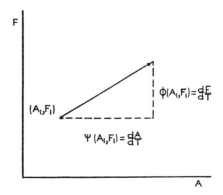

FIG. I

Through any point (A_1, F_1), draw a short line segment with slope $\phi/\psi = \dfrac{dF}{dA}$. Then this segment points along the path on which our system would begin to move if started from (A_1, F_1).

By drawing such a line segment for each point of the (A,F)-plane, and connecting these into continuous curves, we find the paths the system will follow from any initial positions to the subsequent position (and possibly to equilibrium). The collection of all such paths is commonly called the "direction field" of the system (see Figure 2).[9]

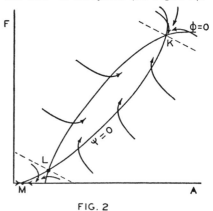

FIG. 2

[9] For a more detailed explanation of the construction of the direction field, see Lester R. Ford, *Differential Equations*, New York: McGraw-Hill, 1933, pp. 9–11. The direction field corresponding to the linear system of this paper is discussed and illustrated by Ford on pp. 48–52. His Figure 14, page 51, corresponds to the case of stable equilibrium.

Now consider the set of points

(2.5) $\dfrac{dA}{dt} = \psi(A,F;E) = 0$

at which A is not changing. Equation (2.5) will, in general define a curve in the (A,F)-plane. At any point on this curve, since ψ is zero and hence A is constant, but not F, the path of the system will be vertical (either upward or downward as $\phi > 0$ or $\phi < 0$, respectively).

Consider next the sets of points

(2.6) $\dfrac{dF}{dt} = \phi(A,F) = 0$

at which F is not changing. At all points on this curve, since ϕ is zero, the path of the system will be horizontal (either to right or left as $\psi > 0$ or $\psi < 0$, respectively).

At the point, or points, where (2.5) and (2.6) hold simultaneously—that is, where the two curves intersect—the system will be in stable or unstable equilibrium. The equilibrium will be stable if any path very close to the point of equilibrium leads toward it and unstable if any path very close to it leads away from it. (This definition of stability can be shown to be equivalent to a suitable generalization of the analytic definition we employed in the linear case.) Figure 2 illustrates the direction field and the curves $\psi = 0$ and $\phi = 0$. There are two points of equilibrium, K and L. Equilibrium at K is stable, at L unstable.

It should be remarked that if the system starts off at any point *above* the lower of the two broken lines in the figure, it will, in time, approach the point of stable equilibrium, K; while if the system starts off below this broken line, F and A will ultimately decline and approach the point M—the group will, in fact, dissolve.

Now the paths taken by the system from various initial points will depend on the locations of the curves $\psi = 0$ and $\phi = 0$, and their points of intersection. The particular shapes and positions of the curves, as drawn in Figure 2, represent empirical assumptions as to the shapes of the functions ψ and ϕ. What can we legitimately assume about these functions? To answer this question we must ascertain the empirical significance of the two curves $\psi = 0$ and $\phi = 0$.

Equation (3.3) says, in effect, that for a given amount of external pressure (a given value of E) the amount of activity undertaken by the group (A) will tend to adjust itself to the level of friendliness (F). Our empirical assumption is that, given E, greater friendliness will tend to produce greater activity. If this is so, then the equilibrium value of A must increase as F increases; that is, the curve $\psi = 0$ must have a positive slope. We now make the second empirical assumption: that there is a saturation phenomenon—that as F continues to increase, A will increase only at a diminishing rate. If this is so, the curve $\psi = 0$ must be concave upward as we have drawn it. In the particular case illustrated in Figure 2, it is assumed that E is sufficiently great so that there will be some activity even in the absence of friendliness. This is represented by the fact that the curve cuts the x-axis to the right of the origin. Later, we will consider the case also where this condition does not hold.

Equation (2.4) says that the amount of friendliness in the group (F) will tend to adjust itself to the amount of group activity (A). Again we assume that greater activity will tend to produce greater friendliness; hence that the curve $\phi = 0$ must have a positive slope. If we now assume that this mechanism is also subject to saturation, the curve must be concave downward. Finally, we assume that unless the activity is above a certain minimum value there is no tendency at all for friendliness to develop ($\phi = 0$ cuts the x-axis to the right of origin).

In the particular case shown, $\phi = 0$ cuts the x-axis to the right of $\psi = 0$. If this were not so, the point L would disappear and the system would move toward the stable equilibrium, K, from *any* initial point, including the origin. We will consider this case later. In the particular case shown, $\psi = 0$ is sufficiently far to the right that it intersects $\phi = 0$. If this were not so, the system would move toward the origin from *any* initial point. This case also will be considered later.

Finally, it should be mentioned that the particular assumptions we have made about the curves do not depend in any essential way upon the precise indexes used to measure F and A. For any given scale used to measure F or A, we can substitute another scale, provided only that the second scale has the same zero point as the first and does not reverse the *direction* of change (i.e., that we do not have $F_1 > F_2$ on the first scale but $F'_1 < F'_2$ for corresponding situations measured on the second). To be more precise, our concavity properties may be altered but not the order or character of the equilibrium points or the presence or absence of the region below the lower broken line. Since the conclusions we shall draw depend only on these properties of the graph, a change in the index employed cannot affect our results.

Suppose now that we begin with the system in equilibrium at K, and progressively reduce E, the external pressure to activity. A reduction in E may be assumed empirically to reduce (through the mechanism of equation (2.3)) the equilibrium value of A associated with each value of F—i.e., to move the curve $\psi = 0$ to the left. In the simplest case (in first approximation) we may assume that the shape of the curve is unchanged. Then, as $\psi = 0$ moves to the left, its intersection, K, with $\phi = 0$ will move downward and to the left along $\phi = 0$. We have shown:

Proposition 2.1. As E is decreased the equilibrium levels of A and F will be decreased.

This proposition also held in our linear system.

As $\psi = 0$ continues to move to the left (continued reduction in E) the two curves will eventually intersect at a single point of tangency. Let us call the value of E corresponding to this position of tangency E_T. As E is reduced below E_T, the two curves will no longer intersect and all paths of the direction field will lead to the x-axis and, if $\psi = 0$ now intersects with the y-axis, the system will come to rest at the origin. We have shown:

Proposition 2.2. As E is decreased below some critical value, E_T, F will go to zero; and for some sufficiently small value of E (equal to or less than E_T depending on the location of the intersection of $\psi(A,F;E_T)$ with the x-axis) A will go to zero.

Here we find, in the non-linear case, a new phenomenon—a dissolution of the group. It might be supposed that if a group has been dissolved by reducing E below E_T it can be restored by again increasing E to E_T. This does not follow. For if the system is initially at the origin, its path will lead

toward K only if $\psi = 0$ intersects the x-axis to the right of $\phi = 0$. But the smallest value of E for which this condition holds is obviously greater than E_T. From this follows:

Proposition 2.3. The level of E required to bring a group into existence is greater than the minimum value, E_T, required to prevent the group, once formed, from dissolution.

To illustrate Proposition 2.3 we show, in Figure 3, the path that will be followed by F and A when E is (1) reduced from some initial value, E_K, to E_T, (2) then to some lower value, E_L, (3) then increased to E_0, where $\psi = 0$ intersects the origin, (4) finally increased to E_M where $\psi = 0$ intersects the x-axis just to the right of $\phi = 0$. In the descending portion of the path, the decrease in F lags behind the decrease in A; while in the ascending portion of the path the increase in F again lags behind the increase in A. Hence the whole path forms a loop in the counter-clockwise direction in the (A,F)-plane.

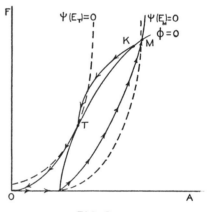

FIG. 3

Notice also that the system remains at rest at the origin so long as E is below E_0 and that A increases, but not F, as E increases from E_0 to E_M.

In the linear model we studied the effects upon the equilibrium values of A and F of certain shifts in the parameters, a_1, a_2, γ, and β of the system. With E fixed, an increase in interdependence of tasks (increase in a_1 and a_2), an increase in congeniality (decrease in β) and an increase in spontaneity (decrease in γ), within the limits imposed by the stability conditions, all resulted in an increase in the equilibrium values of A and F.

In the non-linear model an increase in interdependence of tasks or an increase in congeniality would be represented by a shift upward of the curve $\phi=0$; an increase in spontaneity would be represented by a clockwise rotation of the curve $\psi=0$ about its intersection with the x-axis. In all cases, if we began from a position of equilibrium, the new equilibrium values of A and F would be larger than the initial values.

SOME APPLICATIONS OF THE MODEL

While the model described here was suggested by Homans' analysis of behavior in *The Human Group*, we have attempted to present only part of his system: in particular we have omitted reference to phenomena of hostility, and to interpersonal differentiation (kinship and leadership). On the other hand, the mathematical model is capable of application to some situations that lie outside Homans' analysis. In this section we shall discuss briefly a few of these.

(1) *Formation of Cliques*. Define variables I_1, A_1, F_1, and E_1 to refer to behavior in a specified group, G_I; and I_2, A_2, F_2 and E_2 to refer to behavior in a group, G_{II}, which is a subgroup ("clique") within G_I. Then we might postulate equations of the form:

$$(3.1) \quad \frac{dA}{dt} = \psi_1(A_1, F_1, A_2; E_1)$$

$$(3.2) \quad dF_1/dt = \Phi_1(A_1, F_1)$$

$$(3.3) \quad dA_2/dt = \psi_2(A_2, F_2, A_1; E_2)$$

$$(3.4) \quad dF_2/dt = \Phi_2(A_2, F_2)$$

These equations are similar in form to (2.3) and (2.4) except for the presence of the "coupling" variables: A_2 in (3.1) and A_1 in (3.3). The meaning of this coupling is that activity within the clique (A_2) is assumed to interfere with and depress activity in the larger group (A_1) and activity within the larger group (A_1) is assumed to interfere with clique activity (A_2). We might also have further complicated the model by adding coupling terms to (3.2) and (3.4) ("conflict of loyalties").

The behavior of the system (3.1) to (3.4) can be studied as follows. We take E_1 and E_2 as fixed. Then for any given value of A_2, we can set (3.1) and (3.2) equal to

zero and find the corresponding equilibrium value, A_1^*, of A_1. This value, A_1^*, will depend on A_2, and, under our assumptions will decrease as A_2 increases. Similarly, from (3.3) and (3.4) we can find the equilibrium value, A_2^* of A_2 for each value of A_1. A position of equilibrium of the whole system will be found at the intersection of the two curves $A_1^*=A_1^*(A_2)$ and $A_2^*=A_2^*(A_1)$ in the plane whose x-axis represents A_1 and whose y-axis represents A_2. If the two curves do not intersect, then the clique and the group cannot coexist in equilibrium. Even if the curves intersect, the equilibrium may be unstable, but we cannot here go into the exact conditions of stability.

(2) *Competition of Groups*. Instead of a clique within a group we might have two groups competing for the membership of a single individual. In this case, the variables A_1, F_1, I_1, E_1 would refer to the intensity of his activity in the first group; A_2, F_2, I_2, E_2 to the intensity of his activity in the second group. We can then proceed exactly as in the first case.

(3) *Activity of an Individual*. The variables in equations (2.3) and (2.4) need not be interpreted as group activity. Instead, A might be interpreted as the amount of time per day an individual devotes to *any* particular activity, F as the amount of satisfaction he obtains from the activity, E as the pressure on him to engage in the activity. In this case we might want to make different assumptions as to the shapes of the curves, $\phi=0$ and $\psi=0$ in the phase diagram than in the previous cases, but the general approach is the same. Similarly the model of equations (3.1)—(3.4) might be interpreted to refer to an individual's distribution of attention between two activities.

(4) *Regulatory Enforcement*. Still another application of models of this general class would be to the phenomena associated with the enforcement of a governmental regulation (e.g., gasoline rationing). Here A would be interpreted as the actual degree of conformity to the regulation, F as the social pressure to conform, E as the effect of formal enforcement activity. The reader may find it of some interest to translate the theorems we have previously derived into this new interpretation.

CONCLUSION

In this paper we have constructed a mathematical model that appears to translate with tolerable accuracy certain propositions asserted by Homans to hold for behavior in human groups. We have examined at some length what assumptions the model requires and what further propositions can be deduced from it. In particular, we have seen that it offers an explanation for some of the commonly observed phenomena relating to the stability and dissolution of groups. In the last section we have shown that models of this general class can be applied to a rather wide range of behavioral phenomena beyond those originally examined.

We do not imply from this that the psychological mechanisms involved in all these situations are identical. The underlying similarity appears to be of a rather different character. In all of these situations there are present: (a) an external (positive or negative) motivational force toward some activity, and (b) a secondary "internal" motivational force induced by the activity itself. It is the combined effect of two such motivational forces that produces in each case phenomena of the sort we have observed. And especially when the relations are not linear (and the non-linear must be supposed to be the general case), "persistent" and "gregarious" patterns of behavior can result.

5.5

FRAMEWORK OF A THEORY OF THE FIRM

Herbert A. Simon

APPENDIX B

COMMENTS BY HERBERT A. SIMON

The main purpose of this report is not to propose a theory of the firm but rather to sketch some lines of research that may in time lead to such a theory. But research is a bootstrap operation. Our initial conceptions and theories determine the direction of our investigations, and the results of these in turn cause us to reformulate our theories.

The "framework" of Chapter 2 is one that regards the firm, for the most part, as a singular rather than a plural actor. This is evident both in the central role attributed to the "command," and in the conception of the firm as something that "acts" in relation to an environment. Given this conception of the firm, it appears quite natural that in seeking to understand the business enterprise the overt actions of firms should be the major focus of research. If we examine Chapter 3, we see that this is precisely where the analysis leads.

Now in employing such a framework I think we need to take special care lest we again create for ourselves the very difficulties that have plagued the traditional theory of the firm. The phenomena that the traditional theory of the firm has had no success in explaining are precisely those arising from the fact that a business enterprise is made up of many interacting flesh-and-blood human beings instead of a single profit-maximizing entrepreneur. If we wish to explain these phenomena, we need to be careful not to recreate the mythical entrepreneur either in the form of a "command" or by a personalization of the firm itself.

Let me try to sketch briefly my alternative formulation of the framework and the directions in which my formulation would channel research. In my attempts to formulate a theory of the firm, I find that it tends to divide into two large parts: (1) the explanation of the motivations that induce various groups to participate as customers, employees, owners, etc.—i.e., to assume their "roles"; (2) the explanation of the behavior of the full-time participants—employees and executives—during the period in which they have accepted participation. There are interactions, of course, between the two parts of the theory; but in first approximation I believe they can and should be separated for two reasons: (a) individuals generally view their behavior in relation to the firm in one or the other of these frames of reference, but seldom in both simultaneously; (b) agreement of an employee to join an organization is essentially agreement to accept a role, i.e., to view his behavior while he is in the organization in the second frame of reference. This seems to me the crucial property of the authority relationship, and the property that gives formal organizations their important idiosyncratic characteristics.

If we divide the problem in this particular way, there are several consequences for the organization of research. First, we would probably put substantially more emphasis on research areas relating to internal conditions than Bowen does. It is precisely because the explanation of internal conditions is essential to the prediction of overt behavior that we are driven to look inside the firm. In particular, I would place a high priority on research directed at obtaining a highly detailed and precise picture of the processes that are involved in decision making in organizations.

Second, the approach suggested here would tend to define research problems in terms of the psychological mechanisms and processes involved rather than in economic categories. If, for example, one wished to understand how decisions are made in the face of uncertainty about the future, almost any business function —finance, marketing, production, or any other—would provide relevant situations for investigation. Since I have elaborated on these matters elsewhere,[1] I will not try to set forth in detail here the categories that seem most fruitful for the analysis of the decision-making process.

Any preference for Bowen's emphasis or the one suggested here will depend, I think, partly on our research objectives. Bowen speaks primarily as an economist who would like to see a more satisfactory theory of the firm because such a theory is needed for economic analysis. My position is that of one who is interested in understanding human behavior in organizations and who sees in the business enterprise one of the important types of organizations in our society. But more important than the difference in emphasis suggested by these goals is the existence of a large area of human behavior that economists, organizational theorists, and other social scientists need to understand. This common area of interest brought together the group of scholars, with the most diverse professional backgrounds, who make up the Committee on Business Enterprise Research.

Bowen has indicated somewhat more fully why economists should be interested in this area than why it is significant for other social scientists. I should like to suggest one reason—certainly not the only one—why human behavior in organizations may be expected to supply particularly high grade ore for psychological and

1 "Comments on the Theory of Organizations," *American Political Science Review,* 46:1130–1139 (December 1952).

sociological research. Social psychology has made remarkable progress in the past several decades, but this progress has related much more to an understanding of attitudes, motivations, and emotions than to an understanding of rational and cognitive processes. The psychology of human thinking and human learning is still largely individual psychology. Now if the business enterprise is not the completely rational, profit-maximizing entity that it was at one time supposed to be, still it is fair to characterize a large part of the behavior that goes on in the business enterprise as intendedly rational. If the entrepreneur does not always maximize profit, it may be that he does not want to, but it is more likely that he cannot—that he has neither the computational ability nor the information that would be required for profit maximization in the traditional sense. Hence in organizations there is opportunity to see how human beings handle problems that are too complex to be grasped completely or solved exactly. And since decision making in organizations requires a great deal of communication, there is better opportunity to see precisely what is involved in the problem-solving and decision-making processes than if these were taking place inside an individual human brain. If these conjectures are correct, the study of human behavior in organizations should prove to be highly fruitful for learning more about the complex problem-solving processes.[2]

Speculations about research methodology are not exempt from the law of diminishing marginal utility. Whatever theory of the firm is taken as a starting point, we will almost certainly exhaust our research resources long before we run out of fruitful problems for investigation. The best we can hope for from a theory of the firm in the present state of knowledge is that it be productive enough of research suggestions to guarantee its own obsolescence in a short time.

[2] My views as to the nature of rational decision-making within the limits of human capabilities are set forth in "A Behavioral Model of Rational Choice," *Quarterly Journal of Economics*, 69:99–118 (February 1955).

5.6
The Compensation of Executives[1]

HERBERT A. SIMON, Graduate School of Industrial Administration

Carnegie Institute of Technology

In a recent analysis of the available data on the compensation of business executives, David R. Roberts (4) has shown that the compensation of the highest paid official in a company is related to size of company and to virtually no other variables (in particular, not to profit) after the effect of size has been partialed out. Specifically, the relation that Professor Roberts finds in his data is a logarithmic one. Let C be total annual compensation of the highest paid official, S, annual dollar sales, and a and k constants. Then the observed relation is:

[1] $$C = kS^a$$

or, on a logarithmic scale:

[2] $$\log C = a \log S + k'.$$

Fitting the data to equation [2] by the method of least squares, we find a value of about .37 for a. The data are homoscedastic on the logarithmic scale.

Professor Roberts discusses the implications of these data for the theory of executive compensation and advances an explanation based on marginal productivity theory. In the present paper I should like to develop an alternative theory of a more sociological character. This explanation has the advantage that, unlike the one based on the marginal productivity theory, it predicts not only a positive relation between size of company and compensation, but also the logarithmic form of the function and the approximate value of the coefficient a.

Businesses, like all large-scale organizations, are roughly pyramidal in form, because of the hierarchical structure induced by the authority relation. Each executive has a certain number, n, of subordinates at the level immediately below him, and this number varies within only moderate limits in a given company, and even among a number of companies. At executive levels it is seldom less than three, and seldom more than ten, and usually lies within narrower bounds—particularly if we take averages over all executives in an organization at a given level.

There is a widely accepted attitude in industry that an appropriate dif-

[1] This work has been carried out in the program of organizational studies at the Graduate School of Industrial Administration under a research grant from the Ford Foundation.

ferential in salary exists between an executive and his immediate subordinates, measured not in absolute terms but as a ratio. That is, an executive's salary "should" be b times the salary of his immediate subordinates, no matter what his level.[2] Again, the value of b undoubtedly varies from situation to situation, but one can find figures quoted in the range of 1.25 to 2. While we would expect to encounter instances of larger or smaller ratios, averages can be expected to be relatively stable.

Now, consider an idealized organization in which each executive has exactly n immediate subordinates, and in which he receives a salary b times the salary of his immediate subordinates. Let S be the number of executives in the organization[3] and let L be the number of levels in the executive hierarchy. Then, we have the following relation between S and L:

$$[3] \qquad S = 1 + n + n^2 + \cdots + n^{L-1} = \frac{n^L - 1}{n - 1} \simeq \frac{n^L}{n - 1}$$

Now suppose that executives at the first, or lowest, level are brought in at a salary of A. Again, if this lowest level represents recent college graduates, there is good reason to suppose that there is a recruitment salary that does not vary widely from one position or one company to another. We then have the following equation to determine C, the salary of the top executive:

$$[4] \qquad C = Ab^{L-1} = Bb^L$$

Taking logarithms in [3], we get:

$$[5] \qquad \log S = L \log n + \text{const.}$$

Similarly, from [4] we get:

$$[6] \qquad \text{Log } C = L \log b + \text{const.}$$

Eliminating L between [5] and [6], we find:

$$[7] \qquad \log C = \frac{\log b}{\log n} \log S + \text{const.}$$

But equation [7] becomes identical with equation [2] if we take:

$$[8] \qquad a = (\log b)/(\log n)$$

[2] This "rule of proportionality" receives prominent attention in most discussions of executive compensation, and its correctness as a norm is accepted more or less as a truism. See for example reference (3), and reference (2, pp. 319–321).

[3] In the data we have available, the size of companies is measured by their dollar sales. We assume here an exact proportionality between dollar sales and total number of executives—which, of course, will hold only in an average sense. For this reason, we use the variable S indiscriminately to refer to both measures of company size.

We can test equation [8] further by seeing whether the observed value, .37, for a is consistent with reasonable values of b and n. Equation [8] defines b as a function of n, and vice versa, so that a whole set of possible pairs of values of the latter two variables will be compatible with a given value of a. We could have, for example, $n = 7$, $b = 2$, $n = 5$, $b = 1.75$, or $n = 3$, $b = 1.5$. All these pairs lie within the range we have postulated.[4]

There is one small additional piece of confirming evidence for our hypothesis. In 1936, General Motors made available data on the number of executives at various compensation levels. H. T. Davis (1), p. 49, found that this distribution could be described by the equation:

[9] $$C' = mN^{-.33}$$

where N is the number of executives receiving compensation C', and where m is a constant.

Under our previous assumptions, the number of persons at L' levels from the top is:

[10] $$N(L') = n^{L'-1}$$

From the proportionality assumption, the compensation, C' of persons at this level is:

[11] $$C'(L') = Mb^{1-L'}$$

Taking logarithms, and eliminating L' between [10] and [11], we get:

[12] $$\log C' = -\frac{\log b}{\log n} \log N + \text{const.}$$

which becomes identical with the logarithm of [9] if we set $(\log b)/(\log n) = a = .33$. This new estimate of a is not very different from that obtained from the regression of salaries on size of company.

SUMMARY

In summary, I have proposed a theory of executive compensation that assumes that salaries are determined by requirements of internal "consistency" of the salary scale with the formal organization and by norms of proportionality between salaries of executives and their subordinates. Three mechanisms are postulated: (a) economic determination, through competition, of the salaries at the lowest executive levels where new em-

---

[4] It is worth observing that if we try to estimate n and b directly in a particular firm, we will find the notion of "level" somewhat ambiguous, and will have difficulty distinguishing "levels" from "half-levels." However, any errors we make in estimating n will lead to proportional errors in our estimates of b, so that the ratio of $\log b$ to $\log n$ will be only slightly affected. For this reason, the test of our theory does not depend in any critical way upon the definition of level we employ.

ployees are hired from outside the organization; (b) social determination of a norm for the "steepness" of organizational hierarchies (usually called the span of control); and (c) social determination of a norm for the ratio of an executive's salary to the salaries of his immediate subordinates. Where these mechanisms operate, a relation will exist between the salaries of top executives and the sizes of their companies that matches very well with the observed relation. Moreover, if we take values that appear reasonable for the norms (b) and (c), we obtain a prediction of the slope of the relation between salary and company size that is in good quantitative agreement with the empirical data. Further, the same parameter values are obtained from data on the frequency distribution of executive salaries in a single company.

If the proposed theory is correct, it calls into question the usual economic explanation of compensation—that the executive is paid at a rate roughly equal to his marginal contribution to company profits. While the present theory is consistent with a positive correlation between compensation and ability, only an improbable coincidence would bring about equality between salaries determined by the mechanism described here and salaries determined by the marginal productivity mechanism. Hence, it would appear that the distribution of executive salaries is not unambiguously determined by economic forces, but is subject to modification through social processes that determine the relevant norms.

Manuscript received: August 1, 1956
Revised manuscript received: August 20, 1956
    Herbert A. Simon
    Graduate School of Industrial Administration
    Carnegie Institute of Technology
    Pittsburgh 13, Pennsylvania

REFERENCES

1. Davis, H. T., *The Theory of Econometrics*, Bloomington, Ind.: The Principia Press, 1941.
2. Koontz, H., and C. O'Donnell, *Principles of Management*, New York: McGraw-Hill, 1955.
3. Patton, A., "Current Practices in Executive Compensation," *Harvard Business Review*, 1951, vol. 29, no. 1, pp. 56–64.
4. Roberts, D. R., "A General Theory of Executive Compensation Based on Statistically Tested Propositions," *Quarterly Journal of Economics*, 1956, 20, 270–294.

5.7
Decision Making and Planning

by Herbert Simon

Graduate School of Industrial Administration, Carnegie Institute of Technology

In the construction and organization of a city, as in the design and organizing of industries into a coordinated economy, it is possible to fit individual decisions together to create a pattern through a highly decentralized decision-making process. This process relies largely on individuals pursuing their own interests to make the component decisions. We know that in some areas of human activity this is a satisfactory method of doing business.

The mere fact that something has gotten itself organized does not mean that it is necessarily good or that we like the organization that has resulted; however, anything we propose to do about the city, any way which we propose to modify the design has to be accomplished against the background of a highly decentralized decision-making system. We are not in the position where there are just a few dials which control the planning

188

process. The planner is playing a far more complicated game than the architect. The architect can determine the details as soon as he can get the contractor to read his blueprints and the client to agree. These are minor problems compared to the consensus goal of the urban planner.

Decentralized decision-making has further consequence. Whenever we make decisions through our central powers to modify the pattern of the city, the hundreds and thousands of other decision-makers, who are pursuing their own interests, will respond to the situation created by our planning decisions. For example, planners may provide new transportation facilities, but as a result of the new facilities, the community wants to carry out different activities because they are responding to the new facilities. People in any metropolitan area have a capacity for creating problems at least as fast as we have for solving them.

There are two difficulties of a theory of urban planning which considers it a process in which you lay out a design of the city and then you take the action which will implement that design. First, nobody has really asked you to design a city. At best, they have given you certain very limited powers to modify the design. Secondly, when you do intervene to modify the city, the people in that city, who control the other variables, are going to react to your decision. As a result, any adequate approach to city planning and decision-making has to substitute this kind of dynamic notion of the planning process for the notion of a static city plan or city design. This does not mean that the design does not play a role in a city planning, but it will have to play a much more complicated and sophisticated role than it has in the past.

We live in a culture in which it is appropriate to

189

look to the future, to think about the future, and to act today with a view to the future. I am not really disagreeing with this point of view, but I am saying that the only decisions we really make, ought to make, or ought to be worried about making, are the decisions for what we are going to do *now*. When we plan for a city, I think we have to ask how far we want to carry our visualization of the future. There are many things about the future that are completely irrelevant in the present. I do not mean that all decisions are only decisions for the present. There are certain decisions that are either absolutely or relatively irrevocable. Many of the decisions with which city planners are concerned have a certain irrevocability about them. One of the reasons why planning activities tend to be preoccupied with the physical aspects of the plan is that the decisions we make about the physical plan are the least reversible parts of the plan.

I do not want to overemphasize the relation between the need for looking toward the future and the tangibility of the things about which you make your decisions, but in our planning efforts we need to make some decisions about our planning horizon. One of the criticisms that can be directed against the master planning activity of the past is that planners expended a great deal of energy predicting and estimating things that really didn't have any bearing on what actual projects were to be undertaken in the future. Ordinarily, the amount of effort we have available for planning is not unlimited. As a result it is necessary to be sophisticated about the things that we carry out to the fourth decimal place.

I can provide a striking example of this point from a field quite separate from city planning. Since before World War I, the United States military departments

190

have been prepared for every war with a set of rather complete mobilization plans. In the two World Wars, these mobilization plans were largely unused because the plans were conceived as specific and definite patterns of activity which would be undertaken in an emergency. If you ask yourself what kind of a mobilization plan would be likely to have influence on governmental action during an emergency, I think you would conclude that the plan should explore the central issues of organizing a nation for a wartime economy, should digest out of this analysis some basic principles about methodology, and should attempt to train a large number of people to understand these principles with the hope that some of them would be among those who would do the actual organizing and planning during a subsequent emergency.

In contrast to mobilization for war, city planning, and the execution of city planning, is not normally accomplished under emergency planning pressures, but is accomplished with the participation of a large number of people of whom the professionals are only a small fraction. Planning is completed with the enlistment of extensive public support and understanding; therefore, the preparation of detailed and specific plans constitutes only a small part of the planning effort. A large part of planning must be devoted to the determination of a few guiding principles and the dissemination of these principles to key figures who may be involved in providing a basis of public support and public understanding for the implementation of the plan. In the past, we have been more successful in learning how to create detailed plans than in learning how to communicate some of the basic objectives and goals to influential members of the community with the expectation that

191

if they understood the goals, the eventual product would be reasonable and desirable.

The professional decision-maker, in city planning or in any field where he is in the role of technical adviser to a consumer, is in a position where, through his planning and projecting activities, he can propose alternatives. He can suggest new ways of building a city. He doesn't simply select out of a kit of existing designs the one that he thinks is going to be the best for the city. His job is to formulate alternatives which have not been proposed previously. Any theory of decision-making, which would be relevant to the city planning process, would have to insure that alternatives are generated, so that the professional planners and the opinion leaders could decide among meaningful alternatives.

Social science theories of decision-making have been weak and inadequate in failing to recognize the very large role that has to be played by the professional planner in creating images of cities for the contemplation and consideration of the opinion leaders who must make decisions related to the selected image.

In closing, I would like to refer to the development of technical procedures in the decision-making art which has occurred in the past decade. These techniques promise to contribute a great deal to the power of the designer in any complicated field. For example, operations research techniques have been applied to the design of highways and to problems of traffic congestion. Operations research enlarges the range of technical matters that the planner can encompass in his plan and the complexity of the situation with which he must deal, but I do not think that the new techniques will fundamentally affect the relationship between the decision-making process and city planning.

192

5.8

INVITED LECTURE

NEW DEVELOPMENTS IN THE THEORY OF THE FIRM*

By Herbert A. Simon

Carnegie Institute of Technology

Economics has often been defined as the study of the allocation of scarce resources. Shubik has observed that the definition is so broad as to fit psychiatry about as well as economics. In spite of his stricture, which is probably right, I shall use this very broad definition to delimit the area of my remarks. I shall have something to say about both the normative aspects—the optimal allocation of resources—and the positive—the processes whereby resources actually are allocated. There are many well-known reasons why neither of these two aspects can easily be discussed without some attention to the other.

Economics and Administration. Economics (or psychiatry, if we accept Shubik's observation) is not the only science that claims an interest in resource allocation. A standard, often quoted definition of public administration reads:[1]

> Public administration is the management of men and materials in the accomplishment of the purposes of the state. . . . The objective of public administration is the most efficient utilization of the resources at the disposal of officials and employees.

If we delete the word "public" and substitute "firm" for "state," we arrive at a statement that could serve very well as a definition of normative microeconomics.

In international law, sweeping territorial claims are only made good by effective occupation. Similarly, definitions set the boundaries of a science only if they spell out the concepts it actually uses, the tools of analysis it has developed, and the knowledge it has attained. When we come to describe economics and administration, respectively, in these more specific terms, we soon see that they occupy very different territories within the general domain of resource allocation.

Mechanisms for Resource Allocation. As a general rule, economics and administration have limited their investigations to particular, and distinct, classes of mechanisms and processes for resource allocation. Economics discovered the institution of the market, the price mech-

---

*I have borrowed freely from a forthcoming study, *The Behavioral Theory of the Firm*, by my colleagues Richard W. Cyert and James G. March, and have benefited also from their comments on earlier drafts of this paper.

[1] Leonard D. White, *Introduction to the Study of Public Administration* (Macmillan, 1926), p. 2.

1

anism as a market-regulating process, and marginal analysis as a means of calculation. Administration discovered the institution of the formal organization, the mechanisms of authority and interpersonal influence to secure co-ordination, and planning as a means of decision making. The business firm became the boundary—I am tempted to say, the no man's land—between economics and administration. In our society—and perhaps even more generally in Western society of the last century—market mechanisms have been largely responsible for allocating resources among firms and among sectors of the economy, while authority and influence mechanisms have been largely responsible for allocating resources within firms.

To these two classes of allocative mechanisms we can add two more: democratic political processes and bargaining, which have received some attention in both economics and administration.[2] Viewing these four mechanisms as functional equivalents, all concerned with resource allocation, raises all sorts of possibilities for investigation, and suggests numerous hypotheses, both normative and descriptive, about allocation. It also suggests a possible framework for classifying and interpreting the developments that have been taking place in the theory of the firm.

For example, we may consider explaining allocation in oligopolistic industries by bargaining rather than classical market mechanisms, as Galbraith, Shubik, and others have done. Conversely, we may pursue Anthony Downs's path of interpreting political behavior in terms of a generalized marginal analysis. We may seek parallels between the problems of control over political and administrative leaders by voters in a political democracy, and control over boards of directors and management by stockholders in a corporation. We may examine alternative arrangements for the joint use of prices and administrative controls to allocate resources in a wartime economy; or the consequences of using internal prices and divisional balance sheets to manage large multiproduct corporations.

Much of what is new in the theory of the firm has come from viewing allocation broadly, and from experimenting with the descriptive and normative application of the several allocative mechanisms outside the realms where they were initially discovered and employed.

Prospectus. In my remarks I am going to describe developments in the theory of the firm under two main headings: first, developments arising out of the vigorous activity since the second World War in management science and operations research; second, developments

[2] Robert A. Dahl and Charles E. Lindblom, in *Politics, Economics, and Welfare* (Harper, 1953), organize their analysis of resource allocation in terms of these four major types of processes: the price system, hierarchy (organization), polyarchy (democracy), and bargaining.

arising out of descriptive, positive research on human behavior in organizations.

In each of these areas of work—management science and organization theory—I shall comment on what the new developments imply (1) for our theoretical models of the business firm, (2) for our understanding of allocative mechanisms, and (3) for techniques of investigating behavior in the business firm.

Finally, I shall take the liberty of adding a brief epilogue to the draft of this paper I sent to my discussants before the meeting—I shall be my own first discussant, as it were. In the epilogue I should like to indicate what consequences the new developments in the theory of the firm are likely to have for economic policy and welfare economics.

Management Science and Operations Research. In sheer quantity, the man-hours that have been devoted to normative microeconomics— under such titles as "managment science," "operations research," and "managerial economics"—outnumber those that have been applied to any other aspect of the theory of the firm in recent decades. Whether this has been an optimal allocation of effort is hard to say. It has certainly been productive. If optimizers are uncertain of its worth, satisficers can be content.

Since a whole session of last year's meetings of this Association was devoted to evaluating managerial economics' contributions to economic theory and vice versa, we need not go over the ground again in detail, but can base our conclusions on that previous discussion. The central fact is very simple: management science has brought economists in contact with the facts of business life, and businessmen in contact with the tools of economic analysis on a large scale, to the mutual advantage and surprise of both.

One of Mr. Wallis' colleagues has written that he already knows what an economist will find when he looks into a business firm, and that even if he finds something quite different it does not matter for economics.[3] He may be right on both counts, but since the looking will continue to go on, for quite practical reasons, we have no need to prejudge the result.

Management scientists are not concerned with systematic surveys of business practice. Their activity has not produced sample data from which one can extrapolate or aggregate a model of the behavior of firms in the economy. We should not underestimate, however, the impact upon economic theory of the anecdotal accounts of business decision making made available to economics by contact with business problems and practice.

[3] Milton Friedman, *Essays in Positive Economics,* Chap. 1.

The Role of Information in the Model of the Firm. An example of this impact is the growing attention to search for information and transmission of information as vital steps in the decision-making process. Uncertainty is, of course, a venerable economic variable, but the treatment of reduction of uncertainty as an economic activity is a relatively recent development. As Stigler observes:

> One should hardly have to tell academicians that information is a valuable resource: knowledge is power. And yet it occupies a slum dwelling in the town of economics. Mostly it is ignored: the best technology is assumed to be known; the relationship of commodities to consumer preferences is a datum. And one of the information-producing industries, advertising, is treated with a hostility that economists normally reserve for tariffs or monopolists.[4]

There is no difficulty in tracing this rediscovery of the economic significance of information back to activity in management science and operations research over the past two decades. Without attempting to reconstruct the history, I list some studies that gave information a central role and that are available to the economic theorist who wishes to re-examine the significance of this variable for the theory of the firm. An early example of the use of operations research techniques to solve a military problem was the application, discussed at length in the book of Morse and Kimball, of the theory of search to submarine warfare. Out of this application grew a more general theory of optimal search, developed by B. O. Koopman, Charnes and Cooper, and others.

Contemporaneously, consideration of games of imperfect information within the general framework of the theory of games led Marschak and Radner to develop an economic theory of teams, in which the cost of information and the value of information are the key variables.

Because management scientists became keenly aware of the imperfections of the data with which they worked, they early developed an interest in "sensitivity analysis." Sensitivity analysis is aimed at estimating the costs of making decisions with bad data and, correlatively, at estimating the value of procedures to improve the data. Cooper and Charnes and Dantzig developed techniques of sensitivity analysis as part of the apparatus for applying linear programming to management decisions. Sensitivity analysis and techniques for estimating the costs of inaccurate forecasts were developed for certain classes of dynamic programming models by Holt, Modigliani, Muth, and Simon in the United States and by Theil in the Netherlands. Out of this and similar work came a new understanding of forecast horizons: the degree of

---

[4] George J. Stigler, "The Economics of Information," *J.P.E.,* June, 1961. Even a casual perusal of the current journals will provide evidence for the rapidly growing popularity of information as an economic variable. The most recent example to come to my attention is Malmgren's paper, "Information, Expectations, and the Theory of the Firm," *Q.J.E.,* Aug., 1961.

independence of current decisions from information about distant events.

The examples cited are a sample, neither random nor systematic, of those that could be mentioned—almost all arising initially in the context of genuine practical decision problems. I might equally appropriately have mentioned the invention and development of sequential sampling theory by Wald, or Terborgh's analyses of optimal equipment replacement policies. (Professor Lintner, in the discussion, mentions another important example: the Renaissance of Bayesian statistical decision theory.) Or I could describe advances in the economic theory of distribution and advertising, no longer quite the neglected orphans that Stigler implies them to be in the passage quoted above.[5]

Now any or all of these developments could have come about without contact with practical decision-making problems. The theories are normative, not requiring data for their formulation or (in one sense, at least) their testing. The historical fact is that they were not discovered from an armchair. A proposition from search theory itself suggests the explanation for this historical fact: search begins when we are confronted with a problem for which no satisfactory solution presents itself.

Economists, statisticians, mathematicians, and natural scientists thrown up against concrete management problems discovered that the classical economic models paid little attention to the variables that were, in fact, crucial to rational practical action. All of us—economic theorists, management scientists, organization theorists—are satisficers when it comes to building our theories. We introduce new variables when we become aware that these variables are essential for explaining what we want to explain or solving what we want to solve. If information seeking is becoming significant for economic theory, it is because attempts to apply theory to the actual decision-making problems of the business firm have shown what a crucial role is played in decision by imperfections in our information and limits on our ability to calculate.

Attention to acquiring and processing information is only one way in which the decision models of management science have introduced new emphases into the theory of the firm. I may mention a few others. The new models are, of course, very much more detailed and disaggregated than the classical models. They introduce many decision variables in addition to the quantities and prices of standard commodities. The multitudinous consequences of decisions are incorporated partly in the criterion function—usually a cost or profit function. They are incor-

[5] See, for example, Frank M. Bass *et al.* (eds.), *Mathematical Models and Methods in Marketing* (Irwin, 1961).

porated also in policy constraints that can be introduced flexibly to handle "factors not elsewhere classified"—long-range considerations that are difficult to quantify, certain aspects of uncertainty, complications arising from external economies or diseconomies, and others.

Implications for Resource Allocation Processes. What do the management science models tell us about the general theory of resource allocation, and the relative advantages of prices as compared with other allocative mechanisms? On balance, the introduction of formalized decision procedures incorporating such tools as linear programming and dynamic programming has tended to centralize the decision-making process. To be sure, the optimal solution of a linear programming problem can be interpreted in terms of classical marginalist principles, and quantities appear in the solution that have all the properties of prices. Nevertheless, in practice solutions are invariably obtained by centralized computations using algorithms like the simplex method and not by the *tatonnement* of a market. What are the reasons for this? Two are fairly obvious. First, with modern computing equipment, the solution-finding process is handled centrally at least as readily as it could be through decentralized price mechanisms. The decentralized procedures simply do not yield the savings in information-transmitting cost usually claimed for them. Second, since most of the internal "markets" involve bilateral monopoly, or something close to it, the exchange prices are administered and not competitive prices. Hence, most of the self-policing features of a competitive price system are absent.

There is a third important force toward centralization. In classical Marshallian theory, the principal reason for the existence of the firm, and for the use of administrative rather than market mechanisms for its internal decision making, is the presence of external economics in the operation of its parts. Frequently, the modern quantitative decision models of management science permit more careful attention to these external economies than was possible with simpler decision procedures, with the result that decisions are further centralized. It is common to find, for example, that without formal decision rules, almost independent inventory and production decisions are made by manufacturing and sales departments of companies. The resulting system behavior is far from optimal and often close to being dynamically unstable. Several quantitative studies suggest that such "arms-length" relations of manufacturing and sales departments in inventory policy can cause significant amplification of inventory cycles. Under these conditions, the co-ordination of policy permitted by centralized decision rules constitutes their major contribution to lowered costs.

Experience with the analytic tools of management science shows that the area in which marginalist principles are applicable is not coterminous with the area within which market mechanisms can be used effectively. The latter area is generally much narrower than the former. Under many circumstances, central planning authority and the other resources of organization are needed to secure the application of marginalist analysis to business decisions. Thus, the application of sophisticated marginal analysis within the firm is providing us with a great deal of information about the potentialities and limitations of prices and markets as allocative mechanisms—information whose usefulness for evaluating broader questions of institutional structure has yet to be exploited.

Organization Theory. I turn now to research of a less normative kind that has been directed largely toward understanding goal-forming, predicting, choosing, and control behavior in business firms. The classical theory has been criticized severely under all these heads. It has been asserted that the behavior of firms cannot be explained in terms of a profit-maximization goal; that classical frameworks for analyzing uncertainty are faulty; that the classical models falsify the process of choice; and that they ignore control processes entirely.

What are the facts? The central fact is that the facts are very scanty, indeed. Let us inventory them briefly:

1. There are anecdotal facts derived from the contacts of economists with business firms. Everything we know about how preconceptions color observations should lead us to mistrust these.

2. There are facts derived from sample studies of American business behavior. We have such facts on a variety of topics—business expectations and pricing practices, to mention two examples. The chief defect of these facts, and a very serious one it is, is that they are derived from questionnaires and, to a limited extent, interviews, and are consequently extremely sketchy. In surveys of practices, the facts are generally reports by businessmen as to how they make decisions, lacking independent checks of actual behavior.

3. There are facts obtained by intensive interviews and, to a limited degree, actual observations of behavior in individual business firms. The costs of intensive studies and the degree of co-operation required of the firms usually limit such studies to small and unrepresentative samples of firms. Hence, there are major difficulties in extrapolating the findings to American business as a whole.

4. There are facts obtained by studying in the laboratory behavior that is (intendedly and allegedly) comparable to the behavior that occurs in business firms. The problem with such data is to establish the validity of the extrapolations.

In addition, simulation techniques—with or without computers—

can be used to infer from any of these kinds of facts their implications for organizational behavior. (In his discussion of my paper, Professor Lazarsfeld has made some extremely valuable comments on several areas of sociological theory and method that are relevant to research on the business firm. Professor Lazarsfeld's suggestions are illustrative of the wealth of ideas for methods of investigation and theoretical concepts that the economist who wishes to study the firm at first hand can obtain from his colleagues in sociology.)

In enumerating the kinds of data that are available, I have emphasized limitations and gaps. There is a brighter side to the picture, to which I shall turn in a moment. First, however, I should like to emphasize strongly that neither the classical theory of the firm nor any of the amendments to it or substitutes for it that have been proposed have had any substantial amount of empirical testing. If the classical theory appeals to us, it must be largely because it has a certain face validity (e.g., "only those firms that maximize profits will survive in the long run") rather than because profit maximizing behavior has actually been observed. If we reject the classical theory, it must be largely because it appears to us to have a very low a priori probability (e.g., "firms don't have the information that would permit them to make profit maximizing calculations") rather than because any large body of data clearly refute it. As empirical scientists, we can only hope that in time the case will be different, that we will have the facts to test competing theories; it would be extravagant to claim that the time is now.

Developments in the theory of the firm have largely been of two kinds: (1) proposals for the revision of the theory to take care of objections that have been raised to it; (2) a variety of new techniques for securing data that would permit such proposals to be tested. These explorations have not yet been carried to the point where they give more than scattered indications of what the substantive answers will be.[6] Thus, in any assessment of the progress that has been made over the past two decades, we need to emphasize progress in methods for studying human behavior in the business firm empirically, quite as much as the new facts discovered or the new theories to which these facts give rise.

To give substance to these general comments, I should like to review briefly four specific empirical studies, chosen to illustrate the

[6] Perhaps I am bending over backward in disclaiming knowledge of which version of the theory is correct. Obviously, I have my opinions, and even a certain amount of data that I regard as supporting them. However, one of the characteristics of the scientific endeavor is that it is not necessary to settle issues until enough evidence comes in—and even then they can always be reopened. In the present instance nothing is gained by claiming that the evidence is sufficient when it is so patently inadequate.

range of techniques available for empirical research. In the first example, interviews in the business firm are the primary source of data; the second employs a laboratory experiment; the third includes direct observation of the decision-making process; in the fourth, computer simulation is used as a means of analyzing and interpreting the data.[7]

Pricing Decisions. The setting of prices plays a central role in classical theories of allocation—especially in theories of imperfect competition. It is not surprising, therefore, that pricing decisions have been studied empirically more than almost any others. The approach has generally been simple and straightforward: if you want to know how a businessman sets prices, ask him.

Obvious objections can be—and have been—raised to finding out about a decision-making process by asking the decision-maker. Does he know; and will he tell. Perhaps much of what the decision-maker does is "intuitive" and judgmental, resides in his subconscious when he does it; and perhaps not all, or most, of it can be recaptured even by retrospection. Moreover, how is the businessman motivated to reveal to the researcher his *modus operandi*? In certain circumstances, does not he even lay himself open to risks of antitrust prosecution if he describes how prices are set?

An increasing number of studies based upon extensive interviews in business firms show that these problems can usually be solved satisfactorily. For studies of pricing decisions, interviewing has many advantages over less intensive techniques using questionnaires. To be sure, both methods elicit answers to questions posed by the researcher. But the information gathered through interviewing in a firm can be orders of magnitude more detailed than the information obtained from questionnaires. Respondents probably provide less deliberate misinformation in a face-to-face interview than in a mail questionnaire, and when they consciously warp the facts, they are more easily found out. The interview need not rely on general statements of practice but can probe these by applying them in detail to concrete examples or instances. The interviewer can explore, for example, the exact sequence of decisions and events in the most recent price changes the firm has made. He can see whether these events are consistent with the replies he has received about general pricing practices and procedures, and can ask for—and usually get—clarification when there are apparent discrepancies.

Finally, the interviewer need not rely on a single respondent in the

---

[7] I have drawn most of my examples from work I know at first hand. Hence my discussion may well sound parochial. It is in no way intended as a survey of the field and I hope my discussants will help correct my myopia by citing some of the important work that has been done on other campuses.

firm but can usually get access to a number of executives and functionaries who participate in different aspects of the pricing decision. Almost everyone who does this for the first time is surprised to find how diffusely information about policies and practices is scattered among individual participants in a large business organization, and what a fragmentary picture each single individual has of the whole process. Thus, a major consequence of the use of interview techniques is to replace the classical reification of the firm as a single "entrepreneur" with a model of a complex organization comprised of many interacting parts. It is at this stage of inquiry that organizational considerations begin to play a major role in interpretations of the decision-making process.

For example, the authors of the Brookings study, *Pricing in Big Business*, make the observation that in large multiproduct firms it is one thing to adopt a policy of "maximizing return on investment" or even of "securing a satisfactory return and share of market"; it is quite a different matter to set up procedures that will reflect these and other relevant policies in setting the prices of the individual items the company sells.

The difficulties in relating procedures for pricing items to general price policies do not reside solely or mainly in conflicts of interest between the owners of the firm and subordinate managers. Even apart from such conflicts, price setting involves an enormous burden of information gathering and computation that precludes the use of any but simple rules of thumb as guiding principles. Through detailed study of pricing by multiple interviews throughout the firm we begin to get a picture of the informational and computational constraints that hedge in the pricing process and give it form. We learn, for example, that whatever the shape of the real world, the world that his accounting figures reveal to the businessman is usually one of constant marginal costs, virtually up to the point where output equals full capacity. With this knowledge, the businessman's wariness of price competition takes on a new interpretation, quite different from that given it by classical theories of monopoly and imperfect competition.

Laboratory Experiments on Organizational Decisions. Discovery of major discrepancies between the classical theory of the firm and the decision-making process as revealed by interviews whets the appetite for explanation. We can conjecture why these things are so—as we have just done in the last paragraph. But how test our hypotheses? The laboratory offers one possibility. From interviews, we reach the conclusion that executives who occupy particular positions in firms acquire estimating biases induced by, and characteristic of, those positions. We should be able to abstract the essential characteristics of the positions, say, of sales executives and production executives, respectively, and to create abstract analogues of these positions under laboratory conditions. If the explanation of the estimating biases is correct, then the corresponding biases should appear under the laboratory conditions. As in the natural sciences, we can sometimes test our understanding of a phenomenon by trying to produce that phenomenon in the laboratory.

Some experiments by Cyert, Dill, and March illustrate this approach. In one experiment, subjects were asked to estimate a quantity on the basis of two previous estimates purportedly made by other persons. Under one experimental condition the subjects were told they were "cost analysts" and that the numbers were predicted costs of a new product. Under the other condition, they were told they were "market analysts" and that the numbers were predicted sales of a new product. Both groups were given the same data from which to make their estimates. The "cost analysts" consistently made higher estimates than the "market analysts." In a somewhat more complex experimental design, the same investigators were able to induce estimating bias by motivating subjects to estimate high or low, but also to induce corrective processes as subjects anticipated and adjusted for the biases of the others who were collaborating with them.

Notice that in this way of using the laboratory as a data-generating device complementary to the field study, we meet halfway the usual objections against extrapolating casually from laboratory to real-life situations. Generalizations are not extrapolated from laboratory to field. Rather the laboratory is used as a further check on our understanding of phenomena that we have already observed, and tried to explain, in the field.

The Observation of Decision Making. Students who have progressed from the arm chair, to the questionnaire, to the interview, to the laboratory in their desire to discover how decisions are actually made in the business firm find it relatively easy to take the next step—actually to watch decisions in the course of their manufacture.

Decision-makers are, in fact, unconscious of many of their own judgmental processes. Moreover, even when their motives are of the best, they are unreliable witnesses about what has happened in the past. The very positional biases that the study of executive thinking has revealed make their testimony suspect when it rests on memory of events that have passed through the selective filters of perception and interpretation. These deficiencies in the data can be reduced greatly if decisions are studied contemporaneously rather than retrospectively.

But what does it mean to "observe" decision making? The decision-making process is at best a stream of words and at worst a stream of thoughts. The former, if not the latter, can be captured and recorded. And now the fact that many persons participate in a business decision comes to the aid of the researcher. In individual human problem solving and decision making, the whole process can often take place inside a human skull, completely screened from observation. In organization problem solving, the stream of thoughts cannot go on very long without being accompanied by a stream of words. If the words can be recorded, a great deal can be learned about the process.[8]

As we proceed from the questionnaire through the interview to the observational study, we gain a great deal in the richness of the detail of process that we can observe. The price we pay is to give up any notion of sampling a universe of decisions in favor of making a careful record of one or a few. Both the cost of such studies and the problems of finding business firms that can and will permit them to be carried out make formal sampling notions inapplicable. Hence this approach rests on the assumption that we can reach an understanding of mechanisms through detailed study of processes without sampling in the ordinary way.

An example of this kind of intensive study of decision making is an investigation by Cyert, Dill, and March. They studied decisions by a steel company to invest in new capital equipment, in order to determine how expected return on the investment was estimated and how this factor was weighed against others in determining priorities among projects. The summary of this particular study will illustrate the picture of the decision-making process that is emerging from such work.

Three major features of this decision process are particularly interesting from the point of view of the place of expectations in a theory of business making. First, it is clear that search behavior by the firm was apparently initiated by an exogenous event, was severely constrained, and was distinguished by "local" rather than "general" scanning procedures. Second, the noncomparability of cost expectations and expected returns led to estimates that were vague and easily changed and made the decision exceptionally susceptible to the factors of attention focus and available organizational slack. Third, the firm considered resources as fixed and imposed feasibility tests rather than optimality tests on the proposed expenditure.

Clearly, we are viewing a resource allocating process here that is decidedly different from the price mechanism. One of its significant

---

[8] In point of historical fact, some of the social psychologists who pioneered in the study of problem solving and decision making in groups did so not because they were interested in organizational phenomena, but as a means of externalizing the phenomena and making them accessible to observation.

characteristics is that it is capable of operating in situations, like this one, where the relevant marginal quantities are not thought to be computable.

Computer Simulation of Decision Making. As research moves toward more and more intensive and detailed observation of the decision process, it is soon faced with the historian's dilemma. How can this vast mass of fact be reduced to order as a first step toward interpreting it and generalizing from it? Although it is some centuries since astronomers have thought of the matter in this way, they too were once faced with the same dilemma. They had voluminous data on the locations of the heavenly bodies at many points of time. The first step was to describe these in terms of geometrical paths—the cycles and epicycles of the Ptolemaic system. A little later these paths were simplified to the circles of Copernicus and the elipses of Kepler. But the great simplification came, of course, with Newton, who showed that the scheme of the heavens could be represented far more parsimoniously by replacing the time paths of planets with the differential equations that generated those paths.

For centuries after Newton, systems of differential or difference equations provided the model of "ideal" scientific explanation of dynamic systems. The modern digital computer, with its very general capacities for representing symbol-manipulating systems, opens to us the same possibility for explaining the time stream of a decision-making process by means of a computer program for simulating—i.e., generating—that stream.

The feasibility of reducing detailed historical data on decisions to programs capable of generating them has now been demonstrated by actually carrying it out in a number of instances. (On a much more macroscopic scale, the same approach has been adopted for theorizing about the economy. Orcutt's model of household behavior stands midway between classical macroeconomic dynamic models and the detailed microeconomic models we are discussing here.)

A program to explain the processes of a company deciding to install a digital computer was sketched out by Cyert, Simon, and Trow. A much more detailed program has been flow-diagrammed to represent the decision-making processes of a department store buyer. And recently, Clarkson has produced a computer program that predicts in great detail the decisions of the investment officer of the trust department of a bank. Although there are not yet many examples in the literature, investigations of a comparable kind have now been carried out by other workers.

Thus, with the advent of the high-speed digital computer, economics has acquired a new theory-building and theory-testing tool that will enable it to handle far more detail of the firm's behavior than could be treated in the past. With optimism we may even hope that the demands of the institutionalists for faithfulness to the facts will no longer seem irreconcilable with the demands of theorists for facts that are manageable. We will feel less constrained to believe in a particular kind of world just because it happens to be a world that is easily theorized about.

Conclusion. In painting this picture of what has been transpiring in the theory of the firm, I have faced a difficult problem of selection and sampling, which I have solved largely by emphasizing the work with which I am most closely familiar. I have discussed a few general trends and developments that seem especially significant: the contact with problems of the firm that was induced by the growth of management science, and the increasing attention to problems of information flows that was engendered by that contact; the growth of techniques for studying the decision-making process in great detail and from vantage points within the firm; the study of the firm as a multiperson complex organization; the first steps toward exploring the use of computer programs as a new way of theorizing about complex systems.

On the substantive side, our new knowledge of the decision-making process betokens a major advance over the next few years in the general theory of allocation. Two centuries ago, economic theory discovered, in the price mechanism, an allocative procedure possessing quite remarkable properties. These properties and their application to the regulation of an economy have been pretty thoroughly explored by successive generations of economists. We are now becoming increasingly aware that the price mechanism is just one—although an exceedingly important one—of the means that humans can and do use to make rational decisions in the face of uncertainty and complexity. We are beginning to understand what some of the other mechanisms are and how they are used.

Epilogue. Those economists who are not specialists in the theory of the firm may well ask what implications these developments have for general economics—and particularly for the traditional core of the profession's interest in public policy and welfare economics. I think there are at least three kinds of implications that deserve attention.

First, conclusions about welfare in such areas as tax and antitrust policy depend in an important way upon the underlying postulates about the behavior of the individual firm. The picture of the firm that is emerging from the new research is that of a searching, information processing, satisficing, allocating mechanism. It is doubtful that the propositions that hold with the assumption of static, profit maximizing firms under conditions of certainty also hold for such firms. Professor Baumol has already provided examples of how conclusions about tax incidence have to be modified if we assume the firm to be a sales maximizer rather than a profit maximizer.

Second, the great plan versus no plan debate hinges in considerable measure upon empirical propositions about how price mechanisms and planning mechanisms in fact operate: what costs they impose of information gathering and computing; how stably and rapidly they adjust the system to environmental change. Studies inside the business firm are providing us with a great deal of factual information about the costs and administrative problems associated with various allocative mechanisms. These facts are already calling into question beliefs that allocation through markets simplifies information processing as compared with centralized allocative processes.

Third, when we try to apply classical models to actual decision-making problems within the firm, we find that important modifications and improvements have to be made in these models if they are to operate successfully with the kinds of imperfect information that are available in the real world. From these necessities have emerged inventions like linear programming and modified concepts of rationality like the satisficing concept. As we move from the decision-making tasks of the individual firm to the greater complexities of public decision making for the economy, we discover an even more pressing need for the improvement of the classical tools of analysis. The tool-building innovations in management science are already providing answers to some of these needs—witness, for example, the applications of linear programming to economic development by Tinbergen and his colleagues. The "new realism" in the approach to the firm's decision problems may also prove a major force toward moving welfare economics back from the position of rather excessive formalism it has reached in recent years to a more direct concern with, and ability to handle, concrete policy problems.

For these reasons, we may expect rather confidently that the rapid progress that has been taking place in our understanding of the business firm will induce secondary changes of considerable magnitude in the other branches of economic theory.

VI

THE ECONOMICS OF INFORMATION PROCESSING

My close association with computers since the middle 1950s has prodded me to understand their larger import for society. My inquiries have followed two main lines: First, I have been interested in characterizing information as a factor of production and in asking whether information, regarded as an economic resource, has any peculiar properties that require it to be given special treatment in economic analysis. Second, I have felt some responsibility to gaze, from time to time, into my crystal ball, and to report what I saw there about the future impact of the computer revolution on the economy, on business organizations, and on Man's view of Man. Clearly, these two enterprises are related but distinguishable.

THE USES OF INFORMATION

Although chapter 6.1 deals with the pre-computer world, it is included here because it emphasizes how the design of information systems must rest on a thorough analysis of the uses to which information is put in decision making. The chapter is a summary article drawn from a monograph reporting the results of an extensive field study we carried out in the early 1950s of the organization of corporate controller's departments and the ways in which accounting information produced by such departments was used in managing the corporations. In the standard theory of the firm, information comes to the firm in the form of external prices, to be substituted in the equations for profit maximization, or in the form of data for use in estimating the parameters of cost curves or demand functions. When we examined how accounting information was actually used in the management of six large business firms, we found the reality to be quite different from what is described in the textbooks. To be sure, some information was used in ways that would be predicted from the standard account. We called these *problem solving* uses. But data were most extensively used, by far, for what we called *attention directing*.

Attention directing data are used, first of all, to answer the question

"How well are we doing?" The answer to that question may be used, in turn, to set bonuses, to promote or replace managers, or to readjust goals if they seem either unattainable or too easy to attain. These uses fit an aspiration-level model of the firm better than a profit-maximization model.

Even more important, attention-directing data are used to identify the particular aspects of operations that deserve scarce managerial attention. In chapter 6.6 I will argue that effective allocation of attention is a prime requirement for good management. Again, in this application, data are used qualitatively rather than quantitatively to detect when something is "out of line" or "out of control." Beyond localizing problems, attention-directing data are not used much for diagnosing the cause of the problem or for solving it.

Beyond its discussion of the uses of data, chapter 6.1 provides an example of the way in which organizational designs can be analyzed and evaluated by looking first at the decision making processes and information flows that are required for doing the organization's job, then fitting the information system to these processes.

INFORMATION AS AN ECONOMIC RESOURCE

Chapters 6.2, 6.4, 6.5, and 6.6 can best be classified as "thinkpieces." Chapter 6.2 might be called a computer scientist's description of human capital. The closing pages of the chapter, which predict steady or increasing rates of technological progress, may today seem to have been refuted by the events since 1973, but I share with Denison (1979) the view that we do not really know the reasons for the deceleration of productivity growth since that date or the prospects that the lull will continue. I would go further to say that the probability is substantial that it will all turn out to have been a statistical artifact. However that may be, I continue to see in operations research, electronic data processing, research on human thinking, and heuristic programming enormous prospects for large future gains in productivity.

Chapter 6.4 compares and contrasts human capital — programs in people's heads — with computer software capital, finding one very fundamental difference: Computer programs, once constructed, can be copied almost costlessly; human programs can be copied only by the arduous process of learning. The chapter suggests but does not develop at length some of the economic consequences of this difference.

Chapter 6.5 continues in much the same spirit, studying in what ways the introduction of computers affects the economics of storing information versus recomputing it as needed, updating information stores, allocating scarce attention, and retrieving information in organizations. The paper concludes with applications of the analysis to understanding the "information explosion" that is being brought about by computers.

Chapter 6.6 takes up the argument that a main effect of the advent of computers has been to make capacity for attention rather than information the critical scarce factor in most organizational (and personal) decision making. Up to the present time, most information systems have been designed around the idea of preserving, elaborating, and disseminating information. If information is nearly a free good, as is argued here, then information systems need to be designed around the idea of conserving managerial attention. This argument is developed somewhat further in my *New Science of Management Decision.*

IMPLICATIONS OF COMPUTERS FOR SOCIETY

This is a topic to which I feel an obligation to return periodically, both to see whether the world is ready to understand computers at a little deeper level than in the past and to see whether my own ideas on their import need revising and updating. As early as 1950, in an article entitled "Modern Organization Theories" (1950), I predicted an important future role in management for computers and the mathematical tools of operations research. The managers to whom I directed this prediction were more entertained than convinced. In 1958, Allen Newell and I tried prediction again in "Heuristic Problem Solving: the Next Advance in Operations Research," a paper that generated a heated but not especially light-giving public discussion. A second paper, "What Have Computers to do With Management?," which we did in the following year, was more calmly received. In 1960, on the occasion of a tenth anniversary symposium of the Graduate School of Industrial Administration, I wrote a fourth paper on the same general topic, "The Corporation: Will it be Managed by Machine?" In the same year, I delivered some lectures at New York University that were published as *The New Science of Management Decision.* These were expanded to treat more fully the macroeconomic implications of the introduction of computers in a new edition, published in 1965 as *The Shape of Automation.* A third edition, considerably revised, of the same book, appeared under its original title in 1977.

Chapters 6.5 and 6.7 summarize the main lines of argument that will be found in *The New Science.* Chapter 6.5 is based on lectures commissioned in 1966 by the Canadian Imperial Bank of Commerce; chapter 6.7 is a paper commissioned in 1977 by *Science* for a special issue on computers.

It is frequently urged that scientists have a professional responsibility for acquainting the lay public with the social implications of new scientific advances in their fields. I have found that this is not an easy responsibility to discharge. The well-known T. C. Mits (The Common Man in the Street) is not usually gullible. He tests new ideas conservatively against those he already has and does not feel obliged to accept an argument simply because he cannot answer it at once. Thus, for example, if something is a "machine," then it seems a priori unlikely that it can think; and a writer who uses the phrase "thinking machine" *must* intend a metaphor. Since T. C. Mits does not have time or expertness to explore in depth each new idea presented to him, he generally maintains an attitude of open-minded skepticism. In areas of controversy, this skepticism is reinforced by his hearing conflicting arguments from the experts and supposed experts on both sides. His most likely reaction is to maintain the view that conforms most closely to his preexisting beliefs — or sometimes, his wishes.

Nothing in this posture of T. C. Mits seems to me irrational. It is my own posture in areas outside of my sphere of expertness. However, it makes Futurism one of the most unrewarding of the world's occupations. I find that today my views on the capabilities and potential of computers are fairly widely accepted. These same views were just as sound (and only slightly more speculative) twenty-five years ago but hardly accepted at all. The only moral I would draw is that we must try harder but be satisfied with modest success. Above all, we must guard against judging the validity of our own predictions by the magnitude of the public response to them. A strong feedback loop from public to prophet breeds demagoguery.

T. C. Mits does not always distinguish as carefully as he should the time scale of the technologically feasible from the time scale of the economically feasible. Once he overcomes his conservative doubts about the in-principle possibility of computers thinking, he is in danger of expecting an instantaneous computer revolution. The two chapters printed here emphasize the need to keep these two judgments separate.

REFERENCES

Denison, E. F. *Accounting for slower economic growth.* Washington, D. C.: The Brookings Institution, 1979.

Newell, A., and Simon, H. A. Heuristic problem solving: The next advance in operations research. *Operations Research* 6 (1958): 1-10.

Newell, A., and Simon, H. A. What have computers to do with management? In G. P. Shultz and T. L. Whisler, eds., *Management organizaton and the computer,* pp. 39-60. Glencoe: The Free Press, 1960.

Simon, H. A. Modern organization theories. *Advanced Management* 15 (1950): 2,4.

Simon, H. A. *The new science of management decision.* Englewood Cliffs, NJ: Prentice-Hall, 1960 (rev. ed., 1977).

Simon, H. A. The corporation: Will it be managed by machine? In M. Anshen and G .L. Bach, eds., *Management and corporations, 1985.* New York: McGraw-Hill, 1960.

Simon, H. A. *The shape of automation.* New York: Harper & Row, 1965.

Simon, H. A., Kozmetsky, G., Guetzkow, H., and Tyndall, G. *Centralization vs. decentralization in organizing the controller's department.* New York: The Controllership Foundation, 1954.

6.1

ORGANIZING FOR CONTROLLERSHIP: CENTRALIZATION AND DECENTRALIZATION

Herbert A. Simon, George Kozmetsky, Harold Guetzkow, and Gordon Tyndall

A major responsibility of modern controllership is to provide management with information and analysis that is essential for making sound business decisions.

How shall the controller organize his department to perform these tasks effectively?

How centralized or decentralized should the account structure be in order to provide information of maximum value to management for reducing costs and increasing profits?

Which controllership functions should be performed in the company home office, and which should be geographically decentralized to factories and regional sales offices?

Shall there be a "solid" or a "dotted" line of authority from the factory controller to the company controller?

How shall functions be allocated within the controller's department — should the same units be responsible for record-keeping and analytic functions, or should these be assigned to separate units?

The answer — a very wise one — that the experienced controller will give to these questions is: "It depends." No single pattern of organization will meet the needs of the wide variety of business organizations in our country. But a careful observation of how accounting data are used and how controller's staff operate in different companies can cast light on the strong and weak points of alternative organization plans, and on the conditions under which a particular plan might be expected to work well. The findings reported here are based on such observations — including interviews in seven companies with some 400 accounting and operating executives.

Decentralized Profit-and-Loss Accounting

How can decentralization contribute to the development of profit-consciousness and a broad management outlook in the ranks of middle management? One solution, that has grown in popularity in recent years, is to treat each major division or department of the company as a business in its own right, to expect it to earn profits on its "investment," and to reflect the performance of each of these units in a formal profit-and-loss statement. A related solution is to build up the structure of accounts to parallel the organization structure, so that each part of the company can be charged with the costs it incurs.

The findings of this study suggest that the device of decentralized profit-and-loss statements is likely to be of much greater value in a company made up of separate product divisions, each making and selling its own products and having a considerable degree of independence, than in a company with "functional" divisions — procurement, production, marketing — or with production divisions that are highly interdependent. In the latter cases, it appears difficult to convince a divisional executive of the realism of his profit-and-loss statement when he knows that many of the variables that determine his "profit" depend on decisions made in other parts of the organization, and hence are to a considerable extent outside his control.

Where there are *in fact* important dependencies between parts of a company or of an organizational unit, the method that appears most effective in securing cost- and profit-consciousness is to decentralize accounting to the point where the statements received by each executive reflect those elements of cost and income over which he has a substantial measure of control. Charging cost elements that are agreed to be uncontrollable, or including in the responsibility statements elaborate analyses of recirculated overhead costs appears to discourage, rather than encourage, attention to costs on the part of the responsible executives.

Even though the findings all point in this direction, it would be dangerous to generalize too far from a study of but seven companies. What the study *does* suggest, however, is that decentralized profit-and-loss accounting is not a universal prescription, but one that is to be used with realistic attention to the company structure and to the kinds of responsibilities that are actually placed on executives at various levels.

How Data are Used

These observations on decentralized profit-and-loss accounting are part of a more general conclusion to which we were led: An effective account structure, and an effective system of accounting reports for operating executives have to take into account the ways in which accounting data are used as an aid to operating decisions. An important distinction emerged from the interviews between *attention-directing* uses of data, on the one hand, and *problem-solving* uses, on the other. When a red variance on a monthly operating statement leads a department head to ask, *"Why am I running over on my operating supplies?"*, it is performing an attention-directing function. When data on repair costs are used in determining when trucks should be replaced, these data are performing a problem-solving function.

Different organizational patterns are required to meet these two distinct needs for data. Attention-directing data are provided principally through periodic — daily, weekly, and monthly — reports. These reports (or rather, the appropriate portions of them) need to reach the levels of the company where responsibility for action lies — at least down to the general foreman level in most factories. They need to be prepared promptly. They need to be sufficiently detailed so as to genuinely direct attention.

The constructive use of accounting data for attention-directing purposes requires that the operating executives have confidence in the standards and in the performance reports that come to them, and that go to their superiors. In all cases, a close and direct relationship between accounting personnel and operating personnel appeared to be the most important factor in producing this confidence. This relationship needed to be close in the standard-setting procedure in order that the operating man might have an opportunity to negotiate a standard that he could regard as a reasonable and attainable forecast of his operations. The relationship needed to be close in the reporting process in order that the operating man might have help in interpreting his variances, and might have a part in developing the explanations of off-standard performance that were presented to his superior. Hence it is essential for effective service of the controller's department in the area of attention-directing to develop direct and active channels of communication with the operating executives at the major levels of the organization whose operations are being measured.

To use data effectively for problem-solving purposes — equipment purchases, selective selling, plant location decisions, and the like — the data must fit the problem. Periodic, routine accounting reports, however useful they may be as attention-directing devices, seldom provide the numbers that are needed when a specific problem comes up for study, and seldom provide these numbers in the most useful form. It was our observation that important special problems generally call for special analysis, and that these analyses must go behind the reports and examine the basic data. The controller's department that wishes to increase its usefulness in the problem-solving area will generally find it more useful to develop staff and facilities for special studies, than to further elaborate its periodic accounting reports with the view to anticipating in those reports the data that will be needed for an unpredictable range of future problems.

In the operating departments, problem-solving activities to which special accounting studies can make an important contribution are likely to be more centralized than the day-to-day operating activities that call for attention-directing reports. Hence, the controller's department can contribute most effectively to the solution of important policy problems through the development of small and relatively centralized special analysis units that are carefully kept free from a constant load of routine assignments. One such unit may be needed in the home office of the controller's department, and, in companies with decentralized plants, similar small units at the factory level will find plenty of opportunities for constructive and important analytic work. It was our observation that cross-departmental teams, drawn from accounting, industrial engineering, and operating personnel (or other appropriate units), provided an effective means for the investigation of special problems as they arose. Analytic units in the controller's department can probably do their most effective work through participation in such formal or informal teams.

Implications for Centralization and Decentralization

How would a controller organize his department to follow the general lines sketched out in the preceding paragraphs?

As already noted, he would create units for current analysis (attention-directing services) at relatively decentralized levels of the organization, and units for special studies (problem-solving services) at somewhat more centralized levels. He would have to pay special attention to the creation of communications "bridges" between these units in his own department and the points in the operating organization that the analytic units are intended to serve. Some of the devices that companies have found effective in creating and strengthening such bridges include actually locating the controller's units close to the operating units they are serving and creating regular tasks (like the preparation of monthly variance analyses) that can be performed only by the cooperative effort of controller's and operating personnel.

Thus far we have said nothing about the activities of the controller's department that bulk largest in terms of numbers of personnel and workload — the record-keeping and report-preparation functions. It was our general observation that those controller's departments operated most effectively which provided a considerable measure of separation between these functions on the one hand, and the analytic functions on the other. When important responsibilities for analytic duties and important responsibilities for the supervision of record-keeping and report preparation rested on a single man or a single unit, the former tended to suffer in the time and attention that was given them. The pressure of regular deadlines and the tasks of supervising clerical personnel gave the day-to-day activities priority over equally important, but postponable, analytic tasks. The simplest — and perhaps the only practicable — way to maintain a balanced allocation of effort appeared to be to vest these responsibilities in separate units.

If this is done a problem is created for the long-range development of executives in the controller's department. Unless special attention is given to the problem, supervisory personnel in the controller's department will tend to specialize too exclusively either in supervision of records and reports activities or in analytic work. When careers have been too much specialized along these lines, it will be difficult to find men for promotion who have the breadth needed by a factory controller or by a division head in the company controller's office. Hence, an organization plan like the one outlined here needs to be accompanied by a careful and definite program to provide for periodic lateral transfers — from supervisory to analytic positions and vice versa — of men who show promise for subsequent promotion to executive responsibilities. We observed at least one company in which a carefully administered plan of this kind appeared to be successful in avoiding the dangers of overspecialization.

With respect to the records and reports functions themselves, we found the balance of advantages to lie on the side of a relatively high degree of decentralization. To provide adequate access of operating personnel to documents from which they need information calls for decentralization to levels of the organization where the major use is made of the data. Furthermore, the reliability of data will generally be higher when they are compiled close to the source, for this makes it easier to check them against the physical realities they are suposed to reflect, and to avoid, among other things, some obvious kinds of clerical errors.

These advantages of decentralization have to be balanced against the advantages of mechanization and specialization of clerical operations that centralization permits. We found, however, that most of the important economies could be obtained with units centralized no farther than the factory or regional sales level. Presumably as the use of modern electronic computing devices becomes more common, at least in large companies, this conclusion will have to be re-examined and methods will have to be devised for the efficient use of computers that do not sacrifice the advantages of "grass roots" access to and processing of data.

The Chain of Command

One of the questions we explored was whether it was better to have a "dotted line" or a "solid line" of authority from the factory controller or regional sales accounting executive to the company controller. In most of the companies we studied, the formal authority arrangements did not appear to make much difference. Whatever the formal arrangement, the factory controller, for example, generally looked to the home office controller's department for instructions on the technical aspects of his job, and to the factory manager for special assignments and activities to improve controllership service to the factory.

In a few instances where the operating executives were skeptical of the usefulness of accounting services, and where the sales and manufacturing heads at the vice-presidential level did not give strong support to the controller's department, the distinction between "dotted line" and "solid line" did appear to make some differences. In these situations, the factory accountant appeared to have a more solid base for the development of his program and for working with the factory manager if it was understood that he was directly and formally responsible to the company controller. This observation may be of some significance for companies where the controller is undertaking the task of broadening the scope of his department's services, and where he has not yet succeeded in winning the full support of the top-level operating executives.

We observed another organizational problem that is related to the chain of command. In some companies there appeared to be an excessive number of supervisory "layers" in the controller's department. Where this occured, it was usually due to the fact that a level had been created in the controller's department to parallel each level in the operating departments. If a serious attempt is made to discover the points in the operating organization where the services of the controller's department are needed on a regular basis, it will often be found that certain levels can be omitted. For example, if the sales organization has both regional and district offices, it may be found that one or the other of these levels can be skipped in the organization of the controller's department.

The Future of the Controller's Department

The effectiveness of an organization can be assessed only after the organization's task has been defined. One reason, we believe, why considerable continuing attention is being given in many controller's departments to the organizational problems is that the conception of a controller's role has steadily been changing from a role limited to rather narrowly defined accounting functions to a role that involves important services to operating management and significant participation in the formulation of policy. We suspect — although this goes beyond the evidence of our study — that a particular business function will broaden its scope to the extent that it draws upon a profession capable of performing broader functions, and performing them well. If this is so, the future organizational patterns of the controller's department will be much influenced by what the industrial accounting profession makes of itself. If it can attract superior competence and provide superior training, these are likely to lead in time to larger responsibilitie for the profession, and to organizational arrangements appropriate to these responsibilities.

6.2
Decision Making as an Economic Resource

THE BULK OF THE PRODUCTIVE WEALTH of our economy is not embodied in factories and machines but is to be found in the knowledge and skills stored in men's minds. In a highly developed economy like ours, technological progress depends primarily on accumulation of this knowledge and skill, and only secondarily on the accumulation of physical wealth. I predict that the store of knowledge and skill in our economy is going to increase—both in quantity and quality—even more rapidly than it has in the recent past. I shall set forth presently the evidence on which that prediction is based.

Introductory Comments

Before I develop my central thesis, that our productive wealth is to be found in the skills stored in men's minds, I need to make some introductory reference to the social consequences of technological change and explain what I mean by "decision making."

In dealing with very familiar things, we take their main properties for granted—hardly troubling to mention them—and attend mostly to the qualifying details. Thus, when we think about technological change and automation, we are likely to slur over the central fact of our economy, that it is immensely productive precisely because of its advanced technology. We take that for granted, and hasten on to worry about the dangers of unemployment

71

resulting from continuing technological progress, or the problems of a future society so affluent that it will be buried under the goods it produces.

Consequences of Technological Progress

In any discussion of economic progress let us not lose sight of the central fact. Let us be quite clear that whatever problems the human species faces—in this country, in the underdeveloped countries, in the relations among nations—a necessary condition for the solution of its problems is the achievement of the high productivity levels that advancing technology is making increasingly possible. I say a "necessary condition," for of course it is not sufficient. High productivity, by itself, solves no problems and may even create new ones. Without it, however, the future of humanity would look bleak indeed. The United States of our generation has proved to the world that extreme scarcity of basic goods and services need not be an irremediable fact of human existence. The importance of that demonstration cannot be overestimated.

In order to keep productivity at the center of our attention, I am going to ignore the very legitimate worries that are so often aroused by technological progress. Unemployment is a legitimate worry, not only for the man who faces it but for the whole society in which he lives. Excessive affluence is a worry that seems more remote to most of us, but that can be real enough to someone familiar with the history of the leisured classes in our own and earlier societies.

I am going to ignore these worries because they refer to solvable problems. Both history and economic theory argue unequivocally that technological change may pro-

72

duce transient but not permanent unemployment, and societies are increasingly able to remove the burdens of that unemployment from the individual. We need to accept a fuller responsibility for these burdens than we have in the past, but it does not appear unduly difficult to do so, whenever the conscience of society demands that it be done.[1] The problem of affluence is a subtler one, and I am afraid I can only oppose my optimism to the pessimism of those who see original sin at the root of human behavior. The evidence is not really very convincing that increased leisure in moderate doses will be used badly by those who fall heir to it.

Whatever may be the best solution to either of these problems, the slowing or cessation of technological progress is no solution at all. Quite apart from the fact that it isn't going to happen, the misery it would produce would be out of all proportion to the ills it was intended to remedy. Let us agree, then, that technological progress is the one form of progress that humanity can reliably produce, that it is vitally important to the future of humanity, and that if it sometimes has harmful side effects, these can be mitigated without surrendering its main benefits.

Decision Making, Problem Solving, Thinking

One more introductory comment is needed—an explanation of the term "decision making" in my title. I have used it as a shorthand phrase to denote the whole range of problem solving, thinking, and choosing activities that are involved in productive work. I shall regard all work as "decision making" except the actual, final application of physical energy. I shall include everything under the rubric that takes place in the central nervous

73

system of the worker. My reason for lumping together in this way all the activities of workers' minds will become apparent as we proceed. I observe in passing that what contemporary research is teaching us about the human mind suggests that the processes involved in the "decision making" of the worker on the assembly line are not really very different from the decision-making processes of executives. All thinking appears to have some fundamental characteristics in common that justify treating it as a single economic resource.

Human Capital and Productivity

Traditionally, economists have classified the factors of production as land, labor, and capital. When we think of technology, it is the quantity and quality of the capital employed in production that comes first to mind. We classify primitive technologies as Stone Age, Bronze Age, and Iron Age, and take the steam engine and the blast furnace as our symbols for the Industrial Revolution.

In what does the transition from a pre-industrial to an industrial culture consist? Most obviously, it consists in the introduction of a multitude of new forms of capital equipment—machinery, tools, means of transportation. A major aspect of the change is replacing man (and his domestic animals) by inanimate nature as the main source of physical energy for productive processes. Man remains the controller and the director of that energy, although he no longer provides it with his own muscles.

Physical and Human Capital

But this description of the process conceals the intimacy of man's relation with his artifacts. When man do-

74

mesticated the horse, he did more than give up the use of his legs for locomotion. He learned a whole host of new skills—skills of riding and controlling horses, and skills of caring for horses. Again, when he acquired the automobile, he did not simply give up tasks he had previously performed; he took on new tasks—quite taxing ones they sometimes are.

Entomologists can often distinguish different moths by differences in the cocoons they make for themselves. But of course the essential difference is in the moths, not in the cocoons. The cocoons are different *because* the moths are different—that is, have different programs for making their cocoons. In the same way, changes in the physical equipment for production are symptoms of the corresponding changes in man himself. They are symptoms, in particular, of two kinds of internal changes in skill: changes in the skills of making such artifacts, and changes in the skills of using them.

During the initial stages of industrialization, spectacular changes generally take place in the capital equipment used in production. The amount of physical capital per employed worker increases enormously. The visibility of this phenomenon often leads to the erroneous conclusion that the accumulation of physical capital is the cause, or at least the principal cause, of the increases in productivity that accompany the industrialization. This interpretation, however plausible, is wrong—as we shall see. The increases in productivity must be interpreted as resulting from changes in the technique of production, in which changes in amount of physical equipment are one aspect, but in which changes in the nature of that equipment and in the skills of the work force are equally necessary, and more fundamental to the process.

75

The evidence is quite clear. Although the first stages in industrialization are accompanied by rapid capital accumulation, continuing increases in productivity in countries that have already reached a relatively high level of industrialization—the United States, Canada, Australia, New Zealand, Great Britain and Western Europe—have not depended to any large extent on further net increases in capital plant. Let us consider the American data.[2] Real output per man-hour has approximately doubled since the beginning of World War I. Over this same period, capital per employed worker, measured in constant dollars, has remained almost constant, growing exceedingly slowly. Several careful econometric estimates have been made to determine what part of the overall doubling in productivity could be attributed to the small increase in physical capital that occurred, and what part to improvement in the techniques of production. These estimates agree in attributing no more than 10 per cent of the increase to the growth of capital and the remaining 90 per cent to the shift in the production function—that is, to improvement in the quality of capital and to increase in the skills of the labor force.

Let me dwell for a moment on these facts, for I think they contradict rather sharply the picture that most laymen—and even a great many economists—have as to the nature and conditions of economic progress. Contrary to much of the talk about mechanization and automation, the overall capital-labor mix in our economy today is about what it was a generation ago.

If we look at the data for individual industries, of course, we will see that there has been an increase in the capital-labor ratio in most of these over the same period.

76

I would have a hard time convincing an audience in Detroit that this was not so. But an increasing capital-labor ratio in *all* individual industries is not contradictory with a constant capital-labor ratio for the whole economy. These two facts can coexist provided that the industries that are capital-intensive (e.g., manufacturing) grow less rapidly than the industries that are labor intensive (e.g., services), so that the latter have an increasing weight in the average for the economy.[3] And this is what appears to have happened. In particular, service industries that at present use a relatively small amount of capital per worker have grown more rapidly than manufacturing industries that use a relatively large amount.

Moreover, attention to factory mechanization and automation should not lead us to conclude—for we would be wrong—that productivity has increased more rapidly in capital-intensive spheres than in those where capital-labor ratio is low. An example will make the point clear. The practice of medicine is a labor-intensive occupation. Perhaps the most expensive piece of equipment required by a physician is a means of transportation. But the introduction of the automobile and the telephone enormously increased the hourly output of physicians (even before they shifted the transportation costs to their patients by becoming increasingly reluctant to make house calls). The savings from this increased productivity have not yet been shifted in any great degree to consumers, but that is another story. My present point is that improvements in the quality of capital may have as large effects on productivity in labor-intensive industries as in capital-intensive ones.

We should not be too hasty in applying these facts on capital and productivity to the problems and policies of

77

the underdeveloped countries. There are still large sections of the world, inhabited by the bulk of the world's population, where capital scarcity is a major obstacle to rapid economic progress. Even these countries, in their development plans, have perhaps been excessively preoccupied with capital accumulation as a key strategic consideration. But that, too, is another story. I am primarily concerned here with the future of economies which, like our own, are already highly industrialized. In an industrialized economy, the quality of capital and the quality of the work force are the main determinants of productivity.

The Quality of the Work Force

We must be careful not to equate improvement in the quality of labor with formal education or training.[4] It is true that most industrialized societies have moved very far toward universal literacy, and have depended largely on the formal school system to bring this about. The schools have assumed some of the training burden, also, that was formerly the responsibility of apprenticeship systems, or even of the home (e.g., training in cooking). But the vast bulk of the skill acquisition we are considering takes place almost automatically through direct contact with the productive equipment itself.

The passenger automobile in the United States affords a striking example of how the ubiquitous presence in a society of a piece of complex equipment allows most adult members of that society to obtain the skills of operating the equipment with a minimum of formal training facilities. (With the rise of driver education, this is less true than it was in a previous generation when even most

78

automobile mechanics, as well as drivers, learned by doing.) The capital investment in the physical device produced—almost by mere contact—is an enormous fund of skills of automobile driving, automobile repair, and even automobile design throughout the population exposed to the device.

The same phenomenon can be seen today as the electronic digital computer diffuses through our society. Hundreds of thousands of persons are acquiring new knowledge and skills relating to computers—skills of operating card punches and data processing equipment, skills of writing computer programs, skills of designing and producing computers. If we could measure it, the total economic value of these skills would probably be several times the total value of the computers themselves.

At least a rough measure can be obtained simply by capitalizing the stream of income attributable to labor and capital, respectively, at the same rate of interest. In our society as a whole, about two-thirds of the national product is paid out in the form of salaries and wages, most of the remaining one-third as payments for the use of physical capital. Since most of the effectiveness of the work force in production derives from the kinds of skills we have been discussing—the skills of using the available physical capital—we can say that, at least in rough terms, the total national wealth invested in those skills is two or three times the total national wealth in physical capital.

Now we have already noted that we can have a steady increase in the *productive capacity* of physical capital without any net increase in the *amount* of that capital— simply through the gradual replacement of worn-out

79

capital with more advanced forms. Similarly, to increase steadily the store of society's human skills does not necessarily mean that we must devote more resources in each generation to training and education. Men growing up in our society today often learn about computers, something their fathers never conceived of. But one reason they have time to learn about computers is because they do not have to learn about horses and plows. Skills matched to our present technology are substituted for skills matched to the technology of the past. And all of this comes about with relatively little forethought or planning—primarily through exposure to the technology itself. Machines become their own change agents, carrying with them the information needed for their use.

Human Skills as Programs

To talk about the mass of productive skills that are stored in the minds of members of the labor force of an industrialized society, it is useful to borrow the term *program* from digital computer technology. When a computer is delivered from the factory it is just a big electronic "black box" having the potentiality to perform all kinds of complex symbol-manipulating activities. To change this potentiality into an actuality the computer has to be programmed—provided with complex sequences of instructions that tell it how to perform a variety of tasks. In practice, a computer is often separately instructed for each task it is assigned, but increasingly there are stored permanently in memory (on a magnetic tape, for example) a whole set of relatively general-purpose programs that can be called upon, singly or in combination, as they are needed to solve particular problems. A computer *with* its

80

stored programs is a black box that has acquired the skills necessary for solving a range of problems (inverting matrices, for example, solving regression equations, doing factor analysis, and what not).

We can also think of the whatever-it-is that is stored in the mind of a human being, which enables him to perform tasks or solve problems of certain kinds, as his program. Various parts of this program can be invoked, singly or in combination, to perform a variety of tasks. Two characteristics of human programs deserve special comment. First, *learning programs,* programs having the function and the capability of modifying the remaining programs in memory in an adaptive way, constitute a vitally important component of the set of programs stored in human memory. In fact, most human performance programs—i.e., those that are not learning programs—are acquired not by explicit "programming" the human mind, but through the mediation of the learning programs, which have the task of elaborating and modifying the performance programs.

Second, while most of the performance programs stored in digital computers are relatively specific, and efficacious over only a very narrow range of tasks, the human memory contains, in addition to programs embodying specific skills, some important programs of a rather general-purpose nature. These *general-purpose programs* provide, for example, certain problem-solving skills, such as means-ends analysis, that appear to be used in handling problems in almost every subject-matter domain.

In our society, then, the bulk of the productive wealth consists of programs, corresponding to skills, stored in

81

human minds. Many of these programs are quite specific in application, and hence are intimately interwoven with the structure of the physical technology. Other programs provide rather general capacities for problem solving in domains that are new, and provide learning capacity. When new physical equipment is introduced into production, the learning programs, operating by exploration of the properties and behavior of the equipment, enable human beings to acquire rapidly the new performance programs that are needed to operate the equipment effectively, to maintain it, and even to develop it further. Technology, in these terms, is symbiosis of programs with artifacts.

Referring to human skills as programs is less metaphorical than it might at first appear to be. During the past five years, a number of programs have been written for digital computers that permit the computers to simulate, in considerable degree, the behavior of humans performing relatively complex tasks. Detailed comparisons of the behavior of the programmed computers with the behavior of human subjects show the similarities to be very strong, in several of these cases. Hence, we now have reason to believe that skills are in fact stored in the human mind in forms that parallel closely the corresponding computer programs.[5]

Some Rapid Productivity Increases

Before turning to the future of productivity in the United States, we may use the analysis we have developed to explain several historical examples of rapid productivity increase: the conversion of the United States to a wartime economy from 1939 to 1943, and the postwar recoveries of Germany and Japan. These examples cast

82

additional light on the way in which human skills enter into the processes of production.

The ability of the United States to increase its production after 1939 was of course due in part to the fact that its resources were substantially under-utilized before that time. A considerable part of the labor force was still unemployed, and capital plant was being operated well below capacity levels. Moreover, the war brought many new workers into the labor force. But to attribute the whole increase to these factors would be wrong. The existing capital plant—except for some parts of heavy industry—had not been designed to produce the new military products required by the wartime economy—ships, planes, and tanks. New plant and equipment were required for these and not simply the utilization of existing plant. Similarly, the skills of the unemployed workers, or of the persons newly entered into the labor force, were not the skills needed for the new production.

The design and construction of new capital equipment (itself a task making heavy demands on skills), and the acquisition of production skills by the labor force were the principal processes required to convert to the wartime economy. We may conclude that the principal under-utilized resources that made the conversion possible were the *learning programs* of the employed population. In most societies, human learning capacities are utilized heavily in the child's progress to adulthood, but very much under-utilized in adult life. Learning programs atrophy rather slowly, if at all. In other words, there exists in the adult population a huge reservoir of "standby" learning capacity that can be called upon, by proper organization, to meet rapid or cataclysmic changes in the

83

environment. In spite of constant references to the speed of change in our modern society, it is doubtful that more than a small portion of this learning capacity is used at any given time. The conversion to wartime production at the beginning of World War II was one of the rare periods when a large part of the adult population was called on to acquire important new skills in a relatively short time, and when, as a consequence, this hidden resource became partly visible.

My second example is the postwar economic recovery of Japan and West Germany. Both recoveries took place at rates that are a little difficult to account for in view of the extensive destruction of physical capital that had taken place. Most analysts of the process have commented on the "vigor" and "energy" of the population. The theoretical framework we have developed enables us to describe a little more concretely the nature of this vigor and energy. As in the case of American rearmament, the situation was one in which great use could be made of the populations' learning capacities. But another factor was present also. Much of the recovery involved restoring activities that had been present in the pre-war economy. Here the skills already existed, in large part, for designing, building, and using the capital plant, and hence the physical reconstruction could be carried out with high efficiency by drawing upon these existing skills. Provided the human programs are preserved, the destruction of the physical plant of an industrial economy wipes out only a small fraction of its total capital resources. Its recovery can be expected to be much more rapid than where the human programs must be developed from whole cloth at the same time.

84

Productivity of the American Economy

We have seen that the increases in productivity of the American economy over the past fifty years can be viewed largely as improvements in the programs of production. Partly, these improvements were imbedded in physical equipment—in new and more efficient tools and machines to replace older and less efficient ones—but without a significant net increase in physical capital per worker. But the new production equipment had the dual role of tool and of teacher. At the same time it turned out new goods, it provided the technological environment in which the learning of new skills could take place.

There is every reason to suppose that this same process will continue to be the basis for productivity increases in our economy at rates at least as great as those experienced in the recent past. Indeed, within the last fifteen years, four developments have taken place that are likely to accelerate the process and to bring the programs of men into even closer relation with the machines they use in their work. All four developments make essential use of the modern electronic computer.[6] They are, first, the use of advanced mathematical and other analytical techniques to improve business decision-making processes; second, electronic data processing, the automation of clerical processes; third, the use of computers to investigate human thought processes, and ultimately, to discover ways to improve the human programs for problem solving, decision-making, and learning; and fourth, the development of so-called heuristic programming methods that extend the possibilities of automating decision making far beyond the

85

boundaries of the quantitative and the routine. Let us examine these four developments in turn.

Operations Research

Formal analytic techniques, drawing upon advanced mathematical knowledge, first entered industry in the area of engineering design. They did not extend much beyond the boundaries of that area until after World War II. Then, under such labels as operations research and management science, the revolutionary idea was proposed that many management decision problems could profitably be captured in formal models and solved by the application of mathematical analysis in much the same way that engineering design problems were. Within a surprisingly few years, esoteric tools with such names as linear programming, queuing theory, statistical decision theory, and dynamic programming had been developed and applied to problems of inventory and production control, marketing strategy, equipment replacement policy, and other management decision areas, mostly in the middle-management range.

Many of the real-life problems proved, when captured in formal models, to be beyond the limits of hand calculation. The digital computer fortuitously appeared on the scene to take over the computational work. In many cases, too, finding general solutions for the formal models exhausted the resources of classical mathematics. In these cases the computer again came to the rescue. By means of simulation techniques and so-called Monte Carlo methods, the behavior of the model could be explored numerically over a range of assumed situations.

In terms of our earlier discussion of the bases of

86

productivity, we may say that operations research and management science added to the existing repertoire of programs for making middle-management decisions a whole new collection of such programs, drawing their effectiveness from the analytic power of mathematics and the computational power of modern computers. Because this revolution in technique did not require new physical equipment, except the computer, which was introduced to perform other functions as well, it was not nearly as visible nor as often commented upon as, for example, factory automation. The former may well turn out to have substantially the greater long-range impact of the two.

Electronic Data Processing

Electronic data processing is simply a form of automation applied to the office instead of the factory. Like some modern forms of factory automation, it excites particular interest because it transfers mental rather than physical functions from man to the machine. Thus the program for a computerized payroll preparation scheme is stored in the computer and not in the heads of bookkeepers and clerks. In the new symbiotic relation between man and machine, the man maintains the machine, supplies it with performance programs, and improves and modifies these programs as conditions and needs change. The programs themselves are executed by the machine without the intercession of the man. One might say that the man holds the learning programs, the machine the performance programs. With this division of labor, the capital-labor ratio can vary widely, depending on how great and frequent is the need for program change.

87

The Study of Human Thinking

Under the two preceding headings I have described two contrasting methods for improving production programs. The first improves the human programs by incorporating in them more powerful formal analytic tools. The second transfers some of the programs from the labor force to the physical equipment. Are there other ways of enhancing the efficiency of the thinking, deciding, and problem-solving programs that enter into the production process? In particular, are there ways that can be applied to areas of decision that do not lend themselves readily to quantification and mathematization?

New techniques for improving decision making in non-quantitative, non-formalized, ill-structured realms have indeed been emerging; and surprisingly enough, it is again the electronic computer that provides the basis for them. I say "surprisingly," because most people think of the computer as a device that is peculiarly and necessarily quantitative and numerical. Historically, computers were developed as devices for doing arithmetic operations very rapidly. But in order to do this, they had to be given the power of interpreting and executing whole sequences of instructions stored in their own memories. In this important respect they differ from desk calculators—the program of operations for the desk calculator is stored in the head of its operator, and executed by him; the program of the computer is stored in and executed by the computer itself.

But the program instructions in the computer do not stand for numbers, they stand for sentences in the imperative mode—the computer circuitry interprets them and acts on them as such. When the instruction says "Add a to

88

b," the computer must take the numbers a and b, and do to them exactly what the human operator of the calculator would call "adding." Only sophistry would deny us the right to say that the computer is dealing with the *meaning* of the word "add," and with the symbol-manipulating process denoted by that word.

Thus, a modern digital computer is not an adding machine or a desk calculator. It is a quite general-purpose symbol-manipulating device that happens, historically, to have been pressed into the task of doing arithmetic. But we know now, as the result of research over the past decade, that its symbol-manipulating processes are sufficiently broad and powerful in scope to allow it to carry out the same kinds of manipulations that humans carry out when they think, solve problems, make decisions.[7]

Computers have been programmed to design motors, to write music, to play checkers and chess, to discover proofs for mathematical theorems, to form concepts, to solve the missionaries and cannibals puzzle, to learn, to recognize patterns, to select a portfolio of stocks for a trust fund, to balance an assembly line, and to execute a number of other complex problem-solving tasks. Moreover, a number of these programs have been demonstrated to parallel or simulate, in considerable detail, the processes that humans use to solve the same kinds of problems. We are beginning to have, for the first time, a detailed, testable, and partially tested theory of human thinking processes. We can now begin to say what it is that a man is doing when he is "exercising judgment," "abstracting," "using intuition," or "thinking creatively." Even "aha!" experiences have been simulated on computers and the mechanism underlying them explained.

When we understand human thinking processes we

89

take a long step toward being able to improve them. Of course, that is no new undertaking. Teaching and training are time-honored activities aimed at the improvement, specific and general, of the programs humans use in their thinking. But teaching and training are activities that have had to proceed in the face of rather complete ignorance of the processes they were aimed at improving. As we come to know what kind of a problem-solving program a good thinker must possess, we will find all sorts of new and powerful techniques for aiding people to attain such programs. The instructional process will give up the shotgun spray of its traditional techniques for much more carefully aimed procedures.

If the bulk of the productive capital in our economy lies in the minds of our work force, as I contend that it does, the new advances in our understanding of human thinking promise improvement of first magnitude in the quality of labor, and corresponding rapid gains in productivity. My guess would be—and it is only a guess—that the findings of fundamental research in this area will begin to make themselves felt in application within a decade or less.

Heuristic Programming

We come finally to a fourth major development. As we begin to understand the methods that human beings use to solve problems not quantitative or formalizable in nature, still another prospect opens for using this knowledge to increase productivity. We can enlist computers in the decision-making process, not just with the classical analytic methods or operations research, but by writing computer programs that simulate some of the non-

90

quantitative, non-formal, heuristic procedures that human beings use to solve problems. Such programs are commonly called *heuristic programs,* because of the important use they make of rules of thumb, or heuristics, in order to solve problems by highly selective trial-and-error techniques, as people have been shown to do.[8]

To be sure, man did not learn to fly by a slavish imitation of birds. When art seeks to replace nature, it is sometimes best not to imitate her too closely. In spite of these cautions, the prospect of writing computer programs that simulate human heuristic problem-solving processes holds out great promise for extending the range of activities that can be automated. Nor is this entirely a prospect for the future. Computers have already been programmed to do engineering design work (that is, actual synthesis of motors, generators, and transformers; not simply analysis of their performance characteristics) that formerly was handled by professional engineers. Heuristic programs have been devised for investing trust funds and for balancing assembly lines, to mention two that appear to be sufficiently effective to be used in practice.

The Economics of Heuristic Programs

In estimating the role that heuristic programs for computers might play in production, and the extent to which such programs may prove more economical than human decision making, we have to pay attention to the way in which programs are acquired or learned. The human being acquires his programs partly (perhaps largely) in an environment where he can try things and get feedback about the results of his action—he learns by

91

doing. Partly, he acquires programs by reading or listening to other human beings. Usually some combination of these is required for efficient program acquisition.

If a human being invents a new program or improves an existing one, the two learning processes already described are the only ones available for transferring the improvement to other human beings. To the extent that he can write out a description of the program in a book, the printing press provides a cheap means for duplication of the description. But another human being still has to transform that description into a program stored in his own mind before he can apply it—usually not a simple process, for we are talking of skill acquisition and not simply memorization of verbal material.

Heuristic programs are usually acquired by a computer as a result of the efforts of one or more human beings who write the programs. However, some small experience has now been gained in writing learning programs for computers—programs, that is, that permit the computer to develop and modify performance programs by experience in trying to perform a task. Although computer learning is still far from much practical application, we may expect that in the future this will become an important means for developing new programs.

Once a computer program has been developed—whether by a human programmer or through learning processes—the economics of transferring it to another computer is quite different from the economics of transferring a program from one human being to another. The computer program can simply be duplicated—on punched cards or on magnetic tape—with as many copies as desired. Just as a new and more efficient organism,

92

produced initially by a random mutation, can be reproduced through the copying of the genetic material, so new and more efficient computer programs, however they originate, can be copied almost costlessly. We have here a process for the multiplication of knowledge that will in time prove as important as the invention of printing.

The Division of Labor Between Man and Machine

Since man invented and manufactured his first tools, the boundary line between the part of the productive process he carried out himself and the part he assigned to his tools has been steadily shifting. But in the past, the area we call thinking was largely debarred from the tools. The governor that regulated the speed of the steam engine and the thermostat that maintained the house temperature at a comfortable level were important exceptions, but it was most unclear how they could be generalized to broad ranges of the functions performed by mind.

Now we know, at least in broad outline, how the generalization can be made. The division of labor between man and his machines will be increasingly governed by criteria of economic efficiency rather than limitations of technical capability.

And what do these changes mean to the future of our society? I find that many people are troubled at the idea that we shall understand the processes of human thinking, that we shall be able to simulate these processes with computers, and that in simulating them, we shall also be able to automate them. Some people find these prospects so worrisome that they refuse to examine and assess the extent of the progress that has already been made, or the

93

evidence that this progress is likely to continue at a very rapid pace.

I personally find it difficult to share these worries. First, the idea that extensive automation must be or will be a source of human misery is based on fallacious economic reasoning. There is no connection, as I have already indicated, between the level of technology in a society and the level of employment.

Second, however painful it may be for the human species to acquire a deeper understanding of itself and of its mental processes, I cannot believe that its present ignorance is a blessing. It is a commonplace to observe that our knowledge of physical nature has far outstripped our knowledge of society and human behavior. But to understand society and human behavior requires us to understand how the human mind works. Surely the dignity of man cannot depend upon an unawareness of his own impulses and his own modes of thought.

Conclusion

My central theme has been that the main productive resource in an economy are programs—skills, if you prefer—that in the past have been partly frozen into the design of machines, but largely stored in the minds of men. While industrialization of an economy requires the accumulation of a substantial amount of physical capital, machines and equipment are more the external evidences than the real core of a technology. Moreover, technologically advanced economies like our own have long passed the point where further increases in productivity depend primarily upon new increases in the

94

already high capital-labor ratio. Technological progress depends now upon improvement in the quality of capital and of the work force.

The modern digital computer introduces a significant new factor into technological progress. The computer, appropriately programmed, can share with human beings many parts of the job of production that earlier machines could not. Moreover, it can be used as a powerful research tool to gain a deeper understanding of the structure and development of human thinking. Hence it has strategic importance in two directions. It makes fluid the line that defines the division of work between machines and human beings, and brings machines to the aid of man's muscle. It also creates new knowledge about human performance that will enable us to improve greatly the programs that human beings use in production. Over the next generation, the digital computer will play a central role in increasing the productivity of the most important resource our economy possesses—its power of thinking, solving problems, making decisions.

95

6.3

THE IMPACT OF NEW INFORMATION-PROCESSING TECHNOLOGY

Herbert A. Simon

1. ON MANAGERS

The term "automation" is so widely current, and has become, as a result, so vague that it does not require or admit precise definition. Two or three hundred years ago — after two thousand years of relative stability — the techniques and technical equipment that man used to meet his needs, began to undergo continuous, accelerating change and improvement. These changes, starting on a large scale in Western Europe and America, are still in the process of diffusing to other parts of the world.

Even today, in many hundreds of thousands of villages around the world, these great trends are known to the peasants only as vague rumors, borne to them by an offcourse airplane, a truck bumping over a rutted trail, or, too often, a band of marauding soldiers. These peasants — a majority of the world's population — would feel quite at home with the tools and artifacts used by a Greek farmer at the time of Alexander the Great (and he with theirs).

In the Western world, however, with its expanding boundaries, it is change that has become commonplace. In the Western child's vocabulary, "olden times" does not mean classical Greece, Medieval knighthood, or even frontiersmen and Indians. It means the world of his parents. For Western man, the Industrial Revolution holds more significance than any political revolution (unless, as in Russia, he confuses the two).

At the heart of the increases in productivity that mark the Industrial Revolution is a great burst of tool-building activity. After having been satisfied for thousands of years with his domestic cattle, draft animals, and crops, and with his hand implements of stone, bronze, and iron, he discovered fire for the second time — this time as a source of energy many times more powerful than his own.

With mechanical energy came mechanization — the devising of tools for applying that energy to the processes of production. The human worker remained an essential part of the system of production, but his main function became that of guiding non-human forces rather than applying his own. In very recent years, in speaking of "automation" rather than "mechanization," we mean to note the fact that man's tool-building ingenuity has not limited itself to capturing and harnessing mechanical energy, but has now extended also to the processes of guiding and controlling that energy. Automation, to paraphrase Clausewitz, is a continuation of the Industrial Revolution by other means.

From the earliest times, the productive resource in human economies has always been man-with-tool. In pre-industrial societies, the tool may be inconspicuous — a stone blade held in the fist — but it is always there, and essentially there. Fly over India at 15,000 feet, and see how slightly man has scratched the earth's surface. Man's green crops and earthen huts need no camouflage to merge into the landscape. Fly lower, and man becomes visible. However superficially, he has changed the natural environment to facilitate growing his food, moving about and sheltering himself. Land your plane and walk into the village, and you see that man almost never lives in a natural environment, but always in an environment of his fellow men and his own artifacts and implements.

Man's economy, his whole culture, even in peasant societies, is less accurately viewed as an interaction of man with nature than as a *man-tool system*, a system that increasingly shields man from a direct, naked confrontation with nature. With the Industrial Revolution and mechanization, the man-tool system becomes a man-machine system; and by the time we reach the contemporary stage of automation, the intermingling, in the productive process, of man and his tools is almost complete.

Viewing from this perspective, we are less struck by the differences between peasant and industrial cultures than by their similarities. Both the peasant economy and the modern industrial economy are man-tool systems. In both, man lives and works surrounded by his own artifacts. When westernization reaches his village, it poses no particular problem for the peasant to learn to live in a man-made environment; he has been living in one all his life. It may pose a real problem to learn to live in a *different* environment than the one to which he has become accustomed, and an even more difficult problem to adjust to massive changes in that environment between the "artificiality" of an automated economy, which presents no essential novelty at all, and its changeability, which does, in fact, represent something new under the sun. I will have occasion to return to this distinction at later points in my talks.

Technological Change and Job Content

Before I turn to the particular effects of automation upon the shape of the industrial firm, I should like to call attention to the subtle and indirect ways in which advances in technology sometimes alter the processes of production. Since these indirect consequences are often more important than the direct impact, we must keep our eyes open for them. An illustration will make the point.

We do not usually think of the physician's profession as one that is highly mechanized — capital-intensive in the economist's language. Perhaps, classifying it as a service occupation, we do not regard its productivity as having been much affected by technological change. But let us take a closer look.

At the turn of the century, the most-used skill of a Canadian or American physician was the skill of driving a horse. That is how he spent ninety per cent of his working time, driving from farm to farm. The invention of the automobile and the construction of a system of farm roads probably multiplied the productivity of the rural doctor by a factor of at least two, and perhaps four or five. More recently, the invention and widespread use of antibiotics caused a second large leap in medical productivity. Not only is the pneumonia patient far more likely to recover than he was in 1900, but while he is doing so, he takes only five or ten per cent as much of the physician's time. (That is why we in the United States have only very recently become aware of the failure of the number of physicians to keep pace with the growth of our population and affluence.)

The medical profession may at present be on the brink of an automation and mechanization that will be far more visible and direct than this earlier one. I refer not only to the increasingly elaborate equipment employed in diagnosis and treatment, to the point where it becomes difficult to be sure whether one is in a hospital or a factory, but to the imminence of effective automated techniques for diagnosis, and the already developed methods for monitoring automatically the condition of post-operative patients. It is not clear whether this newer automation will bring about productivity increases any more dramatic than those produced in less direct ways by the earlier ones I have described.

When we turn our attention to corporate automation, we must be on the alert for comparably indirect effects. Thus, to use a hypothetical example, selling will become a very different and more efficient occupation when video-telephone communication largely replaces air travel. (So, I might add, will lecturing.)

Thinking as a Factor of Production

We can still accept the classical list of factors of production — land, labor, and capital. But the content of several of the items, notably labor and capital, has greatly changed. As "capital" became "power-driven machinery," "labor" became "thinking." What a modern worker — whether blue collar or white — rents out when he accepts employment is his brain, its sensors — eyes and ears — and its effectors — mouth and hands. It is seldom, and increasingly seldom, of importance what shoulder and leg muscles are thrown into the bargain.

It was traditional to conceptualize a factory in terms of flows of energy and materials. Raw materials were received; power was applied to them through machines; the finished product came out at the other end, to be shipped to customers. Workmen controlled the process, and continued to do those parts of it that demanded the kind of flexibility and dexterity that is best provided by the coordination of hand with eye.

But often there isn't a physical product, except in the sense that books and advertising flyers are physical products. Many businesses produce services, not goods. And even where there is a tangible product, the physical and energy flows are paralleled by an equally indispensable flow of words and symbols: the words and symbols that represent the organization's decisions, that transmit its information, that constitute its accounts and records. A factory that takes wheat and manufactures flour also takes in vast quantities of words and transforms them into other words. Most of the working force, and an increasing proportion of the machines in any corporation are engaged, not directly in the manufacture of a physical product, but in the manufacture of words.

Often, in our old-fashioned physiocratic way, we regard the physical product as "real," while we regard the words as some kind of epiphenomenon, perhaps indispensable, but certainly regrettable. Most of our ways of referring to them are pejorative: "red tape," "bureaucracy," "paperwork," "overhead." (Prefix the adjective "unnecessary" to each term, and we have all the makings of an efficiency expert's report or a legislative investigation.)

Of course it is an illusion to suppose that the words are any less real than the things, or that any human endeavor, substantial or slight, can go on without a vast production of symbols. We use the term "thinking," or more commonly now, the term "information processing," as a name for the whole collection of processes involved in manufacturing finished words from symbolic raw materials. Thus, a corporation is, among other things, a vast information-processing system, and its production machinery consists largely of information-processing machines.

Until recently, almost the only information-processing machines available for symbol production were human brains. For a long time there have been minor exceptions — steam engine governors and thermostats, for example — but these were few and inconsequential. Taking account of the manufacture of both symbols and physical products, the human brain has been by far the most important factor of production in the modern economy. About three-quarters of the total cost of doing business goes to the payment of labor, with only about one-quarter to the rental and replacement of machines.

What is most novel about automation — as contrasted with the earlier phases of mechanization — is the extent to which it introduces non-human machinery to complement and supplement human resources in information processing. Again, I must qualify the claims of novelty, lest I be convicted of gross historical inaccuracy. Many thousands of years ago, man discovered that his thinking was much impeded by his exceedingly small short-term memory — he could only hold on to a half-dozen things at a time in his thoughts. Moreover, the reliability of his long-term memory was mediocre. The difficulty in short-term memory slowed him down in doing sums, while the inaccuracy of long-term memory made him forget how many bushels of corn his neighbor owed him. Then he discovered that he could store symbols outside his own brain by recording them in physical form — by writing. The brain still had to do all the active information processing, but it could supplement its insufficient memories with the papyrus and clay tablet.

Much more recently, only five hundred years ago, man found a way in which he could manufacture cheaply an indefinite number of copies of the contents of a memory: printing. In this instance, the mechanization encompassed only the simplest — copying — of the basic information processes, leaving the more complicated transformations to human brains. Still more recently, a century ago, man discovered a way of communicating copies of symbols, by telegraph, radio, and telephone, in a moment over vast distances. Still, this new invention was only a means for distant copying, not for the transformation of information.

A more accurate way, then, of saying what is novel, is to observe that automation represents the first large-scale mechanized *active* information processing that goes beyond simple recording, copying, and transmission of copies. The inventions of writing and of printing have always been regarded as among the most significant and consequential human discoveries. From the importance that has been attached to the mechanization of these simplest aspects of information·processing, we obtain a scale that helps us assess the prospective significance of the invention, about twenty years ago, of quite general-purpose, information-processing machinery.

Public discussion of automation has focussed mainly on the blue collar worker. We see that automation has even greater import for the symbol factory than for the factory that produces physical products. In the petroleum and chemical industries, we are already very close to the automatic factory for physical production. But we need to pay even more attention to the prospects of using the modern electronic digital computer to equip automatic information processing factories. To evaluate this prospect, we must understand the nature of the computer.

The Electronic Digital Computer

I have referred to the modern computer as a general-purpose information-processing machine. The term "general-purpose" is meant to imply that a computer is capable of carrying out all of the basic kinds of information processes that are carried out by the human brain. It is not limited to storing symbols, as paper and pencil is; nor to copying symbols, as is printing; nor to transmitting symbols, as is telegraph and radio. In addition to these, it can carry out the other processes that are essential if a system is to think — that is, to make decisions, recognize patterns, solve problems, translate information from one lannguage or encoding to another, and so on. The main additional capability that appears essential for thinking is the ability to match two symbols, to determine whether they are the same or different, and to make subsequent processing conditional on the outcome of the matching process.

How do we know this? How do we know what information processing takes place when a human being thinks, or what processes a machine would need to accomplish thinking? First, it should be said that we don't know completely, or with certainty. What we do know is that computers have been programmed to perform a wide range of tasks that require thinking when performed by human beings. With respect to some of these programs, we know that the paths they follow in seeking problem solutions or in making decisions parallel very closely the paths followed by human subjects performing the same tasks when we study

114

them in the laboratory.[1]

We have found this out by asking people to think aloud while solving problems of various kinds in the laboratory, and by recording their verbalizations. We then compared their tape-recorded verbal protocols with the step-by-step output of a computer that had been programmed to solve problems of the same kinds, the programs having been constructed to use the same processes we thought people used. When a close match was achieved between the computer output and the human protocol, we could conclude that we had explained at least some of the main features of the human thinking. The computer program most certainly contained a *sufficient* set of processes for problem solving — or it would not solve the problems or parallel the human verbalization. And since the computer programs contained only basic processes of the sorts mentioned earlier, we could know that these processes, appropriately organized, are sufficiently powerful to permit a system processing them to solve problems like some solved by people.

Thus, there exists today a theory of human thinking relating to at least several tasks of real-life complexity; and, moreover, a theory that passes some rather severe tests of its sufficiency to explain the phenomena. It is a sufficiently powerful theory so that computer programs based on it can perform non-trivial thinking tasks; and it is sufficiently powerful so that some of the programs use information-processing methods in performing these tasks very similar to the processes used by people.

This development of the past decade, which continues to unfold rapidly, has two quite distinct implications. In our fascination with either one of them, we must not ignore the other. First, it opens up the prospect, already mentioned, of complementing and supplementing human labor with machinery in our symbol factories. But, second, it also opens up the prospect of greatly enhancing the effectiveness of the human information-processing in those factories. Since the latter prospect is less obvious than the former, I should like to examine it in a little more detail.

---

[1]Readers who wish a closer acquaintance with the research on computer simulation of human thinking that is the basis for these assertions will find a fuller description in E. Feigenbaum and J. Feldman (eds.) *Computers and Thought*, McGraw-Hill, New York, 1963. There is a briefer discussion in the last half of my book, *The Shape of Automation*, Harper and Row, New York, 1965.

The Improvement of Human Thinking

Human thinking, we have seen, is an important — the most important — economic resource. For some people, under some conditions, thinking is also fun. When we talk about increasing the effectiveness of human thinking, we must not forget its dual character; and we might well be willing to forego greater efficiency of thought if we could only improve thought by dehumanizing it. I mention this caveat at the outset so that we will not lose sight of it in the course of this discussion. I will anticipate my own personal conclusion to the extent of saying that I believe we can improve human thinking without making it less fun.

Volumes on improving thinking are staple items on the shelf of how-to-books. Evidently, lots of people want to improve their thinking. Experience in improving other kinds of things carries one important lesson for anyone who wants to improve his thinking: to improve something, more than superficially, you must understand it. If your automobile uses too much gas, burns oil, or doesn't run at all, you are unlikely to remedy matters much unless you know something about the mechanics of an automobile, and how its parts operate. If you are suffering from chronic digestive ills, you are unlikely to find a cure except at the hands of someone who understands the anatomy and physiology of the human digestive system.

In the past, the improvement of human thinking has foundered on the rock of understanding. We could tell when a human being had been thinking effectively because he produced an output — a solved problem, a design, a decision. We could measure the relative effectiveness of different thinkers by noting the speed with which they could solve problems, or the difficulties of the problems they could handle. But we didn't know *why* one was more effective than another, or precisely what to do to improve either.

I am exaggerating our ignorance, of course. For a long time we have had processes called "teaching," "learning," and "education" which seem sometimes to improve the quality of thinking. But we haven't quite understood why or when they work. They have been a sovereign remedy, like blood-letting was for an eighteenth century physician, that we could apply when we didn't know what else to do.

The most widely accepted theory of the educational process was largely an information-inventory theory. Clearly, most kinds of thinking required information; improvements in the amounts and quality of relevant information should improve the thinking. Hence to educate was to fill the information granaries against the day of knowledge drought. An educated brain was a library shelved centrally for handy access.

There were competing theories of education, particularly after printing raised the question of whether book knowledge was not better left in well-indexed books. Some thought that the task of education was not simply to store the raw materials for information processing, but to improve the processes themselves. "Mental discipline" was one of the forms this doctrine took. Empirical evidence later showed that courses in Latin or logic did not necessarily produce straight thinking, and this finding was extrapolated into skepticism about the possibility of teaching people how to think better.

Skepticism, or at least pessimism, is quite unjustified today. We are beginning to get precise information as to how, for example, a high school student processes information to solve a word problem in his algebra class. We understand why one student, given a description of a physically impossible situation, will proceed to set up his equations as though nothing were wrong; while another, with precisely the same information, will discover the physical incongruity. Understanding this, we can design remedial treatment for the first student.

While the range of human thinking tasks for which this kind of analysis has been carried out in detail is still very small, it includes not only tasks at the level of school courses, but also certain tasks taken from the work of middle-level business executives and professional engineers. I am not referring to situations where executive decision making has been automated by submitting for it complex mathematical models, and then using computers to solve the resulting arithmetic problems. This has been done too, on a large scale, but it has nothing to do, directly, with human thinking. Humans do not do high-speed arithmetic as a computer does when it is planning production for a refinery by solving a linear programming problem. People use quite different methods, not requiring high-speed calculation, when they have to plan production without computer assistance.

But a computer's processing is not limited to high-speed arithmetic. (This is just another talent it has, in addition to those possessed by people.) It is, as I said earlier, a general-purpose information-processor; and the programs that are interesting for an understanding of human thinking are those that do not require high-speed arithmetic. To have a name for them, let's call them "heuristic programs," and — those requiring rapid calculation — "operations research" programs. A number of operations research programs have been written to carry out the factory scheduling task known as assembly-line balancing. But

Tonge wrote a heuristic assembly-line balancing program that, instead of doing complex arithmetic, simulates closely the processes that were used by a human industrial engineer, experienced in performing that scheduling task.

Similarly, all electrical manufacturers now possess programs for *designing* (not just evaluating the designs of) many kinds of motors, generators, and transformers — programs that resemble closely the design processes formerly used by professional engineers. These are not highly "creative" design activities, but they are activities that had until recently been thought to require the thinking of a college-educated engineer.

Finally, Clarkson has written a program that simulated remarkably closely the decision-making behavior of a bank trust officer whose job it was to buy stocks and bonds for trust funds. The program predicted, with a high degree of accuracy, what specific stocks and bonds he would buy for a trust with specified assets and goals, and how many shares of each.[2] Other programs have been written more recently to simulate the pricing behavior of a department store buyer.

Some of the computer programs I have mentioned were aimed at improving the human performance by automating it; the others simply at understanding it. It is the latter goal with which we are concerned here. The programs are part of the growing body of evidence about the nature of human thought processes, evidence that is leading us to a deep understanding of these processes, and that will lead us from understanding to their improvement.

The Information-Processing Factory

I think we can now being to put the pieces of the puzzle together. I do not mean by this that we can expect to attain a perfectly clear, detailed picture. But I believe we can see some ways for thinking clearly and productively about the future, a frame for viewing it.

1. Physical production is becoming a less important aspect of management than the production of symbols. The significant factory is the information-processing factory.

2. The information-processing factory is becoming a man-machine system involving a close symbiosis between human thinkers and information-processing machines — especially digital computers.

---

[2]Clarkson's program is described in Feigenbaum and Feldman, op. cit., pages 347-371.

3. As computers become cheaper and more plentiful, and as we learn to program them to behave more flexibly, they will be able to assume a larger part of the task of day-to-day operation of the information-processing factory.

4. The division of labor between men and computers will be gradually modified as a function of the relative availabilities and capabilities of the two. In the short-run and middle-run, we may expect the executive's task to become more and more a designing and planning task. That is, he will have less to do with the actual running of the system on an hour-to-hour basis, and more and more with improving the system itself by modifying and redesigning it.

5. We may expect our understanding of human thinking, and our ability to improve it, to advance nearly as rapidly as our understanding of computers. Hence, technological progress in the manufacture of information will result from improvements in both the human and machine processing.

If you want a more concrete picture of what the information-processing factory will look like a few years hence, you will probably not be too badly misled if you examine two analogous situations that can be observed in our economy today. There are already nearly-automated factories for manufacturing physical products in the chemical industry, and there are already nearly-automated electronic data processing departments in insurance companies, banks, and large corporations generally.

When you visit either of these kinds of establishments — the automatic factory or the computerized office — you are struck first by the fact that the human workers are outside the direct work stream. The chemicals are produced untouched by human hands, as are the documents in the modern computer installation. The humans, in fact, can go away, at least for short intervals of time, without disrupting the work. They seem to be little concerned with doing the "work," much concerned with detecting unusual situations, performing preventive and corrective maintenance, and considering how the system can be altered for its improvement. They are, in fact, performing the kinds of functions that we may expect executives in the future to perform in the larger organizations to which these components belong.

It is worth noting that these nearly-automated establishments do not at all resemble the stereotype of the assembly line, with the human worker locked to the machine and forced to its work pace. If the assembly line was a thoroughly bad human environment, as many think, we need not worry that it has any similarity to the automated factory. On the contrary, the kinds of automation we have been discussing appear to permit an "interface" between man and machine that is much more adaptive to the needs and nature of each than the linkages that bound man to his tools in the past.

The Education of the Executive

We have pictured the executive as a designer and maintainer of man-machine systems that process information. We have argued that he and other human beings can expect to understand their own thought processes much more fully than they have understood them in the past. If these propositions are correct, they carry clear implications for the education of executives. One major stem of that education will be devoted to the improvement of thinking and decision-making. Another stem will be concerned with the theory and technique of designing information-processing systems.

In trying to spell out the curriculum at the next level of detail, matters become much more conjectural. It is easiest to make some statements about what it will *not* be. In the light of our analysis, and taking account of the rapid change in our society, specific factual content will become a less important part of it. We will not fill the granary with current institutional knowledge of marketing, production, and finance, because most of that knowledge is almost sure to spoil before the drought comes when we want to use it. I do not mean that people do not need to know anything in order to think and make good decisions.. They need to know a great deal, but what they need to know changes, and cannot be taught — because it is not known — a decade before use. What people most need to know is how to continue to acquire new knowledge and revise old knowledge throughout their careers.

It turns out, then, that learning how to think and learn, and learning how to design an information-processing system are not really separate and distinct topics. They are parts of the same topic. A human thinker is an organization of memories combined with a system of basic information processes that uses those memories, together with new information, to solve problems. But that is a definition of a business organization, too, whose components — men and computers — are, in turn, systems of the same general sort. This is the kind of system — at the level of the individual, and at the level of the organization — that we must understand if we are to continue our technical progress.

Conclusion

I have tried to indicate what seem to me some of the main implications of the contemporary trends in automation for business and for management in the future. My remarks have been less a sketch of the future than a suggestion of a framework for thinking about it. I have had little to say about the implications of these trends for the wider society in which organizations operate; and I should like to devote my second lecture to those broader implications.

2. ON THE ECONOMY

There still appear to be doubts in some intellectual circles whether the Industrial Revolution conferred a great blessing on man, or whether it simply brought about a series of disasters. The man on the street does not often share these doubts, nor do I. He and I believe that the Industrial Revolution was a great thing — the best thing that had happened to man in several thousands of years.

In taking this position, we are not being Pollyannas; we do not even necessarily subscribe to the doctrine of perfectibility of man. We recognize that industrialization in Europe and America imposed heavy costs — by hindsight, often avoidable costs — on large numbers of peasants and workmen who were victims of land enclosures or the cruelties of the early factory system. We recognize that the industrial revolution did not at first lay the spectre of Malthus; although it temporarily relieved the population pressure of the West, and ultimately provided the technology that will allow us to stabilize populations at reasonable levels. Finally, we recognize that an increase in material well-being is not synonymous with human happiness, that hunger is the first, but not the last, of human problems.

No, the claim for the Industrial Revolution does not deny any of these facts. It is a very simple claim. For the first time in the history of man, it has created the possibility of a world in which all can be free from hunger without some being the slaves of the others. If freedom from hunger is not a sufficient condition for happiness — and it surely is not — it is a necessary condition. It is a measure of our progress that reasonable men can now be seriously worried — at least in the United States, Canada, and a few countries of Western Europe — about the human problems that will be created by plenty.

What are these problems? How serious are they? And what effect is the new information-processing technology having on them? The problem usually mentioned first is that continuing technological advance and automation will cause large-scale unemployment. The second is that if a large part of the population is *not* removed from the labor market, by unemployment or otherwise, the society will be unable to consume what it produces — it will become a "vomitorium," to use John Theobald's vivid term.

The third problem is that if a large part of the population *is* removed from the labor market (by unemployment or a short work week) people will experience almost unendurable quantities of leisure. The fourth is that, while these problems can perhaps be solved for part of the population, many people will be unable to find employment because they lack any skills that will have economic value with the new technology. The fifth problem that is mentioned is that whatever the long-term results, rapid -technological change will cause intolerable transitional hardships. I am sure that other problems beside these are sometimes mentioned, but these are the ones that are raised most often. I will consider them in turn, but before doing so, I should like to set forth some quantitative estimates of the rate at which productivity is likely to increase.[3]

The Prospective Increase in Productivity

As far as the increase in productivity is concerned, automation represents no sharp break with the past. We have been experiencing in Canada and America — a growth in per capita production for at least a century and a half at an average rate of perhaps two per cent per year. The current rate may be slightly higher, but it is almost certainly less than three and one-half per cent. (We are all familiar now with the magic number 3.2, and some of us may be old enough to remember that, in the United States, that same magic number designated the legal boundary between the percentage of alcohol in intoxicating and non-intoxicating beverages, respectively. Perhaps the idea is that technological progress will not make us giddy as long as it does not exceed 3.2 per cent per annum.)

But is there any reason for thinking that as automation proceeds, productivity will not increase much more rapidly — at a four or five per cent rate, say. If the rate of innovation were the sole determiner of productivity change, there would be no reason for postulating a ceiling. But there is one other crucial limit. Invention transforms itself into productivity only as it becomes embodied in machines and the skills needed to use them. The rate of investment in capital and training is the main regulator of technological change.

Today in the United States, new investment (gross, not net) in computers and associated equipment accounts for well under one per cent of the gross national product. Rapid automation would require, among other things, a rapid increase in that percentage. But such an increase can only come about as a result of decreases in other forms of investment — unlikely in an expanding economy — or increases in the

---

[3]The economic theory underlying this discussion is set forth at greater length in the first chapter of *The Shape of Automation*, op. cit.

rate of saving. All the evidence suggests that capital and skilled manpower will continue to be scarce resources that will limit technological change to rates that will not differ greatly from the present one.

We can expect, therefore, something like a doubling of average family incomes measures in constant-value dollars each generation. The percentage of families in our society with incomes of less than $5,000 a generation hence can be expected to be similar to the percentage with incomes less than $2,500 at present. Provided that our standards of what constitutes poverty don't change, the number of families experiencing severe poverty in the United States and Canada will decline sharply. But of course our standards *have* changed, and will continue to change. I will be surprised if our children and grand children will apply the adjective "affluent" to families with incomes of, say, $15,000. Perhaps we are already past the point where we consider such an income to represent affluence.

I have spoken of the United States and Canada, and could have spoken in a somewhat similar vein about Australia and much of Western Europe. But of course the rest of the world has no such prospect of Twentieth Century affluence. *If* the developing countries succeed in using the available technology to control population growth, and *if* they succeed in achieving saving rates comparable to those in the industrialized nations, they may look forward to the luxury of worrying about affluence a century — four or five generations — hence. A corollary is that if we in the West are genuinely doubtful about our ability to consume what we produce, there are plenty of ways to use the surplus to help the rest of the world solve its problems of production. But I am getting ahead of my story; I will come back later to the question of our capacity to consume. I must first discuss unemployment.

Is There a Danger of Unemployment?

There is a generalization in economics, known as Say's Law, which asserts that there cannot be overproduction, because the income from the sales of goods and services, distributed to the workers and investors who contributed to its production, is precisely the amount needed to purchase those same goods and services. It's a simple matter of arithmetic to show that an economy can't produce more goods than it can purchase with its collective incomes.

Those of us who can rememember the Great Depression have had experiences, immune to any counter-argument, that prove to us that there must be some fallacy in Say's Law. John Maynard Keynes, among others, showed precisely what was wrong, and what must be done to amend the law. The revised Say's Law asserts that it is always possible for government by regulating the money supply, interest rates, and the public deficit or surplus, to maintain incomes at a level adequate to purchase the goods and services that are produced. With proper government monetary and fiscal policies, overproduction can always be prevented, at any level of employment, including substantially full employment.

[4] Everything that has happened in the past twenty-five years gives us reason to believe that the revised Say's Law is correct. The American economy needs to provide two million new jobs each year to balance the increase in the working force, and two million additional new jobs for workers "displaced" by increasing productivity. But of course, basically, it is the entrance of new population into the labor force that creates their new jobs — for they represent not only an addition to labor but an equivalent addition to prospective demand. In the same way, productivity growth creates new jobs by releasing purchasing power for new products and services. It is a matter of chickens and eggs, or, more literally of a dynamic steady state whose equilibrium can be guaranteed by government policy.

Alarm about widespread unemployment to be created by automation rises and falls inversely with the business cycle. The latter-day Luddites, who think we must smash the machines to prevent unemployment, have been rather quiet the past couple of years in the face of statistics of rising employment. They will become noisy again whenever the economy experiences a recession. They are right to object to unemployment; they are wrong in directing their protests at automation, instead of urging the correction of the situation by proper government policies. Two centuries of technological progress have demonstrated that any level of employment is compatible with any level of productivity.

---

[4] Substantially the same conclusion is reached in *Technology and the American Economy*, the report of the (U.S.) National Commission on Technology, Automation and Economic Progress (U.S. Government Printing Office, Washington, 1966).

Can Production be Consumed?

I have already touched on the question of whether rising productivity, combined with full production, will lead to a situation where all that is produced cannot be consumed, even if purchasing power is adequate. I look forward with hope, not with foreboding, to a next generation in the United States that will have an average family income of $14,000 instead of $7,000. For I know that the median income — the income attained by half the families — is less than the arithmetic average, and I do not regard $14,000 as an excessive *upper* limit for the incomes of more than half the families in the United States. I have no doubt that the bills for straightening children's teeth or paying their college tuitions will cause month-end crises in family budgets then as now.

Even the average figure $28,000, projected for two generations hence, fills me with no alarm. There are plenty of people in Pittsburgh, as I am sure there are in Toronto, who manage to have financial worries with incomes that large and larger.

Nor is it necessary to be snobbish about what money can buy. Let us not confuse productive power with materialism. Very few things of the spirit are free — some of them call for vast quantities of human resources and human effort. The most obvious example is beauty in man's environment. It costs us nothing (except the plane fare to India!) to stand on the banks of the Jumna and view the graceful towers of the Taj Mahal; but it cost the subjects of Shah Jahan enormous toil. It costs little to drive out from Paris to Chartres; but the cathedral we admire so much absorbed the whole economic surplus of that community for a century. But I hardly need to lecture the citizens of Toronto, with your dramatic new skyline, on the economic costs of creating beauty in the urban environment.

It is probably healthy for us to be embarrassed by the tail-fins of our cars, the garishness of our neon lights, and the unrelieved banality (at least in the United States) of our television. But in our embarrassment, let us not be unnecessarily snobbish, and let us not misinterpret the evidence. These excrescences probably indicate merely that we are suffering, collectively, from the tastelessness of the *nouveau riche*. They do not prove that our aesthetic and spiritual needs will be satisfied costlessly when our tastes improve. Bach stereo records cost as much as Rock and Roll, and while I haven't priced a harpsichord recently, I wouldn't be surprised to find them as expensive as electric guitars. There are many of us who would not accept extreme asceticism as a definition of the good life, for ourselves or for man in general. And I would be sorry to think that the human desire to build great new spires and towers to rival the Taj and Chartres should be interpreted as materialism.

We can only conclude that human imagination will not fail to create outlets — including some that are vulgar, some innocuous, and many that are admirable — for our ability to produce. And, of course, as incomes rise, a portion of the increased productivity will be taken in the form of additional leisure through a shortened work wek. Notice, however, that the additional leisure is not a makeshift make-work expedient to prevent unemployment; rather, it reflects our several decisions as to the forms in which we prefer to take our increased income.

Does Leisure Represent a Threat?

Our work-oriented culture still sees a close connection between idleness and deviltry. Our suspicion of leisure is reinforced also by the kind of snobbishness I decried in talking of materialism. Leisure, we fear, may mean that someone will sit on his back porch and whittle; or go fishing; or drink beer and engage in idle conversation with his friends; or do any one of a multitudinous other tedious or inane things that don't happen to be *our* particular hobbies or vices.

Undoubtedly all of those things will happen. As more leisure is placed at our disposal, we will do many things with it that can hardly be described as "useful," "creative," or even "harmless." Somehow, I do not find this prospect alarming, and am even willing to argue that you should not find it alarming. As an intellectual and an academician, I happen to place a rather high value on reading books, listening to or producing music, viewing paintings, sailing boats, and talking — especially talking. Only snobbishness could lead me to want to impose these particular tastes on others.

It is true that history tells us some rather unappealing tales about the lives of the few, restricted leisured classes that have existed in the past. We should treat these histories as warnings; they are not necessarily omens. We cannot even be sure that the leisured classes were *worse* off than their contemporaries, morally or spiritually.

A more tenable conclusion than either the hypothesis that humans only need more affluence and leisure to be happy, or the hypothesis that affluence and leisure will destroy them, is the notion that Man has a very stable capacity for moderate happiness and unhappiness in a wide range of environments. As the world treats him better, he begins to expect more from it, and to be disappointed when his expectations are not met.

127

If the world smiles less often, he gradually adapts himself to a more austere life, and balances what he has lost against the blessings that remain to him.

In psychologists' language, life is always measured against aspirations, which themselves gradually adapt to realities. No matter what happens to the economy, once we have reached the point where acute physical needs are satisfied, and most physical pain alleviated, we can expect the sum total of human happiness — could we measure it at all — to be a rather stable quantity. We should not expect further changes in the amounts of goods or leisure to make much change in that. Whether you regard that as an optimistic or pessimistic conclusion will depend on your aspirations for mankind.

A Place for the Unskilled

So far we have been talking about averages: what technological change means for the society as a whole, or for the "average man" in it. The fear is sometimes expressed, however, that in the nearly automated economy only electricians, engineers, scientists, and computer programmers will have employable skills. Are there any grounds for this fear?

The rising average educational level of the labor force is often taken as evidence for the future unemployability of the unskilled, as is the strong correlation between educational levels and low/high unemployment rates. This diagnosis almost certainly confuses cause and effect. To understand trends in labor markets, we must understand the supply situation as well as the demand situation. The educational attainments demanded of job applicants depend as much on the supply of candidates with various amounts of schooling as upon the skill requirements of the job.

Other things being equal, if an employer has a choice between a college graduate, a high school graduate, and a school dropout, he will pick them in that order. He has good reasons for doing so. In the first place, prospective employees may have learned certain things in school that enhance their competence as employees. At the risk of disloyalty to my profession, however, I am constrained to say that it is easy to exaggerate the vocational or professional value of what is taught in schools, and especially in universities, except possibly in some very specific professional curricula (and probably only for small fragments of these). "Education" is such an obviously good thing that we overestimate the skill requirements of most jobs and the time required to obtain those skills on the job.

A second, and more valid, reason for preferrring the educated for employment is that diplomas provide the employer with a cheap and relatively efficient device for singling out those who, on the average, have a little more drive and are a little brighter than the usual run of job applicants. It is probably safe to say that those who drop out of school represent a generally less well motivated and less intelligent labor pool than those who persevere. It may even be that the college graduates are a smarter, more eager group than the high school students, although I think the evidence here is a little less clear, at least in the United States where the decision to go to college is simply a sign of acceptance of middle class standards.

It is at least as true that the skills demanded by jobs adapt to the distribution of skills in the labor force as that the skills in the labor force adapt to the job demands. Both an unautomated and a highly automated economy are possible with quite widely varying levels of educational attainment in a society. For example, Germany, Japan, and England operate modern industrial economies today with a labor force whose average years of education is far less than the American average. Of course, they are also less productive, per unit of labor input, than the American economy; but it is unlikely that the difference can be attributed in any large extent to differences in the quality of labor. Moreover, we are not concerned here with the question of whether an educated labor force is more productive than an uneducated labor force, but whether unskilled labor is employable at all in an automated economy. The weight of theory and evidence suggests that it is — that man is the measure of all things, including jobs, and that the spectrum of jobs will adapt to the spectrum of available skills and abilities.

Given the large and rapid increase that is occurring in the supply of highly educated employees, it is not even clear that the spread of wages between unskilled and highly skilled labor will increase. Perhaps the more serious question we face is whether college students will become demoralized if they find that they cannot earn much more than high school graduates.

Such evidence as is available from actual instances of factory and office automation also supports the view that automation does not greatly change the range of skills that is demanded. The studies that have been made to date show rather uniformly that average skill requirements remain about the same.

Of course, evidence of what happenes at the point of automation is not conclusive. We must also consider the skill requirements of the new jobs that are created by the income generated by technological progress.

Here we know that employment in service industries is increasing, while employment in manufacturing and agriculture continues to decline. But "service industries" are a mixed bag, including both highly skilled and demanding professional occupations, like physician and professor, and relatively unskilled occupations, like waiter and salesgirl. The rate at which automation proceeds in these several occupations (I refer you to my discussion in the previous talk of the "indirect" mechanization of medical services) will respond, in turn, to the relative abundance or scarcity of suitable personnel.

A man from Mars, visiting the Earth for the first time, might well be surprised to discover that the doors on buildings are tall enough to allow almost all people to pass through them without bumping their heads. He might conclude that this is evidence of natural selection in the evolution of the human species. He would be wrong, of course, because it has been the doors that have evolved in adaptation to the changing height of people, and not vice versa.

Our man from Mars might also be surprised to find that the population possessed, collectively, just about the right spectrum of skills to fill the jobs available in the economy. After reading the discussion above, he might conclude that in this case also, the whole burden of adaptation was not borne by man.

Who Pays for Change?

The fifth question, who bears the transition costs in a society undergoing rapid technological progress, is not as easily dismissed as the other four. A wheat farmer in western Canada is pleased to learn, I am sure, that rapid increases in agricultural productivity over two centuries have been the indispensable condition for Europe's and America's escape from Malthus. He would be even more pleased if he had not had to pay for this desirable result by long hours of hard work at low rates of pay. (His prospects are better at present than they have been for years, but only because of conditions of world population pressure that we all hope are temporary.)

Societies undergoing industrialization have been singularly inept in transferring transition costs from the shoulders of the few and distributing them among the many beneficaries of progress. Part of the difficulty is built into the market mechanism itself, which is an important part of the machinery for regulating the economy.

Adam Smith's "unseen hand" — prices and markets — is a remarkable mechanism for motivating people to produce the goods that other people want, and to stop producing the goods they don't want.

There are few of us today who believe so devoutly in laissez faire that we think the market mechanism can regulate the economy unaided by other tools and an appropriate legal framework. There are few of us, however (even in Socialist economies, with the recent reinvention of prices behind the Iron Curtain), who think an economy can be regulated, and human effort directed into productive channels, without any use of the mechanism.

Low agricultural prices, in laissez faire terms, are simply a signal to farmers that they should get out of the business of producing excess wheat — or whatever it is that is in excess — and find something else that is sufficiently wanted that they can produce at a profit. For a long time, that "something else" was not something that could be produced on a farm; hence farmers were faced with the alternative of living in genteel poverty on the homestead, or starting again at the bottom of the ladder in the city.

In countries where farmers have had considerable political power — and have not had to rely primarily on export markets — governments have responded by subsidizing production that wasn't wanted, or wasting resources by restricing output without restricting inputs. If we decry such politics as bad economics, we should not ignore the problems that gave rise to them. Our task is to find ways of eliminating agricultural (or any other) overproduction without imposing serious hardship on farm families.

We generally prefer, with good reason, to motivate people with rewards than with punishments. We should prefer to pull them from the farms — if that's where too many are — by the attraction of alternatives, rather than to push them from the farms with poverty. An affluent society can afford to do that, and hardly any society can afford not to. The place for us to apply our imagination, then, is in devising schemes that will make it easy for people to acquire new skills in occupations where labor is scarce, to move to places where labor is wanted, and to move jobs to places where labor is available. This hardly seems too difficult an undertaking if we put our minds to it, and make it a central objective of public policy.

Problems and Opportunities

Some apology is due for such a lengthy exposition of "problems." Nevertheless, when we face an uncertain future, it is usually necessary to still our apprehensions before we can think clearly and confidently about the opportunities open to us. few people enjoy an airplane ride if thy think the wings are about to drop off. I hope that I have been able to persuade you that if continuing, rapid, technological change presents problems, they are solvable problems; and that having dealt with them, we are free to turn our eyes to the opportunities.

The material opportunities are obvious and have already been discussed. Briefly, we can gradually eliminate acute poverty as a source of human unhappiness. We can devote an increasing part of our resources to meeting needs of the spirit — both trivial and significant.

Over and above these uses of our increased production, I don't see how we can regard technological progress as anything but inevitable — not just inevitable in the sense that we wouldn't know how to prevent it, but inevitable in the sense that it is the characteristic form of expression, in our modern world, of our sense of exploration and adventure. For a couple of centuries now, there hasn't been much fun left in voyages of exploration on the globe. Too much of it is too well known. Mount Everest was perhaps the last of the great targets of terrestrial adventure.

The conquest of Everest was almost simultaneous with the new adventure of outer space. The broad appeal that space exploration has had, the willingness of the public to pay the cost of such "impractical" adventures, proves how deeply ingrained the spirit of exploration is. I hope I am not just an academic special pleader in suggesting that intellectual adventures have almost as broad an appeal as adventures in space. Not everyone wants to be, or can be, an active participant, any more than everyone of us can or wants to float outside a spaceship. But both science and art can have broad appeal as spectator sports — as expressions of the sense of adventure.

Among the scientific adventures going on at the present time, two have an especially close relation to the information-processing revolution. One of these is molecular biology, which has discovered, within the past five years, how genetic information is encoded in the cells, and which is beginning to discover how that information is used by organisms as a blueprint for growing from birth to maturity.

The second relevant adventure is the growth of information-processing psychology that I discussed briefly in my first lecture. Man is making great strides in the exploration of the most fascinating world of all — himself. Just as Man grown by the long, intricate processes of evolution seems to many of us more interesting and more valuable than Man cast in the mold of special creation, so Man whose thinking involves explainable, but intricate, organizations of information processes seems more worthy of admiration than Man whose thinking is a product of cloudy, unintelligible processes that we name "intuition" or "judgment."

Managers will be in an especially good position to join, both as spectators and participants, in this adventure of exploration into Man's mind. For the very core of their job is to design, develop, and maintain those complex information-processing systems called organizations that we count on to carry out most of Man's economic work.

6.4
PROGRAMS AS FACTORS OF PRODUCTION

HERBERT A. SIMON

Carnegie Institute of Technology

As a member of that rapidly-growing happy band who spend our days trying to find ways of inducing computers to do interesting new things, I feel a good deal of responsibility for understanding the probable economic and social consequences of introducing these new devices into our society and widening the range of their applications. From an economic and social standpoint, are computers and automation something new under the sun, or are they to paraphrase Clausewitz, simply "a continuation of the Industrial Revolution by other means?" Do they call for a new chapter in the economic textbooks, or are they merely details in the chapters on capital and distribution?

In a series of essays published under the title of THE SHAPE OF AUTOMATION,[1] I explored some of the macroeconomic aspects of these questions—in particular, the implications of automation for full employment, real wages, and the demand for unskilled labor. I will not repeat my conclusions here except to observe that I ended my investigation with more optimism than I began with. From the standpoints considered, automation does, indeed, seem a natural continuation of the Industrial Revolution, fully compatible with full employment, creating a high probability that labor will reap all or most of the gains of rising productivity.

The present essay is an inquiry in a different direction. It begins with the observation that what we generally call a "computer" includes both a hardware component and a software component—both a collection of electronic gear, and a collection of programs and data that are stored in the hardware memory. During the first five years that computers were obtainable commercially, to buy or rent a computer meant to buy or rent the hardware. Since that time, during the last decade or so, the merchandise on the market has generally included a substantial software as well as hardware component. In fact, the software represents a steadily increasing part of the total purchase or

---

[1] Harper & Row, 1965. I have been reinforced in the conclusions reached in those essays by noting their agreement with the subsequent report of the National Commission on Technology, Automation, and Economic Progress, *Technology and the American Economy*. Washington: Government Printing Office, 1966, and the recent book by Charles Silberman, *The Myths of Automation*. New York: Harper & Row, 1966.

[1]

rental cost, and no computer of any size could be marketed today without being accompanied by appropriate software.

Computer software falls into a number of categories, including: (1) monitor programs and scheduling algorithms, to make the system available to a multitude of users, and to allocate and schedule its facilities among them; (2) programming languages, such as assembly languages and user-oriented languages (e.g., FAP, FORTRAN, COBOL, SIMSCRIPT); (3) utility routines, such as linear programming algorithms, standard statistical packages, and programs for solving differential equations. For the most part, computer users either employ these pre-cooked programs, or write their programs in user-oriented languages. Few users program in machine language, and almost none in large installations run their programs outside monitor and scheduling systems. Some current suggestions that, because of economies of scale, large central computing hardware systems will take on the character of public utilities will, if realized, accentuate and hasten these trends.

If computers, regarded as a factor of production, are to be classified with capital, they are capital with a difference. To be sure, there are precursers, such as the Jacquard loom, which was as truly programmed as the most modern solid-state machine. But the software component of modern computers is so prominent in comparison with anything that went before that we must treat the difference as having qualitative significance.

Computer Programs as a Form of Labor

An alternative to regarding computers as a new form of capital is to regard them as a new form of labor. This, too, is a familiar idea which we might call the R.U.R. hypothesis. The label is apt provided that it does not evoke spectres of computers "taking over," but is merely used to denote their applicability to a widening range of humanoid tasks. I should like to introduce an allegory for exploring further the reasonableness and limitations of regarding computers as labor. Like most allegories, this one will involve certain simplifications of real life.[2]

[2] The technological developments that underlie the possibilities of using human and computer programs interchangeably in a wide range of tasks are discussed in my paper "Decision Making as an Economic Resource," in Lawrence H. Seltzer (ed.), *New Horizons of Economic Progress* (Detroit: Wayne State University Press. 1964), pp. 71–95.

[2]

In the time of Columbus, devices for ocean transportation incorporated both a hardware component—a sailing ship—and a software component—a navigator. A shift in the production function for ocean transportation could result from an improvement either in sailing ships or in the skills of navigators. Improvements in hardware were incorporated in the production function as new ships were launched. I suppose that the economics of the matter were handled by using Terborgh-like replacement formulas to determine when ships had become obsolete and should be replaced by improved ones.

Improved navigational technology, however, could be incorporated in the production function *either* by replacing navigators or by retraining the present ones. At a cost, an experienced navigator might be trained to use a magnetic compass to find North, or, some centuries later, a chronometer to determine his longitude.

One important *difference,* then, between the hardware and software components in ocean navigation lay in the greater opportunities for revising and improving the latter without complete replacement. One important *similarity* was that, even in the absence of technological change, both hardware and software gradually wore out and had to be replaced anyway. In both cases, the replacement cost was not negligible. Ships were obviously costly to build, and navigators could only be produced by years of training and experience.

Let us now introduce an automated navigator into this technology, in the form of a programmable computer. Only one thing has changed in the economic structure of the situation, but a rather significant one thing: many technological changes in the art of navigation can now be introduced, almost without cost, by replacing the present program in the automated navigator with a copy of a program incorporating the improved method. The automated technology is an example of a technology that can be copied almost without cost.[3] To understand the significance of the difference, we must consider the economics of copying.

THE ECONOMICS OF COPYING

The significance of cheap copying processes is that when they are available, the cost of developing improvements need be paid only once. Among the crucial events in human evolution have been the introduction of five important advances in the technique of copying and

[3] *Ibid.,* pp. 91–93.

[3]

storing information: (1) organismic reproduction with duplication of genetic material, (2) indirect programming through learning, (3) preservation of artifacts, (4) writing, and (5) printing. Each of these has its characteristic structure of costs. None of them allows "instant" reprogramming of existing hardware. The third and fourth are simply storage devices; the fifth allows cheap copying; but all these last three contribute to production only through the second— learning, hence do not avoid its costs.

Direct copying of computer software has characteristics, therefore, quite different from any of these earlier copying techniques. When an improved program has been invented for the automatic navigator, it cannot only be installed in new navigators at no addition to cost, but it can also be provided to existing navigators instantly and substantially without cost. The comparative advantage of automatic navigators relative to human navigators will increase in any field where the technology is advancing rapidly, since improvements can be incorporated in the former sooner than in the latter.[4]

THE COSTS OF SOFTWARE DEVELOPMENTS

In the case of any copyable technique, there is a problem of how the costs of developing improvements are to be recovered. In the absence of adequate opportunity for recovery, there will, of course, be underinvestment in research and development. In a competitive economy, the problem becomes the more severe the less expensive and more rapid the copying process.

Patent and copyright laws are the usual modern procedures for returning rewards to the authors of technological advances that can

[4] As a first approximation, if the navigational technology is advancing at a linear rate of B units per year, and if P_N is the cost of replacing a navigator's program, then the optimal interval, T^*, for replacing programs is given by:

$$T^* = ((2\ P_N)/B)^{1/2}$$

That is, the optimal replacement period varies directly with the square root of the cost of program replacement, inversely with the square root of the rate of change of the technology. This approximation was first derived for equipment replacement policy by George Terborgh, *Dynamic Equipment Policy* (New York: McGraw-Hill, 1949), p. 254. See also, *ibid.*, p. 283.

Thus, because of program copying costs, the technology actually employed will lag, on the average, $T^*/2$ time units behind the best available technology. It is easy to see that if human and automated programs have been just competitive (with a lower copying cost for the latter than the former), the latter will be substituted for the former if B increases.

We can similarly derive optimal replacement intervals, T^*_s and T^*_w, for ships and shipwrights' programs, respectively. The lag in the technology incorporated in ships will then average: $(T^*_s + T^*_w)/2$.

be copied. Secrecy is another method still widely used, but not applicable when the improvement can be copied from artifacts embodying it. (Study of artifacts may permit copying not only the objects themselves, but even improved methods of manufacture, evidences of which are preserved in the manufactured object.) At an earlier point in history (and even today in the military sphere), governments intervened to prevent the export of technological improvements, whether in the form of machinery or of programs recorded in the memories of artisans.

Because of the cheapness of the copying process, and the potential value of even single exemplars, the protection of inventors' interests in improved computer programs is a matter of great technical difficulty. Here we must distinguish programs written to run on a particular type of machine, on the one hand, from programs written in higher-level languages that are easily transferred to different machines. The machine manufacturer can recover investments in software developments of the former kind, since they can only be used with his machine. On the other hand, the improvements are then not used everywhere they might be, and competing manufacturers must duplicate development investments, both sources of misallocation of resources.

With progress in software technology, programs have tended to become more independent of hardware. Hence, the more serious problem from a social point of view appears to be to secure a sufficiently high rate of investment in software development.

HUMAN AND COMPUTER PROGRAMS

Labor's contribution to production is achieved by the coordination of a system of sensory organs—eyes and ears—with a system of effectors—principally hand and mouth—by means of those stored programs we call "skills." [5] In our Columbian ocean transport technology there are both the skills of the navigator—whether human or automated—and the skills, or technical know-how, of the shipbuilders. Evidence from wartime destruction tells us that an economy that has lost a large part of its physical capital, but retained its pool of technology, can restore previous levels of productivity relatively rapidly.

[5] See "Decision Making as an Economic Resource," *op. cit.*, pp. 80–82.
"The Economic Implications of Learning by Doing" are examined in Kenneth Arrow's well-known essay with that title (*Review of Economic Studies*, 29: 155–173, June 1962) and in the references cited there.

[5]

The stored skills in a pre-computer economy must be replaced each generation, even if there is no technological change, since these skills must exist in human brains in order to be useful for production. The replacement costs are by no means the same as the costs of formal education in the economy. In the first place, the entire time, not just the school time, of children prior to their entrance into the labor market should be charged as part of the replacement cost. Whether in school or out, children learn to speak, become acquainted with the common artifacts of their culture and, at least in simple economies, learn one or more relevant production technologies.

In the second place, in societies with formal educational systems, a large part of what is taught and learned in the schools has no productive significance. This is certainly true of most of the curriculum of the contemporary American school system. Schooling is best regarded, under such circumstances, primarily as a consumption good that has as a small by-product the storage of a certain amount of production skill.[6] If I were given a contract, at a fixed price, to produce research scientists, I would certainly turn the finished product out of my educational institution at an age earlier than 25!

In the third place, much of the transmission of programs takes place through on-the-job training and experience. These training costs do not show up in the social accounts, but are hidden as direct costs of production.

In a peasant culture, the avoidable cost of replacing programs each generation is probably very small, because by the time children are physically capable of doing hard manual work they have already learned most of the skills they will use. On the other hand, the absence of mechanisms for cheap transmission of programs and for reliable storage of programs probably operates to slow technical progress or even cause the loss of discoveries, so that improvements need to be repeatedly re-invented.

We observe, for example, that there was only minor technological advance in peasant cultures from pre-Christian times to the Industrial

[6] My intention here is simply to state a fact, not to offer social criticism. In particular, I do not mean to argue that transmission of production programs *should* be the sole, or even a major goal of formal education. I simply observe that it is easy to jump to the conclusion that this is what education is all about. The jumping has been encouraged by studies of American education that have made much of the, largely spurious, correlation between amount of education and earnings. The correlations are spurious because they have been uncorrected, or inadequately corrected, for differences in ability, in ambition, and in family status.

[6]

Revolution. We may conjecture that the technologies of these cultures remained in a state of dynamic equilibrium—they were able to maintain just that level of technology at which the forgetting from one generation to the next was balanced by reinvention. Increases in the density of population, and improvements in the security or economy of travel and transportation would allow increases in specialization, hence permit a larger stock of programs to be transmitted. Nomadism, on the other hand, through increasing the difficulty of retaining numerous physical possessions, would decrease the stock of the culture's artifacts, hence degrade an important store of technological information.

It is not my purpose here to rewrite cultural history in terms of the problems a society faces in maintaining and transmitting stored programs. It might be a rewarding thing to do, but I will leave it to others better informed than I about the facts. The notion of a learning-forgetting equilibrium of technology is not relevant, however, only to peasant cultures. It is equally applicable, for example, to the problem that a university department faces in remembering its own policies, and all of the subtle considerations that went into their formulation. As faculty come and go, secretaries marry and are replaced, files are lost, and conditions change, the subtleties vanish, and the policy tends to reduce to a few general (though not necessarily sound) principles, plus some specific regulations that happen to have been recorded in documents that continue to be referred to. Often, the documents themselves become inoperative because the "retrieval" programs that would cause them to be referred to on appropriate occasions are lost.

In sum, the costs of maintaining a store of human programs over periods during which personnel turnover is substantial are very large. Storing technology in the form of computer programs rather than human programs opens up new possibilities for greatly reducing such costs.

Learning Programs

Learning is needed not only to transmit programs from generation to generation, and to modify programs to incorporate new technology, but also simply to adapt programs to problems posed by a constantly changing environment. The potential economic gains to be realized from cheap copying will be inconsequential if new programs have to be devised *ad hoc* for each small change in circumstances.

The program of the navigator may make use of large amounts of information about tides, currents, winds, coastlines, and harbors in

[7]

different parts of the world. The program, to be workable, must be factorable into two parts: (a) a store of information, that can be augmented readily by simple processes of memorization, and by simple programs for consulting available reference sources; and (b) a general-purpose program that can apply appropriate parts of this data store to any given specific navigational problem.

The economy of automated programs will depend on their having comparable features. They must be learning programs, at least in the sense that they can apply new information to new situations, and probably also in the stronger sense that they are capable of some adaptive modification in their own structures. Without such features, each program would be applicable to only a narrow range of situations; hence little would be gained from the availability of cheap means for producing copies.

DIFFUSION OF NEW TECHNOLOGY

The ocean transportation technology of our allegory depends both on the programs stored in the navigator, and on the programs for the manufacture of ships. All of our discussion of the costs of programming and improving the programs of human or automatic navigators applies quite as well to the programs of human or automated shipwrights.

Technological advance requires the invention of new techniques, but also the development and storage of the programs necessary to apply these techniques. For any extensive technological change, a whole series of "reprogramming" decisions have to be made—by managers, engineers, and workmen. In evaluating these decisions, numerous externalities will be encountered, because the effectiveness of the new technology in comparison with the old will depend on what programs have already been stored. Thus, the productivity of capital in the form of automobiles will depend on the commonness of driving and mechanics' programs in the population, as well as the presence or absence of such material artifacts as roads and gas stations.

One particular difficulty in the diffusion of new technologies is that the new programs have to be ingested, at least in considerable part, in order to evaluate them. Hence, much of the reprogramming cost must be borne before an accurate evaluation can be made—or acceptance of the new technology must be postponed until its advantages are obvious even to the untutored eye. To the extent that the

[8]

programs of the new technology are computerized, the costs of developing the programs will have to be borne, but not borne anew in each application. We would expect more rapid diffusion of new technologies under these conditions.

THE RETRIEVAL OF PROGRAMS

Automation of the programs that constitute a technology will make explicit not only the problem of modifying programs to take advantage of advances in knowledge, but also the problem of bringing existing programs to bear in the situations where they are relevant. Before considering the form that this problem will take in an automated technology, let us examine it in the context of our present culture.

Specialization increases the repertory of programs that are available within the economy taken as a whole. It does not guarantee, however, that the sophisticated programs stored in the specialist's brain will be used whenever relevant. Someone, at the point of problem impact, must note the relevance, and must have an effective procedure for locating the specialist. Even when he has been located, there may be difficult problems of compatibility between his programs and those of the persons consulting him—what we call nowadays an "interface" problem. The specialist may fail to understand the problem properly, and those consulting him may fail to understand his solution, or how to combine his knowledge with aspects of the problem that fall outside his specialty.

There is much talk today about the "knowledge explosion," and how this explosion makes it more difficult to locate relevant knowledge. Much of this alarm is ill-considered, for the advance of knowledge is not primarily an additive (or multiplicative) accumulation of knowledge. It is primarily the reorganization of knowledge to make it more parsimonious and more applicable. To become a research chemist should involve less learning today than it did fifty years ago, because physical chemistry and quantum mechanics have provided such powerful tools for organizing facts, and indeed making them derivable from theory.

This is not the place to pursue this particular issue. It is raised simply to put into perspective current alarm about the stock of knowledge. In this age as in any other, an important part of the programs that define the technology are programs for retrieving

[9]

142

knowledge from its storage places. Among the important prospective consequences of automation are its consequences for retrieval techniques.

The cost of retrieving relevant programs depends, first, on finding them, second, on making them usable in the application situation. Finding costs depend, in turn, on the structure of available indexes and on the power of the available search programs. As illustration, consider the following problem: One of the functions of the National Academy of Sciences is to provide agencies of the National government with expert scientific advice when needed. What kind of processing system is required for the offices of the National Academy to perform this function?

One can dream up designs for elaborate indexes of specialists. One such index, the National Register, actually exists. However, there is a much simpler and fully adequate device available to the staff of the National Academy: the telephone. Any given inquiry can be roughly classified by the field of knowledge to which it belongs. The appropriate members of the Academy staff can carry around in memory indexes to the names of a few persons who are knowledgeable in each of these fields. Each of the knowledgeable respondents, in turn, has a more detailed map of specialties within the general area, and an index of names of the corresponding specialists. These specialists will have their own indexes, and so on. A series of three or four phone calls can hardly fail to locate the best program in the United States to address itself to the problem at hand.

When we look at this retrieval scheme in detail to determine what would be involved in automating it, we see that there is nothing very complicated about the processing. Each of the memories employed contains, among other things, a taxonomy. We may visualize each choice point in the classification key as containing questions to be answered in order to make the choice (i.e., questions the specialized informant can ask in order to pin down the nature of the inquiry).

In spite of the apparent simplicity of a scheme for retrieving specialized information, retrieval in our present technology is by no means a perfected art. A good example of the inadequacies is provided by the lag between the level of sophistication of the statistical techniques applied by data users, and the level of sophistication among experts in statistics. The more sophisticated programs are not retrieved when they would be appropriate because (a) the user is not

[10]

aware of their potential relevance, and (b) his access to the existing knowledge through appropriate inquiry procedures has not been institutionalized. (Among other things, he may have no way to recompense the expert properly for his time and trouble on a problem that is only a matter of "application," hence not of direct professional interest to the technique-oriented expert.)

Automation of technologies will cause the problem of retrieving relevant programs from the stock of existing ones to become more explicit than it has been in the past. The computer technology—both hardware and software—will also provide new means for retrieval. It will also create interesting new problems for economists, relating to the design of efficient retrieval systems.

One question that will arise repeatedly is the question of how far information should be processed when stored, and to what extent, on the other hand, it should be processed on demand. Should executives, for example, have "instantly" available the answers to large numbers of questions they might conceivably ask, should they have available the programs that will seek out and compute the answers in a short time, or should they have available programming languages that will allow them to write programs that, in turn, will find the answers? The cost structures of automated information systems are so different from those of manual systems that all of these issues will have to be rethought as the new technology develops.

Conclusion

The preceding pages develop the viewpoint that a technology exists largely in the minds of its labor force, and in the future will be distributed between those minds and the memories of computers. If programs, stored in one or the other of these forms, constitute the core of a technology, then important consequences are likely to follow from the fact that automation greatly decreases the cost of making copies of such programs.

One of the obvious consequences of cheaper copying is that there will be underinvestment in program improvement unless steps are taken to reward inventors of programs or to subsidize invention. A second consequence is that the comparative advantage of automation will tend to be particularly great in situations where frequent and rapid program change is called for, and will tend to be relatively less in areas where only a few copies of a program can be used. Since

[11]

human programs are at least modestly capable of on-the-job learning and adaptation to specific situations, the range of feasible automation will depend heavily on the extent to which similar learning and adaptive features can be incorporated in automated programs.

The concept of technology as consisting of stored programs gives us a somewhat novel framework for theory about the rate of technological progress and the rate of diffusion of new technology. The level of technology that a society can maintain will depend heavily—indeed, in the past may *have* depended heavily—on the costs of transmitting programs from each generation to the next. It will depend also on the possibility of economizing transmission costs through specialization.

To the extent that there is specialization of programs within an economy, retrieval programs for locating relevant knowledge and skill become an important element in productive capacity. When copying costs are high, locating a relevant specialist will be useless if his time is fully occupied. With techniques for copying programs cheaply, the numbers of specialist programs will respond flexibly to demands, hence retrieval programs will take on an even greater importance than they have at present.

I am sure that the automation of programs will have many consequences beyond those I have identified here. If there is anything we can say with confidence about a new technology, it is that we will not really understand its implications until we have lived with it for a few generations. Now that we have perhaps achieved some understanding of the First Industrial Revolution—the revolution of power—we are already in the midst of the Second—the revolution in the processing of information. It is important that we identify the salient characteristics—like cheap copying techniques—of the new technology, and the consequences of those characteristics for the economy.

[12]

6.5

INFORMATION STORAGE AS A PROBLEM IN ORGANIZATION DESIGN

Herbert A. Simon

When I selected the title for this paper, I was not aware that it reads as well backwards as forwards — I might just as well have taken the topic of "organization design as a problem in information storage" as the topic of "information storage as a problem in organization design." Since organizations are best viewed as complex systems for processing information, posing either topic leads, in the end, to the same thing.

Nineteenth century economics focussed attention upon the process of converting factors of production — land, labor, and capital, say — into commodities which were then sold and consumed. Commodities were sometimes intangible — "services" — but more commonly tangible — "goods." A manufacturing concern purchased factors of production, converted them into commodities, and sold them.

Twentieth century organization theory has taught us that most of the man-hours contributed by the employees of a business enterprise are only indirectly concerned with the actual process of converting factors of production into commodities. With mechanization, the largest fraction of the direct labor inputs into that process have been eliminated. Today, "labor" is largely employed to process the information that is used, in turn, to make the decisions that govern and control the commodity conversion process. The white collar worker (and, to an increasing extent, the blue collar worker also) is primarily an information processor. The commodities he produces are symbols.

In the past twenty-five years, the human information processor — white collar labor — has been joined, in the manufacture of symbols, by a new form of capital, the digital computer. As we know today, the digital computer bears the same relation to the processing of information that the steam engine bears to the processing of physical materials. Economic analysis must be generalized to encompass information processes as central processes, and information-processing labor and capital as central factors of production. It may turn out that the principles of classical economics apply to information in exactly the same way as they apply to more traditional goods and services. We will not know whether this is so until we carry out the analysis.

INTRODUCTION

As one part of our analysis of information as an economic good, we must understand the economics of information within the business firm itself. The function that relates inputs of information and of information processors to outputs of decisions is the twentieth century production function, *par excellence*. Rationalization of the organization and operation of the firm is, first and foremost, rationalization of this production function. My title, then, "Information Storage as a Problem in Organization Design," and its converse, "Organization Design as a Problem in Information Storage," refer to the rationalization of the business firm, viewed as an information-processing system.

The time is not ripe — or at least I am not ripe — for a general, comprehensive approach to the problem. It would seem more fruitful to identify some manageable subproblems, and then to formulate and attack those subproblems. This is the approach that Professor Jacob Marschak has also adopted. In his work on the theory of teams, he has analysed the economics of message transmission in organizations, taking account of the balance between the costs of communication, in the one hand, and the improvements in decision making that may be brought about through reduction of uncertainty, on the other. I should like to borrow Professor Marschak's strategy, but apply it to a number of different information-processing and information-storage questions. To make a little more concrete the nature of the questions we shall be dealing with, I will begin with a bit of history that has considerable illustrative value.

An Example: The Storage of Mathematical Tables

Before the invention of the modern digital computer (B.C., let us say), applied mathematicians — engineers, navigators, surveyors, astronomers — depended heavily, in their numerical calculations, upon the availability of printed tables of the values of important mathematical functions. The most important of these were the tables of logarithms, which allowed the calculator to replace multiplication with addition. Tables were also computed and published of the trigonometric functions and their logarithms, of compound interest and present value, of elliptic functions, and so on.

At a level of common sense, it is obvious why it was efficient to use such tables, but at the danger of elaborating the obvious, I should like to look at the matter in rather more microscopic detail. Suppose I want to know how much money I shall have at the end of five years if I invest $100 at 5% interest, compounded annually. With paper and pencil, I can solve that problem in a couple of minutes, arriving (if I didn't make a mistake) at the answer: $127.64. In carrying out the calculation, I had to write down some 93 digits — exclusive of the "carry" digits.

If I want to make a cost-benefit analysis of what I gain by using a compound interest table, instead of carrying out the calculation by hand, the balance runs as follows:

(1)   Cost Without Tables
       = cost of a sequence of five multiplications
       (by hand methods) = $5\,C_M$

(2)   Cost With Tables
       = cost of one multiplication (by mass-production
       methods) + interest and depreciation on book of
       tables + cost of retrieving one entry from
       tables = $C'_M + C_T + C_R$

I can trace the costs one step further back by observing that the cost of the tables, on which the interest and depreciation charges are based, depends on the costs of making the original calculations plus the costs of recording, printing, publishing, and distributing them. If a person had occasion to make such a calculation frequently enough, he could amortize the cost of the tables over a large number of calculations, and hence incur only a small unit cost. Moreover, if a large number of persons made such calculations, the cost of preparing the tables could be spread over many copies, thus reducing the unit cost of a copy. Notice, however, that the cost of retrieving an entry from the tables is a cost incurred by each user at each use.

After the development of the modern computer (A.D., let us say), it seemed obvious that an important use of the new device would be to produce tables of mathematical functions that had not heretofore been available. This would be possible economically because the computer could make the calculations of the table entries much more cheaply than they could be made by more primitive methods (reduction in C_M). The other costs would be unaffected.

I must interrupt my account at this point to add a word about accuracy. A substantial part of the cost of making calculations as well as the cost of retrieving information from tables is incurred in taking various precautions against error. Simple copying errors are among the most frequent and most costly to detect and correct. Hence, the economies of producing tables by computer depended heavily on the computer being able to output the table entries in photo-reproducible form, and without copying. The savings from error reduction and elimination of proof-reading steps may, in many applications, be more important than the direct savings from faster methods of computation.

Now, with trivial exceptions, the modern computer has not, in fact, been used to prepare tables of mathematical functions. For it was soon discovered that the cost, C_R, of retrieving an entry from a book of tables may exceed the cost of computing the value of that entry when and as needed. Hence, the retrieval cost should be avoided by not publishing the book, but instead simply storing in the computer the algorithm for computing its entries, so that it will be available to anyone wishing to find a particular value.

This was the first — modest but important — step toward using the computer, not just to carry out old processes with faster and cheaper machinery but to replace the old processes with new processes better suited to the new machinery. In the case of the mathematical tables, it proved possible to take even a second step. Storing the algorithms in the computer allowed one to compute only those functions for which algorithms had been written. If a convenient language were available for expressing algorithms, then the user could instruct the computer to produce any value of any function as needed. And thus the notion of "program library" was supplemented, though not displaced, by the notion of "compiling language."

Implications of the Example

Our historical example illustrates a very important point about the economics of technological change, a point that has long been familiar to industrial engineers. Let me call it the "horseless-carriage fallacy." In evaluating the economic effects of a new technology — particularly one that represents a major innovation — it is not enough to estimate how much the new technology will reduce the cost of existing processes. The far more important question is what existing processes the new technology will displace, what new processes it will introduce, and what the economic consequences will be of these new processes. If we try to estimate the effects of the invention of the automobile by treating it as a horseless carriage — a means for doing with a new instrument the tasks we had previously done with a horse — we will miss completely its principal economic and social significance.

In assessing the significance of the contemporary innovations in information processing also, we must avoid the horseless-carriage fallacy — I suppose we could call it the "fast abacus fallacy." A computer is not simply a device for producing mathematical tables by other means; it is a device, in this instance, for postponing the generation of table entries until those entries are needed, and for avoiding entirely the storing of those entries in anticipation of future use.

Who Needs to Know?

There is another very important point to be learned from our example of the mathematical tables: that we must be very careful and precise in defining what we mean when we say that someone "has" certain information. What does it mean to say that I "have" the information that $100 invested at 5% for five years yields $127.64. Do I "have" the information if I have memorized it and can give it to someone on request? Do I also have it, if I haven't memorized it, but have it on a piece of paper before me, where I can read it off? Do I have it, if the piece of paper is in my desk drawer? Do I have it, if I have a book of compound interest tables on my shelf? And what if the book is not on my shelf but in the library? Do

I have it if I have a computer console in my office, and know the formula for compound interest?

There is a very strong preconception in our culture that one only "has" information when it is in his head. This preconception is inherited, I suspect, from a preliterate culture, or at least from one in which books and other written material were not readily available — when the human head was, in fact, the largest and cheapest large-scale memory available. The assumption that information needs to be in the head to be possessed needs careful re-examination in the context of today's technology.

To "have" information, it is neither necessary nor sufficient that it be stored in the human head. The example has already shown why it is not necessary. It is not sufficient because information in the head, like information anywhere, must be retrieved in order to be used. How retrievable it is depends on the form in which it was stored, and upon how it was indexed when it was stored. "I *know* his name, but I can't think of it," is one frequent form that the retrieval problem takes. Another common form, all too familiar to teachers, involves information that has been memorized, but not understood. Such information can be retrieved in literal form, but cannot be used in any of the problem-solving processes for which it was intended.

The question of where and how information has to be stored in order to be known becomes one stage more complicated when we are concerned with information in organizations. Over the past twenty-five years, for example, electric power utilities have had to become knowledgeable about atomic power, and in recent years have had to make choices between atomic and fossil fuels in designing new central generating stations. Who, in the electric utility, has to "know" about the atomic technology in order for these decisions to be made wisely? And if expert advice is accepted from those who do know, how are the experts legitimated and their knowledge accepted in the decision process? And, finally, how do those who make decisions in the organization "know" what expert knowledge is available in the organization, where it is located, and how reliable it is? In considering information storage in organizations, then, we shall have to give special consideration to the issues of legitimating "expert" information sources, and of indexing such information sources for retrieval by other parts of the organization.

Plan of the Paper

As I indicated earlier, I do not know how to launch a comprehensive attack on the whole problem of information storage and information processing in organizations. Instead, I will take up a number of particular problems, each of which represents a partial approach, but which, in aggregate, may cast light on many facets of the total problem. The remaining sections of the paper will consider, in turn:

1) The economics of updating information stores;
2) The economics of attention-directing and "intelligence" functions;
3) The retrieval of information in organizations;
4) The information explosion reconsidered.

UPDATING INFORMATION STORES

In my paper, "Programs as Factors of Production," I showed that the economics of updating information stores is really a quite conventional problem in optimal equipment investment policy under technological change. The argument goes through in a straightforward way independently of whether the information in question consists of a body of data or a set of programs for solving problems or making decisions. It provides us with an approach to the economics of learning.

Let me review the method for calculating the optimal time interval for updating an information store under steady-state conditions. We assume that the value of the information store ($\underline{V}$) remains constant as long as the system is not updated, but is increased to $\underline{V}_0 + \alpha\underline{T}$ if its previous value was $\underline{V}_0$ and it is updated after a time interval, $\underline{T}$. The assumption is equivalent to supposing that the production function, $\alpha t + \beta$, increases linearly with time, through technological change, and that the production function of the information store is equal to the best function technologically attainable at the time it was last updated. (Obviously, if we assumed that the productivity of the non-updated store deteriorated linearly with time, this would increase the coefficient α correspondingly but would not otherwise change our model.)

Let us suppose that, when the updating interval is $\underline{T}$, a cost $\underline{K} + b\underline{T}$ is incurred each time the store is updated. $\underline{K}$ is the fixed cost of updating, $\underline{b}$ is the variable cost for the quantity of changed information that accumulates during one time period. Then the updating cost per unit of time is (T/K + $\underline{b}$), while the cost of using an outdated store is $\alpha T/2$ (since, on average, the time since the last updating will be $T/2$). Hence, we wish to determine the particular value of $\underline{T}$, say $\underline{T}^*$, that minimizes:

1. $c = \dfrac{K}{T} + b + \dfrac{\alpha T}{2}$

We find:

2. $\dfrac{dc}{dt} = -\dfrac{K}{T^2} + \dfrac{\alpha}{2} = 0$

from which,

3. $T^* = \left(\dfrac{2K}{\alpha}\right)^{1/2}$

This formula is already familiar from Terborgh's work on equipment replacement policy. (George Terborgh, *Dynamic Equipment Policy*. (New York: McGraw-Hill, 1949; pp. 254, 283)).

From equation (3) we read off the implications, which are intuitively obvious, that the optimal interval between updatings of an information store will increase with an increase in the fixed cost of an updating, and will decrease with an increase in the rate at which information is changing. By examining more closely the parameters, K and α, we can derive from these further implications that are perhaps not quite so obvious.

It is only the fixed cost, $\underline{K}$, of updating, and not the variable cost, $\underline{b}$, per unit of elapsed time, that enters into the equation determining $\underline{T}^*$. In actual situations, the volume of updating may not increase proportionately with the time, $\underline{T}$, since the last updating. For example, the information store may contain only the most recent value of a frequently-changing datum. Then we must replace the expression ($\underline{K}$ + $\underline{b}T$) with ($\underline{K}$ + $\underline{b}_0$ + $b(\underline{T})$), where $\underline{b}_0$ is a constant and $\underline{b}(T)$ is a monotonically decreasing function of $\underline{T}$ which goes asymptotically to zero as T goes to infinity. Then, setting $\underline{K}$ = $\underline{K + b_0}$, we replace (1) by:

4. $c = \dfrac{K'}{T} + \dfrac{b(T)}{T} + \dfrac{\alpha T}{2}$

Taking the derivative with respect to $\underline{T}$, and setting it equal to zero, we get

5. $T^2 + Tb'(T) - b(T) = \frac{2K'}{\alpha}$

where $\underline{b}'(\underline{T}) = \underline{db}(\underline{T})/\underline{dT}$. Since, by assumption, $\underline{b}'(\underline{T})$ is negative, while $\underline{b}(\underline{T})$ is positive, the new equilibrium value will be larger than the $\underline{T}^*$ of equation (3) — the optimal updating interval will now be longer, in order to avoid repeated updating of the same items.

Information on Current States of Phenomena versus Information in Their Structure

Equation (5) contains a warning against expending a large part of the resources of an information processing system in "staying current." In most real-life situations, at least two kinds of memory contents are relevant to decision making: (a) current data about the situation, and (b) understanding of the general principles and laws that govern the behavior of the phenomena of concern. The latter kind of information usually changes relatively slowly, the former rapidly and repeatedly. Efficient use of the information-processng resources requires an allocation between effort devoted to storing and updating these two kinds of information.

It is my strong and distinct impression that most human executives, professionals and scientists devote far too much time and effort to information in category (a) relative to what they devote to information in category (b). One might call this disease the "daily newspaper syndrome." It should be cured.

It is my further impression that, even with respect to category (b), most persons update their information in areas close to their professional disciplines more frequently than the change in knowledge justifies, and in other areas seldom or not at all. The allocation of efforts could usually be improved if updating were scheduled periodically — and for a wider range of information — rather than attempted continually. As I shall point out later, much of the concern with the "information explosion" stems from these misconceived strategies.

Acquisition by Scanning

Returning to the simpler cost function, $K + bT$, the division of the cost between its fixed and variable parts will depend sensitively upon the form in which information is acquired. Suppose, for example, that it is acquired by scanning a large body of data, some of which may have changed since the last scanning, but the remainder of which is unchanged. The magnitude of K now depends on the size of the body of data to be scanned, while b depends on the frequency with which items change. Obviously, the optimal updating interval depends only on K and is independent of b. This may appear paradoxical, since we might suppose that it would be desirable to update more often as the information changed more frequently. However, the value of improved information is already absorbed in the parameter α. If we wish to make explicit the dependence of T^* on the rate at which the body of information changes, we might write: $b = b(r)$, and $\alpha = \alpha(r)$, where r is the rate at which information changes. Equation (3) would remain unchanged, except that α in that equation would not be a function of r.

As the parameter K becomes smaller, more frequent updating becomes efficient. In the limit, if new data are acquired without scanning, continuous updating is efficient. From the standpoint of organizational reporting practices this implies that reports based on the principle of exceptions — i.e., where only information that requires notice is reported — should be issued as nearly continuously as possible, while reports that have to be scanned by their recipients should appear less frequently.

Multiple Copies

Next, consider situations where we store multiple copies of the same information. We may have a large number of persons in the organization who are performing the same or similar functions in parallel. In this case, the cost of updating may take the form:

6. $K = K_1 + nK_2$

where K_1 is the cost of storing information once, K_2 is the cost of producing a copy in the memory of one person, and n is the number of persons in whose memories it must be stored. We arrive again at equation (3), with K given by (6). To make the assumptions realistic, we probably should also assume that the value of information is proportional to $\underline{n}$ — i.e., that $\alpha = \underline{n}\beta$, where $\underline{\beta}$ is a constant parameter. Rewriting (3) in terms of $\underline{K}_1$, $\underline{K}_2$, $\underline{\beta}$, and $\underline{n}$, a straightforward calculation gives:

7. $dT^*/dn = -K_1/(n^2\beta T^*)$

Thus, as we would expect, with an increasing number of copies, it pays to update more frequently because the fixed cost, $\underline{K}_1$ is spread over all copies. As $\underline{K}_1/\underline{n}$ goes to zero, $\underline{T}^*$ reaches the asymptotic value:

8. $T^* = (2K_2/\beta)^{1/2}$

One of the most important characteristics of modern digital computers is that the cost of storing a copy of information that already exists in one machine in the memories of other machines *of the same kind* is exceedingly small compared with the cost of storing a copy of information in a human memory. (As a matter of fact, we do not possess processes capable of producing close copies of information — particularly information in the form of programs or in a form suitable for input to programs — in human memories. The only process we have for making rough copies is one called "learning", which is slow, costly, and subject to immense, often undetectable, errors.)

From the comparative advantage that computers possess in copying information, we conclude that information that is to be stored in organizations in multiple copies, and especially information that is to be updated frequently, is best stored in computers rather than in people. (In some cases, books and other printed material may be more economical stores than computers; and they offer the same advantage in cheapness of copying. Increasingly, computer memories will offer advantages over conventional "hard copy" memories in efficiency of retrieval, but costs for bulk storage in random-access computer memories are still very high compared with bulk storage costs for printed information.)

Concluding Note

In concluding this section, I should remind the reader again that the term "information" is used here to mean anything that may be stored in a memory. Information includes not only data, numerical or non-numerical, but also active programs — e.g., programs for solving problems and making decisions. These programs, in turn, may operate not only on specific data, but also on empirical laws — e.g., there may be programs that use the laws of mechanics to calculate orbits of rockets. Hence "updating an information store" is equivalent to "learning."

At the present time, we know relatively little about the forms in which information is stored in human memory. As the example, given in the introductory section, of the computation of values of mathematical functions shows, information retrieved by table-lookup of specific data in one memory may be retrieved by a program to compute the value of a function in another. Similarly, when a shop foreman and a college-educated industrial engineer produce similar or identical schedules, their mental processes and the stored data and programs employed in them may be quite different.

To design efficient information processing systems that employ both computers and people, we shall have to know much more than we now do about the parameters associated with human storage and processing of information.

ATTENTION DIRECTING AND INTELLIGENCE FUNCTIONS

In the title of this section, the term "intelligence" is used in its military sense. Human beings and organizations live out their lives immersed in a vast sea of information, which is accessible to them through their senses either as phenomena or as language inputs. The information-processing capacity of a human being or an organization has to be divided between "noticing" — i.e., selecting the portions of this environment of information that are to be processed — and "acting" — i.e., processing information to achieve goals. As with the learning processes in the previous section, a simple mathematical model will help us see what is involved in allocating information processing resources between noticing and acting.

In many contexts, the noticing process can be represented with some realism as a random search through an essentially infinite population of opportunities for action. Each opportunity has a value attached to it, so that we can describe the population of opportunities as a probability distribution of these values. Search consists of a sequence of independent, random choices of members from this population. Clearly, these are not the only assumptions we might adopt, but they lead to an interesting formulation of the attention-directing function.

Let v be the value associated with an opportunity discovered by search, and $f(v)$ be the probability density of values, where

$$9. \quad \int_{\infty}^{\infty} f(v)dv = 1$$

Let S be the average search time required to discover a new opportunity, and A (generally much larger than S) be the average time required to extract the value, v, from the opportunity if it is acted upon. Let b be the fraction of the total available time that is spent in search, so that $(1-b)$ is the fraction of time spent in action. Then the number of opportunities that will be discovered in a unit time interval is b/S, and the number of opportunities that will be acted upon in a unit time interval is $(1-b)/A$. The total payoff, or value received, during a unit time interval will be:

$$10. \quad P = \overline{v}(1-b)/A$$

where $\overline{v}$ is the expected value of the opportunities acted upon. Now the opportunities acted upon will be those, among the opportunities discovered, that have the highest v, under the restriction that of the b/S discovered only $(1-B)/A$ can be acted upon. Let v^* be the lower bound of the values of the opportunities acted upon. Then, the number acted upon will be:

$$11. \quad \frac{(1-b)}{A} = \frac{b}{S} \int_{v^*}^{\infty} f(v)dv$$

Equation (11) determines the lower bound, v^*, as a function of b and the parameters A and S. Once v^* has been fixed, the expected value, v, of opportunities acted upon can be found from the definitional equation:

$$12. \quad \overline{v} = [\int_{v^*}^{\infty} vf(v)dv] / [\int_{v^*}^{\infty} f(v)dv]$$

Substituting this value of $\overline{v}$ in (10), we can then determine P. From

(11), we can write the fraction of discovered opportunities that are acted upon thus:

13. $\dfrac{S}{A} \dfrac{(1-b)}{b} = \displaystyle\int_{v^*}^{\infty} f(v)dv$

and substituting the left-hand side of (13) for the right-hand side in (12), we obtain

14. $\bar{v} = [bA / (1-b)S] \displaystyle\int_{v^*}^{\infty} vf(v)dv$

Finally, from (14) and (10), we get:

15. $P = \dfrac{b}{S} \displaystyle\int_{v^*}^{\infty} vf(v)dv$

The allocation problem is the problem of finding a value of $\underline{b}$, say b_M, that maximizes $\underline{P}$ for fixed values of $\underline{A}$ and $\underline{S}$ — i.e., $\underline{P}(\underline{b}_M) = \underline{P}_{max}$. From (10),

16. $\dfrac{dP}{db} = \bar{v}/A + [(1-b) / A][d\bar{v} / db] = 0$

whence,

17. $\bar{v}_M = (1-b_M)[d\bar{v}_M/db_M]$

From (12),

18. $d\bar{v} / db$

$= [A / (1-b)^2 S]\displaystyle\int_{v^*}^{\infty} vf(v)dv - [bA / (1-b)S] v^*f(v^*)\left(\dfrac{dv}{db}\right)^*$

$= [1 / b(1-b)]\bar{v} - [bA / (1-b)S] v^*f(v^*)\left(\dfrac{dv}{db}\right)^*$

the last substitution employing (14). But from (13),

19. $f(v^*)\left(\dfrac{dv}{db}\right)^* = [S / Ab^2]$

whence

20. $d\bar{v} / db = [\bar{v} / b(1-b)] - [v^* / b(1-b)] = [(\bar{v} - v^*) / b(1-b)]$

Finally, combining (20) with (17), we obtain:

21. $\bar{v}_M = [(\bar{v}_M \cdot v^*_M) / b_M]$

Since $\underline{v}^*$ is a function of $\underline{b}$ by equation (13), and $\bar{v}$ a function of $\underline{v}^*$ by equation (12), these two equations combined with (21) suffice to determine the $\underline{b}_M$ that maximizes P. From equation (21), we can derive explicit expressions for $\underline{b}_M$ and $(1-b_m)$:

22. a. $b_M = [(\bar{v}_M \cdot v^*_M) / \bar{v}_M]$ b. $(1-b_M) = [v^*_M / \bar{v}_M]$

Hence, the fraction of total time spent on action will equal the ratio of the value of the marginal opportunity acted upon to the value of the average opportunity acted upon. We can also arrive at (21) heuristically by the following consideration. If one unit of processing capacity is added to the system, the increment of capacity can be used either to increase search — hence replace marginal opportunities of value $\underline{v}^*$ with average opportunities of value $\underline{v}$ — or to increase the number of opportunities at the margin acted upon. Using equation (13), the expected marginal yield from the former is $(\bar{v} - v^*)/S(S/A(1-b/b))$, while the expected marginal yield from the latter is simply v^*/A. Equating these two quantities, since the yields must be equal at the optimum, we readily derive (21) or (22).

The equilibrium value of $\underline{b}$, therefore, is an explicit function only of $\bar{v}$ and $\underline{v}^*$. From (12), we know that $\underline{v}$ is a function of $\underline{v}^*$ (and obviously a monotonic-increasing function). Since (13) is homogeneous of zero degree is $\underline{S/A}$, $\underline{b}$ also depends only on the ratio, $\underline{S/A}$. The dependence of $\underline{b}_M$ on $\underline{S}$ or $\underline{A}$ separately is more complex. Let us consider, first, the special case where $\underline{f(\underline{v})}$ is the exponential distribution:

23. $f(v) = Ae^{-kv}$

Then, we find immediately that

24. $\int_{v^*}^{\infty} f(v)dv = [A^{-kv^*} / k^e]$, and

25. $\int_{v^*}^{\infty} vf(v)dv = [A(kv^* + 1) / k^2] e^{-kv^*}$, whence

26. $\bar{v} = [(kv^* + 1) / k] = v^* + 1/k$

In this special case, then $\underline{b}_M$ is independent of both $\underline{A}$ and $\underline{S}$, for

27. $(1-b_M) = [v^* / \overline{v}] = [v^* / (v^* + 1/k)]$

In the general case, b_M may either increase or decrease with an increase, say, in $\underline{S}$, the cost of search. From (13), we see that, with $\underline{v}^*$ constant, an increase in $\underline{S}$ must increase $\underline{b}$ (if the cost of search increases, the same quality of opportunity can only be maintained by increasing search); but to attain the new optimum, $\underline{v}^*$ will not, in general, remain constant, but may even decrease more than enough to compensate for the increase in $\underline{S}$. All depends on the shape of $\underline{f}(\underline{v})$. Heuristically, one can see that if $\underline{f}(\underline{v}^*)$ is large, an increase in $\underline{S}$ can be compensated, without change in $\underline{b}$, by a relatively small decrease in $\underline{v}^*$.

This analysis of a highly simplified model serves to show how the question can be approached of allocating resources between intelligence, or attention-directing processes, on the one hand, and problem-solving or action processes, on the other. Professor Henri Theil has analysed a somewhat similar model in his paper on "Organization Size and Efficiency: The Choice Between Reading and Writing";[1] and one can construct a large number of other variants to fit particular sets of circumstances. The particular assumptions I have used have some interesting features, however — particularly the fact that decreasing returns are not introduced explicitly, but derive from the total processing resource combined with the freedom to select the most valuable opportunities from among those that are available. Hence, these assumptions seem suitable to a world containing an essentially unbounded population of undiscovered alternatives, and to a steady-state description of the dynamics of intelligence and action in such a world.

RETRIEVAL FROM MEMORY

The third topic I should like to explore is the retrieval of information from storage. In the introductory section of this paper it was shown that no hard-and-fast line can be drawn between the retrieval of information that is already stored and the generation of new information by inductive or deductive reasoning from the information already available. When the desired information already resides somewhere in memory, more or less in the form in

---

[1] *Management Science*, 1962, 9, 9-15.

which we want it, and the task is first to locate it in the memory, then to copy it, we speak of "retrieval." When the stored information has to be reworked into a new form suitable for our use, we speak of "inference" or "problem solving." Hence, we shall now be concerned primarily with the former end of this continuum of techniques for providing information.

To obtain information from a store, the information must be *located* and *identified* — that is, we must find our way to the place where it is stored, and when we reach it, we must recognize it as the information we want. We may call any device that helps us locate information an *index*; and any device that helps us identify it a *label*. The efficiency of a retrieval system may be associated with the efficiencies of its indexing and labelling systems.

Labels

At one extreme, information in memory may be self-labelled. Consider the retrieval system called SYNTHEX, developed by Robert Simmons and others at the System Development Corporation. Stored in the system's memory is the text of an encyclopedia. In response to the inquiry, "What do worms eat?", the system scans the text, matching sentences against the template, "Worms eat   ." If it finds a match, it takes the part of the sentence corresponding to the blank in the template as the desired information. (This account does not do justice to some of the sophistications of SYNTHEX, but illustrates the relation of self-labelling to simple matching.)

More commonly, information is labelled explicitly: books have titles, as do chapters, sections, and paragraphs, tables of data, and so on. In this case, the matching process that identifies the desired information operates upon the label rather than upon the information itself. In most existing information stores, labels are attached to information by humans — generally, either those who generated the information initially, or those who access it to the information store.

By organizing labels hierarchically, they can be made to perform a locating as well as an identifying function. Thus, a book may be located by a general label, its title. A chapter in the book by a more specific label; a section by a third, and still more specific, label. The desired information, which is self-labelled may then be located and identified by scanning the section.

Indexes

We have seen that labels are merely a limiting case of indexes. A primitive information store might consist of self-labelled items arranged in a sequence. Information is retrieved by a sequential search, each item being matched against a template to identify the desired one. This is essentially the way SYNTHEX works.

If items are only labelled, and not otherwise indexed, then the expected time of search for a unique item increases linearly with the size of the store. If, however, there were some way of determining without scanning whether the desired item is to be found in the first half or the second half of the store; and then, in the first half or the second half of that half; and so on — then we know that the number of steps to search a store of $\underline{n}$ items could be reduced, in the limit, to $\log_2 \underline{n}$. With this twenty-questions or split-halves technique, the index takes the form of a decision tree. In the more general case, the tree need not be binary, but may have several branches at each node.

There is a more general way to look at an index. Suppose we have a "retriever" that is fated always to examine items from an information store in some sequence. By a *simple index* we mean a function whose range is the set of items in the store, and whose domain is any set of labels. Suppose now that the retriever can generate appropriate sequences of labels — where "appropriate" means that labels for items containing the desired information are likely to appear early in the sequence. Then, using the index, the retriever can find items in the store in the same sequence that he generates them, instead of some arbitrary, pre-determined sequence.

Each item in the store can, of course, correspond to several items in the index. Hence, the only limit on the richness and completeness of the index is the cost of preparing it. It might be thought that it would only be economical to provide those index entries that could be expected to be used a number of times. But this is not so, since preparing all the index entries may require each item in the store to be analysed only once, while, in the absence of an index, each inquiry may require a search through the entire sequence of items in the store (or, on average, half the items).

A simple index works well so long as the retriever can generate early in his sequence, an appropriate label for the item he is seeking. His chance of doing so will depend both on the completeness of the index and upon his own understanding of the structure of the index and the kinds of labels used in it.

The titles of positions and the names of units in an organization serve as an index to retrieve appropriate information from the organization. Especially when an organization has many contacts with "outsiders" — i.e., persons who do not have an intimate knowledge of the operation of the organization — the index it presents to the environment in the form of these labels may have a strong effect upon its pattern of communication with the environment, hence, in the long run, upon the structure of the organization itself.

Associative Indexes

A desirable characteristic of an index is that its effectiveness not depend very much upon the user's knowledge of its structure. A related desirable characteristic is that it adapt continuously to changes in the content of the store and the labelling habits of indexers and users. The weakness inherent in Roget's *Thesaurus* or Dewey's library classification scheme was that they required an anticipation of the ways in which information would be classified in the future.

An *associative index* is a system that avoids some of these difficulties of anticipation and change. The associative index consists of a set of nodes connected with (labelled or unlabelled) relations. Each such relation, or pointer, may point either to another node or to an item of information in the store. (The index need not be separate from the store; the information items may themselves constitute the nodes.) The retriever enters the system at some node; chooses one or more of the pointers at that node and retrieves the nodes pointed at. As each node is retrieved, it is placed on a *try list* (in an order yet to be described), and new nodes are explored in the order in which they appear on the try list.[2]

The associative search will be efficient to the extent that the retriever can apply some criterion for placing new nodes on the try list in a priority order that has some relation to the likelihood of their

---

[2]The try list is only one of several methods for implementing a search through an associative store. It will make matters more concrete to talk in terms of this specific scheme.

leading to the desired information. This implies that there must be associated with each node some kind of information from which the retriever can compute this criterion. He must be able to judge, at least approximately, whether the node makes him "warmer" or "cooler" in relation to the goal. If the information stored in the system is held at the nodes, then this information may itself be the input to the process that computes the criterion.

A set of journal articles, each with a bibliography appended, is an example of a store that can be searched associatively. The retriever begins by picking up a journal article and placing a "value" on it in terms of its relevance to the information he is seeking. He then examines the article's bibliography, selects one or more items (also on the basis of the criterion of relevance — but judged this time from information on authors, titles, and journals alone), and places them in some order on the try list. He now picks the top item on the try list and repeats until he finds what he wants, or gives up.

What was referred to above as a criterion or relevance, is a relation of similarity along some dimension or dimensions. Now similarity relations are not, in general, transitive. A's being similar to B, and B's being similar to C does not imply A's being similar to C. The effectiveness of associative search does require, however, some weak analogue to transitivity of the similarity relation — some metric that gives at least statistical guarantees that if R is a template for assessing relevance, and T is the target node, then A's being closer than B to N implies A's being closer than B to T. The distance measure is the number of associative links between a pair of nodes. If the criterion for assigning nodes to their positions on the try list is closely correlated with distances from T, and if the net is reasonably well connected, then the search will discover short paths from the starting point to T.

A major strength of an associative index is that the distance function is not fixed, once and for all, but can be chosen anew for each search. Hence, there is also no requirement of fixed dimensions along which similarity is measured. The scheme can therefore be expected to be quite robust in the face of changing habits of classification and changing contents of the information store.

The associative index also allows for self-modification, although in the past advantage has been taken of this possibility only with information stored in the human head. Suppose that the retriever keeps a record of the search tree during any single search. If he finds the desired information, he can then reconstruct the successful path: say, A-B-D-T. A new pointer can now be inserted in the system directly from A to T or from B to T. In this way, the system will respond adaptively to the search habits and needs of retrievers. By ordering pointers at any node in terms of recency of use, or some such criterion, obsolescent links can gradually be phased out in favor of others in more active use.

Associative searches are conducted with great frequency by human beings, but not much progress has yet been made in automating them. The technical problem that has to be solved, of course, is to provide the retrieving program with enough intelligence to compute the relevance measure. Since this problem is common to all scan-and-search schemes for automated problem solving, we may expect progress to be made toward its solution along with general progress in artificial intelligence. Both problem solving and retrieval from an associative store become applications of the theory of heuristic search.

THE INFORMATION EXPLOSION RECONSIDERED

The currently popular notion that organizations are faced with an information explosion takes on a new aspect if we adopt the view toward information that has been espoused in this paper. If one accepts the assumption that information must be processed simply because it is "there," it is easy to be overwhelmed by the processing task. The solution to the problem lies not in increasing processing capabilities, but in asking at a more fundamental level just why and when information must be processed.

An organization consists of a system of memories, interconnected by channels and processors, and connected to the environment (i.e., other memories outside any arbitrary boundary we care to draw) by receptors or sensors that are capable of receiving information, and effectors that are capable of acting on the environment. The organization problem is to allocate the memory capacity and processing capacity in such a way as to facilitate the use of the effectors in accomplishing desired modifications on the environment.

For many purposes, it is reasonable to assume that the available memory capacity is infinite, but that each type of memory has associated with it certain characteristics that determine the forms in which information can be stored in it, and the times and costs of storage and retrieval. The times and costs of storage and retrieval can then be expressed, in turn, in terms of the demands they make upon the limited processing capacity.

For example, as far as our evidence goes, the human brain has inexhaustible storage capacity. One reason the storage is inexhaustible is that a significant time (perhaps five seconds) is required to store a single new item semi-permanently with a minimum of indexing for later access to it. Since our evidence also indicates that the processor which does the storing and retrieving is basically a serial device, the total amount that can be stored in a lifetime is modest — perhaps 200 million items if the entire processing capacity throughout life were devoted entirely to storage. Hence, the problem for the human being is to allocate his very limited processing capacity among the several functions of noticing, storing, and indexing, on the input side, and retrieving, reorganizing, and controlling his effectors on the output side.

If a human being lives in a rich environment of information, this does not imply that he must devote more of his processing capacity to inputting information. Instead, it implies that he can be more selective in inputting only that information which is potentially most valuable to him. In fact, with a little redefinition of terms, we can apply our earlier analysis of the intelligence function to his situation. A rich information environment might be interpreted, for example, as an environment in which the search parameter, $\underline{S}$, is low, or one in which $\underline{f(v)}$ is large for high values of $\underline{v}$.

The point applies to organizations as well as to individuals. Although organizations have parallel processing capabilities that individuals lack, the fundamental resource limit they face is the limit on their processing capacity. Acquiring and storing information is only one of the functions to which that capacity must be devoted. As with any resource allocation situation, processing capacity should not be used to acquire new information beyond the point where the capacity becomes marginally more valuable in other applications.

Redundancy of Information

Thus far, information has been treated as a homogeneous commodity, to which some kind of scalar measure can be applied. This abstraction overlooks the most important means for conserving processing capacity in obtaining and storing new information — the fact that the information is usually highly redundant, and, because it is redundant, can be compressed by recoding.

I would outrage anyone with even the slightest esthetic sensibilities if I were to say, "When you've seen one snowflake, you've seen them all." And yet it us true, if we leave esthetics aside, that we know a great deal about all possible snowflakes as soon as we know that a snowflake is a plane pattern with hexagonal symmetry. And if we want to store information about snowflakes, it probably would be better to store the fact of the symmetry together with, say, the pictures of a dozen varied snowflakes, than it would be to store the pictures of a million snowflakes without the statement of symmetry. Even better, perhaps, would be to store a program for generating hexagonally-symmetric plane figures. (Such a program is stored by Nature, so if we live in Sweden or the Northern United States, during much of the year we can obtain information about snowflakes almost any time we want it, without going to the trouble or expense of storing it.)

The advance and accumulation of human knowledge can mean either or both of two things. It can mean that we are taking more and more photographs of snowflakes and storing them in human memories, or books, instead of in Nature. Or it can mean that we are storing in memories and books certain general propositions from which the properties of snowflakes can be inferred and even examples generated. The latter is, of course, a process for exploiting the enormous redundancy of the information in Nature in order to know more while storing less. Science is very much concerned with the accumulation of information — with taking photographs of snowflakes. But it is concerned with accumulation largely as a first step toward exploiting redundancy through discovering scientific laws. Accumulation is simply a means for sampling Nature sufficient to permit those laws to be discovered and verified.

During the past thirty years, management science has provided us with examples of this process as it applied to human organizations. Critics of management science sometimes object that scheduling algorithms have seldom been shown to outperform experienced human schedulers significantly. The claim may or may not be true, but even if true, it does not show what it purports to show. For what the scheduling algorithm permits is the substitution of a powerful generalization for years of observation and experience. With a small input of formal training, a human processor — perhaps aided by a computer — can now do what previously could be done only after a very much longer process of acquiring information. Information, far from exploding, is squeezed down by theory into very small pellets, from which the redundancy has been expelled. Some would say that the pellets are sometimes hard and indigestible, but examination of that difficulty would lead us far afield.

The same attention to redundancy can give us new approaches to handling information internal to the business firm. Typically, information is extracted from the accounting system for certain decision-making purposes via the cost accounting procedures. But the cost accounting data are largely descriptive — they are based on only a very primitive and atheoretical model of the business firm and its operations. As we understand the firm better, and how to model it, we will certainly move from these crude data-using scheme to a more sophisticated one. In that more sophisticated scheme, the accounting data will be used largely to build a *theory* of the firm's operations, and that theory, rather than the raw data, will become the main input to the decison-making process. We already see this kind of development taking place in the use, for example, of linear programming models for planning.

Permanence of Information

It may be objected that unless we store raw data it will be lost forever — that the world changes and never regenerates the same data twice. To take this Heraclitean argument literally is to deny that the world is lawful and hence redundant. It is true that in building theories, we have to make strategic decisions about what data from the past will be most useful in discovering and testing pattern. But our storage of data will then stem from the strategic decision and not from a general policy that everything must be saved.

Just as the acquisition of new information must be regulated in terms of the limits of acquisition capacity, so the retention of stored information must be regulated in terms of the limits of retrieval capacity. Suppose that we have a system with constant retrieval capacity, say r items per minute. Suppose that the memory of the system is growing at an acquisition rate of, say, a items per minute.

Then the total size of the store will be $\underline{a}(\underline{t} - \underline{t}_0)$, and a continually declining fraction of the items, $\underline{r}/(\underline{a}(\underline{t} - \underline{t}_0))$, will be retrieved per unit of time.

Suppose that the frequency with which an item is retrieved declines exponentially with age: $\underline{f}(\underline{T}) = \underline{A}e^{T}/k$ where $\underline{T}$ is the time since the item was accessed, and $\underline{k}$ is a constant. Then, over its total lifetime, an item will be retrieved $\underline{a}\underline{K}$ times. On the other hand, with a steady access rate of $\underline{a}$ items per minute, an average of $\underline{a}\underline{A}k$ items will be retrieved per minute. Hence, if we set the retrieval rate so that $\underline{r} = \underline{a}\underline{A}k$, the system will remain in steady-state equilibrium. There is no explosion here, but a relation among three terms — the rate of acquisition of new information, the rate of retrieval of information, and the number of times, on average, an item of information is used after it has been stored.

CONCLUSION

I have tried, in these pages, to illustrate how one can think about organizations in information-processing terms, and about information-processing systems in organizational terms. Information processing in organizations seems best approached as a problem in resource allocation, where the scarce resource is processing capacity that must be allocated among information acquisition, inference and problem-solving, indexing, retrieval, and application tasks.

By way of example, I have sketched approaches to four problem areas: the economics of updating information stores, the allocation of processng resources to intelligence functions, the structure of indexes, and the balance among acquisition, storage, and retrieval functions. Even in their present sketchy and abstract form, these examples appear to cast some useful light on the issues that arise in designing organizations to operate in a world that is rich in information.

6.6

DESIGNING ORGANIZATIONS FOR AN
INFORMATION RICH WORLD

Herbert A. Simon

SIMON. If men do not pour new wine into old bottles, they do something almost as bad: they invest old words with new meanings. "Work" and "energy" are venerable English words, but since the Industrial and Scientific Revolutions they have acquired entirely new definitions. They have become more abstract and divorced from directly sensed qualities of human activity; and they have become more precise, finding expression in quantitative units of measurement (foot-pound, erg) and exact scientific laws (Conservation of Energy). The word "energy" uttered in a contemporary setting may represent quite different concepts and thought processes from the word "energy" uttered in the eighteenth century.

Old word meanings do not disappear; they tend to persist alongside the new. This is perhaps the most insidious part of what C. P. Snow has dubbed the problem of the two cultures. To know what a speaker means by "energy" it is not enough to know what century he is speaking in, but also whether his talk belongs to the common culture or the scientific culture. If the former, his words should not be credited with the quantitative precision that belongs to the latter; and if the latter, his words should not be interpreted vaguely or metaphorically.

Old Words in New Meanings

All of this is preliminary to raising a difficulty I must hurdle to communicate. I intend to use familiar words like "information," "thinking," and "organization," but not with the meanings that the common culture has attached to them over the centuries. During the past twenty-five years these words have begun to acquire new, increasingly precise and quantitative meanings. Words associated with the generation and conversion of information are today undergoing a change of meaning as drastic as that experienced by words associated with the generation and conversion of energy in the eighteenth and nineteenth centuries.

Within the common culture, one cannot carry on a twentieth-century conversation about energy with a physicist or engineer. Similarly, it is increasingly difficult to carry on a twentieth-century conversation about information with a social scientist who belongs to the humanistic rather than scientific subculture of his discipline. The difficulty does not stem from jargon but from a complete disparity of meanings hidden behind a superficially common language.

What do I mean when I say: "Machines think"? The word "machine" seems obvious enough: a modern electronic digital computer. But "machine" has all sorts of unintended humanistic overlays. A machine, in the common culture, moves repetitively and monotonously. It requires direction from outside. It is inflexible. With the slightest component failure or mismanagement it degenerates into senseless or random behavior.

A computer may exhibit none of these mechanical properties. While retaining the word "machine" in the scientific culture as a label for a computer, I have revised drastically the associations stored with the word in my memory. When I say "Machines think," I am *not* referring to devices that behave repetitively and inflexibly, require outside guidance, and often become random.

The word "think" itself is even more troublesome. In the common culture it denotes an unanalyzed, partly intuitive, partly subconscious and unconscious, sometimes creative set of mental processes that sometimes allows humans to solve problems, make decisions, or design something. What do these mental processes have in common with the processes computers follow when they execute their programs?

The common culture finds almost nothing in common between them. One reason is that human thinking has never been described, only labeled. Certain contemporary psychological research, however, has been producing computer programs that duplicate the human information processing called thinking in considerable detail.[3] When a psychologist who has been steeped in this new scientific culture says "Machines think," he has in mind the behavior of computers governed by such programs. He means something quite definite and precise that has no satisfactory translation into the language of the common culture. If you wish to converse with him (which you well may not!) you will have to follow him into the scientific culture.

As the science of information processing continues to develop, it will not be as easy to sequester it from the main stream of managerial activity (or human social activity) as it was to isolate the physical sciences and their associated technologies. Information processing is at the heart of executive activity, indeed at the heart of all social interaction. More and more we are finding occasion to use terms like "information," "thinking," "memory," and "decision making" with twentieth-century scientific precision. The language of the scientific culture occupies more and more of the domain previously reserved to the common culture.

Make no mistake about the significance of this change in language. It is a change in thought and concepts. It is a change of the most fundamental kind in man's thinking about his own processes—about himself.

The Scarcity of Attention

My title speaks of "an information-rich world." How long has the world been rich in information? What are the consequences of its prosperity, if that is what it is?

Last Easter, my neighbors bought their daughter a pair of rabbits. Whether by intent or accident, one was male, one female, and we now live in a rabbit-rich world. Persons less fond than I am of rabbits might even describe it as a rabbit-overpopulated world. Whether a world is rich or poor in rabbits is a relative matter. Since food is essential for biological populations, we might judge the world as rabbit-rich or rabbit-poor by relating the number of rabbits to the amount of lettuce and grass (and garden flowers) available for rabbits to eat. A rabbit-rich world is a lettuce-poor world, and vice versa.

The obverse of a population problem is a scarcity problem, hence a resource-allocation problem. There is only so much lettuce to go around, and it will have to be allocated somehow among the rabbits. Similarly, in an information-rich world, the wealth of information means a dearth of something else: a scarcity of whatever it is that information consumes. What information consumes is rather obvious: it consumes the attention of its recipients. Hence a wealth of information creates a poverty of attention and a need to allocate that attention efficiently among the overabundance of information sources that might consume it.

To formulate an allocation problem properly, ways must be found to measure the quantities of the scarce resource; and these quantities must not be expandable at will. By now, all of us have heard of the *bit*, a unit of information introduced by Shannon in connection with problems in the design of communication systems.[4] Can we use the bit as a measure of an information-processing system's capacity for attention?

Unfortunately, it is not the right unit. Roughly, the trouble is that the bit capacity of any device (or person) for receiving information depends entirely upon how the information is encoded. Bit capacity is not an invariant, hence is an unsuitable measure of the scarcity of attention.

A relatively straightforward way of measuring how much scarce resource a message consumes is by noting how much time the recipient spends on it. Human beings, like contemporary computers, are essentially serial devices. They can attend to only one thing at a time. This is just another way of saying that attention is scarce. Even the modern time-sharing systems which John Kemeny described are really only doing one thing at a time, although they seem able to attend to one hundred things at once.[5] They achieve this illusion by sharing their time and attention among these hundred things. The attention-capacity measure I am proposing for human beings applies as well to time-sharing systems and also to an organization employing many people, which can be viewed as a time-sharing system.

Scarcity of attention in an information-rich world can be measured in terms of a human executive's time. If we wish to be precise, we can define a standard executive (IQ of 120, bachelor's degree, and so on) and ask Director Lewis Branscomb to embalm him at the National Bureau of Standards. Further, we can work out a rough conversion between the attention units of human executives and various kinds of computers.

In an information-rich world, most of the cost of information is the cost incurred by the recipient. It is not enough to know how much it costs to produce and transmit information; we must also know how much it costs, in terms of scarce attention, to receive it. I have tried bringing this argument home to my friends by suggesting that they recalculate how much the *New York Times* (or *Washington Post*) costs them, including the cost of reading it. Making the calculation usually causes them some alarm, but not enough for them to cancel their subscriptions. Perhaps the benefits still outweigh the costs.

Having explained what I mean by an information-rich world, I am now ready to tackle the main question. How can we design organizations, business firms, and government agencies to operate effectively in such a world? How can we arrange to conserve and effectively allocate their scarce attention?

I shall proceed with the help of three examples, each illustrating a major aspect of the problem of organizational design. I make no attempt to cover all significant problem areas, and any fancied resemblance of my hypothetical organizations to real organizations, living or dead, in the city of Washington, are illusory, fortuitous, and the product of the purest happenstance.

Information Overload

Many proposals for eliminating *information overload* (another phrase to describe life in an information-rich world) call for a new computing system. There is good precedent for this. The Hollerith punched card is a creative product of the Census Bureau's first bout with information overload, and a series of crises in the central exchanges of the phone company led to the invention of automatic switching systems.

Today, some argue that the postal service is doomed to collapse from information overload unless means are found to automate the sorting operations. This cannot be so. There is no reason why mail-sorting costs should increase more than proportionally with the volume of mail, nor why unit costs should rise with volume. A major cause of the problem is that certain information-processing services are almost free, resulting in an explosive demand for them. The Post Office is not really prepared to provide this implicit subsidy and reneges by performing the services badly, with insufficient resources. The crisis in the Post Office does not call for computers; it calls for a thoroughgoing application of price and market mechanisms.

This is not to argue that any particular manual Post Office operation, such as sorting, cannot be made more economical by computer. This kind of technical question is settled by cost-benefit analysis within reasonable limits of error and debate. But there is no magic in automation that allows it to resolve dilemmas posed by an organization's unwillingness or inability to allocate and price scarce information-processing resources, whether the resources are sorting clerks or electronic devices. Free or underpriced resources are always in desperately short supply. What is sometimes alleged to be technological lag in the Post Office is really failure of nerve.

A computer is an information-processing system of quite general capability. It can receive information, store it, operate on it in a variety of ways, and transmit it to other systems. Whether a computer will contribute to the solution of an information-overload problem, or instead compound it, depends on the distribution of its own attention among four classes of activities: listening, storing, thinking, and speaking. A general design principle can be put as follows:

An information-processing subsystem (a computer or new organization unit) will reduce the net demand on the rest of the organization's attention only if it absorbs more information previously received by others than it produces—that is, if it listens and thinks more than it speaks.

To be an attention conserver for an organization, an information-processing system (abbreviated IPS) must be an information condenser. It is conventional to begin designing an IPS by considering the information it will *supply*. In an information-rich world, however, this is doing things backwards. The crucial question is how much information it will allow to be *withheld* from the attention of other parts of the system.

Basically, an IPS can perform an attention-conserving function in two ways: (1) it can receive and store information that would otherwise have to be received by other systems, and (2) it can transform or *filter* input information into output that demands fewer hours of attention than the input.

To illustrate these two modes of attention conservation, let me talk about some of the information needs of a nation's Foreign Office. (Since the United States has a State Department and not a Foreign Office, I am obviously talking about some other country.) The bulk of information that enters a system from the environment is irrelevant to action at the time of entry. Much of it will never be relevant, but we cannot be sure in advance which part this is.

One way to conserve Foreign Office attention is to interpose an IPS (human, automated, or both) between environment and organization to index and store information on receipt. A second way is to have an IPS analyze, draw inferences from, and summarize the information received, then index and store the products of its analyses for use by the rest of the system.

This proposal has a familiar ring about it. I have simply described in unconventional language the conventional functions of a conventional intelligence unit. Moreover, I have solved the information-overload problem simply by adding information processors. I eliminated scarcity by increasing the supply of scarce resources. Any fool with money can do that.

But the very banality of my solution carries an important lesson. The functional design an IPS must have to conserve attention is largely independent of specific hardware, automated or human. Hardware becomes a concern only later in economic considerations.

My proposal, however, is actually far less conventional than it sounds. If the IPS is to be even partly automated, we must provide precise descriptions (in the language of the scientific culture) of the processes denoted by vague terms like "analyze" and "summarize." Even if we do *not* intend to automate the process, the new information-processing technology still will permit us to formulate the programs of human analysts and summarizers with precision so that we can predict reliably the relation between inputs and outputs. Looking more closely at the structure and operation of the IPS, we see it really will not resemble a traditional intelligence unit very closely at all. (My thinking on this problem has benefited greatly from acquaintance with the analyses that have been made over the past several years of information-processing requirements in the U.S. State Department.

These planning activities have been laudably free from premature obsession with automated hardware.)

The purpose of the intelligence IPS I have proposed is not to *supply* the Foreign Office with information but to *buffer* it from the overrich environment of information in which it swims. Information does not have to be attended to (*now*) just because it exists in the environment. Designing an intelligence system means deciding: when to gather information (much of it will be preserved indefinitely in the environment if we do not want to harvest it now); where and in what form to store it; how to rework and condense it; how to index and give access to it; and when and on whose initiative to communicate it to others.

The design principle that attention is scarce and must be preserved is very different from a principle of "the more information the better." The aforementioned Foreign Office thought it had a communications crisis a few years ago. When events in the world were lively, the teletypes carrying incoming dispatches frequently fell behind. The solution: replace the teletypes with line printers of much greater capacity. No one apparently asked whether the IPS's (including the Foreign Minister) that received and processed messages from the teletypes would be ready, willing, and able to process the much larger volume of messages from the line printers.

Everything I have said about intelligence systems in particular applies to management information systems in general. The proper aim of a management information system is not to bring the manager all the information he needs, but to reorganize the manager's environment of information so as to reduce the amount of time he must devote to receiving it. Restating the problem this way leads to a very different system design.

The Need to Know

That brings me to the question of *the need to know*. How do we go about deciding where information should be stored in an information-rich world and who should learn about it?

Those of us who were raised during the Great Depression sometimes do not find it easy to adapt to an affluent society. When we ate potatoes, we always ate the peel (which my mother insisted was the best part of the potato). Nonreturnable containers seem to us symbols of intolerable waste.

Our attitudes toward information reflect the culture of poverty. We were brought up on Abe Lincoln walking miles to borrow (and return!) a book and reading it by firelight. Most of us are constitutionally unable to throw a bound volume into the wastebasket. We have trouble enough disposing of magazines and newspapers. Some of us are so obsessed with the need to know that we feel compelled to read everything that falls into our hands, although the burgeoning of the mails is helping to cure us of this obsession.

If these attitudes were highly functional in the world of clay tablets, scribes, and human memory; if they were at least tolerable in the world of the printing press and the cable; they are completely maladapted to the world of broadcast systems and Xerox machines.

The change in information-processing technology demands a fundamental change in the meaning attached to the familiar verb "to know." In the common culture, "to know" meant to have stored in one's memory in a way that facilitates recall when appropriate. By metaphoric extension, "knowing" might include having access to a file or book containing information, with the skill necessary for using it.

In the scientific culture, the whole emphasis in "knowing" shifts from the storage or actual physical possession of information to the process of using or having access to it. It is possible to have information stored without having access to it (the name on the tip of the tongue, the lost letter in the file, the unindexed book, the uncatalogued library); and it is possible to have access to information without having it stored (a computer program for calculating values of the sine function, a thermometer for taking a patient's temperature).

If a library holds two copies of the same book, one of them can be destroyed or exchanged without the system's losing information. In the language of Shannon's information theory, multiple copies make the library *redundant*. But copies are only one of three important forms of redundancy in information. Even if a library has only one copy of each book, it still has a high degree of informational overlap. If half the titles in the Library of Congress were destroyed at random, little of the world's knowledge would disappear.

The most important and subtle form of redundancy derives from the world's being highly lawful. Facts are random if no part of them can be predicted from any other part—that is, if they are independent of each other. Facts are lawful if certain of them *can* be predicted from certain others. We need store only the fraction needed to predict the rest.

This is exactly what science is: the process of replacing unordered masses of brute fact with tidy statements of orderly relations from which these facts can be inferred. The progress of science, far from cluttering up the world with new information, enormously increases the redundancy of libraries by discovering the orderliness of the information already stored. With each important advance in scientific theory, we can reduce the volume of explicitly stored knowledge without losing any information whatsoever. That we make so little use of this opportunity does not deny that the opportunity exists.

Let me recite an anecdote that illustrates the point very well. We are all aware that there is a DDT problem. DDT is one of technology's mixed blessings. It is very lethal to noxious insects, but uncomfortably persistent and cumulatively harmful to eagles, game fish, and possibly ourselves. The practical problem is how to enjoy the agricultural and medical benefits afforded by the toxicity of DDT without suffering the consequences of its persistence.

A distinguished chemist of my acquaintance, who is a specialist neither in insecticides nor biochemistry, asked himself this question. He was able to write down the approximate chemical structure of DDT by decoding its name. He could recognize from general theoretical principles the component radicals in the structural formula that account for its toxicity. The formula also told him on theoretical grounds why the substance is persistent and why the molecule does not decompose readily or rapidly. He asked, again on theoretical grounds, what compound would have the toxicity of DDT but decompose readily. He was able to write down its formula and saw no theoretical reason why it could not easily be produced. (All of this took ten minutes.)

A phone call to an expert in the field confirmed all his conjectures. The new compound he had "invented" was a well-known insecticide, which had been available commercially before DDT. It is not as lethal as DDT over as broad a band of organisms but is nearly so, and it decomposes fairly readily. I do not know if the new-old chemical "solves" the DDT problem. The durability of DDT was intended by its inventors to avoid frequent respraying and reduce the costs of treatment. There may be other economic issues, and even chemical and biological ones.

What the story illustrates is that good problem-solving capacities combined with powerful (but compact) theories (and an occasional telephone call) may take the place of shelves of reference books. It may often be more efficient to leave information in the library of nature, to be extracted by experiment or observation when needed, than to mine and stockpile it in man's libraries, where retrieval costs may be as high as the costs of recreating information from new experiments or deriving it from theory.

These considerations temper my enthusiasm for using new technology to store and retrieve larger and larger bodies of data. I do not mean to express a blanket disapproval of all proposals to improve the world's stores of information. But I do believe we must design IPS's with data-analysis capabilities able to keep up with our propensities to store vast bodies of data.

Today's computers are moronic robots, and they will continue to be so as long as programming remains in its present primitive state. Moronic robots can sop up, store, and spew out vast quantities of information. They do not and cannot exercise due respect for the scarce attention of the recipients of this information. Computers must be taught to behave at a higher level of intelligence. This will take a large, vigorous research and development effort.

In a knowledge-rich world, progress does not lie in the direction of reading and writing information faster or storing more of it. Progress lies in the direction of extracting and exploiting the patterns of the world so that far less information needs to be read, written, or stored. Progress depends on our ability to devise better and more powerful thinking programs for man and machine.

Technology Assessment

Attention is *generally* scarce in organizations, *particularly* scarce at the tops, and *desperately* scarce at the top of the organization called the United States Government. There is only one President. Although he is assisted by the Budget Bureau, the Office of Science and Technology, and other elements of the Executive Office, a frightening array of matters converges on this single, serial, human information-processing system.

There is only one Congress of the United States. It can operate in parallel through committees, but every important matter must occupy the attention of many Congressmen. Highly important matters may claim the time and attention of all.

There is only one body of citizens in the United States. Large public problems such as the Vietnam War, civil rights, student unrest, the cities, and environmental quality (to mention five near the top of the current agenda) periodically require a synchrony of public attention. This is more than enough to crowd the agenda to the point of unworkability or inaction.

Congressman Daddario has devoted a great deal of thought in recent years to improving the procedures in society and government for dealing with the new technology we produce so prodigiously. At the request of his House Subcommittee on Science, Research, and Development, a panel of the National Academy of Sciences on which I served recently prepared the report on technology assessment to which he referred.

Technology assessment is not just a matter of determining the likely good and bad effects of new technological developments. Even less is it a matter of making sure, before new technology is licensed, that it will have no undesirable effects. The dream of thinking everything out before we act, of making certain we have all the facts and know all the consequences, is a sick Hamlet's dream. It is the dream of someone with no appreciation of the seamless web of causation, the limits of human thinking, or the scarcity of human attention.

The world outside is itself the greatest storehouse of knowledge. Human reason, drawing upon the pattern and redundancy of nature, can predict some of the consequences of human action. But the world will always remain the largest laboratory, the largest information store, from which we will learn the outcomes, good and bad, of what we have done. Of course it is costly to learn from experience; but it is also costly, and frequently much less reliable, to try through research and analysis to anticipate experience.

Technology assessment is an intelligence function. If it operated perfectly, which it is certain not to, it would do two things for us. First, it would warn us before our taking action of the really dangerous (especially the irreversibly dangerous) consequences possible from proposed innovations. Second, it would give us early warning of unanticipated consequences of innovations as they became visible, before major irreversible damage had been done. In performing both of these functions, technology assessment would be mindful of the precious scarcity of attention. It would put on the agenda only items needing attention and action (including the action of gathering information to evaluate the need for further attention).

A phrase like "technology assessment" conjures up a picture of scientific competence and objectivity, deliberateness and thoughtfulness, concern for the long run, and a systems view that considers all aspects and consequences. But these desirable qualities of a decision-making system cannot be imposed without considering the organizational and political environment of the system.

As our scientific and engineering knowledge grows, so does the power of our actions. They have consequences ramifying over vast reaches of space and time. The growth of knowledge allows us to recognize consequences we would have been ignorant of or ignored before. We are able to make bigger waves and at the same time have more sensitive instruments to detect the rocking of the boat. Today we sterilize and quarantine everything that travels between earth and moon. Less than five hundred years ago we diffused tuberculosis, smallpox, and syphilis throughout the Americas in happy ignorance.

The injunction to take account of *all* effects conjures up the picture of an integral stretching out through space and time without ever converging. We must assume, as mankind has always assumed, that a reasonable allocation of our limited attention and powers of thought will solve the crucial problems facing us at least as fast as new ones arise. If that assumption is wrong, there is no help for us. If it is right, then technology assessment becomes part and parcel of the task of setting an agenda for society and government.

To bring the notion of technology assessment out of the realm of abstraction, let me go back to the example of DDT. Although I have not researched the history of DDT, I believe it was introduced on a large scale without thorough (or at least adequate) study of its potential cumulative danger in the atmosphere and in organisms (especially predators). It was hailed for its agricultural and medical benefits as one of technology's miracles. Now, some decades later, we learn that the miracle has a flaw.

The possible adverse effects of DDT have been known to specialists for some time. They were probably even known, but ignored, at the time DDT was introduced. If so, this would underscore my fundamental theme of the scarcity of attention.

Suppose the dangers of DDT were not known beforehand but were discovered only in the laboratory of nature. Then, with apologies to eagle lovers, I am not sure that we (or even the eagles) have suffered unconscionable or irreversible loss by letting actual use tell us about DDT rather than trying to anticipate this experience in advance. Technology assessment has been (and is being) made by the environment. We are getting signals from the environment calling attention to some of its findings, and these signals are strong enough to deserve and get our attention. The DDT issue has been claiming attention intermittently for some months, with the loudest environmental signal being the detection of DDT in Great Lakes game fish. The issue is now high enough on the agenda of newspapers, courts, and committees to bring action.

I know this sounds complacent, and I really do not feel complacent. But it serves no useful social purpose to treat with anguish and hand-wringing every public problem which by hindsight might have been avoided if we had been able to afford the luxury of more foresight. Now that we *know* the problems, we should address them rather than hold inquests about who should have seen the problems earlier.

Our information about the effects of DDT and of long-continued diffuse contamination is in many respects unsatisfactory. (So is our information about almost any issue of public policy.) But this does not mean we could improve the situation by massive collection of data. On the contrary, we mainly need carefully aimed, high-quality biological investigations of the cause and effect mechanisms underlying the diffusion and metabolism of DDT. After we understand better the chemistry and biology of the problem we might make sense of masses of data, but then we probably would not need as much.

First-rate biologists and chemists capable of doing the required research are in as short supply as most other high-quality information-processing systems. Their attention is an exceedingly scarce commodity, and we are unlikely to capture much of it soon. The practical question, as always, is how to deal with the situation given the scrappy, inadequate data we now have.

We begin to ask questions like these: Assuming the worst possible case for the harmful effects of DDT, what is the magnitude of the effects in human, economic, and ecological terms, and to what extent are these effects irreversible? In the same terms, what would it cost us to do without DDT? What is the next best alternative?

These are common-sense questions. We do not have to know anything about the technology to ask them, although we might learn something about it from the answers. The most effective IPS for getting answers consists of a telephone, a Xerox machine (to copy documents the telephone correspondents suggest), and some very bright professionals (not necessarily specialists) who do know something about the technology. With this retrieval system, just about anything in the world now known on the problem can be extracted in a few man-weeks of work. (The time required goes up considerably if hearings and briefings are held or a research project is organized.)

There are numerous locations inside and outside the federal government where the questions may be asked. They may be asked by the Office of Science and Technology, the National Academy of Sciences, the National Academy of Engineering, the RAND Corporation, Resources for the Future, or a Congressional committee. (An excellent example of the last is the recent series of reports on steam-powered automobiles.)

The location of the investigating group is significant from only one standpoint, which may be crucial. The location of the group can determine the attention it commands and the legitimacy accorded its findings. These are interdependent but by no means identical matters.

Legitimacy may sometimes be achieved (and even attention secured) by the usual credentials of science: the right degrees, professional posts, and reputations. But many an impeccable report is ignored, and many a report without proper credentials gains a high place on the agenda. The Ralph Naders of the world demonstrate that writing and speaking forcefully, understanding the mass media, and being usually right about the facts can compensate for missing union cards and lack of access to organizational channels. Rachel Carson showed that even literary excellence is sometimes enough to turn the trick.

I agree with Congressman Daddario that we can and should strengthen and make more effective the processes of technology assessment in our country. We shall still need the world itself as a major laboratory, but we may be able to substitute foresight for hindsight to a modest extent. Did we have to wait until all Los Angeles wept before doing anything about automobile exhausts? Well-financed institutions for technology assessment should be spending a hundred million dollars a year instead of ten million to find out whether the steam automobile offers a long-term solution to the smog problem. Our current measures are temporary expedients at best.

Strengthening technology assessment means improving our procedures for setting the public agenda. It does not mean pressing more information and problems on an already burdened President, Congress, and public. In an information-rich world, there is no special virtue in prematurely early warnings. Let the world store information for us until we can focus attention and thought on it.

Assessing Information-Processing Technology

The final issue I should like to address is itself a problem in technology assessment. The science and technology of information processing is only a quarter-century old, and we have merely the faintest glimmerings of what it will be like after another quarter-century. How shall we assess it and make sure it develops in socially beneficial ways?

The most visible and superficially spectacular part of the technology is its hardware: computers, typewriter consoles, cathode-ray tubes, and associated gadgets. These devices give us powerful new ways for recording, storing, processing, and writing information to improve and replace the human IPS's with which we had to make do throughout man's history.

By itself, the hardware does not solve any organizational problems, including the problems of attention scarcity. The hardware boxes will begin to make inroads on these problems only as we begin to understand information-processing systems well enough to conceive sophisticated programs for them—programs that will permit them to think at least as well as man does.

Each step we take toward increasing our sophistication and scientific knowledge about the automated IPS also increases our sophistication and scientific knowledge about the human IPS, about man's thought processes. What we are acquiring with the new technology is something of deep significance—a science of human thinking and organization.[6]

The armchair is no more effective a scientific instrument for understanding this new technology than it was for previous technologies. If we are to understand information processing, we must study it in the laboratory of nature. We must construct, program, and operate many kinds of information-processing systems to see what they do and how they perform.

Our first systems have performed and will perform in all sorts of unexpected ways (most of them stupid), and by hindsight they seem incredibly crude. They will never pass a cost-effectiveness test on their operating performance, and we shall have to write them off as research and development efforts. From their behavior, we may learn that the new technology contains dangers as well as promises. There already is considerable concern about threats to privacy that the new technology might create. Such concerns will be mere armchair speculations until they are tested against a broad base of experience.

Very early in the computer era, I advised several business firms not to acquire computers until they knew exactly how to use them and pay for them. I soon realized this was bad advice. Computers initially pay their way by educating large numbers of people about computers. They are the principal forces for replacement of the vague, inadequate common-culture meanings of words in the information-processing vocabulary by the sharp, rich, scientific meanings these words must have in the future.

I think this points to a clear public policy for understanding and assessing the new technology. We need greatly increased public support for research and development efforts of as varied a nature as possible. They should certainly include network experiments of the sort John Kemeny envisages. They should include data-bank experiments. Above all, they should include experiments in robotry, large-scale memory organization, and artificial intelligence, leading to a basic foundation for a science of information processing.

Past experience suggests that a program pursued in the experimental spirit I have indicated will have valuable by-products. List processing is an esoteric development of computer-programming languages that was motivated initially about fifteen years ago by pure research interests in artificial intelligence. Today, its concepts are deeply imbedded in the design of large programming and operating systems regularly used in accounting and engineering computation.

The exploration of the moon is a great adventure. After the moon, there are objects still farther out in space. But man's inner space, his mind, is less well known than the space of the planets. It is time we establish a national policy to explore this inner space systematically, with goals, timetables, and budgets. Will you think me whimsical or impractical if I propose that one of these goals be a world-champion chess-playing computer program by 1975; and another, an order-of-magnitude increase by 1980 in the speed with which a human being can learn a difficult school subject, such as a foreign language or arithmetic?

If we are willing to dedicate ourselves to national goals of this kind (if you do not like my two, substitute your own), set deadlines for them, and commit resources to them (as we have committed resources to exploration of outer space), I think we soon shall have an understanding of both the information processors we call computers and those we call man. This understanding will enable us to build organizations far more effectively in the future than has ever been possible before.

3. Edward A. Feigenbaum and Julian Feldman, *Computers and Thought*, McGraw-Hill, 1963.
4. Claude Shannon, *Mathematical Theory of Communication*, University of Illinois Press, 1949.
5. John G. Kemeny, "Large Time-Sharing Networks," this volume.
6. National Academy of Sciences, *Technology*; Herbert A. Simon, *The Shape of Automation*, Harper & Row, 1965; Herbert A. Simon, *The Sciences of the Artificial*, MIT Press, 1969.

6.7

WHAT COMPUTERS MEAN FOR MAN AND SOCIETY

Herbert A. Simon

Energy and information are two basic currencies of organic and social systems. A new technology that alters the terms on which one or the other of these is available to a system can work on it the most profound changes. At the core of the Industrial Revolution, which began nearly three centuries ago, lay the substitution of mechanical energy for the energy of man and animal. It was the revolution that changed a rural subsistence society into an urban affluent one and touched off a chain of technological innovations that transformed not only production but also transportation, communication, warfare, the size of human populations, and the natural environment.

It is easy, by hindsight, to see how inexorably these changes followed one another, how "natural" a consequence, for example, suburbia was of cheap, privately owned transportation. It is a different question whether foresight could have predicted these chains of events or have aided in averting some of their more undesirable outcomes. The problem is not that prophets were lacking — they have been in good supply at almost all times and places. Quite the contrary, almost everything that has happened, and its opposite, has been prophesied. The problem has always been to pick and choose among the embarassing riches of alternative projected futures; and in this, human societies have not demonstrated any large foresight. Most often we have been constrained to anticipate events just a few years before their occurrence, or even while they are happening, and to try to deal with them as best we can, as they are engulfing us.

We are now in the early stages of a revolution in processing information that shows every sign of being as fundamental as the earlier energy revolution. Perhaps we should call it the Third Information Revolution. (The first produced written language, and the second, the printed book.) This third revolution, which began more than a century ago, includes the computer but many other things as well. The technology of information comprises a vast range of processes for storing information, for copying it, for transmitting it from one place to another, for displaying it, and for transforming it.

Photography, the moving picture, and television gave us, in the course of a century, a whole new technology for storing and displaying pictorial information. Telegraphy, the telephone, the phonograph, and radio did the same for storing and transmitting auditory information. Among all of these techniques, however, the computer is unique in its capacity for manipulating and transforming information and hence in carrying out, automatically and without human intervention, functions that had previously been performable only by the human brain.

As with the energy revolution, the consequences of the information revolution spread out in many directions. First, there are the economic consequences that follow on any innovation that increases human productivity. As we shall see, these are perhaps the easiest effects of technological change to predict. Second, there are consequences for the nature of work and of leisure — for the quality of life. Third, the computer may have special consequences for privacy and individual liberty. Fourth, there are consequences for man's view of himself, for his picture of the universe and of his place and goals in it. In each of these directions, the immediate consequences are, of course, the most readily perceived. (It was not hard to foresee that Newcomen's and Watt's engines would change the economics of mining in deep pits.) It is far more difficult to predict what indirect chains of effects these initial impacts will set off, for example, the chain that reaches from the steam engine through the internal-combustion engine to the automobile and the suburb.

Prediction is easier if we do not try to forecast in detail the time path of events and the exact dates on which particular developments are going to occur, but to focus, instead, upon the steady state toward which the system is tending.[1] Of course, we are not so much interested in what is going to happen in some vague and indefinite future as we are in what the next generation or two holds for us. Hence, a generation is the time

---

[1] A few years ago, Newell and I erred in predicting that certain specific developments in artificial intelligence were going to take place "within 10 years." The fact that we were optimistic about the time scale has blinded a number of critics to the basic soundness of our characterization of the nature and directions of artificial intelligence. I shall try not to make the same mistake here of predicting that very specific things will occur at very specific times. See H. A. Simon and A. Newell, *Oper. Res.* 6, 1 (1958).

span with which I shall be concerned.

My discussion will be divided into five parts, the last four corresponding to domains of prediction: economics, the nature of work and leisure, social consequences, and how men and women view themselves. These essays in prediction need to be preceded, however, by some analysis of the computer itself, and particularly its capabilities and potential in the area that is usually called artificial intelligence. This subject is taken up in the next section.[2]

Computer Capabilities

The computer is a device endowed with powers of utmost generality for processing symbols. It is remarkable not only for its capabilities but also for the simplicity of its underlying processes and organization. Of course, from a hardware standpoint it is not simple at all but is a highly sophisticated electronic machine. The simplicity appears at the level of the elementary information processes that the hardware enables it to perform, the organization for execution and control of those processes, and the programming languages in terms of which the control of its behavior is expressed. A computer can read symbols from an external source, output symbols to an external destination, store symbols in one or more memories, copy symbols, rearrange symbols and structures of symbols, and react to symbols conditionally — that is, follow one course of action or another, depending on what symbols it finds in memory or in its input devices. The most general symbol-manipulating system that has been defined, the so-called Turing machine, requires no broader capabilities than these. The important limits on the powers of a computer are limits on the sizes of its memories and the speed of its elementary processes, and not on the generality of those processes.

There is great dispute among experts as to what the generality of the computer implies for its ability to behave intelligently. There is also dispute as to whether the computer, when it is behaving more or less intelligently, is using processes similar to those employed by an intelligent human being, or quite different processes. The views expressed here will reflect my own experience in research with computers and my interpretation of the scientific literature. First, no

---

[2]For more detailed discussions of these topics, see H. A. Simon, *The New Science of Management Decision* (Prentice-Hall, Englewood Cliffs, N.J., ed. 3, 1977).

limits have been discovered to the potential scope of computer intelligence that are not also limits on human intelligence. Second, the elementary processes underlying human thinking are essentially the same as the computer's elementary information processes, although modern fast computers can execute these processes more rapidly than can the human brain.[3] In the past, computer memories, even in large computers, have probably not been as capacious as human memory, but the scale of available computer memories is increasing rapidly, to the point where memory size may not be much longer an effective limit on the capacity of computers to match human performance. Any estimate of the potential of the computer in the near or distant future depends on one's agreement or disagreement with these assumptions.

One common objection to the beliefs just expressed is that "computers can only do what you program them to do." That is correct. The behavior of a computer at any specific moment is completely determined by the contents of its memory and the symbols that are input to it at that moment. This does not mean that the programmer must anticipate and prescribe in the program the precise course of its behavior. A program is not a scenario; it is a strategy of of action, and what actions actually transpire depends on the successive states of the machine and its inputs at each stage of the process — neither of which need be envisioned in advance either by the programmer or by the machine. A problem-solving program applied to a particular puzzle situation does not prescribe all the steps to solve that puzzle; it prescribes a selective search strategy that, when followed, may lead the computer to discover a path to a solution. But selective search, under the guidance of strategies, is also the process that people use to solve puzzles.

Of course humans, through the processes called learning, can improve their strategies by experience and instruction. By the same token, computers can be, and to some extent have been, provided with programs (strategies) for improving their own strategies. Since a computer's programs are stored in the same memories as data, it is entirely possible for programs to modify themselves — that is, to learn.

Probably the most fundamental differences between today's

---

[3]The position that computers can be programmed to simulate an indefinite range of human thinking processes is developed in detail, and a large body of supporting evidence is examined in A. Newell and H. A. Simon, *Human Problem Solving* (Prentice-Hall, Englewood Cliffs, N.J., 1972); and J. R. Anderson and G. H. Bower, *Human Associative Memory* (Winston, Washington, D.C., 1973).

computers and the human information-processing system have to do with the input organs that provide the interface between the system and its environment. Simulating the capabilities of human eyes and ears has proved to be a much more difficult task than simulating the thinking processes that go on in the central nervous system. Computer capabilities in both visual and auditory domains, and particularly the former, fall far short of human capabilities.

Over the past two decades a moderate amount of work has been carried on in the field usually called artificial intelligence to explore the potentialities of the computer that have been outlined above. Some of this research has been aimed at programming computers to do things which, if done by a person, would be regarded as intelligent. Another part of the research has been directed at simulating not only the human capabilities but also the processes that human beings use in exercising these capabilities. The considerable progress that has been made in understanding the nature of both of artificial and of human intelligence has hardly begun to translate itself into applications, and has been reflected to only a small degree in the actual practical uses of computers. Artificial intelligence research has had an impact upon the search algorithms that are used to solve large combinatorial problems, it is on the verge of practical application in the realm of medical diagnosis, and it has had an important influence upon certain computer programming techniques (for example, list processing). But its main significance for practical affairs lies in the future.

How, then, have computers actually been used to date? At present, computers typically spend most of their time in two main kinds of tasks: carrying out large-scale engineering and scientific calculations and keeping the financial, production, and sales records of business firms and other organizations. Although precise statistics are not available, it would be safe to estimate that 95 percent of all computing power is allocated to such jobs. Now these tasks belong to the horseless-carriage phase of computer development. That is to say, they consist in doing things rapidly and automatically that were being done slowly and by hand (or by desk calculator) in the precomputer era.

Such uses of computers do not represent new functions but only new ways of performing old functions. Of course, by greatly lowering the cost of performing them, they encourage us to undertake them on a larger scale than before. The increased analytic power provided by computers has probably encouraged engineers to design more complex structures (for example, some of the very tall new office buildings that have gone up in New York and Chicago) than they would have attempted if their analytic aids were less powerful. Moreover, by permitting more sophisticated analyses to be carried out in the design process, they have also brought about significant cost reductions in the designs themselves. In the same way, the mechanization of business record-keeping processes has facilitated the introduction of improved controls over inventories and cash flows, with resulting savings in costs. Thus, the computer not only reduces the costs of the information-processing operations that it automates but also contributes to the productivity of the activities themselves.

The remaining 5 percent of computer uses are more sophisticated. Let us consider two different ways in which a computer can assist an engineer in designing electric motors. On the one hand, the engineer can design the motor using conventional procedures, then employ the computer to analyze the prospective operation of the design — the operating temperature, efficiency, and so on. On the other hand, the engineer can provide the computer with the specifications for the motor, leaving to the computer the task of synthesizing a suitable design. In the second, but not the first, case the computer, using various heuristic search procedures, actually discovers, decides upon, and evaluates a suitable design. In the same way, the role of the computer in managing inventories need not be limited to record-keeping. The computer program may itself determine (on the basis of usage) when items should be reordered and how large the orders should be. In these and many other situations, computers can provide not only the information on which decisions are made but can themselves make the decisions. Process-control computers, in automated or semi-automated manufacturing operations, play a similar role in decision-making. Their programs are decision strategies which, as the system's variables change from moment to moment, retain control over the ongoing process.

It is the capability of the computer for solving problems and making decisions that represents its real novelty and that poses the greatest difficulties in predicting its impact upon society. An enormous amount of research and development activity will have to be carried out before the full practical implications of this capability will be understood and available for use. In the single generation that modern computers have been in existence, enough basic research has been done to reveal some of the fundamental mechanisms. Although one can point to a number of applications of the computer as decision-maker that are already 20 or 25 years old, development and application on a substantial scale have barely begun.

Economic Effects of Computers

The direct economic effects of introducing computers as numerical calculators and decision-makers are like those of introducing any new form of capital that raises productivity and also improves the quality of the product. The computer (its hardware together with the associated system-programming costs) represents an investment in a capital-intensive, laborsaving device that has to justify itself, in competition with other possible forms of investment, through savings in clerical and other personnel costs together with the improvements it brings about in organizational decisions.

When the main motive of introducing the computer is to mechanize existing clerical operations — in the actuarial department of an insurance firm, say, or the accounting department of a manufacturing concern — then its main economic advantage stems from the reduction in clerical costs. When it is introduced to mechanize decision processes — engineering design, for example, or control of stock or cash inventories — then its direct effect shows up as some form of productivity increase in the organization's operations. In either case, there is nothing special about the computer that distinguishes it, in its economic effects, from any other capital investment. Any such investment can be expected to have a direct effect upon employment in the organizational components where it is introduced. When the accounting system is mechanized, fewer clerks and bookkeepers are needed, else there would be no economic motivation for mechanizing. Of course, if part of the motivation for the change is to improve the quality of the system's output, the operation may be expanded, and the net reduction in personnel may be smaller than would be estimated solely from the increase in efficiency. If there is sufficient elasticity of demand for the activity, personnel may actually increase.

The most important question, however, is what the reduction in personnel at the poin of impact means for the total level of employment in the economy. Again, this is a general economic issue — of technological unemployment — that does not depend on any special properties of computers. They are simply one among the many laborsaving devices that have been appearing since the beginning of the Industrial Revolution (and before).

Both standard economic analysis and a large body of empirical evidence demonstrate that there is no relation, positive or negative, between the technological sophistication of an economy and the level of employment it maintains. From a systems standpoint, a cost reduction in any part of the system releases resources that can be employed to increase the output of goods and services elsewhere in the system. At any level of employment, from 0 to 100 percent, the total revenue received by wage earners and owners of capital and land as wages, interest, and rent is just sufficient to purchase the total bundle of goods and services that is produced. Economists sometimes disagree as to why economies do not always operate at or near full employment, but they are unanimous in agreeing that the reason is not that they produce more than they can consume. (Even Marxists agree with this proposition, although they argue that full employment cannot be maintained within the institutions of capitalism.)

An even stronger statement can be made about the system effects of costsaving technological innovations. We usually describe devices like computers (and most other machinery) as laborsaving because they require a lower ratio of labor to capital than the methods they displace. But if we measure savings relative to output, they are usually both laborsaving and capital-saving. That is to say, a smaller capital investment per passenger mile is required to transport people by jet plane than to transport them by ox cart. Similarly, a smaller capital investment per multiplication is required if a large modern computer is used to do the arithmetic than if it is done on a desk calculator or with pencil and paper. (Do not forget to include the capital cost of the desk at which the clerk sits and the heated or air-conditioned room in which he or she works.) Now it is easy to show, for economic equilibrium and under reasonable assumptions about the supply of capital, that the introduction of capital-intensive, cost-saving innovations will raise the level of real wages and increase the fraction of the total revenue that goes to wages. This prediction from economic theory is amply supported by the histories of the industrialized economies over the present century. As productivity has increased (mainly as a consequence of technological innovation), real wages have steadily risen, as has labor's share in the total national product.[4]

Now the rate of technological change depends both upon the rate of discovery of new innovations and upon the availability of capital to turn them into brick and steel (or wire and glass). In this process, computers compete with other forms of technology for the available capital. Hence, the process of computerization is simply a part, currently an important

---

[4]For a fuller discussion of this evidence, see reference, footnote 2, chap. 4.

part, of the general process of technological change. It might be described, paraphrasing Clausewitz, as "a continuation of the Industrial Revolution by other means."[5]

In taking this very global and bird's-eye view of the economics of mechanization, we should not ignore the plight of the worker who is displaced by the computer. His plight is often genuine and serious, particularly if the economy as a whole is not operating near full employment, but even if it is. Society as a whole benefits from increased productivity, but often at the expense of imposing transient costs on a few people. But the sensible reponse to this problem is not to eschew the benefits of change; it is rather to take institutional steps to shift the burdens of the transition from the individual to society. Fortunately, our attitudes on these questions appear to be maturing somewhat, and our institutional practices improving, so that the widespread introduction of the computer into clerical operations over the past generation has not called forth any large-scale Ludditism. In fact, during the depression that we are currently experiencing, in contrast to some earlier ones, technology has not been accused as the villain.

Effects on the Nature of Work

We see that, so far as economic effects are concerned, the computer simply provides a particular path toward higher productivity through industrialization. Whatever benefits it produces, it produces in this way; whatever problems it creates, it creates as other capital-intensive innovations do. We must be careful, however, not to evaluate social change solely in terms of its impact on wages and employment. Of equal importance are the effects it may have on the workplace, and even on leisure. Today we frequently hear the claim that computers and automation dehumanize work and that dehumanization, in turn, causes alienation from work and society. These charges have been laid not only against contemporary developments in automation but against the whole process of industrialization. They were stated eloquently in the *Communist Manifesto* more than a century ago and by numerous social critics before and since. There has been a new surge of concern with the alienation issue in the past 10 years.

Three questions need to be asked about alienation. First, how much alienation is there — is there evidence that alienation has been increased

---

[5]K. von Clausewitz, *On War* (Modern Library, New York, 1943), p. 596.

by computers and automation or, for that matter, by other forms of industrialization and mechanization? Second, in what ways is the nature of work, and the satisfactions derivable from it, changed by automation of the workplace? Third, as automation eliminates certain kinds of jobs in favor of others, what are the net effects upon the profile of jobs in the economy — are the jobs that are eliminated, on balance, more or less satisfying than the new ones that are created to replace them?

Objective data on national trends in job satisfaction are available only for about the last 20 years. About 15 national surveys have been conducted since 1958 by professional polling organizaions that included questions on job satisfaction. Although 20 years is a short time, it does cover almost the whole period of the introduction of computers; hence these data should help answer the question before us. The polls provide absolutely no evidence for a decrease in job satisfactions over this period. If alienation has been increased by automation, the increase somehow does not show up in answers by workers to questions about their attitudes toward their jobs.[6] Notice that the polls do not show that workers are enthusiastic about their jobs, only that they do not seem to like them less today than they did in 1958.

Unfortunately, comparable data are not available to measure the longer trends in job satisfaction over the whole past two centuries or so of industrialization. Perhaps even if computers and automation do not intensify alienation, they confirm and complete a loss of satisfactions that was produced by the rise of the factory system. The answer to that question must be mainly speculative. Clayre, however, recently threw some interesting light on it by examining the attitudes toward work expressed in preindustrial folk literature and popular ballads.[7] He finds few indications of a Golden Age in which work was generally regarded as pleasurable and satisfying. He concludes that, in general, daily work was the same burdensome necessity for peasants and craftsmen as it is for factory workers and that life's satisfactions and pleasure were mainly sought, then as now, in leisure, not work.

---

[6]The polls under discussion were conducted by the Survey Research Centers of the Universities of Michigan and California, the National Opinion Research Center, and the Gallup Poll. For a detailed analysis of these data, see R. P. Quinn and L. J. Shepard, *The 1972-1973 Quality of Employment Survey* (Institute for Social Research, University of Michigan, Ann Arbor, 1974).

[7]A. Clayre, *Work and Play* (Harper & Row, New York, 1974).

Perhaps, however, we should not try to detect alienation in this indirect way but should look directly at the workplaces where computers have been introduced, in order to see how they have changed the nature of work and its environment. Sizable differences have been found in worker satisfaction among blue-collar workers in different kinds of factories, some of the important variables being job variety and worker control over the timing of work. It is not the case, however, that the most advanced forms of industrialization and automation produce the most tedious and restrictive jobs. On the contrary, those forms of work organization that appear to have been most alienating — typified by the auto assembly line or large-scale hand assembly operations — are declining in importance relative to other forms of mechanization. Blauner, for example, studied four industries in depth; printing, a traditional craft industry; textiles, a machine-tending industry; automobile assembly, highly mechanized with highly specialized jobs; and a highly automated continuous-process chemical manufacturing industry.[8] He found few indications of alienation in printing and chemicals, considerably more in textiles, and most of all in automobile assembly. The industry that best typifies modern automation — chemicals — was substantially less alienating than the two that typify older kinds of mechanization.

If we look at office automation, we see that, here too, the kinds of jobs that are displaced tend to be those that are most repetitive and restricting. Whisler, who studied about 20 companies in the insurance industry, found that computerization had produced only small and conflicting changes in the nature of clerical and supervisory jobs.[9] The new jobs placed greater demands on the employees for accuracy and reliability in performance, but they were not generally perceived as being significantly more or less pleasant or more or less boring than before. And, perhaps most important of all, whatever effects were produced

---

[8]R. Blauner, *Alienation and Freedom: The Factory Worker and His Industry* (Univ. of Chicago Press, Chicago, 1964).

[9]T. L. Whisler, *The Impact of Computers on Organizations* (Praeger, New York, 1970). I. R. Hoos [in *Automation in the Office* (Public Affairs Press, Washington, D.C.; 1961)] reaches more pessimistic conclusions than Whisler about the impact of computers, but she mainly observed transient effects at the time the new technology was being introduced, and not the longer-term effects after the changes had been digested.

were small effects. Automation and computerization do not appear to change the nature of work in a fundamental way.

Again we must look not just at immediate impact but at system effects. Factory and office automation are laborsaving technologies. The jobs they eliminate are mostly jobs that were already relatively routine. Therefore, when we look at the impact on the labor force as a whole, we expect to see automation bringing about an overall decrease in the percentage of persons engaged in routine work of these kinds. Correspondingly, there will be a larger percentage of employees than before in service occupations and probably also in technical occupations. The work-satisfaction studies discussed earlier show differences among occupational groups of precisely this kind. From these data it appears that if factory operatives and clerical workers decline as a fraction of the labor force, while service workers, sales personnel, and professional and technical workers increase, there will be a net increase in reported job satisfaction — unless, of course, a compensating shift takes place in aspirations, a possibility we must not dismiss.

On all counts, then, we must acquit the computer technology of the charges that it has been and will be a cause of widespread alienation from work. Empirically, we find no signs of a downward trend in work satisfaction, and when we look at the actual impact of automation upon the workplace and the work force, we find no reason why such a trend should be expected. On the contrary, the newer technologies may even have a modest humanizing effect on the nature of work. The notion of a Golden Age of work prior to the Industrial Revolution must also be dismissed as romanticism, unsupported by such evidence as has been examined.

Control and Privacy

The potential of computers for increasing the control of organizaitons or society over their members and for invading privacy of those members has caused considerable concern. The issues are important but are too complex to be discussed in detail here. I shall therefore restrict myself to a few comments which will serve rather to illustrate this complexity than to provide definitive answers.

A first observation is that our concern here is the competitive aspects of society, the power of one individual or group relative to others. Technologies tend to be double-edged in competitive situations, particularly when they are available to both competitors. For example, the computerization of credit information about individuals facilitates the assembly of such information from many sources, and its indefinite retention and accessibility. On the other hand, it also facilitates auditing such information to determine its sources and reliability. With appropriate legal rules of the game, an automated system can provide more reliable information than a more primitive one and can be surrounded by more effective safeguards against abuse. Some of us might prefer, for good reasons or bad, not to have our credit checked at all. But if credit checking is a function that must be performed, a strong case can be made for making it more responsible by automating it, with appropriate provision for auditing its operation.

Similarly, much has been said of the potential for embezzlement in computerized accounting systems, and cases have occurred. Embezzlement, however, was known before computers, and the computer gives auditors as well as embezzlers powerful new weapons. It is not at all clear which way the balance has been tilted.

The privacy issue has been raised most insistently with respect to the creation and maintenance of longitudinal data files that assemble information about persons from a multitude of sources. Files of this kind would be highly valuable for many kinds of economic and social research, but they are bought at too high a price if they enhance the opportunities of blackmailers. While such dangers should not be ignored, it should be noted that the lack of comprehensive data files has never been the limiting barrier to the suppression of human freedom. The Watergate criminals made extensive, if unskillful, use of electronics, but no computer played a role in their conspiracy. The Nazis operated with horrifying effectiveness and thoroughness without the benefits of any kind of mechanized data processing.

Making the computer the villain in the invasion of privacy or encroachment on civil liberties simply diverts attention from the real dangers. Computer data banks can and must be given the highest degree of protection from abuse. But we must be careful, also, that we do not employ such crude methods of protection as to deprive our society of important data it needs to understand its own social process and to analyze its problems.

Man's View of Man

Perhaps the most important question of all about the computer is what it has done and will do to man's view of himself and his place in the universe. The most heated attacks on the computer are not focused on its possible economic effects, its presumed destruction of job satisfactions, or its threats to privacy and liberty, but upon the claim that it causes people to be viewed, and to view themselves, as "machines."[10]

To get at the real issues, we must first put aside one verbal confusion. All of us are familiar with a wide variety of machines, most of which predated the computer. Consequently, the word "machine" carries with it many connotations: of rigidity, of simplicity, of repetitive behavior, and so on. If we call anything a machine, we implicitly attribute these characteristics to it. Hence, if a computer is a machine, it must behave rigidly, simply, and repetitively. It follows that computers cannot be programmed to behave like human beings.

The fallacy in the argument, of course, lies in supposing that, because we have applied the term "machine" to computers, computers must behave like older forms of machines. But the central significance of the computer derives from the fact that it falsifies these earlier connotations. It can, in fact, be programmed to behave flexibly, in complex ways, and not repetitively at all. We must either get rid of the connotations of the term, or stop calling computers "machines."

There is a more fundamental question behind the verbal one. It is essentially the question that was raised by Darwinism, and by the Copernican revolution centuries earlier. The question is whether the dignity of man, his sense of worth and self-respect, depends upon his being something special and unique in the universe. As I have said elsewhere (2, p. 27):

> The definition of man's uniqueness has always formed the kernel of his cosmological and ethical systems. With Copernicus and Galileo, he ceased to be the species located at the center of the universe, attended by sun and stars. With Darwin, he ceased to be the species created and specially endowed by God with soul and reason. With Freud, he ceased to be the species whose behavior was — potentially — governable by rational mind. As we begin to produce

---

[10]Two books that attack artificial intelligence on this ground are H. L. Dreyfus, *What Computers Can't Do* (Harper & Row, New York, 1972) and J. Weizenbaum, *Computer Power and Human Reason* (Freeman, San Francisco, 1976). The two books have little in common except a shared antipathy against the "machine" view of human thinking, and an eloquent contempt for those who hold that view. Weizenbaum's book is the technically more competent of the two, with respect to its understanding of the current state of the computer programming art.

mechanisms that think and learn, he has ceased to be the species uniquely capable of complex, intelligent manipulation of his environment.

What the computer and the progress in artificial intelligence challenge is an ethic that rests on man's apartness from the rest of nature. An alternative ethic, of course, views man as a part of nature, governed by natural law, subject to the forces of gravity and the demands of his body. The debate about artificial intelligence and the simulation of man's thinking is, in considerable part, a confrontation of these two views of man's place in the universe. It is a new chapter in the vitalism-mechanism controversy.

Issues that are logically distinct sometimes become stuck together with the glue of emotion. Several such issues arise here:

To what extent can human behavior be simulated by computer?

In what areas of work and life should the computer be programmed to augment or replace human activities?

How far should we proceed to explore the human mind by psychological research that makes use of computer simulation?

The first of these three issues will only be settled, over the years, by the success or failure of research efforts in artificial intelligence and computer simulation. Whatever our beliefs about the ultimate limits of simulation, it is clear that the current state of the art has nowhere approached those limits.

The second question will be settled anew each year by a host of individual and public decisions based on the changing computer technology, the changing economics of computer applications, and our attention to the social consequences of those applications.

The answer to the third question depends upon our attitudes toward the myths of Pandora and Prometheus. One viewpoint is that knowledge can be dangerous — there are enough historical examples — and that the attempt to arrive at a full explanation of man's ability to think might be especially dangerous. A different point of view, closer to my own, is that knowledge is power to produce new outcomes, outcomes that were not previously attainable. To what extent these outcomes will be good or bad depends on the purposes they serve, and it is not easy, in advance, to predict the good and bad uses to which any particular technology will be put. Instead, we must look back over human history and try to assess whether, on balance, man's gradual emergence from a state of ignorance about the world and about himself has been something we should celebrate or regret. To believe that knowledge is to be preferred to ignorance is to believe that the human species is capable of progress and, on balance, has progressed over the centuries. Knowledge about the human mind can make an important contribution to that progress. It is a belief of this kind that persuades researchers in artificial intelligence that their endeavor is an important and exciting chapter in man's great intellectual adventure.

Summary

From an economic standpoint, the modern computer is simply the most recent of a long line of new technologies that increase productivity and cause a gradual shift from manufacturing to service employment. The empirical evidence provides no support for the claim sometimes made that the computer "mechanizes" and "dehumanizes" work. Perhaps the greatest significance of the computer lies in its impact on Man's view of himself. No longer accepting the geocentric view of the universe, he now begins to learn that mind, too, is a phenomenon of nature, explainable in terms of simple mechanisms. Thus the computer aids him to obey, for the first time, the ancient injunction, "Know thyself."

VII

ECONOMICS AND PSYCHOLOGY

A large fraction of the papers in this volume could be included, appropriately, under the heading of "economics and psychology." Most of the papers of section V had a strong psychological content, but at the level of organizational behavior. In the present section, the emphasis is largely (although not exclusively) on individual behavior, and especially individual decision making.

MODELING RATIONAL AND ADAPTIVE BEHAVIOR

Chapters 7.1 and 7.4 are largely of methodological interest. The former explores the relation between the way in which choice is modeled in sociology (compare chapter 5.4) and the way in which it is modeled in economics. The models considered here foreshadow the contrast of procedural with substantive rationality that is developed at length in section VIII. This chapter was written for Paul Lazarsfeld's seminar in mathematical social science at Columbia University.

Chapter 7.4 was written somewhat with tongue in cheek to show that, with sufficient flexibility in the "utility function," almost any kind of more or less patterned behavior could be interpreted as rational. In this case, certain peculiar but very common patterns of betting behavior were interpreted as minimaxing regret. Although I expressed in the published article my skepticism about the validity of this "explanation" of the behavior, my skepticism did not come through to readers, and I found, somewhat to my dismay, that my analysis was being taken seriously and literally.

I am not the first prankster to suffer this fate, and undoubtedly not the last. Let me say loudly here that I think the true explanation for the event-matching behavior of human subjects in the binary choice experiment was provided, a few years after my article was published, by Julian Feldman in his doctoral dissertation, *Simulation of Behavior in the Binary Choice Experiment,* a summary of which appears as a chapter in Feigenbaum and Feldman (eds.), *Computers and Thought* (McGraw-Hill, 1963).

Feldman showed that when subjects are presented with random sequences and asked to forecast their continuations, they search for patterns that they can extrapolate. Limits on short-term memory permit them to overlook the fact that the patterns they use conform for only a short distance with the past histories of the sequences. To be sure, this is far from an irrational strategy if the sequences are in fact patterned but noisy, but it leads to behavior that is quite different from most of the strategies (except the minimax regret strategy) that would be deemed rational for predicting a biased but not autocorrelated random series.

BOUNDED RATIONALITY

Chapters 7.2 and 7.3 seek to formalize the basic model of bounded rationality that was developed in *Administrative Behavior*. They may be regarded as mathematizations of chapters 4 and 5 of that volume in the same sense that chapter 5.4 here is a mathematization of George Homans's *The Human Group*. These two chapters provide a good basis for comparing the fundamental assumptions and structure of a theory of bounded rationality with those of the theories of perfect rationality embodied in classical economic theory and in statistical decision theory. If I were asked to select just two of my publications in economics for transmission to another galaxy where intelligent life had just been discovered, these are the two I would choose. Since essentially all they assume about the rational actor is seriality of computation in the face of great complexity, I believe that the recipients of the communication would have no difficulty understanding them and applying them to their own affairs. But, of course, I wrote these chapters to explain how matters are on Earth, not in some other world.

We discover how things are on Earth by making empirical studies there. Chapter 7.4 reports one small sample of the studies of organizational decision making that were carried out at Carnegie-Mellon University during the 1950s, serving to illustrate one kind of empirical evidence that supports the theory of bounded rationality and the behavioral theory of the firm. The methodology of these studies reflects a conviction, held by most of us who were then developing this theory, that decision making has to be studied longitudinally, as a process, and that concern for sampling the universe of decisons adequately has to be preceded by a basic qualitative understanding of the process. We believed (and I continue to believe) that this understanding must be sought through microscopic analysis rather than through indirect and remote interpretation of gross aggregative data.

REVIEWS OF DECISION-MAKING THEORIES

On several occasions in the late 1950s and early 1960s I was asked to write survey articles on theories of decision making in economics and psychology and on computer simulation of human behavior. Chapter 7.6, an invited paper for the *American Economic Review*, was addressed to economists, while chapter 7.7, published as a chapter in *Psychology: A Study of a Science*, was addressed to an audience of psychologists. Consequently, though the two chapters cover somewhat the same ground, their emphases are different.

Chapter 7.8, a rather early survey of computer simulation, seeks to compare simulation techniques with standard econometric techniques and to survey progress in microsimulation, especially simulation using non-numerical models.

All three of these chapters set the stage for the more recent papers on these topics in section VIII. Hence, they are probably mostly of archival interest. However, in conjunction with section VIII, they would provide useful materials for anyone wishing to see how (or whether) my general outlook on the relation between economics and psychology has changed in the past twenty years.

THE REALISM OF ASSUMPTIONS

In general, I prefer discussing methodology in the context of concrete examples rather than in abstraction. On one occasion, however, I undertook to discuss explicitly Milton Friedman's position on the realism or unrealism of assumptions. Chapter 7.9 reports that discussion, which took place at a session of the meetings of the AEA.

As I reread my brief comments, I have no wish to revise them, although I might like to expand them. If we ignore the micro-level evidence on the invalidity of our assumptions, we leave ourselves open to serious errors whenever the structure of the system we are studying changes. For example, our present difficulties with business cycle theory (and public policy relating to it) are in considerable part traceable, in my view, to the absence of any solid empirical foundation for our hypotheses about how expectations are formed. If we had been taking George Katona's advice more seriously over the past thirty years, about studying expectations at the micro level, we might now have such a foundation. Armchair speculation about expectations, rational or other, is not a satisfactory substitute for factual knowledge as to how human beings go about anticipating the future, what factors they take into account, and how these factors, rather than others, come within the range of their attention. To quote Katona (1978, p. 18).

The basic difference between the traditional methods of economic theory and behavioral economics may be found in the mental set of the practitioners of the two scientific methodologies. Theorists abhor surprises; behaviorists rejoice when they are surprised. For instance, Milton Friedman began his Nobel lecture in December 1976 (see *Journal of Political Economy,* June 1977) by acknowledging the surprise caused by the acceleration of both inflation and unemployment in 1974-75: then he proceeded to minimize the surprise and explained the developments by a "modest elaboration" of the original hypothesis. On the other hand, this author, surprised by a large increase in purchases of one-family houses in 1977 following great advances in their prices and in interest rates, proceeded to study the behavior of home buyers. The Survey Research Center found that the expectation of further large price increases motivated a substantial proportion of home buyers, and the author was delighted to have obtained an additional instance of the powerful impact of expectations on demand.

CHOICE UNDER UNCERTAINTY

Chapters 7.10 and 7.11 contain some ruminations on the treatment of expectations in economic theory but do not supply the empirical research that I have just said is needed. What these chapters do is to suggest a number of different ways in which economic actors might formulate their problems of addressing uncertainty in future events. Since both were written (the first with William W. Cooper) at a time when I was much interested in dynamic programming and servomechanism approaches to uncertainty, both chapters reflect this interest. This predilection for adaptive feedback processes was motivated, of course, by considerations of bounded rationality.

If bounded rationality is assumed, then forming expectations is only one of several strategies for dealing with uncertainty. Another is to construct an environment in which the impact of uncertainty is buffered, so that robust strategies can be constructed that are relatively insensitive to how the uncertainty is resolved. In particular, in chapter 7.11, I argue that a major function of social institutions (one that they do not always perform well, however) is to do this buffering for their participants.

Given this wide range of possible modes of adaptation to uncertainty, I come back again to the concern expressed earlier: it is hard to see how we can have a satisfactory theory of the business cycle or of such phenomena as inflation and stagflation, until we have an empirically grounded theory of expectation formation and reaction to uncertainty.

REFERENCES

Denison, E. F. *Accounting for slower economic growth.* Washington, D.C.: The Brookings Instituion, 1979.

Feldman, J. *An analysis of predictive behavior in a two-choice situation.* Unpublished doctoral dissertation, Carnegie Institute of Technology, Pittsburgh, 1959.

Feldman, J. Simulation of behavior in the binary choice experiment. In E. Feigenbaum and J. Feldman, eds., *Computers and thought,* New York: McGraw-Hill, 1963.

Katona, G. Behavioral economics. *Challenge* (September-October 1978): 14-18.

7.1

Some Strategic Considerations in the Construction of Social Science Models

Herbert A. Simon

Section I. MODELS OF OPTIMIZATION

It is my aim in this paper to discuss some problems of strategy in theory construction in the social sciences. To put the matter more modestly, I should like to set forth, illustrate, and discuss some of the basic strategic considerations that have guided my own work in the formulation of theories -- and particularly mathematical theories -- of various aspects of human behavior.

The undertaking requires some preface. First, I should like to rule out of bounds the question of whether mathematics has any business in the social sciences. I will simply assert, with J. Willard Gibbs, that mathematics is a language; it is a language that sometimes makes things clearer to me than do other languages, and that sometimes helps me discover things that I have been unable to discover with the use of other languages. What the contribution of mathematics will be to the social sciences can perhaps be more fruitfully evaluated some generations hence when that contribution -- if any -- has been made.

Second, we shall be concerned with *applied* mathematics, and hence we shall be as concerned with the field of application as with mathematics itself. The strategy of mathematical theorizing must come primarily from the field about which the theorizing is to be done. The aim of a language is to say something -- and not merely to say something about the language itself. Mathematical social science is, first and foremost, social science. If it is bad social science (i.e., empirically false), the fact that it is good mathematics (i.e., logically consistent) should provide little comfort.

In the first section, I should like to comment, in a completely unmathematical fashion, upon certain current trends in social science research that have an important bearing upon the strategy

388

209

of theory construction. In succeeding sections of this and the
following chapter I shall attempt to draw out more specifically the
implications of these basic trends, illustrating the discussion with
a few of the relatively primitive mathematical social science
models that are now in existence.[2]

THE REINTEGRATION OF THE SOCIAL SCIENCES

The social sciences -- weakened by a half-century of schisms
among economists, political scientists, sociologists, anthropologists,
and social psychologists -- are undergoing at present a very rapid
process of reintegration. This development is so rapid, and so obvious from even a casual survey of the journals and new books in
these fields, that it hardly requires documentation.[3] The common
diplomatic language for the scientists participating in the process
is the language of sociology and social psychology, and the common
core of theory -- the rules of international law, if you like -- is
theory drawn primarily from those two fields.

An important cause of this development is that, in attempting
to understand and analyse the large events in the political and
economic scene -- the wars, elections, and depressions -- the
social scientist has been forced to a recognition that all such events
are aggregated from the interrelated behavior of human beings.
The theoretical models, and the predictions based on models, of
the larger scene have required him to make assumptions (explicit
or implicit) about the motives, understandings, and abilities of
these human beings. Critical attention to these assumptions, and a
desire to validate them in a scientifically respectable manner, has
gradually and inexorably driven social science back to the molecular phenomena of human behavior in a social environment.

Of course, psychological postulates -- generally contrived
in the comfort of the armchair -- have long been a part of social
science theory. What is new in the present situation is that the
student of aggregative phenomena is now confronted with a growing body of social psychological and sociological theory and empirical verification that places a check on his free imagination and
requires him to reconcile his postulates with this theory and these
data. To state the matter in a more constructive way, social psychology and sociology are, perhaps for the first time, reaching a
stage of development where they can make a positive contribution
toward the foundations on which the more aggregative theories are
built.

MODELS OF EXISTING SOCIO-PSYCHOLOGICAL THEORY

It is from these important trends that I would derive a first canon of strategy. If mathematics is to play an important role in the development of social science theory, then a great deal of experience must be gained as to what kinds of mathematics are likely to be useful, and as to what are some of the promising ways of imbedding fundamental psychological and sociological concepts and phenomena in mathematical models. What form shall human motives take in such models, how shall the rational and the non-rational aspects of human behavior be represented, what kind of mathematical schemes will conveniently represent the interactions of human groups, and so on?

The starting point, if this strategy is adopted, is the task of translating into the language of mathematics some of the concepts and some of the propositions that appear promising and fundamental in the growing body of social-psychological theory. In one sense, such translations will not say anything that is not already known -- they will merely say it in another language. In another sense it is improbable that any great amount of translation of verbal theories into mathematical language can take place without significant advances in the clarity of the concepts imbedded in the theory.

The few areas where any considerable amount of activity of this sort has already been undertaken will suggest what might be accomplished. The most important of these is economics, where, to cite one example from many, the attempt to construct mathematical models of utility theory has rubbed off a great deal of fuzziness from the concept of "rational behavior," and has laid bare some of the basic methodological problems in the operational definition and measurement of "utility."[4] Perhaps these advances could have been made without mathematics, but the fact is that they weren't.

A widespread effort to translate into mathematical language the core of existing social science theories will make another, and very direct, contribution to the reintegration of the social sciences. By translating from the specialized languages of the several social sciences to the common language of mathematics, unsuspected relationships will be discovered among theories that have been developed independently in these several sciences. In later sections of this paper I shall cite some examples of this -- notably an example of two closely related theories, one drawn from the economist's theory of the firm, the other from the notion of organizational equilibrium discussed by administrative theorists.

NEED FOR A PLURALITY OF MODELS

A second canon of strategy is suggested by the magnitude of the task proposed. In social psychology today -- much less the other social sciences -- we do not have a theory, but theories -- disconcertingly many of of them. *Realism would suggest that we attempt to construct, not a mathematical model, but a plurality of mathematical models.* Once we have learned to imbed particular pieces of social reality in particular pieces of theoretical models, the interconnections among these will begin to suggest themselves. This has been the path of development of even the most successful of the sciences.

In the succeeding sections of this paper I shall suggest a number of central concepts that, I believe, should receive the attention of model builders and I shall survey some of the approaches that have been employed already to incorporate these concepts in models.

MODELS OF RATIONAL BEHAVIOR

As far as economic and administrative theory are concerned, man has been conceived primarily as a rational animal. The concept of rationality has played a prominent, but much less central, role in the other social sciences. Since economics, of all the social sciences, has had by far the greatest assistance from mathematics, it is not surprising that models of rational behavior are far more advanced than mathematical models of other aspects of behavior.

The most advanced theories, both verbal and mathematical, of rational behavior are those that employ as their central concepts the notions of: (1) a set of alternative courses of action presented to the individual's choice; (2) knowledge and information that permit the individual to predict the consequences of choosing any alternative; and (3) a criterion for determining which set of consequences he prefers. [5] In these theories rationality consists in selecting that course of action which leads to the set of consequences most preferred. (At a later point of our discussion we will see that this definition of rationality is somewhat too restrictive, but we may accept it temporarily as a starting point for analysis.)

Practically the whole of classical economic theory is constructed within the framework of this model. As an example of a mathematical version of it, which will serve to indicate how a verbal theory can be mathematized, we may take a very simple model of the theory of the firm. In this simple example there is a single rational human being, an "entrepreneur" who is operating a firm that manufactures a single product from a single raw material. (1) The alternatives open to the entrepreneur are to employ more or less of the raw material. (2) The consequences of a given course of action are that he will incur a cost (determined by the price of the raw material, and the quantity used), and he will receive a revenue (determined by the price of the product, and the quantity produced with the given amount of raw material). We assume that he knows the price at which any specified amount of raw material can be bought, the price at which any specified amount of product can be sold, and the maximum amount of product that can be produced from a given amount of raw material. That is, he knows his "supply curve, " his "demand curve," and his "production function." (In this model, the supplier and the consumer need not be regarded as rational human beings, their behavior being specified and known.) (3) The entrepreneur's criterion is that he wishes the largest possible profit -- the largest attainable difference between total revenue and cost of production.

THE MATHEMATICAL TRANSLATION

In the language of mathematics, let y be the quantity of product made, and x the quantity of raw material bought. Let $p = p(y)$ be the price of the product, which is assumed to depend on the quantity sold; and $P = P(x)$ be the price of the raw material, assumed to depend on the quantity bought. Let the quantity of product obtainable from a given quantity of raw material be given by $y = f(x)$. Then the entrepreneur's alternatives are a range of values of x. The revenue, $yp(y) = f(x)p(f(x))$, and the cost $xP(x)$, are the consequences which can be calculated when x is known. The criterion is to maximize the profit, $\pi = yp(y) - xP(x)$, regarded as function of x. The rational behavior is given by the well-known "marginal" condition,

$$\frac{d\pi}{dx} = \frac{df}{dx} p[f(x)] + f(x) \frac{dp}{dy} \frac{df(x)}{dx} - P(x) - x\frac{dP}{dx} = 0 \qquad (1)$$

Translating this equation back into English, it says that the rational entrepreneur will fix his output at the point where marginal cost equals marginal revenue.

Several features of this model deserve notice, as generally characteristic of models of rational behavior. Certain variables -- in this case x -- are regarded as "strategic" variables, controllable by a rational being. Other variables -- in this case π -- are the criterion, and measure of the goal he is seeking. The limits of attainment are set by conditions outside his control -- relationships he must accept -- which determine the value of the criterion as a function of the strategic variable. The problem of rationality then becomes a problem in maximization -- to find the greatest value of the criterion, regarded as a function of the strategic variables.

SIGNIFICANCE OF THE LIMITS OF RATIONALITY

If we regard this model as a description of the actual behavior of some entrepreneur, we see that if we are to predict his behavior, the knowledge that he is rational is only a small part -- almost an insignificant part -- of the information that we require. His intention to be rational leads to particular behavior only in the context of conditions in which his behavior takes place. These conditions include both (1) the limits expressed by the demand curve, the supply curve, and the production function -- we might regard these as the limits of his "abilities" in the situation -- and (2) the limits expressed by the criterion function. The criterion (regarded as a "final end") is itself not an object of rational calculation, but a given. The model would be equally a model of rational behavior if the entrepreneur chose to maximize his losses, or his gross revenue instead of his profit.

Indeed, our principal use for such models is in predicting how the entrepreneur's behavior will be affected by a change in the environment that conditions or "bounds" his rationality. For example, we may wish to predict how the price and output of the product will be altered, assuming the entrepreneur always to behave rationally, if there occurs a shift in the demand function. To do this, we can regard the price of the product, p, as depending both on the quantity sold, y, and upon a parameter (i.e., a coefficient regarded as constant in the short run, but as possibly varying in the long run), a, which may vary, for example, with changes in consumers' tastes: $p = p(y,a)$. Each change in a shifts the whole demand curve -- relating p to y -- to right or left. If we follow the maximizing procedure previously described for finding

the optimal value of x, this value will now depend on a --
that is, a will in general appear in equation (1). Hence, we can
regard equation (1) as a statement of relationship between x
and a -- a statement of how production, under the assumption
of the entrepreneur's rationality, will vary with shifts in
demand.[6]

We may summarize our discussion to this point by saying:
that a simple model of rational behavior leads quite naturally to
maximizing procedures and, in mathematical translation, to the
methods of the differential calculus; and that the specific features
of interest in any particular model arise primarily from the particular conditions under which rationality is exercised. This second point perhaps deserves to be dignified as a third canon of
strategy: *In mathematical models incorporating rational and non-
rational aspects of behavior, the non-rational aspects can be imbedded in the model as the limiting conditions that "bound" the
area of rational adjustment.*[7]

QUALIFICATIONS ON THE MODEL
OF RATIONAL BEHAVIOR

The previous paragraph registers my conviction that improvement in the model of rational behavior will come primarily
through careful attention to the boundaries of the area of rationality. In the remaining sections of this paper, I shall try to make
this recommendation more explicit. We can begin our examination
of these boundaries by looking at some of the extensions and
amendments to the rational model that economists have been led to
by their attempts to extend that model to broader and broader
classes of phenomena.

RATIONALITY OF MORE THAN ONE

The rationality of the classical maximizing procedures is
essentially the rationality of Robinson Crusoe. For each rational
individual in the model must take as fixed "givens" the patterns of
behavior of the other individuals -- he must regard these others
not as rational beings, but as some kind of responsive or unrespon-
sive mechanism. The classical theory found three paths that gave
promise of leading out of this wilderness:

(1) *Perfect Competition.* In the theory of perfect competition, each participant assumes that what he does is such an

insignificant part of the total picture that it will have no effect on the others. Hence, if he can predict the behavior of the others, and adjust his own behavior to the prediction, his adjustment will not have repercussions that would disturb the prediction.

(2) *Imperfect Competition.* If the participants will adjust their behavior to each other, but each participant can predict what the adjustments of the others to his behavior will be, then he can determine which of his own behavior alternatives will be optimal in the light of the prediction. This was our procedure in the simple model used in the previous section. The demand curve and the supply curve each constitutes a prediction of the price that the customer or supplier, respectively, will pay or require for the quantity of product or raw material the entrepreneur decides upon. The customer and supplier are supposed to regard the price as something given -- as something they cannot influence.

(3) *Cournot's Oligopoly Theory.* If the customer and the supplier in the previous case were just one whit cleverer, the solution there given would be untenable. If the entrepreneur assumes they are going to adjust to his behavior, and acts in anticipation of that adjustment, why do not they, in turn, assume that he is going to adjust to their behavior and act in anticipation of that adjustment? The imperfect competition model admits rationality of all participants, but does not permit the same level of cleverness in the customer or supplier as in the entrepreneur. The limits on his rationality, as it is postulated, are broader and less restricting than the limits on theirs -- he tries to outguess them, but they do not try to outguess him.

Cournot sought a way out of this difficulty by permitting *each* participant, in a two-person model, to guess at the reaction of the other, and to behave accordingly. Equality of cleverness was restored, and if dynamic stability was present the actual behaviors would in fact conform to the predicted behavior. (At the equilibrium point, the participants would predict correctly on a wrong basis.) But the Cournot model, while consistent with the assumptions of rationality, is not a model of unlimited cleverness. For either participant, if he knew the other was following the Cournot procedure, could form some new, and more accurate, expectations of that other's reactions to his choices, and use this new prediction to better his position. This way lies madness, for it leads to an infinite regress of prediction in which A predicts what B will predict as to A's prediction of B's reaction to A's behavior -- and so on, ad infinitum. [8]

The conclusion we reach from our examination of models of rationality involving the behavior of more than one person is that

we must adopt one of two alternatives: (a) on the one hand, we can
assume that not more than one participant is unlimitedly clever in
predicting the reactions of the other participants to his behavior;
(b) on the other hand, we can seek a new definition of rationality
that does not identify rationality with a simple maximization process. The first approach -- assumptions of rationality and maximization, but limited cleverness -- is the one involved in all three
paths described above: perfect competition, imperfect competition,
and oligopoly theory. The second approach, abandonment of simple
maximization, was adoped by von Neumann and Morgenstern in
their pioneering work on the theory of games.[9] By replacing the
maximum, in the definition of rationality, with a more sophisticated
mathematical concept, the minimax, the difficulty is avoided[10]--
at the expense of attributing to human beings a cleverness they
have perhaps not often exhibited outside the more successful poker-
playing circles.

No attempt will be made here to evaluate the respective merits of the two approaches to rationality. The von Neumann model
may be the more useful appraoch to the question of optimal be-
vior -- i.e., for a book on how to play successful poker. The model
of limited cleverness may be more useful in the description of
actual rational behavior -- at least until such time as most people
have learned to minimax rather than to maximize.

REACTION TIME--RATIONALITY AND DYNAMICS

The outguessing difficulty is only one of the problems that
can be raised in connection with the classical model. Another is
the question of speed of adjustment. In our simple model of the
theory of the firm, the entrepreneur is assumed to know not only
the shape of the demand curve, but also its position at any given
time -- i.e., the value of the parameter a . For many situations a
more realistic assumption would be that he does not have this detailed knowledge, but only discovers his optimal position by experimenting and learning on the basis of his experience and his
mistakes. For example, he might have some information about
marginal costs and marginal revenue, but only in the neighborhood
of the position in which he is actually operating. He might then
adopt the rule of behavior that he will continue to increase his output so long as his marginal revenue is in excess of marginal cost,
and decrease it whenever he finds marginal cost in excess of marginal revenue. In equations, the assumption is:

$$\frac{dx}{dt} = b \left\{ \frac{df}{dx} \ p \ [f(x)] + f(x) \ \frac{dp}{dy} \ \frac{df(x)}{dx} - P(x) - x \frac{dP}{dx} \right\}, \ (b > 0). \quad (2)$$

Now if "other conditions" like the parameter a remain reasonably steady, and if the system satisfies certain other stability
requirements, it turns out that the optimal solution, in the sense
of equation (1), is actually the stable equilibrium position of the
time path described by equation (2)[11]. When this is true, equation
(2) may be taken as a definition of rational behavior under the restrictions of information that have been assumed. *How* rational
it is, will depend, of course, on the size of the coefficient b, which
measures the adjustment rate, for if this coefficient is large the
adjustment and the approach to the equilibrium will be rapid,
while if b is small, the approach will be slow. If, now, a fluctu-
ates moderately (there are shifts from time to time in demand), a
large b will prevent the entrepreneur from ever departing very
widely from the optimal output, while a small b may permit very
wide departures, and consequent loss of profit.

The difference between the kind of rationality depicted in
equation (1) and the kind depicted in equation (2) might be described as follows. Two popcorn men are vending their wares on a very
large county fair ground. Their profits will depend on keeping
their wagons in the part of the fair ground where as dense a crowd
as possible has assembled. The crowd is in continual motion. The
first popcorn man has radio equipment on his wagon on which he
has arranged to receive from all parts of the fair ground frequent
reports on the size of the crowd. As soon as he learns where it is
densest, he speeds to that part of the ground. The second popcorn
man has less modern equipment. He keeps his cart in motion in
the direction of increasing density of the crowd, and away from the
direction of decreasing density.

Amount of Information and Speed of Adjustment. Now if one is
willing to include amount of information and speed of adjustment
among the boundaries of rationality, a large number of interesting
possibilities offer themselves. In the first place, while it seems
to be almost always possible to construct a stable dynamic system
whose equilibrium position corresponds to the maximum of a given
static system, it is often possible to construct more than one such
dynamic system. In terms of our "dynamic" definition of rationality, it would then occur that there would be more than one rational
pattern of behavior in a given situation.

For example, in the usual dynamization of the theory of markets -- leading to the well-known cobweb phenomena -- it is assumed that when supply is out of balance with demand, a price adjustment will take place in the short-run to "clear the market,"
while in the long run, an adjustment in the quantity supplied will

restore the suppliers to their position of profit maximization. An alternative dynamic mechanism can be constructed in which a lack of balance between supply and demand leads to an adjustment in the quantity supplied, while if the current price does not provide suppliers with a "reasonable" profit, a price adjustment takes place. With suitable assumptions, this second model has the same position of equilibrium, and virtually the same stability conditions as the first.

To predict an individual's behavior under these circumstances, we would have to know, not only that he was being rational, but also whether he was exhibiting rationality of species A (corresponding to one dynamic system) or rationality of species B (corresponding to another). In the long run -- in equilibrium -- it would not make any difference, but as Keynes has pointed out, in the long run we are all dead.

Optimizing versus Adaptive Behavior. As we move from the static model to the dynamic, our original definition of rationality (selection of that course of action which leads to the set of consequences most preferred) becomes somewhat too restrictive. On the one hand, we may build the concept of rationality, as in the earlier models, upon the ability of the individual to discover a "best" situation and to move toward it, either instantaneously (as in the static models) or gradually (as in the dynamic). On the other hand, we can base an alternative notion of rationality on the ability of the individual to distinguish "better" (or "preferred") from "worse" directions of change in his behavior and to adjust continually in the direction of the "better." A rational process in which the choice of a "best" is central we will call optimization; a rational process in which movement toward a "better" is central we will call adaptation. Clearly, as is shown by the models of dynamic adjustment toward an optimal equilibrium, the two species of rationality are not mutually exclusive. In spite of the overlap, however, we will find the distinction useful in progressing through the whole continuum of models of rational behavior from those, on the one extreme, incorporating instantaneous optimization to those, at the other extreme, requiring only that minimum of adaptation which may be essential for survival.

Now, taking the next step along the continuum, and freeing the dynamic model we have already discussed from its ties with the corresponding static system, we may view it as follows:

An individual has a certain criterion, by means of which he judges his situation. Call the criterion θ_s. He measures his actual situation, θ_0, and its departure, $(\theta_s - \theta_0)$, from the criterion.

He then adjusts his behavior at a rate that is proportional to the difference between the actual and the criterion. In the model previously discussed, for example, the criterion is that the marginal revenue should equal the marginal cost; the actual situation is described by the difference between the (actual) marginal revenue and the (actual) marginal cost. He then adjusts his behavior -- the variable x -- at a rate assumed to be proportional to this difference. In equations, the system is:

$$\theta_s = 0 \tag{3}$$

$$\theta_0 = \left\{ \frac{df}{dx} \, p \, [f(x)] + f(x) \, \frac{dp}{dy} \, \frac{df(x)}{dx} - P(x) - x \, \frac{dP}{dx} \right\} \tag{4}$$

$$\epsilon = \theta_s - \theta_0 = -\theta_0 \tag{5}$$

$$\frac{dx}{dt} = b\epsilon \tag{6}$$

An engineer looking at this model would recognize in it something he is accustomed to call a "servomechanism" or a "closed-loop control system." If we follow the engineer's terminology in calling the difference between the actual state of the system and the criterion an "error," then we may say that the system is an adaptive one in which the individual measures the error in his behavior, and adjusts the behavior seeking to eliminate the error. Norbert Wiener has argued persuasively that the servomechanism model may be a useful model for describing physiological, psychological, and sociological adaptive systems.[12]

There is yet another sense in which the notion of an adaptive system is broader than the notion of optimizing behavior. Optimization carries at least the connotation of conscious deliberation, foresight, and intention. Adaptation, on the other hand, more generally connotes appropriateness for survival, movement toward equilibrium. Now the two notions of optimization and survival are combined in the classical economic theory of pure competition in an ingenious fashion. But there is no reason why we cannot consider systems that are adaptive, in the sense of possessing a stable equilibrium position toward which the system continually moves, without postulating an optimizing mechanism (in the conscious sense) that explains the adaptation. As a matter of fact, refusal to consider such systems would make all of biology hopelessly anthropomorphic. It may be argued that a similar refusal in the social sciences would make those sciences hopelessly economomorphic.

At any rate it would appear that there is a large number of possible dynamic models of social behavior that deserve to be examined quite apart from their possible linkage to models of static optimizing behavior, and quite apart from any insistence that the "criterion" in terms of which the system adjusts need be a conscious goal of rational action. In the next chapter we shall proceed to an examination of several such models, but before we do so, some concluding comments need to be added under the present heading of "Qualifications on the Model of Rational Behavior."

INCOMPLETE INFORMATION AND UNCERTAINTY

In the previous section, we examined one way in which the model of rational behavior can be altered to take account of limits on information and speed of adjustment. In that section we were concerned primarily with the individual's information about the behavior of other individuals. He may also, of course, have incomplete information about the non-human conditions that surround his activity. We may sketch briefly a number of schemes for handling the problem:

(1) We can incorporate the individual's expectations into the behavior model. Then we require a theory of how he forms those expectations -- a theory of his forecast model. His expectations may take the form of specific predictions, or of probability distributions of the predicted variable. If we take the latter alternative, then we may wish to define rational choice as the choice that maximizes the expected value (in the statistical sense) of the criterion variable. This approach adds nothing essentially new to our optimization model. It is the approach that, in combination with the von Neumann game theory, dominates modern statistical theory -- e.g., the Neyman-Pearson theories of testing hypotheses and the sequential analysis theories of Wald.[13]

(2) We can assume that the individual adjusts to his changing situation without forecasting. This leads again to dynamic models of the servo-mechanism type.[14]

(3) We can assume that the individual balances the costs of postponing decisions against the advantages of obtaining additional information before he makes them. Then we are led to the theory of the timing of decisions. J. Marschak has shown how such an approach can be used to explain certain aspects of liquidity preference -- the preference for holding assets in relatively liquid form -- and I have shown that the same approach can be used as a basis for explaining, on rational grounds, the authority relationship

between employer and employee and the comparative advantages of an employment or a sales contract for accomplishing a particular task.[15]

PREFERENCE FIELDS

In our initial model of optimizing behavior, we assumed that a criterion function exists. In the case of the entrepreneur, the criterion function has traditionally been his profit, in the case of the consumer, his "utility." This has led to the question of whether such a function exists, and this question, in turn, to some very fruitful examinations of the whole subject of preference fields. In those cases where we are willing to admit that an unambiguous field exists -- where at the very least, each possible outcome can be judged as "better," "the same," or "worse" than each other possible outcome -- we are assuming again a very global kind of rationality. We are assuming that the individual possesses a very wide span of attention, and a single consistent system of values that he applies simultaneously to the whole range of action.

There has been only a little exploration into the possibilities of models that make less global assumptions about the consistency, comprehensiveness, and stability of the individual's preference field.[16] Yet these limits of rationality -- limits on the consistency of choice -- certainly have empirical importance in many areas of behavior. I can offer at the moment no concrete suggestions as to the way in which such limits can effectively be incorporated in a model, but simply call to the reader's attention this potentially significant area for theoretical work.

CONCLUSION

This completes our survey of the various directions that have been pursued in the construction of models of that species of rational behavior we have called optimization. We have seen that as soon as we begin to introduce limits upon the speed of adjustment and upon the range of alternatives over which choice is exercised, we begin to move from models of optimization to models of adaptation. The next section will be devoted to a further investigation of this latter class of models.

Section II. MODELS OF ADAPTIVE BEHAVIOR

Theory construction, largely the work of mathematical economists, in the area of rational human behavior has been developing, as we have just seen, in the direction of more and more explicit attention to the various limitations upon the capacity of human beings to behave in a "perfectly" rational fashion. Of the various amendments to the classical model, perhaps the most radical is the one -- leading to dynamics -- that shifts the focus from "optimal" behavior to "adaptive" behavior. In the present section I shall explore some of the implications of this shift. Rather than to speculate about the problem in the abstract, our procedure will be to exhibit several models that show how various kinds of behavior, viewed as an adaptive process, can be handled. We will begin with a model of individual behavior, and proceed to some models of behavior in groups.

MOTIVATION AND LEARNING

In psychological formulations of adaptive human behavior, the concepts of motivation and learning are central.[17] The notion of motivation is closely connected with the "criterion" in the models of optimization, while learning is connected with changes in such limitations on rationality as "state of information" and "technology." In the present model we shall not attempt any further exact translation from the previous concepts, but will start afresh.

THE "BERLITZ" MODEL

We suppose that there is an activity in which an individual engages from time to time, and that he can engage in varying amounts of it each day. As he engages in it, it becomes progressively easier for him (this is our "learning" assumption). To the extent that he finds it pleasant, he engages in it more frequently; to the extent he finds it unpleasant, he engages in it less frequently. Its pleasantness depends on how easy it is for him. (The latter two statements comprise our "motivation" assumption.)

As a concrete example, we may suppose that our individual has subscribed to a correspondence course to learn French by the Berlitz method. Each day he spends a certain amount of time in practice. As he practices, the language becomes easier; so long as the difficulty is greater than a certain level, he finds the work

unpleasant, and tends to shorten his practice sessions. (We assume our student to be a kind of hedonist.) If he reaches a certain level of skill, however, the work becomes pleasant, and he
will tend to practice for a longer period.[18]

Let x be the rate (say, in hours per day) at which the activity is performed. Let D be the level of difficulty, and let us assume (learning) that the difficulty decreases logarithmically with
practice:

$$dD/dt = -aDx \qquad (7)$$

Let us assume that at any given level of difficulty, practice is
pleasurable up to a certain point, and unpleasant beyond that point,
and that $x = \bar{x}(D)$ is this satiation level of activity. We assume
then (motivation) that:

$$dx/dt = -b(x - \bar{x}) \qquad (8)$$

The two equations for dD/dt and dx/dt permit us to predict the
time paths of D and x if we know their initial values, D_0 and x_0
at time t_0. Several representative time paths are shown in
Figure 1.

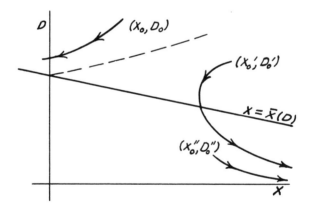

Figure 1.

The figure shows that whether our student eventually becomes discouraged and fails to complete his course, or whether
he is successful in learning French depends on his starting point

(and, of course, on the relative magnitudes of a and b and the shape of $\overline{x}(D)$). The value of D_0 represents the difficulty of the language to him at the outset, and x_0 the amount of time he initially devotes to practice. If the point (x_0, D_0) lies above the dotted line, he will ultimately become discouraged and give up his lessons; if, instead, he begins at (x_0', D_0'), between the dotted line and the line $x = \overline{x}(D)$, he will suffer some discouragement at the outset, but practice will ultimately become pleasant and he will learn the language. If he begins at (x_0'', D_0''), practice will be pleasant from the outset, and he will learn.

Clearly one would want to refine this model before trying to verify it from actual situations, but even in its highly simple form it exhibits some of the qualitative features we would expect to find in such situations, and illustrates in what a natural manner differential equations can be employed in a model of adaptive behavior.

Prediction and Verification. One interesting feature of a model of this sort is that it permits qualitative predictions to be made that are very easy to test empirically. We do not need to trace out in detail the time path of the system, but merely to observe whether the activity terminates before learning was completed, or whether it ends in mastery of the language. With such observations we can test, over a sample of cases, a prediction like: the activity is likely to persist until learning has been achieved only if the initial rate of practice is above a certain critical level.

Multiple Equilibria. Another feature of importance is that the model allows us to deal with behavioral or social systems in which both intermittent forces, which act for a brief period, and continuously acting forces are at play. The intermittent force in this case would be the individual's decision to subscribe to the language course and devote a certain amount of time to practice (i.e., the determinants of the initial position). The continuous forces would be the process of learning and the varying motivation as the resolution was actually carried out (i.e., the forces determining the path from the initial position). A Spencer would say that the final outcome is determined by the continuous interplay of forces immanent in the behavioral interaction itself; a Bentham would say that the outcome is determined by the intermittent intervention -- the determination of the initial conditions.[19] The two views are in fact not contradictory provided the system has more than one position of final equilibrium. In this case an intervention can "jar" the system from one position of equilibrium to another.

A possible application of this notion is to the theory of political and social "reform" movements. It is notorious that such movements are short-lived, at least in their active and influential phases. If they are effective, it must be through disturbance of a system of forces previously in equilibrium, and a sufficient shift in initial conditions to permit the system to move toward a new equilibrium with a different stable constellation of forces.

There would seem to be a wide class of social phenomena that could be studied in terms of a model embodying this feature of multiple equilibria. Gunnar Myrdal's theory of social change appears to be of this sort, as do most theories of revolution.[20] The relationship between "formal" organization (which operates in considerable part through intermittent pressures) and "informal" organization might also be expressed in these terms.[21]

A Social Interpretation of the "Berlitz" Model. It might appear that we are not justified in discussing the applicability to social systems of a model that represents, after all, the behavior of a single human being. In fact, however, the writer was originally led to construct this model in order to represent a social situation. In an organization where accountants were given the task of providing accounting information to operating executives, it was found that if understanding between accountants and operators was good, they tended to communicate frequently with each other; when it was bad, less frequently. Moreover, frequent communication, by helping them understand each others' languages, made communication easier. By renaming the variable x "frequency of communication between accountants and operators," and the variable D "difficulty of communication between accountants and operators," we obtain in the model a clear representation of this social system.

FURTHER COMMENTS ON MOTIVATION

If we compare the notion of motivation in the present model with the notion of a preference field, discussed earlier, we find one important difference that has not been mentioned. In a preference field we can say that one alternative is preferable or "more pleasant" than another, but there is no natural zero-point for pleasantness: we can distinguish more or less of pleasantness, but cannot speak of pleasantness and unpleasantness in any absolute sense. In the "Berlitz" model, the function $\bar{x}(D)$ does define such a dividing line, or zero separating pleasantness from unpleasantness.

We can reconcile the present viewpoint with the earlier one by supposing that our student, if he does not study his language, can engage in some other activity which, when $x > \bar{x}$, is more pleasant than the work on his language. Then to say that an activity is "unpleasant" simply means that there is an alternative that is preferable. The zero-point of preference for an activity is defined by what the economist would call the "opportunity cost" of the activity.[22]

From the standpoint of psychological theory, however, it would appear that a "natural" zero-point can be defined with respect to motivation. This zero-point arises from two related psychological mechanisms. The first of these is the dependence of strength of motivation upon the relationship between the level of aspiration and the level of achievement.[23] The second of these is the qualitative change in motivation that takes place under conditions of frustration.[24]

We take as our independent variable the difference between the actual level of skill of an individual in performing a task and the level of skill to which he aspires. If achievement exceeds aspiration, this variable will be positive; if the two are equal, zero; if aspiration exceeds achievement, negative. Now the psychological evidence would appear to indicate that the strength of drive toward the activity is related to achievement in somewhat the fashion indicated in Figure 2.

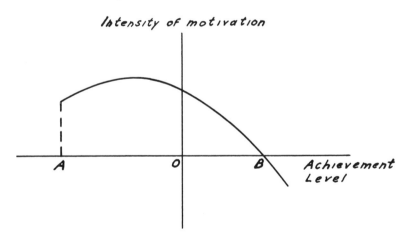

Figure 2.

As the achievement level exceeds B, the drive toward improvement of skill disappears. We may call this "satiation." On the other hand, as the achievement level falls below A, the drive changes its character. Instead of engaging in rational, adaptive behavior, the individual in his frustration engages in behavior best described as non-adaptive or "neurotic."

The evidence generally indicates that frustration will not occur if there are alternative activities available that are regarded as desirable. In this case the aspiration level for the first activity will simply fall, until point B is reached. Frustration occurs when *all* alternatives are regarded by the individual as distinctly unpleasant -- when he is faced with a dilemma rather than a choice. But this distinction between dilemma and choice suggests, again, a natural zero of motivation which is distinct from the zero of satiation. The latter would seem to correspond best with the notion of zero opportunity cost.

EQUILIBRIUM IN GROUP INTERACTION

The previous section suggests that in the study of human and social adaptive systems we may be interested not only in the mechanism of adaptation, but also in the possible states of equilibrium of the system. In the present section we will examine a system of social interaction with primary emphasis on equilibrium, and will return more specifically to the question of adaptation in the next section.

THE HOMANS MODEL

The system to be examined has some intrinsic interest in that it appears to represent fairly well in a formal model some of the theoretical relations postulated by George Homans in *The Human Group*.[25] Homans' system contains four variables (his treatment of them is, of course, verbal rather than mathematical):

(1) The intensity of interaction (or communication) among the members of a group; we will designate it by $T(t)$.

(2) The amount of friendliness (or group identification) among group members; we will designate it by $I(t)$.

(3) The total amount of activity carried on by a member of the group; we will designate it by $W(t)$.

(4) The amount of activity imposed on the group by its external environment (the amount required for its survival); we will designate it by $F(t)$. (Homans also calls it the activity required for survival, the "external system.")

Each of the variables is written as a function of time, and each of the first three is supposed to be some kind of average of the levels for the individual members of the group. Homans nowhere explicitly states his postulates regarding the interrelations of these variables, but the postulates he actually employs would seem to be contained in the following statements:

"If the scheme of activities is changed, the scheme of interaction will, in general, change also, and vice versa."[26]

"Persons who interact frequently with one another tend to like one another."[27]

"If the interactions between the members of a group are frequent in the external system, sentiments of liking will grow up between them, and these sentiments will lead in turn to further interaction over and above the interactions of external system."[28]

"Persons who feel sentiments of liking for one another will express those sentiments in activities over and above the activities of the external system, and these activities may further strengthen the sentiments of liking."[29]

"The more frequently persons interact with one another, the more alike in some respects both their activities and their sentiments tend to become."[30]

A MATHEMATICAL TRANSLATION

Now these five statements can be approximately translated into three equations among our four variables. The first equation will be algebraic -- representing an "instantaneous" or very rapid adjustment. The other two will be differential equations determining paths over time.

$$T = a_1 I + a_2 W \tag{9}$$

$$\frac{dI}{dt} = b (T - \beta I) \tag{10}$$

$$\frac{dW}{dt} = c_1 (I - \tau W) + c_2 (F - W) \tag{11}$$

The first equation may be translated, roughly: interaction will be produced by friendliness and/or group activity. The second: friendliness will tend to increase or decrease as the amount of interaction is disproportionately large or disproportionately small, respectively, in relation to the existing level of friendliness. (The two variables will be in adjustment when $T = \beta I$) The third:

group activity will tend to increase as the level of friendliness is high relative to the existing level of activity (the two being in equilibrium when $I = \gamma W$), and as the requirements of the external system are high relative to the existing level of activity, otherwise group activity will tend to decrease.

By studying these translations -- or better, by studying the equations themselves -- in relation to Homans' postulates, the reader can judge for himself how well we have succeeded in capturing the essential features of Homans' system in our equations. In any event it is unnecessary to concern ourselves here with the exactness of the representation or the empirical correctness of his postulates.

Now systems of the kind we have just written down (linear differential equations with constant coefficients) are well known to the mathematician, and he can provide us with a well-stocked kit of tools for analysing their behavior. Without going into details of method or result, it may be stated that he can easily find: (1) the equilibrium position of this system, (2) the conditions under which this equilibrium is stable and unstable, and (3) the precise time path the system will follow from any initial position.[31]

Social Disintegration. Among the conclusions that can be drawn from the purely mathematical properties of the system is the following:

If the system represented by equations (9) - (11) is dynamically stable, then as the system of externally imposed activities, F, decreases toward zero, the amounts of interaction, friendliness, and group activity will decrease toward zero (with a lag).

But this is precisely the hypothesis that Homans employs to explain social disintegration in Hilltown,[32] and to explain the difference in extension between the primitive and modern family.[33] Our formal model permits us to demonstrate rigorously that this is not an independent hypothesis, but follows logically from the other postulates if only the system is assumed to be dynamically stable.

Morale and "Anomie". We will cite one further example of the conclusions that mathematical reasoning permits us to draw from the model. One of Homans' empirical statements is that a social group will tend to develop a system of activities more elaborate than that needed to satisfy the requirements of the external system. In one sense we have already incorporated this statement in equation (11) -- for this equation says that W will tend to increase not only if F is greater than W, but also when I is greater than γW.

That is, friendliness, as well as external requirements can be a source of group activity. But does it follow from this that, when the system has attained equilibrium, W will be greater than F?

Let us define a group as possessing "positive morale" if, when the group is in a state of equilibrium, W exceeds F -- the actual level of activity is higher than that required for survival. When this condition is not satisfied, we will say that the group possesses "negative morale." It can be shown from equations (9) - (11) that the group will possess positive morale if and only if $a_2 > \gamma(\beta - a_1)$. To see what the condition means we note that, in particular, it will be satisfied if a_2 is sufficiently large -- that is, if the amount of interaction required per unit of group activity is large. This can be stated in still another way: group morale will be positive if there is a sufficiently high degree of interrelation among the members' tasks, requiring much communication for their performance. But this is, in substance, the central proposition of Durkheim's theory of *anomie* -- a proposition that has received considerable empirical verification in work situations from the Hawthorne studies and their successors.[34]

RELATION TO THE EARLIER MODEL

These two examples will serve, I hope, to whet, if not to satisfy, the reader's appetite for empirically verifiable propositions derivable from our three mathematical postulates. We will leave this system with a final observation as to its possible relation to the motivation-learning model discussed in the previous section. Equations (9) and (11) may be regarded as statements of motivation: the former says that interaction is motivated by friendliness and group activity, the latter that activity is motivated by friendliness and the requirements of group survival. Equation (10) may be regarded as a learning process: Interaction develops friendliness. Hence the two systems may be interpreted as special cases of a broader class of systems in which group relationships are determined by a system of motivational and learning processes.

GROUP SURVIVAL

In the "Berlitz" model, motivation to perform a task was assumed to depend on the pleasantness of the task (i.e., the task was assumed to be pleasant if it was not too difficult). In the "Homans" model, one of our motivational assumptions was that the

necessity of group activity for group survival provided an inducement to group activity (this is incorporated, as has been pointed
out, in the last term of equation (11)). The first ("Berlitz") assumption is plausible from the standpoint of individual psychology,
but the second has no immediate explanation in these terms. To
provide a psychological basis for deriving the proposition that
"members of a group will be motivated to activity" from the proposition that "activity is essential to survival," we must postulate
that the members of the group wish it to survive. What kind of
model of the relation of the individual to the group can we construct that will make such a postulate plausible?

TWO THEORIES OF SURVIVAL

Two general paths appear to be open. On the one hand we
can adopt a "sociological" hypothesis that the values an individual
possesses are, in large part, the internalization of values the society inculcates in him. If this is so, then those societies would
tend to survive that inculcated in their members values conducive
to the society's survival. In the "selection of the fittest" among
societies, there would tend to be present among the survivors motivational forces like those expressed in equation (11).

On the other hand we can adopt the "economic" hypothesis
that each member of a group calculates, on the basis of given values, whether he prefers to remain in the group or leave it. Those
groups would then tend to survive that provided satisfaction to the
values of their individual members. Moreover, if certain members
of a group found a great advantage, from the standpoint of their
values, in the continued existence of a group, their rational effort
to secure its survival would provide a specific adaptive mechanism.

It is probable that a complete theory of group and organizational survival will have to incorporate elements of both mechanisms. The mechanism first mentioned may predominate in groups
characterized by face-to-face contact, opportunities for thorough
and long-term indoctrination of members, and a relative weakness
of individualistic values. The second mechanism may predominate
in the secondary associations of a modern society, characterized
by freedom of association and rationalistic calculation in terms of
individual values. It may be suggested, parenthetically, that the
difference between the theories of the "human relations" school in
contemporary industrial sociology and the classical theory of
"economic man" is closely related to the difference between these
two motivational mechanisms.

THE BALANCE OF INDUCEMENTS AND CONTRIBUTIONS.

Having described in the two previous sections some "sociological" models of group behavior, we return in the present section to a model in which individual values are determined outside the group process.

We postulate for each member of a group a *satisfaction function*. We assume that his satisfaction increases with the amount of inducement, y, the group provides him, and decreases with the amount of contribution, x, the group requires from him. Thus, we write for the ith member:

$$S_i = \phi(y_i) - \psi(x_i), \quad (i = 1, . . , n). \tag{12}$$

In a business firm, for eample, customers receive products in return for money; employees receive money in return for labor; and so forth. The organizational activity consists in taking the contributions of the several members and transforming these into the inducements that it then distributes among the same members. Since something can seldom be made out of nothing, the quantities of inducements that can be "manufactured" are limited by the quantities of contributions that can be obtained. This limitation can be stated in the form of a set of transformation functions:

$$\xi_j(x_1, . . . , xn; y_1, . . . , y_m) = 0, \quad (j = 1, . . . , k). \tag{13}$$

Let us now measure the zero of each member's satisfaction function from the point where he is just indifferent between remaining in the organization or leaving. Then the organization can survive if we can find a set of members, and a set of inducements and contributions for these members satisfying the limitations (13), such that $S_i > 0$ for all i. For the case of a business, this requirement can be translated: the business must be able to produce its product cheaply enough (as determined from some of the limitations (13)) so that it can sell the product at a price customers are willing to pay, and receive enough money from the sale (another limitation--the business is not generally permitted to manufacture additional money on a printing press) to pay employees for their services, and so forth.

When the organization more than satisfies this condition-- when each member receives a positive net satisfaction -- then the net satisfactions of members, taken together, can be regarded as a "surplus" which can be distributed in a variety of ways without endangering survival. This suggests elaboration of the model in a number of directions:

(1) We might wish to add to it a description of the processes whereby the surplus actually gets divided. This might take the form, for example, of a theory of bargaining between employer and employee, or between buyer and seller. As a matter of fact, it can be shown that if we assume (1) that this bargaining takes place in incremental units (rather than on an all-or-none basis of participation or non-participation), and (2) that the entire surplus is captured by the entrepreneur, then we obtain as a special case of the present organizational model the theory of imperfect competition discussed earlier in this paper. (The "surplus" in this case becomes the "profit" in the earlier model.)

(2) When a surplus exists, the organization is not committed to a single course of action -- a number of paths are compatible with survival. This situation provides one psychological basis for a theory of authority--members of an organization may be willing to accept authority over their activities provided that the exercise of this authority is limited to the area in which these members receive a net balance of inducements over contributions. Authority may be directed by its possessors toward various goals. For example, if the persons who control the organization are strongly motivated towards its survival, they may employ the range of choice permitted them in such a way as to enhance the chances of future survival and growth.

Since this model is described at length elsewhere,[35] we will not carry its analysis further here.

CONCLUSION

The main aim of these chapters has been to show how the essential elements of a wide range of postulates about human behavior, individual and social, can be translated into mathematical models; and to suggest how this translation can be employed both to clarify the similarities and differences among theories and to draw new conclusions, by mathematical means, from the postulates. In doing this, we have been guided by the canons of strategy that were set forth at the beginning of the first section. In conclusion, I should like to refer again to those canons, to see what help they give us in overall appraisal of the systems we have surveyed.

The canons were three in number:

(1) We should begin by translating into mathematics concepts and postulates that lie in the central core of existing social science theory;

(2) We should not attempt to incorporate all of these concepts and postulates in a single model, but should be satisfied at the outset with constructing a number of partial models;

(3) Significant models can be constructed by singling out for attention, and for embodiment in them, the significant limiting conditions that serve as boundaries to the area of rationality in human behavior.

Our general procedure in this paper has been to start with theories of optimizing behavior -- theories that incorporate the fewest possible limits on rationality. We have then progressively diluted the requirements of rationality -- or stated otherwise, have imposed successive limitations. In this way we have progressed from simple processes of maximization to much more complex processes of adaptive (and even of "motivated" and "learned") behavior.

With each additional limitation we have been confronted with choices - we have had to make more and more assumptions as to the characteristics of actual human behavior. Hence it is not surprising that at each step we have (at least potentially) gained realism, but lost certainty. Empirical research has not progressed to the point where we can make assured choices among alternative assumptions; and mathematical analysis of the models has not progressed to the point where we can handle simultaneously all of the complications we should like to incorporate.

What can we conclude about the present state and future prospects of this kind of model-building? We do not pretend to have surveyed all, or even most, of the existent attempts at mathematization. Many not mentioned here are discussed in other contributions to this volume. We can, however, draw several conclusions. Formalization of the systems in which highly rational and individualistic behavior is postulated has already reached a point of development where mathematical theory is displacing literary theory on the frontiers of research. Most of the things that can be said in economics can be said more easily and clearly with the language of mathematics than without it. Moreover, mathematics has already made important contributions not only to substantive theory but also to the clarification of central concepts. In particular, we have seen that the attempt to set down in mathematical form the precise assumptions of "rationality" has led to important advances in the understanding of that concept and its various possible meanings.

In areas of a more distinctly sociological or psychological character, much less has been accomplished. Even here we have seen that rather simple mathematical tools permit us to study with a high degree of clarity and rigor the assumptions underlying particular theories, the conclusions that follow from these assumptions, and the interrelations of competing theories. The tentative explorations made thus far give sufficiently good prospect of rich reward to justify further work on a much larger and more systematic scale.

1. I am indebted to a number of colleagues and others for helpful comments on an earlier draft of this paper. Among these are Messrs. G. L. Bach, Read Bain, W. W. Cooper, R. M. Cyert, H. Guetzkow, P. Lazarsfeld and members of the University Seminar on Organization at Columbia University.

2. Since I have taken as my central theme the canons of strategy that have guided my own work, I hope I may be pardoned for including a disproportionate number of footnote citations to others of my own publications where particular topics have been treated at greater length. More adequate references to predecessors, contemporaries, and collaborators will be found in these other publications.

3. The economist who is still practising intellectual isolationism can begin to reform himself by reading a book like George Katona, *Psychological Analysis of Economic Behavior* (McGraw-Hill, 1951); the political scientist can try David B. Truman, *The Governmental Process* (Knopf, 1951); the organization theorist, Herbert A. Simon, Donald W. Smithburg, and Victor A. Thompson, *Public Administration* (Knopf, 1950).

4. Further elaboration of this point will be found in the section below on preference fields.

5. For an extended (verbal) discussion of this model, and a comparison with the less satisfactory "means-ends" model employed by Parsons, Tolman and others, see H. A. Simon, *Administrative Behavior* (Macmillan, 1947), ch. 4. *Cf.* Paul A. Samuelson, *Foundations of Economic Analysis* (Harvard U. Press, 1947), pp. 21-3, 97-8.

6. The method just illustrated is the method of comparative statics. See Samuelson, *op. cit.*, pp. 7-20 for a more complete discussion.

7. This "canon of strategy" was first proposed by the author as a basic principle for the guidance of research in administrative theory. See *Administrative Behavior*, pp. 39-41, 240-4.

8. For a description of the Cournot model see R. G. D. Allen, *Mathematical Analysis for Economists* (Macmillan, 1938), pp. 200-204; 345-347. The Cournot model has an obvious affinity to sociological models, like those of Mead and Cooley, which involve "taking the role of the other." These models are discussed in Theodore M. Newcomb, *Social Psychology* (Dryden Press, 1950), ch. 9.

9. J. von Neumann and O. Morgenstern, *The Theory of Games and Economic Behavior* (Princeton U. Press, 1944), pp. 8-15, 31-45. For a nontechnical introduction to the theory of games, see John McDonald, *Strategy in Poker, Business and War* (Norton, 1950), particularly the Introduction and Part 2.

10. Von Neumann and Morgenstern, *op. cit.*, pp. 88-95.

11. The specific requirements with respect to stability have been discussed in full by Samuelson, *op. cit.*, ch. 9, and do not need to be reviewed here.

12. Norbert Wiener, *Cybernetics* (Wiley, 1948), particularly ch. 4. An introduction to servomechanisms will be found in H. Lauer, R. Lesnick, and L. E. Matson, *Servomechanism Fundamentals* (McGraw-Hill, 1947), ch. 1. The idea of biological and human feedback systems goes back to the physiologist Claude Bernard. See Alfred J. Lotka, *Elements of Physical Biology* (Williams and Wilkins, 1925), pp. 362-416.

13. These theories are discussed by Jacob Marschak elsewhere in this volume.

14. H. A. Simon, "On the Application of Servomechanism Theory in the Study of Production Control," *Econometrica*, Vol 20, 1952, pp. 247-268.

15. Jacob Marschak, "Role of Liquidity under Complete and Incomplete Information," Papers and Proceedings, *American Economic Review*, vol. 39, May, 1949, pp. 182-195; H. A. Simon, "A Formal Theory of the Employment Relationship," *Econometrica*, July 1951, vol. 19, pp. 293-305.

16. For an example of some recent work in this field, see Kenneth J. Arrow, *Social Choice and Individual Values* (Wiley, 1951), pp. 9-21.

17. The contrast between the optimizing man of the economists and the adaptive man of the psychologists is discussed in Simon, *Administrative Behavior*, chapter 4 (previously referred to), and chapter 5.

18. There are other less trivial situations that exhibit the characteristics of this model, as will be shown later, but this one is simple, and will serve to illustrate the point.

19. See William Archibald Dunning, *A History of Political Theories: From Rousseau to Spencer* (Macmillan, 1920), pp. 211-24, 395-402. As Carl Becker puts it: "Whereas the 18th century held that man

can by taking thought add a cubit to his stature, the 19th century held that a cubit would be added to his stature whether he took thought or not." (Article on "Progress" in *Encyclopedia of the Social Sciences*, vol. 12, p. 498.)

20. See Gunner Myrdal, *An American Dilemma* (Harper, 1944), Appendix 3. While Myrdal does not speak explicitly of multiple equilibria this seems to an implicit element of his model. For a mathematical model, along these lines of revolutionary change see Nicolas Rashevsky, *Mathematical Biology of Social Behavior* (Chicago U. Press, 1951), chapter 13. I might add that I am greatly indebted to Professor Rashevsky's work, which he discusses elsewhere in this volume, for stimulating my thinking along the general lines of this and the following section.

21. For definitions of "formal" and "informal" see Simon, Smithburg, and Thompson, *op. cit.*, pp. 85-90.

22. *Ibid.*, pp. 492-8.

23. Norman R. F. Maier, *Psychology in Industry*, pp. 244-7.

24. *Ibid.*, pp. 57-70.

25. George Homans, *The Human Group* (Harcourt, Brace, 1950). A more detailed discussion of the formal model of Homans' system is presented in "A Formal Theory of Interaction in Social Groups," *American Sociological Review*, Vol. 17, 1952, p. 202-211.

26. Homans, *op. cit.*, p. 102.

27. *Ibid.*, p. 111.

28. *Ibid.*, p. 112.

29. *Ibid.*, p. 118.

30. *Ibid.*, p. 120.

31. See any standard textbook on differential equations, e.g., Lester R. Ford, *Differential Equations* (McGraw-Hill, 1933), ch. 8.

32. Homans, *op. cit.*, pp. 356-62, 450.

33. *Ibid.*, pp. 263-5.

34. *Ibid.*, ch. 13.

35. H. A. Simon, "A Comparison of Organization Theories" *Review of Economic Studies*, *20*, 19, p. 40-48. See also, Simon, Smithburg, and Thompson, *op. cit.*, pp. 498-503.

7.2

A BEHAVIORAL MODEL OF RATIONAL CHOICE

By Herbert A. Simon*

Traditional economic theory postulates an "economic man," who, in the course of being "economic" is also "rational." This man is assumed to have knowledge of the relevant aspects of his environment which, if not absolutely complete, is at least impressively clear and voluminous. He is assumed also to have a well-organized and stable system of preferences, and a skill in computation that enables him to calculate, for the alternative courses of action that are available to him, which of these will permit him to reach the highest attainable point on his preference scale.

Recent developments in economics, and particularly in the theory of the business firm, have raised great doubts as to whether this schematized model of economic man provides a suitable foundation on which to erect a theory — whether it be a theory of how firms *do* behave, or of how they "should" rationally behave. It is not the purpose of this paper to discuss these doubts, or to determine whether they are justified. Rather, I shall assume that the concept of "economic man" (and, I might add, of his brother "administrative man") is in need of fairly drastic revision, and shall put forth some suggestions as to the direction the revision might take.

Broadly stated, the task is to replace the global rationality of economic man with a kind of rational behavior that is compatible with the access to information and the computational capacities that are actually possessed by organisms, including man, in the kinds of environments in which such organisms exist. One is tempted to turn

* The ideas embodied in this paper were initially developed in a series of discussions with Herbert Bohnert, Norman Dalkey, Gerald Thompson, and Robert Wolfson during the summer of 1952. These collaborators deserve a large share of the credit for whatever merit this approach to rational choice may possess. A first draft of this paper was prepared in my capacity as a consultant to the RAND Corporation. It has been developed further (including the Appendix) in work with the Cowles Commission for Research in Economics on "Decision Making Under Uncertainty," under contract with the Office of Naval Research, and has been completed with the aid of a grant from the Ford Foundation.

99

to the literature of psychology for the answer. Psychologists have certainly been concerned with rational behavior, particularly in their interest in learning phenomena. But the distance is so great between our present psychological knowledge of the learning and choice processes and the kinds of knowledge needed for economic and administrative theory that a marking stone placed halfway between might help travellers from both directions to keep to their courses.

Lacking the kinds of empirical knowledge of the decisional processes that will be required for a definitive theory, the hard facts of the actual world can, at the present stage, enter the theory only in a relatively unsystematic and unrigorous way. But none of us is completely innocent of acquaintance with the gross characteristics of human choice, or of the broad features of the environment in which this choice takes place. I shall feel free to call on this common experience as a source of the hypotheses needed for the theory about the nature of man and his world.

The problem can be approached initially either by inquiring into the properties of the choosing organism, or by inquiring into the environment of choice. In this paper, I shall take the former approach. I propose, in a sequel, to deal with the characteristics of the environment and the interrelations of environment and organism.

The present paper, then, attempts to include explicitly some of the properties of the choosing organism as elements in defining what is meant by rational behavior in specific situations and in selecting a rational behavior in terms of such a definition. In part, this involves making more explicit what is already implicit in some of the recent work on the problem — that the state of information may as well be regarded as a characteristic of the decision-maker as a characteristic of his environment. In part, it involves some new considerations — in particular taking into account the simplifications the choosing organism may deliberately introduce into its model of the situation in order to bring the model within the range of its computing capacity.

I. Some General Features of Rational Choice

The "flavor" of various models of rational choice stems primarily from the specific kinds of assumptions that are introduced as to the "givens" or constraints within which rational adaptation must take place. Among the common constraints — which are not themselves the objects of rational calculation — are (1) the set of alternatives open to choice, (2) the relationships that determine the pay-offs ("satisfactions," "goal attainment") as a function of the alternative that is chosen, and (3) the preference-orderings among pay-offs. The selection of particular constraints and the rejection of others for incorporation in the model of rational behavior involves implicit assumptions as to what variables the rational organism "controls" — and hence can "optimize" as a means to rational adaptation — and what variables it must take as fixed. It also involves assumptions as to the character of the variables that are fixed. For example, by making different assumptions about the amount of information the organism has with respect to the relations between alternatives and pay-offs, optimization might involve selection of a certain maximum, of an expected value, or a minimax.

Another way of characterizing the givens and the behavior variables is to say that the latter refer to the organism itself, the former to its environment. But if we adopt this viewpoint, we must be prepared to accept the possibility that what we call "the environment" may lie, in part, within the skin of the biological organism. That is, some of the constraints that must be taken as givens in an optimization problem may be physiological and psychological limitations of the organism (biologically defined) itself. For example, the maximum speed at which an organism can move establishes a boundary on the set of its available behavior alternatives. Similarly, limits on computational capacity may be important constraints entering into the definition of rational choice under particular circumstances. We shall explore possible ways of formulating the process of rational choice in situations where we wish to take explicit account of the "internal" as well as the "external" constraints that define the problem of rationality for the organism.

Whether our interests lie in the normative or in the descriptive aspects of rational choice, the construction of models of this kind should prove instructive. Because of the psychological limits of the organism (particularly with respect to computational and predictive ability), actual human rationality-striving can at best be an extremely crude and simplified approximation to the kind of global rationality that is implied, for example, by game-theoretical models. While the approximations that organisms employ may not be the best — even at the levels of computational complexity they are able to handle — it is probable that a great deal can be learned about possible mechanisms from an examination of the schemes of approximation that are actually employed by human and other organisms.

In describing the proposed model, we shall begin with elements it has in common with the more global models, and then proceed to introduce simplifying assumptions and (what is the same thing) approximating procedures.

1.1 Primitive Terms and Definitions

Models of rational behavior — both the global kinds usually constructed, and the more limited kinds to be discussed here — generally require some or all of the following elements:

1. A set of *behavior alternatives* (alternatives of choice or decision). In a mathematical model, these can be represented by a point set, A.

2. The subset of *behavior alternatives that the organism "considers"* or "perceives." That is, the organism may make its choice within a set of alternatives more limited than the whole range objectively available to it. The "considered" subset can be represented by a point set $\mathring{A}$, with $\mathring{A}$ included in A ($\mathring{A} \subset A$).

3. *The possible future states of affairs*, or outcomes of choice, represented by a point set, S. (For the moment it is not necessary to distinguish between actual and perceived outcomes.)

4. A *"pay-off"* function, representing the "value" or "utility" placed by the organism upon each of the possible outcomes of choice. The pay-off may be represented by a real function, $V(s)$ defined for all elements, s, of S. For many purposes there is needed only an ordering relation on pairs of elements of S — i.e., a relation that states that s_1 is preferred to s_2 or vice versa — but to avoid unnecessary complications in the present discussion, we will assume that a cardinal utility, $V(s)$, has been defined.

5. *Information as to which outcomes in S will actually occur* if a particular alternative, a, in A (or in $\mathring{A}$) is chosen. This information may be incomplete — that is, there may be more than one possible outcome, s, for each behavior alternative, a. We represent the information, then, by a mapping of each element, a, in A upon a subset, S_a — the set of outcomes that may ensue if a is the chosen behavior alternative.

6. *Information as to the probability that a particular outcome will ensue* if a particular behavior alternative is chosen. This is a more precise kind of information than that postulated in (5), for it associates with each element, s, in the set S_a, a probability, $P_a(s)$ — the probability that s will occur if a is chosen. The probability $P_a(s)$ is a real, non-negative function with $\sum_{S_a} P_a(s) = 1$.

Attention is directed to the threefold distinction drawn by the definitions among the set of behavior alternatives, A, the set of outcomes or future states of affairs, S, and the pay-off, V. In the ordinary representation of a game, in reduced form, by its pay-off matrix, the set S corresponds to the cells of the matrix, the set A to the strategies of the first player, and the function V to the values in the cells. The set S_a is then the set of cells in the ath row. By keeping in mind this interpretation, the reader may compare the present formulation with "classical" game theory.

1.2 *"Classical" Concepts of Rationality*

With these elements, we can define procedures of rational choice corresponding to the ordinary game-theoretical and probabilistic models.[1]

A. *Max-min Rule.* Assume that whatever alternative is chosen, the worst possible outcome will ensue — the smallest $V(s)$ for s in S_a will be realized. Then select that alternative, a, for which this worst pay-off is as large as possible.

$$\hat{V}(\hat{a}) = \underset{s \epsilon S_{\hat{a}}}{\text{Min}} \ V(s) = \underset{a \epsilon A}{\text{Max}} \ \underset{s \epsilon S_a}{\text{Min}} \ V(s)$$

Instead of the maximum with respect to the set, A, of actual alternatives, we can substitute the maximum with respect to the set, $\overset{\circ}{A}$, of "considered" alternatives. The probability distribution of outcomes, (6) does not play any role in the max-min rule.

B. *Probabilistic Rule.* Maximize the expected value of $V(s)$ for the (assumed known) probability distribution, $P_a(s)$.

$$\hat{V}(\hat{a}) = \underset{s \epsilon S_{\hat{a}}}{\Sigma} \ V(s)P_{\hat{a}}(s) = \underset{a \epsilon A}{\text{Max}} \ \underset{s \epsilon S_a}{\Sigma} \ V(s)P_a(s)$$

C. *Certainty Rule.* Given the information that each a in A (or in $\overset{\circ}{A}$) maps upon a specified s_a in S, select the behavior alternative whose outcome has the largest pay-off.

$$\hat{V}(\hat{a}) = V(S_{\hat{a}}) = \underset{a \epsilon A}{\text{Max}} \ V(S_a)$$

II. The Essential Simplifications

If we examine closely the "classical" concepts of rationality outlined above, we see immediately what severe demands they make upon the choosing organism. The organism must be able to attach definite pay-offs (or at least a definite range of pay-offs) to each possible outcome. This, of course, involves also the ability to specify the exact nature of the outcomes — there is no room in the scheme for "unanticipated consequences." The pay-offs must be completely ordered —

1. See Kenneth J. Arrow, "Alternative Approaches to the Theory of Choice in Risk-Taking Situations," *Econometrica*, XIX, 404–37 (Oct. 1951).

it must always be possible to specify, in a consistent way, that one outcome is better than, as good as, or worse than any other. And, if the certainty or probabilistic rules are employed, either the outcomes of particular alternatives must be known with certainty, or at least it must be possible to attach definite probabilities to outcomes.

My first empirical proposition is that there is a complete lack of evidence that, in actual human choice situations of any complexity, these computations can be, or are in fact, performed. The introspective evidence is certainly clear enough, but we cannot, of course, rule out the possibility that the unconscious is a better decision-maker than the conscious. Nevertheless, in the absence of evidence that the classical concepts do describe the decision-making process, it seems reasonable to examine the possibility that the actual process is quite different from the ones the rules describe.

Our procedure will be to introduce some modifications that appear (on the basis of casual empiricism) to correspond to observed behavior processes in humans, and that lead to substantial computational simplifications in the making of a choice. There is no implication that human beings use all of these modifications and simplifications all the time. Nor is this the place to attempt the formidable empirical task of determining the extent to which, and the circumstances under which humans actually employ these simplifications. The point is rather that these are procedures which appear often to be employed by human beings in complex choice situations to find an approximate model of manageable proportions.

2.1 *"Simple" Pay-off Functions*

One route to simplification is to assume that $V(s)$ necessarily assumes one of two values, $(1, 0)$, or of three values, $(1, 0, -1)$, for all s in S. Depending on the circumstances, we might want to interpret these values, as (a) (satisfactory or unsatisfactory), or (b) (win, draw or lose).

As an example of (b), let S represent the possible positions in a chess game at White's 20th move. Then a $(+1)$ position is one in which White possesses a strategy leading to a win whatever Black does. A (0) position is one in which White can enforce a draw, but not a win. A (-1) position is one in which Black can force a win.

As an example of (a) let S represent possible prices for a house an individual is selling. He may regard $15,000 as an "acceptable" price, anything over this amount as "satisfactory," anything less as "unsatisfactory." In psychological theory we would fix the boundary at the "aspiration level"; in economic theory we would fix the boundary at the price which evokes indifference between selling and not selling (an opportunity cost concept).

The objection may be raised that, although $16,000 and $25,000 are both "very satisfactory" prices for the house, a rational individual would prefer to sell at the higher price, and hence, that the simple pay-off function is an inadequate representation of the choice situation. The objection may be answered in several different ways, each answer corresponding to a class of situations in which the simple function might be appropriate.

First, the individual may not be confronted simultaneously with

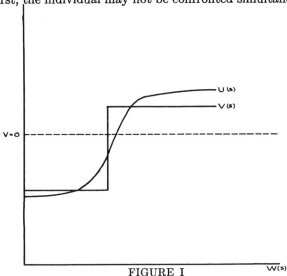

FIGURE I

a number of buyers offering to purchase the house at different prices, but may receive a sequence of offers, and may have to decide to accept or reject each one before he receives the next. (Or, more generally, he may receive a sequence of pairs or triplets or n-tuples of offers, and may have to decide whether to accept the highest of an n-tuple before the next n-tuple is received.) Then, if the elements S correspond to n-tuples of offers, $V(s)$ would be 1 whenever the highest offer in the n-tuple exceeded the "acceptance price" the seller had determined upon at that time. We can then raise the further question of what would be a rational process for determining the acceptance price.[2]

2. See the Appendix. It might be remarked here that the simple risk function, introduced by Wald to bring problems in statistical decision theory within the bounds of computability, is an example of a simple pay-off function as that term is defined here.

Second, even if there were a more general pay-off function, $W(s)$, capable of assuming more than two different values, the simplified $V(s)$ might be a satisfactory approximation to $W(s)$. Suppose, for example, that there were some way of introducing a cardinal utility function, defined over S, say $U(s)$. Suppose further that $U(W)$ is a monotonic increasing function with a strongly negative second derivative (decreasing marginal utility). Then $V(s) = V\{W(s)\}$ might be the approximation as shown on page 107.

When a simple $V(s)$, assuming only the values $(+1, 0)$ is admissible, under the circumstances just discussed or under other circumstances, then a (fourth) rational decision-process could be defined as follows:

D. (i) Search for a set of possible outcomes (a subset, S' in S) such that the pay-off is satisfactory ($V(s) = 1$) for all these possible outcomes (for all s in S').

(ii) Search for a behavior alternative (an a in $\overset{\circ}{A}$) whose possible outcomes all are in S' (such that a maps upon a set, S_a, that is contained in S').

If a behavior alternative can be found by this procedure, then a satisfactory outcome is assured. The procedure does not, of course, guarantee the existence or uniqueness of an a with the desired properties.

2.2 *Information Gathering*

One element of realism we may wish to introduce is that, while $V(s)$ may be known in advance, the mapping of A on subsets of S may not. In the extreme case, at the outset each element, a, may be mapped on the whole set, S. We may then introduce into the decision-making process information-gathering steps that produce a more precise mapping of the various elements of A on nonidentical subsets of S. If the information-gathering process is not costless, then one element in the decision will be the determination of how far the mapping is to be refined.

Now in the case of the simple pay-off functions, $(+1, 0)$, the information-gathering process can be streamlined in an important respect. First, we suppose that the individual has initially a very coarse mapping of A on S. Second, he looks for an S' in S such that $V(s) = 1$ for s in S'. Third, he gathers information to refine that part of the mapping of A on S in which elements of S' are involved. Fourth, having refined the mapping, he looks for an a that maps on to a subset of S'.

Under favorable circumstances, this procedure may require the individual to gather only a small amount of information — an insignificant part of the whole mapping of elements of A on individual elements of S. If the search for an a having the desirable properties is successful, he is certain that he cannot better his choice by securing additional information.[3]

It appears that the decision process just described is one of the important means employed by chess players to select a move in the middle and end game. Let A be the set of moves available to White on his 20th move. Let S be a set of positions that might be reached, say, by the 30th move. Let S' be some subset of S that consists of clearly "won" positions. From a very rough knowledge of the mapping of A on S, White tentatively selects a move, a, that (if Black plays in a certain way) maps on S'. By then considering alternative replies for Black, White "explores" the whole mapping of a. His exploration may lead to points, s, that are not in S', but which are now recognized also as winning positions. These can be adjoined to S'. On the other hand, a sequence may be discovered that permits Black to bring about a position that is clearly not "won" for White. Then White may reject the original point, a, and try another.

Whether this procedure leads to any essential simplification of the computation depends on certain empirical facts about the game. Clearly all positions can be categorized as "won," "lost," or "drawn" in an objective sense. But from the standpoint of the player, positions may be categorized as "clearly won," "clearly lost," "clearly drawn," "won or drawn," "drawn or lost," and so forth — depending on the adequacy of this mapping. If the "clearly won" positions represent a significant subset of the objectively "won" positions, then the combinatorics involved in seeing whether a position can be transformed into a clearly won position, for all possible replies by Black, may not be unmanageable.[4] The advantage of this procedure over the more common notion (which may, however, be applicable in the opening) of a general valuation function for positions, taking on values from -1 to 1, is that it implies much less complex and subtle evaluation criteria. All that is required is that the evaluation func-

3. This procedure also dispenses with the necessity of estimating explicitly the cost of obtaining additional information. For further discussion of this point see the comments on dynamics in the last section of this paper.

4. I have estimated roughly the actual degree of simplification that might be realized in the middle game in chess by experimentation with two middle-game positions. A sequence of sixteen moves, eight by each player, might be expected to yield a total of about 10^{24} (one septillion) legally permissible variations. By following the general kind of program just described, it was possible to reduce the number of lines of play examined in each of these positions to fewer than 100 variations — a rather spectacular simplification of the choice problem.

tion be reasonably sensitive in detecting when a position in one of the three states — won, lost, or drawn — has been transformed into a position in another state. The player, instead of seeking for a "best" move, needs only to look for a "good" move.

We see that, by the introduction of a simple pay-off function and of a process for gradually improving the mapping of behavior alternatives upon possible outcomes, the process of reaching a rational decision may be drastically simplified from a computational standpoint. In the theory and practice of linear programming, the distinction is commonly drawn between computations to determine the *feasibility* of a program, and computations to discover the *optimal* program. Feasibility testing consists in determining whether a program satisfies certain linear inequalities that are given at the outset. For example, a mobilization plan may take as given the maximum work force and the steel-making capacity of the economy. Then a feasible program is one that does not require a work force or steel-making facilities exceeding the given limits.

An optimal program is that one of the feasible programs which maximizes a given pay-off function. If, instead of requiring that the pay-off be maximized, we require only that the pay-off exceed some given amount, then we can find a program that satisfies this requirement by the usual methods of feasibility testing. The pay-off requirement is represented simply by an additional linear inequality that must be satisfied. Once this requirement is met, it is not necessary to determine whether there exists an alternative plan with a still higher pay-off.

For all practical purposes, this procedure may represent a sufficient approach to optimization, provided the minimum required pay-off can be set "reasonably." In later sections of this paper we will discuss how this might be done, and we shall show also how the scheme can be extended to vector pay-off functions with multiple components (Optimization requires, of course, a complete ordering of pay-offs).

2.3 *Partial Ordering of Pay-Offs*

The classical theory does not tolerate the incomparability of oranges and apples. It requires a scalar pay-off function, that is, a complete ordering of pay-offs. Instead of a scalar pay-off function, $V(s)$, we might have a vector function, $V(s)$; where V has the components $V_1, V_2, \ldots$ A vector pay-off function may be introduced to handle a number of situations:

1. In the case of a decision to be made by a *group of persons*, components may represent the pay-off functions of the individual

members of the group. What is preferred by one may not be preferred by the others.

2. In the case of an individual, he may be trying to implement a number of *values that do not have a common denominator* — e.g., he compares two jobs in terms of salary, climate, pleasantness of work, prestige, etc.;

3. Where each behavior alternative, *a*, maps on a set of *n possible consequences*, S_a, we may replace the model by one in which each alternative maps on a single consequence, but each consequence has

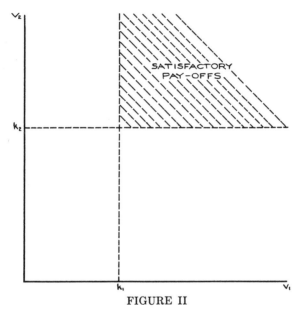

FIGURE II

PARTIAL ORDERING OF PAY-OFFS

as its pay-off the *n*-dimensional vector whose components are the pay-offs of the elements of S_a.

This representation exhibits a striking similarity among these three important cases where the traditional maximizing model breaks down for lack of a complete ordering of the pay-offs. The first case has never been satisfactorily treated — the theory of the *n*-person game is the most ambitious attempt to deal with it, and the so-called "weak welfare principles" of economic theory are attempts to avoid it. The second case is usually handled by superimposing a complete ordering on the points in the vector space ("indifference curves"). The third case has been handled by introducing probabilities as weights for summing the vector components, or by using principles like minimaxing satisfaction or regret.

An extension of the notion of a simplified pay-off function permits us to treat all three cases in much the same fashion. Suppose we regard a pay-off as *satisfactory* provided that $V_i \geqslant k_i$ for all i. Then a reasonable decision rule is the following:

E. Search for a subset S' in S such that $V(s)$ is satisfactory for all s in S' (i.e., $\underset{s \epsilon S'}{V(s)} \geqslant k$).

Then search for an a in A such that S_a lies in S'.

Again existence and uniqueness of solutions are not guaranteed. Rule E is illustrated in Figure II for the case of a 2-component pay-off vector.

In the first of the three cases mentioned above, the satisfactory pay-off corresponds to what I have called a *viable* solution in "A Formal Theory of the Employment Relation" and "A Comparison of Organization Theories."[5] In the second case, the components of V define the *aspiration levels* with respect to several components of pay-off. In the third case (in this case it is most plausible to assume that all the components of k are equal), k_i may be interpreted as the *minimum guaranteed pay-off* — also an aspiration level concept.

III. EXISTENCE AND UNIQUENESS OF SOLUTIONS

Throughout our discussion we have admitted decision procedures that do not guarantee the existence or uniqueness of solutions. This was done in order to construct a model that parallels as nearly as possible the decision procedures that appear to be used by humans in complex decision-making settings. We now proceed to add supplementary rules to fill this gap.

3.1 *Obtaining a Unique Solution*

In most global models of rational choice, all alternatives are evaluated before a choice is made. In actual human decision-making, alternatives are often examined sequentially. We may, or may not, know the mechanism that determines the order of procedure. When alternatives are examined sequentially, we may regard the first satisfactory alternative that is evaluated as such as the one actually selected.

If a chess player finds an alternative that leads to a forced mate for his opponent, he generally adopts this alternative without worry-

5. *Econometrica*, XIX (July 1951), 293–305 and *Review of Economic Studies*, XX (1952–53, No. 1), 40–49.

ing about whether another alternative also leads to a forced mate. In this case we would find it very hard to predict which alternative would be chosen, for we have no theory that predicts the order in which alternatives will be examined. But in another case discussed above — the sale of a house — the environment presents the seller with alternatives in a definite sequence, and the selection of the *first* satisfactory alternative has precise meaning.

However, there are certain dynamic considerations, having a good psychological foundation, that we should introduce at this point. Let us consider, instead of a single static choice situation, a sequence of such situations. The *aspiration level*, which defines a satisfactory alternative, may change from point to point in this sequence of trials. A vague principle would be that as the individual, in his exploration of alternatives, finds it *easy* to discover satisfactory alternatives, his aspiration level rises; as he finds it *difficult* to discover satisfactory alternatives, his aspiration level falls. Perhaps it would be possible to express the ease or difficulty of exploration in terms of the cost of obtaining better information about the mapping of A on S, or the combinatorial magnitude of the task of refining this mapping. There are a number of ways in which this process could be defined formally.

Such changes in aspiration level would tend to bring about a "near-uniqueness" of the satisfactory solutions and would also tend to guarantee the existence of satisfactory solutions. For the failure to discover a solution would depress the aspiration level and bring satisfactory solutions into existence.

3.2 *Existence of Solutions: Further Possibilities*

We have already discussed one mechanism by which the existence of solutions, in the long run, is assured. There is another way of representing the processes already described. Up to this point little use has been made of the distinction between A, the set of behavior alternatives, and $\mathring{A}$, the set of behavior alternatives that the organism considers. Suppose now that the latter is a proper subset of the former. Then, the failure to find a satisfactory alternative in $\mathring{A}$ may lead to a search for additional alternatives in A that can be adjoined to $\mathring{A}$.[6] This procedure is simply an elaboration of the information-

6. I might mention that, in the spirit of crude empiricism, I have presented a number of students and friends with a problem involving a multiple pay-off — in which the pay-off depends violently upon a very contingent and uncertain event — and have found them extremely reluctant to restrict themselves to a set of behavior alternatives allowed by the problem. They were averse to an alternative that promised very large profit or ruin, where the relevant probability could not be computed, and tried to invent new alternatives whose pay-offs were less sensitive to the contingent event. The problem in question is Modigliani's "hot-

gathering process previously described. (We can regard the elements of A that are not in A^o as elements that are initially mapped on the whole set, S.)

In one organism, dynamic adjustment over a sequence of choices may depend primarily upon adjustments of the aspiration level. In another organism, the adjustments may be primarily in the set A^o: if satisfactory alternatives are discovered easily, A^o narrows; if it becomes difficult to find satisfactory alternatives, A^o broadens. The more *persistent* the organism, the greater the role played by the adjustment of A^o, relative to the role played by the adjustment of the aspiration level. (It is possible, of course, and even probable, that there is an asymmetry between adjustments upward and downward.)

If the pay-off were measurable in money or utility terms, and *if* the cost of discovering alternatives were similarly measurable, we could replace the partial ordering of alternatives exhibited in Figure II by a complete ordering (an ordering in terms of a weighted sum of the pay-off and the cost of discovering alternatives). Then we could speak of the optimal degree of persistence in behavior — we could say that the more persistent organism was more rational than the other, or vice versa. But the central argument of the present paper is that the behaving organism does *not* in general know these costs, nor does it have a set of weights for comparing the components of a multiple pay-off. It is precisely because of these limitations on its knowledge and capabilities that the less global models of rationality described here are significant and useful. The question of how it is to behave "rationally," given these limitations, is distinct from the question of how its capabilities could be increased to permit action that would be more "rational" judged from the mountain-top of a more complete model.[7]

The two viewpoints are not, of course, completely different, much less antithetical. We have already pointed out that the organism may possess a whole hierarchy of rational mechanisms — that, for example, the aspiration level itself may be subject to an adjustment process that is rational in some dynamic sense. Moreover, in many situations we may be interested in the precise question of whether one decision-making procedure is more rational than another, and to answer this question we will usually have to construct a broader criterion of rationality that encompasses both procedures as approximations. Our whole point is that it is important to make explicit what level we are considering in such a hierarchy of models, and that

dog stand" problem described in *American Economic Review, Proceedings*, XXXIX (1949), 201–8.

7. One might add: "or judged in terms of the survival value of its choice mechanism."

for many purposes we are interested in models of "limited" rationality rather than models of relatively "global" rationality.

IV. Further Comments on Dynamics

The models thus far discussed are dynamic only in a very special sense: the aspiration level at time t depends upon the previous history of the system (previous aspiration levels and previous levels of attainment). Another kind of dynamic linkage might be very important. The pay-offs in a particular trial might depend not only on the alternative chosen in that trial but also on the alternatives chosen in previous trials.

The most direct representation of this situation is to include, as components of a vector pay-off function, the pay-offs for the whole sequence of trials. But then optimization would require the selection, at the beginning of the sequence, of a strategy for the whole sequence (see the Appendix). Such a procedure would again rapidly complicate the problem beyond the computational capacity of the organism. A possible middle ground is to define for each trial a pay-off function with two components. One would be the "immediate" pay-off (consumption), the other, the "position" in which the organism is left for future trials (saving, liquidity).

Let us consider a chess game in which the players are paid off at the end of each ten moves in proportion to arbitrarily assigned values of their pieces left on the board (say, queen, 1; rook, 10; etc.). Then a player could adopt some kind of planning horizon and include in his estimated pay-off the "goodness" of his position at the planning horizon. A comparable notion in economics is that of the depreciated value of an asset at the planning horizon. To compute such a value precisely would require the player actually to carry his strategy beyond the horizon. If there is time-discounting of pay-offs, this has the advantage of reducing the importance of errors in estimating these depreciated values. (Time-discounting may sometimes be essential in order to assure convergence of the summed pay-offs.)

It is easy to conjure up other dynamic complications, which may be of considerable practical importance. Two more may be mentioned — without attempting to incorporate them formally. The consequences that the organism experiences may change the pay-off function — it doesn't know how well it likes cheese until it has eaten cheese. Likewise, one method for refining the mapping of A on S may be to select a particular alternative and experience its consequences. In these cases, one of the elements of the pay-off associated with a particular alternative is the information that is gathered about the mapping or about the pay-off function.

V. Conclusion

The aim of this paper has been to construct definitions of "rational choice" that are modeled more closely upon the actual decision processes in the behavior of organisms than definitions heretofore proposed. We have outlined a fairly complete model for the static case, and have described one extension of this model into dynamics. As has been indicated in the last section, a great deal remains to be done before we can handle realistically a more completely dynamic system.

In the introduction, it was suggested that definitions of this kind might have normative as well as descriptive value. In particular, they may suggest approaches to rational choice in areas that appear to be far beyond the capacities of existing or prospective computing equipment. The comparison of the I.Q. of a computer with that of a human being is very difficult. If one were to factor the scores made by each on a comprehensive intelligence test, one would undoubtedly find that in those factors on which the one scored as a genius the other would appear a moron — and conversely. A survey of possible definitions of rationality might suggest directions for the design and use of computing equipment with reasonably good scores on some of the factors of intelligence in which present computers are moronic.

The broader aim, however, in constructing these definitions of "approximate" rationality is to provide some materials for the construction of a theory of the behavior of a human individual or of groups of individuals who are making decisions in an organizational context. The apparent paradox to be faced is that the economic theory of the firm and the theory of administration attempt to deal with human behavior in situations in which that behavior is at least "intendedly" rational; while, at the same time, it can be shown that if we assume the global kinds of rationality of the classical theory the problems of internal structure of the firm or other organization largely disappear.[8] The paradox vanishes, and the outlines of theory begin to emerge when we substitute for "economic man" or "administrative man" a choosing organism of limited knowledge and ability. This organism's simplifications of the real world for purposes of choice introduce discrepancies between the simplified model and the reality; and these discrepancies, in turn, serve to explain many of the phenomena of organizational behavior.

8. See Herbert A. Simon, *Administrative Behavior* (Macmillan, 1947), pp. 39–41, 80–84, 96–102, 240–44.

APPENDIX

Example of Rational Determination of an Acceptable Pay-Off

In the body of this paper, the notion is introduced that rational adjustment may operate at various "levels." That is, the organism may choose rationally within a given set of limits postulated by the model, but it may also undertake to set these limits rationally. The house-selling illustration of Section 2.1 provides an example of this.

We suppose that an individual is selling a house. Each day (or other unit of time) he sets an acceptance price: $d(k)$, say, for the kth day. If he receives one or more offers above this price on the day in question, he accepts the highest offer; if he does not receive an offer above $d(k)$, he retains the house until the next day, and sets a new acceptance price, $d(k + 1)$.

Now, if he has certain information about the probability distribution of offers on each day, he can set the acceptance price so that it will be optimal in the sense that it will maximize the expected value, $V[d(k)]$, of the sales price.

To show this, we proceed as follows. Let $p_k(y)$ be the probability that y will be the highest price offered on the kth day. Then:

$$(A.1) \qquad P_k(d) = \int_{d(k)}^{\infty} p_k(y)dy$$

is the probability that the house will be sold on the kth day if it has not been sold earlier.

$$(A.2) \qquad \mathcal{E}_k(d) = \int_{d(k)}^{\infty} y\, p(y,k)dy$$

will be the expected value received by the seller on the kth day if the house has not been sold earlier. Taking into account the probability that the house will be sold before the kth day,

$$(A.3) \qquad E_k(d) = \mathcal{E}_k(d) \prod_{j=1}^{k-1} (1 - P_j(d))$$

will be the unconditional expected value of the seller's receipts on the kth day; and

(A.4)
$$V\{d(k)\} = \sum_{k=1}^{\infty} E_k(d)$$

will be the expected value of the sales price.

Now we wish to set $d(k)$, for each k, at the level that will maximize (A.4). The k components of the function $d(k)$ are independent. Differentiating V partially with respect to each component, we get:

(A.5)
$$\frac{\partial V}{\partial d(i)} = \sum_{k=1}^{\infty} \frac{\partial E_k(d)}{\partial d(i)} \qquad (i = 1, \ldots, n).$$

But:

(A.6)
$$\frac{\partial E_i(d)}{\partial d(i)} = \frac{\partial \mathcal{E}_i(d)}{\partial d(i)} \prod_{j=1}^{i-1} (1 - P_j(d)), \quad \text{and}$$

(A.7)
$$\frac{\partial E_k(d)}{\partial d(i)} = \mathcal{E}_k(d) \prod_{\substack{j \neq i \\ j=1}}^{k-1} (1 - P_j(d)) \left(-\frac{\partial P_i(d)}{\partial d(i)} \right) \text{ for } i < k \text{ and}$$

(A.8)
$$\frac{\partial E_k(d)}{\partial d(i)} = 0 \qquad \text{for } i > k.$$

Hence for a maximum:

(A.9)
$$\frac{\partial V}{\partial d(i)} = -d(i)p_i(d) \prod_{j=1}^{i-1} (1 - P_j(d))$$
$$+ \sum_{k=i+1}^{\infty} \mathcal{E}_k(d) \prod_{\substack{j \neq i}}^{k-1} (1 - P_j(d))p_i(d) = 0.$$

Factoring out $p_i(d)$, we obtain, finally:

(A.10)
$$d(i) = \frac{\displaystyle\sum_{k=i+1}^{\infty} \mathcal{E}_k(d) \prod_{j \neq i}^{k-1} (1 - P_j(d))}{\displaystyle\prod_{j=1}^{i-1} (1 - P_j(d))}$$
$$= \sum_{k=i+1}^{\infty} \mathcal{E}_k(d) \prod_{j=i+1}^{k-1} (1 - P_j(d)).$$

For the answer to be meaningful, the infinite sum in (A.10) must converge. If we look at the definition (A.2) for $\mathcal{E}_k(d)$ we see this would come about if the probability distribution of offers shifts downward through time with sufficient rapidity. Such a shift might correspond to (a) expectations of falling prices, or (b) interpretation of y as the *present value* of the future price, discounted at a sufficiently high interest rate.

Alternatively, we can avoid the question of convergence by assuming a reservation price $a(n)$, for the nth day, which is low enough so that $P_n(d)$ is unity. We shall take this last alternative, but before proceeding, we wish to interpret the equation (A.10). Equation (A.10) says that the rational acceptance price on the ith day, $d(i)$, is equal to the expected value of the sales price if the house is not sold on the ith day and acceptance prices are set optimally for subsequent days. This can be seen by observing that the right-hand side of (A.10) is the same as the right-hand side of (A.4) but with the summation extending from $k = (i + 1)$ instead of from $(k = 1)$.[9]

Hence, in the case where the summation is terminated at period n — that is, the house will be sold with certainty in period n if it has not been sold previously — we can compute the optimal $d(i)$ by working backward from the terminal period, and without the necessity of solving simultaneously the equations (A.10).

It is interesting to observe what additional information the seller needs in order to determine the rational acceptance price, over and above the information he needs once the acceptance price is set. He needs, in fact, virtually complete information as to the probability distribution of offers for all relevant subsequent time periods.

Now the seller who does not have this information, and who will be satisfied with a more bumbling kind of rationality, will make approximations to avoid using the information he doesn't have. First, he will probably limit the planning horizon by assuming a price at which he can certainly sell and will be willing to sell in the nth time period. Second, he will set his initial acceptance price quite high, watch the distribution of offers he receives, and gradually and approximately adjust his acceptance price downward or upward until

9. Equation (A.10) appears to have been arrived at independently by D. A. Darling and W. M. Kincaid. See their abstract, "An Inventory Problem," in the *Journal of Operations Research Society of America*, I, 80 (Feb. 1953).

he receives an offer he accepts — without ever making probability calculations. This, I submit, is the kind of rational adjustment that humans find "good enough" and are capable of exercising in a wide range of practical circumstances.

HERBERT A. SIMON.

CARNEGIE INSTITUTE OF TECHNOLOGY

7.3
RATIONAL CHOICE AND THE STRUCTURE
OF THE ENVIRONMENT [1]

HERBERT A. SIMON

Carnegie Institute of Technology

A growing interest in decision making in psychology is evidenced by the recent publication of Edwards' review article in the *Psychological Bulletin* (1) and the Santa Monica Conference volume, *Decision Processes* (7). In this work, much attention has been focused on the characterization of *rational* choice, and because the latter topic has been a central concern in economics, the theory of decision making has become a natural meeting ground for psychological and economic theory.

A comparative examination of the models of adaptive behavior employed in psychology (e.g., learning theories), and of the models of rational behavior employed in economics, shows that in almost all respects the latter postulate a much greater complexity in the choice mechanisms, and a much larger capacity in the organism for obtaining information and performing computations, than do the former. Moreover, in the limited range of situations where the predictions of the two theories have been compared (see [7, Ch. 9, 10, 18]), the learning theories appear to account for the observed behavior rather better than do the theories of rational behavior.

Both from these scanty data and from an examination of the postulates of the economic models it appears probable that, however adaptive the behavior of organisms in learning and choice situations, this adaptiveness falls far short of the ideal of "maximizing" postulated in economic theory. Evidently, organisms adapt well enough to "satisfice"; they do not, in general, "optimize."

If this is the case, a great deal can be learned about rational decision making by taking into account, at the outset, the limitations upon the capacities and complexity of the organism, and by taking account of the fact that the environments to which it must adapt possess properties that permit further simplication of its choice mechanisms. It may be useful, therefore, to ask: How simple a set of choice mechanisms can we postulate and still obtain the gross features of observed adaptive choice behavior?

In a previous paper (6) I have put forth some suggestions as to the kinds of "approximate" rationality that might be employed by an organism possessing limited information and limited computational facilities. The suggestions were "hypothetical" in that, lacking definitive knowledge of the human decisional processes, we can only conjecture on the basis of our everyday experiences, our introspection, and a very limited body of psychological literature what these processes are. The suggestions were intended, however, as empirical statements, however tentative, about some of the actual mechanisms involved in human and other organismic choice.[2]

Now if an organism is confronted

[1] I am indebted to Allen Newell for numerous enlightening conversations on the subject of this paper, and to the Ford Foundation for a grant that permitted me leisure to complete it.

[2] Since writing the paper referred to I have found confirmation for a number of its hypotheses in the interesting and significant study, by A. de Groot, of the thought processes of chess players (3). I intend to discuss the implications of these empirical findings for my model in another place.

129

with the problem of behaving approximately rationally, or adaptively, in a particular environment, the kinds of simplifications that are suitable may depend not only on the characteristics— sensory, neural, and other—of the organism, but equally upon the structure of the environment. Hence, we might hope to discover, by a careful examination of some of the fundamental structural characteristics of the environment, some further clues as to the nature of the approximating mechanisms used in decision making. This is the line of attack that will be adopted in the present paper.

The environment we shall discuss initially is perhaps a more appropriate one for a rat than for a human. For the term *environment* is ambiguous. We are not interested in describing some physically objective world in its totality, but only those aspects of the totality that have relevance as the "life space" of the organism considered. Hence, what we call the "environment" will depend upon the "needs," "drives," or "goals" of the organism, and upon its perceptual apparatus.

THE ENVIRONMENT OF THE ORGANISM

We consider first a simplified (perhaps "simple-minded") organism that has a single need—food—and is capable of three kinds of activity: resting, exploration, and food getting. The precise nature of these activities will be explained later. The organism's life space may be described as a surface over which it can locomote. Most of the surface is perfectly bare, but at isolated, widely scattered points there are little heaps of food, each adequate for a meal.

The organism's vision permits it to see, at any moment, a circular portion of the surface about the point in which it is standing. It is able to move at some fixed maximum rate over the surface. It metabolizes at a given average rate and is able to store a certain amount of food energy, so that it needs to eat a meal at certain average intervals. It has the capacity, once it sees a food heap, to proceed toward it at the maximum rate of locomotion. The problem of rational choice is to choose its path in such a way that it will not starve.

Now I submit that a rational way for the organism to behave is the following: (a) it explores the surface at random, watching for a food heap; (b) when it sees one, it proceeds to it and eats (food getting); (c) if the total consumption of energy during the average time required, per meal, for exploration and food getting is less than the energy of the food consumed in the meal, it can spend the remainder of its time in resting.[3]

There is nothing particularly remarkable about this description of rational choice, except that it differs so sharply from the more sophisticated models of human rationality that have been proposed by economists and others. Let us see what it is about the organism and its environment that makes its choice so simple.

1. It has only a single goal: food. It does not need to weigh the respective advantages of different goals. It requires no "utility function" or set of "indifference curves" to permit it to choose between alternatives.

2. It has no problem of maximization. It needs only to maintain a certain average rate of food intake, and additional food is of no use to it. In

---

[3] A reader who is familiar with W. Grey Walter's mechanical turtle, *Machina speculatrix* (8), will see as we proceed that the description of our organism could well be used as a set of design specifications to assure the survival of his turtle in an environment sparsely provided with battery chargers. Since I was not familiar with the structure of the turtle when I developed this model, there are some differences in their behavior—but the resemblance is striking.

the psychologist's language, it has a definite, fixed aspiration level, and its successes or failures do not change its aspirations.

3. The nature of its perceptions and its environment limit sharply its planning horizon. Since the food heaps are distributed randomly, there is no need for pattern in its searching activities. Once it sees a food heap, it can follow a definite "best" path until it reaches it.

4. The nature of its needs and environment create a very natural separation between "means" and "ends." Except for the food heaps, one point on the surface is as agreeable to it as another. Locomotion has significance only as it is a means to reaching food.[4]

We shall see that the first point is not essential. As long as aspirations are fixed, the planning horizon is limited, and there is a sharp distinction between means and ends, the existence of multiple goals does not create any real difficulties in choice. The real complications ensue only when we relax the last three conditions; but to see clearly what is involved, we must formulate the model a little more precisely.

PERCEPTUAL POWERS, STORAGE CAPACITY, AND SURVIVAL

It is convenient to describe the organism's life space not as a continuous surface, but as a branching system of paths, like a maze, each branch point representing a choice point. We call the selection of a branch and locomotion to the next branch point a "move." At a small fraction of the branch points are heaps of food.

Let p, $0 < p < 1$, be the percentage of branch points, randomly distributed, at

which food is found. Let d be the average number of paths diverging from each branch point. Let v be the number of moves ahead the organism can see. That is, if there is food at any of the branch points within v moves of the organism's present position, it can select the proper paths and reach it. Finally let H be the maximum number of moves the organism can make between meals without starving.

At any given moment, the organism can see d branch points at a distance of one move from his present position, d^2 points two moves away, and in general, d^k points k moves away. In all, it can see $d + d^2 + \cdots + d^v = \dfrac{d}{d-1}(d^v - 1)$ points. When it chooses a branch and makes a move, d^v new points become visible on its horizon. Hence, in the course of m moves, md^v new points appear. Since it can make a maximum of H moves, and since v of these will be required to reach food that it has discovered on its horizon, the probability, $Q = 1 - P$, that it will *not* survive will be equal to the probability that no food points will be visible in $(H - v)$ moves. (If p is small, we can disregard the possibility that food will be visible inside its planning horizon on the first move.) Let ρ be the probability that none of the d^v new points visible at the end of a particular move is a food point.

Then:

$$\rho = (1 - p)^{d^v}. \qquad [2.1]$$

$$1 - P = Q = \rho^{(H-v)} = (1 - p)^{(H-v)d^v}. \qquad [2.2]$$

We see that the survival chances, from meal to meal, of this simple organism depend on four parameters, two that describe the organism and two the environment: p, the richness of the environment in food; d, the richness of the environment in paths; H, the storage capacity of the organism; and v, the range of vision of the organism.

---

[4] It is characteristic of economic models of rationality that the distinction between "means" and "ends" plays no essential role in them. This distinction *cannot* be identified with the distinction between behavior alternatives and utilities, for reasons that are set forth at some length in the author's *Administrative Behavior*, Ch. 4 and 5 (5).

To give some impression of the magnitudes involved, let us assume that p is 1/10,000, $(H - v)$ is 100, d is 10 and v is 3. Then the probability of seeing a new food point after a move is $1 - \rho = 1 - (1 - p)^{1000} \sim 880/10,000$, and the probability of survival is $P = 1 - \rho^{100} \sim 9999/10,000$. Hence there is in this case only one chance in 10,000 that the organism will fail to reach a food point before the end of the survival interval. Suppose now that the survival time $(H - v)$ is increased one-third, that is, from 100 to 133. Then a similar computation shows that the chance of starvation is reduced to less than one chance in 100,000. A one-third increase in v will, of course, have an even greater effect, reducing the chance of starvation from one in 10^{-4} to one in 10^{-40}.

Using the same values, $p = .0001$, and $(H - v) = 100$, we can compute the probability of survival if the organism behaves completely randomly. In this case $P' = [1 - (1 - p)^{100}] = .009$. From these computations, we see that the organism's modest capacity to perform purposive acts over a short planning horizon permits it to survive easily in an environment where random behavior would lead to rapid extinction. A simple computation shows that its perceptual powers multiply by a factor of 880 the average speed with which it discovers food.

If p, d, and v are given, and in addition we specify that the survival probability must be greater than some number close to unity $(P \geq 1 - \epsilon)$, we can compute from [2.2] the corresponding minimum value of H:

$$\log (1 - P) = (H - v) \log \rho \quad [2.3]$$

$$H \geq v + \frac{\log \epsilon}{\log \rho}. \quad [2.4]$$

For example, if $\rho = .95$ and $\epsilon = 10^{-10}$, then $\log \rho = - .022$, $\log \epsilon = - 10$ and $(H - v) \geq 455$. The parameter, H, can be interpreted as the "storage capacity" of the organism. That is, if the organ-

ism metabolizes at the rate of α units per move, then a storage of αH food units, where H is given by Equation 4, would be required to provide survival at the specified risk level, ϵ.

Further insight into the meaning of H can be gained by considering the average number of moves, M, required to discover food. From Equation 1, the probability of making $(k - 1)$ moves without discovering food, and then discovering it on the kth is:

$$P_k = (1 - \rho)\rho^{(k-1)}. \quad [2.5]$$

Hence, the average number of moves, M, required to discover food is:

$$M = \sum_{k=1}^{\infty} k(1 - \rho)\rho^{k-1}$$

$$= \frac{(1 - \rho)}{(1 - \rho)^2} = \frac{1}{(1 - \rho)}. \quad [2.6]$$

Since $(1 - \rho)$ is the probability of discovering food in any one move, M is the reciprocal of this probability. Combining [2.3] and [2.6], we obtain:

$$\frac{M}{H - v} = \frac{\log \rho}{(1 - \rho)} \frac{1}{\log (1 - P)}. \quad [2.7]$$

Since ρ is close to one, $\log_e \rho \simeq (1 - \rho)$, and [2.7] reduces approximately to:

$$\frac{M}{H - v} \simeq \frac{1}{\log_e (1 - P)}. \quad [2.8]$$

For example, if we require $(1 - P) = \epsilon \leq 10^{-4}$ (one chance in 10,000 of starvation), then $M/(H - v) \leq .11$. For this survival level we require food storage approximately equal to $\alpha(v + 9M)$—food enough to sustain the organism for nine times the period required, on the average, to discover food, plus the period required to reach the food.[5]

[5] I have not discovered any very satisfactory data on the food storage capacities of animals, but the order of magnitude suggested above for the ratio of average search time to storage capacity is certainly correct. It may be noted that, in some cases at least, where the "food" substance is ubiquitous, and hence the search time negligible, the storage capacity is also small.

CHOICE MECHANISMS FOR MULTIPLE GOALS

We consider now a more complex organism capable of searching for and responding to two or more kinds of goal objects. In doing this we could introduce any desired degree of complexity into the choice process; but the interesting problem is how to introduce multiple goals with a minimum complication of the process—that is, to construct an organism capable of handling its decision problems with relatively primitive choice mechanisms.

At the very least, the presence of two goals will introduce a consistency requirement—the time consumed in attaining one goal will limit the time available for pursuit of the other. But in an environment like the one we have been considering, there need be no further relationship between the two goals. In our original formulation, the only essential stipulation was that H, the storage capacity, be adequate to maintain the risk of starvation below a stipulated level $(1 - P)$. Now we introduce the additional stipulation that the organism should only devote a fraction, λ, of its time to food-seeking activities, leaving the remaining fraction, $1 - \lambda$, to other activities. This new stipulation leads to a requirement of additional storage capacity.

In order to control the risk of starving, the organism must begin its exploration for food whenever it has reached a level of H periods of food storage. If it has a total storage of $(\mu + H)$ periods of food, and if the food heaps are at least $\alpha(\mu + H)$ in size, then it need begin the search for food only μ periods after its last feeding. But the food research will require, on the average, M periods.

Thus, in terrestrial animals there is little oxygen storage and life can be maintained in the absence of air for only a few minutes. I am not arguing as to which way the causal arrow runs, but only that the organisms, in this respect, are adapted to their environments and do not provide storage that is superfluous.

Hence, if a hunger threshold is established that leads the organism to begin to explore μ periods after feeding, we will have:

$$\lambda = \frac{M}{M + \mu}. \qquad [3.1]$$

Hence, by making μ sufficiently large, we can make λ as small as we please. Parenthetically, it may be noted that we have here a close analogue to the very common two-bin system of controlling industrial inventories. The primary storage, H, is a buffer stock to meet demands pending the receipt of new orders (with risk, $1 - P$, of running out); the secondary storage, μ, defines the "order point"; and $\mu + M$ is the average order quantity. The storage μ is fixed to balance storage "costs" against the cost (in this case, time pressure) of too frequent reordering.

If food and the second goal object (water, let us say) are randomly and independently distributed, then there are no important complications resulting from interference between the two activities. Designate by the subscript 1 the variables and parameters referring to food getting (e.g., μ_1 is the food threshold in periods), and by the subscript 2 the quantities referring to water seeking. The organism will have adequate time for both activities if $\lambda_1 + \lambda_2 < 1$.

Now when the organism reaches either its hunger or thirst threshold, it will begin exploration. We assume that if *either* of the goal objects becomes visible, it will proceed to that object and satisfy its hunger or thirst (this will not increase the number of moves required, on the average, to reach the other object); but if *both* objects become visible at the same time, and if S_1 and S_2 are the respective quantities remaining in storage at this time, then it will proceed to food or water as M_1/S_1 is greater or less than M_2/S_2. This choice will maximize its survival probability. What is required, then, is a mechanism that produces a drive proportional to M_i/S_i.

A priority mechanism of the kind just described is by no means the only or simplest one that can be postulated. An even simpler rule is for the organism to persist in searching for points that will satisfy the particular need that first reached its threshold and initiated exploratory behavior. This is not usually an efficient procedure, from the standpoint of conserving goal-reaching time, but it may be entirely adequate for an organism generously endowed with storage capacity.

We see that an organism can satisfy a number of distinct needs without requiring a very elaborate mechanism for choosing among them. In particular, we do not have to postulate a utility function or a "marginal rate of substitution."

We can go even further, and assert that a primitive choice mechanism is adequate to take advantage of important economies, if they exist, which are derivable from the interdependence of the activities involved in satisfying the different needs. For suppose the organism has n needs, and that points at which he can satisfy each are distributed randomly and independently through the environment, each with the same probability, p. Then the probability that no points satisfying *any* of the needs will be visible on a particular move is ρ^n, and the mean number of moves for discovery of the *first* need-satisfying point is:

$$m_n = \frac{1}{(1-\rho^n)}. \qquad [3.2]$$

Suppose that the organism begins to explore, moves to the first need-satisfying point it discovers, resumes its exploration, moves to the next point it discovers that satisfies a need other than the one already satisfied, and so on. Then the mean time required to search for all n goals will be:

$$M_n = m_n + m_{n-1} + \cdots$$
$$= \sum_{i=1}^{n} \frac{1}{(1-\rho^i)} \ll \frac{n}{(1-\rho)}. \qquad [3.3]$$

In particular, if ρ is close to one, that is, if need-satisfying points are rare, we will have:

$$M_n - M_{n-1} = \frac{1}{(1-\rho^n)}$$
$$= \frac{1}{(1-\rho)} \cdot \frac{1}{\sum_{i=0}^{n} \rho^i} \simeq \frac{M_1}{n}, \qquad [3.4]$$

and

$$M_n \simeq M_1 \sum_{i=1}^{n} \frac{1}{i}. \qquad [3.5]$$

Now substituting particular values for n in [3.5] we get: $M_2 = 3/2 \ M_1$; $M_3 = 11/6 \ M_1$; $M_4 = 25/12 \ M_1$, etc. We see that if the organism has two separate needs, its exploration time will be only 50 per cent greater than—and not twice as great as—if it has only one need; for four needs the exploration time will be only slightly more than twice as great as for a single need, and so on. A little consideration of the program just described will show that the joint exploratory process does not reduce the primary storage capacity required by the organism but does reduce the secondary storage capacity required. As a matter of fact, there would be no necessity at all for secondary storage.

This conclusion holds only if the need-satisfying points are *independently* distributed. If there is a negative correlation in the joint distribution of points satisfying different needs, then it may be economical for the organism to pursue its needs separately, and hence to have a simple signaling mechanism, involving secondary storage, to trigger its several exploration drives. This point will be developed further in the next section.

A word may be said here about "avoidance needs." Suppose that certain points in the organism's behavior space are designated as "dangerous." Then it will need to avoid those paths that lead to these particular points. If r per cent of all points, randomly distributed, are dangerous, then the number of available paths, among those visible at a given move, will be reduced to $(1 - r)d^v$. Hence, $\rho' = (1 - p)^{(1-r)d^v}$ will be smaller than ρ (Equation 2.1), and M (Equation 2.6) will be correspondingly larger. Hence, the presence of danger points simply increases the average exploration time and, consequently, the required storage capacity of the organism.

Further Specification of the Environment: Clues

In our discussion up to the present point, the range of the organism's anticipations of the future has been limited by the number of behavior alternatives available to it at each move (d), and the length of the "vision" (v). It is a simple matter to introduce into the model the consequences of several types of learning. An increase in the repertoire of behavior alternatives or in the length of vision can simply be represented by changes in d and v, respectively.

A more interesting possibility arises if the food points are not distributed completely at random, and if there are clues that indicate whether a particular intermediate point is rich or poor in paths leading to food points. First, let us suppose that on the path leading up to each food point the k preceding choice points are marked with a food clue. Once the association between the clue and the subsequent appearance of the food point is learned by the organism, its exploration can terminate with the discovery of the clue, and it can follow a determinate path from that point on. This amounts to substituting $v' = (v + k)$ for v.

A different kind of clue might operate in the following fashion. Each choice point has a distinguishable characteristic that is associated with the probability of encountering a food point if a path is selected at random leading out of this choice point. The organism can then select at each move the choice point with the highest probability. If only certain choice points are provided with such clues, then a combination of random and systematic exploration can be employed. Thus the organism may be led into "regions" where the probability of goal attainment is high relative to other regions, but it may have to explore randomly for food within a given region.

A concrete example of such behavior in humans is the "position play" characteristic of the first phase of a chess game. The player chooses moves on the basis of certain characteristics of resulting positions (e.g., the extent to which his pieces are developed). Certain positions are adjudged richer in attacking and defensive possibilities than others, but the original choice may involve no definite plan for the subsequent action after the "good" position has been reached.

Next, we turn to the problem of choice that arises when those regions of the behavior space that are rich in points satisfying one need (p_1 is high in these regions) are poor in points satisfying another need (p_2 is low in these same regions). In the earlier case of goal conflict (two or more points simultaneously visible mediating different needs), we postulated a priority mechanism that amounted to a mechanism for computing relative need intensity and for responding to the more intense need. In the environment with clues, the learning process would need to include a conditioning mechanism that would attach the priority mechanism to the response to competing clues, as well as to the response to competing visible needs.

Finally, we have thus far specified the environment in such a way that there is only one path leading to each point. Formally, this condition can always be satisfied by representing as two or more points any point that can be reached by multiple paths. For some purposes, it might be preferable to specify an environment in which paths converge as well as diverge. This can be done without disturbing the really essential conditions of the foregoing analysis. For behavior of the sort we have been describing, we require of the environment only:

1. that if a path is selected *completely* at random the probability of survival is negligible;

2. that there exist clues in the environment (either the actual visibility of need-satisfying points or anticipatory clues) which permit the organism, sufficiently frequently for survival, to select specific paths that lead with certainty, or with very high probability, to a need-satisfying point.

CONCLUDING COMMENTS ON MULTIPLE GOALS

The central problem of this paper has been to construct a simple mechanism of choice that would suffice for the behavior of an organism confronted with multiple goals. Since the organism, like those of the real world, has neither the senses nor the wits to discover an "optimal" path—even assuming the concept of optimal to be clearly defined— we are concerned only with finding a choice mechanism that will lead it to pursue a "satisficing" path, a path that will permit satisfaction at some specified level of all of its needs.

Certain of the assumptions we have introduced to make this possible represent characteristics of the organism. (*a*) It is able to plan short purposive behavior sequences (of length not exceeding *v*), but not long sequences. (*b*) Its needs are not insatiable, and hence it does not need to balance marginal increments of satisfaction. If all its needs are satisfied, it simply becomes inactive. (*c*) It possesses sufficient storage capacity so that the exact moment of

satisfaction of any particular need is not critical.

We have introduced other assumptions that represent characteristics of the environment, the most important being that need satisfaction can take place only at "rare" points which (with some qualifications we have indicated) are distributed randomly.

The most important conclusion we have reached is that blocks of the organism's time can be allocated to activities related to individual needs (separate means-end chains) without creating any problem of over-all allocation or coordination or the need for any general "utility function." The only scarce resource in the situation is time, and its scarcity, measured by the proportion of the total time that the organism will need to be engaged in *some* activity, can be reduced by the provision of generous storage capacity.

This does not mean that a more efficient procedure cannot be constructed, from the standpoint of the total time required to meet the organism's needs. We have already explored some simple possibilities for increasing efficiency by recognizing complementarities among activities (particularly the exploration activity). But the point is that these complications are not essential to the survival of an organism. Moreover, if the environment is so constructed (as it often is in fact) that regions rich in possibilities for one kind of need satisfaction are poor in possibilities for other satisfactions, such efficiencies may not be available.

It may be objected that even relatively simple organisms appear to conform to efficiency criteria in their behavior, and hence that their choice mechanisms are much more elaborate than those we have described. A rat, for example, learns to take shorter rather than longer paths to food. But this observation does not affect the central argument. We can introduce a mechanism that leads the organism to choose time-conserving paths, where multiple paths are available for satisfying a given need, without any assumption of a mechanism that allocates time among *different* needs. The former mechanism simply increases the "slack" in the whole system, and makes it even more feasible to ignore the complementarities among activities in programming the over-all behavior of the organism.

This is not the place to discuss at length the application of the model to human behavior, but a few general statements may be in order. First, the analysis has been a static one, in the sense that we have taken the organism's needs and its sensing and planning capacities as given. Except for a few comments, we have not considered how the organism develops needs or learns to meet them. One would conjecture, from general observation and from experimentation with aspiration levels, that in humans the balance between the time required to meet needs and the total time available is maintained by the raising and lowering of aspiration levels. I have commented on this point at greater length in my previous paper.[6]

Second, there is nothing about the model that implies that the needs are physiological and innate rather than sociological and acquired. Provided that the needs of the organism can be specified at any given time in terms of the aspiration levels for the various kinds of consummatory behavior, the model can be applied.

The principal positive implication of the model is that we should be skeptical in postulating for humans, or other

organisms, elaborate mechanisms for choosing among diverse needs. Common denominators among needs may simply not exist, or may exist only in very rudimentary form; and the nature of the organism's needs in relation to the environment may make their nonexistence entirely tolerable.

There is some positive evidence bearing on this point in the work that has been done on conflict and frustration. A common method of producing conflict in the laboratory is to place the organism in a situation where: (*a*) it is stimulated to address itself simultaneously to alternative goal-oriented behaviors, or (*b*) it is stimulated to a goal-oriented behavior, but restricted from carrying out the behaviors it usually evinces in similar natural situations. This suggests that conflict may arise (at least in a large class of situations) from presenting the animal with situations with which it is not "programmed" to deal. Conflict of choice may often be equivalent to an absence of a choice mechanism in the given situation. And while it may be easy to create such situations in the laboratory, the absence of a mechanism to deal with them may simply reflect the fact that the organism seldom encounters equivalent situations in its natural environment.[7]

CONCLUSION

In this paper I have attempted to identify some of the structural characteristics that are typical of the "psychological" environments of organisms. We have seen that an organism in an environment with these characteristics requires only very simple perceptual and choice mechanisms to satisfy its several needs and to assure a high probability of its survival over extended periods of

[6] See (6, pp. 111, 117–18). For an experiment demonstrating the adjustment of the rat's aspiration levels to considerations of realizability, see Festinger (2).

[7] See, for example, Neal E. Miller, "Experimental Studies of Conflict" in (4, Ch. 14).

time. In particular, no "utility function" needs to be postulated for the organism, nor does it require any elaborate procedure for calculating marginal rates of substitution among different wants.

The analysis set forth here casts serious doubt on the usefulness of current economic and statistical theories of rational behavior as bases for explaining the characteristics of human and other organismic rationality. It suggests an alternative approach to the description of rational behavior that is more closely related to psychological theories of perception and cognition, and that is in closer agreement with the facts of behavior as observed in laboratory and field.

REFERENCES

1. EDWARDS, W. The theory of decision making. *Psychol. Bull.,* 1954, **51**, 380–417.
2. FESTINGER, L. Development of differential appetite in the rat. *J. exp. Psychol.,* 1953, **32**, 226–234.
3. DE GROOT, A. *Het Denken van den Schaker.* Amsterdam: Noord-Hollandsche Uitgevers Maatschapij, 1946.
4. HUNT, J. McV. *Personality and the behavior disorders.* New York: Ronald, 1944.
5. SIMON, H. A. *Administrative behavior.* New York: Macmillan, 1947.
6. SIMON, H. A. A behavioral model of rational choice. *Quart. J. Econ.,* 1955, **59**, 99–118.
7. THRALL, R. M., COOMBS, C. H., & DAVIS, R. L. (Eds.). *Decision processes.* New York: Wiley, 1954.
8. WALTER, W. G. *The living brain.* New York: Norton, 1953.

(Received March 28, 1955)

7.4
A COMPARISON OF GAME THEORY AND LEARNING THEORY

HERBERT A. SIMON

CARNEGIE INSTITUTE OF TECHNOLOGY

It is shown that Estes' formula for the asymptotic behavior of a subject under conditions of partial reinforcement can be derived from the assumption that the subject is behaving rationally in a certain game-theoretic sense and attempting to minimax his regret. This result illustrates the need for specifying the frame of reference or set of the subject when using the assumption of rationality to predict his behavior.

Learning theory and game theory (together with the closely related statistical decision theory) purport to provide theories of *rational* behavior. Implicit in any theory of learning is a motivational assumption that learning consists in the acquisition of a pattern of behavior appropriate to *goal achievement, need reduction,* or the like. In parallel fashion game theory and statistical decision theory are concerned with discovering the course of action in a particular situation that will optimize the attainment of some objective pay-off.

In order to gain a better understanding of the concepts of *rationality* underlying these two bodies of theory, it would be interesting to construct a situation in which predictions made from these theories could be compared and then checked against experimental data on actual behavior. One situation of this kind received considerable attention at the Santa Monica Conference on Decision Processes (**2, 3, 4**). The experiment is one involving partial reinforcement. At each trial the subject chooses between two alternatives. Each alternative is rewarded on a certain per cent of the trials in which it is chosen (the trials rewarded being randomly determined) and not rewarded on the remaining trials in which it is chosen; the per cent of rewarded trials is in general different for the two alternatives. The learning theory advanced by Estes provides a prediction as to the frequency (in the limit as the number of trials increases) with which the first alternative will be chosen in preference to the second (**2**). The same frequency is predicted by the Bush-Mosteller theory when certain assumptions of symmetry are made with respect to the parameters that appear in their model (**1**, ch. 8). Estes reports several experiments that confirm predictions from his theory.

When this experimental situation was described to a number of game theorists at the Santa Monica conference, they pointed out that a *rational* individual would first estimate, by experimenting, which of the two alternatives had the greatest probability of reward, and would subsequently always select that alternative which would not be predicted by the Estes theory. Flood has defended the choices predicted by the Estes theory against the charge of irrationality, basing his defense on two points (4, p. 288):

(a) The proper definition of payoff utilities would be unclear in attempts to apply game-theoretic arguments to a real case, and there is a reasonable payoff matrix that would rationalize the reported behavior. Thus, if the organism's object were to maximize its score rather than its expectation, then it should sometimes not tend to use a pure strategy . . .

(b) The von Neumann-Morgenstern game theory is inapplicable in this situation unless the organism can assume safely that the experimental stimulus is generated by a stationary stochastic process. For example, if the organism believes that there may be some pattern (non-stationarity) over time, in the stimulus, then it can often do better by using a mixed strategy rather than a pure one, for the latter would give it no way to discover any pattern effect.

In the next section, by combining in an appropriate fashion the two considerations advanced by Flood—that is, by assuming (a) the subject is trying to maximize something other than expected payoff, and (b) the subject does not believe or expect that the probability of reward from each alternative is fixed—it will be shown that the behavior predicted by the Estes theory and actually observed in experiments is rational in the sense of game theory (or at least in one of the many senses consistent with game theory). In a final section, the implications of this result will be discussed briefly.

Game-Theoretical Derivation of Estes' Result

Consider a partial reinforcement experiment in which there are two alternatives of behavior, A_1 and A_2. If A_1 is chosen on a particular trial, it is rewarded with probability π_1 ; if A_2 is chosen, it is rewarded with probability π_2 . Let $p_1(t)$ be the probability that the subject chooses A_1 on the tth trial; $p_2(t) = (1 - p_1)$ the probability that he chooses A_2 . From the postulates of his learning model, Estes (2) predicts that the asymptotic value of p_1 as the number of trials increases will be p_1^* ,

$$p_1^* = \frac{1 - \pi_2}{(1 - \pi_1) + (1 - \pi_2)}. \tag{1}$$

This value for p_1^* may be obtained as the steady state of the stochastic process

$$\bar{p}(t + 1) = \Pi\bar{p}(t), \quad \text{where} \quad \Pi = \begin{pmatrix} \pi_1 & (1 - \pi_2) \\ (1 - \pi_1) & \pi_2 \end{pmatrix}; \tag{2}$$

for

$$p_1(t + 1) = \pi_1 p_1(t) + (1 - \pi_2)[1 - p_1(t)], \tag{3}$$

so that, if $p_1(t + 1) = p_1(t) = p_1^*$,

$$(1 - \pi_1 + 1 - \pi_2)p_1^* = (1 - \pi_2),\qquad(4)$$

from which (1) follows immediately.

We see that in Estes' theory π_1 is the probability that A_1 will be rewarded; but it is also the asymptotic probability that, having chosen A_1 on a given trial, the subject will choose it again on the next succeeding trial. A similar interpretation can be given to π_2. Hence, we may interpret π_1 and π_2 as the conditional probabilities of *persistent* behavior when the subject has just chosen A_1 or A_2, respectively; while $(1 - \pi_1)$ and $(1 - \pi_2)$ are the corresponding conditional probabilities of a *shift* in behavior.

For specificity, let us consider the case where $\pi_1 > \pi_2$. Then the game-theoretical objection to regarding as rational the asymptotic behavior predicted by the Estes model is that the subject could increase his expected reward by always choosing A_1. For then the expected reward would be

$$\pi_1 > p_1^*\pi_1 + (1 - p_1^*)\pi_2,\qquad(5)$$

where the terms on the right-hand side of the inequality are easily seen to be the expected reward for the Estes model.

But the rationality of this game-theoretical solution is compelling only under the assumption that the reward probabilities are known to the subject, and known to be constant. These are the assumptions that Flood challenges. Let us consider an alternative set of assumptions which, while not the only possible such set, has some plausibility.

(*i*) The subject takes as given and fixed the π corresponding to the alternative he has chosen on the last trial. That is, he assumes the probability of reward to be π_1 or π_2, if he persists in choosing again A_1 or A_2, as the case may be.

(*ii*) The subject expects that if he *shifts* from the alternative just chosen to the other one, the probability of reward is unknown and dependent on a strategy of nature.

(*iii*) The subject does not wish to persist in his present behavior if there is a good chance of increased reward from shifting. He measures his success on each trial not from the reward received, but from the difference between the reward actually received and the reward that *could* have been attained if he had outguessed nature. In the terminology of L. J. Savage, he wishes to minimize his *regret*.

We may formalize these assumptions as follows: On each trial, the subject chooses between (*i*) *persisting* or (*ii*) *shifting* his choice. If he persists, he is rewarded with probability π (where $\pi = \pi_1$, or $\pi = \pi_2$ depending on whether the previous choice was A_1 or A_2, respectively), irrespective of the strategy adopted by nature. If he shifts, he will receive a reward of 0 if nature adopts her strategy (α), and a reward of 1 if nature adopts her strategy

(β). The payoff matrix corresponding to these assumptions is:

	(α)	(β)
(i)	π	π
(ii)	0	1

where rows correspond to the subject's strategies and columns to nature's strategies. *Regret* is defined as the difference between the actual payoff for a given pair of strategies [e.g. (i), (β)], and the payoff that *could* have been realized, if the strategy actually employed by nature had been anticipated [e.g., (ii), (β)]. Performing the indicated subtractions, the regret matrix is:

	(α)	(β)
(i)	0	$(\pi - 1)$
(ii)	$-\pi$	0

(This was obtained from the first matrix by subtracting from each element the largest element in the same column).

Now let ρ be the probability that the subject uses strategy (i), i.e., persists, μ be the probability that nature uses strategy (α). Then the expected regret will be

$$R = \rho\mu\cdot 0 + \rho(1 - \mu)(\pi - 1) + (1 - \rho)\mu(-\pi) + (1 - \rho)(1 - \mu)\cdot 0 \qquad (6)$$

$$= \rho(1 - \mu)(\pi - 1) - (1 - \rho)\mu\pi.$$

The conditions that the regret be minimum (strictly, *minimax*) are given by

$$\frac{\partial R}{\partial \rho} = \frac{\partial R}{\partial \mu} = 0. \qquad (7)$$

Using the second of these equations, we obtain from (6)

$$0 = -\rho(\pi - 1) - (1 - \rho)\pi, \qquad (8)$$

whence

$$\rho = \pi. \qquad (9)$$

Hence the subject would persist with probability π and shift with probability $(1 - \pi)$. But this is precisely the postulate contained in (2).

Hence, we have shown that the behavior predicted by Estes' theory is identical with that which would be exhibited by a *rational* subject intent on *minimaxing* his regret.

Comments on the Derivation

We need not try to decide whether the subjects who behave in conformity with the predictions of Estes' theory are minimaxing regret, or whether they are simply behaving in the adaptive fashion implied by the usual learning mechanisms. Most economists and statisticians would be tempted to accept the former interpretation, most psychologists the latter. It is not immediately obvious what source, other than introspection, would provide evidence for deciding the issue.

Perhaps the most useful lesson to be learned from the derivation is the necessity for careful distinctions between *subjective* rationality (i.e., behavior that is rational, given the perceptual and evaluational premises of the subject), and *objective* rationality (behavior that is rational as viewed by the experimenter). Because this distinction has seldom been made explicitly by economists and statisticians in their formulations of the problem of rational choice, considerable caution must be exercised in employing those formulations in the explanation of observed behavior.

To the experimenter who knows that the rewards attached to the two behaviors A_1 and A_2 are random, with constant probabilities, it appears unreasonable that the subject should not learn to behave in such a way as to maximize this expected gain—always to choose A_1. To the subject, who perceives the situation as one in which the probabilities may change, and who is more intent on outwitting the experimenter (or nature) than on maximizing expected gain, rationality is something quite different. If rationality is to have any meaning independent of the perceptions of the subject we must distinguish between the rationality of the perceptions themselves (i.e., whether or not the situation as perceived is the real situation) and the rationality of the choice, given the perceptions.

If we accept the proposition that organismic behavior may be subjectively rational but is unlikely to be objectively rational in a complex world then the postulate of rationality loses much of its power for predicting behavior. To predict how economic man will behave we need to know not only that he is rational, but also how he perceives the world—what alternatives he sees, and what consequences he attaches to them (**5**). We should not jump to the conclusion, however, that we can therefore get along without the concept of rationality. While the Estes model predicts the behavior of naive subjects under partial reinforcement, we observe (**3**) that persons trained in game theory and placed in the same situation generally learn to choose A_1 consistently. It appears simpler to postulate here a change in set— a change in the perceptual model—rather than to attempt to explain this behavior in terms of simpler learning-theoretic models. If anything was learned during the series of trials by the subjects who were game theorists, it was the appropriate perceptual model and not the appropriate behavior once that model is assumed.

REFERENCES

1. Thrall, R. M., Coombs, C. H., and Davis, R. L. (Eds.) Decision processes. New York: Wiley, 1954.
2. Estes, W. K. Individual behavior in uncertain situations: an interpretation in terms of statistical association theory. In (1), chap. 9.
3. Flood, M. W. Game-learning theory and some decision-making experiments. In (1), chap. 10.
4. Flood, M. W. Environmental non-stationarity in a sequential decision-making experiment. In (1), chap. 18.
5. Simon, H. A. A behavorial model of rational choice. *Quart. J. Econ.*, **69**, 1955, 99–118.

Manuscript received 4/18/55

Revised manuscript received 5/28/55

7.5
OBSERVATION OF A BUSINESS DECISION

RICHARD M. CYERT, HERBERT A. SIMON, AND DONALD B. TROW*

DECISION-MAKING — choosing one course of action rather than another, finding an appropriate solution to a new problem posed by a changing world—is commonly asserted to be the heart of executive activity in business. If this is so, a realistic description and theory of the decision-making process are of central importance to business administration and organization theory. Moreover, it is extremely doubtful whether the only considerable body of decision-making theory that has been available in the past—that provided by economics—does in fact provide a realistic account of decision-making in large organizations operating in a complex world.

In economics and statistics the rational choice process is described somewhat as follows:

1. An individual is confronted with a number of different, specified alternative courses of action.

2. To each of these alternatives is attached a set of consequences that will ensue if that alternative is chosen.

3. The individual has a system of preferences or "utilities" that permit him to rank all sets of consequences according to preference and to chose that alternative that has the preferred consequences. In the case of business decisions the criteri-

on for ranking is generally assumed to be profit.

If we try to use this framework to describe how real human beings go about making choices in a real world, we soon recognize that we need to incorporate in our description of the choice process several elements that are missing from the economic model:

1. The alternatives are not usually "given" but must be sought, and hence it is necessary to include the search for alternatives as an important part of the process.

2. The information as to what consequences are attached to which alternatives is seldom a "given," but, instead, the search for consequences is another important segment of the decision-making task.

3. The comparisons among alternatives are not usually made in terms of simple, single criterion like profit. One reason is that there are often important consequences that are so intangible as to make an evaluation in terms of profit difficult or impossible. In place of searching for the "best" alternative, the decision-maker is usually concerned with finding a *satisfactory* alternative—one that will attain a specified goal and at the same time satisfy a number of auxiliary conditions.

4. Often, in the real world, the problem itself is not a "given," but, instead, searching for significant problems to which organizational attention should be turned becomes an important organizational task.

Decisions in organizations vary widely

* Graduate School of Industrial Administration, Carnegie Institute of Technology. This is a preliminary report on research carried out under a grant from the Ford Foundation for studies in organization and decision-making. The authors are grateful to the Foundation for its support, to the executives of the company that opened its doors to them, and to colleagues and graduate students who have assisted at various stages of data collection and analysis.

237

with respect to the extent to which the decision-making process is *programmed*. At one extreme we have repetitive, well-defined problems (e.g., quality control or production lot-size problems) involving tangible considerations, to which the economic models that call for finding the best among a set of pre-established alternatives can be applied rather literally. In contrast to these highly programmed and usually rather detailed decisions are problems of a non-repetitive sort, often involving basic long-range questions about the whole strategy of the firm or some part of it, arising initially in a highly unstructured form and requiring a great deal of the kinds of search processes listed above. In this whole continuum, from great specificity and repetition to extreme vagueness and uniqueness, we will call decisions that lie toward the former extreme *programmed*, and those lying toward the latter end *non-programmed*. This simple dichotomy is just a shorthand for the range of possibilities we have indicated.

It is our aim in the present paper to illustrate the distinctions we have introduced between the traditional theory of decision, which appears applicable only to highly programmed decision problems, and a revised theory, which will have to take account of the search processes and other information processes that are so prominent in and characteristic of non-programmed decision-making. We shall do this by recounting the stages through which an actual problem proceeded in an actual company and then commenting upon the significance of various items in this narrative for future decision-making theory.

The decision was captured and recorded by securing the company's permission to have a member of the research team present as an observer in the company's

offices on substantially a full-time basis during the most active phases of the decision process. The observer spent most of his time with the executive who had been assigned the principal responsibility for handling this particular problem. In addition, he had full access to the files for information about events that preceded his period of observation and also interviewed all the participants who were involved to a major degree in the decision.

THE ELECTRONIC DATA-PROCESSING DECISION

The decision process to be described here concerns the feasibility of using electronic data-processing equipment in a medium size corporation that engages both in manufacturing and in selling through its own widely scattered outlets. In July, 1952, the company's controller assigned to Ronald Middleton, an assistant who was handling several special studies in the accounting department, the task of keeping abreast of electronic developments. The controller, and other accounting executives, thought that some of the current developments in electronic equipment might have application to the company's accounting processes. He gave Middleton the task of investigation, because the latter had a good background for understanding the technical aspects of computers.

Middleton used three procedures to obtain information: letters to persons in established computer firms, discussions with computer salesmen, and discussions with persons in other companies that were experimenting with the use of electronic equipment in accounting. He also read the current journal literature about computer developments. He informed the controller about these matters principally through memorandums that described the current status of equipment and some of the procedures that would be necessary for an applications study in the company. Memorandums were written in November, 1952, October, 1953, and January, 1954. In them, in addition to summarizing developments, he recommended that two computer companies be asked to propose possible installations in the company and that the company begin to adapt its accounting procedures to future electronic processing.

In the spring of 1954 a computer company representative took the initiative to propose and make a brief equipment application study. In August he submitted a report to the company recommending an installation, but this was not acted upon—doubt as to the adequacy of the computer company's experience and knowledge in application being a major factor in the decision. A similar approach was made by another computer company in September, 1954, but terminated at an early stage without positive action. These experiences convinced Middleton and other executives, including the controller, that outside help was needed to develop and evaluate possible applications of electronic equipment.

Middleton drew up a list of potential consultants and, by checking outside sources and using his own information, selected Alpha as the most suitable. After preliminary meetings in October and November, 1954, between representatives of Alpha and the company accounting executives, Alpha was asked to develop a plan for a study of the application of electronic data-processing to sales accounting. Additional meetings between Alpha and company personnel were held in February, 1955, and the proposal for the study was submitted to the controller in March.

Although the proposal seemed competent and the price reasonable, it was felt that proposals should be obtained from another consulting firm as a double check. The controller agreed to this and himself selected Beta from Middleton's list. Subsequently representatives of Beta met with Middleton and other department executives. Middleton, in a memorandum to the controller, listed criteria for choosing between the two consultants. On the assumption that the written report from Beta was similar to the oral proposal made, the comparison indicated several advantages for Beta over Alpha.

After the written report was received, on May 2, the company's management committee authorized a consulting agreement with Beta, and work began in July, 1955. The controller established a committee, headed by Middleton, to work on the project. Middleton was to devote full time to the assignment; the other two committee members, one from sales accounting and one from auditing, were to devote one-third time.

The consulting firm assigned two staff members, Drs. Able and Baker, to the study. Their initial meetings with Middleton served the purpose of outlining a general approach to the problem and planning the first few steps. Twenty-three information-gathering studies were defined, which Middleton agreed to carry out, and it was also decided that the consultants would spend some time in field observation of the actual activities that the computer might replace.

During July, Middleton devoted most of his time to the twenty-three studies on volume of transactions and information flow, obtaining data from the sales department and from the field staffs of the other two committee members. Simultaneously, steps were taken to secure the co-operation of the field personnel who would be visited by the consultants early in August.

On July 22 Middleton submitted a progress report to the controller, describing the data-gathering studies, estimating completion dates, and summarizing the program's objectives. On July 25 the consultants met with Middleton and discussed a method of approach to the design of the data-processing system. The field trip took place early in August. The consultants obtained from field personnel information as to how accounting tasks were actually handled and as to the use actually made of information generated by the existing system.

On August 8 Middleton submitted another progress report, giving the status of the data-gathering studies and recording some ideas originating in the field trip for possible changes in the existing information-processing system. On August 10 he arranged with the assistant controller to obtain clerical assistance on the data-gathering studies, so that the consultants would not be held up by lack of this information, and on August 17 this work was completed.

On the following day the consultants met with the company committee to review the results of the twenty-three studies. They then listed the outputs, files, and inputs required by any sales accounting system the company might adopt and drew a diagram showing the flow of the accounting information. The group also met with the assistant controller and with the controller. The latter took the opportunity to emphasize his basic decentralization philosophy.

Upon returning from his vacation early in September, Middleton discussed the flow diagram in greater detail with Able and Baker, and revisions were made on the basis of information Middleton supplied about the present accounting system. Baker pointed out that all the alternative systems available to the company could be defined by the location of seven principal functions and records. Further analysis reduced this number to three: stock records, pricing of orders, and accounts receivable. The possible combinations of locations of these gave eighteen basic alternative systems, of which eight that were obviously undesirable were eliminated. Middleton was to make a cost analysis of the existing system and the most decentralized of the proposed systems, while the consultants were to begin costing the most centralized system.

Middleton reviewed these tentative decisions with the other members of the company committee, and the group divided up the work of costing. Middleton also reported to the controller on the conference, and the latter expressed his attitudes about the location of the various functions and the resulting implications for the development of executive responsibility.

During the next week, in addition to working on his current assignments, Middleton gave an equipment salesman a preliminary overview of the probable requirements of a new system. Next, there was a two-day meeting of the consultants and the company's committee to discuss the form and implications of a centralized electronic system. The consultants presented a method of organizing the records for electronic processing and together with the committee calculated the requirements which this organization and company's volume of transactions would impose on a computer. The group then discussed several problems raised by the system, including the auditing problems, and then met with the assistant controller to review the areas they had discussed.

On the following day, Middleton summarized progress to date for the controller, emphasizing particularly the work that had been done on the centralized system. The controller expressed satisfaction with several new procedures that would be made possible by an electronic computer. During the next several days the committee members continued to gather the information necessary to determine the cost of the present system. Middleton also checked with the assistant controller on the proposed solutions for certain problems that the consultants had indicated could not be handled readily by a computer and relayed his reactions to the consultants.

A week later the consultants returned for another series of meetings. They discussed changes that might be necessary in current practices to make centralized electronic processing possible and the way in which they would compare the centralized and decentralized proposals. The comparison presented some difficulties, since the data provided by the two systems would not be identical. A general form for a preliminary report was cleared with the assistant controller, and a date was set for its submission. The processing, outputs, and costs for the two alternatives would be described, so that additional information required for a final report could be determined.

During the next week Middleton continued collecting cost data. He phoned to the consultants to provide them with important new figures and to inform them of the controller's favorable reaction to certain proposed changes in the system that had implications for the company's policies.

On October 17 Baker met with Middleton to review the content of the accounting reports that would be produced by the centralized system, to discuss plans for the preliminary report, and to discuss the relative advantages and disadvantages of the centralized and decentralized systems. On the next day, Middleton checked on their decisions relative to the report with the controller and assistant controller and raised the possibility of an outside expert being retained by the company to review the final report submitted by Beta. During the last days of this week, Middleton attended the national meeting of a management society, where he obtained information about the availability of computers and computer personnel and the existence of other installations comparable to that contemplated for the company.

Work continued on the planning and costing of the two systems—Middleton worked primarily on the decentralized plan, and the consultants on the centralized. On October 27 the two consultants met with Middleton and they informed each other of the status of their work. Baker discussed methods for evaluating system reliability. Plans for the preliminary report were discussed with the company committee and the assistant controller. Since the controller strongly favored decentralization of authority, the question was raised of the compatibility of this with electronic processing in general and with the centralized system in particular. The groups concluded, however, that centralization of purely clerical data-processing operations was compatible with decentralization of responsibility and authority.

After several meetings between the committee and the consultants to iron out details, the preliminary report was presented to the company committee, the controller, and the assistant controller on November 3. The report was devoted primarily to the centralized system. The following points were made in the oral presentation: (1) that both the centralized and decentralized proposals would yield substantial and roughly equivalent savings but that the centralized system would provide more and better accounting data; (2) that the alternatives had been costed conservatively; (3) that the centralized system involved centralization of paper work, not of management; (4) that not all problems raised by the centralized system had been worked out in detail but that these did not appear insurmountable; (5) that the centralized system would facilitate improved inventory control; and (6) that its installation would require nine to twelve months at a specified cost. At this meeting the group decided that in the final report only the two systems already considered would be costed, that the final report would be submitted on December 1, and that investigation of other accounting applications of the system would be postponed.

In informal conversations after the meeting the controller told Middleton he had the impression that the consultants strongly favored the centralized system and that he believed the cost considerations were relatively minor compared with the impact the system would have on executives' operating philosophies. The assistant controller told Middleton he thought the preliminary report did not adequately support the conclusions. The committee then reviewed with the assistant controller the reasons for analyzing in detail only the two extreme systems: the others either produced less information or were more costly.

The next day the committee met with the controller and assistant controller to determine what additional information should be requested for the final report. The controller outlined certain questions of practicability that the final report should answer and expressed the view that the report should contain a section summarizing the specific changes that the system would bring about at various levels of the organization. He thought the comparison between systems in the preliminary report had emphasized equivalence of savings, without detailing other less tangible benefits of the centralized system.

Middleton reported these discussions to the consultants and with them developed flow charts and organization charts for inclusion in the final report, settled on some intermediate deadlines, and worked up an outline of the report. Within the company he discussed with the controller and assistant controller the personnel and organizational requirements for installation of an electronic system and for operation after installation. Discussion focused on the general character and organizational location of the eventual electronic-data-processing group, its relation to the sales accounting division, and long-term relations with manufacturing accounting and with a possible operations research group.

On November 14 the controller, on recommendation of Middleton, attended a conference on automation for company senior executives. There he expressed the view that three to five years would be required for full installation of a centralized electronic system but that the fear of obsolescence of equipment should not deter the company in making the investment. He also concluded that a computer installation would not reverse his long-range program for decentralizing information and responsibility.

Middleton, his suggestion being accepted, made tentative arrangements with an independent expert and with two large computer companies for the review of the consultants' report. Middleton presented to the controller and assistant controller a memorandum he had prepared at the latter's request, establishing a new comparison of the centralized and a modified decentralized system. The modification made the two systems more nearly comparable in data-processing capacity, hence clarified the cost comparison, which was now in favor of the centralized system. Consideration of the possibility of starting with a partially electronic decentralized system as a step toward a completely electronic system led to the decision that this procedure had no special advantages. The controller reported that conversations with the sales manager and the president had secured agreement with the concept of removal of stock record-keeping from field locations—an aspect of the plan to which it had been assumed there would be sales department opposition. The group discussed several other specific topics and reaffirmed that the final report should discuss more fully the relative advantages and disadvantages of centralized and decentralized systems.

Toward the end of November there was further consultation on the report, and final arrangements for its review were made with the two equipment companies and the independent expert. Each equipment company was expected to determine the method for setting up the proposed system on its computer and to check the consultants' estimates of computer capacity. During this week the controller informed the company's management committee that the report from the consultants would be submitted shortly and would recommend a rather radical change to electronic data-processing.

The final report, which recommended installation of the centralized system, was submitted on December 1. The report consisted of a summary of recommendations, general description of the centralized system, a discussion of the

installation program, and six appendixes: (1) statistics on volume of transactions (the twenty-three studies); (2) costs of the present system; (3) the requirements of a fully centralized system; (4) changes in allocation of functions required by the system; (5) an outline of the alternative decentralized system; and (6) a description of the existing system in verbal and flow-chart form. When the report was received and reviewed initially, the company's committee members and the consultants made some further computations on installation costs.

At a meeting the following Monday the assistant controller proposed an action program: send copies of the report to equipment companies, send copies to the sales department, and await the report of the independent expert. The controller decided that the second and third steps should be taken before giving the report to the machine companies, and the assistant controller indicated to Middleton some points requiring further clarification and elaboration.

By January 7 Middleton had prepared an outline for a presentation of the report to the sales department. This was revised on the basis of a meeting with the other interested accounting executives. A final outline was agreed upon after two more revisions and three more meetings. The report was presented on January 28 to the president and to six of the top executives of the sales department. The presentation discussed large-scale computers briefly, described with flow charts the proposed system, emphasized the completeness and accuracy of the information produced, discussed costs and savings, and mentioned the current trend in other companies toward electronic data-processing.

At Middleton's recommendation the same presentation was made subsequently to top members of the accounting department and still later to a group from the manufacturing department. At the same time the preliminary report of the independent expert was received, agreeing that the electronic installation seemed justifiable and stating that there might not be any cost savings but that it would make possible numerous other profitable applications of the computer. The consultants' report was then distributed to the computer companies, and Middleton began more detailed planning of the installation.

Middleton, the assistant controller, and the controller now met with the independent expert, who reported his conclusions: the feasibility study was excellent, the estimates of processing time were probably optimistic, the installation program should provide for an early test run, and the two principal available computers were highly competitive. Independent confirmation had been obtained on the last two points from another outside source. Middleton now proposed that the company proceed with its planning while awaiting the final written report from the independent expert and the proposals of the equipment companies. The assistant controller preferred to wait until these reports were actually in hand.

During the next week the equipment companies proceeded with their analysis, meeting several times with Middleton. Baker sent a memorandum on his estimates of processing time to meet the criticism of the independent expert. Middleton prepared two charts, one proposing a schedule and the staffing requirements for the installation phase, the other proposing organizational arrangements for the computer center. Middleton and the assistant controller presented these to the controller at the beginning of February, discussion centering responsibility for accuracy of input information.

Middleton and the assistant controller also had a meeting with sales executives who reported that on the basis of their own internal departmental discussions of the consultants' report they were in general agreement with the program. Middleton and one of the other committee members then spent two days inspecting computer installations in two other companies.

In the middle of February the two equipment companies presented their reports, each bringing a team of three or four men to present their recommendations orally. The two recommendations were substantially alike (except for the brand of the machine recommended!), but one report emphasized the availability of its personnel to give help during the installation planning stage.

Discussions were held in the accounting department and with consultant Baker about these reports and the next steps to be taken. The question was debated whether a commitment should be made to one equipment company or whether a small group should continue planning the system in detail, postponing the equipment decision until fall. Most of the group preferred the former alternative.

On February 15 the controller, in conference with the assistant controller and Middleton, dictated a letter to the company's president summarizing the conclusions and recommendations of the study and requesting that the accounting department be authorized to proceed with the electronics program.

On the following day the controller read the letter to the management committee. The letter reviewed briefly the history of the project and summarized the conclusions contained in the consultants' report: that there was ample justification for an electronic-data-processing installation; that the installation would warrant use of the largest computers; and that it would produce savings, many intangible benefits, and excess computer capacity for other applications. The letter quoted the consultants' estimate of the cost of the installation and their recommendation that the company proceed at once to make such a conversion and to acquire the necessary equipment. It then cited the various cross-checks that had been made of the consultants' report and concluded with a repetition of the conclusions of the report—but estimating more conservatively the operating and installation costs—and a request for favorable management committee action. Supplementary information presented included a comparison of consultant and equipment company cost estimates and a list of present and proposed computer installations in other companies. After a few questions and brief discussion, the management committee voted favorably on the recommendation, and the controller informed Middleton of the decision when the meeting ended.

THE ANATOMY OF THE DECISION

From this narrative, or more specifically from the actual data on which the narrative is based, one can list chronologically the various activities of which the decision process is composed. If we wish to describe a program for making a decision of this kind, each of these activities might be taken as one of the steps of the program. If the rules that determined when action would switch from one program step to another were specified, and if the program steps were described in enough detail, it would be possible to replicate the decision process.

The program steps taken together define in retrospect, then, a program for an originally unprogrammed decision. The program would be an inefficient one because it would contain all the false starts and blind alleys of the original process, and some of these could presumably be avoided if the process were repeated. However, describing the process that took place in terms of such a program is a useful way of organizing the data for purposes of analysis.

In order to make very specific what is meant here by a "program," Chart I has been prepared to show the broad outlines of the actual program for the first stages of the decision process (through the first seven paragraphs of the narrative).

CHART I

PROGRAM STEPS FROM INCEPTION OF THE
PROBLEM TO SELECTION OF
A CONSULTANT

KEEPING-UP PROGRAM (paragraphs 1 and 2 of narrative):
  Search for and correspond with experts;
  Discuss with salesmen and with equipment users;
  Search for and read journals;
PROCUREMENT PROGRAM (paragraph 3):
  Discuss applications study with salesmen who propose it;
  Choice: accept or reject proposed study;
  (If accepted) transfer control to salesmen;
  Choice: accept or reject applications proposal;
  (If rejected) switch to consultant program;
CONSULTANT PROGRAM (paragraphs 4 through 7):
  Search for consultants;
  Choice: best consultant of several;
  Transfer control to chosen consultant;
  Choice: accept or reject proposal;
  (If accepted): begin double-check routine;
  Request expenditure of funds;
  (If authorized) transfer control to consultants;
  And so on.

Subprograms.—The various program steps of the decision process fall into several subprograms, some of which have been indicated in Chart I. These subprograms are ways of organizing the activities *post factum*, and in Chart I the organizing principle is the method of approach taken by the company to the total problem. It remains a question as to whether this organizing principle will be useful in all cases. As in the present example, these subprograms may sometimes be false starts, but these must be regarded as parts of the total program, for they may contribute information for later use, and their outcomes determine the switching of activity to new subprograms.

In this particular case the reasons for switching from one subprogram to another were either the proved inadequacy of the first one or a redefinition of the problem. Other reasons for switching can be imagined, and a complete theory of the decision process will have to specify the conditions under which the switch from one line of attack to another will occur.

Common processes.—In the whole decision-making program there are certain steps or "routines" that recur within several of the subprograms; they represent the basic activities of which the whole decision process is composed. For purposes of discussion we have classified these common processes in two categories: the first comprises processes relating to the communication requirements of the organization; the second comprises processes relating directly to the solution of the decisional problem.

Communication processes.—Organizational decision-making requires a variety of communication activities that are absent when a decision is made in a single human head. If we had written out the program steps in greater detail, many more instances of contacts among different members of the organization would be recorded than are now explicit in the narrative. The contacts may be oral or written. Oral contacts are used for such purposes as giving orders, transmitting information, obtaining approval or criticism of proposed action; written communications generally take the form of memorandums having the purpose of transmitting information or proposing action.

The information-transmitting function is crucial to organizational decision-making, for it almost always involves acts of selection or "filtering" by the information source. In the present instance, which is rather typical in this respect, the consultants and subordinate executives are principal information sources; and the controller and other top executives must depend upon them for most of their technical information. Hence, the subordinate acts as an information filter and in this way secures a large influence over the decisions the superior can and does reach.

The influence of the information source over communications is partly controlled by checking processes—for example, retaining an independent expert to check consultants—which give the recipient an independent information source. This reduces, but by no means eliminates, filtering. The great differences in the amounts and kinds of information available to the various participants in the decision process described here emphasize the significance of filtering. It will be important to determine the relationship of the characteristics of the information to the resultant information change and to explore the effects of personal relations between people on the filtering process and hence upon the transmission of information.

Problem-solving processes.—Alongside the organizational communication processes, we find in the narrative a number of important processes directed toward the decision problem itself. One of the most prominent of these is the search for alternative courses of action. The first activities recounted in the narrative—writing letters, reading journals, and so on—were attempts to discover possible action alternatives. At subsequent points in the process searches were conducted to obtain lists of qualified consultants and experts. In addition to these, there were numerous searches—most of them only implicit in the condensed narrative—to find action alternatives that would overcome specific difficulties that emerged as detail was added to the broader alternatives.

The data support strongly the assertion made in the introduction that searches for alternative courses of action constitute a significant part of non-programmed decision-making—a part that is neglected by the classical theory of rational choice. In the present case the only alternatives that became available to the company without the expenditure of time and effort were the systems proposals made early in the process by representatives of two equipment companies, and these were both rejected. An important reason for the prominent role of search in the decision process is that the "problem" to be solved was in fact a whole series of "nested" problems, each alternative solution to a problem at one level leading to a new set of problems at the next level. In addition, the process of solving the substantive problems created many procedural problems for the organization: allocating time and work, planning agendas and report presentations, and so on.

Examination of the narrative shows that there is a rich variety of search processes. Many questions remain to be answered as to what determines the particular character of the search at a particular stage in the decision process: the possible differences between searches for procedural alternatives, on the one hand, and for substantive alternatives, on the other; the factors that determine how many alternatives will be sought before a choice is made; the conditions under which an alternative that has tentatively been chosen will be subjected to further check; the general types of search strategies.

The neglect of the search for alternatives in the classical theory of decision would be inconsequential if the search were so extensive that most of the alternatives available "in principle" were generally discovered and considered. In that case the search process would have no influence upon the alternative finally selected for action. The narrative suggests that this is very far from the truth—that, in fact, the search for alternatives terminates when a satisfactory solution has been discovered even though the field of possibilities has not been exhausted. Hence, we have reason to suppose that changes in the search process or its outcome will actually have major effects on the final decision.

A second class of common processes encompasses information-gathering and similar activity aimed at determining the consequences of each of several alternatives. In many decisions, certainly in the one we observed, these activities account for the largest share of man-hours, and it is through them that subproblems are discovered. The narrative suggests that there is an inverse relation between the cost or difficulty of this investigational task and the number of alternative courses of action that are examined carefully. Further work will be needed to determine if this relation holds up in a broader range of situations. The record also raises numerous questions about the *kinds* of consequences that are examined most closely or at all and about the conditions under which selection of criteria for choice is prior to, or subsequent to, the examination of consequences.

Another set of common processes are those concerned with the choices among alternatives. Such processes appear at many points in the narrative: the selection of a particular consulting firm from a list, the choice between centralized and decentralized electronic-data-processing systems, as well as numerous more detailed choices. These are the processes most closely allied to the classical theory of choice, but even here it is notable that traditional kinds of "maximizing" procedures appear only rarely.

In some situations the choice is between competing alternatives, but in many others it is one of acceptance or rejection of a single course of action—really a choice between doing *something·* at this time and doing nothing. The first such occasion was the decision by the controller to assign Middleton to the task of watching developments in electronics, a decision that initiated the whole sequence of later choices. In decisions of this type the consequences of the single alternative are judged against some kind of explicit or implicit "level of aspiration"—perhaps expressed in terms of an amount of improvement over the existing situation—while in the multiple-alternative situations, the consequences of the several alternatives are compared with each other. This observation raises a host of new questions relating to the circumstances under which the decision will be formulated in terms of the one or the other of these frameworks and the personal and organizational factors that determine the aspiration levels that will be applied in the one-alternative case.

Another observation derivable from our data—though it is not obvious from the condensed narrative given here—is that comparability and non-comparability of the criteria of choice affects the decision processes in significant ways. For one thing, the criteria are not the same from one choice to another: one choice may be made on the basis of relative costs and savings, while the next may be based entirely on non-monetary criteria. Further, few, if any, of the choices were based on a single criterion. Middleton and the others recognized and struggled with this problem of comparing consequences that were sometimes measured in different, and incomparable, units, and even more often involved completely intangible considerations. The narrative raises, but does not answer, the question of how choices are made in the face of these incommensurabilities and the degree to which tangible considerations are overemphasized or underemphasized as compared with intangibles as a result.

CONCLUSION

We do not wish to try to transform one swallow into a summer by generalizing too far from a single example of a decision process. We have tried to illustrate, however, using a large relatively nonprogrammed decision in a business firm, some of the processes that are involved in business decision-making and to indicate the sort of theory of the choice mechanism that is needed to accommodate these processes. Our illustration suggests that search processes and information-gathering processes constitute significant parts of decision-making and must be incorporated in a theory of decision if it is to be adequate. While the framework employed here—and particularly the analysis of a decision in terms of a hierarchical structure of *programs*—is far from a complete or finished theory, it appears to provide a useful technique of analysis for researchers interested in the theory of decision as well as for business executives who may wish to review the decision-making procedures of their own companies.

7.6

THEORIES OF DECISION-MAKING IN ECONOMICS AND BEHAVIORAL SCIENCE

By HERBERT A. SIMON*

[*Editor's note:* This is the first of eight survey articles on recent developments in economics scheduled for appearance in the *Review* over the next few years. Financial support of the series has been generously provided by the Rockefeller Foundation. The managing editor is particularly grateful for the personal interest which the late Dr. Norman S. Buchanan, Director for the Social Sciences at the Foundation, took in the planning of the project.]

Recent years have seen important new explorations along the boundaries between economics and psychology. For the economist, the immediate question about these developments is whether they include new advances in psychology that can fruitfully be applied to economics. But the psychologist will also raise the converse question—whether there are developments in economic theory and observation that have implications for the central core of psychology. If economics is able to find verifiable and verified generalizations about human economic behavior, then these generalizations must have a place in the more general theories of human behavior to which psychology and sociology aspire. Influence will run both ways.[1]

I. *How Much Psychology Does Economics Need?*

How have psychology and economics gotten along with little relation in the past? The explanation rests on an understanding of the goals toward which economics, viewed as a science and a discipline, has usually aimed.

Broadly speaking, economics can be defined as the science that

* The author is professor of administration at the Carnegie Institute of Technology. This paper draws heavily upon earlier investigations with his colleagues in the Graduate School of Industrial Administration, carried out in library, field, and laboratory, under several grants from the Ford Foundation for research on organizations. He is especially indebted to Julian Feldman, whose wide-ranging exploration of the so-called binary choice experiment [25] has provided an insightful set of examples of alternative approaches to a specific problem of choice.

[1] The influence of economics upon recent work in the psychology of higher mental processes is well illustrated by Bruner, Goodnow and Austin [14, Ch. 3 and 4]. In this work, game theory is used to throw light on the processes of concept formation.

describes and predicts the behavior of several kinds of economic man—notably the consumer and the entrepreneur. While perhaps literally correct, this definition does not reflect the principal focus in the literature of economics. We usually classify work in economics along two dimensions: (a) whether it is concerned with industries and the whole economy (macroeconomics) or with individual economic actors (microeconomics); and (b) whether it strives to describe and explain economic behavior (descriptive economics), or to guide decisions either at the level of public policy (normative macroeconomics) or at the level of the individual consumer or businessman (normative microeconomics).

The profession and literature of economics have been largely preoccupied with normative macroeconomics. Although descriptive macroeconomics provides the scientific base for policy prescription, research emphases have been determined in large part by relevance to policy (e.g., business cycle theory). Normative microeconomics, carried forward under such labels as "management science," "engineering economics," and "operations research," is now a flourishing area of work having an uneasy and ill-defined relation with the profession of economics, traditionally defined. Much of the work is being done by mathematicians, statisticians, engineers, and physical scientists (although many mathematical economists have also been active in it).[2]

This new area, like the old, is normative in orientation. Economists have been relatively uninterested in descriptive microeconomics—understanding the behavior of individual economic agents—except as this is necessary to provide a foundation for macroeconomics. The normative microeconomist "obviously" doesn't need a theory of human behavior: he wants to know how people *ought* to behave, not how they *do* behave. On the other hand, the macroeconomist's lack of concern with individual behavior stems from different considerations. First, he assumes that the economic actor is rational, and hence he makes strong predictions about human behavior without performing the hard work of observing people. Second, he often assumes competition, which carries with it the implication that only the rational survive. Thus, the classical economic theory of markets with perfect competition and rational agents is deductive theory that requires almost no contact with empirical data once its assumptions are accepted.[3]

Undoubtedly there is an area of human behavior that fits these assumptions to a reasonable approximation, where the classical theory

[2] The models of rational decision-making employed in operations research are surveyed in Churchman, Ackoff, and Arnoff [16]; Bowman and Fetter [11]; and Vazsonyi [69].

[3] As an example of what passes for empirical "evidence" in this literature, I cite pp. 22-23 of Friedman's *Essays in Positive Economics* [27], which will amaze anyone brought up in the empirical tradition of psychology and sociology, although it has apparently excited little adverse comment among economists.

with its assumptions of rationality is a powerful and useful tool. Without denying the existence of this area, or its importance, I may observe that it fails to include some of the central problems of conflict and dynamics with which economics has become more and more concerned. A metaphor will help to show the reason for this failure.

Suppose we were pouring some viscous liquid—molasses—into a bowl of very irregular shape. What would we need in order to make a theory of the form the molasses would take in the bowl? How much would we have to know about the properties of molasses to predict its behavior under the circumstances? If the bowl were held motionless, and if we wanted only to predict behavior in equilibrium, we would have to know little, indeed, about molasses. The single essential assumption would be that the molasses, under the force of gravity, would minimize the height of its center of gravity. With this assumption, which would apply as well to any other liquid, and a complete knowledge of the environment—in this case the shape of the bowl—the equilibrium is completely determined. Just so, the equilibrium behavior of a perfectly adapting organism depends only on its goal and its environment; it is otherwise completely independent of the internal properties of the organism.

If the bowl into which we were pouring the molasses were jiggled rapidly, or if we wanted to know about the behavior before equilibrium was reached, prediction would require much more information. It would require, in particular, more information about the properties of molasses: its viscosity, the rapidity with which it "adapted" itself to the containing vessel and moved towards its "goal" of lowering its center of gravity. Likewise, to predict the short-run behavior of an adaptive organism, or its behavior in a complex and rapidly changing environment, it is not enough to know its goals. We must know also a great deal about its internal structure and particularly its mechanisms of adaptation.

If, to carry the metaphor a step farther, new forces, in addition to gravitational force, were brought to bear on the liquid, we would have to know still more about it even to predict behavior in equilibrium. Now its tendency to lower its center of gravity might be countered by a force to minimize an electrical or magnetic potential operating in some lateral direction. We would have to know its relative susceptibility to gravitational and electrical or magnetic force to determine its equilibrium position. Similarly, in an organism having a multiplicity of goals, or afflicted with some kind of internal goal conflict, behavior could be predicted only from information about the relative strengths of the several goals and the ways in which the adaptive processes responded to them.

Economics has been moving steadily into new areas where the power of the classical equilibrium model has never been demonstrated, and where its adequacy must be considered anew. Labor economics is such an area, oligopoly or imperfect competition theory another, decision-making under uncertainty a third, and the theory of economic development a fourth. In all of these areas the complexity and instability of his environment becomes a central feature of the choices that economic man faces. To explain his behavior in the face of this complexity, the theory must describe him as something more than a featureless, adaptive organism; it must incorporate at least some description of the processes and mechanisms through which the adaptation takes place. Let us list a little more concretely some specific problems of this kind:

(a) The classical theory postulates that the consumer maximizes utility. Recent advances in the theory of rational consumer choice have shown that the existence of a utility function, and its characteristics, if it exists, can be studied empirically.

(b) The growing separation between ownership and management has directed attention to the motivations of managers and the adequacy of the profit-maximization assumption for business firms. So-called human relations research has raised a variety of issues about the motivation of both executives and employees.

(c) When, in extending the classical theory, the assumptions of perfect competition were removed, even the definition of rationality became ambiguous. New definitions had to be constructed, by no means as "obvious" intuitively as simple maximization, to extend the theory of rational behavior to bilateral monopoly and to other bargaining and outguessing situations.

(d) When the assumptions of perfect foresight were removed, to handle uncertainty about the environment, the definition of rationality had to be extended in another direction to take into account prediction and the formation of expectations.

(e) Broadening the definition of rationality to encompass goal conflict and uncertainty made it hard to ignore the distinction between the objective environment in which the economic actor "really" lives and the subjective environment that he perceives and to which he responds. When this distinction is made, we can no longer predict his behavior—even if he behaves rationally—from the characteristics of the objective environment; we also need to know something about his perceptual and cognitive processes.

We shall use these five problem areas as a basis for sorting out some recent explorations in theory, model building, and empirical testing. In Section II, we will examine developments in the theory of utility and consumer choice. In Section III, we will consider somewhat parallel issues relating to the motivation of managers. In Section IV, we will deal with conflict of goals and the phenomena of bargaining. In Section V, we will survey some of the work that has been done on uncertainty and the formation of expectations. In Section VI, we will explore recent developments in the theory of human problem-solving and other higher mental processes, and see what implications these have for economic decision-making.

II. *The Utility Function*

The story of the re-establishment of cardinal utility, as a consequence of the introduction of uncertainty into the theory of choice, is well known.[4] When Pareto and Slutsky had shown that the theory of consumer demand could be derived from the properties of indifference curves, without postulating a cardinal utility function underlying these curves, it became fashionable to regard utility as an ordinal measure— a ranking of alternatives by preference. Indeed, it could be shown that only ordinal utility had operational status—that the experiments that had been proposed, and even tried in a couple of instances, to measure an individual's utilities by asking him to choose among alternatives could never distinguish between two cardinal utility functions that were ordinally equivalent—that differed only by stretchings and contractions of the unit of measurement.

It was shown by von Neumann and Morgenstern, as a byproduct of their development of the theory of games, that if the choice situation were extended to include choices among uncertain prospects—among lottery tickets, say—cardinal utilities could be assigned to the outcomes in an unequivocal way.[5] Under these conditions, if the subject's behavior was consistent, it was possible to measure cardinally the utilities that different outcomes had for him.

A person who behaved in a manner consistent with the axioms of choice of von Neumann and Morgenstern would act so as to maximize the expected value—the average, weighted by the probabilities of the alternative outcomes of a choice—of his utility. The theory could be tested empirically, however, only on the assumption that the probabilities assigned to the alternatives by the subject were identical with the "objective" probabilities of these events as known to the experimenter. For example, if a subject believed in the gamblers' fallacy, that after a run of heads an unbiased coin would be more likely to fall tails, his choices might appear inconsistent with his utility function, while the real difficulty would lie in his method of assigning probabilities. This

---

[4] Ward Edwards [23] provides an account of these developments from the psychologist's point of view; Chapter 2 of Luce and Raiffa [43] is an excellent introduction to the "new" utility theory. Arrow [5] contains a nonmathematical survey of this and related topics.

[5] The second edition of von Neumann and Morgenstern [50] contains the first rigorous axiomatic demonstration of this point.

difficulty of "subjective" versus "objective" probability soon came to light when attempts were made to test experimentally whether people behaved in accordance with the predictions of the new utility theory. At the same time, it was discovered that the problem had been raised and solved thirty years earlier by the English philosopher and mathematician Frank Ramsey.[6] Ramsey had shown that, by an appropriate series of experiments, the utilities and subjective probabilities assigned by a subject to a set of uncertain alternatives could be measured simultaneously.

Empirical Studies

The new axiomatic foundations of the theory of utility, which show that it is possible at least in principle to determine empirically whether people "have" utility functions of the appropriate kind, have led to a rash of choice experiments. An experimenter who wants to measure utilities, not merely in principle but in fact, faces innumerable difficulties. Because of these difficulties, most experiments have been limited to confronting the subjects with alternative lottery tickets, at various odds, for small amounts of money. The weight of evidence is that, under these conditions, most persons choose in a way that is reasonably consistent with the axioms of the theory—they behave as though they were maximizing the expected value of utility and as though the utilities of the several alternatives can be measured.[7]

When these experiments are extended to more "realistic" choices—choices that are more obviously relevant to real-life situations—difficulties multiply. In the few extensions that have been made, it is not at all clear that the subjects behave in accordance with the utility axioms. There is some indication that when the situation is very simple and transparent, so that the subject can easily see and remember when he is being consistent, he behaves like a utility maximizer. But as the choices become a little more complicated—choices, for example, among phonograph records instead of sums of money—he becomes much less consistent [21, Ch. 3] [47].[8]

We can interpret these results in either of two ways. We can say that consumers "want" to maximize utility, and that if we present

[6] Ramsey's important essay [57] was sufficiently obscure that it was overlooked until the ideas were rediscovered independently by de Finetti [26]. Valuable notes on the history of the topic together with a thorough formal treatment will be found in the first five chapters of Savage [58].

[7] Some of the empirical evidence is reviewed in [23]. A series of more recent empirical studies is reported in Davidson and Suppes [21].

[8] Some more recent experiments [57a], show a relatively high degree of transitivity. A. G. Papandreou, in a publication I have not yet seen (University of California Publications in Economics) also reports a high degree of transitivity.

them with clear and simple choices that they understand they will do so. Or we can say that the real world is so complicated that the theory of utility maximization has little relevance to real choices. The former interpretation has generally appeared more attractive to economists trained in classical utility theory and to management scientists seeking rules of behavior for normative microeconomics; the latter to behavioral scientists interested in the description of behavior.

Normative Applications

The new utility theory has provided the formal framework for much recent work in mathematical statistics—i.e., statistical decision theory.[9] Similarly (it would be accurate to say "synonymously"), this framework provides the basis for most of the normative models of management science and operations research designed for actual application to the decision-making problems of the firm.[10] Except for some very recent developments, linear programming has been limited to decision-making under certainty, but there have been far-reaching developments of dynamic programming dealing with the maximization of expected values of outcomes (usually monetary outcomes) in situations where future events can be predicted only in terms of probability distributions.[11]

Again, there are at least two distinct interpretations that can be placed on these developments. On the one hand, it can be argued: "Firms would like to maximize profits if they could. They have been limited in doing so by the conceptual and computational difficulties of finding the optimal courses of action. By providing powerful new mathematical tools and computing machines, we now enable them to behave in the manner predicted by Alfred Marshall, even if they haven't been able to in the past." Nature will imitate art and economic man will become as real (and as artificial) as radios and atomic piles.

The alternative interpretation rests on the observation that, even with the powerful new tools and machines, most real-life choices still lie beyond the reach of maximizing techniques—unless the situations are heroically simplified by drastic approximations. If man, according to this interpretation, makes decisions and choices that have some ap-

[9] The systematic development of statistics as decision theory is due largely to A. Wald [70] on the basis of the earlier work of J. Neyman and E. Pearson. Savage [58] carries the development further, erecting the foundations of statistics solidly on utility and probability theory.

[10] This work relates, of course, to profit maximization and cost minimization rather than utility maximization, but it is convenient to mention it at this point. See [11] [16] [69].

[11] Arrow, Harris and Marschak [3] were among the first to treat inventory decisions dynamically. A general treatment of the theory of dynamic programming will be found in Bellman [9].

pearance of rationality, rationality in real life must involve something simpler than maximization of utility or profit. In Section VI, we will see where this alternative interpretation leads.

The Binary Choice Experiment

Much recent discussion about utility has centered around a particularly simple choice experiment. This experiment, in numerous variants, has been used by both economists and psychologists to test the most diverse kinds of hypotheses. We will describe it so that we can use it as a common standard of comparison for a whole range of theories and empirical studies.[12]

We will call the situation we are about to describe the *binary choice* experiment. It is better known to most game theorists—particularly those located not far from Nevada—as a two-armed bandit; and to most psychologists as a partial reinforcement experiment. The subject is required, in each of a series of trials, to choose one or the other of two symbols—say, plus or minus. When he has chosen, he is told whether his choice was "right" or "wrong," and he may also receive a reward (in psychologist's language, a reinforcement) for "right" choices. The experimenter can arrange the schedule of correct responses in a variety of ways. There may be a definite pattern, or they may be randomized. It is not essential that one and only one response be correct on a given trial: the experimenter may determine that both or neither will be correct. In the latter case the subject may or may not be informed whether the response he did not choose would have been correct.

How would a utility-maximizing subject behave in the binary choice experiment? Suppose that the experimenter rewarded "plus" on one-third of the trials, determined at random, and "minus" on the remaining two-thirds. Then a subject, provided that he believed the sequence was random and observed that minus was rewarded twice as often as plus, should always, rationally, choose minus. He would find the correct answer two-thirds of the time, and more often than with any other strategy.

Unfortunately for the classical theory of utility in its simplest form, few subjects behave in this way. The most commonly observed behavior is what is called *event matching*.[13] The subject chooses the two alternatives (not necessarily at random) with relative frequencies roughly proportional to the relative frequencies with which they are rewarded.

---

[12] My understanding of the implications of the binary choice experiment owes much to conversations with Julian Feldman, and to his unpublished work on the experiment. See also, Bush and Mosteller [15] particularly Chapter 13.

[13] An example of data consistent with event-matching behavior is given on page 283 of [15].

Thus, in the example given, two-thirds of the time he would choose minus, and as a result would make a correct response, on the average, in 5 trials out of 9 (on two-thirds of the trials in which he chooses minus, and one-third of those in which he chooses plus).[14]

All sorts of explanations have been offered for the event-matching behavior. The simplest is that the subject just doesn't understand what strategy would maximize his expected utility; but with adult subjects in a situation as transparent as this one, this explanation seems far-fetched. The alternative explanations imply either that the subject regards himself as being engaged in a competitive game with the experimenter (or with "nature" if he accepts the experimenter's explanation that the stimulus is random), or that his responses are the outcome of certain kinds of learning processes. We will examine these two types of explanation further in Sections IV and V respectively. The important conclusion at this point is that even in an extremely simple situation, subjects do not behave in the way predicted by a straightforward application of utility theory.

Probabilistic Preferences

Before we leave the subject of utility, we should mention one recent important development. In the formalizations mentioned up to this point, probabilities enter only into the estimation of the consequences that will follow one alternative or another. Given any two alternatives, the first is definitely preferable to the second (in terms of expected utility), or the second to the first, or they are strictly indifferent. If the same pair of alternatives is presented to the subject more than once, he should always prefer the same member of the pair.

One might think this requirement too strict—that, particularly if the utility attached to one alternative were only slightly greater or less than that attached to the other, the subject might vacillate in his choice. An empirical precedent for such vacillation comes not only from casual observation of indecision but from analogous phenomena in the psychophysical laboratory. When subjects are asked to decide which of two weights is heavier, the objectively heavier one is chosen more often than the lighter one, but the relative frequency of choosing the heavier approaches one-half as the two weights approach equality. The probability that a subject will choose the objectively heavier weight depends, in general, on the ratio of the two weights.

Following several earlier attempts, a rigorous and complete axiom system for a utility theory incorporating probabilistic preferences has been constructed recently by Duncan Luce [cf. 43, App. 1]. Although

---

[14] Subjects tend to choose the more highly rewarded alternative slightly more frequently than is called for by event matching. Hence, the actual behavior tends to be some kind of average between event matching and the optimal behavior. See [15, Ch. 13].

the theory weakens the requirements of consistency in preference, it is empirically testable, at least in principle. Conceptually, it provides a more plausible interpretation of the notion of "indifference" than does the classical theory.

III. *The Goals of Firms*

Just as the central assumption in the theory of consumption is that the consumer strives to maximize his utility, so the crucial assumption in the theory of the firm is that the entrepreneur strives to maximize his residual share—his profit. Attacks on this hypothesis have been frequent.[15] We may classify the most important of these as follows:

(a) The theory leaves ambiguous whether it is short-run or long-run profit that is to be maximized.

(b) The entrepreneur may obtain all kinds of "psychic income" from the firm, quite apart from monetary rewards. If he is to maximize his utility, then he will sometimes balance a loss of profits against an increase in psychic income. But if we allow "psychic income," the criterion of profit maximization loses all of its definiteness.

(c) The entrepreneur may not care to maximize, but may simply want to earn a return that he regards as satisfactory. By sophistry and and adept use of the concept of psychic income, the notion of seeking a satisfactory return can be translated into utility maximizing but not in any operational way. We shall see in a moment that "satisfactory profits" is a concept more meaningfully related to the psychological notion of aspiration levels than to maximization.

(d) It is often observed that under modern conditions the equity owners and the active managers of an enterprise are separate and distinct groups of people, so that the latter may not be motivated to maximize profits.

(e) Where there is imperfect competition among firms, maximizing is an ambiguous goal, for what action is optimal for one firm depends on the actions of the other firms.

In the present section we shall deal only with the third of these five issues. The fifth will be treated in the following section; the first, second, and fourth are purely empirical questions that have been discussed at length in the literature; they will be considered here only for their bearing on the question of satisfactory profits.

Satisficing versus Maximizing

The notion of satiation plays no role in classical economic theory, while it enters rather prominently into the treatment of motivation in psychology. In most psychological theories the motive to act stems from

[15] For a survey of recent discussions see Papandreou [55].

drives, and action terminates when the drive is satisfied. Moreover, the conditions for satisfying a drive are not necessarily fixed, but may be specified by an aspiration level that itself adjusts upward or downward on the basis of experience.

If we seek to explain business behavior in the terms of this theory, we must expect the firm's goals to be not maximizing profit, but attaining a certain level or rate of profit, holding a certain share of the market or a certain level of sales. Firms would try to "satisfice" rather than to maximize.[16]

It has sometimes been argued that the distinction between satisficing and maximizing is not important to economic theory. For in the first place, the psychological evidence on individual behavior shows that aspirations tend to adjust to the attainable. Hence in the long run, the argument runs, the level of aspiration and the attainable maximum will be very close together. Second, even if some firms satisficed, they would gradually lose out to the maximizing firms, which would make larger profits and grow more rapidly than the others.

These are, of course, precisely the arguments of our molasses metaphor, and we may answer them in the same way that we answered them earlier. The economic environment of the firm is complex, and it changes rapidly; there is no a priori reason to assume the attainment of long-run equilibrium. Indeed, the empirical evidence on the distribution of firms by size suggests that the observed regularities in size distribution stem from the statistical equilibrium of a population of adaptive systems rather than the static equilibrium of a population of maximizers.[17]

Models of satisficing behavior are richer than models of maximizing behavior, because they treat not only of equilibrium but of the method of reaching it as well. Psychological studies of the formation and change of aspiration levels support propositions of the following kinds.[18] (a) When performance falls short of the level of aspiration, search behavior (particularly search for new alternatives of action) is induced. (b) At the same time, the level of aspiration begins to adjust itself downward until goals reach levels that are practically attainable. (c) If the two mechanisms just listed operate too slowly to adapt aspirations to performance, emotional behavior—apathy or aggression, for example—will replace rational adaptive behavior.

---

[16] A comparison of satisficing with maximizing models of decision-making can be found in [64, Ch. 14]. Katona [40] has independently made similar comparisons of economic and psychological theories of decision.

[17] Simon and Bonini [66] have constructed a stochastic model that explains the observed data on the size distributions of business firms.

[18] A standard psychological reference on aspiration levels is [42]. For applications to economics, see [61] and [45] (in the latter, consult the index under "aspiration levels").

The aspiration level defines a natural zero point in the scale of utility—whereas in most classical theories the zero point is arbitrary. When the firm has alternatives open to it that are at or above its aspiration level, the theory predicts that it will choose the best of those known to be available. When none of the available alternatives satisfies current aspirations, the theory predicts qualitatively different behavior: in the short run, search behavior and the revision of targets; in the longer run, what we have called above emotional behavior, and what the psychologist would be inclined to call neurosis.[19]

Studies of Business Behavior

There is some empirical evidence that business goals are, in fact, stated in satisficing terms.[20] First, there is the series of studies stemming from the pioneering work of Hall and Hitch that indicates that businessmen often set prices by applying a standard markup to costs. Some economists have sought to refute this fact, others to reconcile it— if it is a fact—with marginalist principles. The study of Earley [22a, pp. 44-70] belongs to the former category, but its evidence is suspect because the questions asked of businessmen are leading ones—no one likes to admit that he would accept less profit if he could have more. Earley did not ask his respondents how they determined marginal cost and marginal revenue, how, for example, they estimated demand elasticities.

Another series of studies derived from the debate over the Keynesian doctrine that the amount of investment was insensitive to changes in the rate of interest. The general finding in these studies has been that the rate of interest is not an important factor in investment decisions [24] [39, Ch. 11] [71].

More recently, my colleagues Cyert and March, have attempted to test the satisficing model in a more direct way [19]. They found in one industry some evidence that firms with a declining share of market strove more vigorously to increase their sales than firms whose shares of the market were steady or increasing.

Aspirations in the Binary Choice Experiment

Although to my knowledge this has not been done, it would be easy to look for aspiration-level phenomena in the binary choice experiment.

[19] Lest this last term appear fanciful I should like to call attention to the phenomena of panic and broken morale, which are well known to observers of the stock market and of organizations but which have no reasonable interpretation in classical utility theory. I may also mention that psychologists use the theory described here in a straightforward way to produce experimental neurosis in animal and human subjects.

[20] A comprehensive bibliography of empirical work prior to 1950 will be found in [37]. Some of the more recent work is [19] [24] [39, Ch. 11].

By changing the probabilities of reward in different ways for different groups of subjects, we could measure the effects of these changes on search behavior—where amount of search would be measured by changes in the pattern of responses.

Economic Implications

It has sometimes been argued that, however realistic the classical theory of the firm as a profit maximizer, it is an adequate theory for purposes of normative macroeconomics. Mason, for example, in commenting on Papandreou's essay on "Problems in the Theory of the Firm" [55, pp. 183-222] says, "The writer of this critique must confess a lack of confidence in the marked superiority, *for purposes of economic analysis*, of this newer concept of the firm over the older conception of the entrepreneur." The italics are Mason's.

The theory of the firm is important for welfare economics—e.g., for determining under what circumstances the behavior of the firm will lead to efficient allocation of resources. The satisficing model vitiates all the conclusions about resource allocation that are derivable from the maximizing model when perfect competition is assumed. Similarly, a dynamic theory of firm sizes, like that mentioned above, has quite different implications for public policies dealing with concentration than a theory that assumes firms to be in static equilibrium. Hence, welfare economists are justified in adhering to the classical theory only if: (a) the theory is empirically correct as a description of the decision-making process; or (b) it is safe to assume that the system operates in the neighborhood of the static equilibrium. What evidence we have mostly contradicts both assumptions.

IV. Conflict of Interest

Leaving aside the problem of the motivations of hired managers, conflict of interest among economic actors creates no difficulty for classical economic theory—indeed, it lies at the very core of the theory —so long as each actor treats the other actors as parts of his "given" environment, and doesn't try to predict their behavior and anticipate it. But when this restriction is removed, when it is assumed that a seller takes into account the reactions of buyers to his actions, or that each manufacturer predicts the behaviors of his competitors—all the familiar difficulties of imperfect competition and oligopoly arise.[21]

The very assumptions of omniscient rationality that provide the basis for deductive prediction in economics when competition is present lead

[21] There is by now a voluminous literature on the problem. The difficulties in defining rationality in competitive situations are well stated in the first chapter of von Neumann and Morgenstern [50].

to ambiguity when they are applied to competition among the few. The central difficulty is that rationality requires one to outguess one's opponents, but not to be outguessed by them, and this is clearly not a consistent requirement if applied to all the actors.

Game Theory

Modern game theory is a vigorous and extensive exploration of ways of extending the concept of rational behavior to situations involving struggle, outguessing, and bargaining. Since Luce and Raiffa [43] have recently provided us with an excellent survey and evaluation of game theory, I shall not cover the same ground here.[22] I concur in their general evaluation that, while game theory has greatly clarified the issues involved, it has not provided satisfactory solutions. Not only does it leave the definition of rational conduct ambiguous in all cases save the zero-sum two-person game, but it requires of economic man even more fantastic reasoning powers than does classical economic theory.[23]

Power and Bargaining

A number of exploratory proposals have been put forth as alternatives to game theory—among them Galbraith's notion of countervailing power [30] and Schelling's bargaining theory [59] [60]. These analyses draw at least as heavily upon theories of power and bargaining developed initially to explain political phenomena as upon economic theory. They do not lead to any more specific predictions of behavior than do game-theoretic approaches, but place a greater emphasis upon description and actual observation, and are modest in their attempt to derive predictions by deductive reasoning from a few "plausible" premises about human behavior.

At least four important areas of social science and social policy, two of them in economics and two more closely related to political science, have as their central concern the phenomena of power and the processes of bargaining: the theory of political parties, labor-management relations, international politics, and oligopoly theory. Any progress in the basic theory applicable to one of these is certain to be of almost equal importance to the others. A growing recognition of their common concern is evidenced by the initiation of a new cross-disciplinary journal, *Journal of Conflict Resolution*.

[22] Chapters 5 and 6 of [43] provide an excellent survey of the attempts that have been made to extend the theory of games to the kinds of situations most relevant to economics.

[23] In a forthcoming volume on *Strategy and Market Structure*, Martin Shubik approaches the topics of imperfect competition and oligopoly from the standpoint of the theory of games.

Games against Nature

While the binary choice experiment is basically a one-person game, it is possible to interpret it as a "game against nature," and hence to try to explain it in game-theoretic terms. According to game theory, the subject, if he believes in a malevolent nature that manipulates the dice against him, should minimax his expected utility instead of maximizing it. That is, he should adopt the course of action that will maximize his expected utility under the assumption that nature will do her worst to him.

Minimaxing expected utility would lead the subject to call plus or minus at random and with equal probability, regardless of what the history of rewards has been. This is something that subjects demonstrably do not do.

However, it has been suggested by Savage [58] and others that people are not as interested in maximizing utility as they are in minimizing regret. "Regret" means the difference between the reward actually obtained and the reward that could have been obtained with perfect foresight (actually, with perfect hindsight!). It turns out that minimaxing regret in the binary choice experiment leads to event-matching behavior [64, Ch. 16]. Hence, the empirical evidence is at least crudely consistent with the hypothesis that people play against nature by minimaxing regret. We shall see, however, that event-matching is also consistent with a number of other rules of behavior that seem more plausible on their face; hence we need not take the present explanation too seriously—at least I am not inclined to do so.

V. The Formation of Expectations

While the future cannot enter into the determination of the present, expectations about the future can and do. In trying to gain an understanding of the saving, spending, and investment behavior of both consumers and firms, and to make short-term predictions of this behavior for purposes of policy-making, economists have done substantial empirical work as well as theorizing on the formation of expectations.

Empirical Studies

A considerable body of data has been accumulated on consumers' plans and expectations from the Survey of Consumer Finances, conducted for the Board of Governors of the Federal Reserve System by the Survey Research Center of the University of Michigan [39, Ch. 5]. These data, and similar data obtained by others, begin to give us some information on the expectations of consumers about their own incomes, and the predictive value of their expenditure plans for their actual subsequent behavior. Some large-scale attempts have been made, notably by Modigliani and Brumberg [48, pp. 388-436] and, a little later, by Friedman [28] to relate these empirical findings to classical utility theory. The current empirical research on businessmen's expectations is of two main kinds:

1. Surveys of businessmen's own forecasts of business and business conditions in the economy and in their own industries [24, pp. 165-88] [29, pp. 189-98]. These are obtained by straightforward questionnaire methods that assume, implicitly, that businessmen can and do make such forecasts. In some uses to which the data are put, it is also assumed that the forecasts are used as one basis for businessmen's actions.

2. Studies of business decisions and the role of expectations in these decisions—particularly investment and pricing decisions. We have already referred to studies of business decisions in our discussion of the goals of the firm.[24]

Expectations and Probability

The classical way to incorporate expectations into economic theory is to assume that the decision-maker estimates the joint probability distribution of future events.[25] He can then act so as to maximize the expected value of utility or profit, as the case may be. However satisfying this approach may be conceptually, it poses awkward problems when we ask how the decision-maker actually estimates the parameters of the joint probability distribution. Common sense tells us that people don't make such estimates, nor can we find evidence that they do by examining actual business forecasting methods. The surveys of businessmen's expectations have never attempted to secure such estimates, but have contented themselves with asking for point predictions— which, at best, might be interpreted as predictions of the means of the distributions.

It has been shown that under certain special circumstances the mean of the probability distribution is the only parameter that is relevant for decision—that even if the variance and higher moments were known to the rational decision-maker, he would have no use for them.[26] In these cases, the arithmetic mean is actually a certainty equivalent, the optimal decision turns out to be the same as if the future were known with certainty. But the situations where the mean is a certainty equival-

[24] See the references cited [12, p. 160].

[25] A general survey of approaches to decision-making under uncertainty will be found in [2] and in [43, Ch. 13].

[26] The special case in which mean expectations constitute a certainty equivalent is treated in [62]. An alternative derivation, and fuller discussion is given by Theil [67, Ch. 8, sect. 6].

ent are, as we have said, very special ones, and there is no indication that businessmen ever ask whether the necessary conditions for this equivalence are actually met in practice. They somehow make forecasts in the form of point predictions and act upon them in one way or another.

The "somehow" poses questions that are important for business cycle theory, and perhaps for other problems in economics. The way in which expectations are formed may affect the dynamic stability of the economy, and the extent to which cycles will be amplified or damped. Some light, both empirical and theoretical, has recently been cast on these questions. On the empirical side, attempts have been made: (a) to compare businessmen's forecasts with various "naïve" models that assume the future will be some simple function of the recent past, and (b) to use such naïve models themselves as forecasting devices.

The simplest naïve model is one that assumes the next period will be exactly like the present. Another assumes that the change from present to next period will equal the change from last period to present; a third, somewhat more general, assumes that the next period will be a weighted average of recent past periods. The term "naïve model" has been applied loosely to various forecasting formulae of these general kinds. There is some affirmative evidence that business forecasts fit such models. There is also evidence that elaboration of the models beyond the first few steps of refinement does not much improve prediction; see, for example, [20]. Arrow and his colleagues [4] have explored some of the conditions under which forecasting formulae will, and will not, introduce dynamic instability into an economic system that is otherwise stable. They have shown, for example, that if a system of multiple markets is stable under static expectations, it is stable when expectations are based on a moving average of past values.

The work on the formation of expectations represents a significant extension of classical theory. For, instead of taking the environment as a "given," known to the economic decision-maker, it incorporates in the theory the processes of acquiring knowledge about that environment. In doing so, it forces us to include in our model of economic man some of his properties as a learning, estimating, searching, information-processing organism [65].

The Cost of Information

There is one way in which the formation of expectations might be reincorporated in the body of economic theory: by treating information-gathering as one of the processes of production, so to speak, and applying to it the usual rules of marginal analysis. Information, says price theory, should be gathered up to the point where the incremental cost of additional information is equal to the incremental profit that can be earned by having it. Such an approach can lead to propositions about optimal amounts of information-gathering activity and about the relative merits of alternative information-gathering and estimating schemes.[27]

This line of investigation has, in fact, been followed in statistical decision theory. In sampling theory we are concerned with the optimal size of sample (and in the special and ingenious case of sequential sampling theory, with knowing when to stop sampling), and we wish to evaluate the efficiencies of alternative sampling procedures. The latter problem is the simpler, since it is possible to compare the relative costs of alternative schemes that have the same sampling error, and hence to avoid estimating the value of the information.[28] However, some progress has been made also toward estimating the value of improved forecast accuracy in situations where the forecasts are to be used in applying formal decision rules to choice situations.[29]

The theory of teams developed by Marschak and Radner is concerned with the same problem (see, e.g., [46]) It considers situations involving decentralized and interdependent decision-making by two or more persons who share a common goal and who, at a cost, can transmit information to each other about their own actions or about the parts of the environment with which they are in contact. The problem then is to discover the optimal communication strategy under specified assumptions about communication costs and payoffs.

The cost of communication in the theory of teams, like the cost of observations in sampling theory, is a parameter that characterizes the economic actor, or the relation of the actor to his environment. Hence, while these theories retain, in one sense, a classical picture of economic man as a maximizer, they clearly require considerable information about the characteristics of the actor, and not merely about his environment. They take a long stride toward bridging the gap between the traditional concerns of economics and the concerns of psychology.

Expections in the Binary Choice Experiment

I should like to return again to the binary choice experiment, to see what light it casts on the formation of expectations. If the subject is told by the experimenter that the rewards are assigned at random, if he

---

[27] Fundamental and applied research are examples of economically significant information-gathering activities. Griliches [34] has recently made an attempt to estimate the economic return from research on hybrid corn.

[28] Modern treatments of sampling theory, like Cochran [17] are based on the idea of minimizing the cost of obtaining a fixed amount of information.

[29] For the theory and an application to macroeconomics, see Theil [67, Ch. 8, sects. 5 and 6].

is told what the odds are for each alternative, *and if he believes the experimenter*, the situation poses no forecasting problem. We have seen, however, that the behavior of most subjects is not consistent with these assumptions.

How would sequential sampling theory handle the problem? Each choice the subject makes now has two consequences: the immediate reward he obtains from it, and the increment of information it provides for predicting the future rewards. If he thinks only of the latter consequences, he is faced with the classical problem of induction: to estimate the probability that an event will occur in the future on the basis of its frequency of occurrence in the past. Almost any rule of induction would require a rational (maximizing) subject to behave in the following general manner: to sample the two alternatives in some proportion to estimate the probability of reward associated with each; after the error of estimate had been reduced below some bound, always to choose the alternative with the higher probability of reward. Unfortunately, this does not appear to be what most subjects do.

If we give up the idea of maximization, we can make the weaker assumption that the subject is adaptive—or learns—but not necessarily in any optimal fashion. What do we mean by adaptation or learning? We mean, gradually and on the basis of experience responding more frequently with the choice that, in the past, has been most frequently rewarded. There is a whole host of rules of behavior possessing this characteristic. Postulate, for example, that at each trial the subject has a certain probability of responding "plus," and the complementary probability of responding "minus." Postulate further that when he makes a particular response the probability of making the same response on the next trial is increased if the response is rewarded and decreased if the response is not rewarded. The amount of increment in the response probability is a parameter characterizing the learning rate of the particular subject. Almost all schemes of this kind produce asymptotic behaviors, as the number of trials increases, that are approximately event-matching in character.

Stochastic learning models, as the processes just described are usually called, were introduced into psychology in the early 1950's by W. K. Estes and Bush and Mosteller [15] and have been investigated extensively since that time. The models fit some of the gross features of the observed behaviors—most strikingly the asymptotic probabilities—but do not explain very satisfactorily the fine structure of the observations.

Observation of subjects in the binary choice experiment reveals that usually they not only refuse to believe that (or even to act as if) the reward series were random, but in fact persist over many trials in searching for systematic patterns in the series. To account for such behavior, we might again postulate a learning model, but in this case a model in which the subject does not react probabilistically to his environment, but forms and tests definite hypotheses about systematic patterns in it. Man, in this view, is not only a learning animal; he is a pattern-finding and concept-forming animal. Julian Feldman [25] has constructed theories of this kind to explain the behavior of subjects in the binary choice experiment, and while the tests of the theories are not yet completed, his findings look exceedingly promising.

As we move from maximizing theories, through simple stochastic learning theories, to theories involving pattern recognition our model of the expectation-forming processes and the organism that performs it increases in complexity. If we follow this route, we reach a point where a theory of behavior requires a rather elaborate and detailed picture of the rational actor's cognitive processes.

VI. *Human Cognition and Economics*

All the developments we have examined in the preceding four sections have a common theme: they all involve important modifications in the concept of economic man and, for the reasons we have stated, modifications in the direction of providing a fuller description of his characteristics. The classical theory is a theory of a man choosing among fixed and known alternatives, to each of which is attached known consequences. But when perception and cognition intervene between the decision-maker and his objective environment, this model no longer proves adequate. We need a description of the choice process that recognizes that alternatives are not given but must be sought; and a description that takes into account the arduous task of determining what consequences will follow on each alternative [63, Ch. 5] [64, Part 4] [14].

The decision-maker's information about his environment is much less than an approximation to the real environment. The term "approximation" implies that the subjective world of the decision-maker resembles the external environment closely, but lacks, perhaps, some fineness of detail. In actual fact the perceived world is fantastically different from the "real" world. The differences involve both omissions and distortions, and arise in both perception and inference. The sins of omission in perception are more important than the sins of commission. The decision-maker's model of the world encompasses only a minute fraction of all the relevant characteristics of the real environment, and his inferences extract only a minute fraction of all the information that is present even in his model.

Perception is sometimes referred to as a "filter." This term is as misleading as "approximation," and for the same reason: it implies that what comes through into the central nervous system is really quite a bit like what is "out there." In fact, the filtering is not merely a passive selection of some part of a presented whole, but an active process involving attention to a very small part of the whole and exclusion, from the outset, of almost all that is not within the scope of attention.

Every human organism lives in an environment that generates millions of bits of new information each second, but the bottleneck of the perceptual apparatus certainly does not admit more than 1,000 bits per second, and probably much less. Equally significant omissions occur in the processing that takes place when information reaches the brain. As every mathematician knows, it is one thing to have a set of differential equations, and another thing to have their solutions. Yet the solutions are logically implied by the equations—they are "all there," if we only knew how to get to them! By the same token, there are hosts of inferences that *might* be drawn from the information stored in the brain that are not in fact drawn. The consequences implied by information in the memory become known only through active information-processing, and hence through active selection of particular problem-solving paths from the myriad that might have been followed.

In this section we shall examine some theories of decision-making that take the limitations of the decision-maker and the complexity of the environment as central concerns. These theories incorporate some mechanisms we have already discussed—for example, aspiration levels and forecasting processes—but go beyond them in providing a detailed picture of the choice process.

A real-life decision involves some goals or values, some facts about the environment, and some inferences drawn from the values and facts. The goals and values may be simple or complex, consistent or contradictory; the facts may be real or supposed, based on observation or the reports of others; the inferences may be valid or spurious. The whole process may be viewed, metaphorically, as a process of "reasoning," where the values and facts serve as premises, and the decision that is finally reached is inferred from these premises [63]. The resemblance of decision-making to logical reasoning is only metaphorical, because there are quite different rules in the two cases to determine what constitute "valid" premises and admissible modes of inference. The metaphor is useful because it leads us to take the individual *decision premise* as the unit of description, hence to deal with the whole interwoven fabric of influences that bear on a single decision—but without being bound by the assumptions of rationality that limit the classical theory **of choice.**

Rational Behavior and Role Theory

We can find common ground to relate the economist's theory of decision-making with that of the social psychologist. The latter is particularly interested, of course, in social influences on choice, which determine the *role* of the actor. In our present terms, a role is a social prescription of some, but not all, of the premises that enter into an individual's choices of behavior. Any particular concrete behavior is the resultant of a large number of premises, only some of which are prescribed by the role. In addition to role premises there will be premises about the state of the environment based directly on perception, premises representing beliefs and knowledge, and idiosyncratic premises that characterize the personality. Within this framework we can accommodate both the rational elements in choice, so much emphasized by economics, and the nonrational elements to which psychologists and sociologists often prefer to call attention.

Decision Premises and Computer Programs

The analysis of choice in terms of decision premises gives us a conceptual framework for describing and explaining the process of deciding. But so complex is the process that our explanations of it would have remained schematic and hypothetical for a long time to come had not the modern digital computer appeared on the scene. The notion of decision premise can be translated into computer terminology, and when this translation has been accomplished, the digital computer provides us with an instrument for simulating human decision processes —even very complex ones—and hence for testing empirically our explanations of those processes [53].

A fanciful (but only slightly fanciful) example will illustrate how this might be done. Some actual examples will be cited presently. Suppose we were to construct a robot incorporating a modern digital computer, and to program (i.e., to instruct) the robot to take the role of a business executive in a specified company. What would the program look like? Since no one has yet done this, we cannot say with certainty, but several points are fairly clear. The program would not consist of a list of prescribed and proscribed behaviors, since what an executive does is highly contingent on information about a wide variety of circumstances. Instead, the program would consist of a large number of *criteria* to be applied to possible and proposed courses of action, of routines for *generating* possible courses of action, of computational procedures for *assessing* the state of the environment and its implications for action, and the like. Hence, the program—in fact, a role prescription—would interact with information to produce concrete behavior adapted to the situation. The elements of such a program take the form of what we have called decision premises, and what the computer specialists would call instructions.

The promise of constructing actual detailed descriptions of concrete roles and decision processes is no longer, with the computer, a mere prospectus to be realized at some undefined future date. We can already provide actual examples, some of them in the area of economics.

1. *Management Science.* In the paragraphs on normative applications in Section II, we have already referred to the use of such mathematical techniques as linear programming and dynamic programming to construct formal decision processes for actual situations. The relevance of these decision models to the present discussion is that they are not merely abstract "theories" of the firm, but actual decision-making devices. We can think of any such device as a simulation of the corresponding human decision-maker, in which the equations and other assumptions that enter into the formal decision-making procedure correspond to the decision premises—including the role prescription—of the decision-maker.

The actual application of such models to concrete business situations brings to light the information-processing tasks that are concealed in the assumptions of the more abstract classical models [65, pp. 51-52]:

(1) The models must be formulated so as to require for their application only data that are obtainable. If one of the penalties, for example, of holding too small inventories is the loss of sales, a decision model that proposes to determine optimal inventory levels must incorporate a procedure for putting a dollar value on this loss.

(2) The models must call only for practicable computations. For example, several proposals for applying linear programming to certain factory scheduling problems have been shown to be impracticable because, even with computers, the computation time is too great. The task of decision theory (whether normative or descriptive) is to find alternative techniques—probably only approximate—that demand much less computation.

(3) The models must not demand unobtainable forecast information. A procedure that would require a sales department to estimate the third moment of next month's sales distribution would not have wide application, as either description or prescription, to business decision-making.

These models, then, provide us with concrete examples of roles for a decision-maker described in terms of the premises he is expected to apply to the decision—the data and the rules of computation.

2. *Engineering Design.* Computers have been used for some years to carry out some of the analytic computations required in engineering design—computing the stresses, for example, in a proposed bridge

design. Within the past two years, ways have been found to program computers to carry out synthesis as well as analysis—to evolve the design itself.[30] A number of companies in the electrical industry now use computers to design electric motors, transformers, and generators, going from customer specifications to factory design without human intervention. The significance of this for our purpose here is that the synthesis programs appear to simulate rather closely the processes that had previously been used by college-trained engineers in the same design work. It has proved possible to write down the engineers' decision premises and inference processes in sufficient detail to produce workable computer programs.

3. *Human Problem Solving*. The management science and engineering design programs already provide examples of simulation of human decision-making by computer. It may be thought that, since in both instances the processes are highly arithmetical, these examples are relevant to only a very narrow range of human problem-solving activity. We generally think of a digital computer as a device which, if instructed in painful detail by its operator, can be induced to perform rather complicated and tedious arithmetical operations. More recent developments require us to revise these conceptions of the computer, for they enable it to carry out tasks that, if performed by humans, we would certainly call "thinking" and "learning."

Discovering the proof of a theorem of Euclid—a task we all remember from our high school geometry course—requires thinking and usually insight and imagination. A computer is now being programmed to perform this task (in a manner closely simulating the human geometer), and another computer has been successfully performing a highly similar task in symbolic logic for the past two years.[31] The latter computer is programmed to learn—that is to improve its performance on the basis of successful problem-solving experience—to use something akin to imagery or metaphor in planning its proofs, and to transfer some of its skills to other tasks—for example, solving trigonometric identities—involving completely distinct subject matter. These programs, it should be observed, do not involve the computer in rapid arithmetic—or any arithmetic for that matter. They are basically nonnumerical, involving the manipulation of all kinds of symbolic material, including words.

Still other computer programs have been written to enable a computer to play chess.[32] Not all of these programs, or those previously

[30] A nontechnical description of such a program will be found in [33].

[31] The program for proving theorems in logic is discussed in [51] and [52], Gelernter and Rochester's geometry program in [31].

[32] A survey of computer chess programs can be found in [54].

mentioned, are close simulations of the processes humans use. However, in some direct attempts to investigate the human processes by thinking-aloud techniques and to reproduce in computer programs the processes observed in human subjects, several striking simulations have been achieved.[33] These experiments have been described elsewhere and can't be reviewed here in detail.

4. *Business Games.* Business games, like those developed by the American Management Association, International Business Machines Corporation, and several universities, represent a parallel development.[34] In the business game, the decisions of the business firms are still made by the human players, but the economic environment of these firms, including their markets, are represented by computer programs that calculate the environment's responses to the actions of the players. As the games develop in detail and realism, their programs will represent more and more concrete descriptions of the decision processes of various economic actors—for example, consumers.

The games that have been developed so far are restricted to numerical magnitudes like prices and quantities of goods, and hence resemble the management science and engineering design programs more closely than they do those we have described under the heading of human problem solving. There is no reason, however, to expect this restriction to remain very long.

Implications for Economics

Apart from normative applications (e.g., substituting computers for humans in certain decision-making tasks) we are not interested so much in the detailed descriptions of roles as in broader questions: (1) What general characteristics do the roles of economic actors have? (2) How do roles come to be structured in the particular ways they do? (3) What bearing does this version of role theory have for macroeconomics and other large-scale social phenomena?

Characterizing Role Structure. Here we are concerned with generalizations about thought processes, particularly those generalizations that are relatively independent of the substantive content of the role. A classical example is Dewey's description of stages in the problem-solving process. Another example, of particular interest to economics, is the hypothesis we have already discussed at length: that economic man is a *satisficing* animal whose problem solving is based on search activity to meet certain aspiration levels rather than a *maximizing* animal whose problem solving involves finding the best alternatives in terms of specified criteria [64]. A third hypothesis is that operative goals (those

[33] Much of this work is still unpublished, but see [53] and [54].
[34] Two business games are described by Andlinger [1].

associated with an observable criterion of success, and relatively definite means of attainment) play a much larger part in governing choice than nonoperative goals (those lacking a concrete measure of success or a program for attainment) [45, p. 156].

Understanding How Roles Emerge. Within almost any single business firm, certain characteristic types of roles will be represented: selling roles, production roles, accounting roles, and so on [22]. Partly, this consistency may be explained in functional terms—that a model that views the firm as producing a product, selling it, and accounting for its assets and liabilities is an effective simplification of the real world, and provides the members of the organization with a workable frame of reference. Imitation within the culture provides an alternative explanation. It is exceedingly difficult to test hypotheses as to the origins and causal conditions for roles as universal in the society as these, but the underlying mechanisms could probably be explored effectively by the study of less common roles—safety director, quality control inspector, or the like—that are to be found in some firms, but not in all.

With our present definition of role, we can also speak meaningfully of the role of an entire business firm—of decision premises that underlie its basic policies. In a particular industry we find some firms that specialize in adapting the product to individual customer's specifications; others that specialize in product innovation. The common interest of economics and psychology includes not only the study of individual roles, but also the explanation of organizational roles of these sorts.

Tracing the Implications for Macroeconomics. If basic professional goals remain as they are, the interest of the psychologist and the economist in role theory will stem from somewhat different ultimate aims. The former will use various economic and organizational phenomena as data for the study of the structure and determinants of roles; the latter will be primarily interested in the implications of role theory for the model of economic man, and indirectly, for macroeconomics.

The first applications will be to those topics in economics where the assumption of static equilibrium is least tenable. Innovation, technological change, and economic development are examples of areas to which a good empirically tested theory of the processes of human adaptation and problem solving could make a major contribution. For instance, we know very little at present about how the rate of innovation depends on the amounts of resources allocated to various kinds of research and development activity [34]. Nor do we understand very well the nature of "know how," the costs of transferring technology from one firm or economy to another, or the effects of various kinds and amounts of education upon national product. These are difficult questions to answer from aggregative data and gross observation, with the result that our views have been formed more by arm-chair theorizing than by testing hypotheses with solid facts.

VII. *Conclusion*

In exploring the areas in which economics has common interests with the other behavioral sciences, we have been guided by the metaphor we elaborated in Section I. In simple, slow-moving situations, where the actor has a single, operational goal, the assumption of maximization relieves us of any need to construct a detailed picture of economic man or his processes of adaptation. As the complexity of the environment increases, or its speed of change, we need to know more and more about the mechanisms and processes that economic man uses to relate himself to that environment and achieve his goals.

How closely we wish to interweave economics with psychology depends, then, both on the range of questions we wish to answer and on our assessment of how far we may trust the assumptions of static equilibrium as approximations. In considerable part, the demand for a fuller picture of economic man has been coming from the profession of economics itself, as new areas of theory and application have emerged in which complexity and change are central facts. The revived interest in the theory of utility, and its application to choice under uncertainty, and to consumer saving and spending is one such area. The needs of normative macroeconomics and management science for a fuller theory of the firm have led to a number of attempts to understand the actual processes of making business decisions. In both these areas, notions of adaptive and satisficing behavior, drawn largely from psychology, are challenging sharply the classical picture of the maximizing entrepreneur.

The area of imperfect competition and oligopoly has been equally active, although the activity has thus far perhaps raised more problems than it has solved. On the positive side, it has revealed a community of interest among a variety of social scientists concerned with bargaining as a part of political and economic processes. Prediction of the future is another element common to many decision processes, and particularly important to explaining business cycle phenomena. Psychologists and economists have been applying a wide variety of approaches, empirical and theoretical, to the study of the formation of expectations. Surveys of consumer and business behavior, theories of statistical induction, stochastic learning theories, and theories of concept formation have all been converging on this problem area.

The very complexity that has made a theory of the decision-making process essential has made its construction exceedingly difficult. Most approaches have been piecemeal—now focused on the criteria of choice, now on conflict of interest, now on the formation of expectations. It seemed almost utopian to suppose that we could put together a model of adaptive man that would compare in completeness with the simple model of classical economic man. The sketchiness and incompleteness of the newer proposals has been urged as a compelling reason for clinging to the older theories, however inadequate they are admitted to be.

The modern digital computer has changed the situation radically. It provides us with a tool of research—for formulating and testing theories—whose power is commensurate with the complexity of the phenomena we seek to understand. Although the use of computers to build theories of human behavior is very recent, it has already led to concrete results in the simulation of higher mental processes. As economics finds it more and more necessary to understand and explain disequilibrium as well as equilibrium, it will find an increasing use for this new tool and for communication with its sister sciences of psycology and sociology.

REFERENCES

1. G. R. Andlinger, "Business Games—Play One," Harvard Bus. Rev., Apr. 1958, 36, 115-25.
2. K. J. Arrow, "Alternative Approaches to the Theory of Choice in Risk-Taking Situations," Econometrica, Oct. 1951, 19, 404-37.
3. K. J. Arrow, T. E. Harris, and J. Marschak, "Optimal Inventory Policy," Econometrica, July 1951, 19, 250-72.
4. K. J. Arrow and M. Nerlove, "A Note on Expectations and Stability," Econometrica, Apr. 1958, 26, 297-305.
5. K. J. Arrow, "Utilities, Attitudes, Choices," Econometrica, Jan. 1958, 26, 1-23.
6. D. Bakan, "Learning and the Principle of Inverse Probability," Psych. Rev.," Sept. 1953, 60, 360-70.
7. A. Bavelas, "A Mathematical Model for Group Structures," Applied Anthropology, Summer 1948, 7, 16-30.
8. M. Beckmann, "Decision and Team Problems in Airline Reservations," Econometrica, Jan. 1958, 26, 134-45
9. R. Bellman, Dynamic Programming. Princeton 1957.
10. H. R. Bowen, The Business Enterprise as a Subject for Research. New York 1955.
11. E. H. Bowman and R. B. Fetter, Analysis for Production Management. Homewood, Ill., 1957.
12. M. J. Bowman, ed., Expectations, Uncertainty, and Business Behavior. New York 1958.
13. H. Brems, "Response Lags and Nonprice Competition," in Bowman [12], Ch. 10, pp. 134-43.

14. J. Bruner, J. J. Goodnow and G. A. Austin, *A Study of Thinking.* New York 1956.

15. R. R. Bush and F. Mosteller, *Stochastic Models for Learning.* New York 1955.

16. C. W. Churchman, R. L. Ackoff and E. L. Arnoff, *Introduction to Operations Research.* New York 1957.

17. W. G. Cochran, *Sampling Techniques.* New York 1953.

18. R. M. Cyert and J. G. March, "Organizational Structure and Pricing Behavior in an Oligopolistic Market," *Am. Econ. Rev.,* Mar. 1955, *45,* 129-39.

19. ――― and ―――, "Organizational Factors in the Theory of Oligopoly," *Quart. Jour. Econ.,* Feb. 1956, *70,* 44-64.

20. W. Darcovich, "Evaluation of Some Naive Expectations Models for Agricultural Yields and Prices," in Bowman [12], Ch. 14, pp. 199-202.

21. D. Davidson and P. Suppes, *Decision Making: An Experimental Approach.* Stanford 1957.

22. D. C. Dearborn and H. A. Simon, "Selective Perception: A Note on the Departmental Identification of Executives," *Sociometry,* June 1958, *21,* 140-44.

22a. J. S. Earley, "Marginal Policies of 'Excellently Managed' Companies," *Am. Econ. Rev.,* Mar. 1956, *66,* 44-70.

23. W. Edwards, "The Theory of Decision Making," *Psych. Bull.,* Sept. 1954, *51,* 380-417.

24. R. Eisner, "Expectations, Plans, and Capital Expenditures," in Bowman [12], Ch. 12, 165-88.

25. J. Feldman, "A Theory of Binary Choice Behavior," Carnegie Inst. of Tech., Grad. Sch. Indus. Admin., Complex Information Processing Working Paper No. 12, rev., May 5, 1958. Unpublished ditto.

26. B. de Finetti "La prevision: ses lois logiques, ses sources subjectives," *Annales Inst. Henri Poincare,* 1937, *7,* 1-68.

27. M. Friedman, *Essays in Positive Economics.* Chicago 1953.

28. ―――, *A Theory of the Consumption Function.* New York 1956.

29. I. Friend, "Critical Evaluation of Surveys of Expectations, Plans, and Investment Behavior," in Bowman [12], Ch. 13, pp. 189-98.

30. J. K. Galbraith, *American Capitalism: The Concept of Countervailing Power.* Boston 1952.

31. H. L. Gelernter and N. Rochester, "Intelligent Behavior in Problem-Solving Machines," *IBM Jour. Research and Develop.,* Oct. 1958, *2,* 336-45.

32. N. Georgescu-Roegen, "The Nature of Expectation and Uncertainty" in Bowman [12], Ch. 1, pp. 11-29.

33. G. L. Godwin, "Digital Computers Tap Out Designs for Large Motors—Fast," *Power,* Apr. 1958.

34. Z. Griliches, "Hybrid Corn: An Exploration in the Economics of Technological Change," *Econometrica,* Oct. 1957, *25,* 501-22.

35. H. Guetzkow and H. A. Simon, "The Impact of Certain Communication

Nets in Task Oriented Groups," *Management Sci.*, July 1955, *1*, 233-50.

36. B. F. Haley, ed., *A Survey of Contemporary Economics*, Vol. II. Homewood, Ill. 1952.

37. S. P. Hayes, "Some Psychological Problems of Economics," *Psych. Bull.*, July 1950, *47*, 289-330.

38. C. C. Holt, F. Modigliani and H. A. Simon, "A Linear Decision Rule for Production and Employment Scheduling," *Management Sci.*, Oct. 1955, *2*, 1-30.

39. G. Katona, *Psychological Analysis of Economic Behavior*. New York 1951.

40. ———, "Rational Behavior and Economic Behavior," *Psych. Rev.*, July 1953, *60*, 307-18.

41. H. J. Leavitt, "Some Effects of Certain Communication Patterns on Group Performance," *Jour. Abnormal and Soc. Psych.*, Feb. 1951, *46*, 38-50.

42. K. Lewin, and others, "Level of Aspiration," in J. McV. Hunt, *Personality and the Behavior Disorders*, New York 1944, pp. 333-78.

43. R. D. Luce and H. Raiffa, *Games and Decisions*. New York 1957.

44. R. Mack, "Business Expectations and the Buying of Materials," in Bowman [12], Ch. 8, pp. 106-18.

45. J. G. March and H. A. Simon, *Organizations*. New York 1958.

46. J. Marschak, "Elements for a Theory of Teams," *Management Sci.*, Jan. 1955, *1*, 127-37.

47. K. O. May, "Intransitivity, Utility, and the Aggregation of Preference Patterns," *Econometrica*, Jan. 1954, *22*, 1-13.

48. F. Modigliani and R. E. Brumberg, "Utility Analysis and the Consumption Function," in K. K. Kurihara, *Post Keynesian Economics*, New Brunswick, N.J., 1954, pp. 388-436.

49. F. Mosteller and P. Nogee, "An Experimental Measurement of Utility," *Jour. Pol. Econ.* Oct. 1951, *59*, 371-404.

50. J. von Neumann and O. Morgenstern, *Theory of Games and Economic Behavior*. Princeton 1947.

51. A. Newell and H. A. Simon, "The Logic Theory Machine," *IRE Transactions of Information Theory*, Sept. 1956, IT-2, 61-79.

52. A. Newell, J. C. Shaw and H. A. Simon, "Empirical Explorations of the Logic Theory Machine," *Proceedings of the Western Joint Computer Conference, Feb. 26-28, 1957*, pp. 218-30.

53. ———, ———, ———, "Elements of a Theory of Human Problem Solving," *Psych. Rev.* May 1958, *65*, 151-66.

54. ———, ———, ———, "Chess-Playing Programs and the Problem of Complexity," *IBM Jour. Research and Develop.*, Oct. 1958, *2*, 320-35.

55. A. G. Papandreou, "Some Basic Problems in the Theory of the Firm," in Haley [36], Ch. 5, pp. 183-222.

56. M. J. Peck, "Marginal Analysis and the Explanation of Business Behavior Under Uncertainty," in Bowman [12], Ch. 9, pp. 119-33.

57. F. P. Ramsey, "Truth and Probability," in the *Foundations of Mathematics and Other Logical Essays*, London 1931, pp. 156-98.

57a. A. M. Rose, "A Study of Irrational Judgments," *Jour. Pol. Econ.*, Oct. 1957, *65*, 394-402.

58. L. J. Savage, *The Foundations of Statistics*. New York 1954.

59. T. C. Schelling, "Bargaining, Communication, and Limited War," *Jour. Conflict Resolution*, Mar. 1957, *1*, 19-36.

60. ———, "An Essay on Bargaining," *Am. Econ. Rev.*, June 1956, *46*, 281-306.

61. S. Siegel, "Level of Aspiration and Decision Making," *Psych. Rev.*, July 1957, *64*, 253-62.

62. H. A. Simon, "Dynamic Programming Under Uncertainty with a Quadratic Criterion Function," *Econometrica*, Jan. 1956, *24*, 74-81.

63. ———, *Administrative Behavior*. New York 1957.

64. ———, *Models of Man*. New York 1957.

65. ———, "The Role of Expectations in an Adaptive or Behavioristic Model," in Bowman [12], Ch. 3, pp. 49-58.

66. H. A. Simon and C. P. Bonini, "The Size Distribution of Business Firms," *Am. Econ. Rev.*, Sept. 1958, *48*, 607-17.

67. H. Theil, *Economic Forecasts and Policy*. Amsterdam 1958.

68. L. L. Thurstone, "The Indifference Function," *Jour. Soc. Psych.* May 1931, *2*, 139-67.

69. A. Vazsonyi, *Scientific Programming in Business and Industry*. New York 1958.

70. A. Wald, *Statistical Decision Functions*. New York 1950.

71. T. Wilson and P. W. S. Andrews, *Oxford Studies in the Price Mechanism*. Oxford 1951.

7.7
Economics and Psychology

Herbert A. Simon

INTRODUCTION

In discussing the mutual relations of psychology and economics, I shall generally use psychological categories to divide the analysis. After considering the extent to which the two fields have areas of common interest, the next three sections are concerned with the motivation of the consumer, of the producer or entrepreneur, and of the employee, respectively. There follows a discussion of *oligopoly* (competition among the few) viewed as a conflict phenomenon. The sixth section reviews the cognitive aspects of economic behavior, including some important recently proposed modifications in the characterization of rational economic action.

The relations between psychology and economics run both ways. We are not concerned merely with possible applications of psychological methods *to* economics, but equally with the use of economic theory and data about economic behavior *in* psychology.

Economic behavior, family behavior, political behavior, and organizational behavior are all forms of human behavior. Each can be explained partly in relatively general terms that cut across these categories, and partly in terms that apply only to a particular area of behavior. The fruitfulness of the interaction between economics and other social sciences hinges on whether the same mechanisms operate in all these areas of behavior, and on how far human behavior in one area is relevant for testing theories in the others. The question is a pragmatic one that has to be asked and reasked as the sciences of man develop, and as our understanding of their interrelationship deepens.

The Subspecies of Economic Man

Psychology enters economics through the characteristics that are postulated for the several subspecies of economic man. These subspecies include (1) the buyer or seller of commodities in a market, (2) the entrepreneur or producer, (3) the consumer, and (4) the worker. In certain areas of economic theory the categories overlap, but they are convenient for classifying and examining economic man.

We must look first at the distinction between producer and consumer. When we understand this, we can study the motivations of each kind of economic man, and then the cognitive aspects of his behavior.

The separation of producer and consumer. It is not strictly accurate to say that in economic theory there are producers and consumers. Each person is, of course, assumed to be both, but each role is kept rather distinct from the other. The line between them is defined by the clock: during the working day, economic man is a producer; during the remainder of the twenty-four hours, he is a consumer.

Interactions between producer and consumer. In a strict version of the theory, there are only two possibilities of interaction between John Doe, producer, and John Doe, consumer. First, the length of the work day—and hence, the time boundary between his two roles—may depend on an economic decision that weighs the utility of the income obtainable by working longer against the disutility of substituting work for leisure. This decision is an essential part of any economic theory that seeks to explain the length of the work week.

Second, when he makes decisions as a consumer, John Doe's income is one determinant of his spending and saving behavior. Theories of consumer choice take income as a given, determined by the production segment of the economy.

The masters of classical economic theory were well aware that separating producer from consumer, and vice versa, oversimplified the facts of the real world—but still permitted a tolerable approximation to human behavior throughout most of the economic sphere. Alfred Marshall, for example, was careful to discuss the possible "psychic income" that the entrepreneur received from his activity, and was also quite aware that the daily work activity of the laborer might alter his tastes, and hence his utility function [39; 63, chap. 15]. Ricardo assumed that, in the long run, wages must sink to a subsistence level; hence, the wage rate might really be regarded as a "marginal cost of producing labor" [63, chap. 6]. In the Ricardian theory, the consumer was almost swallowed by the producer.

A few important economic theorists have rejected all or most of this classical analysis—Veblen and John R. Commons being prominent examples. The vast majority of contemporary economic theorists may be regarded, however, as disciples of the classical tradition; and, like most disciples, they sometimes ignore or underemphasize the qualifications that the masters were careful to acknowledge. In extreme cases, the result has been to change economics from an empirical science to a vast tautology in which entrepreneurs maximize profit by definition—for profit is defined as "that which entrepreneurs maximize"—and consumers maximize utility by definition—for the same reason.

The other subspecies. I have mentioned four subspecies of economic man. One of these is the consumer, who tends not to be further differentiated in the theory. On the production side of the economy, however, the distinction between the entrepreneur and the worker is significant. About the buyer and seller, little needs to be said except that they observe the classical maxim "Buy cheap and sell dear." For the rest, they do not require separate discussion. I have omitted the investor as a separate subspecies. As a person who saves, his behavior is part of that of the consumer. As a person who lends to others, he is buyer and seller of the services of capital. As a person who holds the residual equity in a business in anticipation of profit, he is an entrepreneur.

What distinguishes the worker from the entrepreneur is that the former sells to the latter the right to apply his time and effort during working hours to the goals of the enterprise [55]. In agreeing to accept authority in the workplace, the laborer's productive services become "disembodied" from him, so to speak, and are turned over to the entrepreneur. In terms of this distinction, the hired executive, however exalted his position in the administrative hierarchy, is a worker and not an entrepreneur. We shall see that economists have become increasingly uneasy with this classification of roles—both with its factual accuracy and with its economic consequences, if accurate.

The Goals of Economic Science

Economics can be defined as the science that describes and predicts the behavior of the various kinds of economic man I have mentioned. This definition, while perhaps literally correct, conveys a false impression of the principal goals and focus in the literature of economics.

Work in economics may be classified as dealing with (1) the economy or industries as a whole (*macroeconomics*), or behavior of the individual economic man and individual firm (*microeconomics*); or (2) description of the economy and economic behavior within it, or norms either for purposes of public policy (*normative macroeconomics*) or advice to the consumer or businessman (*normative microeconomics*).

The dominant viewpoint in economics has been that of normative macroeconomics. Descriptive macroeconomics is, of course, the essential basis for policy prescription—but the specific research emphases have been determined in considerable part by relevance to policy (e.g., business-cycle theory). Normative microeconomics, while it has only been very recently cultivated on any extensive scale, is now a flourishing area of economic research having many contacts with statistical decision theory and other new areas, such as "management science," "logistics," and "operations research."

Economists have usually been interested in descriptive microeconomics—understanding the behavior of individual economic agents—only to the extent necessary to provide a foundation for macroeconomics. Hence, economic research at the microlevel has stemmed from a recognition that some aspect of the economy could be understood only by explaining a particular sector of individual behavior. We shall see this mechanism operating with particular clarity when we come to the topic of expectations.

Two economic principles operate to keep at a minimum the macro-economist's concern with individual behavior [6, pp. 6–8]. The first is the assumption of objective rationality, which permits strong predictions to be made about human behavior without the painful necessity of observing people. The second is the assumption of competition, for where competition prevails, the individuals and firms that behave in conformity with the principle of rationality will survive at the expense of the others. Hence, the classical economic theory of markets with perfect competition and rational agents is deductive theory that requires almost no contact with empirical data—once the underlying assumptions are accepted or verified—to establish its propositions.

This preoccupation of economists with the economy as a whole (or with normative rules for individual agents), and the sealing off of macro- from microphenomena by the mechanisms of rationality and competition help to explain why there has been little interaction between economists and psychologists, and little dependence by either upon the literature of the other field. As we proceed, we shall consider how far this independence of economics from the behavioral sciences is justified by the present state of knowledge in these fields.

Our task, then, is to explore what has been a no man's land between economics and behavioral science—the area of descriptive microeconomics. Of course, we are not the first explorers and we shall be guided by what has already been learned of the territory—particularly by the economists who are usually called "institutionalists." The assumptions of economic theory that have been most challenged are its motivational assumptions—particularly the consistency of preferences of humans and their exclusive preoccupation with monetary rewards. In fact, there has been perhaps an excessive preoccupation with motivation and insufficient attention to the cognitive aspects of economic behavior. Hence, I shall pay particular attention to the psychological study of the limits of humans —regarded as learning and information-processing organisms—in their capacities for rational choice.

MOTIVATION: THE CONSUMER

I shall discuss separately the motivation of the consumer and the motivation of the producer, taking up the consumer first. A first section describes the apparatus—based on the concept of utility function—used by the economist to discuss consumer behavior. The second section explores psychology to determine what concepts in that field, if any, correspond to the economist's "utility." A third section considers the economist's interest in consumer behavior and the possible relevance of psychological research in answering his questions.

The Utility Function

The fundamental postulate in microeconomics about the consumer is that he possesses a *utility function*. This is roughly equivalent to saying that, for any pair of alternatives of action presented to him, he can tell which he prefers. In some variants of the theory, alternatives are assumed to be presented in the form of "bundles of commodities"; in others, as alternative courses of action with consequences attached.

For example, F. Modigliani and E. Brumberg [41] have developed a theory of consumption and saving that assumes that each consumer estimates the present value of his expected future stream of income; he then chooses among all possible time patterns of saving and spending consistently with his assumption. The consumer, in this theory is assumed to be able to ascertain his preferences among these alternative streams of spending and saving.

Cardinal and ordinal utility.[2] There has been much discussion as to whether a *cardinal* utility function should be postulated, or only an *ordinal* function. Suppose that we assign the utility x_1 to one of the consumer's alternatives, and the utility x_2 to another where x_1 is greater than x_2 and the first alternative is the one he prefers. We say that the utility function is *ordinal* if the numbers x_1 and x_2 could equally well be replaced by any numbers y_1 and y_2, such that y_1 is greater than y_2. The set of functions y that have this property in relation to the function x are called the *monotonic increasing transformations* of x. By "equally well," we mean that the new function y leads to exactly the same predictions of the consumer's behavior as the function x.

Suppose, on the contrary, that only *linear transformations* of x preserve all the properties of the consumer's behavior

$$y_i = ax_i + b$$

where a is a positive constant and b is an arbitrary constant. In this case, the quantity of utility attached to alternatives is uniquely defined, except for the unit of measurement a and the zero point of the scale, fixed by b.

---

[2] A rather comprehensive discussion of the literature and issues on the topics considered in this and the following section will be found in Ward Edwards [22]. While I have departed from Professor Edward's interpretations in a number of particulars, the analysis that follows owes a great deal to his review. See also Arrow's chapter in this volume and his review [2].

It is defined to just the same extent that temperature is defined by the Fahrenheit and centigrade scales. When utility is defined up to a linear transformation, we say that the utility function is *cardinal*.

Let us suppose that four alternatives are open to a consumer. If he has only an ordinal utility function, then a statement such as "The first alternative has greater utility than the third," is meaningful; but a statement such as "The advantage of the first alternative over the second is greater than the advantage of the third over the fourth," is not meaningful. For, by monotonic transformations of the utility scale, we can make the difference in utility between one pair of alternatives greater or less, as we please, than the difference between another pair of alternatives.

It follows that, if utility is ordinal, statements about increasing or decreasing marginal utility[3] are meaningless, i.e., we cannot say that a man gets more or less utility from his sixth dollar than from his one million and sixth. Conversely, it can be shown that if such statements are meaningful, then—implicitly or explicitly—a cardinal utility function has been defined.

Until about a decade ago, there was a tendency to prefer the ordinal function on grounds of parsimony and because Slutsky, Hicks, and other economists had demonstrated that no significant proposition in the accepted theory of consumer choice depended on the cardinal measurement of utility. This trend was reversed in 1944 with the publication by J. von Neumann and O. Morgenstern of *The Theory of Games and Economic Behavior* [62]. Up to that time, the theory of consumer choice had been concerned primarily with choice where no uncertainty about future events was involved. Von Neumann and Morgenstern treated the more general case where uncertainty was admitted. They showed that if a decision maker could make consistent choices among uncertain prospects (e.g., lottery tickets at various odds for various bundles of commodities), then cardinal utilities could be assigned to the commodity bundles after observing a sufficient variety of such choices [see also 34, 38, 48a].

The Von Neumann-Morgenstern proposal provided cardinal utility with the same operational status that had previously been held by ordinal utility—utilities could be measured simply by observing acts of choice. Further study has shown that, where uncertain prospects are involved, there is an important interaction between subjective probabilities and cardinal utilities; to measure either one operationally calls for an experimental design that, in effect, permits the measurement of both. In the next paragraphs we shall consider this point more fully.

---

[3] The *marginal* utility of a commodity or money is the amount the utility will be increased by an increase of one unit in the amount of the commodity or money; that is, it is the first derivative of utility with respect to the other variable.

Utility and subjective probability. To understand the issues involved in utility measurement and their implications for psychology, let us consider them in a psychophysical framework. We confront a subject with a number of alternatives (e.g., we offer him any one of several phonograph records or, as suggested above, a choice among lottery tickets, each having different odds and different payoffs) and we observe the choices he makes. We wish to construct scales to measure the probabilities he has assigned to the occurrence of the various possible outcomes and the utilities he attaches to them.

Now if there were *objective* probabilities attached to each of the possible outcomes, and if the subject accepted these probabilities as the basis for his choices, then we would be faced with a straightforward task of constructing a utility scale. However, we must consider the possibility that there are no objective probabilities attached to events or that, if there are, they are not identical with the subjective probabilities that the subject himself attaches to the same events. A subject may prefer a particular risky alternative because one of the possible outcomes has a low subjective probability but a very high utility, or because this same outcome is judged to have a high probability of occurrence but only a moderately high utility.

It is not at all obvious that this interacting expectational-preference system can be analyzed into its components, but a rigorous formal examination of the question shows that in fact it can be. If we propose an appropriate set of alternatives to the subject, we can measure operationally both his probability estimates and his utility.[4]

There is one important "if" to be attached to this statement—an "if" involved in all psychophysical measurement. The scales can be measured operationally *provided that* the subject can make consistent choices. For example, no utility scale would be compatible with a preference for *A* over *B*, for *B* over *C*, and for *C* over *A*. By adopting a statistical viewpoint (i.e., percentage of trials in which *A* is preferred to *B*), we can weaken somewhat the requirements of consistency, but basically the possibility of constructing such a scale hinges on the consistency of the subject, and his consistency hinges on the transitivity and the stability of his choices [33, 35].

Thus the issue has been shifted. The question is no longer one of cardinal versus ordinal utility. If a utility scale can be defined, the additional assumption that it can be defined for choices among uncertain prospects guarantees its cardinality. The question now is whether a utility scale "exists" at all—is the behavior of consumers over the range of situa-

---

[4] This was first shown some decades ago by the English philosopher Frank Ramsey [48], but his proposal was not clearly understood and was largely neglected until the rediscovery of cardinal utility by von Neumann and Morgenstern.

tions relevant for economics sufficiently consistent and are consumer choices sufficiently transitive, to make the concept of utility empirically meaningful?

Joining the issue in these terms has given it interest for both economists and psychologists—and a number of philosophers and mathematical statisticians as well—with the result that several empirical investigations of these questions are going forward at the present time [an important study is 18; 38, including references]. The earliest investigation predates the present surge of interest; it was an attempt in 1931 by the psychologist L. L. Thurstone [61] to establish the ordinal utility function of a single subject.

The evidence available at the present moment is too scanty to permit very definite conclusions. The following observations are at least consistent with the experimental results:

1. Under a number of experimental conditions, significant differences can be observed between the probability estimates used by the subjects (subjective probabilities) and the objective probabilities known to the experimenter.

2. A fairly high degree of consistency is observed in choices when the payoff is in money; consistency is much lower with multidimensional payoffs (e.g., choice among phonograph records or among marriageable young ladies).

Psychological Analogs of Utility

The term "utility" has until recently had little currency in psychology —either because psychologists had not found a use for the concept, or because it was used, but under an alias. The truth lies somewhere between these extremes.

A construct like the utility function is needed to explain choice in the face of complex alternatives when the subject is trying to select the "best" alternative. If the alternatives can all be scaled along a single dimension (e.g., are all measured in money), or if the subject is merely looking for a "good" alternative, a theory of choice can be constructed that dispenses with a utility scale [57]. In *most* laboratory experiments where the subject is faced with a choice among alternatives, the situation is one of reward versus no reward, and even where alternative rewards are present, the consistency of the subject's preferences is not usually tested over a wide range of circumstances or a long stretch of time.

Contemporary work in the behavioral sciences aimed at defining and measuring "values" will undoubtedly raise questions of the relative strength of values as soon as attempts are made to predict behavior from a knowledge of a subject's value profile. Since little has yet been done empirically to make the jump from verbal attitudes about values to their behavioral consequences, this issue has not yet been faced. When the time arrives for dealing with it, social psychologists will find that the basic issues are precisely the ones that have arisen in the definition and measurement of utility.

Lewin, in his theory of "valences," treated choice with competing rewards and punishments as analogous to the situation in physics where a number of nonparallel forces converge on the same body. If the analogy were carried out strictly, the net valences of the Lewinian theory would have the formal properties of utilities. Lewin and those who have used his theoretical formulations as the basis for empirical work have not actually followed this path to its conclusion. If there are attached to a particular course of action *both* a large reward and a smaller punishment, for example, Lewinians and most other psychologists would predict that behavior will be different from what it would be if only a small reward— representing the difference between the original reward and the punishment—were attached to the action [31]. In contrast, utility theory would predict that, corresponding to any combination of punishments and rewards attached to an action, there would exist an exactly equivalent simple net punishment or reward.

We see, then, that although the Lewinian valence bears some resemblance to utility; the actual properties attributed to it on the basis of empirical study are quite different. The empirical facts—rather consistently observed with both human and animal subjects—are these: Choices bearing mixed consequences and choices where all alternatives have unpleasant consequences represent *conflict* situations for the subject, and behavior in a conflict situation is qualitatively different from behavior when conflict is absent [57]. For example, one kind of behavior has no place in classical utility theory, but it is frequently observed in conflict situations—this is the subject's refusal to accept the alternatives as given and his search for new alternatives [see 15 for an application of this notion in the theory of the firm]. Where the conflict is stronger, various kinds of neurotic behavior come into evidence—fixation, regression, aggression, withdrawal, and so on.

The empirical findings on choice in conflict situations challenge the validity of the utility function as a basis for conceptualizing decision-making behavior. Any microeconomic description of behavior that purports to fit empirical data will have to deal with this evidence. The study of choice under conflict may prove to be even more fruitful for reexamining the utility concept than the experiments on choice under uncertainty that were mentioned earlier.

The Economist's Interest in Utility

Returning now to macroeconomics, we may ask how much of the theory of utility and of consumer behavior is really needed to explain the operation of the economy. The answer is that the macroeconomist is ordinarily rather uninterested in detailed information about the shapes of consumers' utility functions—either the functions of individuals or aggregated functions. The broad aspects of consumer behavior with which he is actually concerned are discussed in the following paragraphs.

Consumer rationality. An important policy application of economic theory is to determine under what circumstances economic mechanisms lead to an efficient allocation of resources. This is the main topic of the branch of economic theory known as welfare economics. The important postulate about consumers required for welfare economics is rationality—that consumers maximize utility, that they attempt to allocate their income so as to purchase—from all possible baskets—the basket that will give them the greatest satisfaction. Hence the welfare economist has ordinarily no particular interest in the shape of the utility function, but a strong interest in its existence as the criterion of consumer choice.

Elasticity of demand. In economics, the consumer enters the market through his demand schedule—the schedule of quantities of a commodity he will buy at various prices. The summation of these quantities for all consumers gives the market-demand schedule. For many applications, it must be assumed that the market-demand schedule has a negative slope—that the quantity demanded decreases as price increases. For other purposes, it may be necessary to know the elasticity of demand—how sensitively the quantity demanded depends on price. The tendency even in these matters is to deal in generalities; only occasionally is the economist concerned with the numerical measurement of the elasticities of demand for specific commodities.

Many attempts have been made to derive certain characteristics of the demand schedule by deductive reasoning from the theory of consumer choice. However, where it is necessary to measure the elasticity of demand numerically, the usual procedure is to infer the elasticity from direct measurements of quantities purchased in the market at various prices. Hence the empirical study of demand has rested much more on the direct accumulation and analysis of data than on inferences from underlying psychological principles [50].

Saving and spending. In the modern post-Keynesian theory of the business cycle and national income, the consumer's decision as to what proportion of his income he will spend and what proportion he will save is of very great importance. The number of cents he will spend out of each additional dollar of income is the "marginal propensity to consume" of Keynes. In certain versions of Keynesian theory, one crucial assumption is that spending increases less than proportionately as income increases. Much effort has been devoted, over the last decade, to testing this assumption [29, chaps. 7, 8].

On the one hand, there have been attempts to measure spending and saving behavior by obtaining empirical data from consumers or analyzing secondary data from the economy. On the other hand, there have been attempts to deduce the spending and saving behavior of the consumer from the theory of rational consumer choice. The first course involves no particular framework of theory and, while it may yield data of interest to psychologists, it has borrowed little or nothing from psychology.

The second course, the deduction of the theory of saving from the theory of consumer choice, has also evolved almost independently of work in psychology. It illustrates the characteristic approach of the economist to individual behavior and the reason why he can formulate his assumptions with so little dependence on empirical observation (even though he may use aggregative data to test the consequences derived from his assumptions).

Modigliani and Brumberg [41], assume that the only motive for saving is retirement income and that the consumer adjusts his saving to give him a level annual expenditure over his lifetime. During periods of high income, he saves; during periods of low or no income, he dissaves. These are plausible assumptions—at least as approximations—and it is their introspective plausibility that the economist takes as his justification for adopting them. From these assumptions, together with assumptions as to how income expectations are formed and data on length of life and length of adult earning period, numerical estimates can be made of the fraction of total income that will be saved—that is to say, the saving-consumption function can be deduced from these assumptions. Up to the present time, the model has held up fairly well in explaining the actually observed data on consumer expenditures and savings.

Similar approaches have been used by economists to explain the fact —or supposed fact—that some individuals both gamble in lotteries and buy insurance [22, p. 393]. The explanation—like that outlined above— consists in showing that circumstances exist (i.e., can be postulated) under which the behavior in question *would be* rational behavior for a consumer bent on maximizing his utility. It is quite uncharacteristic of the economic theorist to test his explanation further by studying the consumer's attitudes or subjecting him to experimental situations. On the other hand, the psychological assumptions that underlie theories of this kind are not difficult to identify, and there are many possibilities here for direct testing by psychologists of the economic models.

Expectations.[5]   The third aspect of the consumer's behavior in which the macroeconomist has substantial interest is the formation of expectations. In a world of uncertainty, a theory cannot make a consumer's expenditure depend on future income, but only on *expectations* of future

[5] Expectations really belong to the cognitive rather than the motivational sphere, but it is convenient to discuss them here to round out our picture of contemporary research. For a panorama of recent approaches to the theory of expectations, see Bowman [7].

income. Hence the predictions of the theory will depend on assumptions about the formation of expectations.

Over the past decade, considerable data have been accumulated on consumers' plans and expectations from the Survey of Consumer Finances conducted for the Board of Governors of the Federal Reserve System by the Survey Research Center of the University of Michigan [7; 29, chap. 5]. These and similar data obtained by others begin to inform us to what extent consumers plan their expenditures in advance and for what kinds of purchases; what expectations they hold about their own income, and how well the expenditure plans predict actual behavior. It can hardly be said that these data have been linked with psychological generalizations from other areas of behavior; at present, they simple stand as brute facts.

Marketing. Thus far we have left out of account the study of consumer behavior that has been carried out for its practical utility to the business firm—market research. The literature on selling and advertising has generally had a closer tie to psychology than has the economic literature on consumer demand. There have been attempts to apply principles of motivation and learning to the design of effective selling procedures.

The validity of general psychological principles applied to marketing behavior has had limited empirical test. There have been, for example, a number of controlled experiments comparing the relative effectiveness of different advertising copy or methods. An interesting development of the past few years has been the application of projective techniques to the study of consumer motivation. An early study of this sort, carried out by Mason Haire, showed that housewives had a quite different perception of an (otherwise unidentified) woman who bought instant coffee from a woman who bought ground coffee.

Much of the data of market research does not see the light of day, since it is gathered and analyzed for proprietary purposes. Hence, in spite of the great amount of discussion in the marketing field concerning "motivation research" and other applications of psychology to marketing; the number of good empirical studies in the literature is not large.

An important study, which may be a prototype of research to come on innovation and consumer adoption of new commodities, was carried out by the Bureau of Applied Social Research at Columbia University to determine the influence processes involved in the adoption of a new antibiotic by physicians [13]. While this study will hardly fit within the traditional static framework of utility theory, it points the way to possible approaches to the dynamics of consumer choice.

Summary: Consumer Motivation

Macroeconomics does not require for most purposes a detailed theory of consumer choice. The utility function has been the central theoretical construct here, but only a few qualitative features of the function are required for the theories derived from it. Moreover, much of the work on consumer demand—and particularly empirical work—is independent of the concept of utility.

The predisposition of economists to deduce behavior from assumptions of rationality and other "plausible" assumptions about behavior has limited the interaction of economics and psychology in the area of consumer behavior. The greatest potentialities for work of mutual value to the two disciplines lie at present in (1) testing the assumptions of utility theory and the existence of a cardinal utility function, (2) exploring the implications of behavior in conflict situations for economic theory, (3) extending the study of the spending-saving behavior of consumers and the formation of consumer expectations, and (4) extending the study of consumer market behavior in relation to individual products and specific marketing techniques.

MOTIVATION: THE ENTREPRENEUR

The entrepreneur is the man who holds the residual equity in the business firm. After all the other factors of production—including interest on invested capital—have been paid, his share is the remainder, be it large or small. Most important for the theory, he is the man who controls the decision variables of the basic productive unit, the firm.

Just as the central assumption about consumption is that the consumer strives to maximize his utility, so the central assumption about production is that the entrepreneur strives to maximize his residual share—his profit [47, pp. 205–210]. But the assumption of profit maximization is even more essential to the validity of classical economic theory than the assumption of utility maximization; hence the attack upon and the defense of classical theory has tended to focus upon the former postulate.

The hypothesis that the entrepreneur seeks to maximize his profit is a simple corollary to the general postulate of economic rationality. Attacks on the hypothesis have been frequent, and they range over many issues [29, chap. 9; 47]:

1. The theory leaves ambiguous whether short-run or long-run profit is to be maximized. If long-run profit is the criterion, then it is extremely difficult—because of the uncertainty in long-run consequences of action —to determine what course of action maximizes profit or to test whether a particular firm is in fact using the criterion. This is a serious difficulty for both descriptive and normative microeconomics.

2. The entrepreneur may obtain all kinds of "psychic income" from the firm, quite apart from monetary rewards. If he is to maximize his

utility, then he will sometimes balance a loss of profits against an increase in psychic income. For example, the high return from ownership of slum property is sometimes attributed to the negative psychic income attached to such ownership. But if we admit psychic income into the picture, the criterion of profit maximization loses all its definiteness and becomes identical with (and as ambiguous as) utility maximization.

3. The entrepreneur may not care to maximize, but may simply want to earn a return that he regards as "satisfactory." By sophistry and an adept use of the concept of psychic income, the notion of seeking a satisfactory return can be translated into utility maximization—but not in any operational way. As we shall see, the notion of seeking "satisfactory" levels of profits or sales is more meaningfully related to the psychological concept of aspiration levels than to any notion of maximization.

4. Under modern conditions, the equity owners and the active managers of an enterprise are usually separate and distinct groups of persons —the managers are really "labor" and not "entrepreneurs." Under these circumstances, there is no reason to postulate an identity of interests between entrepreneurs and managers or to assume that the latter are motivated to maximize profits.

All of these objections concern motivation; they assume, more or less, that the entrepreneur or the manager *could* aim at profit maximization if he wanted to. We shall see in the section on cognition that there are also serious cognitive questions as to the capacity of economic man to maximize profit, but I shall focus on questions of motivation for the moment.

Few data from psychology outside economics bear directly on the issues at hand. There have been some investigations, however, that are worth mentioning. These fall in two categories: attempts to determine the relative importance of economic and noneconomic motivation and studies of the dynamics of aspiration levels.

In addition to these psychological studies, there have been a number of inquiries directed specifically at these economic issues and carried out primarily by economists. Among these are studies of the formation of expectations by managers and business firms and studies of the making of particular classes of business decisions (pricing decisions, investment decisions, etc.). I shall consider each of these four classes of investigations, the two "psychological" and the two "economic" in turn. In a final part of this section, I shall discuss the identity and conflict of interest between owners and managers.

Economic and Noneconomic Motivation

The past twenty years has seen a strong reaffirmation of the importance of noneconomic as against economic motivation—for employees as well as for managers and entrepreneurs. This is one of the central points—and certainly one of the most widely quoted points—of Barnard's *The Functions of the Executive* [5]. It was earlier emphasized by Veblen and other institutionalists.

It is hard to determine the relative role of noneconomic and economic motivations because we do not have a metric for comparing them. We are really confronted again with the task of constructing a utility function in which monetary gain is one dimension in the commodity space, and status, prestige, power, and all the other things that men are supposed to work for are the other dimensions. Since no one has made the measurements needed to establish the shape of this function, the usual statements about the relative importance of the various motivations are nonoperational. They have about the same semantic status as the assertion "It is later than you think."

Really the situation is not so hopeless if we reject the economists' assumptions, which are implicit above, that there must be some marginal rate of substitution between profit and other goals and that "measuring the importance of the profit motive" is synonymous with measuring this marginal rate of substitution. From an institutionalist point of view, it would be equally satisfactory if we could simply describe the situations where profit would be sacrificed for other goals. Unfortunately, even this descriptive task has not been carried out in any comprehensive fashion. About the best we can say is that enough illustrations of response to other motivations have been collected to rule out the hypothesis that profit maximization (even long-run profit maximization) is an all-encompassing goal of business management. A measure of the "importance" of the deviations remains to be constructed.

Satisficing versus Maximizing

The notion of "satiation" plays no role in classical economic theory. However, in the treatment of motivation in psychology, this concept enters rather prominently. First, there is the widely accepted idea that motivation to act stems from *drives*, and that action terminates when the drive is satisfied. Second, there is the idea that the conditions for satisfaction of a drive are not necessarily fixed, but may be specified by an *aspiration level* that adjusts itself on the basis of experience [32, 52, 57, 60b].

The prevalent psychological treatments of motivation, then, hypothesize that drive satisfaction is an all-or-none phenomenon, but that the boundary between the satisfied and unsatisfied states (the level of aspiration) is variable. If we apply this point of view to the business firm, we would expect its goals to be stated not in terms of maximizing profit, but in terms of reaching a certain level or rate of profit, holding a certain share of the market, a certain level of sales, or the like [15a; 29, chap. 9]. There is considerable empirical evidence—most of it, unfortunately, of an anecdotal kind—that supports this interpretation of the goals of the business firm [21].

Here is one of the most interesting areas of relationship between economics and psychology. First, it does not seem unfeasible to test whether business behavior is governed by maximizing or by satisficing criteria. Second, the economic data required to choose between these hypotheses would extend previous theorizing about aspiration levels to a new area of human behavior.

It has sometimes been argued that the distinction between satisficing and maximizing behavior is not important for economic theory. In the first place, the psychological evidence shows that aspirations tend to adjust to the attainable. Hence, in the long run, the argument runs, the level of aspiration and the attainable maximum will be very close together.

A second argument is that even if some firms behaved in the manner of the aspiration-level hypothesis, they would gradually lose out to the maximizing firms, which would make larger profits and grow more rapidly than the others [1].

Both of these arguments assume that (1) firms know how to go about maximizing if they want to, and (2) the economic environment of firms changes slowly enough that the long-run position of equilibrium will be approached. Both hypotheses are dubious, but their discussion will have to be postponed to a later section where cognitive matters will be considered in detail. If we retain a reasonable skepticism—at least until the evidence is in—toward arguments that lean heavily on long-run equilibriums, then the test of the aspiration-level hypothesis is of substantial interest to economic theory as well as to psychology.

Business Expectations

Business expectations, like consumer expectations, are variables of crucial importance to macroeconomics and—unlike most other psychological concepts—cannot be exorcised from the economic model by assumptions of rationality. A considerable part of business-cycle theory hinges on postulates—most of them constructed in the comfort of armchairs—about the way in which business expectations are formed and how they change under changing environmental circumstances.[6]

Business expectations are currently a very active object of economic research, and several periodic surveys are now being conducted of bus-

---

[6] For an exploration of relations between business forecasting and partial reinforcement situations, see Feldman [23] and Cyert et al. [16].

iness forecasts of business conditions [29, chaps. 9–13]. The current empirical research is of two main kinds:

1. Surveys of businessmen's own forecasts of business conditions in the economy and in their own industries. These are obtained by straightforward questionnaire methods, which assume implicitly that businessmen can and do make such forecasts. In some uses to which the data are put, it is also assumed that these forecasts are used as one basis for businessmen's actions.

2. Studies of business decisions and the role of expectations in these decisions—particularly investment and pricing decisions. These will be the topic of the next paragraphs.

Studies of Business Decisions

I have commented earlier on the significance of Keynesian economics for the empirical study of consumer behavior. The controversy over the correctness of the Keynesian system had a similar impact on the study of business behavior. For one of the heretical doctrines of Keynes was that the amount of investment was very nearly independent of the rate of interest. The debate over this doctrine led to a number of empirical studies in the thirties by a group of Oxford economists who adopted the very direct procedure of asking businessmen whether the rate of interest was an important factor in their investment decisions; they concluded from the answers that it was not. This method of inquiry has been followed in virtually all the studies that have been published dealing with business decision making. A comprehensive list of such studies up to 1950 will be found in Hayes [27].

Stemming from a pioneer study by Hall and Hitch [26], there have also been a number of attempts to determine whether businessmen use marginalist principles in pricing their products,[7] as is predicted by classical theory. Different investigators have returned from their interviews with different conclusions. Hall and Hitch, for example, found average costs to be more significant in determining prices than marginal costs, while Early [21] has found an extensive use of marginalist procedures.

Conflict of Interest

We come finally to the actual or potential conflict of interest between owner and hired manager, a conflict that has been considered at length in the economics literature [47]. Two questions are involved:

1. Is the reward that the top management of modern industrial firms

---

[7] Under classical assumptions, profits will be maximized if the quantity produced is set so that the cost of producing one more unit would just equal the increase in revenue from selling the larger product.

actually receive closely related to the effect of their actions upon the firm's profits?

2. In so far as the correlation between management rewards and company profits is imperfect, what do members of top management in fact maximize?

Gordon [24] was able to show pretty conclusively that the correlation between management rewards and company profits is relatively low. On the second point, the evidence is less clear; it takes us back to some of our earlier questions about measuring the relative strengths of different motivations where there is conflict of interest. A formal comparison between the classical theory of the firm and organizational theories that come out of behavioral science, such as those of Barnard [5] and Simon [54], shows that they differ precisely at this point. Both the economic theories and the organizational theories of the firm assume that the firm will adopt a *viable* course of action, a course that will enable it to satisfy its various groups of participants (customers, investors, employees, suppliers) so that they will continue to participate. In general, any such course of action yields a *surplus*—i.e., income over and above that needed for distribution to the participants. The organizational theories leave indeterminate whether (1) the managers will try to maximize this surplus, or (2) all of it will be captured by the entrepreneur. The classical theory of the firm takes a definite stand on both points, asserting that the firm will be conducted in such a way as to maximize the surplus and that the surplus will go to the entrepreneur [56].

However inconclusive and anecdotal the evidence, most observers are persuaded that the organizational theory provides a more realistic picture of the behavior of large corporations than does the classical theory. The former is also consistent with a satisficing theory of the firm's decision making, while the latter is not.

Perhaps the most interesting psychological aspect of this topic is its connection with role theory. The conclusions of classical economics about the behavior of the firm can be valid in a world in which there is a considerable divorce of management from ownership only if the members of management are willing to play the *role* of profit-maximizing entrepreneurs, even though they do not receive the rewards of the entrepreneur. On the other hand, if the classical conclusions are wrong, then it becomes an empirical question to determine what premises the members of management do, in fact, employ in their decision making. Do they identify with the interests of some particular group of participants (e.g., investors), or do they perceive themselves as arbiters seeking to make a "fair" and acceptable division of the firm's surplus among its various participant's? Again, the answers will have to come out of continuing empirical study of the firm's behavior.

Summary: Entreprenurial Motivation

Over the past twenty years the motivational assertions embedded in the classical theory of the firm have been widely challenged. The challenge has stemmed partly from theory, and partly from a substantial body of data that is far from consistent with the classical theory. First, there has been emphasis on the noneconomic—as contrasted with the economic—motivations of the entrepreneur. Second, there has been argument that firms and individual persons do not maximize, but satisfice. Third, data on actual decision-making processes in firms has failed to confirm the universality or even the prevalence of marginalist principles of choice. Fourth, data on management and ownership has shown that, in large segments of modern business, those who hold active managerial control have no great personal economic inducement to maximize profits.

There has been some resistance among economists to accepting the cogency of the evidence for these assertions—even more resistance to admitting their relevance to normative macroeconomics if they are true. Edward S. Mason, for example, in commenting on Papandreou's essay, "Some Basic Problems in the Theory of the Firm" [47, pp. 221–222], states his defense as follows: "The writer of this critique must confess a lack of confidence in the marked superiority, *for purposes of economic analysis,* of this newer concept of the firm over the older conception of the entrepreneur." The italics are Professor Mason's, and the italicized phrase can be translated—I think without violence—as "for purposes of normative macroeconomics."

The matters discussed in these paragraphs are relevant for business-cycle theory largely for understanding how businessmen form their expectations and how these expectations affect their investment and pricing decisions. This is perhaps the weakest point in the empirical verification of business-cycle theories, and a point at which much on-going empirical work is directed.

The theory of the firm is relevant also for welfare economics—for determining under what circumstances the behavior of the firm will lead to efficient allocation of resources. The departure of the firm's behavior from the classical model vitiates all the conclusions about resource allocation that are derivable from that model when perfect competition is assumed. Hence the indifference of Professor Mason (and numerous other economists) is justified only if the firm's behavior turns out to be about the same in the newer theories as in the old ones. There is no reason so far for supposing that this will be so.

There are other questions of long-run economic policy which have been only slightly investigated in economics and for which an accurate understanding of motivation in the business firm may well have even more important implications than any mentioned thus far. The separation of ownership from control may well affect the risk-taking behavior of the firm. Most commentators on this point—solid evidence is almost completely lacking—assume that "business bureaucrats" will be more conservative in their attitudes toward risk and innovation than entrepreneur-owners. There is no very solid basis in psychological theory for making a definite prediction on this point, and the question can be answered only through empirical work.

MOTIVATION: LABOR

More can be said about the relations of economics and psychology in the area of labor relations than in the two areas previously discussed. By the same token, what has to be said is already well known to the specialists in labor relations, who have been less respectful of disciplinary boundaries than most of their colleagues in psychology and economics. I shall try here to steer a middle course. I shall not attempt a full exposition of the roles of economics, psychology, and sociology in labor economics and industrial relations, but point instead to a few key issues.

The motivation of the employee can be and has been approached from the classical standpoint as a pure question of "labor economics." At the other extreme, the same topic can be and has been approached as a pure question of the psychology of motivation. The field of labor economics and industrial relations is today an area of active communication—although not always complete agreement—for economists, psychologists, and sociologists [14].

The central issues are very similar to those considered in the two previous sections. We are interested in the job-taking and job-leaving behaviors of the employee, in his behavior while employed on the job; and in his activity in and through unions. Numerous predictions can be made about all these segments of behavior if we make the classical assumptions about economic rationality. The classical theory, for example, predicts movement from one job to another in terms of wage-rate differentials, and predicts the absence in equilibrium of differentials in wages for comparable jobs. The classical theory also permits predictions as to how employees will respond to wage incentive schemes—and most of the theorizing about piece rates in the early scientific management movement was thoroughly consistent with classical economic theory.

The empirical evidence, on the other hand, only partly supports these classical predictions. Geographical movements of the labor force, for example, are responsive to many forces other than wage differentials, although the influence of the latter, as one of several factors, is clearly demonstrable. In the matter of wage incentive schemes, employee responses have been shown to be far more complicated and dependent on far more complex relations than can be accounted for by a simple economic calculus. Unfortunately, we have as substitute for the classical model only a mass of empirical specifics that do not permit sharp predictions beyond the particular phenomena to which the data themselves relate. Thus, the situation is similar to that in the area of consumer motivation and entrepreneurial motivation [37].

The Authority Relation

One peculiar feature of the employment relation, which distinguishes it from most other economic arrangements and transactions, is this: The employee sells his "services" to the employer and then becomes a "factor of production" [55]. Here the classical assumption of the separation of production behavior from consumption behavior is clearly open to question.

The economic model of the employee—once the employment bargain has been struck—is that of a passive and neutral agent of production who will accept the authority of the employer. A considerable body of psychological evidence shows that the behavior of employees typically departs from this model of passivity and neutrality in a number of ways [28; 37, chaps. 3, 4]. Among the hypotheses that have been pretty well validated are these:

1. *The Hawthorne effect.* When special attention is given to a group of workers by management (say, by enlisting them in an experimental situation), production is likely to rise independently of changes in actual working conditions.

2. *The interaction hypothesis.* High morale and productivity in organizations are promoted if the employees have opportunities for interaction with each other. Conversely, when the work is organized in such a way as to discourage cooperation, teamwork, or social intercourse, low morale is likely to result.

3. *The participation hypothesis.* Significant changes in human behavior can be brought about rapidly only if the persons who are expected to change participate in deciding what the change shall be and how it shall be made.

4. *The cross-pressures hypothesis.* When the same individual has occasion for frequent and close contact with two or more groups that hold conflicting values and attitudes, he will find himself in internal personal conflict. The conflict is often evidenced by symptoms of frustration—withdrawal, aggressive behavior, and the like.

In view of the prominence of phenomena like these in research data, and in the everyday practice of management as well, there is less tendency to apply the economic calculus to supervisory problems than to most other areas of economic behavior. On the other hand, however significant these phenomena may be for the practice of management, they do not appear to have important implications for macroeconomics. Or to state the conclusion in a more precise way, if this revision of our picture of the employment relation has implications for public policy, these implications cannot be explored via the classical economic model for discussing welfare questions.

Labor Unions

In discussing the employment relation we must give great attention to labor unions. The effect of unions on the relation can be discussed more conveniently in the next section, where we consider the topic of competition among the few. Again, we shall see that the existence of unions provides new reasons for lowering the walls between economics and the other behavioral sciences and for bringing social and political considerations to bear upon an economic relationship.

CONFLICT OF INTEREST: OLIGOPOLY

Economic theory avoids any assumption of common goals and parallel interests among the participants in the economic system. Through the authority relation, employees can agree to accept the goals of their employers as guides to behavior; apart from this, each consumer is assumed to maximize his personal utility, each producer his profit.[8]

The conflict of interests creates no particular problems of theory so long as each participant in the system treats the other participants as parts of his given environment, and doesn't try to predict their behavior and anticipate it. But when this restriction is removed—when it is assumed that a seller takes into account the reactions of buyers to his actions or that each manufacturer predicts the behaviors of his competitors—the precision of prediction of the classical theory vanishes. The only case where the classical theory can then be applied with complete safety is to situations of perfect competition—where the number of competitors is so large that each competitor may safely assume that the market price is a given which is not affected by his own actions. Notice that we are not concerned here with the usual antimonopoly argument that competition is desirable from a welfare standpoint; what we are saying is that competition is an essential condition for unambiguous prediction of behavior from the classical assumptions of economic rationality.

[8] This does not rule out the possibility of nonselfish goals, for one person's pleasure may enter into another person's utility function; but since the utility functions are givens of economic analysis, their content is irrelevant to the theory.

The very assumptions of omniscient rationality that provide the basis for deductive prediction in economics when competition is present lead to ambiguity when they are applied to competition among the few. Awareness of this problem goes back a century to Augustin Cournot, but recognition of its fundamental character and sweeping consequences stems from von Neumann and Morgenstern's *The Theory of Games and Economic Behavior* [62], published in 1944. The central difficulty in competition among the few is familiar to every bridge or poker player: Rational play requires one to outguess one's opponents, but not to be outguessed by them—clearly not a consistent requirement, if it is applied to all the players.

Von Neumann and Morgenstern proposed a solution in the case of a game with two players and a zero-sum payoff—that is, a payoff in which one player would lose what the other won. In this case "omniscient" rationality generally calls for each player to randomize his play in a specified way in order to prevent the opponent from discovering his intentions. If the players accept this definition of rationality and behave this way, then their behavior is predictable at least in an average sense.

But when we attempt to extend the theory to situations that are not zero-sum or that involve more than two players, the ambiguities reappear in new forms (specifically in the form of bargaining among actual or potential coalitions of players), and the theory no longer makes specific predictions of behavior.

A further objection against the theory of games, at least as a descriptive theory, is that it requires of economic man even more fantastic reasoning powers than does classical economic theory. For the elimination of the ambiguities that "outguessing" introduces into prediction, we must seek more realistic assumptions that stem from limitations upon the human capacity for rational calculation [36, chap. 10; 57].

In general, analyses of economic behavior in situations of oligopoly draw at least as heavily upon theories of power and bargaining—initially developed to explain political phenomena—as upon economic theory. This is true of both competition among producers (e.g., the automobile, steel, or aluminum industries) and between unions and employers (particularly industry-wide collective bargaining). This framework does not lead to any more specific predictions of behavior than do other approaches to these phenomena. However, it introduces a greater emphasis upon description and actual observation and is modest in its attempts to derive predictions by deductive reasoning from a few "plausible" premises about human behavior [9, 49, 53].

Four important areas of social science and social policy—two in economics and two more closely related to political science—have as their central concern the phenomena of power and the processes of bargaining, the theory of political parties, labor-management relations, international politics, and oligopoly theory. Any progress in the basic theory applicable to one of these is certain to be almost equally important to the others.

COGNITION: THE CHALLENGE TO RATIONALITY

Up to this point I have emphasized primarily the relations between economics and motivational theory in psychology. It is true that cognitive considerations have not been absent—for example, the formation of expectations by the economic actor—but they have played a secondary role in the discussion. In the present section, cognitive matters will have the central place, while motivation and affect will be considered only as they interact with cognition. This shift in emphasis will allow us to view the relation of economics to psychology from a standpoint suggested by important recent trends in research on both sides of the interdisciplinary boundary.

Classical economics minimized its dependence upon motivational theory in psychology by taking utility maximization (for the consumer) and profit maximization (for the entrepreneur) as the sole motives of economic man. Similarly, economics got along almost without psychological hypotheses about economic man's intellective qualities by assuming him to be "objectively" rational—that is, rational in dealing with a given external environment as viewed by an omniscient being gifted with unlimited powers of computation [54, chap. 4]. Given these basic assumptions, motivational and cognitive, nothing more need be known about economic man to predict his behavior; it suffices to have information about his environment—e.g., the prices in the markets in which he trades, his production function, and so on.

Economists can claim—with considerable justification—that the classical model has had great predictive power in the areas of behavior with which they have been concerned. But economics has been moving steadily into newer areas where the power of the model has never been demonstrated and where its adequacy must be considered anew. Labor economics has been such an area, oligopoly or imperfect competition theory another, decision making under uncertainty a third, and the theory of economic development a fourth. I have already noted some difficulties the theory encountered in these new territories:

1. When the assumptions of perfect competition were removed, even the definition of rationality became ambiguous. New definitions had to be constructed (by no means as "obvious" intuitively as was simple maximization) to extend the theory of rational behavior to bargaining and outguessing situations. Moreover, these new game-theory formula-

tions do not give a univocal prediction of how a rational man would behave.

2. When the assumptions of perfect foresight were removed, the definition of rationality had to be extended in another direction to handle uncertainty about the environment. (There has been a strong tendency, under the influence of game theory, to wrap these two problems into one by treating "nature" as a malevolent opponent. While this solution appeals to some mathematicians and statisticians on aesthetic grounds, its logical or empirical basis is hard to find.)

But extending the classical theory to these new areas requires more than broadening the definition of rationality. In addition, it requires a distinction between the objective environment in which the economic actor "really" lives and the subjective environment that he perceives and to which he responds. When this distinction is made, we can no longer predict his behavior—even if he behaves rationally—from the characteristics of the objective environment; we also need to know something about his perceptual and cognitive processes [57, 58].

The classical model is a theory of a man choosing among fixed and known alternatives to each of which is attached known consequences. When perception and cognition intervene between the decision maker and his objective environment, this model is no longer adequate. Then we need a description of the choice process that recognizes that alternatives are not given but must be sought and a description that takes into account the arduous task of determining what consequences will follow on each of the alternatives [11].

The decision maker's information about his environment is much less than an approximation of the real environment. The term "approximation" implies that the subjective world of the decision maker resembles quite closely the external environment but lacks, perhaps, some fineness of detail. The psychological evidence contradicts this view—the perceived world is fantastically different from the "real" world. The differences involve both omissions and distortions and arise in both perception and inference.

Psychological research has paid most attention to the sins of commission—to the distortions of the external environment in perception and inference. In recent years, experimental work [e.g., Sherif, 51, Asch, 3] has emphasized affect as a cause of distortion. For our purposes, however —understanding the relations of psychology to economics—the sins of *omission* in perception are more important than the sins of *commission*. The decision maker's model of the world encompasses only a minute fraction of all the relevant characteristics of the real environment, and his inferences extract only a minute fraction of all the information that is present, even in his model. Under these circumstances, his choices cannot be predicted from a knowledge of the external environment without a knowledge also of the selective mechanisms that are part of his perceptual and problem-solving processes [37].

Perception is sometimes referred to as a "filter." This term is as misleading as "approximation," and for the same reason: It implies that what comes through into the central nervous system is really quite a bit like what is "out there." In fact, the filtering is not merely a passive selection of some part of a presented whole, but an active process involving attention to a very small part of the whole and exclusion, from the outset, of almost all that is not within the scope of attention. We need not argue the issue of "conscious" and "subconscious" perception; we need simply observe that every human organism lives in an environment that generates millions of bits of new information each second and that the bottleneck of the perceptual apparatus certainly does not admit more than 1,000 bits per second and probably much less.

Equally significant omissions characterize the processing that takes place when information reaches the brain. As every mathematician knows, it is one thing to have a set of differential equations and another to have their solutions. Yet the solutions are logically implied by the equations—they are "all there," if we only knew how to get at them! By the same token, hosts of inferences *might* be drawn from the information stored in the brain but they are not. The consequences implied by information in the memory become known only through active information processing, and hence through active selection of particular problem-solving paths from the myriad that might have been followed.

If we have a rat in a very small maze, with cheese at one branch point, and if we give the rat plenty of time to explore, we can predict where he will finally go without any very deep knowledge of rat psychology. We simply assume that he likes cheese (a given utility function) and that he chooses the path that leads to cheese (objective rationality). If we now transfer the rat to a maze having a number of pieces of cheese in it, but a maze that is several orders of magnitude larger than the largest maze he could possibly explore in a rat's lifetime, then prediction is more difficult. We must now know how a rat solves problems in order to determine where he will go. We must understand what determines the paths he will try and what clues will make him continue along a path or go back.

Classical economics was highly successful in handling small-maze problems without depending on psychology. Labor relations, imperfect competition, uncertainty, and long-run dynamics encase the decision maker in a much larger maze than those considered in classical short-run static theory. In these new areas the economist and the psychologist have numerous common interests in cognitive theory that they have not shared previously.

The Government of Attention: Roles

Short-run predictions of behavior, where there is a large discrepancy between subjective and objective rationality, require information both about the environment and about the frame of reference of the decision maker. In the longer run, the frame of reference may itself become the dependent variable for prediction, but a variable not easily eliminated from the analysis. For even if the environment is one of the long-run determinants of the frame of reference, there is no reason to suppose that there is any simple one-to-one relation between them. Although the individual and the social system to which he belongs must meet long-run tests of survival and efficiency, there are certainly multiple solutions to the survival problem (as evidenced, in another realm, by the large number of distinct biological species).

Although the distinction between the perceived environment and the objective environment is important in many parts of sociology, social psychology, and individual psychology, there has been little consensus as to what terms should be used to denote the perceived environments. Those in common use include "frame of reference," "set," "definition of the situation," and "role." None of these terms is exactly synonymous with the others—at least in the usage of a single writer—but all are used in a variety of meanings, and each has a large area of overlap with the others.

For the purposes of this essay, we need not solve this terminological problem—we can use the four terms above more or less interchangeably. But we must clarify the concepts to which the terms refer. Indeed, this clarification opens important possibilities for contributions of economics to psychology and vice versa.[9] In the following paragraphs I shall propose a revision in the concept of "role" or "frame of reference" that appears to me essential to the fruitful application of that concept.[10] In the next section, the redefined concept will be used to interpret some of the significant relevant current research.

A current definition of *role* [42, p. 278] that is representative of definitions in use in social psychology and sociology reads: "Each position carries with it definite prescriptions for behaving toward other persons in related positions. . . . Such ways of behaving toward others . . . are called *roles*." For brevity, we may say that roles are usually defined as *positionally prescribed sets of behaviors*.

There is, up to the present time, a great poverty of propositions about the characteristics of roles (as distinguished from propositions about how roles are acquired). This poverty can be traced in large part to the un-

---

[9] Bruner et al. provide a somewhat different example of important conceptual borrowing of psychology from economics and game theory [8].

[10] For a more detailed discussion of the proposal set forth here, see Simon [54].

satisfactory nature of the definition of role. The definition provides a name or label for a phenomenon but not a useful tool for its analysis. The difficulty resides in the term "behaviors," which designates the unit for the description of roles. A "behavior" or "action" is not a satisfactory unit for describing the cognitive orientations of persons to their environments.

The inadequacy of this basis for role description becomes apparent when we try to apply the role concept to rational and adaptive behavior. If roles were prescribed sets of behaviors, then there would be no place for rational calculation in role behavior. A person could decide whether he would conform to a role (and this is the topic most prominently discussed in the literature on roles), but having decided that he would conform, the role prescription would itself determine his behavior in that role.

A concept of role that does not admit processes of rational choice is obviously useless for describing the behavior of economic or administrative man. We need something like the role concept, for we need to distinguish between the objective and subjective environments of choice. At the same time, we must avoid substituting, in the theory, socially prescribed sets of behaviors for choice. We need a definition of role that accomplishes the former without implying the latter.

The difficulties with the role concept disappear if we introduce the *decision premise* as the unit of role description in place of the *behavior*. *A role—in terms of this definition—is a social prescription of some, but not all, of the premises that enter into an individual's choices of behaviors* [54, pp. 221–228; 19]. Any particular concrete behavior is the result of a large number of premises, only some of which are prescribed by the role. In addition to role premises, there are premises about the state of the environment based directly on perception, premises representing beliefs and knowledge, and idiosyncratic premises that characterize the personality.

A fanciful (but only slightly fanciful) example will help to make clear both the distinction between the new definition and the usual one—and the reason for making it. Suppose we were to construct a robot incorporating a modern digital computer and to program (i.e., instruct) the robot to take the role of a business executive in a specified company. What would the program look like? Since no one has yet done this [11, 17], we cannot say with certainty. However, several points are fairly clear. The program would *not* consist of a list of prescribed and proscribed behaviors, since what an executive does is highly contingent on information about a wide variety of circumstances. Instead, the program would consist of a large number of *criteria* to be applied to possible and proposed courses of action, of programs for *generating* possible courses of action, of computational procedures for *assessing* the state of the environ-

ment and its implications for action, and the like. Hence, the program—
that is, the role prescription—would interact with information to produce
concrete behavior adapted to the situation. The elements of such a program take the form of what we have called "decision premises," and
what the computer specialist would call "instructions and data" [45].

Roles and the Process of Rational Decision

The definition of role in terms of decision premises is useful not only
for clarifying concepts, but also for constructing actual detailed descriptions of concrete roles preparatory to analyzing the structure of these roles
and their specific content. We can study the form of the role prescription
and the cognitive and other central processes through which it is translated into action; at this point we can expect some genuine congruence
to develop between the "economic" or "administrative" man and the
"problem-solving" man who has been studied in psychology.

This is not a mere prospectus to be realized at some undefined future
date. A substantial number of current research efforts in different fields
are converging toward this point, as the following examples show:

Economics. Normative microeconomics seeks to advise the businessman in his decisions—whether to buy a piece of equipment, how much
inventory to hold, what price to pay for a product, etc. Hence theories in
this field take the form of decision-making procedures for handling particular problems. To mention just one example, linear programing theory
has been used to construct a computational model for determining the
most profitable blending policies in an oil refinery [10].

These decision models are not merely abstract "theories" of the firm,
but actual decision-making devices. We can think of any such a device
as a simulation of the corresponding human decision maker, in which
the equations and other assumptions that enter into the formal decision-
making procedure correspond to the decision premises, including the role
prescription, of the decision maker [10a, 12].

In particular, the problems of subjective rationailty must be faced
in constructing normative decision models: (1) The latter can require
for their application only data that are obtainable; (2) they can call only
for practicable computations; (3) in so far as they utilize forecasts, they
must specify a method of forecasting. These models, then, share many of
the properties of less formal decision-making processes and provide us
with concrete examples of decision-making roles described in terms of
the premises used in deciding, the data, and the rules of computation.

Higher mental processes. Students of human problem solving have
tried to describe in some detail the stages of the process and the steps
taken by the problem solver. Although the studies that have been reported to date fall far short of complete descriptions of the process—in

many respects less complete than the normative economic models mentioned above—they point clearly in the direction of describing the problem solver in terms of his "program," i.e., the premises that determine the course of the process [8, 20].

Electronic computers. Until very recently, the electronic digital computer was a device that, if instructed in painful detail by its operator, could be induced to perform rather complicated and tedious arithmetical operations. Recent research has enabled the computer to interpret and execute instructions given to it in languages that begin to have some of the power and flexibility of natural languages and to carry out tasks that, if performed by humans, we would certainly call "thinking" and "learning."

A few items will illustrate the stage that such research has reached. Several computers have been programmed to design industrial equipment (for example, small motors and transformers), and the persons who have devised these programs believe that their main processes simulate the decision procedures previously followed by the design engineers—hence describe the role of design engineer in these situations. Second, a computer program, the General Problem Solver [44, 46], is able to reason in rather general terms, solving problems of discovering proofs for mathematical theorems, proving trigonometric and algebraic identities, and a variety of other problems by applying means-end analysis. The program has been shown to simulate the main processes used by college students in solving some novel problems of moderate difficulty. Another computer program [10a, 11] simulates the decision processes used by a bank officer in investing the assets of a trust fund. A third [23] shows that the same basic cognitive processes can be used to explain on the one hand, certain economic predictions of businessmen and, on the other, the behavior of subjects in partial reinforcement experiments.

These computer programs contribute to economic theory by providing very concrete explanations of significant economic decision-making processes. At the same time, they are laying the foundations for an operational and rigorous information-processing theory of human thinking and problem solving. They bring promise of a far closer relation between economic and psychological theories of decision making than we have had in the past [60a]. So long as economics emphasized macroscopic events and ignored detailed process within the business firm and so long as psychology avoided the complexities of higher mental process in favor of rigorous experiments on simple learning and choice situations, the two fields had little common ground. With the appearance of computer programming as a tool powerful enough to allow the study of thinking and learning processes in situations as complex as those of everyday life, it will no longer be acceptable to explain the same phenomena with two different, and often contradictory, bodies of theory.

The Structure of Organizational and Economic Roles

We see that the *role* of a person who is behaving rationally or adaptively can be identified in large part with the decision premises he applies to the substance of his problem and the decision premises that govern his problem-solving processes. We see also that rapid progress is being made toward a more accurate and complete description of certain economic, executive, and technical roles (or parts of them). Apart from normative applications (e.g., substituting computers for humans in decision-making tasks), we are not primarily interested—as psychologists or economists—in the detailed description of the roles, but in broader questions—characterizing the structure of roles in general terms, understanding how roles come to be structured in the particular ways they do, and tracing out the implications for macroeconomics and other large-scale social phenomena of this version of role theory.

Characterizing role structure. Here we are concerned with generalizations about cognitive processes, particularly generalizations that are relatively independent of the substantive content of the role. A classical example is Dewey's description of stages in the problem-solving process and its use in Bales's categories for coding group discussions [4, 30]. Another example, of particular interest to economics, is the hypothesis that economic man is a *satisficing* animal whose problem solving is based on search activity to meet aspiration levels, rather than a *maximizing* animal whose problem solving involves finding the best alternatives in terms of specified criteria [57]. A third hypothesis is that *operative goals,* associated with observable criteria of success, and relatively definite means of attainment, play a much larger part in governing choice than *nonoperative goals,* lacking concrete measures of success or programs for attainment [37, chap. 6].

Understanding how roles emerge. Within almost any single business firm, certain characteristic roles will be represented—selling, production, accounting, and so on [16, 19]. Partly, this consistency may be explained in functional terms—a model that views the firm as producing a product, selling it, and accounting for its assets and liabilities simplifies the real world and provides the members of the organization with a workable frame of reference. Imitation within the culture provides an alternative explanation. It is exceedingly difficult to test hypotheses as to the origins and causal conditions for roles as universal in the society as these, but the underlying mechanisms could probably be explored effectively by studying less common roles—safety director, quality control inspector, or the like, that are found in some firms, but not in all.

With our present definition of "role," we can also speak meaningfully of the role of an entire business firm—of decision premises that underlie its basic policies [6, chap. 3; 17]. In a particular industry, we find that some firms specialize in adapting the product to individual customers' specifications; others specialize in product innovation. The common interest of economics and psychology includes not only the study of individual roles, but also the explanation of organizational roles of these sorts.

Tracing the implications for macroeconomics. If basic professional goals remain as they are, the interest of the psychologist and the economist in role theory will stem from somewhat different ultimate aims. The former will use various economic and organizational phenomena as data for studying the structure and determinants of roles; the latter will be primarily interested in the implications or role theory for the model of economic man and, indirectly, for macroeconomics.

Let us consider, by way of example, the economic theory of the size of firms. The classical theory is a static equilibrium theory: Firms of optimum size in terms of average cost per unit of output drive other firms to this size or out of business. Hence the "typical" size of firm in an industry will be that at which average cost per unit is a minimum. Attempts to determine empirically what this size is in specific cases have not been very successful; the theory is further embarrassed by the fact that in almost all industries there is an extremely wide dispersion of firms by size.

The empirical data are more easily reconciled with a model that assumes that the firm searches for growth opportunities than with one that assumes equilibrium at an optimum [6, pp. 72–73]. Thus research at the microlevel on the actual mechanisms of decision making and problem solving has important implications at the macrolevel for the size distributions of firms. The implications extend both to the explanation of the phenomena and the consequences for economic welfare of various kinds of governmental interventions to alter the size distributions of firms [60].

The topics of innovation and technological change provide somewhat more obvious links than the one just discussed between the firm and individual decision maker, on the one hand, and the economy and society, on the other. The factors determining the rate of a nation's economic and technological development are still very much matters of speculation. In particular, classical economics, built upon basically static models of the economy, does not readily handle the processes of invention, growth, and diffusion of knowledge as determinants of productivity or of the rate of capital investment. Some progress has been made in exploring the processes by which innovations are diffused through a culture [13, 25]. However, little or nothing is known of the determinants of the rate and direction of inventive activity or how technical know-how is "stored" and reproduced by a society. A better understanding of these processes would have obvious implications for the decisions that individual firms have to make in budgeting and directing research and development activities, for the decisions of governments relating to economic development, and for the encouragement of technological progress. Hence improved theories of human thinking and problem solving may have a major impact on economic and business policy.

Concluding Comments

This discussion of the mutual interests of economics and the behavioral sciences in cognitive processes—and particularly those of the rational decision maker—has necessarily been more speculative than earlier sections of this article. Here we are examining an area of investigation that is just emerging—just becoming an important element in the social scientist's model of the world. In describing this area, I have tried to point to a number of the diverse research activities that testify to its growing significance and its possible implications for the social sciences.

The relative lack of communication between economists and behavioral scientists on the topic of motivation can be attributed in considerable part to the economist's belief that his purposes are served by a very rudimentary theory of motivational processes, a theory he can construct without much outside help. Cognitive theory has been of great concern both to economics (rationality) and to behavioral scientists (learning, problem solving). What has limited communication here has been the great difference between the models of rational behavior that have prevailed in the several disciplines. There are strong indications today that a more realistic description of human rationality is emerging—one that may serve as common ground for a wide variety of social scientists [8, 20, 46].

METHODOLOGICAL BORROWINGS

A person who has occasion to wander into various territories in the social sciences is struck not only by the diversity of tribal customs relating to substantive matters—concepts and theories—but by the diversity of methodologies as well. If a social scientist is discovered computing a regression coefficient, he is almost certainly an economist; a factor analysis identifies him as a psychologist, probably working with test data, a *t* or chi-square test, or as a social or experimental psychologist, probably working with experimental data, etc. Mathematical statistics has provided a common meeting ground for the statistically sophisticated of all disciplines, but the statistical techniques they have brought back to their own tribes have tended to be somewhat specialized. Scaling techniques and latent structure analysis are hardly known outside social psychology, the country of origin; the work that has been done on the statistical identification problem is an even more closely held secret of the econometricians. The highly technical nature of some of these developments and the language in which they must be described have hindered their diffusion.

The same may be said about empirical methodology. For a traditional economic theorist, an empirical study means going to the reports of the U.S. Census or the Bureau of Foreign and Domestic Commerce. A social psychologist generates new data by experimenting with small groups of college sophomores in a laboratory. The anthropologist-sociologist buys a ticket to New Guinea or Newburyport. The ecologist-sociologist and the demographer-sociologist behave more like the economist, looking largely to official tabulations of aggregative data for their information. The public opinion specialist constructs a stratified random sample and asks questions of a number of respondents. These are some of the principal varieties of social scientists, viewed as data seekers.

Recent years have seen an increasing amount of borrowing of empirical methodologies among disciplines, although the average experience of social scientists trained in one discipline, but using the data-gathering techniques of the others, is very slight. A few economists are now using questionnaires and the interview as a means for learning about economic behavior. An even smaller group is exploring the possibilities of actually observing behavior within the business firm. A few studies, easily counted on the fingers, have attempted to elucidate economic phenomena by laboratory experimentation.

All of these activities seem to be growing—amidst a certain healthy skepticism of traditionally trained economists—and growing not merely in quantity but in their sophistication of technique. For example, the belief that the way to learn how a businessman makes decisions is to ask him (comparable to earlier beliefs in most public opinion polling studies) is gradually waning; one or two of the most carefully designed and controlled studies of utility functions show a high degree of sophistication with respect to introspective evidence.

The borrowing in the other direction—from economics to the behavioral sciences—lies more in the direction of statistics and mathematical formalization than empirical techniques. Mathematical theorizing is undoubtedly most highly developed in economics, where it has been intimately involved in the advance of theory over the last fifty years. Recently, the trend toward mathematical formalization of theories has spread to psychology and, to a lesser extent, sociology [30]. The number of social scientists capable of handling mathematics as consumers and as producers is increasing rapidly, and we may expect it to continue to do so under the impetus it has been given by the Social Science Research Council and the Ford Foundation.

As we survey the various aspects of methodology, then, we observe a slow but significant diffusion of empirical techniques from the behavioral sciences to economics and a return traffic in statistics and mathematics. These streams of diffusion of knowledge are bringing about important advances in the technical level of both empirical and theoretical work in the social sciences.

CONCLUSION

I shall not try to summarize further what is already a compressed survey of an alarmingly wide range of topics. The word "interdisciplinary" is in fashion again in the social sciences, but my review of the literature has not revealed any great excess of interdisciplinary fervor on the whole. On the contrary, the disciplinary boundaries remain rather effective barriers to the sharing of knowledge in areas that are certainly of common concern to economics and the behavioral sciences, and areas to which all these disciplines have much to contribute. It is doubtful whether the existing disciplines constitute a satisfactory frame of reference for the sciences of man. If the subjective rationality of the social scientist is to be adequate to the task of interpreting the objective facts of the real world of social phenomena, a more effective set of role definitions than those in current use needs to be found.

REFERENCES

1. Alchian, A. A. Uncertainty, evolution, and economic theory. *J. polit. Econ.,* 1950, **58**, 58–212.
2. Arrow, K. J. Utilities, attitudes, choices: a review note. *Econometrica,* 1958, **26**, 1–23.
3. Asch, S. E. *Social psychology.* Englewood Cliffs, N.J.: Prentice-Hall, 1952.
4. Bales, R. F. *Interaction process analysis.* Reading, Mass.: Addison-Wesley, 1950.
5. Barnard, C. I. *The functions of the executive.* Cambridge, Mass.: Harvard Univer. Press, 1938.
5a.Borko, H. (Ed.) *Computer applications in the behavioral sciences.* Englewood Cliffs: Prentice-Hall, 1962.
6. Bowen, H. R. *The business enterprise as a subject for research.* New York: Social Science Research Council, 1955.
7. Bowman, M. J. *Expectations, uncertainty, and business behavior.* New York: Social Science Research Council, 1958.
8. Bruner, J. A., Goodnow, J. T., & Austin, G. A. *A study of thinking.* New York: Wiley, 1956.
9. Chamberlin, N. W. *A general theory of economic process.* New York: Harper, 1955.

10. Charnes, A., Cooper, W. W., & Mellon, B. Blending aviation gasolines. *Econometrica*, 1952, **20**, 135–159.

10a. Clarkson, G. P. E. *Portfolio selection: a simulation of trust investment.* Englewood Cliffs: Prentice-Hall, 1962.

11. Clarkson, G. P. E., & Meltzer, A. H. Portfolio selection: a heuristic approach. *J. Finance*, 1960, **15**, 465–480.

12. Clarkson, G. P. E., & Simon, H. A. Simulation of individual and group behavior. *Amer. Econ. Rev.*, 1960, **50**, 920–932.

13. Coleman, J., Katz, E., & Menzel, H. The diffusion of an innovation among physicians. *Sociometry*, 1957, **20**, 253–270.

14. Coleman, J. R. The role of the local industrial union in contemporary collective bargaining. *Proc. eighth Annu. Mtg industr. Relat. Res. Ass.*, 1955. Madison, Wis.: The Association, 1956. Pp. 274–286.

15. Cyert, R. M., & March, J. G. Organizational factors in the theory of oligopoly. *Quart. J. Econ.*, 1956, **70**, 44–64.

15a. Cyert, R. M. & March, J. G. *A behavioral theory of the firm.* Englewood Cliffs: Prentice-Hall, forthcoming, 1962.

16. Cyert, R. M., March, J. G., & Starbuck, W. Two experiments on bias and conflict in organizational estimation. *Management Sci.*, 1961, **7**, 254–264.

17. Cyert, R. M., Simon, H. A., & Trow, D. B. Observation of a business decision. *J. Business*, 1956, **29**, 237–248.

18. Davidson, D., & Suppes, P. *Decision making: an experimental approach.* Stanford, Calif.: Stanford Univer. Press, 1955.

19. Dearborn, D. C., & Simon, H. A. Selective perception: a note on the departmental identifications of executives. *Sociometry*, 1958, **21**, 140–144.

20. de Groot, A. *Het Denken van den Schaker.* Amsterdam: Noord-Hollandsche Uitgevers Maatschapij, 1946.

21. Early, J. S. Marginal policies of "excellently managed" companies. *Amer. Econ. Rev.*, 1956, **46**, 44–70.

22. Edwards, W. The theory of decision making. *Psychol. Bull.*, 1954, **51**, 380–417.

23. Feldman, J. An analysis of predictive behavior in a two choice situation. Unpublished doctoral dissertation, Carnegie Inst. Technol., 1959.

24. Gordon, R. A. *Business leadership in the large corporation.* Washington: Brookings, 1945.

25. Griliches, Z. Hybrid corn: an exploration in the economics of technological change. *Econometrica*, 1957, **25**, 501–522.

26. Hall, R. L., & Hitch, C. J. Price theory and business behavior. *Oxford Econ. Papers*, 1939, No. 2, 12–45.

27. Hayes, S. P., Jr. Some psychological problems of economics. *Psychol. Bull.*, 1950, **47**, 289–330.

28. Homans, G. C. *The human group.* New York: Harper, 1950.

29. Katona, G. *Psychological analysis of economic behavior.* New York: McGraw-Hill, 1951.

30. Lazarsfeld, P. F. (Ed.) *Mathematical thinking in the social sciences.* Glencoe, Ill.: Free Press, 1954.

31. Lewin, K. *Principles of topological psychology.* New York: McGraw-Hill, 1936.

32. Lewin, K., et al. Level of aspiration. In J. McV. Hunt (Ed.), *Personality and the behavior disorders.* Vol. 1. New York: Ronald, 1944. Pp. 333–378.

33. Luce, R. D. A probabilistic theory of utility. *Econometrica,* 1958, **26,** 193–224.

34. Luce, R. D. *Individual choice behavior.* New York: Wiley, 1959.

35. Luce, R. D., & Edwards, W. The derivation of subjective scales from just noticeable differences. *Psychol. Rev.,* 1958, **65,** 222–237.

36. Luce, R. D., & Raiffa, H. *Games and decisions.* New York: Wiley, 1957.

37. March, J. C., & Simon, H. A. *Organizations.* New York: Wiley, 1958.

38. Marschak, J. Binary-choice constraints and random utility indicators. In K. J. Arrow, S. Karlin, & P. Suppes (Eds.), *Mathematical methods in the social sciences.* Stanford, Calif.: Stanford Univer. Press, 1959. Pp. 312–329.

39. Marshall, A. *Principles of economics.* (8th ed.) New York: St. Martin's Press, 1920.

40. Menzel, H., Coleman, J., & Katz, E. On the flow of scientific information in the medical profession. New York: Columbia Univer., Bur. Appl. Soc. Res., 1955. (Mimeographed report)

41. Modigliani, F., & Brumberg, E. Utility analysis and the consumption function. In K. K. Kurihara (Ed.), *Post-Keynesian economics.* New York: Knopf, 1954.

42. Newcomb, T. M. *Social psychology.* New York: Dryden, 1950.

43. Newell, A., Shaw, J. C., & Simon, H. A. Empirical explorations of the logic theory machine. *Proceedings Western Joint Computer Conference.* New York: Institute of Radio Engineers, 1957. Pp. 218–230.

44. Newell, A., Shaw, J. C., & Simon, H. A. Elements of a theory of human problem solving. *Psychol. Rev.,* 1958, **65,** 151–166.

45. Newell, A., & Simon, H. A. The logic theory machine. *Trans. Inf. Theor., Inst. Radio Eng.,* September 1956, **IT-2**(3), 61–79.

46. Newell, A., & Simon, H. A. The simulation of human thought. In *Current trends in psychological theory.* Pittsburgh, Pa.: Univer. Pittsburgh Press, 1960.

47. Papandreou, A. G. Some basic problems in the theory of the firm. In B. F. Haley (Ed.), *A survey of contemporary economics.* Vol. 2. Homewood, Ill.: Irwin, 1952. Chap. 5.

48. Ramsey, F. P. *The foundations of mathematics and other logical essays.* New York: Harcourt, Brace, 1931.

48a. Restle, F. *Psychology of judgment and choice.* New York: Wiley, 1961.

49. Schelling, T. C. An essay on bargaining. *Amer. Econ. Rev.,* 1956, **46,**(3), 281–306.

50. Schultz, H. *The theory and measurement of demand.* Chicago: Univer. Chicago Press, 1938.

51. Sherif, M. *The psychology of social norms.* New York: Harper, 1936.

52. Siegel, S. Level of aspiration and decision making. *Psychol. Rev.,* 1957, **64,** 253–263.

53. Siegel, S., & Fouraker, L. *Bargaining and group decision-making.* New York: Macmillan, 1960.

54. Simon, H. A. *Administrative behavior.* New York: Macmillan, 1947.

55. Simon, H. A. A formal theory of the employment relation. *Econometrica,* 1951, **19,** 293–305. Reprinted in [59, chap. 11].

56. Simon, H. A. A comparison of organization theories. *Rev. Econ. Stud.,* 1952, **20,** 40–48. Reprinted in [59, chap. 10].

57. Simon, H. A. A behavioral model of rational choice. *Quart. J. Econ.,* 1955, **69,** 99–118. Reprinted in [59, chap. 14].

58. Simon, H. A. Rational choice and the structure of the environment. *Psychol. Rev.,* 1956, **63,** 129–138. Reprinted in [59, chap. 15].

59. Simon, H. A. *Models of man.* New York: Wiley, 1957.

60. Simon, H. A., & Bonini, C. P. The size distribution of business firms. *Amer. Econ. Rev.,* 1958, **48,** 607–617.

60a. Sprowls, R. C. Business simulation. In H. Borko (Ed.), *Computer applications in the behavioral sciences.* Englewood Cliffs: Prentice-Hall, 1962. Chap. 23.

60b. Stedry, A. C. *Budget control and cost behavior.* Englewood Cliffs: Prentice-Hall, 1960.

61. Thurstone, L. L. The indifference function. *J. soc. Psychol.,* 1931, **2,** 139–167.

62. Von Neumann, J., & Morgenstern, O. *The theory of games and economic behavior.* Princeton, N.J.: Princeton Univer. Press, 1944.

63. Weisskopf, W. A. *The psychology of economics.* Chicago: Univer. Chicago Press, 1955.

7.8

SIMULATION OF INDIVIDUAL AND GROUP BEHAVIOR

By Geoffrey P. E. Clarkson and Herbert A. Simon*

Simulation is a technique for building theories that reproduce part or all of the output of a behaving system. The system can be an aggregate of behaving units, an entire economy, or a particular unit, a human decision-maker. The output can be one aggregated element, e.g., that interest rate which clears the money market, or the whole host of thoughts, associations, and actions employed by a man while he solves a specified problem.

This paper, with its companion papers, outline some methods for using simulation to study various aspects of an economic system. In our paper, we shall place special emphasis on microeconomic simulation —especially the simulation of individual economic actors and individual firms—leaving to Orcutt and Shubik the discussion of larger units. In an earlier article, one of us has discussed at length the reasons why economists might be interested in analysis of behavior at the level of the decision-making process [23], and we shall not repeat these reasons here.

The process of simulation involves constructing a theory, or model, of a system that prescribes the system's processes. These processes can refer to macro as well as micro elements and the prescriptive detail reflects the researcher's knowledge of and interest in particular parts of the system. By carrying out the processes postulated in the theory, a hypothetical stream of behavior is generated that can be compared with the stream of behavior of the original system.

I. *Simulation and Classical Econometric Analysis*

What is new and what is "classical" in simulation can be illustrated by a simple market theory of the familiar cobweb type. Consider a dynamic model consisting of two equations:

(1)
$$p_t = D(q_t)$$
(2)
$$q_t = S(p_{t-1})$$

where p_t is the price during time-period t, q_t the quantity sold during time-period t, D the demand function, and S the supply function.

* The authors are Ford Foundation fellow and professor of administration, respectively, in the Graduate School of Industrial Administration, Carnegie Institute of Technology.

Henry Schultz dealt extensively with models like this in *The Theory and Measurement of Demand* [22]. What did he do with them? (a) He postulated that the economic relations were of this form. (b) He estimated the parameters of the functions D and S from empirical data for particular commodities (by regression methods). (c) He tested the goodness of fit of the regressions. (d) He compared the qualitative properties of the estimated parameters with certain predictions derived from utility theory.

The last point, (d), requires a word of explanation. As is well known, under certain additional assumptions, the postulate of consumer utility maximization implies that the elasticity of demand is negative. Hence, if the empirically estimated coefficient of the demand function was negative, this would be regarded as confirming the utility theory; if positive, as disconfirming. The method implicit in this analysis has been systematically developed by Samuelson [21, Ch. 9], who calls it the method of comparative statics.

The methodology of steps (a) through (c) is widely employed in econometrics. Cohen and Cyert [8] speak of classical econometrics as using "one-period change models," which they distinguish from the "process models" used in simulation. Since the difference lies not in the models themselves, but in the ways they are manipulated and tested, we prefer to speak of "one-period change analysis," which we shall distinguish from "simulation."

Now consider how simulation techniques may be applied to the simple market theory we are using for illustration:

(a) We postulate that the economic relations are of the form given by the equations. (b) We estimate the parameters of the functions D and S from empirical data for particular commodities (say, by regression methods). (c) Taking the given initial quantity, q_0, by alternate applications of equations (1) and (2) we generate time series for p and q for the system. We compare these hypothetical time series with the actual time series.

Since the equations of the theory certainly do not hold exactly in the real world, it might be supposed that the predicted values of the time series would necessarily diverge more and more from the actual values. Thus, one-period change analysis, since it sets the estimates back on the track each period by comparing them with the actual values, might be expected to give better fits than simulation. This would probably be the case with our simple illustrative model. It need not hold for more sophisticated models—in particular, if the model itself contains "feedback" mechanisms. For example, if quantity produced in a given time-period is a function *both* of last period's price and of inventory at the beginning of the period, errors in the model's supply prediction will tend to be self-correcting for the same reason that suppliers' actual errors are self-correcting—the errors reflect themselves in disequilibrium inventories which affect the supply for the next period. In a particular case—a model of the shoe industry—Cohen [7] has shown that annual averages of the time series yielded by simulation were generally closer to the actual series than were the series yielded by one-period change analysis.

Our purpose here, however, is not to argue for the superiority of simulation over one-period change analysis. We wish simply to explain in what respects they are the same, and in what respects different. Research over the next decade will undoubtedly teach us a great deal about their respective spheres of greatest usefulness.

II. *Some Forms of Simulation*

Simulation has come into economics through at least three routes: (1) dynamic macroeconomics, particularly business cycle theory and "cobweb" theory; (2) operations research and management science; and (3) theory of economic decision-making—including theory of the firm and oligopoly theory.

1. *Dynamic Macroeconomics.* This kind of simulation is exemplified by the models usually found in theories of the business cycle and market behavior.[1] In the past, mathematical models of the business cycle were handled by standard analytic techniques—e.g., solving the differential or difference equations of the model; applying the method of comparative statics to draw qualitative conclusions; and so on. As the models grew in complexity, and as various kinds of nonlinearities were introduced that were relatively impervious to standard analytic methods, greater use was made of numerical analysis—especially one-period change analysis—to study system behavior. In this realm, simulation is simply an additional technique for numerical analysis. Combined with the computer's speed, it permits a study of a system's behavior when initial conditions and parameters are varied. The computer allows much larger systems to be formulated and studied than could be analyzed numerically without this tool.

2. *Management Science.* The models used by the operations researcher or management scientist are normative in intent. They incorporate certain decision variables that the management of the firm can manipulate, and the problem is to find rules for setting these decision variables so as to maximize, minimize, or satisfice with respect to some criterion—e.g., to maximize profits, minimize costs, or achieve a

[1] The classical models of business cycle and market behavior are surveyed in Henderson and Quandt [13]; Klein [15].

desired share of the market. A number of powerful mathematical techniques have been developed for approximating complex business decision-making situations and finding optimal decision rules by straightforward computational algorithms. Linear programming and dynamic programming are among the best known of these techniques [2] [4] [10] [26]

In this as in other realms, the riches of nature often embarrass art, for the complexities of the situations to be handled make inapplicable even such flexible techniques as linear programming. In these cases, simulation provides an alternative route to finding good decision rules. The system can be modeled with little regard to the applicability of known computational schemes, and the behavior of the model studied "empirically," that is, numerically with various decision rules over a range of hypothesized environmental histories. Decision rules can then be chosen that yield satisfactory system behavior under the conditions studied. Of course these techniques—the analytic techniques as well as simulation—can only be employed after adequate estimates have been made of the structural parameters of the system [1].

3. *Economic Decision-Making*. Almost all economic models refer at least implicitly to the decision-making of economic actors—a demand curve, for instance, can be interpreted as a set of hypothetical statements about what buyers would do under a range of circumstances. However, as we move from macroscopic to microscopic models, and as we move into the area of normative economics, the decision-making elements in the models becomes more explicit. In normative economics, our aim is to find rules for making "good"decisions. In positive microeconomics, our aim is to explain the decision-making behavior of economic agents.

Apart from its normative uses, simulation is a peculiarly attractive method for describing and explaining the decision-making processes at a microeconomic level. Its first, and most obvious, advantage is the same one that has led to its wide use in management science—it allows a degree of complexity to be handled that would be unthinkable if inferences could be drawn from the model only by standard analytical techniques. We shall provide, below, an example of an oligopoly theory that attains considerable realism and plausibility by exploiting this tolerance for complexity.

Simulation has a second advantage that may turn out, in the long run, to be even more important. We are beginning to learn that models do not have to be stated in mathematical or numerical form to permit us to simulate their behavior with electronic computers. With computers, we can simulate the behavior of symbol-manipulating and information-processing systems, regardless of whether the symbols these systems handle are numbers, or are English words, phrases and sentences [16] [17].

It has always seemed quite natural to express macroeconomic models in mathematical form. After all, the phenomena with which they are concerned are quantities of goods and services and prices. The further we move, however, toward the detail of microeconomic analysis, the more dubious becomes the assumption that the important factors in the situation can all be represented as real numbers. We try manfully to encompass the phenomena. With great ingenuity, we axiomatize utility as a cardinal quantity; we represent risks by probability distributions. Having done this, we are left with the question of whether we have constructed a theory of how economic man makes his decisions, or instead a theory of how he *would* make his decisions if he could reason only in terms of numbers and had no qualitative or verbal concepts.

The question is still an open one, but the answer need no longer be imposed by the limitations of our analytic techniques. Research in so-called heuristic programming[2] has given us new ways of simulating systems that incorporate some of the kinds of nonnumerical symbol manipulation that, in humans, we call thinking and problem-solving. These technical advances open up new opportunities for building and studying realistic models of economic decision-making at the level of the individual firm and the individual decision-maker. Before we go on to some concrete examples, which will occupy the final part of this paper, we need briefly to discuss these new techniques of nonnumerical simulation.

III. *Nonnumerical Computation*

To appreciate the scope of opportunity for computer simulation of decision-making processes, we must be quite clear as to what a computer is, and what it is capable of doing.

1. Computers are general-purpose devices capable of employing various operations for manipulating symbols. They can read symbols (e.g., sense patterns of holes on punched cards), write symbols (e.g., create magnetic patterns on coated tape), erase symbols (change such patterns), and store symbols (retain patterns in magnetic cores or other kinds of internal memories). They can copy symbols (write patterns identical with patterns that are presented), and compare symbols (determine whether two patterns are identical or different). Finally, and most important, they can behave differentially depending

---

[2] Heuristics are important because they often lead us quickly to solutions which we would otherwise reach much more expensively by algorithmic and analytic techniques. For a more extensive discussion of heuristic programs see [18] [24].

on whether a pair of patterns, when compared, turn out to be identical or different (in computer terminology, they can transfer or branch conditionally). By virtue of this last capacity, they can follow strategies— make decisions that are conditional upon any kind of symbolic information.

2. The symbols, or patterns, that computers can read, write, compare, and process can be interpreted as numbers, as words, as English sentences, or even as geometric diagrams. How they are interpreted depends on the programs that process them. Historically, computers were specifically designed to process symbols as numbers—to perform arithmetical operations on them. The computer "hardware" of standard computers in use today does not incorporate this limitation. If computers are used mainly to do rapid arithmetic, that is because people want to use them in this way and not because this is the only way they can be used.

3. A number of computer programs have been written that process nonnumerical symbols. At least one of these [19] is capable of applying means-end analysis to the solution of a fairly wide range of types of problems. It proceeds somewhat as follows: I am given situation a, and am asked to arrive at b. What is the difference between a and b? One difference I note is d. Do I know of any ways of dealing with differences like d? Yes, using q sometimes removes such differences. Let me, then, apply q to a, and see whether the resulting situation, a', brings me any closed to b. There is a growing body of evidence that this computer program simulates some of the main processes that humans use in solving problems.

4. A number of computer programs have been written that learn— that modify their own programs in an adaptive direction on the basis of experience [20]. The existence of such self-adaptive programs takes most of the meaning out of such statements as: "A computer can only do what you program it to do." The statement becomes exactly parallel to a statement like: "A human being can only do what his genes program him to do."

By reason of these capabilities of computers, we are today in a position to use simulation not only as a means of handling systems of great complexity, but also as a means of incorporating in our theories of human decision-making qualitative aspects of human symbol manipulation that have eluded our attempts at mathematical translation. To write a heuristic program of a decision-making process, we do not first have to construct a mathematical model, and then write a program to simulate the behavior of the model. We can directly write a program that manipulates meaningful symbols in the same ways that (we hypothesize) the human decision-maker manipuates them [11].

IV. *Examples of Microeconomic Simulation*

We shall illustrate our general discussion with three examples of computer simulations of microeconomic systems. Even though the use of simulation for building and testing theories is a recent phenomenon, a number of such models have already been reported in the literature. The particular examples we cite are not intended to be "representative," but are chosen to emphasize some important specific points. The first, a mathematical model of a duopoly situation, illustrates the richness in description of the decision-making process that is attainable with simulation techniques. The second, a normative program for solving an assembly-line balancing problem, shows how heuristic methods grossly modeled on the processes used by skilled human schedulers provide a usable simulation of a situation too complex to be handled by existing mathematical algorithms. The third, a direct simulation of the decision-making processes of an economic agent, shows how simulation can be used to describe and explain decision-making that involves non-numerical as well as numerical symbols and that is dependent in important ways upon the structure of human memory.

A. *A Theory of Duopoly*

Although there are numerous theories of duopoly, the model of Cyert, Feigenbaum and March [9] postulates in much greater detail than earlier ones the decision processes of the firms. In rough outline, each firm is assumed to: (1) forecast the reactions of its competitor, (2) revise its estimate of the demand curve, (3) revise its estimates of its own cost curve, (4) specify its profit goal (on the basis of its profit achievements in the past), (5) evaluate the alternatives available to it. If no alternatives which meet its goal are available, the firm (6) searches for opportunities for cost reduction, (7) re-examines its estimates of demand, and (8) lowers its profit goal to a more modest level. Finally, the firm (9) sets its output for the coming period.

The authors point to a number of important ways in which this theory differs from conventional oligopoly models [9, pp. 93-94]:

(1) The models are built on a description of the decision-making process . . . (2) The models depend on a theory of search as well as a theory of choice. They specify under what conditions search will be intensified. . . . They also specify the direction in which search will be undertaken. . . . (3) The models describe organizations in which objectives change over time as a result of experience. . . . (4) Similarly, the models describe organizations that adjust forecasts on the basis of experience. Organizational learning occurs. . . . (5) The models introduce organizational biases in making estimates. . . . (6) The models all introduce features of "organizational slack."

By specifying particular values for the parameters of the model, the authors were able to generate behavior over time that simulated some of the striking general features of the history of the tin can industry from the time of entry of Continental Can Company as a competitor of the American Can Company.

B. *Balancing an Assembly Line*

F. M. Tonge [25] has built a heuristic model that balances an assembly line. The problem of balancing an assembly line is a member of the class of combinatorial problems in which the elements of a set are ordered or grouped on the basis of some criterion. This class includes such problems as job-shop scheduling, the traveling salesman problem, and the personnel and equipment assignment problems.[3] Although these problems fall within the domain of operations research, they are too large to be solved by the usual algorithmic approaches. As an example of their size, consider the problem of assigning n men to n distinct jobs. If we let $n = 100$ (a relatively small number when you consider the size of the work force in a large company), the number of possible assignments is $n! = 100! = 9.3 \times 10^{157}$. Now if 10^6 orderings are examined in one second (which is the approximate manipulatory speed of current computers) it will take 3×10^{144} years to examine all possible orderings and select the optimal one. Thus, blind search techniques are simply not feasibly methods for solving combinatorial problems of any size. Unfortunately, for these problems efficient algorithms that would reduce the search to practicable dimensions are not known.

The assembly-line balancing problem is essentially a task of assigning the elemental tasks making up the assembly operation to work stations along the line. In his model, Tonge assumes a fixed rate of production, e.g., a fixed conveyor-belt speed, and takes as given the time required to complete each elemental task. The goal of the program is to find the minimum number of workmen consistent with the given rate of production and the partial ordering constraints on the assembling of the product.

Tonge uses heuristics to simplify the problem sufficiently so that it can be solved by simple, straightforward methods. Although the heuristics were devised by observing industrial assembly-line balancers, the program does not attempt to reproduce in detail actual decision-making behavior. The program consists of three main phases. Phase one simplifies the line-balancing problem by constructing a hierarchy of aggregated elements. Thus, the elemental tasks are grouped into large "subassemblies" each of which has partial orderings between the elements and requires a given amount of operating time. The second phase solves

[3] These problems are described in detail in Churchman, Ackoff, Arnoff [4].

the simplified problem by assigning groups of available workmen to the subassemblies generated by phase one. It then treats each subassembly as a simplified line balancing problem and assigns the groups of workmen to the components of each subassembly. Phase three is a "smoothing" operation which transfers the tasks among work stations until the distribution of assigned time is as even as possible.

The program was tested by having it balance 11-, 21-, and 70-element problems. Even though the program does not produce optimal solutions the results of the 70-element test compared very favorably with an industrial engineer's balance of a roughly similar problem. Although the comparison is not too precise, since the industrial engineer had to deal with a few additional constraints, the program assigned 23 men to the assembly task as against the 26 men required by the industrial engineer's plan.

C. *The Investment Decision Process*

Although economists have constructed normative mathematical and statistical theories of investment decision-making, the investment model of G. P. Clarkson [5] is the first that attempts to describe and explain the actual processes of an individual making investment decisions. The goal of this model is two-fold: (a) to develop a model of individual trust investment behavior which incorporates and reproduces observable and inferable human problem-solving processes, and (b) to use the structure of the decision process itself as a method of predicting aggregate trust investment behavior.

The investment decision process is divided into three parts: (a) the analysis and selection of a list of stocks available for investment, (b) the formation of an investment policy, and (c) the selection of a portfolio. Although the selection process (c) contains rules on diversification and on how to select the number of shares to buy, the essence of the whole investment process lies in carrying out the prior analysis—steps (a) and (b). Thus, a major part [step (a)] of the model's function is to convert the information on the economy, industries, and companies as found in financial journals and reports into a list of stocks suitable for current investment. The next part [step (b)] consists of formulating an investment policy from the information on the beneficiary or the trust fund involved, while the final section (c) of the model performs the task of actually selecting the required portfolio.

The model, built by observing the decision processes of individual trust investors, is a theory of decision-making under uncertainty. The major hypotheses of this theory are structural and make strong assertions about the content of decisions as well as the order in which they take place. For example, the model asserts that the formation of expectations is essentially a process of "pattern-recognition." While this is neither an entirely new idea nor the first time it has been asserted as an hypothesis[4] the model asserts in detail how expectations are formulated, adjusted over time, and employed in the investment decision process.

The model, like the human investor, stores information in its memory in lists which contain closely associated pieces of information. These lists are arranged in a hierarchical order, e.g., for each industry there is a list of associated companies, and for each company there is a list of attributes that contain relevant financial information. Detailed information, given to the model from the outside, is processed to form new lists which summarize the basic data. In some cases the summary contains quantitative information, e.g., the average rate of growth of sales or earnings, and in other cases qualitative information, e.g., that the F.R.B. index of industrial production is expected to be above last year's, and last year's was below the index of the year before. These lists are the backbone of the decision-making process, since they provide the information necessary for the concept formation and pattern-recognition processes.

In the course of his work, an investor forms definite concepts of what different industries are like and how they can be expected to perform. Investors also associate different industries with different investment goals. These concepts change with time, but in order to alter them new information must appear that is sufficiently out of keeping with the current concept to force a reappraisal. Thus, small changes are unlikely to affect general concepts and what was a good buy yesterday will probably remain a good buy today and for some time to come. The model simulates these processes by scanner-selector mechanisms which search the summarized lists and match their values against sets of desired criteria. Since new information on the economy, industries, and companies is fed in at regular intervals the scanner-selector mechanisms allow the model to adapt both the criteria by which it selects and the portfolio selections it makes to current economic and market conditions.

Since there can be no theory of human problem-solving unless invariances exist among problem solvers, one cannot develop an aggregate investment model, along these lines, unless one first isolates the structure of the investment decision process that is invariant among investors. Although a general investment model has not been developed, the author suggests that his investment model contains that part of the investment decision process which is invariant among trust investors, and hence provides a basis for an aggregate model of trust investment

[4] See Bruner, Goodnow, Austin [3]; Feldman [12].

behavior. Thus, the program may be viewed as a theory of the "representative investor," analogous to the Marshallian representative firm.

In order to test both assertions—that is, the ability of the model to predict both individual and aggregate trust investment behavior, a series of tests are performed. The first part of these tests consists in having the model select a series of portfolios for a particular set of actual trust accounts. These selections are compared with the actual portfolios chosen by the investment officers of several national banks. The second part of the testing program requires the model to predict the set of stocks purchased by trust funds in the state of Pennsylvania during 1960. The model makes its selections on a quarterly basis and the results are compared with the purchases of trust funds as reported by the Pennsylvania Bankers Association. As yet this testing program has not been completed and the reader can only be referred to the results obtained from an earlier and less complete model [6].

If space permitted, we could describe other instructive examples of microeconomic theories developed by means of simulation. Cohen, for example [7], has studied by simulation techniques an elaborate model of the shoe, leather, and hide industries; while Hoggatt [14] has simulated a perfectly competitive industry allowing entry and exit of firms. These and other examples are described in the papers by Orcutt and Shubik.

V. *Directions of Simulation Research*

We have seen that one advantage of simulation models lies in the complexity they permit. This does not mean that this new technique will relieve us of the task of making careful selection of our variables. The real world is still orders of magnitude more complex than the simulations we can handle on present or prospective computers. We still will need to think, and think hard, about what part of reality needs to be incorporated in the model if it is to provide reasonable answers to the questions we wish to ask of it.

Another advantage of simulation derives from our new-found ability to construct directly computer programs describing human problem-solving and decision-making processes without first going through the intermediate step of constructing mathematical models. We can look forward to theories that will handle the qualitative aspects of human decision-making as readily as the quantitative, and we can already find examples of such theories. These theories incorporate adaptive and learning behavior and include one or more aspects of heuristic reasoning. Since expectations play a central role in economic theory, and since all the evidence suggests that expectations are formed by a process of pattern recognition, this process, incorporated in heuristic programs, will be the object of much research.

Finally, simulation appears to offer new approaches to the aggregation problem. To the extent that whole classes of individual decision units in the economy share relatively invariant structures, aggregation can be attempted by writing programs for individual units, and treating these as representative units, à la Marshall, in the aggregate model. Much work will have to be done before we will be in a position to evaluate the potentialities of this approach. One of its attractions lies in the new opportunities it affords for direct confrontation of the theory with concrete behavior. It does not restrict us to viewing the economic system through the wrong end of a telescope—limiting ourselves to census data and similar kinds of statistics. It permits us to see whether the decision-making processes we observe in the executive and the individual business firm correspond to the postulates about process that we incorporate in our models, and—if we are even moderately successful in finding satisfactory aggregation techniques—to work back and forth in our theory testing between micro-observations and aggregative data.

REFERENCES

1. W. E. ALBERTS, "System Simulation," *Proceedings of the Seventh Annual National Conference of the AIEE*, Washington, D.C., May 17-18, 1956.
2. H. R. BOWMAN AND R. B. FETTER, *Analysis for Production Management*. Homewood, Ill. 1957.
3. J. BRUNER, J. J. GOODNOW, AND G. A. AUSTIN, *A Study in Thinking*. New York 1956.
4. C. W. CHURCHMAN, R. L. ACKOFF, AND E. L. ARNOFF, *Introduction to Operations Research*. New York 1957.
5. G. P. CLARKSON, "Trust Investment: A Study in Decision Making." Unpublished ditto, Carnegie Institute of Technology, 1960.
6. ———— AND A. H. MELTZER, "Portfolio Selection: An Heuristic Approach," *Jour. Finance*, forthcoming.
7. K. J. COHEN, *Computer Models of the Shoe, Leather, Hide Sequence*. Englewood Cliffs, N.J. 1960.
8. ———— AND R. M. CYERT, "Computer Models and Dynamic Economics," *Quart. Jour. Econ.*, forthcoming.
9. R. M. CYERT, E. A. FEIGENBAUM, AND J. G. MARCH, "Models in a Behavioral Theory of the Firm," *Behavior Sci.*, Apr. 1959, *4*, 81-95.
10. R. DORFMAN, "Operations Research," *Am. Econ. Rev.*, Sept. 1960, *50*, 575-623.
11. E. A. FEIGENBAUM, "An Information Processing Theory of Verbal Learning," unpublished Ph.D. thesis, Carnegie Institute of Technology 1959.
12. J. FELDMAN, "An Analysis of Predictive Behavior in a Two-Choice Situa-

tion," unpublished Ph.D. thesis, Carnegie Institute of Technology 1959.
13. J. M. HENDERSON AND R. E. QUANDT, *Microeconomic Theory*. New York 1958.
14. A. C. HOGGATT, "Simulation of the Firm," IBM Research Paper, RC-16, August 1957.
15. L. R. KLEIN, *A Textbook of Econometrics*. Evanston, Ill. 1953.
16. A. NEWELL, J. C. SHAW AND H. A. SIMON, "Empirical Explorations of the Logic Theory Machine," *Proc. Western Joint Computer Conference*, February 26-28, 1957, pp. 218-30.
17. ———, ———, ———, "Chess-Playing Programs and the Problem of Complexity," *IBM Jour. Research and Develop.*, Oct. 1958, *2*, 320-35.
18. ———, ———, ———, "Elements of a Theory of Human Problem Solving" *Psych. Rev.*, May 1958, *65*, 151-66.
19. ———, ———, ———, "Report on a General Problem-Solving Program," *Proc. of the ICIP Paris*, June 1959. (Reprinted in *Computers and Automation*, July 1959, *8*, 10-17, as "A General Problem-Solving Program for a Computer.")
20. A. L. SAMUEL, "Some Studies in Machine Learning, Using the Game of Checkers," *IBM Jour. Research and Develop.*, July 1959, pp. 210-30.
21. P. A. SAMUELSON, *Foundations of Economic Analysis*. Cambridge, Mass. 1947.
22. H. SCHULTZ, *The Theory and Measurement of Demand*. Chicago 1938.
23. H. A. SIMON, "Theories of Decision-Making in Economics," *Am. Econ. Rev.*, June 1959, *49*, 253-83.
24. ——— AND A. NEWELL, "What Have Computers to do with Management?" RAND Pub. P-1708.
25. F. M. TONGE, "A Heuristic Program for Assembly Line Balancing," unpublished Ph.D. thesis, Carnegie Institute of Technology, 1959.
26. A. VAZSONYI, *Scientific Programming in Business and Industry*. New York 1958.

7.9

PROBLEMS OF METHODOLOGY -- DISCUSSION

Herbert A. Simon

HERBERT A. SIMON: I find methodological inquiry interesting and instructive to the extent to which it addresses itself to concrete problems of empirical science. Thus, while I find myself in general agreement with almost everything that has been said in the previous papers and by discussants, I should like to pitch my remarks at a level less abstract than theirs.

The Relation of Premises and Conclusions in Economic Theory. Professor Nagel has pointed out that whether a particular proposition is a fundamental assumption of a theory or one of its derived conclusions is relative to the formulation of the theory. If this were the whole story, then asymmetry between assumptions and derivations in Friedman's position—what Professor Samuelson called the F-Twist, and what I like to think of as Friedman's "principle of unreality"—would be entirely arbitrary. Professor Krupp's remarks on composition laws and the relation of microscopic to macroscopic theories suggest, however, that something more is at issue.

Since the prefixes "micro" and "macro" have rather special meanings in economics, let me talk instead of theories of economic actors and theories of economic markets, respectively. In the present context, the relevant theory at the actor level can be approximated by the propositions: X—businessmen desire to maximize profits; Y—businessmen can and do make the calculations that identify the profit-maximizing course of action. The theory at the market level may be summed up as: Z—prices and quantities are observed at those levels which maximize the profits of the firms in the market. (For simplicity, let us assume that we mean the maximum of perfect competition theory.)

Defending the theory consisting of X, Y, and Z, Friedman asserts that it doesn't matter if X and Y are false, provided Z is true. Professors Nagel and Samuelson have already exposed the logical fallacy in using the validity of Z to support X and Y, or to support consequences of X and Y that do not follow from Z alone. But there are other equally serious difficulties in Friedman's position.

That X and Y are taken as premises and Z as a conclusion is not just a matter of taste in formulation of the theory. The formulation fits our common, if implicit, notions of explanation. We explain the macroscopic by the microscopic (plus some composition laws)—the market by the actors. We do this partly because it satisfies our feeling that individual actors are the simple components of the complex market; hence proper explanatory elements. We do it partly because X and Y, plus the composition laws, allow us to derive other propositions at the market level—say, about shifting of taxes, or other policy matters—which we are not able to test by direct observation.

The logical fallacy in Friedman's principle of unreality has exerted so much fascination—both in this session and elsewhere—that attention has been distracted from its other errors. Most critics have accepted Friedman's assumption that proposition Z is the empirically tested one, while X and Y are not directly observable. This, of course, is nonsense. No one has, in fact, observed whether the actual positions of business firms are the profit-maximizing ones; nor has anyone proposed a method of testing this proposition by direct observation. I cannot imagine what such a test would be, since the tester would be as incapable as business firms are of discovering what the optimal position actually is.

If, under these circumstances, Z is a valid theory, it must be because it follows from empirically valid assumptions about actors together with empirically valid composition laws. Now we do have a considerable body of evidence about X and Y, and the vast weight of evidence with respect to Y, at least, is that it is false. The expressed purpose of Friedman's principle of unreality is to save classical theory in the face of the patent invalidity of Y. (The Alchian survival argument that "only profit-maximizers survive," does not help matters, since it, like Z, cannot be tested by direct observation—we cannot identify the profit-maximizers.)

The remedy for the difficulty is straightforward, although it may involve more empirical work at the level of the individual actors than most conventionally-trained economists find comfortable. Let us make the observations necessary to discover and test true propositions, call them X' and Y', to replace the false X and Y. Then let us construct a new market theory on these firmer foundations. This is not, of course, a novel proposal. The last two decades have seen it carried a long distance toward execution.

Ideal Types and Approximations. My final comment is related to the previous one. There has been much talk at this session of ideal types: perfect vacuums and perfect competition. I am not satisfied with the answers to Friedman's argument that he has as much right as the physicists to make unreal assumptions. Was Galileo also guilty of using the invalid principle of unreality? I think not. I think he was interested in behavior in perfect vacuums not because there aren't any in the real world, but because the real world sometimes sufficiently approximates them to make their postulation interesting.

Let me propose a methodological principle to replace the principle of unreality. I should like to call it the "principle of continuity of approximation." It asserts: if the conditions of the real world approximate sufficiently well the assumptions of an ideal type, the derivations from these assumptions will be approximately correct. Failure to incorporate this principle into his formulation seems to me a major weakness in the interesting approach of Professor

Papandreou's paper. Unreality of premises is not a virtue in scientific theory; it is a necessary evil—a concession to the finite computing capacity of the scientist that is made tolerable by the principle of continuity of approximation.

Working scientists employ the principle of continuity all the time. Unfortunately, it has no place in modern statistical theory. The word "significant" has been appropriated by the statisticians to mean "unlikely to have arisen by chance." Now, in testing extreme hypotheses—ideal types—we do not primarily want to know whether there are deviations of observation from theory which are "significant" in this sense. It is far more important to know whether they are significant in the sense that the approximation of theory to reality is beyond the limits of our tolerance. Until this latter notion of significance has been properly formalized and incorporated in statistical methodology, we are not going to accord proper methodological treatment to extreme hypotheses. The discussion at this session has not provided the solution, but it has identified this problem as one of central methodological importance for economics.

7.10
ECONOMIC EXPECTATIONS AND PLANS OF FIRMS IN RELATION TO SHORT-TERM FORECASTING: COMMENT
W. W. Cooper and H. A. Simon

This paper by Modigliani and Sauerlender is long, interesting, and incomplete. Full and balanced assessment of an empirical study like this must await revelation of much of the background material, which is promised for studies to be released by the Bureau of Business Research at the University of Illinois. These comments will, therefore, be fragmentary and selective and directed toward some of the more novel and interesting findings and ideas contained in the paper.

The analyses of existing expectations data undertaken in this study are valuable for the light they throw on business behavior. Among other matters of interest, to which attention has already been addressed at this Conference,[1] is the question of how forecasts by professional economists compare with those by businessmen. Much more needs to be done before this question can be discussed unequivocally. For example, the need for forecasting accuracy of the professional group and that of the business group should be compared both in terms of the problems to be solved by such forecasts and the (e.g. administrative) mechanisms available to each of the groups for corrective action in the event of mistaken forecasts. Intimately involved in this question are the differences, as well as relations, between forecasting for scientific and forecasting for "practical" purposes. The two are not in all respects comparable; and differences as well as similarities should be recognized in arriving at an assessment. The farmer, with smokepots available in his orchard, needs to meet, for his limited purposes, less exacting requirements in his forecasts of the weather than does the meteorologist in his general-purpose analyses of the weather. The farmer's tolerances are wider and vaguer, requiring him merely to turn the smokepots up or down, more or less, and except at certain critical levels his forecasts do not even have to assume specific numerical form. He can correct, overcorrect, and adjust from moment to moment as he finds conditions altering, and his forecast band is, generally, much shorter than that of the meteorologist. The need for making the forecast and access to corrective instruments will of

[1] See the paper by V Lewis Bassie, "Recent Developments in Short-Term Forecasting," in this volume.

352

course condition, if not determine, the character and the form of the forecast.

Another matter of some interest revealed by Modigliani and Sauerlender's analyses of expectations data is the critical character of the form of the questions by which the expectations are solicited. Much depends on what the respondent is expected to estimate: experiences of his immediate environment or the vast reaches of gross national product. Much also depends on the bases of comparison to which attention is directed, and the estimating form used. Ratio and absolute estimates seem, *ceteris paribus*, to yield quite different results, as Modigliani and Sauerlender note. The clearest case, perhaps, is the forecasts of the regional Shippers' Advisory Boards of the American Association of Railroads. Here the method of estimating is itself subject to the ordinary bias of a ratio estimate.[2] But more, apparently, is involved than this. Judging from Modigliani and Sauerlender's analyses of Dun & Bradstreet and *Fortune* data on expectations, a psychological, as well as a statistical, bias arises when the questionnaire solicits information in ratio form. Evidently the "stability" of ratios has psychological as well as statistical roots.

But, of course, it may be a mistake to accept such estimates of anticipations by businessmen—or others—at face value. "Practical" people frequently behave more intelligently than they speak or write.[3] Closely related to this point is a question of different types

[2] It is also subject to the bias of a "selected" sample intended to give representation to the large shippers. Even in unbiased sampling, however, a ratio estimate will yield biased results. Thus, if X' = parameter for which an estimate is sought, such as shipments in forthcoming quarter; Y' = base to which ratio is to be applied, such as actual shipments in comparable quarter of preceding year; and XY = sample values of corresponding parameter, then what is sought is

$$X' = \frac{EX}{EY}Y'$$

where the expected value $EX = X'$ and the expected value $EY = Y'$. But the ratio is secured in the form

$$E\frac{X}{Y} = \frac{EX}{EY} - \frac{\sigma_{Y\frac{X}{Y}}}{EY} = \frac{X'}{Y'} - \frac{\rho_{Y\frac{X}{Y}}\sigma_Y\,\sigma_{\frac{X}{Y}}}{Y'}$$

the amount of bias being given by the last term on the right. Thus in upturns, where one would expect positive correlation, such a method would tend to underestimate true levels, while in downturns, where one would expect negative correlations, such a method would tend to overestimate true levels.

[3] As Modigliani and Sauerlender are careful to note. Estimates that seem to be grossly unsatisfactory to an outsider may prove to be quite satisfactory for practical operating purposes, and their use more satisfactory than allotting the additional time and expense necessary to secure more precise and reliable estimates.

353

of budgets used by business firms for different purposes. Needless to say, the types (and purposes) of budgeting used by business are legion. But one distinction that should be drawn by persons analyzing such data is between the use of budgets as forecasting or estimating devices—in a sense akin to scientific forecasting—and the use of budgets as instruments of control and coordination. As Hart has reminded us, uncertainty introduces elements into the picture that cannot be resolved by reference to certainty equivalents of uncertainty. One of these elements is the need, in planning, to plan for replanning as events materialize.

Illustrative of this difference in types are the so-called "variable" (or flexible) and "forecast" (or fixed) budgets. Firms using modern budgetary techniques usually choose the former type for their operating budgets, and the latter for their capital budgets. The two are quite different in emphasis, and hence the figures contained in them need to be interpreted differently. A variable budget is a frank recognition of the low probability to be attached to point, as against interval, estimates. It begins by attempting to secure a "best" estimate of, say, sales, cost of sales, etc., but then immediately begins to prepare for deviations from these values. It may be roughly characterized in the following fashion: "If sales are at 100 per cent of the assumed levels then costs should be of such and such a magnitude, but if sales are only 90 per cent of the assumed levels then costs should be of such and such different magnitude," and so on. The emphasis of the flexible, as compared with the forecast, type of budget is thus on control and coordination. If asked to report a single figure of expected or budgeted sales, costs, etc., business firms using this type of budget for operating purposes and those using a fixed or forecast type of budget are likely to attach quite different meanings to this figure.

As has already been noted, the forecast type of budget is generally used for capital expenditures, and, indeed, it is difficult to see how a flexible budget, strictly interpreted, can be used for these purposes. Thus data on capital expenditures, such as those being exploited by Friend and Bronfenbrenner, are likely to be more homogeneous, at least in this respect, than budgetary data covering operating costs. Of course, this is not to say that budgetary data on capital expenditures can be taken at face value. Even in the case of forecast budgets various trigger criteria at critical stages of execution—such as review by a budgetary committee before work orders are issued—are frequently carefully built into the budget or sur-

354

rounding budgetary procedures. As Katona has noted, much more in the way of interviewing work, of the kind that Friend and Bronfenbrenner have now begun, is needed before safe ground can be reached in prediction analyses resting on these types of data. Certainly, no mere questionnaire classification into types of budget from which the data are extracted will prove sufficient, since even so-called forecast, or fixed operating, budgets may have strong co-ordinating and control (corrective or adjustive), as well as forecasting, procedures built into them.

Of some interest in this connection is the use of servomechanism analogies by Modigliani and Sauerlender. These analogies have had a strong appeal to us in work being done at the Carnegie Institute of Technology in connection with a project on intra-firm behavior sponsored by the Air Force. One reason for this appeal is the strong intermixture of control and prediction (or lack of prediction) considerations in the design of such devices.

Here a page may be borrowed from the electrical engineer in his design, say, of a radio. He knows that an undesirable quality in reception is noise or static. He knows that from time to time static will be received, but he does not know when this will occur, or the form it will take. But knowing (or predicting) that it will occur within certain limits, he can build control devices into the mechanism so that these undesirable properties will, within reasonable limits of time and magnitude, be eliminated from the reception.

The basic control process built into such devices is not prediction in the usual sense of that term. It is, rather, a process of continuous correction. The elements of prediction involved are: (1) assessment and statement of goals, (2) recognition that disturbances will occur in the process of attaining these goals, and (3) design (prediction of the properties) of a control system or apparatus that will correct for these disturbances when they occur.

Information is gathered at frequent intervals to determine departures of actual behavior from some norm. The difference between the actual and the norm is regarded as an "error," and corrections are made in order to reduce this "error." Diagram 1 illustrates what is involved. A common example of such a servomechanism is the house thermostat, which does not try to predict the weather, but simply measures deviations of actual from desired room temperature and makes appropriate corrections.

No implication that engineering analogies can or should be imported literally into economics is intended. But the central notion

355

of the servomechanism—that behavior in the face of uncertainty can take the form primarily of adjustment rather than prediction—is certainly suggestive for many areas of business behavior.

As a matter of fact there is no reason why adjustment and prediction cannot be combined, why the servomechanism cannot encompass both "feed-back" (or adjustive) and "feed-forward" (or predictive) control. Indeed, Modigliani and Sauerlender have implicitly recognized this by introducing a feed-forward device in their model of production and inventory behavior. For their model

Diagram 1

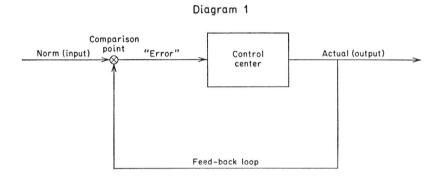

may be pictured as follows: At the present time, t, an estimate is formed of how conditions will appear τ units hence. On the basis of this expectation, and by means of comparison with current outputs, corrective information is carried back to be translated into a change in production or input schedules. A simple pictorial representation of a control system embodying both feed-back and feed-forward is given in diagram 2.[4]

Our investigations have indicated that the introduction of a predictive, feed-forward element into the control system can lead quite easily to unstable behavior in the form of "hunting"—cycles of increasing amplitude—unless the response to the prediction is a highly damped one.

[4] This diagram is drawn from Herbert A. Simon, "On the Application of Servomechanism Theory in the Study of Production Control," *Econometrica*, Vol. 20 (April 1952), pp. 247-268. The use of servomechanisms is suggested in intra-firm analysis by rather strong analogies with the types of administrative control devices and decision rules that are found in many business firms. But judging by Modigliani and Sauerlender's success in applying the analogy to industry analysis, the usefulness of this device is by no means restricted to cases where strong formal administrative apparatuses are present.

356

Servomechanism analogies, with the precautions noted above, should thus provide a useful tool for the study of control systems. Judging from Modigliani and Sauerlender's application to an important segment of the cement industry, such analogies can be successfully applied even in areas where articulate control systems (such as those commonly found on the intra-firm level) are not present in any formal and developed sense.

Diagram 2

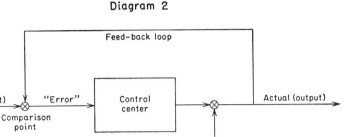

Servomechanical analogies have an additional appeal in suggesting a useful distinction between what might be called "rational" behavior and "adaptive" behavior. The traditional model of economic man has been that of a being who continually strives to attain optimal positions. The behavior of such a creature might be termed "rational." Servomechanism theory suggests, however, the model of an organism that continually adjusts its behavior so that it gets along "well enough"—it adjusts to changes in external conditions rapidly enough and successfully enough to avoid trouble, but it does not in any precise sense maximize or optimize.

Now human behavior probably exhibits elements of both the "rational" and the "adaptive." The notion of adapting to change may well suggest a more realistic model of human behavior in the face of uncertainty than any such sophisticated concept as "maximization of discounted expected gain." If any optimizing principle is involved in the process of adaptation, it is more akin to a "minimax" principle than to a maximum principle. The adaptive system seeks to assure

357

adjustment to the future *whatever it may be*, rather than optimal adjustment to a future that is predicted and described in terms of probability distributions. Even the concept of minimax probably attributes to the adjustive mechanism a more precise criterion of optimality than is generally justifiable.[5]

In any actual organism or organization the effectiveness of adjustment is restricted by, among other factors, limits on the complexity of the problems the system can handle and the cost of securing information. Traditional approaches tend to ignore these costs, or impossibilities, of behaving rationally rather than adaptively. The notion that behavior is necessarily a mixture of the rational and the adaptive suggests the possibility of rephrasing the question of optimality—of asking what is the optimal combination of rational and adaptive behavior rules that should be designed into the system. The advantages to be gained from eliminating or reducing errors can thus be matched against the cost of securing this greater precision—in much the same spirit as this is done in modern theories of sampling.

Even if a model like that employed by Modigliani and Sauerlender is judged to be satisfactory in its handling of uncertainty, it is hard to see how the model deals with mistakes—bona fide mistakes having nothing to do with uncertainty. It would seem preferable to rest models of business and individual behavior on the assumption that mistakes will repeatedly be made and that they will be followed by corrective action looking toward the reduction of undesirable consequences. Again, the mechanism that is suggested is a combination of "adaptive" and "rational" behavior.

One further assumption in this paper should be questioned. This is the assumption, implicitly made, that the system whose behavior is to be predicted is a "given." Now when adaptive behavior must take place in the face of uncertainty, one direction in which optimality can be sought is by reducing the uncertainty—not by gaining

[5] Closely associated with these types of behavior is the distinction between "smooth" and "sudden" adjustments. In complex organisms, including man, mechanisms exist for rational and adaptive adjustment; but also means exist for detecting when the usual adjustment mechanism is inappropriate and for bringing about sudden jumps from one mechanism to another, more appropriate one. A crude example is the behavior of a businessman when he suddenly becomes aware that he is involved in a price war or when, his business having increased rapidly, his working capital position suddenly becomes an acute problem. As Modigliani and Sauerlender note, the use of switching devices by means of which the entire behavioral properties of the system may be changed offers possibilities in this direction.

358

additional information, but by simplifying and stabilizing the system about which information needs to be obtained. An engineering analogy will illustrate the point. Humidity is an important variable in the spinning room of a textile mill. It would be possible to introduce instruments to measure the humidity and continually adjust the machinery to allow for it, but this is not done in modern installations. Instead a relatively uniform humidity is maintained in the room to avoid the necessity for such adjustment.

Many examples can be found in business behavior of adaptation to uncertainty by removing or reducing its sources. The desire often evidenced by oligopolistic firms to maintain a constant share of the market may fall under this head. The costs associated with adjustment to unpredicted or unpredictable variation in sales may be so great that, even from a profit standpoint, it is preferable to seek certainty in sales volume by tacit agreement as to market shares. The drive toward product differentiation and the aversion to price competition in oligopolistic situations may be based, at least partly, on the same motivations.

All of these complications emphasize, as was mentioned at the outset of these comments, that the study of business forecasts, plans, and expectations must take into account the purposes that the prediction mechanisms serve, and the role that they play (in relation to the other mechanisms) in the total process of adjustment to uncertainty and change.

7.11

THE ROLE OF EXPECTATIONS IN AN ADAPTIVE OR BEHAVIORISTIC MODEL

Herbert A. Simon

By this time, I think it is agreed on all sides that the kind of theory of the firm that is required if our interests lie largely in macroeconomics is rather different from the theory required for an understanding of economic behavior at the microlevel. I do not wish to discuss that point at length here. In the present paper I shall take the point of view of microeconomics — that we are interested in understanding, as fully as possible, behavior within the business firm. In particular, I shall discuss what we can learn from psychology and sociology that may prepare us for the facts of life that we will discover when we make actual empirical studies of the formation and use of expectations in business decision-making.

PROGRAMMED AND NONPROGRAMMED DECISION-MAKING

There is no reason to suppose that there is *a* decision-making process to which all instances of rational choice do or should conform. On the contrary, there are good reasons — empirical and theoretical — for believing that humans and organizations of humans are capable of employing a wide variety of choice processes, and that different processes are appropriate to different kinds of decision-making situations.

Two Types of Decision Processes

There is one distinction, in particular, that has attracted the attention of several serious students of organizational decision-making. Katona refers to it as the distinction between "habitual" behavior and "genuine" decisions; in a very similar context, Selznick uses the terms "routine" and "critical"; in our organizational research at Carnegie Institute of Technology, we distinguish between "programmed" and "non-programmed" decisions.

I do not believe that there is an absolute synonymy among the three pairs of terms thus distinguished, but I think that underlying all of them is an observable fact of individual and organizational behavior. Under certain circumstances when an individual or organization is confronted with a situation requiring decision, the decision process goes off quickly and smoothly — almost as though no decision were being made at all, but the matter has been decided previously. Under other circumstances, a choice situation is the occasion for much stirring about, deliberation, discussion, often vacillation. The former kind of behavior is characteristic of decisions that are nonprogrammed.

Whether a particular situation will bring forth programmed or nonprogrammed choice behavior cannot be predicted from the characteristics of the situation alone, but depends also on the previous history of the person or organization confronted with the choice. If we add a liberal dose of *ceteris paribus*, we may say that very complicated choices are more apt to be made in a nonprogrammed way than very simple choices; but that the probability that any particular choice will be made in a programmed way increases rapidly with the number of previous experiences the chooser has had with closely comparable choice problems.

But why do choice situations sometimes elicit behavior that suggests that the choice has been made in advance — that there is no genuine decision-making going on? For the very simple and obvious reason that this is precisely what is happening — for all practical purposes the choice *has* been made in advance. That is to say, in these cases there is a well-established procedure that leads through a series — which may be quite short or very long — of steps to a determinate decision.

I want to stress that a programmed decision may involve a very great amount of computation before a choice is actually made. For an experienced driver, for example, operating an automobile involves almost exclusively programmed decision-making, although a great deal of computation (most of it subconscious) takes place, based on information obtained through the eyes. (A simple experiment that will show that a driver's decisions actually do require a great deal of computing on new information is to blindfold him. We might be willing to predict the outcome of such an experiment without actually trying it.) In the next section, I shall discuss a class of organizational decisions that is quite similar in many ways to driving decisions — the choices are relatively complex, they require an appropriate response to a continuing flow of information, yet they are capable of being almost completely programmed.

Characteristics of Nonprogrammed Decisions

Are there any decisions, then, that are *not* programmed? If we want to be literal, we can take the position that any sequence of events in which each event is determined is some way by the whole collection of its antecedents is "programmed." In these terms, even searching through a haystack for a needle is programmed choice — and perhaps it is. Nevertheless, it is useful to classify or arrange decisions according to the following criteria, and to call decisions at one end of the range "nonprogrammed," those at the other end of the range "programmed." The criteria are these:

(a) To what extent are *search processes* (physical search or search of the memory) involved in the choice; and to what extent is the search *unsystematic* and nonexhaustive — as contrasted with systematic and exhaustive?

(b) To what extent is the process characterized by sudden *switches from one frame of reference* (or "set," in the psychological sense) *to another* frame of reference; and to what extent are these switches themselves relatively unsystematic and dependent on higher-order search processes?

To the extent that a decision process is characterized by unsystematic search and unsystematic change of set, we will call it nonprogrammed. It is immediately evident from the nature of the criteria that the stigmata of nonprogrammed decisions are precisely those visible concomitants of a choice process that we use, when we observe it, to assure ourselves that a genuine choice is being made. Suppose that a friend to whom we posed a question wished to conceal from us that he had already made up his mind. He would take pains to show us that his decision processes were of the nonprogrammed variety. He would hem and haw, produce a sequence of statements as if by free association, view the question now from one "angle," now from another, and finally reach a conclusion.

Decision-Making in the Theory of the Firm

To the extent that we have today a theory of rational choice, it is almost exclusively concerned with programmed decision-making — decision making in a fixed and specified frame of reference, with alternatives given in advance, a determinate set of preferences among consequences, and at worst some uncertainty (often expressed in terms of known probability distributions) as to the connections between alternatives and consequences.[1]

The classical theory of the firm, in its simplest form, is a good example of rational programmed decision-making. The alternatives of action facing the entrepreneur are the different amounts of a commodity he can produce. By means of a cost function and a demand function, he can attach to each alternative of action a set of consequences, and the principle that profits should be maximized provides a complete preference ordering among these consequences. The introduction of uncertainty and expectations into the model (in the demand function, and possibly also in the cost function) does not alter the fundamental structure of the decision. The analysis of such decision processes under circumstances where uncertainty plays an important role has been carried in recent years to a very high level of sophistication, but without altering the fundamentally programmed character of the decision.[2] Characteristic of such theories is Savage's definition of "decision": "To say that a decision is to be made is to say that one of two or more acts is to be chosen, or decided on. In deciding on an act, account must be taken of the possible states of the world, and also of the consequences implicit in each act for each possible state of the world. A consequence is anything that may happen to the person."[3]

It is only a slight exaggeration to say that what an economist or statistical theorist regards as a "rational decision process" is what a psychologist might regard as "habitual behavior"; while what a psychologists regards as "rational choice," an economists would refuse to regard as "rational" at all. The key to the difficulty lies in the contrast between the infinite complexity, on the one hand, of the real world with

---

[1] For some attempts to outline a theory of rational choice that would include important nonprogrammed aspects, see "A Behavioral Model of Rational Choice," *Quarterly Journal of Economics*, February 1955; and "Rational Choice and the Structure of the Environment," *Psychological Review*, July 1956.

[2] See Jacob Marschak, "Probability in the Social Sciences," Chapter 4 in Paul Lazarsfeld, ed., *Mathematical Thinking in the Social Sciences*, Glencoe: Free Press, 1954, particularly pp. 166-187; Kenneth J. Arrow, "Mathematical Models in the Social Sciences," Chapter 9 in Daniel Lerner and Harold D. Lasswell, eds., *The Policy Sciences*, Stanford: Stanford University Press, 1951, pp. 135-137; Leonard J. Savage, *The Foundations of Statistics*, New York: John Wiley & Sons, 1954.

[3] *Op. cit.*, p. 13.

which the choice process, if it is to be genuinely rational, must deal, and the severe simplicity, on the other hand, of even the most complicated models that the human mind can handle in its calculations. A (not completely neutral) summary of the difference in viewpoint between economist and psychologist would allege that the former is concerned with how one can be perfectly rational in an imaginary simple world; the latter with how one can avoid complete and suicidal irrationality in the real complex world.

Since we also, as scientists, are frail humans, we shall probably not succeed in capturing the whole complex phenomena of rational behavior in one simple model. A sophisticated theory of the economist's version of rationality is already in being. It needs to be complemented by an equally sophisticated theory that starts from the psychologist's and sociologist's viewpoint.[4]

All of this is by way of explanation as to why existing knowledge about expectations in psychology and sociology is not easily related to the phenomena of expectations and uncertainty as these appear in economic theory. Even the term "expectations" rarely occurs in the literature of psychology, although the term "set" sometimes takes on closely related meanings and, as we shall see, "levels of aspiration" incorporate certain types of expectations.

In the discussion that follows, we shall maintain the distinction between programmed and nonprogrammed decision-making, since there is no reason to suppose that expectations play the same role in both processes. The next section will be concerned with programmed decision-making; the third section, with the role of institutions in creating for the individual a "simple" world within which his programmed decision-making can take place; the fourth section, with nonprogrammed decisions and the processes of innovation.

---

[4]There is a great danger at the present moment that the economists and statisticians will carry the day even within the territories of psychology and sociology. As can be seen from the recent review article, "The Theory of Decision Making," by Ward Edwards, *Psychological Bulletin*, July 1954, and *Decision Processes*, edited by Robert Thrall et al., John Wiley & Sons, 1954, the behavioral scientists are currently much entranced by the economic models of rationality, and inclined to accept the "definition of the situation" proposed by the latter.

EXPECTATIONS IN PROGRAMMED DECISION-MAKING

As an example of a decision that can conceivably be made in a highly programmed manner, let us consider the monthly aggregate production plan of a factory. We will assume that prices are rigid, and that what the factory manager (or some other executive of the firm) has to decide is how much to produce in total during the coming month and each succeeding month. Only the plan for the first month has to be adhered to, of course, for the plan can be revised at the beginning of the next month on the basis of the additional information about past and expected sales that will then be available.

"Realism" in Decision Models

I shall not discuss at any length whether the decision problem thus posed is "realistic." The term realistic is, in fact, highly ambiguous. It might be intended normatively: is it *rational* to define the decision problem confronting the manager in this way? But this question can only be answered if we have a larger and more comprehensive model of the decision-making program of which the decision before us comprises one part. For example, if we had taken as our starting point the classical theory of the firm, and had assumed further that the elasticity of demand for the product was not infinite, then it would not be rational for the manager to take prices as fixed. For he could presumably make maximum profits only if he regarded the quantity he would sell as a function of price. But the decision model incorporated in the classical theory of the firm is itself an heroic abstraction from reality. It is only in a relative, and not in an absolute sense, that we can refer to a particular framework of decision as "rational" or "nonrational." If we optimize at all, we always suboptimize. Hence, the decision problem posed in the previous paragraph, which assumes fixed prices, cannot be rejected as "unrealistic."

On the other hand, we might interpret the term realistic descriptively. If we take this point of view, we can make a strong argument for the realism of the decision problem we have posed. For it is an absolute fact of business behavior, at least in a large number of firms, that the factory manager's decisions as to how much to produce do not take into consideration the price elasticity of demand, but are based on the assumption that sales are exogenous variables.

A Rational Decision Rule

Under the assumptions of the problem, revenues are fixed, and profit maximization is synonymous with cost minimization. The costs that depend on the production decision are of two main kinds: there are costs associated with having more or less inventory (inventory holding costs and costs associated with stockout), and there are costs associated with the level of production and the fluctuations in that level (e.g., overtime costs, training costs, severance pay).

The problem of setting the optimal level of production under these circumstances has been formulated with great generality, and it has been shown rigorously that solutions exist both under the assumption that future sales are known with certainty and under the assumption that the joint probability distribution of future sales is known.[5]

The Need to Approximate

But the very same analyses that demonstrate the existence and uniqueness of solutions to this dynamic programming problem also show that the task of computing these solutions is in general exceedingly burdensome, even if modern large-scale electronic computers are available. In fact, there are three separate and distinct classes of difficulties that have to be overcome before the "in principle" solutions to the decision problem can actually be applied by flesh-and-blood (or "wire-and-tube") decision makers:

(1) The coefficients of the factory's cost function must be estimated numerically — including such intangibles as the penalty to be attached to stock runouts, the value of lost production associated with the breaking in of new employees, and so on;

(2) The joint probability distribution of future sales must be determined;

(3) The equations obtained for the optimal strategy, with these numerical data substituted in them, must be solved.

Let us consider for the moment the last of these three difficulties. I

---

[5]The fundamental references are: Kenneth J. Arrow, Theodore Harris, and Jacob Marschak, "Optimal Inventory Policy," *Econometrica*, July 1951; Richard Bellman, *An Introduction to the Theory of Dynamic Programming*, RAND Corporation, 1953; and A. Dvoretzky, J. Kiefer, and J. Wolfowitz, "The Inventory Problem," *Econometrica*, April and July, 1952. For an overview, see Herbert A. Simon and Charles C. Holt, "The Control of Inventories and Production Rates — a Survey," *Journal of the Operations Research Society of America*, August 1954.

shall state categorically that the decision problem is not usually within the limits of computational feasibility unless very severe simplifying assumptions are introduced to make it so. An assumption that the cost function is of a particularly simple form (e.g., linear or quadratic) will often do the trick. On the other hand, somewhat more complicated cost functions can sometimes be handled if restrictive assumptions are imposed on the probability density function of the sales — say that this is a product of identical and independent functions for each month, each of which takes the form of a Poisson distribution.

Since heroic simplifications are required in any event to bring the problem within the limits of computability, it is hard to see that there is room for highly sophisticated assumptions about the forecasts of sales or the estimates of the cost coefficients. Companies can and do survive under these circumstances — perhaps because they only have to compete with other companies that are in the same fix. But I should like to suggest that under many circumstances they need not even incur large losses through their inability to deal more exactly with the determination of an optimal production decision. To see why this is so, let us consider a special case where the computations *can* be carried out exactly — the case where the cost function can be approximated by a sum of quadratic and linear terms.

In the special case where the cost function is quadratic, the following may be said:

(1) *Computability.* It is possible, with very little labor, to compute the optimal production each month provided that the cost coefficients can be estimated and a prediction can be made of the expected values of sales, month by month.

(2) *Expected values are sufficient statistics.* The only information about future sales that is relevant is the expected value — the variance and higher moments of the probability distribution of sales are irrelevant, even if known.

(3) *Planning horizon.* For most cost functions one would expect to encounter in practice, the coefficients are such that a relatively short planning horizon can be assumed — that is, future sales have a significant influence on the optimal production level only a few months in advance.

(4) *Feedback correction of forecast errors.* Errors in forecasting sales will ultimately be reflected in excessive or deficient inventories, and the optimal procedure for adjusting for these errors will be to liquidate, over a period of months, this excess or deficiency.

(5) *Sensitivity to estimating errors.* The optimal production level will be

387

relatively insensitive to errors in the production cost coefficients, so that these need to be estimated only very roughly.[6]

We should not lose sight of the number of simplifying assumptions we have had to make in order to bring our problem within the bounds of practical solvability. But the point is that we *can*, by making a series of approximations, each of which has some "reasonable" justification, rephrase this optimization problem so as to bring it within the capacities of humans for making estimates and forming expectations. If we are really interested in a decision model as a realizable model of human decision-making — for either normative or descriptive purposes — then each of the five points mentioned in the previous paragraph deserves serious attention; the computational demands must be modest; we may reasonably expect managers to be able to estimate expected values of variables, but it is dubious whether they can often estimate other characteristics of probability distributions (variances or higher moments); plans should not depend sensitively on forecasts that peer into the future beyond a modest planning horizon; rational adaptation must rely as much upon correction of past errors as upon accurate anticipation of the future; plans must not depend sensitively on data of very limited accuracy.

It may be objected that managers cannot behave rationally if their decision processes are to be limited to those that satisfy the five criteria I have listed. But this objection misses the central point of my argument. We must surrender the illusion that programmed decision-making is a process of discovering the "optimal" course of action in the real, complex world. Even the most enthusiastic exponents of the formal theory of rational decision do not have this illusion. Savage, for example, concedes:

---

[6]These statements are based on a rather extensive program of research into the theory and practice of dynamic programming with a quadratic cost criterion. For a full discussion of the theory and of applications to specific manufacturing situations see: Herbert A. Simon, "On the Application of Servomechanism Theory in the Study of Production Control," *Econometrica*, April 1952; Charles C. Holt and Herbert A. Simon, "Optimal Decision Rules for Production and Inventory Control," *Proceedings of the Conference on Production and Inventory Control*, Case Institute of Technology, Cleveland, January 1954; Herbert A. Simon, "Some Properties of Optimal Linear Filters," *Quarterly Journal of Applied Mathematics*, January 1955; and Charles C. Holt, Franco Modigliani, and Herbert A. Simon, "A Linear Decision Rule for Production and Employment Scheduling," *Management Science*, October 1955.

Carried to its logical extreme, the "Look before you leap" principle demands that one envisage every conceivable policy for the government of his whole life (at least from now on) in its most minute details, in the light of the vast number of unknown states of the world, and decide here and now on one policy. This is utterly ridiculous, not — as some might think — because there might later be cause for regret, if things did not turn out as had been anticipated, but because the task implied in making such a decision is not even remotely resembled by human possibility. It is even utterly beyond our power to plan a picnic or to play a game of chess in accordance with the principle, even when the world of states and the set of available acts to be envisaged are artificially reduced to the narrowest reasonable limits.

We should view programmed decision-making as a process for making choices within the frameworks set by highly simplified models of real-world problems. If we take this viewpoint, it appears entirely reasonable that actual human capacities for computation, for forming expectations about the future, and for estimating parameters be taken into account in constructing our models of the choice problem. These considerations must, in fact, be our principal guidelines in deciding what approximations to make and what simplifying assumptions to admit.

INSTITUTIONS AS SOURCES OF STABLE EXPECTATIONS

In the previous section we directed our attention to a specific programmed decision — the choice of an aggregate production rate for a factory. But the pattern of behavior in a business firm, in which this particular decision represents one small detail, may be regarded as a whole mosaic of such decision-making programs — the pattern being interspersed with a variety of choice processes of a less programmed nature. In fact, it is both possible and useful to view in this way not only the individual business firm but also the whole network of economic interrelationship in which the firm is involved.

---

[7] L. J. Savage. *The Foundations of Statistics*, John Wiley & Sons, 1954, p. 16; by permission.

The Social Environment of Choice

So far as any one of the programmed decision-making processes is concerned, all the other programs that surround it are a part of its environment — in general, just as lawful and just as predictable as the physical environment. When I address a letter and drop it into my mail tray, the reasonableness of my action hinges upon the predictability of a host of programs that collectively constitute the U.S. Post Office Department.

A very large part of the environment of any particular subsystem in our society is made up of the patterns of behavior, more or less regular, of other subsystems. While these patterns are seldom completely reliable or predictable, they are more predictable than many natural phenomena — the weather, say. As a matter of fact a paradoxer, if he were so inclined, could probably maintain with fair success the position that most of the unpredictabilities of human life come not from the social environment but from the natural.[8]

The sociological terms "institution" and "role" refer to these mosaics of programmed behavior that constitute social systems. The point is much emphasized in the sociological literature that the whole system of interlocking roles constituting a society is adaptive, in the sense that it satisfies the functional requirements of the society. What is usually less emphasized is that each role is not a fixed pattern of behavior but a set of ground rules — a program, in the precise sense in which we have been using that term — on the basis of which more or less rational choice can be exercised.

This is the sense in which we must interpret the rationality of *homo oeconomicus* if we are to apply to his behavior psychological and sociological theories of expectations. He does not stand on a mountain-top and, viewing the whole world at his feet, make a global, omniscient, rational choice. He is rational within the bounds set by his social role of economic man. His calculations rest on his expectation that the others with whom he interacts will accept their corresponding social roles. Even

---

[8]I must resist the temptation to pursue further the question of predictability of social events. I should like to observe that there appear to be two quite distinct sorts of regularity in human affairs — the one represented by prediction of the arrival of a train, the other represented by prediction of the number of people who will die in auto accidents over Labor Day weekend. The latter depends, in one form or another, upon the law of large numbers; the former, upon a strict determination of behavior by program.

the "facts" on which he acts obtain their status as facts by a social process of legitimation, and have only a very indirect and tenuous connection with the evidence of his senses.

I am afraid that the economist may find in this description of social behavior too little room for the exercise of rational choice; the sociologist, an excessive emphasis on reason. The former will damn it as "institutionalist," the latter as "rationalist" doctrine. Both will be correct in their characterization; wrong, I think, in their condemnation. For it is precisely this interaction between rational choice and its social boundaries that appears to me — and has so appeared since my first encounters with the phenomena of organization — the most central and significant characteristic of behavior in organized social groups. And it is this same area — so central to organizational behavior — that has been peripheral to each of the social sciences, a sort of no man's land separating economics and statistical decision theory, on the one hand, from sociology and social psychology, on the other.

Let me return from these asides on the present state of the social sciences to a little further exploration of expectations as they are embedded in social institutions. In particular, I should like to make a few comments on each of three topics: (a) the relation of the stability of expectations to the stability of the institutions themselves, (b) institutional stability and forecasting, (c) social pressures toward conformity in expectations.

Stability of Institutions

We do not need a theory of revolution so much as we need a theory of the absence of revolution — what is it that maintains the stability of the patterns of behavior in groups of interacting persons? For most purposes, I find the following kind of explanation the most plausible. Suppose that A's behavior has been rational, *given* B's and C's behaviors; that B's is rational, given A's and C's; and C's is rational, given A's and B's. Suppose now that A changes his behavior, but B and C do not. Then A will discover that he is worse off than he was before, and he will be motivated to revert to his previous pattern. Any one member of the group is acting rationally in maintaining his present pattern of behavior so long as the others do likewise. This is not to say that all members of the group, or some subset of them would not be better off if they all changed their behavior in an appropriate *synchronous* fashion.

The kind of equilibrium I have been describing is, of course, identical with the Nash-Cournot equilibrium of duopoly theory. The present utterly confused state of oligopoly theory is an excellent demonstration of the importance of the stability of expectations — and the equilibrium that depends on that stability — for the exercise of human rationality. Even the collective minds of our very best economists are unable to arrive at agreement as to what constitutes rational behavior when we remove the assumption that the social environment of the chooser will remain constant.

Forecasting

The inventory and production decision that I selected as my example of programmed decision-making does not impose very severe strains on the forecasting abilities of the decision maker. As I explained above, a formal anslysis of this decision problem shows that the planning horizon is quite short, and that the effects of forecast errors are further cushioned by feedback adjustment. But how typical is this of business decision-making in general? What about decisions regarding new plant investment that involve very long-run commitment?

I do not know the general answer to this question, but I should like to hazard a suggestion as to how stable institutional patterns simplify the forecasting problem. As long as it is assumed that governmental policy will be aimed at reasonably full employment of resources in the economy and that the policy will be reasonably effective, the only long-term forecast that a business firm really needs to make is a projection of the growth of the economy, based on population forecasts and projections of productivity increases. Moreover, in a growing economy forecast errors will not be very costly because they will simply mean that new plant will be acquired a little too soon or a little too tardily, and no irrevocable loss will be incurred.

This observation is related to my earlier comments on oligopoly theory, and is quite consistent with the views about planning that are commonly expressed by theorists of business administration — particularly those of the European "rationalization" movement — if not by economists. Applying this viewpoint to price competition and cartelization, we would argue that certain forms of competition are "irrational" because they destroy the very stability of expectations on which rationl calculation rests. It should be noticed that this is very different from the argument that cutthroat competition is irrational because it does not lead to a stable equilibrium short of suicide, or because the competitors are unreasonably foregoing the monopoly profits that would be theirs if they combined.

Social Determination of Expectations

Expectations may be based less on the observation of external realities than on the observation of the expectations of others. Although the term "panic" is somewhat old-fashioned, its synonyms play an important role in contemporary business cycle theory. Economics has been in closer communication with her sister disciplines in this area of investigation than in almost any other, and a number of the empirical studies to be reported at this conference will deal with it.

Facts are the grist for the mill of programmed choice. To determine what is the fact is not simply a matter of observation, but it is in itself a complex social process. In an organization a member does not have a right to choose for himself the facts that he is going to use for making his decisions — the volume of sales next year, or the cost of manufacturing a particular product. There is an official process for establishing such facts which has the function — or at least the aim — of securing uniformity throughout the organization in the factual premises applied to decision and of assuring expertness in the establishment of such premises.

NONPROGRAMMED DECISIONS: THE PROCESS OF INNOVATION

Nonprogrammed decisions were defined earlier as those in which relatively unsystematic search processes and relatively unsystematic shifts in frames of reference were prominent. Decision processes with these characteristics would be "unreasonable" under the conditions usually assumed in formal theories of rational choice. They become "reasonable" when we consider situations where the alternatives of choice are not given in advance, but must be discovered; where the means-ends connections between choices and consequences are imperfectly known, and must be explored; and finally, where a simplified and approximating frame of reference must be choosen before the choice can be brought within the limits of human computation.

Aspiration Levels and Search Processes

I should like to describe a class of simple, but extremely common, decision-making situations in which these characteristics — particularly the first — are prominent, and in which search processes play an important role in choice. In many situations an individual is confronted with a choice of "doing A" or "not doing A." But the second, negative, alternative is not a specific course of action; "not doing A" really stands for the whole class of alternative actions that are available if A is rejected. Before A can be accepted or rejected, the alternative — or rather, this amorphous mass of potential alternatives — must be evaluated.

Speaking in the language of utility theory, what the decision maker wishes to do is to attach a utility to "not doing A" that he can then compare with the utility of "doing A." Equally important, he wishes to assess the former utility without examining in detail all the alternatives that are subsumed under not A. It is this utility — the utility of not A — that economists denote by the phrase "opportunity cost of A," and psychologists by the phrase "aspiration level."

The opportunity cost and the aspiration level — accepting the hypothesis for the moment that they are the same thing — provide a natural zero of utility for the anchoring of choice. Alternative A may be chosen if it yields a utility that is positive, net of the opportunity cost.

But are we correct in identifying opportunity cost with aspiration level? There is a great deal of psychological evidence that the aspirations that influence choice are highly sensitive to success and failure — that persistent failure to attain an aspired level reduces the aspirations; while success raises it. That is to say, in general — if only in the long run — a person aspires to that which he has a reasonable expectation of achieving. Now the opportunity cost of choosing A may be measured by the decision maker's reasonable expectation of a result in case he rejects A — that is, his aspiration level. We have thus reached two important conclusions: first, that "opportunity cost" is a concept that refers to expectations; second, that "aspiration level" is closely related to, if not identical with, opportunity cost.

If the result the decision maker expects from A exceeds or equals his aspiration level, he will presumably choose A; if not, he will choose not A. But what does choosing not A involve? It involves a *search* for a new concrete alternative to replace A. Hence, the aspiration-level mechanism determines whether a course of action will be chosen from among those presently available (those the organization is already programmed to select and execute), or whether a new alternative will be sought that has not previously been part of the repertory.

The mechanisms just described provide, I submit, a plausible psychological basis for such concepts as "reasonable profit." The doctrine that a firm seeks reasonable rather than maximum profits does not mean that the firm prefers less profit to more or even that it is indifferent as between less and more profit. Among the courses of action it perceives as available to it, it may be expected to choose the most profitable. But the point is that failure to earn a reasonable profit will lead to a search for new alternatives, will stimulate the innovative processes.

This does not explain how expectations are formed as to what the reasonable level of profit is. We may conjecture that recently attained levels of profit are an important element of the assessment. We may suppose also that there will be comparisons with other firms in the industry. Whatever the mechanisms, we should be able to test empirically the proposition that failure to earn reasonable profits leads to efforts at innovation.

The Occasions of Innovation

A direct and unsophisticated application of the theory developed in the preceding paragraphs would suggest that we should search for the initiation of innovation largely in the environment of the organization — particularly in adverse changes in the environment that threaten a previously existing level of achievement. Two kinds of adverse conditions come to mind at once: a downturn or anticipated downturn in the business cycle; innovations by competitors that improve their market position. Very few data are available to show whether such circumstances do, in fact, stimulate search activities and innovation, although some confirmatory evidence has been compiled by my colleagues, James March and Richard Cyert.

All sorts of difficulties lie in the path of a test of the hypothesis. As far as the business cycle is concerned, a downturn might stimulate innovative attempts at the same time it deterred actual investment. Hence the latter could not be used as an index of innovative activity. As far as imitation of competitors is concerned, this could be explained on other grounds than the hypothesis of reasonable profit, since the imitators escape most of the costs of originating the innovation. Other difficulties as perplexing as these can be conjured up.

But over and beyond the empirical testing of the hypothesis, we may be skeptical even a priori as to its validity. For an aspiration can become attached to the *rate of change* of a variable just as well as it can to the *level* of the variable. For example, many recent labor contracts have incorporated in them the assumption that productivity will increase, through technological advance, at a more or less steady annual rate. When such an escalator is built into the aspiration-level mechanism, a need for innovation will be generated even in the absence of adverse environmental changes.

There are several ways that are more direct than the general diffusion of a belief in progress in which innovation can become "institutionalized" — i.e., self-generating — in an organization. First, as we move upward through successive levels of an executive hierarchy, we find that executives at higher levels have progressively less to do with the day-to-day programs of the organization that are necessary to maintain activity at current levels. Executives at these higher levels define their tasks more and more in terms of *change* in programs as they are less and less involved in the routine *execution* of programs. The levels of aspirations of executives are, then, generally attached to rates of change, and hence the executive hierarchy may be expected to be a frequent source of demands for innovation.

Second — and this appears to be, on the whole, a relatively modern phenomenon — organizational units may be created with the special aim of producing innovations. They may be almost completely detached from the organization's programmed activity, and their only contribution may reside in the successful innovations they produce. The industrial research department is the most obvious example of such a unit. None of this controverts the general proposition that necessity — in the form of the pressure of applications — really is the mother of invention. But it does argue that adversity is not the only, or perhaps even the most important, source of necessity. The necessity for innovation in large hierarchical organizations may reside in the needs of executives and research personnel, who are seldom indispensable to the organization's programmed activity.

Innovation: The Construction of New Programs

The general tenor of the analysis to this point has been to stress the difficulties of forming accurate expectations about complex affairs, and the consequent tendency of organizations and individuals to minimize the role of expectations in their decision-making processes. In programmed decision-making, this de-emphasis is accomplished by substituting a simplified approximate decision model for the complexities of the "real world." In nonprogrammed decision-making, the de-emphasis is accomplished largely by relying on simple aspiration-level mechanisms to initiate search activities and innovation, thus avoiding the necessity for forming expectations about alternatives and their consequences when existing programs are deemed "satisfactory."

Rational man is a *satisficing* rather than an *optimizing* animal. He is the former, if for no other reason, because he does not have the wits to be the latter. This is almost certainly true, as we have seen, of the way in which he decides *whether to search for new alternatives.* It is also true of the way in which he *selects new alternatives* when he is in an innovative mood.

When a search for a new program is initiated by the failure of the current one to satisfy aspirations, the problem is not to find a best one, but to find one that is "good enough." Even this task is not a light one, for it possesses three intrinsic difficulties, two of which are directly concerned with expectations:

(1) Alternative programs must be discovered. I will not discuss the discovery process here. Little enough is known about it, and it would take us away from our present topic.

(2) The facts of the case must be established. That is, the consequences of adopting any proposed program must be determined.

(3) When a new program adopted by a particular organization unit is dependent on the programs of other units or other organizations, the programs of these other units must be determined simultaneously.

The second and third points have already been discussed, briefly, in the section on institutions as sources of expectations. Let me add a few further comments on their particular implication for nonprogrammed decisions.

A decision-making program in an organization generally not only specifies the decision procedure, but also designates who shall carry it out. In particular, the program usually makes it legitimate for certain persons or organization units to stipulate particular matters of fact as premises of the decision. In nonprogrammed decision-making it is often far from clear in whose jurisdiction particular questions of fact fall, and who has the right to determine them. Hence nonprogrammed choice is often characterized by jurisdictional disputes and by significant conflicts in the expectations and factual assumptions that enter as decision premises.

We may expect that an organization that has occasion for frequent innovations in a particular area (e.g., product innovations in a pharmaceutical company) is likely to institutionalize the processes of forecasting, establishing consequences, and finding the other facts that are relevant to decision. The "experts" and their respective areas of jurisdiction will likely be clearly designated. In areas where this institutionalization has not taken place, we would expect innovation to be a relatively slow and difficult process.

My final observation is that the interdependence of organization units is a strong force toward conservatism in the innovative process. We have seen that the number of variables that can be handled in human decision-making processes is limited — that all sorts of devices are employed to keep the choice process simple. We have seen further that a stable institutional environment is an important source of reliable expectations that can serve as "given" premises in the choice process.

Hence, when a change is contemplated in any particular part of an organization, there are strong reasons for regarding the programs of surrounding organization units as fixed and unchangeable. It is too difficult to form global expectations of the consequences of changing large numbers of programs simultaneously. As a result, the adaptation of organizations to new circumstances is often achieved by local change, rather than by revolutionary innovations that alter organizational programs simultaneously over a wide area.

CONCLUSION

If someone were to ask me whether I expected the next winter to be severe or mild, I would have to reply: "I have no expectations about next winter." This would *not* mean that I had considered the matter and had reached the conclusion that the chances of a mild or severe winter were about even; it would mean that I had not thought about it. So it is with expectations in general, and business expectations in particular. A theory of expectations must be concerned with the way in which expectations are formed; it must be equally concerned with the *conditions under which* expectations are or are not formed.

Expectations play a narrower role in actual business behavior than they do in classical models of rational choice. The devices employed in programmed decision-making to reduce dependence on explicit forecasts are numerous. Rarely are forecasts made in the form of estimates of probability distributions; the future is bounded naturally or artificially by a planning horizon; feedback correction is depended upon for retroactive correction of forecast errors.

Estimates of the behaviors and reactions of the organizations that form the social environment of the decision maker are of great relevance to planning in most situations. In order for the decision maker to be able to cope with the problems of choice, it is essential to him that this environment be relatively static and predictable. Economic instability, whether it stems from business cycles, monetary inflation, or "excessively" vigorous competition in an industry, paralyzes rational action because it destroys most of the customary bases for forming accurate expectations. I would argue that a large part of the discomfort that is felt in the face of instability can be traced to distraction and confusion of choice, rather than to any careful calculation of economic loss.

Stability of expectations can be so essential for decision making that it may be more important, in some circumstances, to have *agreement* on the facts than to be certain that what is agreed upon is really fact. Hence, we often find that the procedures for fact finding and for legitimating facts are themselves institutionalized. A critical step in the innovative process is to secure legitimacy for the facts and expectations that justify the innovation.

A set of expectations of particular importance in organizational decision-making are those that define the aspiration levels of the decision makers. Aspirations are expectations — adjusted in the long run to realities — of the result that can reasonably be attained. They are not formed on the basis of detailed evaluation of alternative courses of action. Indeed, their principal usefulness lies in the fact that they remove the necessity for such evaluations until the failures of existing programs indicate the need for innovation. The innovation process then requires the discovery and elaboration of new programs that can be regarded as satisfactory — that is, as compatible with aspirations.

Even if this theory of the role of aspiration levels is generally correct, we are left wih some important problems in applying it. In particular, we need far more empirical knowledge than we now possess as to the bases on which aspirations are formed and the conditions under which they are modified. There is some indication that innovation can itself be institutionalized by attaching aspirations to rates of change rather than to absolute levels of performance. The expectations created by the "idea of progress" can themselves be powerful innovative forces.

Finally, the need for simplification in order to bring rational choice within the limits of human powers is a powerful force toward conservatism even in the innovative process. Innovation does not dispense with the needs either for the legitimation of facts or for relative stability in the institutional environment of choice.

I believe that the propositions set forth here about the nature of choice and the formation of expectations are consistent with what we know, in a common-sense way, about behavior in organizations and in everyday affairs. But what common sense knows is often very different from what science has tested — particularly in the social sciences. The empirical study of the role of expectations in rational choice can give useful employment to a great many social scientists for a long time to come.

VIII

SUBSTANTIVE AND PROCEDURAL RATIONALITY

While computers and research on the psychology of problem solving mostly took me away from economics after about 1960, I continued to maintain a strong interest — at least an observer's interest — in the continuing development of the theory of the firm. I must confess to some surprise that the behavioral theory, demonstrably so much truer to the facts than had been the classical theory, was not soon embraced by substantial numbers of economists as an obvious step forward and did not rapidly attract dozens or hundreds of graduate students into research that would extend it further. In particular, I was naively unprepared for the claim that the new theory was "irrelevant" and for the expressions of a "lack of confidence in the marked superiority, for purposes of economic analysis, of this newer concept of the firm, over the older conception of the entrepreneur." (The words are E. S. Mason's (1952), but the sentiments that they echo were and are widely shared and frequently expressed in the economics profession.)

Until I was confronted with these expressions of disinterest and with the radical pragmatism of Friedman's methodological essays I had ingenuously supposed that economists, like other species of empirical scientists, were interested in discovering how the world works — in this case the world of human behavior in economic affairs. Now I learned that behavior was of interest to economists (at least to those who were making public methodological pronouncements) only if it had important implications for matters of policy at the level of the economy, or at least of the industry. To claim the attention of neoclassical economists, one had to present not only discoveries about human behavior and evidence for their validity but also evidence that they led to different macroeconomic or market-level consequences than did the classical theory. Nor did I see much indication of patience in the reactions of the skeptics — the relevance should be demonstrated here and now, else the research was not worth pursuing.

In looking back at the research on economics I have undertaken since 1960, and even some I did during the 1950s, I see that a great deal of it can be interpreted as reaction to this resistance of the profession to novelty it regarded as unnecessary. To what extent I was following a conscious strategy of assault on classical theory, to what extent I was driven by those unconscious fonts of energy about which modern psychology is so eloquent, or to what extent my focus on such topics was coincidence I cannot say with any certainty.

The work to which I make reference has three main themes. First, I was concerned with providing theoretical explanations, whether classical or not, for certain significant observed phenomena — notably, the size distribution of business firms, the good fit of the Cobb-Douglas and CES production functions to data that could hardly represent genuine production functions, and the relation between executive salaries and the sizes of firms. The work on business firm sizes can be found in Ijiri and Simon, *Skew Distributions and the Sizes of Business Firms* (1977); the work on production functions is reported in chapters 4.3 and 4.4 of volume 1 of these papers; and the work on executive salaries is contained in chapter 5.6 of this volume.

As a second theme, I was concerned with setting forth the evidence for the behavioral theory and explaining why it is in fact relevant to the traditional concerns of economic theory — as well as interesting in its own right and for its own purposes. Most of the papers of section VII of this volume represent this line of work.

The third theme emerged when I asked myself how economics and psychology, both deeply concerned with human rational behavior, could go their separate ways with almost no concern for each other or mutual communication. In particular, when asked to provide a definition of "rationality" for the *Dictionary of the Social Sciences,* I had to supply two distinct definitions, one to fit the usage in economics, the other to fit the usage in psychology. Out of this discovery came the distinction between the "substantive rationality" assumed in classical economic theory and the "procedural rationality" studied by psychologists, which provides the basis for most of the papers of section VIII.

Chapter 8.2, written, appropriately enough, for a Festschrift in honor of Jacob Marschak, reviews the case for bounded rationality and serves, thereby, as a bridge from section VII. An earlier version of chapter 8.3 was given on the occasion of the twenty-fifth anniversary of the economics department in Groningen, The Netherlands, but was later developed further and presented at a symposium on the philosophy of science at Navplion, Greece. Three later festive occasions allowed me to develop the theme further and to expose a wider audience of economists to it: my Ely Lecture at the meetings of the American Economic Association (chapter 8.4), a conference given in my honor by my economics colleagues at Carnegie-Mellon University (chapter 8.5), and my Nobel Lecture (chapter 8.6).

Chapter 8.6 provides a suitable conclusion to this volume, for in it I have tried to survey, albeit briefly, the whole development in the study of procedural rationality and the behavioral theory of the firm since the Second World War. Readers will see that I am unshaken in my belief that the processes of human thought as well as its products are topics of basic importance for the continuing progress of economic theory and knowledge — for the theory of the firm in particular, but also for business cycle theory and other topics in macroeconomics. From recent developments surveyed in the chapter, I see new signs that this belief is shared by a growing (though growing too slowly, perhaps) segment of the economics profession.

REFERENCES

Ijiri, Y., and Simon, H. A. *Skew distributions and the sizes of business firms.* Amsterdam: North-Holland, 1977.

Mason, E. S: Comment. In B. T. Haley, ed., *A survey of contemporary economics,* vol. 2, pp. 221-222. Homewood: Irwin, 1952.

Simon, H. A. Rationality. In J. Gould and W. L. Kolb, eds., *A dictionary of the social sciences,* pp. 573-574. Glencoe: The Free Press, 1964.

8.1

RATIONALITY

Herbert A. Simon

1.   In a broad sense, *rationality* denotes a style of behavior (A) that is appropriate to the achievement of given goals, (B) within the limits imposed by given conditions and constraints.

2.   In particular contexts, (A) and (B) of the definition may receive more exact specification.   Some of the more important of these specialized uses are:

a.   The goal may be assumed to take the form of maximizing (or, in game theory, minimaxing) the expected value, over some time interval, of a utility function. Further, the existence of the utility function may be derived from postulates about the ordering and consistency of the choosing organism's preferences. Thus, the rational consumer of formal economic theory maximizes his expected utility, and the rational entrepreneur maximizes his expected profit. If a distinction is wanted between this very strict species of rationality and more general forms, the former may be termed *optimality*, the latter *adaptiveness* or *functionality*.

b.   The goal may be assumed to consist of criteria to be satisfied in an all-or-none way (e.g. attainment of the level of aspiration).

c.   The conditions and constraints referred to in the general definition may be *objective characteristics* of the environment external to the choosing organism, they may be *perceived characteristics*, or they may be *characteristics of the organism itself* that it takes as fixed and not subject to its own control. The line between the first case and the other two is sometimes drawn by distinguishing *objective rationality*, on the one hand, from *subjective* or *bounded rationality*, on the other.

d.   The goals referred to in the definition may be goals of the choosing organism, goals of a social system to which he belongs, or goals imputed by the observer.

e.   An unambiguous use of the term *rationality* requires the user to specify what assumptions he is making about both goals and conditions.

3.   *Rationality* and its synonyms were important in the vocabulary of philosophy and ethics before the social sciences emerged as independent

disciplines. The modern usage of rationality is very close to Aristotle's concept of calculative or deliberative intellectual virtue. In this sense, the rationality of an action involves its derivation by logical processes from valid premises. Rationality sometimes refers to processes of choice that employ the intellective faculty; sometimes to the choices themselves. The former emphasis is typical of earlier usage in psychology, logic, and ethics; the latter emphasis predominates in economics and sociology.

a. Thus, W. James (*Principles of Psychology*, New York: Holt, 1890, ch. 22) uses rationality as synonymous with "the peculiar thinking process called reasoning". In this view, the rationality of a choice depends on the process of making it. Correspondingly, *irrationality* in psychological literature denotes domination of choice by affective mechanisms (emotion, drive, instinct, impulse) rather than intellective mechanisms (G. Allport, "The Historical Background of Modern Social Psychology", in G. Lindzey (ed.), *Handbook of Social Psychology*, Cambridge, Mass.: Addison-Wesley, 1954, pp. 15-18). Because of this historical identification of rationality with the doctrine of *rationalism*, recent psychological writing tends to prefer terms like *cognitive process* (J. S. Bruner, J. V. Goodnow, & G. A. Austin, *A Study of Thinking*, New York: J. Wiley, 1956, p. viii) or *intellective process*. Hence *rationality*, in reference to the process of choice, appears to be disappearing from social science literature.

b. Economists have generally used *rationality* to denote an attribute of an action selected by a choice process, rather than an attribute of the process. Thus R. A. Dahl and C. E. Lindblom (*Politics, Economics, and Welfare*, New York: Harper & Brothers, 1953, p. 38) say: "An action is rational to the extent that it is 'correctly' designed to maximize goal achievement, given the goal in question and the real world as it exists". In sociology, similar definitions can be found in M. Weber (*The Theory of Social and Economic Organization*, trans. by A. M. Henderson & T. Parsons, New York: Oxford University Press, 1947, p. 117), K. Mannheim (*Man and Society in an Age of Reconstruction*, London: Kegan Paul, Trench, Trubner, 1940, pp. 51-7), and T. Parsons (*The Social System*, Glencoe, Ill: The Free Press, 1951, pp. 549-50). (Pareto prefers the term *logical* to *rational*.) The term is used rather loosely in sociology, while in mathematical economics and statistical decision theory it has received exact axiomatic treatment (see 2. above).

c. There is a somewhat distinct usage of *rational* in the writing of Weber (*The Theory of Social and Economic Organization*, pp. 329-41) and others on bureaucracy. In the ideal type of "rational legal authority", rationality means the conscious adaptation of the organization to goals, and its operation through the impersonal application of rules without deflection by the personal goals of the functionaries. An approximate synonym is Mannheim's phrase, *functional rationality* (*Man and Society in an Age of Reconstruction,* p. 53).

8.2
THEORIES OF BOUNDED RATIONALITY

HERBERT A. SIMON

1. Introduction. – 2. Approaches to rational choice in chess. – 3. Bounded rationality in design. – 4. Bounded rationality in management science. – 5. Conclusion.

1. Introduction

Rationality denotes a style of behavior that is appropriate to the achievement of given goals, within the limits imposed by given conditions and constraints. Theories of rational behavior may be normative or descriptive – that is, they may prescribe how people or organizations should behave in order to achieve certain goals under certain conditions, or they may purport to describe how people or organizations do, in fact, behave. This essay will be concerned with the structure of theories of rational behavior, whether they are intended prescriptively or descriptively.

Individual and organizational rationality. A theory of rational behavior may be concerned with the rationality of individuals or the rationality of organizations. In fact, the two bodies of theory are not wholly distinct.[1] One plausible distinction between them is that a theory of organizational rationality must treat the phenomena of goal conflict, while a theory of individual rationality need not. This is only partly correct, for goal conflict may be important in individual as in group behavior – it is a major theme of so-called "dissonance theory" in psychology. (See N. P. CHAPANIS and J. A. CHAPANIS (1964).) A theory of individual behavior microscopic enough to concern itself with the internal organization (neurological or functional) of the central nervous system will have a significant organizational component. A theory of organizational behavior macroscopic enough to treat the organization as a monolith will be a theory of an "individual." Although this chapter will be aimed primarily at understanding individual rationality, I shall not hesitate to use the theory of the firm – classically, the theory of a

---

[1] This point was made by J. MARSCHAK (1955) in his first paper on teams, "Elements for a Theory of Teams." I shall follow his good precedent.

monolithic entrepreneur – as a convenient and enlightening illustrative example.

From the standpoint of this chapter, then, the distinction between individual and organization will not be very important. A more significant taxonomy of theories of rational behavior, for our purposes, differentiates them by the assumptions they make about the "givens" – the given goals and given conditions. Particularly important is the distinction between those theories that locate all the conditions and constraints in the environment, outside the skin of the rational actor, and those theories that postulate important constraints arising from the limitations of the actor himself as an information processor. Theories that incorporate constraints on the information-processing capacities of the actor may be called *theories of bounded rationality*.

Rationality in the classical theory of the firm. The classical theory of the firm in its simplest form provides a useful standard for comparing and differentiating theories of rationality. In the theory of the firm, the given objective is to maximize profits, where profit is defined as the difference between gross receipts from sales and cost of production. The given conditions are two in number:

(I) *the demand function*: the quantity demanded is a function of price:

(1) $$q_d = D(p), \text{ or } p = D^{-1}(q_d).$$

Since gross receipts equal price times quantity, the demand function determines gross receipts:

(2) $$R = pq_d.$$

(II) *the cost function*: the cost of production is a function of the quantity produced:

(3) $$C = C(q_s).$$

If the quantity produced equals the quantity demanded,

(4) $$q_s = q_d,$$

then the profit, to be maximized, is simply the difference between gross receipts and the cost of production:

(5) $$\text{Profit} = R - C = pq - C(q),$$

and, under appropriate assumptions regarding differentiability, we will have for the maximum profit:

(6) $\qquad d(R-C)/dq = p + q d(D^{-1}(q))/dq - dC(q)/dq = 0.$

The constraints in this theory, the demand and cost functions, D and C, are both located in the actor's environment. He is assumed to find the solution of equation (6). To do this, he must have perfect knowledge of these constraints, and must be able to perform the necessary calculations – to set the derivative of profit with respect to quantity equal to zero and to solve the resulting algebraic equation.

The limits of rationality. Theories of bounded rationality can be constructed by modifying these assumptions in a variety of ways. *Risk and uncertainty* can be introduced into the demand function, the cost function, or both. For example, certain parameters of one or both of these functions can be assumed to be random variables with known distributions. Then the assumption of the actor's perfect knowledge of these functions has been replaced by the assumption that he has perfect knowledge of their distributions. This change in assumptions may, in turn, make it easier or more difficult to carry out the calculations for finding the optimum – usually it becomes much more difficult than in the corresponding case of certainty.

Another way in which rationality can be bounded is by assuming that the actor has only *incomplete information about alternatives*. Fewer models have been constructed to deal with this situation than with the situation in which he has incomplete information about consequences. However, in certain search models it is assumed that the actor knows the probability distribution of profits in a population of possible alternative actions. Specific actions become available to him – say, by random sampling from this population – as a function of the amount of resources he devotes to search. His task is to find the alternative that maximizes his expected profit net of the search cost. In this class of models, selecting the best alternative from among those already discovered is assumed to be a trivial problem; the decision question has been switched to the question of how much of the actor's resources should be allocated to search.[2]

---

[2] For an example, see STIGLER (1961). Theories of the allocation of resources to search can also be constructed to deal with incomplete information about consequences. Sequential sampling theory falls into this category, for it answers the question: shall I make a decision now, or wait until I have gathered additional information? The question is answered by comparing the incremental cost of enlarging the sample with the expected gain through the resulting average improvement in the decision.

Finally, rationality can be bounded by assuming *complexity* in the cost function or other environmental constraints so great as to prevent the actor from calculating the best course of action. Limits on rationality stemming from this source have not been prominent in classical theories of rational behavior. However, in numerical analysis, the theory of approximation provides analogues, for it is concerned with the rate at which an approximation can be expected to improve as a function of amount of computational effort. By introducing explicitly into that theory the cost of computational effort, it can be transformed into a theory of optimal approximation.

Alternatives to the classical goals. The classical theory can be modified not only by altering the nature of the conditions and constraints, but also by altering the nature of the given goals. Some modern theories of the firm depart from the classical theory, not along any of the dimensions mentioned above, but by postulating different goals from the classical goal of profit maximization.

BAUMOL (1959, pp. 45–53), for example, has developed a model in which the firm maximizes sales subject to the constraint that profit should not be less than a specified "satisfactory" level. According to this theory of Baumol, equation (6) in the classical model should be replaced by:

(6′)
$$dR/dq = p + q\,d(D^{-1}(q))/dq = 0,$$

subject to the constraint that

(7)
$$P = R - C \geq P^*.$$

It may be observed that the informational and computational requirements for applying Baumol's theory to concrete situations are not very different from the requirements of the classical model.

This essay will not be concerned with variants of the theory of rationality that assume goals different from profit or utility maximization, except to the extent that there is significant interaction between the assumptions about goals and the assumptions about conditions and constraints. We shall see, however, that this is a very important exception. In actual fact, most of the variants of the theory that make significant modifications in the assumptions about conditions and constraints also call for assumptions about goals that are different from the classical assumptions of profit or utility maximization. The reasons for this interaction will appear as we proceed.

2. Approaches to Rational Choice in Chess

A number of the persons who have engaged in research on rational decision-making have taken the game of chess as a microcosm that mirrors interesting properties of decision-making situations in the real world. The research on rational choice in chess provides some useful illustrations of alternative approaches to rationality.

The problem confronting a chess player whose turn it is to move can be interpreted in either of two ways. First, it can be interpreted as a problem of finding a good (or the best) strategy – where "strategy" means a conditional sequence of moves, defining what move will be made at each successive stage after each possible response of the opponent.

Second, the problem can be interpreted as one of finding a set of accurate evaluations for the alternative moves immediately before the player.

From a classical standpoint, these two problems are not distinguishable. If the player has unlimited computational power, it does not matter whether he selects a complete strategy for his future behavior in the game, or selects each of his moves, one at a time, when it is his turn to play. For the way in which he goes about evaluating the next move is by constructing alternative complete strategies for the entire future play of the game, and selecting the one that promises the best return (i.e., the best return under the assumption that the opponent will also do *his* best to win). This is the approach taken in the von Neumann-Morgenstern theory of games (VON NEUMANN and MORGENSTERN (1953)).

The game-theoretical definition of rationality in chess. As von Neumann and Morgenstern observed, chess is a trivial game. "... if the theory of Chess (i.e., the complete tree of possible games) were really fully known there would be nothing left to play" (*ibid.*, p. 125). Each terminus of the tree of possible games represents a win, loss, or draw for White. Moving backward one branch on the tree, the player whose move it is at that branch can examine the termini to which it could lead by his choice of move, and can choose the move having the preferred terminus. The value of that terminus becomes, then, the value of the branch that leads to it. Working backward in this way, a value – win, lose, or draw for White – can be assigned to each position, and ultimately to each of the initial legal moves for White. Now each player can specify an optimal strategy – a strategy that will guarantee him at least as good an outcome as any other – by specifying which move he would select at each branch point in the tree whenever it is his move.

Unfortunately, as von Neumann and Morgenstern also observed, the triviality of chess offers no practical help to a player in actually choosing a move. "But our proof, which guarantees the validity of one (and only one) of these three alternatives [that the game must have the value of win lose or draw for White], gives no practically usable method to determine the true one. This relative, human difficulty necessitates the use of those incomplete, heuristic methods of playing, which constitute 'good' Chess; and without it there would be no element of 'struggle' and 'surprise' in that game" (*ibid.*).

What "impracticality" means becomes more vivid when we calculate how much search would be involved in finding the game-theoretically correct strategy in chess. On the average, at any given position in a game of chess, there are about 30 legal moves – in round numbers, for a move and its replies, an average of about 10^3 continuations. Forty moves would be a not unreasonable estimate of the average length of a game. Then there would be perhaps 10^{120} possible games of chess. Obviously the exact number does not matter: a number like 10^{40} would be less spectacular, but quite large enough to support the conclusions of the present argument.

Studies of the decision-making of chess players indicate strongly that strong players seldom look at as many as one hundred possibilities – that is one hundred continuations from the given position – in selecting a move or strategy. One hundred is a reasonably large number, by some standards, but somewhat smaller than 10^{120}! Chess players do not consider all possible strategies and pick the best, but generate and examine a rather small number, making a choice as soon as they discover one that they regard as satisfactory (see DE GROOT (1965)).

Before we consider in detail how they do it, let us return to the classical model and ask whether there is any way in which we could make it relevant to the practical choice problem, taking account of the size of the problem space, in a game like chess. One possible way would be to replace the actual problem space with a very much smaller space that approximates the actual one in some appropriate sense, and then apply the classical theory to the smaller approximate space.

This approach was taken in some of the early computer programs for playing chess and checkers. In the Los Alamos program, for example, the computer generated all legal moves, all legal replies to each, and so on, two moves deep. Each of the terminal positions thus generated (about a million in a two-move analysis) was evaluated, and the minimax procedure applied, working backwards, to find the best first move. Thus, a space of about

10^6 elements was substituted for the space of 10^{120} elements that represents the "real" world of chess.

The scheme was approximate, because the actual chess values of the million terminal positions were not known, and could not be known accurately without returning to the space of 10^{120} elements – that is, returning to the game-theoretical analysis of the full game. In place of these unknown true values, approximate values were computed, using rules of thumb that are commonly employed by chess players – conventional numerical values for the pieces, and measures of mobility. Thus, the approximate scheme was not guaranteed to select the objectively best move, but only the move leading to the positions that appeared best, in terms of these heuristic criteria, after an analysis two moves deep. Experience indicates that it is not possible to make such approximate evaluations accurately enough to enable the program to play good chess. The optimal decision in the approximated world is not necessarily even a good decision in the real world.

Satisficing processes in chess thinking. Chess programs now exist that take the alternative course, trying to emulate the human chess player in looking at only a very few continuations. The effectiveness of such a scheme depends critically on three components: the *move generators*, processes that select the continuations to be explored; the *evaluators*, processes that determine how good each continuation is; and the *stop rules*, criteria that determine when the search should be terminated and a move selected.

By scanning a chess position, features of the position can be detected that suggest appropriate moves. To take an extreme case, suppose a chess player discovers, when it is his move, that one of his Pawns attacks the opponent's Queen. Obviously, the capture of the Queen by the Pawn is one move that deserves consideration. It may turn out to be a poor move – another piece will checkmate him, say, if he captures the Queen – but its superficial merits are obvious, and its deficiencies can only be detected by considering it and evaluating it dynamically. A simple process that would generate this move, and others like it, would consist in determining which of the opponent's pieces were attacked by a piece of lesser value, or were undefended and attacked by any piece. Thus, a suitable set of move-generating processes might identify for further analysis all or most of the moves deserving serious consideration. If the generators were ordered appropriately, they might usually identify first the most promising moves, then the ones slightly less promising, and so on.

Possible moves, produced by the move generators, can be evaluated by a combination of static and dynamic criteria. Static criteria are features of the position, or differences between successive positions. Thus, one of the important static evaluators used by all chess players is the piece count: each piece is assigned a conventional value (say, Pawn = 1, Knight and Bishop = 3, Rook = 5, Queen = 9), and the sums of the values for the two players are compared. In general, if the piece count of one player exceeds that of the other by more than one point (or even, in many cases, by a single point), the player with the higher count can find a winning continuation *unless* the balance is very quickly redressed by a sequence of forceful moves. (Thus, it does not matter being 5 points down if you can capture the opponent's Queen on the next move without further reprisals.)

The short-run tactical considerations are handled by carrying out dynamic analysis of plausible continuations until a position is reached that is sufficiently quiet or "dead" that it can safely be evaluated by means of the static evaluators. These static evaluators are then propagated backwards to the move under consideration by the familiar minimax procedure.

Two kinds of stop rules are needed in a program having this structure: rules to stop exploration at dead positions that can be evaluated statically, and rules to stop the entire process and select a move when a satisfactory one has been found. The former class of stop rules has already been discussed; the latter needs to be examined more closely. If the alternatives in a choice situation are not given, but have to be discovered or invented, and if the number of possible alternatives is very large, then a choice has to be made before all or most of them have been looked at. It was precisely this difficulty in the classical requirement of comparing all alternatives that led to the approach described here. But if all alternatives are not to be examined, some criterion must be used to determine that an adequate, or satisfactory, one has been found. In the psychological literature, criteria that perform this function in decision processes are called *aspiration levels*. The Scottish word "satisficing" (= satisfying) has been revived to denote problem solving and decision making that sets an aspiration level, searches until an alternative is found that is satisfactory by the aspiration level criterion, and selects that alternative (SIMON (1957), Part IV).

In satisficing procedures, the existence of a satisfactory alternative is made likely by dynamic mechanisms that adjust the aspiration levels to reality on the basis of information about the environment. Thus, in a chess-playing program, the initial aspiration level can be set (preferably with a little upward bias) on the basis of a static evaluation of the position. As alternative moves are considered and evaluated by dynamic and static analysis, the evaluation of the position can gradually be reduced until the best move discovered so far reaches or exceeds in value the aspiration level.

The limits of rationality in chess. In the introductory section of this paper, three limits on perfect rationality were listed: uncertainty about the consequences that would follow from each alternative, incomplete information about the set of alternatives, and complexity preventing the necessary computations from being carried out. Chess illustrates how, in real world problem-solving situations, these three categories tend to merge.

If we describe the chess player as choosing a *strategy*, then his difficulty in behaving rationally – and the impossibility of his behaving as game theory says he should – resides in the fact that he has incomplete information as to what alternatives (strategies) are open to him. He has time to discover only a minute fraction of these strategies, and to specify the ones he discovers only incompletely.

Alternatively, if we describe the chess player as choosing a *move*, his difficulty in behaving rationally lies in the fact that he has only rough information about the consequences of adopting each of the alternatives (moves) that is open to him. It would not be impossible for him to generate the whole set of his legal moves, for they seldom number more than about thirty. However, he can evaluate them, even approximately, only by carrying out further analysis through the immense, branching, move tree. Since only a limited amount of processing time is available for the evaluation, he must allocate the time among the alternative moves. The practical facts of the matter are that it is usually better to generate only a few of the entire set of legal moves, evaluating these rather thoroughly, than it is to generate all of them, evaluating them superficially. Hence the good chess player does not examine all the moves open to him, but only a small fraction of them. (Data presented by DE GROOT (1965) suggest that typically a half dozen to a dozen of a set of thirty legal moves may be generated and explored by the chess player.)

From still a third standpoint, the chess player's difficulty in behaving rationally has nothing to do with uncertainty – whether of consequences or alternatives – but is a matter of complexity. For there is no risk or uncertainty, in the sense in which those terms are used in economics or statistical decision theory, in the game of chess. As von Neumann and Morgenstern observe, it is a game of perfect information. No probabilities of future events need enter the calculations, and no contingencies, in a statistical sense, arise.

From a game-theoretical standpoint, the presence of the opponent does not introduce contingencies. The opponent can always be counted on to do his worst. The point becomes clear if we replace the task of playing chess with the task of proving theorems. In the latter task, there is no opponent. Nor are there contingencies: the true and the derivable theorems reside eternally in Plato's heaven. Rationality in theorem proving is a problem only because the maze of possible proof paths is vast and complex.

What we refer to as "uncertainty" in chess or theorem proving, therefore, is uncertainty introduced into a perfectly certain environment by inability – computational inability – to ascertain the structure of that environment. But the result of the uncertainty, whatever its source, is the same: approximation must replace exactness in reaching a decision. In particular, when the uncertainty takes the form of an unwieldy problem space to be explored, the problem-solving process must incorporate mechanisms for determining when the search or evaluation will stop and an alternative will be chosen.

Satisficing and optimizing. The terms satisficing and optimizing, which we have already introduced, are labels for two broad approaches to rational behavior in situations where complexity and uncertainty make global rationality impossible. In these situations, optimization becomes approximate optimization – the description of the real-world situation is radically simplified until reduced to a degree of complication that the decision maker can handle. Satisficing approaches seek this simplification in a somewhat different direction, retaining more of the detail of the real-world situation, but settling for a satisfactory, rather than an approximate-best, decision. One cannot predict in general which approach will lead to the better decisions as measured by their real-world consequences. In chess at least, good players have clearly found satisficing more useful than approximating-and-optimizing.

A satisficing decision procedure can often be turned into a procedure for optimizing by introducing a rule for optimal amount of search, or, what amounts to the same thing, a rule for fixing the aspiration level optimally. Thus, the aspiration level in chess might be adjusted, dynamically, to such a level that the expected improvement in the move chosen, per minute of additional search, would just balance the incremental cost of the search.

Although such a translation is formally possible, to carry it out in practice requires additional information and assumptions beyond those needed for satisficing. First, the values of alternatives must be measured in units comparable with the units for measuring search cost, in order to permit comparison at the margins. Second, the marginal productivity of search – the expected increase in the value per unit of search time – must be estimated on some basis or other. If one were designing a chess-playing program, it is doubtful whether effort spent in attempting to imbed the program in such a dynamic optimizing framework would be nearly as worthwhile as equivalent effort spent in improving the selectivity of the program's move-generating and move-evaluating heuristics.

Another quite different translation between optimizing and satisficing schemes has also been suggested from time to time. A chess program of the "classical" type, which makes optimal decisions in an approximated world, can be regarded as a particular kind of satisficing program, in which "satis-factory" is defined by the approximating procedure that is used. Hence, it is difficult to draw a formal distinction between optimizing and satisficing procedures that is so iron-clad as to prevent either from being reinterpreted in the frame of the other. The practical difference, however – the difference in emphasis that results from adopting one viewpoint or the other – is often very great.

In research on optimizing procedures, considerable attention has been paid to the formal properties of the evaluation functions, to the existence and efficiency of procedures for computing the optimum, and to procedures for reducing uncertainty (e.g., forecasting methods). The nature of the approximations that are necessary to cast real-world problems into forms suitable for optimization, and the means for choosing among alternative approximations, have been less fully and less systematically studied. Much effort, for example, has gone into the discovery of efficient algorithms for solving linear programming problems. Finding an appropriate way of formulating a concrete real-world decision problem as a linear-programming problem remains largely an art.[3]

Research on satisficing procedures has focussed primarily on the efficiency of search – on the nature of the heuristic methods that enable the rare solutions in enormous spaces of possibilities to be sought and found with moderate amounts of search effort. Since moderate changes in heuristics often make order-of-magnitude changes in search effectiveness, highly accurate means for assessing the quality of solutions or the effort required to find them may be relatively unimportant. It probably does not require delicate evaluation functions or stop rules to change a duffer's chess play to a reasonably effective move-choosing program.

---

[3] The work of A. CHARNES and W. W. COOPER (1961) is full of sophisticated examples of this art. See, for instances, Appendix B and Chapter 11 of Volume I.

3. Bounded Rationality in Design

The engineering activities usually called "design" have not been much discussed under the heading of rational decision-making. The reason for this should be clear from the foregoing discussion: classical decision theory has been concerned with choice among *given* alternatives; design is concerned with the discovery and elaboration of alternatives. Our exploration of the microcosm of chess has indicated, however, how the theory of design can be assimilated to a satisficing theory of rational choice. Let me spell the point out a little more fully.

Consider that interpretation of chess which views the task as one of choosing a strategy, and not just a single move. Specifically, consider a situation where a player is searching for a combination (a strategy) that will definitely checkmate his opponent, even though it may require sacrifices of pieces along the way. A chess player will ordinarily not enter into such a course of action unless he can see it through to the end – unless he can *design*, that is, a water-tight mating combination.

As we have seen already, the evaluations and comparisons that take place during this design process are not, in general, comparisons among complete designs. Evaluations take place, first of all, to guide the search – the elaboration of the design itself. They provide the basis for decisions that the design should be elaborated in one direction rather than another. Complete designs (in this case, mating combinations), when they are finally arrived at, are not generally evaluated by comparing them with alternative designs, but by comparing them with standards defined by aspiration levels. In the chess situation, as soon as the player discovers a strategy that guarantees a checkmate, he adopts it. He does not look for all possible checkmating strategies and adopt the best (H. A. SIMON and P. A. SIMON (1962)).

In the design of complex objects – a bridge, say, or an airplane – the process has an even more involved search structure. Here, the early stages of search take place in highly simplified spaces that abstract most of the detail from the real-world problem, leaving only its most important elements in summarized form. When a plan, a schematized and aggregated design, has been elaborated in the planning space, the detail of the problem can be reintroduced, and the plan used as a guide in the search for a complete design.

More than two spaces may be used, of course; there may be a whole hierarchy of planning spaces, leading from a highly abstract and global design to successive specification of detail. At each of these levels of abstraction, the design process, too, may be differently structured. Since the more abstract spaces tend to be "smoother," it is often possible to use optimization models for planning purposes, reverting to satisficing search models to fill in the detail of the design. Thus, linear programming or dynamic programming may be used for general planning of factory operations, while more heuristic techniques are used for scheduling of individual jobs. In other situations, the overall design process may employ satisficing search procedures, while optimizing techniques may be used to set parameters once the general design has been fixed.[4]

4. Bounded Rationality in Management Science

Most of the formal techniques that constitute the technical backbone of management science and operations research are procedures for finding the best of a set of alternatives in terms of some criterion – that is, they fall in our category of "classical" procedures. Linear and dynamic programming are among the most powerful of these techniques. The dominant approach to problems in this sphere has been to simplify the real-world problems to the point where the formal optimizing models can be used as approximations.

Some industrial problems of a combinatorial sort have not yielded easily to this approach. Typically, the recalcitrant problems involve integer solutions, or, what usually amounts to the same thing, the consideration of possible permutations and combinations of a substantial number of elements. Warehouse location is a problem of this kind. The task is to "determine the geographical pattern of warehouse locations which will be most profitable to the company by equating the marginal cost of warehouse operation with the transportation cost savings and incremental profits resulting from more rapid delivery" (KUEHN and HAMBURGER (1963), p. 643).

A heuristic program devised by KUEHN and HAMBURGER (1963) for locating warehouses has two parts: "(1) the main program, which locates warehouses one at a time until no additional warehouses can be added to the distribution network without increasing total costs, and (2) the bump and shift routine, ..., which attempts to modify solutions ... by evaluating the profit implications of dropping individual warehouses or of shifting them from one location to another" (ibid., p. 645).

---

[4] Some modern semi-automated procedures for the design of chemical processing plants proceed from heuristic techniques for selecting the unit operations and their flow, then employ linear programming to determine the parameters of the system so specified.

This program fits our earlier characterization of design procedures. A possible plan is gradually built up, step by step, through a search procedure, and then possible local modifications are investigated before the final plan is settled upon. In building up the initial plan, locations are tried that are near concentrations of demand, adding at each step the warehouse that produces the greatest cost savings for the entire system. Only a fraction of the possible warehouse sites, which preliminary screening selects as "promising," are evaluated in detail at each stage. Finally, a so-called "bump-shift" routine modifies the programs tentatively arrived at by (1) eliminating warehouses no longer economical because new warehouses have been introduced at later steps of the program, (2) considering shifting warehouses to alternative sites within their territories. The flow diagram of the warehouse location programs, which will serve to illustrate the typical structure of heuristic programs when they are formalized, is shown in Fig. 1.

Kuehn and Hamburger have carried out some detailed comparisons of the heuristic program with optimizing techniques. They conclude that "in theory, a linear programming approach ... could be used to solve the problem. In practice, however, the size and nonlinearities involved in many problems are such that application is not currently feasible" (*ibid.*, p. 658). They attribute the superior performance of the heuristic program to two main causes: "(1) computational simplicity, which results in substantial reductions in solution times and permits the treatment of large-scale problems, and (2) flexibility with respect to the underlying cost functions, eliminating the need for restrictive assumptions" (*ibid.*, p. 656).

Perhaps the technique most widely used in management science to deal with situations too complex for the application of known optimization methods is simulation. The amount of detail incorporated in the simulation of a large system is limited only by computational feasibility. On the other hand, simulation, unaided by other formal tools of analysis, provides no direct means for discovering and evaluating alternative plans of action. In simulation, the trial and error is supplied by the human investigators rather than by the technique of analysis itself (see FORRESTER (1961)).

5. Conclusion

The theory of rational decision has undergone extremely rapid development in the past thirty years. A considerable part of the impetus for this development came, during and since World War II, from the attempt to use formal decision procedures in actual real-world situations of considerable

A HEURISTIC PROGRAM FOR LOCATING WAREHOUSES

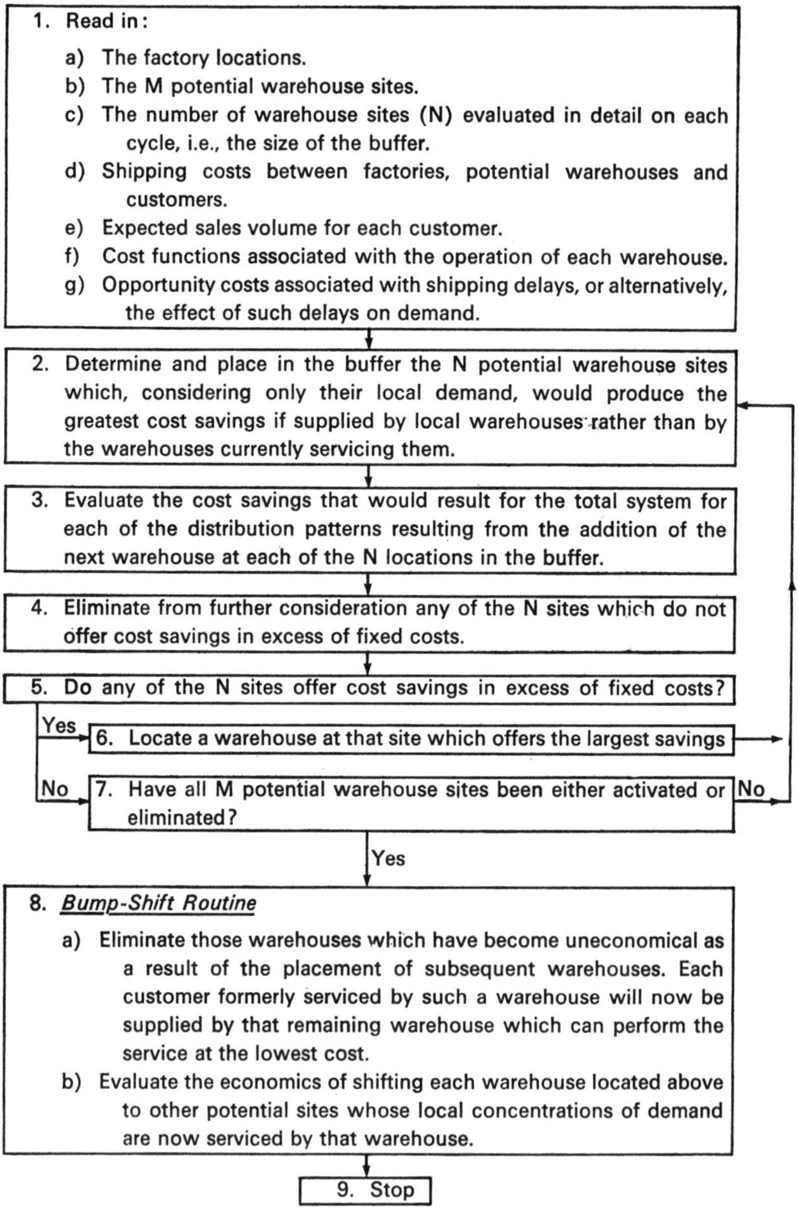

1. Read in:

    a) The factory locations.

    b) The M potential warehouse sites.

    c) The number of warehouse sites (N) evaluated in detail on each cycle, i.e., the size of the buffer.

    d) Shipping costs between factories, potential warehouses and customers.

    e) Expected sales volume for each customer.

    f) Cost functions associated with the operation of each warehouse.

    g) Opportunity costs associated with shipping delays, or alternatively, the effect of such delays on demand.

2. Determine and place in the buffer the N potential warehouse sites which, considering only their local demand, would produce the greatest cost savings if supplied by local warehouses rather than by the warehouses currently servicing them.

3. Evaluate the cost savings that would result for the total system for each of the distribution patterns resulting from the addition of the next warehouse at each of the N locations in the buffer.

4. Eliminate from further consideration any of the N sites which do not offer cost savings in excess of fixed costs.

5. Do any of the N sites offer cost savings in excess of fixed costs?

Yes → 6. Locate a warehouse at that site which offers the largest savings →

No → 7. Have all M potential warehouse sites been either activated or eliminated? No →

Yes

8. *Bump-Shift Routine*

    a) Eliminate those warehouses which have become uneconomical as a result of the placement of subsequent warehouses. Each customer formerly serviced by such a warehouse will now be supplied by that remaining warehouse which can perform the service at the lowest cost.

    b) Evaluate the economics of shifting each warehouse located above to other potential sites whose local concentrations of demand are now serviced by that warehouse.

9. Stop

Fig. 1.   Flow diagram

complexity. To deal with this complexity the formal models have grown in power and sophistication. But complexity has also stimulated the development of new kinds of models of rational decision that take special account of the very limited information-gathering and computing capacity of human beings and their associated computers.

One response to the concern with uncertainty, with the difficulties of discovering or designing alternatives, and with computational complexity has been to introduce search and information transmission processes explicitly into the models. Another (not exclusive) response has been to replace optimization criteria with criteria of satisfactory performance. The satisficing approach has been most often employed in models where "heuristic" or trial-and-error methods are used to aid the search for plausible alternatives.

As a result of all these developments, the decision maker today, in business, government, universities, has available to him an unprecedented collection of models and computational tools to aid him in his decision-making processes. Whatever the compromises he must make with reality in order to comprehend and cope with it, these tools make substantially more tractable the task of matching man's bounded capabilities with the difficulty of his problems.

References

BAUMOL, W. J. (1959), *Business Behavior, Value and Growth*, Macmillan, New York, pp. 45–53.

CHAPANIS, N. P. and J. A. CHAPANIS (1964), "Cognitive Dissonance: Five Years Later," *Psychological Bulletin, 61*, 1023.

CHARNES, A. and W. W. COOPER (1961), *Management Models and Industrial Applications of Linear Programming*, Wiley, New York, (2 volumes).

DE GROOT, A. (1965), *Thought and Choice in Chess*, Mouton, The Hague.

FORRESTER, J. W. (1961), *Industrial Dynamics*, M.I.T. Press, Cambridge.

KUEHN, A. A. and M. J. HAMBURGER (1963), "A Heuristic Program for Locating Warehouses," *Management Science, 9*, 643-666.

MARSCHAK, J. (1955), "Elements for a Theory of Teams," *Management Science, 1*, 127–137

SIMON, H. A. (1957), Part IV in *Models of Man*, Wiley, New York, pp. 196–279.

SIMON, H. A. and P. A. SIMON (1962), "Trial and Error Search in Solving Difficult Problems," *Behavioral Science, 7*, 425–429.

STIGLER, G. J. (1961), "The Economics of Information," *Journal of Political Economy, 69*, 213–225.

VON NEUMANN, J. and O. MORGENSTERN (1953), *Theory of Games and Economic Behavior*, (3rd ed.), Princeton University Press, Princeton, pp. 125.

8.3
From substantive to procedural rationality[1]

HERBERT A. SIMON
CARNEGIE-MELLON UNIVERSITY

In his paper on 'Situational Determinism in Economics',[2] Spiro J. Latsis has described two competitive research programs dealing with the theory of the firm, one of which he calls 'situational determinism', the other, 'economic behavioralism'. A basic contrast between these two programs is that the latter does, but the former does not, require as an essential component a psychological theory of rational choice. Both situational determinism and economic behavioralism postulate behavior that is, in a certain sense, rational, but the meaning of the term 'rational' is quite different for the two programs.

The conflict between situational determinism and economic behavioralism has been most often discussed from the vantage point of the discipline of economics, and as though the discrepant views of rationality associated with the two programs were both indigenous to economics. In point of fact, situational determinism is indigenous to economics, but economic behavioralism is largely an import from psychology, brought into economics to handle certain problems that appeared not to be treated satisfactorily by the situational approach. Thus, the concept of rationality employed in the program of economic behavioralism is not merely an

---

[1] An earlier version of this paper was presented in the Autumn of 1973 at the University of Groningen, The Netherlands, on the occasion of the twenty-fifth anniversary of the faculty of economics there. The Nafplion Colloquium provided me with a welcome opportunity to revise it and make more explicit its relation to the competition among research programs in economics that is discussed in the Colloquium papers of Messrs Coats, Hutchison and Latsis.

[2] Latsis [1972].

adaptation of the concept previously used by economists following the program of situational determinism. It is a distinct concept that has its own independent origins within psychology. I shall use the phrase 'substantive rationality' to refer to the concept of rationality that grew up within economics, and 'procedural rationality' to refer to the concept that developed within psychology.

A person unfamiliar with the histories and contemporary research preoccupations of economics and cognitive psychology might imagine that there were close relations between them – a constant flow of theoretical concepts and empirical findings from the one to the other and back. Mr Coats, in his chapter in this volume, describes a whole series of earlier attempts, mostly unsuccessful, to bring the findings of psychology to bear upon economic theory. At the present time there is still little communication between the two fields. In the United States, at least, there seem to be no doctoral programs in economics that require their students to master the psychological literature of rationality, and no psychology programs that insist that their students become acquainted with economic theories of rationality. (I would be gratified to learn that such programs exist, but if they do, they are inconspicuous in the extreme.) This state of mutual ignorance becomes understandable when we recognize that the two fields of economics and psychology are interested in answering rather different sets of research questions, and that each has adopted a view of rationality that is more or less appropriate to its own research concerns. As these concerns change, of course, so must the underlying concepts and the research programs that imbed them.

In this paper, I will undertake, first, to explain the two terms 'substantive rationality' and 'procedural rationality' – the differences between them as well as their relations. I shall then try to document the growing interest, during the past twenty-five years, of economists in procedural rationality and in the associated program of economic behavioralism. Finally, I will set forth some reasons for thinking that procedural rationality will become an even more central concern of economics over the next twenty-five years. These changes, past and predicted, are a response to changes in the central research questions with which economics is occupied. The new research questions bring new empirical phenomena into the focus of attention, and the explanation of the new phenomena calls, in turn, for an understanding of the processes that underlie human rationality.

1. Substantive rationality

Behavior is substantively rational when it is appropriate to the achievement of given goals within the limits imposed by given conditions and constraints.[3] Notice that, by this definition, the rationality of behavior

[3] Cf. the entry under 'rationality' in Gould & Kolb [1964], pp. 573–4.

130

depends upon the actor in only a single respect – his goals. Given these goals, the rational behavior is determined entirely by the characteristics of the environment in which it takes place.

Suppose, for example, that the problem is to minimize the cost of a nutritionally adequate diet, where nutritional adequacy is defined in terms of lower bounds on intakes of certain proteins, vitamins, and minerals, and upper and lower bounds on calories, and where the unit prices and compositions of the obtainable foods are specified. This diet problem can be (and has been) formulated as a straightforward linear-programming problem, and the correct solution found by applying the simplex algorithm or some other computational procedure. Given the goal of minimizing cost and the definition of 'nutritionally adequate', there are no two ways about it – there is only one substantively rational solution.

Classical economic analysis rests on two fundamental assumptions. The first assumption is that the economic actor has a particular goal, for example, utility maximization or profit maximization. The second assumption is that the economic actor is substantively rational. Given these two assumptions, and given a description of a particular economic environment, economic analysis (descriptive or normative) could usually be carried out using such standard tools as the differential calculus, linear programming, or dynamic programming.

Thus, the assumptions of utility or profit maximization, on the one hand, and the assumption of substantive rationality, on the other, freed economics from any dependence upon psychology. As long as these assumptions went unchallenged, there was no reason why an economist should acquaint himself with the psychological literature on human cognitive processes or human choice. There was absolutely no point at which the findings of psychological research could be injected into the process of economic analysis. The irrelevance of psychology to economics was complete.

2. Procedural rationality

Behavior is procedurally rational when it is the outcome of appropriate deliberation. Its procedural rationality depends on the process that generated it. When psychologists use the term 'rational', it is usually procedural rationality they have in mind. William James, for example, in his *Principles of Psychology*,[4] uses 'rationality' as synonymous with 'the peculiar thinking process called reasoning'. Conversely, behavior tends to be described as 'irrational' in psychology when it represents impulsive response to affective mechanisms without an adequate intervention of thought.

Perhaps because 'rationality' resembles 'rationalism' too closely, and because psychology's primary concern is with process rather than outcome, psychologists tend to use phrases like 'cognitive processes' and

[4] James [1890], chapter 22.

131

'intellective processes' when they write about rationality in behavior. This shift in terminology may have contributed further to the mutual isolation of the concepts of substantive and procedural rationality.

(a) *The study of cognitive processes*

The process of rational calculation is only interesting when it is non-trivial – that is, when the substantively rational response to a situation is not instantly obvious. If you put a quarter and a dime before a subject and tell him that he may have either one, but not both, it is easy to predict which he will choose, but not easy to learn anything about his cognitive processes. Hence, procedural rationality is usually studied in problem situations – situations in which the subject must gather information of various kinds and process it in different ways in order to arrive at a reasonable course of action, a solution to the problem.

Historically, there have been three main categories of psychological research on cognitive processes: learning, problem solving, and concept attainment. Learning research is concerned with the ways in which information is extracted from one problem situation and stored in such a way as to facilitate the solving of similar problems subsequently. Problem-solving research (in this narrower sense) focuses especially upon the complementary roles of trial-and-error procedures and insight in reaching problem solutions. Concept attainment research is concerned with the ways in which rules or generalizations are extracted from a sequence of situations and used to predict subsequent situations. Only in recent years, particularly since the Second World War, has there been much unification of theory emerging from these three broad lines of research.

(b) *Computational efficiency*

Let us return for a moment to the optimal diet problem which we used to illustrate the concept of substantive rationality. From a procedural standpoint, our interest would lie not in the problem solution – the prescribed diet itself – but in the method used to discover it. At first blush, this appears to be more a problem in computational mathematics than in psychology. But that appearance is deceptive.

What is the task of computational mathematics? It is to discover the relative efficiencies of different computational processes for solving problems of various kinds. Underlying any question of computational efficiency is a set of assumptions about the capabilities of the computing system. For an omniscient being, there are no questions of computational efficiency, because the consequences of any tautology are known as soon as the premises are stated; and computation is simply the spinning out of such consequences.[5]

[5] This statement is a little over-simple in ignoring the distinction between induction and deduction, but greater precision is not needed for our purposes.

132

Nowadays, when we are concerned with computational efficiency, we are concerned with the computing time or effort that would be required to solve a problem by a system, basically serial in operation, requiring certain irreducible times to perform an addition, a multiplication, and a few other primitive operations. To compare the simplex method with some other method for solving linear programming problems, we seek to determine how much total computing time each method would need.

The search for computational efficiency is a search for procedural rationality, and computational mathematics is a normative theory of such rationality. In this normative theory, there is no point in prescribing a particular substantively rational solution if there exists no procedure for finding that solution with an acceptable amount of computing effort. So, for example, although there exist optimal (substantively rational) solutions for combinatorial problems of the travelling-salesman type, and although these solutions can be discovered by a finite enumeration of alternatives, actual computation of the optimum is infeasible for problems of any size and complexity. The combinatorial explosion of such problems simply outraces the capacities of computers, present and prospective.

Hence, a theory of rationality for problems like the travelling-salesman problem is not a theory of best solutions – of substantive rationality – but a theory of efficient computational procedures to find good solutions – a theory of procedural rationality. Notice that this change in viewpoint involves not only a shift from the substantive to the procedural, but a shift also from concern for optimal solutions to a concern for good solutions. I shall discuss this point later.

(c) Computation: risky decisions

But now it is time to return to psychology and its concern with computational efficiency. Man, viewed as a thinker, is a system for processing information. What are his procedures for rational choice?

One method of testing a theory of human rational choice is to study choice behavior in relatively simple and well-structured laboratory situations where the theory makes specific predictions about how subjects will behave. This method has been used by a number of investigators – including W. Edwards, G. Pitts, A. Rapaport, and A. Tversky – to test whether human decisions in the face of uncertainty and risk can be explained by the normative concepts of statistical decision theory. This question is particularly interesting because these norms are closely allied, both historically and logically, to the notions of substantive rationality that have prevailed in economics, and make no concessions to computational difficulties – they never choose the computable second-best over the non-computable best.

Time does not permit me to review the extensive literature that this line

133

of inquiry has produced. A recent review by Rapaport[6] covers experimental tests of SEU (subjective expected utility) maximization, of Bayesian strategies for sequential decisions, and of other models of rational choice under uncertainty. I think the evidence can be fairly summarized by the statements (i) that it is possible to construct gambles sufficiently simple and transparent that most subjects will respond to them in a manner consistent with SEU theory; but (ii) the smallest departures from this simplicity and transparency produce behavior in many or most subjects that *cannot* be explained by SEU or Bayesian models. I will illustrate this statement by just three examples, which I hope are not atypical.

The first is the phenomenon of event matching.[7] Suppose that you present a subject with a random sequence of X's and 0's, of which 70 per cent are X's and 30 per cent 0's. You ask the subject to predict the next symbol, rewarding him for the number of correct predictions. 'Obviously' the rational behavior is always to predict X. This is what subjects almost never do.[8] Instead, they act as though the sequence were patterned, not random, and guess by trying to extrapolate the pattern. This kind of guessing will lead X to be guessed in proportion to the frequency with which it occurs in the sequence. As a result, the sequence of guesses has about the same statistical properties as the original sequence, but the prediction accuracy is lower than if X had been predicted each time (58 per cent instead of 70 per cent).

In a recent study by Kahneman and Tversky,[9] a quite different phenomenon showed up. The rational procedure for combining new information with old is to apply Bayes's theorem. If a set of probabilities has been assigned to the possible outcomes of an uncertain event, and then new evidence is presented, Bayes's theorem provides an algorithm for revising the prior probabilities to take the new evidence into account. One obvious consequence of Bayes's theorem is that the more extensive and reliable the new evidence, the greater should be its influence on the new probabilities. Another consequence is that the new probabilities should not depend on the new evidence only, but upon the prior probabilities as well. In the experiments conducted by Kahneman and Tversky, the estimates of subjects were independent of the reliability of the new evidence, and did not appear to be influenced by the prior probabilities at all.

On the other hand, Ward Edwards[10] has reviewed a large body of experimental evidence describing quite conservative behavior. In these experiments, subjects did not revise prior probability estimates nearly as

[6] Rapaport and Wallsten [1972].
[7] Feldman [1963].
[8] The sole exceptions of which I am aware were two well-known and expert game theorists who served as subjects in this experiment at the RAND Corporation many years ago!
[9] Kahneman and Tversky [1973].
[10] Edwards [1968].

134

much as would be called for by Bayes's theorem. It appears, then that humans can either over-respond to new evidence or ignore it, depending upon the precise experimental circumstances. If these differences in behavior manifest themselves even in laboratory situations so simple that it would be possible for subjects to carry out the actual Bayes calculations, we should be prepared to find variety at least as great when people are required to face the complexities of the real world.

(d) Man's computational efficiency

If these laboratory demonstrations of human failure to follow the canons of substantive rationality in choice under uncertainty caused any surprise to economists (and I do not know that they did), they certainly did not to experimental psychologists familiar with human information processing capabilities.

Like a modern digital computer's, Man's equipment for thinking is basically serial in organization. That is to say, one step in thought follows another, and solving a problem requires the execution of a large number of steps in sequence. The speed of his elementary processes, especially arithmetic processes, is much slower, of course, than those of a computer, but there is much reason to think that the basic repertoire of processes in the two systems is quite similar.[11] Man and computer can both recognize symbols (patterns), store symbols, copy symbols, compare symbols for identity, and output symbols. These processes seem to be the fundamental components of thinking as they are of computation.

For most problems that Man encounters in the real world, no procedure that he can carry out with his information processing equipment will enable him to discover the optimal solution, even when the notion of 'optimum' is well defined. There is no logical reason why this need be so; it is simply a rather obvious empirical fact about the world we live in – a fact about the relation between the enormous complexity of that world and the modest information-processing capabilities with which Man is endowed. One reason why computers have been so important to Man is that they enlarge a little bit the realm within which his computational powers can match the complexity of the problems. But as the example of the travelling-salesman problem shows, even with the help of the computer, Man soon finds himself outside the area of computable substantive rationality.

The problem space associated with the game of chess is very much smaller than the space associated with the game of life. Yet substantive rationality has so far proved unachievable, both for Man and computer,

---

[11] In my comparison of computer and Man, I am leaving out of account the greater sophistication of Man's input and output system, and the parallel processing capabilities of his senses and his limbs. I will be primarily concerned here with thinking, secondarily with perceiving, and not at all with sensing or acting.

135

even in chess. Chess books are full of norms for rational play, but except for catalogues of opening moves, these are procedural rules: how to detect the significant features of a position, what computations to make on these features, how to select plausible moves for dynamic search, and so on.

The psychology of chess-playing now has a considerable literature. A pioneer in this research was Professor Adriaan de Groot, of the University of Amsterdam, whose book, *Het Denken van den Schaker*, has stimulated much work on this subject both in Amsterdam, and in our own laboratory at Carnegie-Mellon.[12] These studies have told us a great deal about the thought processes of an expert chessplayer. First, they have shown how he compensates for his limited computational capacity by searching very selectively through the immense tree of move possibilities, seldom considering as many as 100 branches before making a move. Second, they have shown how he stores in long-term memory a large collection of common patterns of pieces, together with procedures for exploiting the relations that appear in these patterns. The expert chessplayer's heuristics for selective search and his encyclopedic knowledge of significant patterns are at the core of his procedural rationality in selecting a chess move. Third, the studies have shown how a player forms and modifies his aspirations for a position, so that he can decide when a particular move is 'good enough' (satisfices), and can end his search.

Chess is not an isolated example. There is now a large body of data describing human behavior in other problem situations of comparable complexity. All of the data point in the same direction, and provide essentially the same descriptions of the procedures men use to deal with situations where they are not able to compute an optimum. In all these situations, they use selective heuristics and means–end analysis to explore a small number of promising alternatives. They draw heavily upon past experience to detect the important features of the situation before them, features which are associated in memory with possibly relevant actions. They depend upon aspiration-like mechanisms to terminate search when a satisfactory alternative has been found.

To a moderate extent, this description of choice has been tested outside the laboratory, in even more complex 'real-life' situations; and where it has been tested, has held up well. I will only mention as examples Clarkson's well-known microscopic study of the choices of an investment trust officer,[13] and Peer Soelberg's study of the job search and job choice of graduating management students.[14] I cannot supply you with a large number of more recent examples, possibly because they do not exist, or possibly because my own research has taken me away from the area of field studies in recent years.

[12] Newell and Simon [1972]; Chase and Simon [1973a].
[13] Clarkson [1963].
[14] Soelberg [1967].

136

Contrast this picture of thought processes with the notion of rationality in the classical theory of the firm in its simplest form. The theory assumes that there is given, in addition to the goal of profit maximization, a demand schedule and a cost curve. The theory then consists of a characterization of the substantively rational production decision: for example, that the production quantity is set at the level where marginal cost, calculated from the cost curve, equals marginal revenue, calculated from the demand schedule. The question of whether data are obtainable for estimating these quantities or the demand and cost functions on which they are based is outside the purview of the theory. If the actual demand and cost curves are given, the actual calculation of the optimum is trivial. This portion of economic theory certainly has nothing to do with procedural rationality.

3. *Economics' concern with procedural rationality*

In my introductory remarks, I said that while economics has traditionally concerned itself with substantive rationality, there has been a noticeable trend, since the Second World War, toward concern also with procedural rationality. This trend has been brought about by a number of more or less independent developments.

(a) *The real world of business and public policy*

The first of these developments, which predated the war to some extent, was increasing contact of academic economists with real-world business environments. An early and important product was the 1939 Hall–Hitch paper 'Price Theory and Business Behavior',[15] which advanced the heretical proposition that prices are often determined by applying a fixed mark-up to average direct cost rather than by equating them with marginal cost.

I am not concerned here to determine whether Hitch and Hall, or others who have made similar observations, were right or wrong. My point is that first-hand contact with business operations leads to observation of the procedures that are used in reaching decisions, and not simply the final outcomes. Independently of whether the decision processes have any importance for the questions to which classical economics has addressed itself, the phenomena of problem solving and decision-making cannot help but excite the interest of anyone with intellectual curiosity who encounters them. They represent a fascinating and important domain of human behavior, which any scientist will wish to describe and explain.

In the United States, in the decade immediately after the Second World War, a number of large corporations invited small groups of academic economists to spend periods of a month or more as 'interns' and observers

---

[15] Hall and Hitch [1939].

137

in their corporate offices. Many young economists had their first opportunity, in this way, to try their hands at applying the tools of economic theory to the decisions of a factory department, or a regional sales office.

They found that businessmen did not need to be advised to 'set marginal cost equal to marginal revenue'. Substantive norms of profit maximization helped real decisions only to the extent that appropriate problem-solving procedures could be devised to implement them. What businessmen needed – from anyone who could supply it – was help in inventing and constructing such procedures, including the means for generating the necessary data. How could the marginal productivity of R & D expenditures be measured? Or of advertising expenditures? And if they could not be, what would be reasonable procedures for fixing these quantities? These – and not abstract questions of profit maximization in a simplified model of the firm – were the questions businessmen wrestled with in their decisions.

Matters were no different with the economists who were increasingly called upon by governments to advise on national fiscal and monetary policy, or on economic development plans. We have the notable example in The Netherlands of Tinbergen's schemes for target planning[16] – a pioneering example of 'satisficing', if I may speak anachronistically. In the face of difficult problems of formulating models, designing appropriate and implementable instruments of measurement, taking account of multidimensional criteria and side conditions, questions of optimization generally faded into the background. The rationality of planning and development models was predominately a procedural rationality.

(b) Operations research

With the end of the war also, businessmen and government departments began to exhibit an interest in the tools of operations research that had been developed for military application during the war. At the same time, operations analysts began to cast about for peacetime problems to which their skills might be applicable. Since the rapid burgeoning of operations research and management science in industry, and the even more rapid development of powerful analytic tools during the first decade after the war is familiar to all of you, it does not need recounting.

The coincidence of the introduction of the digital computer at the same time undoubtedly accelerated these developments. In fact, it is quite unclear whether operations research would have made any considerable impact on practical affairs if the desk calculator had been its only tool.

Operations research and management science did not alter the economic theory of substantive rationality in any fundamental way. With linear programming and activity analysis it did provide a way of handling the old problems and their solutions without the differential calculus, and the

---

[16] Tinbergen [1952].

classical theorems of marginalism were soon restated in terms of the new formalism.[17]

What was genuinely new for economics in operations research was the concern for procedural rationality – finding efficient procedures for computing actual solutions to concrete decision problems. Let me expand on the specific example with which I am most intimately familiar: decision rules for inventory and work-force smoothing.[18] Here the problem was to devise a decision rule for determining periodically the production level at which a factory should operate. Since the decision for one period was linked to the decisions for the following periods by the inventories carried over, the problem fell in the domain of dynamic programming.

The nub of the problem was to devise a dynamic programming scheme that could actually be carried out using only data that could be obtained in the actual situation. Dynamic programming, in its general formulations, is notoriously extravagant of computational resources. A general algorithm for solving dynamic programming problems would be a non-solution to the real-world decision problem.

The scheme we offered was an algorithm, requiring only a small amount of computing effort, for solving a very special class of dynamic programming problems. The algorithm required the costs to be represented by a quadratic function. This did not mean that we thought real-world cost functions were quadratic; it meant that we thought that many cost functions could be reasonably approximated by a quadratic, and that the deviations from the actual function would not lead to seriously non-optimal decisions. This assumption must, of course, be justified in each individual case, before an application can safely be made. Not only did the quadratic function provide good computational efficiency, but it also greatly reduced the data requirements, because it could be proved that, with this function, only the expected values of predicted variables, and not their higher moments, affected the optimal decision.[19]

This is only part of what was involved in devising a procedurally rational method for making these inventory and production decisions. The problems had also to be solved of translating an aggregate 'production level' into specific production schedules for individual products. I will not, however, go into these other aspects of the matter.

Observe of our solution that we constructed a quite classical model for profit maximization, but we did not have the illusion that the model reflected accurately all the details of the real-world situation. All that was

[17] Dorfman, Samuelson and Solow [1958].

[18] Holt, Modigliani, Muth and Simon [1960].

[19] It is interesting that this same dynamic programming procedure for quadratic cost functions was invented independently and simultaneously by Henri Theil of the Rotterdam School of Economics. See Theil [1958]. The Rotterdam group was also concerned with concrete applications – in this case to national economic planning in The Netherlands – and hence gave a high priority to the demands of procedural rationality in the solutions it developed.

139

expected of the solution was that the *optimal* decision in the world of the model be a *good* decision in the real world. There was no claim that the solution was substantively optimal, but rather that formal optimization in the dynamic programming model was an effective procedural technique for making acceptable decisions (i.e., decisions better than those that would be made without this formal apparatus).

Some operations research methods take the other horn of this dilemma: they retain more of the real-world detail in the model, but then give up, for reasons of computational feasibility, the goal of searching for an optimum, and seek a satisfactory solution instead.[20]

Thus, the demands of computability led to two kinds of deviation from classical optimization: simplification of the model to make computation of an 'optimum' feasible, or, alternatively, searching for satisfactory, rather than optimal choices. I am inclined to regard both of these solutions as instances of satisficing behavior rather than optimization. To be sure, we can *formally* view these as optimizing procedures by introducing, for example, a cost of computation and a marginal return from computation, and using these quantities to compute the optimal stopping-point for the computation. But the important difference between the new procedures and the classical ones remain. The problem has been shifted from one of characterizing the substantively optimal solution to one of devising practicable computation procedures for making reasonable choices.

(c) Imperfect competition

More than a century ago, Cournot identified a problem that has become the permanent and ineradicable scandal of economic theory. He observed that where a market is supplied by only a few producers, the notion of profit-maximization is ill-defined. The choice that would be substantively rational for each actor depends on the choices made by the other actors; none can choose without making assumptions about how others will choose.

Cournot proposed a particular solution for the problem, which amounted to an assumption about the *procedure* each actor would follow: each would observe the quantities being produced by his competitors, and would assume these quantities to be fixed in his own calculations. The Cournot solution has often been challenged, and many alternative solutions have been proposed – conjectural variations, the kinky demand curve, market leadership, and others. All of them rest on postulates about the decision process, in particular, about the information each decision-maker will take into account, and the assumptions he will make about the reactions of the others to his behavior.

[20] I have already mentioned the pioneering work of Jan Tinbergen in The Netherlands, who employed national planning models that aimed at target values of key variables instead of an optimum.

140

I have referred to the theory of imperfect competition as a 'scandal' because it has been treated as such in economics, and because it is generally conceded that no defensible formulation of the theory stays within the framework of profit maximization and substantive rationality. Game theory, initially hailed as a possible way out, provided only a rigorous demonstration of how fundamental the difficulties really are.

If perfect competition were the rule in the markets of our modern economy, and imperfect competition and oligopoly rare exceptions, the scandal might be ignored. Every family, after all, has some distant relative it would prefer to forget. But imperfect competition is not a 'distant relative', it is the characteristic form of market structure in a large part of the industries in our economy.

In the literature on oligopoly and imperfect competition one can trace a gradual movement toward more and more explicit concern with the processes used to reach decisions, even to the point – unusual in most other areas of economics – of trying to obtain empirical data about these processes. There remains, however, a lingering reluctance to acknowledge the impossibility of discovering at last 'The Rule' of substantively rational behavior for the oligopolist. Only when the hope of that discovery has been finally extinguished will it be admitted that understanding imperfect competition means understanding procedural rationality.[21]

This change in viewpoint will have large effects on many areas of economic research. There has been a great burgeoning, for example, of 'neoclassical' theories of investment – theories that undertake to deduce the rates of investment of business firms from the assumptions of profit-maximization and substantive rationality. Central to such theories is the concept of 'desired capital' – that is, the volume of capital that would maximize profits. Jorgenson, for example, typically derives 'desired capital' by an argument that assumes a fixed price for the firm's products and a production function of the Cobb–Douglas type, all in the absence of uncertainty.[22] Under these assumptions, he shows that the optimal level of capital is proportional to output.

Since the data which Jorgenson and others use to test these theories of investment derive mostly from oligopolistic industries, their definitions of rationality are infected with precisely the difficulties we have been discussing. Can we speak of the capital desired by General Motors or the American Can Company without considering their expectations for size and share of market or the interactions of these expectations with price

---

[21] My colleagues Richard Cyert and Morris de Groot have recently developed some interesting dynamic decision rules for oligopolists, which illustrate further the wide range of alternative formulations of what 'rationality' means in this situation. See Cyert and de Groot [1973].

[22] Jorgenson [1963]. For a thorough critique of Jorgenson's approach, see Kornai [1971]. Kornai's book also develops other arguments about the nature of economic rationality that are much in the spirit of this essay.

141

policies and with the responses of competitors?[23] Under conditions of imperfect competition, one can perhaps speak of the procedural rationality
of an investment strategy, but surely not of its substantive rationality. At
most, the statistical studies of investment behavior show that some business
firms relate their investments to output; they do not show that such
behavior is predictable from an objective theory of profit maximization.
(And if that is what is being demonstrated, what is the advantage of doing
it by means of elaborate statistical studies of public data, rather than by
making inquiries or observations of the actual decision processes in the
firms themselves?)

(d) Expectations and uncertainty

Making guesses about the behavior of a competitor in an oligopolistic
industry is simply a special case of forming expectations in order to make
decisions under uncertainty. As economics has moved from statics to
dynamics – to business cycle theory, growth theory, dynamic investment
theory, theory of innovation and technological change – it has become
more and more explicit in its treatment of uncertainty.

Uncertainty, however, exists not in the outside world, but in the eye and
mind of the beholder. We need not enter into philosophical arguments as
to whether quantum-mechanical uncertainty lies at the very core of
nature, for we are not concerned with events at the level of the atom. We
are concerned with how men behave rationally in a world where they are
often unable to predict the relevant future with accuracy. In such a world,
their ignorance of the future prevents them from behaving in a substantively rational manner; they can only adopt a rational choice procedure, including a rational procedure for forecasting or otherwise
adapting to the future.

In a well-known paper, my former colleague, John F. Muth,[24] proposed to objectify the treatment of uncertainty in economics by removing
it from the decision-maker to nature. His hypothesis is 'that expectations
of firms (or, more generally, the subjective probability distribution of
outcomes) tend to be distributed, for the same information set, about the
prediction of the theory (or the "objective" probability distributions of
outcomes)'. In application this hypothesis involves setting the expected
value (in the statistical sense) of a future economic variable equal to its
predicted value.

Muth's proposal is ingenious and important. Let us see exactly what it
means. Suppose that a producer has an accurate knowledge of the consumer demand function and the aggregate supply function of producers
in his industry. Then he can estimate the equilibrium price – the price at
which the quantities that producers will be induced to offer will just

---

[23] Cyert, Feigenbaum and March [1959].
[24] Muth [1961].

142

balance demand. Muth proposes essentially that each producer takes this equilibrium price as his price forecast. If random shocks with zero expected value are now introduced into the supply equation, and if producers continue to act on price forecasts made in the manner just described, then the forecast price will equal the expected value of the actual price.

Notice that the substantively rational behavior for the producer would be to produce the quantity that would be optimal for the price that is *actually* realized. The assumption of Muth's model that the random shocks are completely unpredictable makes this impossible. The producer then settles for a procedure that under the assumptions of the model will give him an unbiased prediction of the price. Nor, as Muth himself notes, will this procedure be optimal, even under uncertainty, unless the loss function is quadratic.

Uncertainty plays the same innocuous role in the optimal linear production smoothing rule I described earlier,[25] which is closely related to Muth's analysis. Here the explicit assumption of a quadratic cost function makes it possible to prove that only the expected values and not the higher moments of predicted variables are relevant to decision. This does not mean that action based on unbiased estimates is substantively rational, independently of the variances of those estimates. On the contrary, performance can always be improved if estimation errors can be reduced.

Even if it turns out to be empirically true that the forecasts of business firms and other economic actors are unbiased forecasts of future events, this finding will have modest implications for the nature of human rationality. Unbiased estimation can be a component of all sorts of rational and irrational behavior rules.

In an earlier section I commented on the psychological evidence as to human choice in the face of uncertainty. Only in the very simplest situations does behavior conform reasonably closely to the predictions of classical models of rationality. But even this evidence exaggerates the significance of those classical models for human affairs; for all of the experiments are limited to situations where the alternatives of choice are fixed in advance, and where information is available only from precisely specified sources.

Once we become interested in the procedures – the rational processes – that economic actors use to cope with uncertainty, we must broaden our horizons further. Uncertainty not only calls forth forecasting procedures; it also calls forth a whole range of actions to reduce uncertainty, or at least to make outcomes less dependent upon it. These actions are of at least four kinds:

(i) intelligence actions to improve the data on which forecasts are based, to obtain new data, and to improve the forecasting models;

[25] See footnote 19 *supra*.

143

(ii) actions to buffer the effects of forecast errors: holding inventories, insuring, and hedging, for example;

(iii) actions to reduce the sensitivity of outcomes to the behavior of competitors: steps to increase product and market differentiation, for example;

(iv) actions to enlarge the range of alternatives whenever the perceived alternatives involve high risk.

A theory of rational choice in the face of uncertainty will have to encompass not only the topic of forecasting, but these other topics as well. Moreover, it will have to say something about the circumstances under which people will (or should) pursue one or the other of these lines of action.

Confronting a list of contingencies of this sort fills many economists with malaise. How can a unique answer be found to the problem of choice if all of these considerations enter it? How much more attractive is classical economics, in allowing strong conclusions to be drawn from a few *a priori* assumptions, with little need for empirical observation!

Alas, we must take the world as it is. As economics becomes more concerned with procedural rationality, it will necessarily have to borrow from psychology or build for itself a far more complete theory of human cognitive processes than it has had in the past. Even if our interest lies in normative rather than descriptive economics, we will need such a theory. There are still many areas of decision – particularly those that are ill-structured – where human cognitive processes are more effective than the best available optimization techniques or artificial intelligence methods. Every Class A chessplayer plays a far better game than any existing chess-playing computer program. A great deal can still be learned about effective decision procedures by studying how humans make choices.

The human mind is programmable: it can acquire an enormous variety of different skills, behavior patterns, problem-solving repertoires, and perceptual habits. Which of these it will acquire in any particular case is a function of what it has been taught and what it has experienced. We can expect substantive rationality only in situations that are sufficiently simple as to be transparent to this mind. In all other situations, we must expect that the mind will use such imperfect information as it has, will simplify and represent the situation as it can, and will make such calculations as are within its powers. We cannot expect to predict what it will do in such situations unless we know what information it has, what forms of representation it prefers, and what algorithms are available to it.

There seems to be no escape. If economics is to deal with uncertainty, it will have to understand how human beings in fact behave in the face of uncertainty, and by what limits of information and computability they are bound.

144

4. *The empirical study of decision-making*

Since my own recent research has removed me from the study of decision-making in organization settings, I am not in a position to comment on the current state of our empirical knowledge of organizational decision-making. In trying to understand procedural rationality as it relates to economics, we do not have to limit ourselves, however, to organizational studies. I have already commented upon the understanding we have gained, during the past 20 years, of human problem-solving processes – mostly by study in the laboratory, using puzzle-like tasks. Most of these studies have used naive subjects performing tasks with which they had little or no previous experience. In one case, however – the research on chess-playing – an intensive investigation has been made of highly skilled, professional performance, and a body of theory constructed to explain that performance.

Chess may seem a rather esoteric domain, but perhaps business is no less esoteric to those who do not practice it. There is no reason to believe that the basic human faculties that a chess professional of 20 years' experience brings to bear upon his decisions are fundamentally different from the faculties used by an experienced professional businessman. In fact, to the extent that comparable studies of business decision-making have been carried out, they give us positive reasons to believe in the basic similarity of those faculties.

On the basis of the research on chess-players, what appears to distinguish expert from novice is not only that the former has a great quantity and variety of information, but that his perceptual experience enables him to detect familiar patterns in the situations that confront him, and by recognizing these patterns, to retrieve speedily a considerable amount of relevant information from long-term memory.[26] It is this perceptual experience that permits the chess-master to play, and usually win, many simultaneous games against weaker opponents, taking only a few seconds for each move. It is very likely similar perceptual experience about the world of business that enables the executive to react 'intuitively', without much awareness of his own cognitive processes, to business situations as they arise.

There is no reason to suppose that the theory of cognitive processes that will emerge from the empirical study of the chessmaster's or businessman's decision processes will be 'neat' or 'elegant', in the sense that the Laws of Motion or the axioms of classical utility theory are neat and elegant. If we are to draw an analogy with the natural sciences, we might expect the theory of procedural rationality to resemble molecular biology, with its rich taxonomy of mechanisms, more closely than either classical mechanics

[26] de Groot [1965]; Chase and Simon [1973*b*].

145

or classical economics. But as I suggested earlier, an empirical science cannot remake the world to its fancy: it can only describe and explain the world as it is.

A major source of complication in theories of professional decision-making is the dependence of decisions upon large quantities of stored information and previously learned decision procedures. This is true not only at an individual psychological level, but also at a social and historical level. The play of two chess-players differs as a result of differences in what they know about chess: no less do the decisions of two businessmen differ as a result of differences in what they know about business. Moreover, Bobby Fischer, in 1972, played chess differently from Paul Morphy, in 1861. Much of that latter difference was the result of the knowledge of the game that had cumulated over the century through the collective experience of the whole society of professional chess-players.

Economics, like chess, is inevitably culture-bound and history-bound. A business firm equipped with the tools of operations research does not make the same decisions as it did before it possessed those tools. The substantial secular decline over recent years of inventories held by American firms is probably due in considerable part to this enhancement of rationality by new theory and new computational tools.

Economics is one of the sciences of the artificial.[27] It is a description and explanation of human institutions, whose theory is no more likely to remain invariant over time than the theory of bridge design. Decision processes, like all other aspects of economic institutions, exist inside human heads. They are subject to change with every change in what human beings know, and with every change in their means of calculation. For this reason the attempt to predict and prescribe human economic behavior by deductive inference from a small set of unchallengeable premises must fail and has failed.

Economics will progress as we deepen our understanding of human thought processes; and economics will change as human individuals and human societies use progressively sharpened tools of thought in making their decisions and designing their institutions. A body of theory for procedural rationality is consistent with a world in which human beings continue to think and continue to invent; a theory of substantive rationality is not.

5. Conclusion

In this paper I have contrasted the concept of substantive rationality, which has dominated classical economics and provided it with its program of structural determinism, with the concept of procedural rationality, which has prevailed in psychology. I have described also some of the

[27] Simon [1969].

146

concerns of economics that have forced that discipline to begin to concern itself with procedural rationality – with the actual processes of cognition, and with the limits on the human organism that give those processes their peculiar character.

One can conceive of at least two alternative scenarios for the continuation into the future of this gradual change in the program of economics. One involves the direct 'psychologizing' of economics, the explicit adoption of the program of economic behavioralism.[28] The second scenario pictures economists as borrowing the notions of optimal search and computational efficiency from operations research and statistical decision theory, and introducing a wider and wider range of computational considerations into the models of rationality. Since these computational constraints can be viewed (at least formally) as located in the external world rather than in the mind of the decision-maker, they give the appearance of avoiding the need for psychologizing. Of course that need is in fact only postponed, not avoided permanently. It is illusory to describe a decision as 'situationally determined' when a part of the situation that determines it is the mind of the decision-maker. Choosing between alternative models of the situation then calls for determining empirically the processes used by the person or organization making the decisions. Hence, our second scenario leads as inevitably, if not as directly, as does the first to economic behavioralism.

The shift from theories of substantive rationality to theories of procedural rationality requires a basic shift in scientific style, from an emphasis on deductive reasoning within a tight system of axioms to an emphasis on detailed empirical exploration of complex algorithms of thought. Undoubtedly the uncongeniality of the latter style to economists has slowed the transition, and accounts in part for the very limited success of economic behavioralism in the past. For this reason, the second scenario appears more promising than the first, and, indeed, appears to be unfolding visibly at the present time.

In other chapters in this volume, Messrs Coats and Latsis have described the largely successful resistance of economics to earlier attempts at injecting behavioral premises into its body of theory. The present situation is different from the earlier ones because economics is now focusing on new research questions whose answers require explicit attention to procedural rationality. As economics becomes more and more involved in the study of uncertainty, more and more concerned with the complex actuality of business decision-making, the shift in program will become inevitable. Wider and wider areas of economics will replace the over-simplified assumptions of the situationally constrained omniscient decision-maker

[28] This path has already been followed for some distance, for example, in Part IV of my own *Models of Man* [1957], in Cyert and March [1963] and in Katona's *Psychological Analysis of Economic Behaviour* [1951].

with a realistic (and psychological) characterization of the limits on Man's rationality, and the consequences of those limits for his economic behavior.

References

Chase, W. G. and Simon, H. A. [1973a]: 'Skill in Chess', *American Scientist*, **61**, pp. 394–403.

Chase, W. G. and Simon, H. A. [1973b]: 'Perception in Chess', *Cognitive Psychology*, **4**, pp. 55–81.

Clarkson, G. P. E. [1963]: 'A Model of the Trust Investment Process' in E. A. Feigenbaum and J. Feldman (eds.): *Computers and Thought*, pp. 347–71.

Cyert, R. M., Feigenbaum, E. A. and March, J. G. [1959]: 'Models in a Behavioural Theory of the Firm', *Behavioral Science*, **4**, pp. 81–95.

Cyert, R. M. and March, J. G. [1963]: *Behavioral Theory of the Firm*.

Cyert, R. M. and de Groot, M. H. [1973]: 'An Analysis of Cooperation and Learning in a Duopoly Context', *American Economic Review*, **63**, pp. 24–37.

Dorfman, R., Samuelson, P. A. and Solow, R. M. [1958]: *Linear Programming and Economic Analysis*.

Edwards, W. [1968]: 'Conservatism in Human Information Processing', in B. Kleinmuntz (ed.): *Formal Representation of Human Judgment*, pp. 17–52.

Feldman, J. [1963]: 'Simulation of Behaviour in the Binary Choice Experiment' in E. A. Feigenbaum and J. Feldman (eds.): *Computers and Thought*, pp. 329–46.

Gould, J. and Kolb, W. L. (eds.) [1964]: *The Dictionary of the Social Sciences*.

Groot, A. D. de [1965]: *Thought and Choice in Chess*.

Hall, R. L. and Hitch, C. H. [1939]: 'Price Theory and Business Behaviour', *Oxford Economic Papers*, **2**, pp. 12–45.

Holt, H. G., Modigliani, F., Muth, J. F. and Simon, H. A. [1960]: *Planning Production, Inventories and Work Force*.

James, W. [1890]: *Principles of Psychology*.

Jorgenson, D. W. [1963]: 'Capital Theory and Investment Behavior', *American Economic Review Proceedings*, **53**, pp. 247–59.

Kahneman, D. and Tversky, A. [1973]: 'On the Psychology of Prediction', *Psychological Review*, **80**, pp. 237–51.

Katona, G. [1951]: *Psychological Analysis of Economic Behavior*.

Kornai, J. [1971]: *Anti-Equilibrium*.

Latsis, S. J. [1972]: 'Situational Determinism in Economics', *The British Journal for the Philosophy of Science*, **23**, pp. 207–45.

Muth, J. F. [1961]: 'Rational Expectations and the Theory of Price Movements, *Econometrica*, **29**, pp. 315–35.

Newell, A. and Simon, H. A. [1972]: *Human Problem Solving*.

Rapaport, A. and Wallsten, T. S. [1972]: 'Individual Decision Behavior', *Annual Review of Psychology*, **23**, pp. 131–76.

Simon, H. A. [1957]: *Models of Man*.

Simon, H. A. [1969]: *The Sciences of the Artificial*.

Soelberg, P. [1967]: 'A Study of Decision Making: Job Choice'. Unpublished PhD dissertation, Carnegie-Mellon University.

Theil, H. [1958]: *Economic Forecasts and Policy*.

Tinbergen, J. [1952]: *On the Theory of Economic Policy*.

8.4
Rationality as Process and as Product of Thought

By HERBERT A. SIMON*

This opportunity to deliver the Richard T. Ely Lecture affords me some very personal satisfactions. Ely, unbeknownst to him, bore a great responsibility for my economic education, and even for my choice of profession. The example of my uncle, Harold Merkel, who was a student of Commons and Ely at Wisconsin before World War I, taught me that human behavior was a fit subject for scientific study, and directed me to economics and political science instead of high energy physics or molecular biology. Some would refer to this as satisficing, for I had never heard of high energy physics or molecular biology, and hence was spared an agonizing weighing of alternative utiles. I simply picked the first profession that sounded fascinating.

Ely's influence went much further than that. My older brother's copy of his *Outlines of Economics*—the 1930 edition—was on our bookshelves when I prepared for high school debates on tariffs versus free trade, and on the Single Tax of Henry George. It provided me with a sufficiently good grounding in principles that I was later able to take Henry Simons' intermediate theory course at the University of Chicago, and the graduate courses of Frank Knight and Henry Schultz without additional preparation.

The Ely textbook, in its generation, held the place of Samuelson or Bach in ours. If it would not sound as though I were denying any progress in economics over the past half century, I might suggest that Ely's textbook could be substituted for any of our current ones at a substantial reduction in weight, and without students or teacher being more than dimly aware of the replacement. Of course they would not hear from Ely about marginal propensities to do this

*Carnegie-Mellon University.

or that, nor about the late lamented Phillips curve. But monetarists could rejoice in Ely's uncompromising statement of the quantity theory (p. 298, italics), and in his assertion that "the solution of the problem of unemployment depends largely upon indirect measures, such as monetary and banking reform"—Ely does go on to say, however, that "we shall recognize that society must offer a willing and able man an opportunity to work" (p. 528).

I. Rationality in and out of Economics

I have more than personal reasons for directing your attention to Ely's textbook. On page 4, we find a definition of economics that is, I think, wholly characteristic of books contemporary with his. "Economics," he says, "is the science which treats of those social phenomena that are due to the wealth-getting and wealth-using activities of man." Economics, that is to say, concerns itself with a particular subset of man's behaviors—those having to do with the production, exchange, and consumption of goods and services.

Many, perhaps most, economists today would regard that view as too limiting. They would prefer the definition proposed in the *International Encyclopedia of the Social Sciences*: "Economics . . . is the study of the allocation of scarce resources among unlimited and competing uses" (vol. 4, p. 472). If beefsteak is scarce, they would say, so are votes, and the tools of economic analysis can be used as readily to analyze the allocation of the one as of the other. This point of view has launched economics into many excursions and incursions into political science and her other sister social sciences, and has generated a certain amount of hubris in the profession with respect to its broader civilizing mission. I

1

444

would suppose that the program of this meeting, with its emphasis upon the relations between economics and the other social sciences, is at least partly a reflection of that hubris.

A. *Rationality in Economics*

The topic of allocating scarce resources can be approached from either its normative or its positive side. Fundamental to the approach from either side are assumptions about the adaptation of means to ends, of actions to goals and situations. Economics, whether normative or positive, has not simply been the study of the allocation of scarce resources, it has been the study of the *rational* allocation of scarce resources.

Moreover, the term "rational" has long had in economics a much more specific meaning than its general dictionary signification of "agreeable to reason; not absurd, preposterous, extravagant, foolish, fanciful, or the like; intelligent, sensible." As is well known, the rational man of economics is a maximizer, who will settle for nothing less than the best. Even his expectations, we have learned in the past few years, are rational (see John Muth, 1961).[1] And his rationality extends as far as the bedroom for, as Gary Becker tells us, "he would read in bed at night only if the value of reading exceeded the value (to him) of the loss in sleep suffered by his wife" (1974, p. 1078).

It is this concept of rationality that is economics' main export commodity in its trade with the other social sciences. It is no novelty in those sciences to propose that people behave rationally—if that term is taken in its broader dictionary sense. Assumptions of rationality are essential components of virtually all the sociological, psychological, political, and anthropological theories with which I am familiar. What economics has to export, then, is not

rationality, but a very particular and special form of it—the rationality of the utility maximizer, and a pretty smart one at that. But international flows have to be balanced. If the program of this meeting aims at more active intercourse between economics and her sister social sciences, then we must ask not only what economics will export, but also what she will receive in payment. An economist might well be tempted to murmur the lines of the tentmaker: "I wonder often what the Vintners buy—One half as precious as the stuff they sell."

My paper will be much concerned with that question, and before I proceed, it may be well to sketch in outline the path I propose to follow in answering it. The argument has three major steps.

First, I would like to expand on the theme that almost all human behavior has a large rational component, but only in terms of the broader everyday sense of rationality, not the economists' more specialized sense of maximization.

Second, I should like to show that economics itself has not by any means limited itself to the narrower definition of rationality. Much economic literature (for example, the literature of comparative institutional analysis) uses weaker definitions of rationality extensively; and that literature would not be greatly, if at all, improved by substituting the stronger definition for the weaker one.[2] To the extent that the weaker definition is adequate for purposes of analysis, economics will find that there is indeed much that is importable from the other social sciences.

Third, economics has largely been preoccupied with the *results* of rational choice rather than the *process* of choice. Yet as economic analysis acquires a broader concern with the dynamics of choice under uncertainty, it will become more and more essential to consider choice processes. In the past twenty years, there have been im-

---

[1] The term is ill-chosen, for rational expectations in the sense of Muth are profit-maximizing expectations only under very special circumstances (see below). Perhaps we would mislead ourselves and others less if we called them by the less alluring phrase, "consistent expectations."

[2] For an interesting argument in support of this proposition from a surprising source, see Becker (1962). What Becker calls "irrationality" in his article would be called "bounded rationality" here.

portant advances in our understanding of procedural rationality, particularly as a result of research in artificial intelligence and cognitive psychology. The importation of these theories of the processes of choice into economics could provide immense help in deepening our understanding of the dynamics of rationality, and of the influences upon choice of the institutional structure within which it takes place.

We begin, then, by looking at the broader concept of rationality to which I have referred, and its social science applications.

B. *Rationality in the Other Social Sciences: Functional Analysis*

Let me provide some examples how rationality typically enters into social science theories. Consider first so-called "social exchange" theories (see, for example, George Homans). The central idea here is that when two or more people interact, each expects to get something from the interaction that is valuable to him, and is thereby motivated to give something up that is valuable to the others. Social exchange, in the form of the "inducements-contributions balance" of Chester I. Barnard and the author (1947), has played an important role in organization theory, and in even earlier times (see, for example, George Simmel) was a central ingredient in sociological theories. Much of the theorizing and empirical work on the topic has been concerned with determining what constitutes a significant inducement or contribution in particular classes of exchange situations—that is, with the actual shape and substance of the "utility function." Clearly, the man of social exchange theory is a rational man, even if he is never asked to equate things at the margin.

It is perhaps more surprising to discover how pervasive assumptions of rationality are in psychoanalytic theory—confirming the suspicion that there is indeed method in madness. In his *Five Lectures* Sigmund Freud has this to say about neurotic illnesses:

We see that human beings fall ill when, as a result of external obstacles or of an internal lack of adaptation, the satisfaction of their erotic needs *in reality* is frustrated. We see that they then take flight into *illness* in order that by its help they may find a satisfaction to take the place of what has been frustrated . . . We suspect that our patients' resistance to recovery is no simple one, but compounded of several motives. Not only does the patient's ego rebel against giving up the repressions by means of which it has risen above its original disposition, but the sexual instincts are unwilling to renounce their substitutive satisfaction so long as it is uncertain whether reality will offer them anything better.

Almost all explanations of pathological behavior in the psychoanalytic literature take this form: they explain the patient's illness in terms of the functions it performs for him.

The quotation from Freud is illustrative of a kind of functional reasoning that goes far beyond psychoanalysis and is widely used throughout the social sciences, and especially anthropology and sociology. Behaviors are functional if they contribute to certain goals, where these goals may be the pleasure or satisfaction of an individual or the guarantee of food or shelter for the members of a society. Functional analysis in this sense is concerned with explaining how "major social patterns operate to maintain the integration or adaptation of the larger system" (see Frank Cancian). Institutions are functional if reasonable men might create and maintain them in order to meet social needs or achieve social goals.

It is not necessary or implied that the adaptation of institutions or behavior patterns to goals be conscious or intended. When awareness and intention are present, the function is usually called *manifest*, otherwise it is a *latent* function. The function, whether it be manifest or latent, provides the grounds for the reasonableness or rationality of the institution or behavior pattern. As in economics, evolutionary arguments are often adduced to explain the persistence and survival of functional patterns, and to avoid assumptions of deliberate calculation in explaining them.

In practice, it is very rarely that the existence or character of institutions are *deduced* from the functions that must be performed for system survival. In almost all cases it is the other way round; it is empirical observation of the behavior pattern that raises the question of why it persists—what function it performs. Perhaps, in an appropriate axiomatic formulation, it would be possible to *deduce* that every society must have food-gathering institutions. In point of fact, such institutions can be *observed* in every society, and their existence is then rationalized by the argument that obtaining food is a functional requisite for all societies. This kind of argument may demonstrate the sufficiency of a particular pattern for performing an essential function, but cannot demonstrate its necessity—cannot show that there may not be alternative, functionally equivalent, behavior patterns that would satisfy the same need.

The point may be stated more formally. Functional arguments are arguments about the movements of systems toward stable self-maintaining equilibria. But without further specification, there is no reason to suppose that the attained equilibria that are reached will be global maxima or minima of some function rather than local, relative maxima or minima. In fact, we know that the conditions that every local maximum of a system be a global maximum are very strong (usually some kind of "convexity" conditions).

Further, when the system is complex and its environment continually changing (that is, in the conditions under which biological and social evolution actually take place), there is no assurance that the system's momentary position will lie anywhere near a point of equilibrium, whether local or global. Hence, all that can be concluded from a functional argument is that certain characteristics (the satisfaction of certain functional requirements in a particular way) are consistent with the survival and further development of the system, not that these

same requirements could not be satisfied in some other way. Thus, for example, societies can satisfy their functional needs for food by hunting or fishing activities, by agriculture, or by predatory exploitation of other societies.

C. *Functional Analysis in Economics*

Functional analysis of exactly this kind, though with a different vocabulary, is commonly employed by economists, especially when they seek to use economic tools to "explain" institutions and behaviors that lie outside the traditional domains of production and distribution. Moreover, it occurs within those domains. As an example, the fact is observed that individuals frequently insure against certain kinds of contingencies. Attitudes are then postulated (for example, risk aversion) for which buying insurance is a functional and reasonable action. If some people are observed to insure, and others not, then this difference in behavior can be explained by a difference between them in risk aversion.

To take a second example, George Stigler and Becker wish to explain the fact (if it is a fact—their empiricism is very casual) that as people hear more music, they want to hear still more. They invent a commodity, "music appreciation" (not to be confused with time spent in listening to music), and suggest that listening to music might produce not only immediate enjoyment but also an investment in *capacity* for appreciating music (i.e., in amount of enjoyment produced per listening hour). Once these assumptions are granted, various conclusions can be drawn about the demand for music appreciation. However, only weak conclusions follow about listening time unless additional strong postulates are introduced about the elasticity of demand for appreciation.

A rough "sociological" translation of the Stigler-Becker argument would be that listening to music is functional both in producing pleasure and in enhancing the pleasure of subsequent listening—a typical functional argument. It is quite unclear what is gained by dressing it in the garb of marginalism. We might be willing to grant that people would be inclined to invest more in musical appreciation early in life than later in life (because they would have a longer time in which to amortize the investment) without insisting that costs and returns were being equated at the margin, and without gaining any new insights into the situation from making the latter assumption.

A sense of fairness compels me to take a third example from my own work. In my 1951 paper, I defined the characteristics of an employment contract that distinguish it from an ordinary sales contract, and then showed why reasonable men might prefer the former to the latter as the basis for establishing an employment relation. My argument requires a theorem and fifteen numbered equations, and assumes that both employer and employee maximize their utilities. Actually, the underlying functional argument is very simple. An employee who didn't care very much which of several alternative tasks he performed would not require a large inducement to accept the authority of an employer—that is, to permit the employer to make the choice among them. The employer in turn would be willing to provide the necessary inducement in order to acquire the right to postpone his decisions about the employee's agenda, and in this way to postpone some of his decisions whose outcomes are contingent on future uncertain events.[3] The rigorous economic argument, involving the idea of maximizing behavior by employer and employee, is readily translatable into a simple qualitative argument that an employment contract may be a functional ("reasonable") way of dealing with certain kinds of uncertainty. The argument then explains why employment relations are so widely used in our society.

The translation of these examples of economic reasoning into the language of functional analysis could be paralleled by examples of translation scholarship which run in the opposite direction. Political scientists, for example, long ago observed that under certain circumstances institutions of representative democracy spawned a multiplicity of political parties, while under other circumstances, the votes were divided in equilibrium between two major parties. These contrasting equilibria could readily be shown by functional arguments to result from rational voting decisions under different rules of the electoral game, as was observed by Maurice Duverger, in his classic work on political parties, as well as by a number of political scientists who preceded him. In recent years, these same results have been rederived more rigorously by economists and game theorists, employing much stronger assumptions of utility maximization by the voters; it was hard to see that the maximization assumptions have produced any new predictions of behavior.[4]

D. *Summary*

Perhaps these examples suffice to show that there is no such gap as is commonly supposed between the view of man espoused by economics and the view found in the other social sciences. The view of man as rational is not peculiar to economics, but is endemic, and even ubiquitous, throughout the social sciences. Economics tends to emphasize a particular

---

[3]Recently, Oliver Williamson has pointed out that I would have to introduce slightly stronger assumptions to justify the employment contract as rational if one of the alternatives to it were what he calls a "contingent claims" contract, but the point of my example is not affected. To exclude the contingent claims contract as a viable alternative, we need merely take account of the large transaction costs it would entail under real world conditions.

[4]For an introduction to this literature, see William H. Riker and Peter C. Ordeshook, and Riker. Anthony Downs' book belongs to an intermediate genre. While it employs the language of economics, it limits itself to verbal, nonrigorous reasoning which certainly does not make any essential use of maximizing assumptions (as contrasted with rationality assumptions in the broader sense), and which largely translates into economic vocabulary generalizations that were already part of the science and folklore of politics. In the next section, other examples of this kind of informal use of rationality principles are examined to analyze institutions and their behavior.

form of rationality—maximizing behavior—as its preferred engine of explanation, but the differences are often differences in vocabulary more than in substance. We shall see in a moment that in much economic discussion the notion of maximization is used in a loose sense that is very close to the common sense notions of rationality used elsewhere in the social sciences.

One conclusion we may draw is that economists might well exercise a certain amount of circumspection in their endeavors to export economic analysis to the other social sciences. They may discover that they are sometimes offering commodities that are already in generous supply, and which can therefore be disposed of only at a ruinously low price. On the other side of the trade, they may find that there is more of interest in the modes and results of inquiry of their fellow social scientists than they have generally been aware.

II. On Applying the Principle of Rationality

What is characteristic of the examples of functional analysis cited in the last section, whether they be drawn from economics or from the other social sciences, is that they are not focused on, or even much concerned with, how variables are equated at the margin, or how equilibrium is altered by marginal shifts in conditions (for example, shifts in a supply or demand schedule). Rather, they are focused on qualitative and structural questions, typically, on the choice among a small number of discrete institutional alternatives:

Not "how much flood insurance will a man buy?" but "what are the structural conditions that make buying insurance rational or attractive?"

Not "at what levels will wages be fixed?" but "when will work be performed under an employment contract rather than a sales contract?"

If we want a natural science analogy to this kind of theorizing, we can find it in geology. A geologist notices deep scratches in rock; he notices that certain hills of gravel are elongated along a north-south axis, and that the boulders embedded in them are not as smooth as those usually found on beaches. To explain these facts, he evokes a structural, and not at all quantitative, hypothesis: that these phenomena were produced by the process of glaciation.

In the first instance, he does not try to explain the depth of the glacial till, or estimate the weight of the ice that produced it, but simply to identify the basic causative process. He wants to explain the role of glaciation, of erosion, of vulcanization, of sedimentation in producing the land forms that he observes. His explanations, moreover, are after-the-fact, and not predictive.

A. Toward Qualitative Analysis

As economics expands beyond its central core of price theory, and its central concern with quantities of commodities and money, we observe in it this same shift from a highly quantitative analysis, in which equilibration at the margin plays a central role, to a much more qualitative institutional analysis, in which discrete structural alternatives are compared.

In these analyses aimed at explaining institutional structure, maximizing assumptions play a much less significant role than they do typically in the analysis of market equilibria. The rational man who sometimes prefers an employment contract to a sales contract need not be a maximizer. Even a satisficer will exhibit such a preference whenever the difference in rewards between the two arrangements is sufficiently large and evident.

For this same reason, such analyses can often be carried out without elaborate mathematical apparatus or marginal calculation. In general, much cruder and simpler arguments will suffice to demonstrate an inequality between two quantities than are required to show the conditions under which these quantities are equated at the margin. Thus, in the recent works of Janos Kornai, Williamson, and John Montias on economic organization, we find only rather modest and simple applications of mathematical analysis. In the ways in which they involve principles of rationality, the arguments of these authors resemble James March and the author's *Organizations* more closely than Paul Samuelson's *Foundations*.[5]

What is the predominant form of reasoning that we encounter in these theoretical treatments of social institutions? Do they contain arguments based on maximizing assumptions? Basically, they rest upon a very simple form of causal analysis. Particular institutional structures or practices are seen to entail certain undesirable (for example, costly) or desirable (for example, value-producing) consequences. *Ceteris paribus*, situations and practices will be preferred when important favorable consequences are associated with them, and avoided when important unfavorable consequences are associated with them. A shift in the balance of consequences, or in awareness of them, may motivate a change in institutional arrangements.

Consider the following argument from Montias typical of this genre of analysis, which relates to the balance in organizations between centralization and decentralization.

> Decentralizing measures are generally aimed at remedying two shortcom-

[5] A notable exception to this generalization about the economic literature on organizations is the work of Jacob Marschak and Roy Radner on the theory of teams. These authors chose the strategy of detailed, precise analysis of the implications of maximizing assumptions for the transmission of information in organizations. The price they paid for this rigor was to find themselves limited to the highly simplified situations where solutions could be found for the mathematical problems they posed. We need not, of course, make an either-or choice between these two modes of inquiry. While it may be difficult or impossible to extend the formal analysis of the theory of teams to problems of real world complexity, the rigorous microtheory may illuminate the workings of important component mechanisms in the complex macrosituations. The methodological issues in choosing between analytic tractability and realism are quite parallel to those involved in the choice between laboratory and field methods for gathering empirical information about social phenomena. Neither one by itself marks the exclusive path toward truth.

> ings of an 'overcentralized' system structure. (1) Superordinates are overburdened with responsibility for the detailed direction and coordination of their subordinates' activities. (2) This 'petty tutelage' deprives subordinates of the opportunity to make decisions that might increase the payoff of the organization of which they are a part. . . . Why not loosen controls . . . ? . . . When controls are loosened, unless the incentive system is modified to bring about greater harmony between the goals of supervisors and supervisees, it may induce producers to shift their input and output mix in directions that . . . vitiate any benefits that might be reaped by the organization as a whole from the exercise of greater initiative at lower tiers. [p. 215]

Here two costs or disadvantages of centralization (burden on supervisors, restriction of choice-set of subordinates) are set off against a disadvantage of decentralization (goals of subordinates divergent from organization goals). What can we learn about organization from an argument like this? Certainly little or nothing about the optimal balance point between centralization and decentralization in any particular organization. Rather, we might derive conclusions of these kinds:

1. That increasing awareness of one of the predicted consequences may cause an organization to move in the direction of centralization or decentralization. (For example, an egregious case of "suboptimizing" by a subordinate may cause additional centralized controls to be instituted.)

2. That new technical devices may tilt the balance between centralization and decentralization. For example, invention and adoption of divisionalized profit and loss statements led toward decentralization of many large American business firms in the 1950's; while reduction in information costs through computerization led at a later date to centralization of inventory control decisions in those same firms.

Of course Montias' conclusions could also be derived from a more formal optimization analysis—in fact he presents such an analysis on the two pages following the passage quoted above. But it is not clear that anything new is added by the formalization, since the parameters imputed to the system are largely unmeasured and unmeasurable.

There is something to be said for an Ockham's Razor that, eschewing assumptions of optimization, provides an explanation of behavior that is consistent with *either* optimizing or satisficing procedures on the part of the human agents. Parsimony recommends that we prefer the postulate that men are reasonable to the postulate that they are supremely rational when either one of the two assumptions will do our work of inference as well as the other.[6]

B. *Procedural Rationality*

The kind of qualitative analysis I have been describing has another virtue. In complex situations there is likely to be a considerable gap between the real environment of a decision (the world as God or some other omniscient observer sees it) and the environment as the actors perceive it. The analysis can then address itself either to normative questions—the whole range of consequences that *should* enter into decisions in such situations—or descriptive questions, including the questions of which components of the situation are likely to be taken into account by the actors, and how the actors are likely to represent the situation as a whole.

In the precomputer era, for example, it was very difficult for managers in business organizations to pay attention to all the major variables affected by their decisions. Company treasurers frequently made deci-

sions about working capital with little or no attention to their impact on inventory levels, while production and marketing executives made decisions about inventory without taking into account impacts on liquidity. The introduction of computers changed the ways in which executives were able to reach decisions; they could now view them in terms of a much wider set of interrelated consequences than before. The perception of the environment of a decision is a function of—among other things—the information sources and computational capabilities of the executives who make it.

Learning phenomena are also readily handled within this framework. A number of the changes introduced into planning and control procedures in eastern European countries during the 1960's were instituted when the governments in question learned by experience of some of the dysfunctional consequences of trying to control production by means of crude aggregates of physical quantities. An initial distrust of prices and market mechanisms was gradually and partially overcome after direct experience of the disadvantages of some of the alternative mechanisms. These learning experiences could be paralleled with experiences of American steel companies, for example, that experimented with tonnage incentives for mill department superintendents.

A general proposition that might be asserted about organizations is that the number of considerations that are potentially relevant to the effectiveness of an organization design is so large that only a few of the more salient of these lie within the circle of awareness at any given time, that the membership of this subset changes continually as new situations (produced by external or internal events) arise, and that "learning" in the form of reaction to perceived consequences is the dominant way in which rationality exhibits itself.

In a world where these kinds of adjustments are prominent, a theory of rational behavior must be quite as much concerned with the characteristics of the rational actors—the means they use to cope with uncertainty and cognitive complexity—as

[6]Ockham is usually invoked on behalf of the parsimony of optimizing assumptions, and against the additional *ad hoc* postulates that satisficing models are thought to require in order to guarantee uniqueness of solutions. But that argument only applies when we are trying to deduce unique equilibria, a task quite different from the one most institutional writers set for themselves. However, I have no urge to enlarge on this point. My intent here is not polemical, on behalf of satisficing postulates, but rather to show how large a plot of common ground is shared by optimizing and satisficing analysis. Again, compare Becker (1962).

with the characteristics of the objective environment in which they make their decisions. In such a world, we must give an account not only of *substantive rationality*—the extent to which appropriate courses of action are chosen—but also *procedural rationality*—the effectiveness, in light of human cognitive powers and limitations, of the *procedures* used to choose actions. As economics moves out toward situations of increasing cognitive complexity, it becomes increasingly concerned with the ability of actors to cope with the complexity, and hence with the procedural aspects of rationality. In the remainder of my talk, I would like to develop this concept of procedural rationality, and its implications for economic analysis.

III. Mind as the Scarce Resource

Until rather recently, such limited attention as was paid by economists to procedural, as distinct from substantive, rationality was mainly motivated by the problems of uncertainty and expectations. The simple notion of maximizing utility or profit could not be applied to situations where the optimum action depended on uncertain environmental events, or upon the actions of other rational agents (for example, imperfect competition).

The former difficulty was removed to some degree by replacing utility maximization with the maximization of subjective expected utility (*SEU*) as the criterion of rationality. In spite of its conceptual elegance, however, the *SEU* solution has some grave defects as either a normative or a descriptive formulation. In general, the optimal solution depends upon all of the moments of the frequency distributions of uncertain events. The exceptions are a small but important class of cases where the utility or profit function is quadratic and all constraints are in the form of equations rather than inequalities.[7] The empirical

defect of the *SEU* formulation is that when it has been subjected to test in the laboratory or the real world, even in relatively simple situations, the behavior of human subjects has generally departed widely from it.

Some of the evidence has been surveyed by Ward Edwards, and more recently by Daniel Kahneman and Amos Tversky. They describe experimental situations in which estimates formed on the basis of initial information are not revised nearly as much by subsequent information as would be required by Bayes' Theorem. In other situations, subjects respond largely to the information received most recently, and take inadequate account of prior information.

Behavior that is radically inconsistent with the *SEU* framework occurs also in naturalistic settings. Howard Kunreuther et al. have recently carried out extensive studies of behavior and attitudes relating to the purchase of flood insurance by persons owning property in low-lying areas. They found that knowledge of the availability of insurance, or rates, and of objective risks was very imperfect, and that the actual decisions whether or not to insure were related much more to personal experience with floods than to any objective facts about the situation—or even to personal subjective beliefs about those facts. In the face of this evidence, it is hard to take *SEU* seriously as a theory of actual human behavior in the face of uncertainty.[8]

For situations where the rationality of an action depends upon what others (who are also striving to be rational) do again, no consensus has been reached as to what constitutes optimal behavior. This is one of the reasons I have elsewhere called imperfect competition "the permanent and ineradicable scandal of economic theory" (1976b, p. 140). The most imaginative and

[7]In this case the expected values of the environmental variables serve as certainty equivalents, so that *SEU* maximization requires only replacing the unknown true values by these expected values. See the author (1957).

[8]Kunreuther et al. point out that the theory cannot be "saved" by assuming utility to be radically nonlinear in money. In the flood insurance case, that interpretation of the data would work only if we were willing to assume that money has strongly *increasing* marginal utility, not a very plausible escape route for the theory.

ambitious attempt to resolve the difficulty was the von Neumann-Morgenstern theory of games, which is embarrassing in the wealth of alternative solutions it offers. While the theory of games reveals the potential richness of behavior when rational individuals are faced with conflict of interest, the capability of reacting to each other's actions (or expected actions), and possibilities for coalition, it has provided no unique and universally accepted criterion of rationality to generalize the *SEU* criterion and extend it to this broader range of situations.

The so-called "rational expectations" models, currently so popular (and due originally to Muth), pass over these problems rather than solving them. They ignore potential coalitions and attempted mutual outguessing behavior, and correspond to optimal solutions only when the losses are quadratic functions of the errors of estimate.[9] Hence they do not correspond to any classical criterion of rationality, and labeling them with that term, rather than the more neutral "consistent expectations," provides them with a rather unwarranted legitimation.

Finally, it should be remarked that the main motivation in economics for developing theories of uncertainty and mutual expectations has not been to replace substantive criteria of rationality with procedural criteria, but rather to find substantive criteria broad enough to extend the concept of rationality beyond the boundaries of static optimization under certainty. As with classical decision theory, the interest lies not in *how* decisions are made but in *what* decisions are made. (But see, contra, such analyses as Richard Cyert and Morris De-Groot.)

[9]That is, only under the conditions where the uncertainty equivalents of fn. 8 exist. Under other circumstances, a "rational" person would be well advised, if he knew that all others were following the "rational expectations" or "consistent expectations" rule, to recalculate his own optimal behavior on that assumption. Of course if others followed the same course, we would be back in the "outguessing" situation.

A. *Search and Teams*

Decision procedures have been treated more explicitly in the small bodies of work that have grown up in economics on the theory of search and on the theory of teams. Both these bodies of theory are specifically concerned with the limits on the ability of the economic actor to discover or compute what behavior is optimal for him. Both aspire not only to *take account* of human bounded rationality, but to *bring it within the compass* of the rational calculus. Let me explain what I mean by that distinction.

Problems of search arise when not all the alternatives of action are presented to the rational actor *ab initio*, but must be sought through some kind of costly activity. In general, an action will be chosen before the search has revealed all possible alternatives. One example of this kind of problem is the sale of a house, or some other asset, when offers are received sequentially and remain open for only a limited time (see the author, 1955). Another example which has been widely cited is the purchase of an automobile involving travel to dealers' lots (see Stigler, 1961). In both these examples, the question is not how the search is carried out, but how it is decided when to terminate it—that is, the amount of search. The question is answered by postulating a cost that increases with the total amount of search. In an optimizing model, the correct point of termination is found by equating the marginal cost of search with the (expected) marginal improvement in the set of alternatives. In a satisficing model, search terminates when the best offer exceeds an aspiration level that itself adjusts gradually to the value of the offers received so far. In both cases, search becomes just another factor of production, and investment in search is determined by the same marginal principle as investment in any other factor. However cavalierly these theories treat the actual search process, they do recognize explicitly that information gathering is not a free activity, and that unlimited amounts of it are not available.

The theory of teams, as developed by Marschak and Radner, goes a step farther in specifying the procedure of decision. That theory, as is well known, is concerned with the improvement that may be realized in a team's decisions by interchange of information among the team members. But here the theory does not limit itself to determining the aggregate amount of information that should be transmitted, but seeks to calculate what messages should be exchanged, under what conditions, and at what cost. The content of the communication as well as the total amount of information becomes relevant to the theory.

In its attitude toward rationality, the theory of teams is as "classical," however, as is search theory. The bounds on the rationality of the team members are "externalized" and represented as costs of communication, so that they can be folded into the economic calculation along with the costs and benefits of outcomes.

B. *Rational Search Procedures*

To find theories that compare the merits of alternative search procedures, we must look largely outside the domain of economics. A number of such theories have been developed in the past thirty years, mainly by management scientists and researchers in the field of artificial intelligence. An important example is the body of work that has been done on integer programming.

Integer programming problems resemble linear programming problems (to maximize some quantity, subject to constraints in the form of linear equations and inequalities), with the added condition that certain variables can only take whole numbers as their values. The integer constraint makes inapplicable most of the powerful computational methods available for solving linear programming problems, with the result that integer programming problems are far less tractable, computationally, than linear programming problems having comparable numbers of variables.

Solution methods for integer program-ming problems use various forms of highly selective search—for example branch-and-bound methods that establish successively narrower limits for the value of the optimum, and hence permit a corresponding narrowing of search to promising regions of the space. It becomes a matter of considerable practical and theoretical interest to evaluate the relative computational efficiency of competing search procedures, and also to estimate how the cost of search will grow with the size of the problem posed. Until recently, most evaluation of search algorithms has been empirical: they have been tested on sample problems. Recently, however, a body of theory—called theory of computational complexity—has grown up that begins to answer some of these questions in a more systematic way.

I cannot give here an account of the theory of computational complexity, or all of its implications for procedural rationality. A good introduction will be found in Alfred Aho et al. One important set of results that comes out of the theory does require at least brief mention. These results have to do with the way in which the amount of computation required to solve problems of a given class grows with the size of the problems—with the number of variables, say.[10]

In a domain where computational requirements grow rapidly with problem size, we will be able to solve only small problems; in domains where the requirements grow slowly, we will be able to solve much larger problems. The problems that the real world presents to us are generally enormous compared with the problems that we can solve on even our largest computers. Hence, our computational models are always rough approximations to the reality, and we must hope that the approximation will not be too inexact to be useful.

[10]Most of the theorems in computational complexity have to do with the "worst case," that is, with the maximum amount of computation required to solve *any* problem of the given class. Very few results are available for the expected cost, averaged over all problems of the class.

We will be particularly concerned that computational costs not increase rapidly with problem size.

It is customary in the theory of computational complexity to regard problems of a given size as "tractable" if computations do not grow faster than at some fixed power of problem size. Such classes of problems are known as "polynomial complex." Problems that grow exponentially in complexity with size are not polynomial complex, since the rate of growth of computation comes to exceed any fixed power of their size.

A large and important class of problems which includes the general integer programming problem, as well as standard scheduling problems, all have been shown to have the same level of complexity—if one is polynomial complex, then all are; if one is not polynomial complex, then none are. These problems have been labeled "NP-complete." It is conjectured, but not yet proven, that the class of NP-complete problems is not polynomially complex, but probably exponentially complex.

The significance of these findings and conjectures is in showing that computational difficulties, and the need to approximate, are not just a minor annoying feature of our world to be dealt with by manufacturing larger computers or breeding smarter people. Complexity is deep in the nature of things, and discovering tolerable approximation procedures and heuristics that permit huge spaces to be searched very selectively lies at the heart of intelligence, whether human or artificial. A theory of rationality that does not give an account of problem solving in the face of complexity is sadly incomplete. It is worse than incomplete; it can be seriously misleading by providing "solutions" to economic questions that are without operational significance.

One interesting and important direction of research in computational complexity lies in showing how the complexity of problems might be decreased by weakening the requirements for solution—by requiring solutions only to approximate the optimum, or by replacing an optimality criterion by a satisficing criterion. Results are still fragmentary, but it is already known that there are some cases where such modifications reduce exponential or NP-complete problem classes to polynomial-complete classes.

The theory of heuristic search, cultivated in artificial intelligence and information processing psychology, is concerned with devising or identifying search procedures that will permit systems of limited computational capacity to make complex decisions and solve difficult problems. (For a general survey of the theory, see Nils Nilsson.) When a task environment has patterned structure, so that solutions to a search problem are not scattered randomly throughout it, but are located in ways related to the structure, then an intelligent system capable of detecting the pattern can exploit it in order to search for solutions in a highly selective way.

One form, for example, of selective heuristic search, called best-first search, assigns to each node in the search space an estimate of the distance of that node from a solution. At each stage, the next increment of effort is expended in searching from the node, among those already reached, that has the smallest distance estimate (see, for example, the author and J.B. Kadane). As another example, when the task is to find a good or best solution, it may be possible to assign upper and lower bounds on the values of the solutions that can be obtained by searching a particular part of the space. If the upper bound on region A is lower than the lower bound on some other region, then region A does not need to be searched at all.

I will leave the topics of computational complexity and heuristic search with these sketchy remarks. What implications these developments in the theory of procedural rationality will have for economics defined as "the science which treats of the wealth-getting and wealth-using activities of man" remain to be seen. That they are an integral part of economics defined as "the science which treats of the allocation of scarce resources" is obvious. The scarce resource is computational capacity—the mind. The ability of man to solve complex problems, and the magnitude of the resources that have to be allocated to solving them, depend on the efficiency with which this resource, mind, is deployed.

C. Attention as the Scarce Resource

Finally, I would like to turn from the rather highly developed approaches to procedural rationality that I have been discussing back to the more qualitative kinds of institutional issues that were considered in the previous section of this paper. Many of the central issues of our time are questions of how we use limited information and limited computational capacity to deal with enormous problems whose shape we barely grasp.

For many purposes, a modern government can be regarded as a parallel computing device. While one part of its capability for rational problem solving is directed to fire protection, another is directed to paving highways, and another to collecting refuse. For other important purposes, a government, like a human being, is a serial processing system, capable of attending to only one thing at a time. When important new policies must be formulated, public and official attention must be focused on one or a few matters. Other concerns, no matter how pressing, must wait their turn on the agenda. When the agenda becomes crowded, public life begins to appear more and more as a succession of crises. When problems become interrelated, as energy and pollution problems have become, there is the constant danger that attention directed to a single facet of the web will spawn solutions that disregard vital consequences for the other facets. When oil is scarce, we return to coal, but forget that we must then deal with vastly increased quantities of sulfur oxides in our urban air. Or we outlaw nuclear power stations because of radiation hazards, but fail to make alternative provision to meet our energy needs. It is futile to talk of substantive rationality in public affairs without considering what procedural means are available to order issues on the public agenda in a rational way, and to insure attention to the in-direct consequences of actions taken to reach specific goals or solve specific problems.

In a world where information is relatively scarce, and where problems for decision are few and simple, information is almost always a positive good. In a world where attention is a major scarce resource, information may be an expensive luxury, for it may turn our attention from what is important to what is unimportant. We cannot afford to attend to information simply because it is there. I am not aware that there has been any systematic development of a theory of information and communication that treats attention rather than information as the scarce resource.[11] Some of the practical consequences of attention scarcity have already been noticed in business and government, where early designs of so-called "management information systems" flooded executives with trivial data and, until they learned to ignore them, distracted their attention from more important matters. It is probably true of contemporary organizations that an automated information system that does not consume and digest vastly more information than it produces and distributes harms the performance of the organization in which it is incorporated.

The management of attention and tracing indirect consequences of action are two of the basic issues of procedural rationality that confront a modern society. There are others of comparable importance: what decision-making procedure is rational when the basic quantities for making marginal comparisons are simply not known? A few years ago, I served as chairman of a National Academy of Sciences (NAS) committee whose job it was to advise the Congress on the control of automobile emissions (see NAS, Coordinating Committee on Air Quality Studies). It is easy to formulate an SEU model to conceptualize the problem. There is a production function for automobiles that associates different costs with different levels of emissions. The laws govern-

---

[11]Some unsystematic remarks on the subject will be found in the author (1976a, chs. 13, 14).

ing the chemistry of the atmosphere determine the concentrations of polluting substances in the air as a function of the levels of emissions. Biomedical science tells us what effects on life and health can be expected from various concentrations of pollutants. All we need do is to attach a price tag to life and health, and we can calculate the optimum level of pollution control.

There is only one hitch—which will be apparent to all of you. None of the relevant parameters of the various "production functions" are known—except, within half an order of magnitude, the cost of reducing the emissions themselves. The physics and chemistry of the atmosphere presents a series of unsolved problems—particularly relating to the photochemical reactions affecting the oxides of nitrogen and ozone. Medical science is barely able to detect that there *are* health effects from pollutants, much less measure how large these effects are. The committee's deliberations led immediately to one conclusion—one that congressmen are accustomed to hearing from such committees: We need more research. But while the research is being done, what provisions should be incorporated in the Clean Air Act of 1977 (or the Acts of 1978 through 2000, for that matter)? For research won't give us clear answers then either. What constitutes procedural rationality in such circumstances?

"Reasonable men" reach "reasonable" conclusions in circumstances where they have no prospect of applying classical models of substantive rationality. We know only imperfectly how they do it. We know even less whether the procedures they use in place of the inapplicable models have any merit—although most of us would choose them in preference to drawing lots. The study of procedural rationality in circumstances where attention is scarce, where problems are immensely complex, and where crucial information is absent presents a host of challenging and fundamental research problems to anyone who is interested in the rational allocation of scarce resources.

IV. Conclusion

In histories of human civilization, the invention of writing and the invention of printing are always treated as key events. Perhaps in future histories the invention of electrical communication and the invention of the computer will receive comparable emphasis. What all of these developments have in common, and what makes them so important, is that they represent basic changes in man's equipment for making rational choices—in his computational capabilities. Problems that are impossible to handle with the head alone (multiplying large numbers together, for example) become trivial when they can be written down on paper. Interactions of energy and environment that almost defy conceptualization lend themselves to at least approximate modeling with modern computers.

The advances in man's capacity for procedural rationality are not limited to these obvious examples. The invention of algebra, of analytic geometry, of the calculus were such advances. So was the invention, if we may call it that, of the modern organization, which greatly increased man's capacity for coordinated parallel activity. Changes in the production function for information and decisions are central to any account of changes over the centuries of the human condition.

In the past, economics has largely ignored the processes that rational man uses in reaching his resource allocation decisions. This was possibly an acceptable strategy for explaining rational decision in static, relatively simple problem situations where it might be assumed that additional computational time or power could not change the outcome. The strategy does not work, however, when we are seeking to explain the decision maker's behavior in complex, dynamic circumstances that involve a great deal of uncertainty, and that make severe demands upon his attention.

As economics acquires aspirations to explain behavior under these typical conditions of modern organizational and public life, it will have to devote major energy to building a theory of procedural rationality to complement existing theories of substantive rationality. Some elements of such a theory can be borrowed from the neighboring disciplines of operations research, artificial intelligence, and cognitive psychology; but an enormous job remains to be done to extend this work and to apply it to specifically economic problems.

Jacob Marschak, throughout his long career, had a deep belief in and commitment to the interdependencies and complementarity of the several social sciences. I have shared that belief and commitment, without always agreeing with him in detail as to the precise route for exploiting it. The developments I have been describing strengthen greatly, it seems to me, the rational grounds for both belief and commitment. Whether we accept the more restricted definition of economics that I quoted from Ely's textbook, or the wider definition that is widely accepted today, we have every reason to try to communicate with the other social sciences, both to find out what we have to say that may be of interest to them, and to discover what they can teach us about the nature of procedural rationality.

REFERENCES

Alfred V. Aho et al., *The Design and Analysis of Computer Algorithms*, Reading 1974.

Chester I. Barnard, *The Functions of the Executive*, Cambridge 1938.

G. S. Becker, "Irrational Behavior and Economic Theory," *J. Polit. Econ.*, Feb. 1962, *70*, 1–13.

_____, "A Theory of Social Interations," *J. Polit. Econ.*, Nov./Dec. 1974, *82*, 1063–93.

F. M. Cancian, "Functional Analysis," in *International Encyclopedia of the Social Sciences*, 1968, *6*, 29–42.

R. M. Cyert and M. H. Degrott, "Sequential Strategies in Dual Control," *Theory Decn.*, Apr. 1977, *8*, 173–92.

Anthony Downs, *An Economic Theory of Democracy*, New York 1957.

Maurice Duverger, *Political Parties*, rev. ed., New York 1959, (*Les Partis Politiques*, Paris 1951).

W. Edwards, "Conservation in Human Information Processing," in Benjamin Kleinmuntz, ed., *Formal Representation of Human Thought*, New York 1968.

Richard T. Ely, *Outlines of Economics*, rev. ed., New York 1930.

S. Freud, "Five Lectures on Psychoanalysis" (originally "The Origin and Development of Psychoanalysis" 1910) in *The Complete Psychological Works of Sigmund Freud*, Vol. 11, London 1957.

George Homans, *Social Behavior: Its Elementary Forms*, New York 1961.

D. Kahneman and A. Tversky, "On the Psychology of Prediction," *Psychol. Rev.*, July 1973, *80*, 237–51.

Janos Kornai, *Anti-Equilibrium*, Amsterdam 1971.

Howard Kunreuther et al., *Protecting Against High-Risk Hazards: Public Policy Lessons*, New York 1978.

James G. March and Herbert A. Simon, *Organizations*, New York 1958.

Jacob Marschak and Roy Radner, *Economic Theory of Teams*, New Haven 1972.

John M. Montias, *The Structure of Economic Systems*, New Haven 1976.

J. F. Muth, "Rational Expectations and the Theory of Price Movements," *Econometrica*, July 1961, *29*, 315–35.

Nils Nilsson, *Problem-Solving Methods in Artificial Intelligence*, New York 1971.

A. Rees, "Economics," in *International Encyclopedia of the Social Sciences*, 1968, *4*, 472.

William H. Riker, *The Theory of Political Coalitions*, New Haven 1962.

_____ and Peter C. Ordeshook, *An Introduction to Positive Political Theory*, New Jersey 1973.

Paul Samuelson, *Foundations of Economic Analysis*, Cambridge 1947.

George Simmel, *Soziologie*, Berlin 1908.

Herbert A. Simon, "A Formal Theory of the Employment Relation," *Enconometrica*, July 1951, *19*, 293–305.

_____, "A Behavioral Model of Rational

Choice," *Quart. J. Econ.*, Feb. 1955, *69*, 99–118.

_____, "Dynamic Programming Under Uncertainty with a Quadratic Criterion Function," *Econometrica*, Jan. 1956, *24*, 74–81.

_____, (1976a) *Administrative Behavior*, 3d ed., New York 1976.

_____, (1976b) "From Substantive to Procedural Rationality," in Spiro J. Latsis, ed., *Method and Appraisal in Economics*, Cambridge 1976.

_____ and J. B. Kadane, "Optimal Problem-Solving Search: All-or-None Solutions,"

Artificial Intel., Fall 1975, *6*, 235–48.

G. J. Stigler, "The Economics of Information," *J. Polit. Econ.*, June 1961, *69*, 213–15.

_____ and G. S. Becker, "De Gustibus non est Disputandum," *Amer. Econ. Rev.*, Mar. 1977, *67*, 76–90.

Oliver E. Williamson, *Markets and Hierarchies*, New York 1975.

National Academy of Sciences, (*NAS*) Coordinating Committee on Air Quality Studies, *Air Quality and Automobile Emission Control*, Vol. 1 summary rep., Washington 1974.

8.5
On how to decide what to do

Herbert A. Simon
Professor of Psychology
Carnegie-Mellon University

Economics, which has traditionally been concerned with what decisions are made rather than with how they are made, has more and more reason to interest itself in the procedural aspects of decision, especially to deal with uncertainty, and more generally, with nonequilibrium phenomena. A number of approaches to procedural rationality have been developed in such fields as operations research and management science, artificial intelligence, computational complexity, and cognitive simulation which might be of considerable value to economics as it moves in this new direction.

1. Introduction

■ It is commonplace to observe that economics has traditionally been concerned with *what* decisions are made rather than with *how* they are made — with substantive rationality rather than procedural rationality. In other places (Simon, 1976, 1978), I have tried to explain why this is so, and to suggest some reasons why it is changing — why economics is becoming increasingly interested in how people go about deciding what to do, or, in a normative mode, how they *should* go about it. Economics is not the only domain of science that is concerned with questions of procedural rationality; indeed, such questions have been at the very center of attention of several other disciplines, and important progress has been made in finding answers.

Let me start with the most familiar realms, and then go on to those that are more remote. First, I shall take up operations research and management science, then artificial intelligence and the new discipline of computational complexity, and finally, cognitive simulation. I shall also discuss briefly how the new developments might apply to traditional problems in economics. For the most part, however, I shall leave those applications to the reader and to the future, after stating my reasons for thinking that they will be needed for the continuing progress of economic analysis.

2. Operations research and management science

■ What is the goal of basic theory in operations research (OR) and management science? It is to specify good (or best) methods for finding good (or best)

This research was supported by Research Grant MH-07722 from the National Institute of Mental Health.

494

decisions in complex managerial situations. OR theory is a theory of computation, of procedural rationality. It is, to paraphrase Clausewitz (1832), the continuation of classical numerical analysis by other means. The "other means" are such tools as linear, dynamic, integer, and geometric programming, queuing theory, combinatorial analysis, simulation, and search theory. OR theory is normative theory: it tells managers how they ought to use their computers. Of course, as more and more managers follow its advice, it also becomes a positive science, describing some of the actual decision procedures employed by organizations.

I observed in passing that OR theory is normative in a dual sense: it is concerned with good methods for reaching good decisions. Thus, a linear programming (LP) algorithm is a procedure for reaching an optimum in a situation represented as a system of linear equations and inequalities. A good LP algorithm is one that determines the optimum at a relatively low computational cost. Research in LP is directed at inventing new algorithms or new computational paradigms that will reduce this cost.

Conceptually, of course, there is no reason why we need to treat the substantive decision problem and the procedural problem at arm's length, as though they were independent of each other. The global optimization problem is to find the least-cost or best-return decision, *net* of computational costs. We formulate this problem in terms of a tradeoff between the marginal computational cost and the marginal improvement in the substantive decision it is expected to produce (Simon, 1955; Stigler, 1961; Marschak and Radner, 1972).

In practice, this is not always the way we proceed. In writing LP algorithms, we almost always assume that we want to discover the optimal solution, while disregarding computational costs. We then try to devise an algorithm that will find this solution as cheaply as possible. This is a reasonable way even for an optimizer to proceed, since computers are rather cheap these days, and getting cheaper. For $300 one can purchase an hour's attention from a fairly large computer, and if one's interest is in scheduling an oil refinery, the payoff from making correct decisions is several orders of magnitude larger than that.

Why, then, be concerned with the $300 at all? Well, as managers say, it is still money. If one algorithm can compute the solution in an hour, while another takes two, it is worth pocketing the change. But there is a more important reason: there are not only cost constraints on the solutions of problems; there are also real-time constraints. If the refinery has to be rescheduled daily, a scheduling algorithm that takes two weeks to run provides little help or comfort. With each modest increase in the size of the problem the cost of finding a solution with any given algorithm is likely to increase by orders of magnitude. For problems above some limiting size, the algorithm becomes not just expensive but impracticable—it simply will not yield solutions in any reasonable span of time. For this reason, OR researchers concerned with linear programming (or other) algorithms have usually held that their goal is to expand the upper limits of problem size for which solutions can be found, rather than to reduce the cost of finding solutions for problems of a given size. Of course, these are simply the two sides of the same coin, and, in fact, alternative algorithms are frequently evaluated by comparing their speeds of solution on standard sets of test problems.

The evaluation of algorithms is still largely a pragmatic matter, with little theoretical foundation. That is to say, there are today few theorems that prove that a particular LP algorithm is the most efficient, or that one class of algorithms is better than another. Algorithms are usually evaluated, as indicated above, by running them on test problems and recording the amount of computation required for solution. This state of affairs has been a source of understandable unhappiness in OR, and is showing some signs of impending change. Within computer science, a new subdiscipline—computational complexity—has emerged. It addresses problems of precisely this kind. Operations researchers (and a few economists) have begun to make contact with it, and I shall have more to say about it later.

When we shift our attention from LP to the domain of integer problems, or combinatorial problems in general, the criterion of procedural rationality takes a different shape. In these domains, it is easy to frame problems of practical import whose exact solutions are well beyond present and prospective computational resources, even with the most efficient algorithms we have available. Here we must turn again to heuristic procedures that give us reasonable approximate solutions with reasonable amounts of computation, and hence we are faced with the tradeoff of solution quality against computational cost. The classic example of an immense problem is choosing a move in the game of chess. Since chess is a finite, zero-sum game of perfect information, it is trivial to prove that a (not necessarily unique) best strategy exists; but it is also easy to estimate that finding it by systematic, unselective, search would require exploring a tree of some 10^{120} branches. Algorithms for solving problems by selective, heuristic search of large spaces have been studied both in OR and in the discipline of artificial intelligence, and I shall discuss them under the latter heading.

In summary, OR theory is a part of the normative theory of procedural rationality specifying both algorithms for finding optimal or good decisions and procedures, usually empirical and pragmatic, for evaluating such algorithms. Conceptually, these theories are concerned with the tradeoff between the quality of the solution and the cost of finding it, but in most cases, the tradeoff is only implicit. On the one hand, when it is possible to find optimal-solution algorithms that demand only reasonable amounts of computing time, the quality of the solution drops out of the equation, and we are concerned only with the cost of computation. At the other extreme, when the problem spaces to be searched are very large, and we are unable to discover structure in them that would permit the search to be conducted in an efficient way, then costs hardly enter in at all, for we are constrained to seek *any* algorithm that will find acceptable solutions with acceptable amounts of computing effort. In these realms, the exponential explosion of computation with increasing depth of search is a familiar and melancholy fact of life, and "efficiency" means the difference between getting there at all or remaining lost in the maze of possible paths. And that brings us to the topic of artificial intelligence.

3. Artificial intelligence

■ Artificial intelligence is the discipline that is concerned with programming computers to do clever, humanoid things—but not necessarily to do them in a humanoid way. The closely allied field of cognitive simulation (or "cognitive science" as it is more and more being called) is concerned with programming computers to do the clever things that people do, but to do them by using the same information processes that people use. The close relation between artificial intelligence and cognitive science is, in a sense, accidental. Experience of the past twenty years has shown that often (not always) the best way to program a computer to solve complex problems, discover concepts or patterns, or understand natural language is to imitate as closely as possible the way humans handle the same tasks.

Humans and computers do not, however, have the same strengths. People have very small short-term memories but indefinitely large long-term memories (see Section 6); no such distinction need be made in computer memory. People are very poor at doing large amounts of simple arithmetic, but very good at carrying out highly selective searches, using complex criteria of selection; almost the converse is true of computers—they are bears for arithmetic, but short on subtlety. Of course, when I say "computers" here, I mean computers programmed in simple, straightforward ways. The whole aim of cognitive science is to induce cleverness and subtlety into the behavior of computers, not by inventing new hardware, but by writing programs that incorporate the heuristic devices that people use.

The history of chess playing programs for computers illustrates nicely the uneasy alliance between artificial intelligence methods and the methods of cognitive simulation. The earliest chess playing programs largely relied on computer speed (such as it was in the middle 1950s) to explore, to a modest depth, a large number of possibilities in the game tree.[1] In 1958, Newell, Shaw, and I demonstrated a much more humanoid chess program that searched much less (a few hundred or thousand branches), but thought much more. It did not play very good chess (neither do most people), but it was in the same ballpark as the speed-oriented programs contemporary with it.

Today, we have some very good chess playing programs, comparable to human experts in playing strength (hence ranking with the top few hundred players in the United States). These programs resemble neither kinds of the earlier systems. They do a great deal of search, using the power of the computer, and of course they search many times faster, hence more extensively, than the programs of the 1950s. On the other hand, they incorporate a large amount of chess knowledge, so that their searches are in fact conducted quite selectively, and hence to considerable depth in the game tree. So the progress in computer chess has depended upon a blending of the computer's brute force with humanoid intelligence, and the field is likely to retain this hybrid form for some time to come. There is no sign that, in the near future, a strong computer chess program will be able to dispense with either machine speed or heuristic selectivity.

However closely history may have entwined their fates, it should be clear that artificial intelligence and cognitive science have quite distinct goals. Artificial intelligence is a normative discipline. Like OR, its goal is to find powerful problem-solving algorithms, and no holds are barred. In fact, there is no real boundary between these two disciplines, and today the theory of heuristic search is being pursued vigorously by both. Cognitive science, on the other hand, is a positive discipline, a branch of psychology, whose goal is to discover how humans perform complex cognitive tasks. Artificial intelligence (together with OR and parts of statistical decision theory) is a normative science of procedural

---

[1] For a history of these efforts up to 1958, see Newell, Shaw, and Simon (1958).

rationality; cognitive science is a positive science of procedural rationality. Whether the two fields will continue to be associated as closely as they have been in the past will depend on the relative rates of progress of computer speed and power, on the one hand, and our understanding of human heuristics, on the other. For once, I shall be cautious and not offer a prediction. (Al Newell and I are just now celebrating the twentieth anniversary of our 1957 ORSA predictions of the future of artificial intelligence (Simon and Newell, 1958).)

4. The state of the art in artificial intelligence

■ There are a number of areas other than chess where artificial intelligence programs have reached respectable human levels of performance. Some examples go back nearly twenty years—I refer to Tonge's assembly-line balancing program, Clarkson's simulation of an investment trust officer, and some of the heuristic programs for finding good solutions to scheduling problems.[2] Other examples are more recent: the DENDRAL program (Buchanan and Lederberg, 1971), which identifies molecules by analysis of mass spectrogram data; MYCIN (Davis, Buchanan, and Shortliffe, 1977) and INTERNIST (Pople, 1977), which make medical diagnoses in particular areas of disease; the programs for automatic chemical synthesis developed by Corey (Corey and Wipke, 1969), Powers (1972) and Gelernter and his associates (Gelernter et al., 1977). All of these programs share with the chess programs a hybrid reliance on machine power and human selectivity, but with a considerably stronger admixture of the latter than is characteristic of the best existing chess programs.

When I speak of these programs as reaching "respectable human levels of performance," I mean levels like those we expect of professionals in the field. (The progress of chess programs was long obscured by unwisely setting world championship as the goal.) Evaluating such programs is beset with the same difficulties as evaluating OR algorithms. There are few opportunities for proving optimality, or even theoretical dominance of one program over another. For the most part, evaluation is carried out by examining performance in comparison with the performance of other programs and human professionals on standard tasks. In chess, standardized evaluation has been facilitated by the generosity of human chess players in admitting chess playing programs into their tournaments, and by the organization of computer chess tournaments in recent years. In areas like medical diagnosis, no such standardized evaluation procedures are available, and ad hoc methods have had to be devised.

A few islands of theory have begun to appear, however, that enable more general statements to be made about the power of algorithms. The first of these relates to the alpha-beta heuristic, a scheme for pruning search trees in two-person games, and thereby reducing the total search effort. The alpha-beta heuristic belongs to the general class of branch-and-bound methods, which are widely used in integer programming.

The central idea of branch-and-bound is this. Suppose that I can place an accurate upper bound and an accurate lower bound on the payoff obtainable from any of the branches of a search tree that are descendants of a particular

---

[2] A number of the pioneering heuristic search programs are described in Feigenbaum and Feldman (1963).

branch, say A. Suppose that the upper bound on a different branch, B, is lower than the lower bound on A. Then it is obviously futile to search any of the descendants of B, and the tree can be pruned accordingly. The alpha-beta scheme is essentially the same, complicated only by the fact that the optimizing criterion is the minimax criterion, to take account of the opposed goals of the two opponents and their alternating choice of move.

Theoretical analysis of the alpha-beta heuristic shows that, in a tree with B branches at each node, it may be expected to reduce the search to a subtree with a branching factor of about $B^{1/2}$. Results of this kind can be proved either by making simplifying assumptions about the tree (e.g., that payoffs are distributed randomly on the terminal branches), or by carrying out worse-case analysis—that is, computing the amount of search that would be required if the payoffs were arranged in the tree in the most perverse order possible.[3] Results of these kinds belong to a new branch of computer science called computational complexity. I shall have more to say about it in the next section.

A number of theories about optimal algorithms have been constructed in addition to branch-and-bound theory. There are two separate pieces of theory, each applicable to a particular class of problems. In one class of problems of heuristic search, we are interested in finding *shortest paths* to the goal. An example is the traveling salesperson problem: we are seeking the shortest path that will take a person from a starting city, through all of a set of cities, and back to the starting point. Finding *a* path that encompasses all the cities is trivial; finding the shortest path is a difficult combinatorial problem, which we can try to solve with an algorithm for *best-first* search. Suppose that, for any partial path, we have some way of estimating accurately the length of the shortest path for accomplishing the complete goal. Then the optimal path is one for which, at all points along it, the sum of the distance already traveled and the minimum distance yet to be traveled is equal to the shortest total path. With an accurate distance measure, the optimal path can be detected without any extraneous search whatsoever.

In general, of course, we possess no such infallible distance measure, but only some more or less approximate estimate of the distance that remains to be traversed. We can still use this estimate to conduct a best-first search, as follows. First calculate the measure for all cities reached directly from the starting city. Then pick the lowest of these and continue the set of possible paths one city further, evaluating again. Repeat this process, always continuing from the city whose total path estimate is "best so far" until a path is found along which all the cities have been visited, and the goal city reached again.

Now we call a distance estimator *admissible* if it is guaranteed, when used to evaluate best-first search, to find the shortest path. Any distance estimator that never overestimates the distance is clearly admissible, while distance estimators that sometimes overestimate may not be. An admissible estimator need not, of course, be efficient. If the estimator grossly overestimates distances on the true path relative to other paths, until it comes close to the very end, it will make many unnecessary explorations before it finds the solution.[4]

---

[3] These statements are very approximate. A general discussion of the alpha-beta heuristic will be found in Nilsson (1971), pp. 140–149, and analyses of the efficiency of the heuristic in Knuth and Moore (1975) and Newborn (1977).

[4] Further discussion of these matters will be found in Nilsson (1971), pp. 54–71, and in Gaschnig (1977).

In a great many practical problem situations, finding the shortest path that leads to a solution is quite a different matter from finding a path with a minimal expenditure of computing effort. Of course, in the case of the traveling salesperson problem we want the shortest path—that is part of the definition of the solution. On the other hand, when we are searching for the proof of a mathematical theorem, and if we want to find the proof in a reasonable time, we shall not insist upon finding the shortest proof. In most cases where the length of the solution path is irrelevant, the cost of search can be reduced enormously by ignoring path length as a criterion.

A different approach is needed to evaluate search procedures when the task is to find any solution from the one required when the task is to find the shortest-path solution. Suppose we are searching for oil. Oil can only be discovered in certain locations if we have previously explored other locations— that is, we can only drill to the 2,000-foot stratum by first drilling through the 1,000-foot stratum. If there may be oil in either stratum, both possibilities must be taken into account in determining the profitability of drilling to either layer. Such precedence relations complicate greatly the task of devising a good evaluation function for a best-first search in problem domains of this kind. Roughly speaking, we should do our next bit of drilling at the point where the expected return is greatest, taking into account the various outputs that might be obtained from a well penetrating through that point, and the depths at which they may be found. Characterizations of optimal algorithms for a large class of such problems have been obtained by Garey (1973), Simon and Kadane (1975), and Sidney (1975).

5. Computational complexity

■ I have several times referred to computational complexity as a new theoretical approach to the study of problem solving. Some of the results I have just described in the discussion of artificial intelligence—those relating to the optimality of certain search algorithms—could be regarded as part of the theory of computational complexity. However, they lie a little aside from the central focus of that theory.

Classical numerical analysis has long been concerned with goodness of approximation and speed of convergence of computational algorithms. In the case of algorithms that are, sooner or later, guaranteed to find exact solutions, the corresponding concern is with the amount of computing required to find them.

Early in its history, computer science became concerned with the decidability problem: with the question of whether one could be sure that a problem solving program operating in some problem domain would always reach a positive or negative answer to a question from that domain in a finite time. The celebrated theorem of Gödel (1931) showed that no such guarantee could be provided for any domain that was sufficiently rich (which meant a good many domains, many of them deceptively simple in appearance).

It gradually dawned on computer scientists, however, that the decidability question was not usually the right question to ask about an algorithm or a problem domain. (So great was the fascination of automata theory and the prestige of the Gödel theorem that the dawning took several decades.) It really did not matter very much whether the answer to a problem would never be forthcoming,

466

or whether it would be produced only after a hundred years. The important questions for computing were the probabilities that answers would be produced in a reasonable computation time (an hour or a day, depending on the importance of the problem), and what the average computing time would be for those problems from a domain that could be solved at all with reasonable amounts of computation. These are the questions addressed by the theory of computational complexity (Aho, Hopcroft, and Ullman, 1974).

Questions of computational complexity can be approached with either mathematical or computational tools. We can try to prove theorems about the complexity of a certain class of problems, or we can actually compute solution times for samples of problems drawn from the class. Most mathematical results that have been obtained in the theory provide information only about the worst case: they give upper bounds on solution times for all problems in a class. In general, these upper bounds are expressed as functions of problem size. Thus, the statement that a certain class of problems is "exponential" means that as we increase the number of problem elements or components, the maximum time required for solution will rise exponentially. Here "time" really means the number of elementary computational steps that must be executed to solve the problem.

Notice that these are not theorems about the efficiency of particular computational algorithms. They are limits that apply to *any* algorithms used to solve problems of the domain in question. The theorems warn us that we must not aspire to construct an algorithm that will improve upon the worst-case limit. Nor are the theorems usually constructive: they do not tell us how to build an algorithm that will actually reach the limit—the latter is a lower bound.

When it has been proved that a particular class of problems is exponential, we know that we shall sometimes fail to solve problems in this class unless the problems are quite small. If the class of problems is only polynomial—and especially if it is only linear—then we can aspire to solve problems up to very much larger size limits. Several very important classes of problems, including a number of standard OR problem classes, have been shown to be of equivalent complexity—NP-complete. Since it is not yet known whether NP-complete problems are polynomial or exponentially complex (or something in between), we may still be optimistic about finding powerful algorithms to solve them. However, there is a suspicion abroad among specialists in computational complexity that these problems are actually exponentially complex.

Before we become too despondent about these results and prospective results, we should recall that they apply only to the worst case. We might be willing to put up with failing, occasionally, to find the solution to a problem in a reasonable length of time if we could be assured that we *usually* would succeed. Unfortunately, theorems about expected computing times for problems belonging to some class, and, even more relevant, theorems about the fraction of problems that could be solved within some specified time, are hard to come by. Here, we generally have to be satisfied with empirical tests on randomly selected samples of problems from the domain.

In the last couple of years, Rabin has obtained some interesting potentially important results to the effect that we can reduce certain domains from exponential to polynomial complexity if we are willing to settle for approximate solutions. He has also shown that in some theorem-proving domains, complexity is greatly reduced if we permit a small fraction (it need only be an epsilon fraction) of erroneous proofs. Those of us who are faster than we are accurate can take comfort from that.

I have long had a favorite example to show how computational complexity can be greatly reduced if we are willing to accept approximations: it has to do with finding needles in haystacks. If needles are distributed randomly in a haystack of size, H, with an average density of distribution, d, then to find the sharpest needle in the stack, we have to search the entire stack, and the search time will vary with H. Search time will be linear with size, which does not seem too bad until we remember that the haystack of life is essentially infinite.

If we are satisfied with any needle, however (after all, they are all sharp enough to sew with), then the amount of search to find one will vary with d — that is, will be independent of the size of the stack. Complexity independent of the size of the problem domain is a property we badly need in algorithms designed to face the problems of the real world. The theory of computational complexity has not yet really addressed issues of this kind. Its main value at present to persons concerned with the decisionmaking process is to underscore the great complexity even of problems with relatively clean structures (e.g., integer programming problems), and to warn us against abstracting from the costs of computation and the needs for approximation in our theories of problem solving and decisionmaking.

6. Cognitive simulation

■ Thus far we have been discussing normative theories of procedural rationality that have been developed in operations research, artificial intelligence, and computational complexity. There has been a parallel development in the past two decades of a positive theory of procedural rationality in the discipline of cognitive psychology, based primarily on work that uses the computer to simulate human thought processes.

I have already suggested the basic reason that we might expect the positive theory to differ in some respects from the normative theory. Human beings do not have the arithmetic capabilities of computers. There is a striking difference in speed, a difference that increases by an order of magnitude each three to five years. There is also a very important difference in the capacities of short-term memory (STM). Information that is being processed by the human central nervous system has to be held in STM, a memory of notoriously small capacity. STM is the memory we use when we look up a number in the phone book, and retain it long enough to dial it. Most people find that a phone number can be held comfortably in STM, but adding the area code may fill it past overflowing.

Research in recent years has shown that human performance on cognitive tasks (especially, but not exclusively, when they are carried out without paper and pencil) is dramatically sensitive to the limits of STM. For example, in concept attainment tasks, when a generalization is to be derived from a sequence of instances, only a few of the most recent instances (sometimes only one or two) can be held in memory, with the result that hypotheses are often entertained that contradict evidence that was available only a few minutes earlier. The "event matching" behavior that is frequently observed in human attempts to predict time series is largely attributable to this excessive attention to events in the recent past and ignoring of earlier ones. In fact, large anomalies are observed in the ways in which people combine earlier and later evidence in making judgments, so that their inferences are generally inconsistent with Bayesian models of information accumulation (Kahneman and Tversky, 1973). These anomalies are probably attributable in large measure to limits on memory.

The relative slowness of human thought processes (measurable in tens or hundreds of milliseconds, while the primitive processes of contemporary computers are at the microsecond or nanosecond levels) leads people to avoid problem solving methods that require searches of large spaces. The human chess grandmaster probably does not search more than a hundred (just possibly as many as a thousand) possibilities in the course of his consideration of a difficult position. His computer competitor (who is only an expert, at best) will examine several hundred thousand possibilities, or even several million, in the same situation. Clearly the use of selective heuristics, a characteristic of many artificial intelligence programs, is even more highly developed in human thinking.

The study of skilled chess players shows that a body of knowledge stored in long-term memory (LTM) compensates in large measure for the slowness of search. The human expert does not so much *search out* the correct move as *recognize* it (see Chase and Simon, 1973). I do not mean anything mysterious by this. There is now good empirical evidence that a skilled human chessplayer holds in memory perhaps 50,000 different patterns of pieces (i.e., patterns of clusters of three of four pieces) that he will recognize instantly when they are present in a chess position, and that will evoke for him information stored in LTM about possible moves that are relevant when those particular patterns are present. This is the reason why a grandmaster can play fifty or more opponents simultaneously, spending only a few seconds at each move. He simply waits for his weaker opponents to make a mistake (i.e., to create a recognizable feature on the board that denotes a weakness in the position), and then exploits it with the help of the knowledge he has stored in LTM.

This evidence suggests that, for humans, accumulated experience is indeed a very large component of high-level skill (no one, not even Bobby Fischer, reaches grandmaster status in less than about ten years of intense study and effort). This accumulation of experience may allow people to behave in ways that are very nearly optimal in situations to which their experience is pertinent, but will be of little help when genuinely novel situations are presented. That conclusion is consistent with our general belief that the limits of human rationality become particularly important in explaining behavior under uncertainty— where we translate "uncertainty" here to mean any kind of significant novelty.

These, then, are some of the considerations that must be incorporated in any positive theory of procedural rationality that purports to explain how human beings make decisions in complex task domains. The theory must take account of the fact that the human information processor operates serially, being capable of dealing with only one or a few things at a time. The basic processes are slow (by comparison with modern computers), so that the system is incapable of undertaking extensive searches of problem spaces, particularly when it must reach a decision in a matter of minutes or hours. Judging from the chess evidence, consideration of a hundred closely related alternatives could easily occupy a quarter hour's concentrated thinking. The flexibility of search (e.g., the use of best-first search techniques) is further limited by the very small size of human short-term memory. It is not possible to "save" in STM recollections of significant numbers of unexplored branches in the search tree, so that when search along a particular line is unsuccessful, there is very limited capability for backup to more promising lines that were passed up earlier.

On the positive side, the human information processing system is capable of storing large amounts of information in long-term memory, and of retrieving them upon recognition of familiar patterns in stimuli. Direct retrieval of possible courses of action as a result of recognizing familiar features of the problem situation provides a major (one might almost say *the* major) basis for professional performance in complex problem situations. We would predict of a system having this characteristic a very much more sophisticated level of performance in familiar situations, where the recognition mechanism could operate effectively, than in situations possessing any considerable element of novelty.

We would not expect a system like this to perform in a history-free manner, but would expect, instead, to see many evidences of learning in its behavior over any considerable period of time. Thus, we would not necessarily expect a positive economic theory that fit nineteenth century data to fit twentieth century data. For example, there is considerable evidence that, as a result of the availability of computers, methods of determining desired inventory levels changed substantially in large American business firms in the 1950s and 1960s. These changes in decision methods showed up at the level of the economy as changes in the parameters of the inventory cycle. As Franco Modigliani was fond of saying, "If businessmen are not now maximizers, after enough of them have graduated from business school, they will be." So we might even expect that a positive theory of economic behavior will have to include as a subtheory the way in which business schools produce and diffuse decisionmaking techniques.

I do not want to exaggerate, however, the speed of such learning processes. Not only is social diffusion of new techniques a lengthy matter, but the rate at which the invention of new techniques is expanding human cognitive capabilities is modest. For a long time to come, man, even in association with his most powerful computing devices, will be navigating a very small ship in a vast sea of alternatives and their possible consequences.

7. Applications to economics

■ Many questions of economics cannot be answered simply by determining what would be the substantively rational action, but require an understanding of the procedures used to reach rational decisions. Procedural rationality takes on importance for economics in those situations where the "real world" out there cannot be equated with the world as perceived and calculated by the economic agent. Procedural rationality is the rationality of a person for whom computation is the scarce resource—whose ability to adapt successfully to the situations in which he finds himself is determined by the efficiency of his decisionmaking and problem solving processes.

The domains where a theory of computation, normative or descriptive, is likely to prove useful are the domains that are too complex, too full of uncertainty, or too rapidly changing to permit the objectively optimal actions to be discovered and implemented. Nor can we rely on evolutionary arguments to conclude that natural selection will find the optimum where calculation cannot. All we can conclude from natural selection is that the fitter will survive in competition with the less fit. There is no theorem that proves that the process will converge, in historical time, to limit survival to the absolutely fittest—those who have found the objective optimum. It is much more likely, in a world with rapidly advancing human knowledge and technology, with an unpredictably shifting political situation, with recurrent and unforeseen (if not always unforeseeable) impacts of demographic, environmental, and other changes, that the location of the objective optimum has little relevance for the decisionmakers or the situations that their decisions create.[5]

Let us consider, more concretely, some of the specific domains in economics to which a theory of calculation and procedural rationality has something to offer. Normative microeconomics is one, for that is the area where operations research and management science have already made large contributions. American business firms make their inventory decisions, their cash-holding decisions, and their investment decisions in a significantly differently way from that which they did thirty years ago, as the result of the availability of the new algorithms and the new computers. In some cases, the new methods are sufficiently powerful to permit them to achieve at least suboptimization in limited problem domains. In other cases, the new methods simply provide them with more powerful heuristics than they had before for reaching "good enough" decisions. They allow a higher level of procedural rationality to be reached.

What we have learned of the procedural complexities of normative microeconomics underscores the need for introducing procedural considerations—as has already been done to a modest extent—into positive microeconomics. Entering wedges have already been made in labor theory, with models of search processes in the labor market. Similarly, the search and decision processes underlying consumer brand and product decisions are now receiving some attention.

The theory of the business cycle is another important candidate area, for a procedural theory of the forming of expectations and the making of decisions. Our capacity to predict the ups and downs of the economy within the framework of neoclassical theory, even with the help of "rational expectations" (more accurately described as "consistent expectations"), is far from adequate to the needs of policy. One direction of progress is to erect theories that postulate, more explicitly and accurately than the current ones, exactly how expectations for the future are in fact formed by economic actors, and how those expectations enter into the calculations of actions. A realistic procedural theory would almost certainly have to include learning mechanisms, thus leading to historical irreversibilities in behavior (see, for example, Cyert and DeGroot (1971)).

Another candidate area of great importance is the Schumpeterian domain of long-term dynamics. The search for new products or new marketing strategies surely resembles the search for a good chess move more than it resembles the search for a hilltop. Rough stochastic models have been offered to describe the diffusion of innovations among firms, but little has been done to provide these phenomenological models with explanatory theories of the underlying search and decision processes. The computing capabilities and search strategies of

---

[5] For exactly the same reasons—the frequency of major disturbances to equilibrium—many ecologists believe that the plant communities actually observed in nature are quite as often transitional, nonequilibrium states as they are equilibrium climax communities in which only the very fittest have survived. A theory of these communities, then, requires a theory of the dynamic processes of adaptation, as well as a theory of the static optimum. See Connell (1978).

firm managers and engineers are central to any theory of firm growth or of inter-firm competition for markets.

These are some of the areas where the more vigorous introduction and exploitation of procedural considerations appear promising. I am sure they are not the only areas. I am not even sure they are the *most* promising, for I doubt whether we are better optimizers in this domain of speculation about the prospects of economic theory than we are in making economic decisions.

There exist, of course, some standard techniques for avoiding a separate theory of procedural rationality—in particular, the proposal that we simply fold in the costs of computation with all of the other costs in the general optimization problem. While that solution to the problem of scarce computational resources may suffice for certain simple questions in economics, it leaves unanswered all of the fascinating and important questions of what constitutes an efficient decisionmaking procedure, of how the structures of such procedures are related to the structures of particular kinds of decisionmaking environments, of the evolution of computational capabilities in the face of competition, and of the shape of an economic system in which effectiveness in computation is one of the most important weapons of survival.

8. Conclusion

■ In my remarks here, I have tried to survey some of the pieces of a theory of procedural rationality that have been emerging from research in the disciplines of OR, artificial intelligence, computational complexity, and cognitive simulation. All of these disciplines have been making great strides toward identifying powerful problem-solving algorithms, and at the same time, toward identifying the limits of human beings and computers in their efforts to explore large, complex problem spaces.

I have said only a little about the potential application of these results to the standard concerns of economics. Elsewhere, I have argued that there is an urgent need to expand the established body of economic analysis, which is largely concerned with substantive rationality, to encompass the procedural aspects of decisionmaking. As that need is increasingly recognized by the discipline, economists will find that there is available to them a substantial body of relevant work on these topics that has been produced by economics' sister disciplines.

References

AHO, A. V., HOPCROFT, J. E., AND ULLMAN, J. D. *The Design and Analysis of Computer Algorithms*. Reading, Mass.: 1974.

BUCHANAN, B. G. AND LEDERBERG, J. "The Heuristic DENDRAL Program for Explaining Empirical Data." Proceedings of the IFIP Congress 71. Ljubljana, Yugoslavia, 1971.

CHASE, W. G. AND SIMON, H. A. "Skill in Chess." *American Scientist*, Vol. 61 (July/August 1973), pp. 394–403.

CLAUSEWITZ, C. VON. *Vom Kriege*. Berlin: F. Dümmler, 1832.

CONNELL, J. H. "Diversity in Tropical Rain Forests and Coral Reefs." *Science*, Vol. 199 (March 24, 1978), pp. 1302–1310.

COREY, E. J. AND WIPKE, W. T. "Computer-Assisted Design of Complex Organic Synthesis." *Science*, Vol. 166 (October 10, 1969), pp. 178–192.

CYERT, R. M. AND DeGROOT, M. H. "Interfirm Learning and the Kinked Demand Curve." *Journal of Economic Theory*, Vol. 3 (1971), pp. 272–287.

DAVIS, R., BUCHANAN, B., AND SHORTLIFFE, E. H. "Production Rules as a Representation for a

Knowledge-Based Consultation System." *Artificial Intelligence*, Vol. 8 (February 1977), pp. 15–45.

FEIGENBAUM, E. A. AND FELDMAN, J., EDS. *Computers and Thought*. New York: 1963.

GAREY, M. R. "Optimal Task Sequencing with Precedence Constraints." *Discrete Mathematics*, Vol. 4 (1973), pp. 37–56.

GASCHNIG, J. "Exactly How Good Are Heuristics." Proceedings of the 5th IJCAI, Vol. 1 (1977), pp. 434–441.

GELERNTER, H. L., *et al.* "Empirical Explorations of SYNCHEM." *Science*, Vol. 197 (September 1977), pp. 1041–1049.

GÖDEL, K. "Über formal unentscheidbare Sätze der *Principia Mathematica* und verwandter Systeme." *Monatshefte für Mathematik und Physik*, Vol. 38 (1931).

KAHNEMAN, D. AND TVERSKY, A. "On the Psychology of Prediction." *Psychological Review*, Vol. 80 (July 1973), pp. 237–251.

KNUTH, D. E. AND MOORE, R. W. "An Analysis of Alpha-Beta Pruning." *Artificial Intelligence*, Vol. 6 (Winter 1975), pp. 293–326.

MARSCHAK, J. AND RADNER, R. *Economic Theory of Teams*. New Haven: 1972.

NEWBORN, M. M. "The Efficiency of the Alpha-Beta Search on Trees with Branch-Dependent Terminal Node Scores." *Artificial Intelligence*, Vol. 8 (April 1977), pp. 137–154.

NEWELL, A., SHAW, J. C., AND SIMON, H. A. "Chess-Playing Programs and the Problem of Complexity." *IBM Journal of Research and Development*, Vol. 2 (October 1958), pp. 320–335.

NILSSON, N. *Problem-Solving Methods in Artificial Intelligence*. New York: 1971.

POPLE, H. E. "The Formation of Composite Hypotheses in Diagnostic Problem Solving: An Exercise in Synthetic Reasoning." Proceedings of the 5th IJCAI, Vol. 2 (1977), pp. 1030–1037.

POWERS, D. J. "Heuristic Synthesis in Process Development." *Chemical Engineering Progress*, Vol. 68 (1972).

SIDNEY, J. B. "Decomposition Algorithms for Single-Machine Sequencing with Precedence Relations and Referral Costs." *Operations Research*, Vol. 23 (March/April 1975), pp. 283–298.

SIMON, H. A. "A Behavioral Model of Rational Choice." *Quarterly Journal of Economics*, Vol. 69 (February 1955), pp. 99–118.

———. "From Substantive to Procedural Rationality" in S. J. Latsis, ed., *Method and Appraisal in Economics*. Cambridge: 1976.

———. "Rationality As Process and As Product of Thought." *The American Economic Review* (1978).

——— AND KADANE, J. B. "Optimal Problem-Solving Search: All-or-None Solutions." *Artificial Intelligence*, Vol. 6 (Fall 1975), pp. 235–248.

SIMON, H. A. AND NEWELL, A. "Heuristic Problem Solving: The Next Advance in Operations Research." *Operations Research*, Vol. 6 (January/February 1958), pp. 1–10.

STIGLER, G. J. "The Economics of Information." *Journal of Political Economy*, Vol. 69 (June 1961), pp. 213–215.

8.6
Rational Decision Making in Business Organizations

By Herbert A. Simon*

In the opening words of his *Principles*, Alfred Marshall proclaimed economics to be a psychological science:

> Political Economy or Economics is a study of mankind in the ordinary business of life; it examines that part of individual and social action which is most closely connected with the attainment and with the use of the material requisites of wellbeing.
>
> Thus it is on the one side a study of wealth; and on the other, and more important side, a part of the study of man. For man's character has been moulded by his every-day work, and the material resources which he thereby procures, more than by any other influence unless it be that of his religious ideals.

In its actual development, however, economic science has focused on just one aspect of man's character, his reason, and particularly on the application of that reason to problems of allocation in the face of scarcity. Still, modern definitions of the economic sciences, whether phrased in terms of allocating scarce resources or in terms of rational decision making, mark out a vast domain for conquest and settlement. In recent years there has been considerable exploration by economists even of parts of this domain that were thought traditionally to belong to the disciplines of political science, sociology, and psychology.

*Carnegie-Mellon University. This article is the lecture Herbert Simon delivered in Stockholm, Sweden, December 8, 1978, when he received the Nobel Prize in Economic Science. The article is copyright © the Nobel Foundation 1978. It is published here with the permission of the Nobel Foundation.

The author is indebted to Albert Ando, Otto A. Davis, and Benjamin M. Friedman for valuable comments on an earlier draft of this paper.

I. Decision Theory as Economic Science

The density of settlement of economists over the whole empire of economic science is very uneven, with a few areas of modest size holding the bulk of the population. The economic Heartland is the normative study of the international and national economies and their markets, with its triple main concerns of full employment of resources, the efficient allocation of resources, and equity in distribution of the economic product. Instead of the ambiguous and over-general term "economics," I will use "political economy" to designate this Heartland, and "economic sciences" to denote the whole empire, including its most remote colonies. Our principal concern in this paper will be with the important colonial territory known as decision theory. I will have something to say about its normative and descriptive aspects, and particularly about its applications to the theory of the firm. It is through the latter topic that the discussion will be linked back to the Heartland of political economy.

Underpinning the corpus of policy-oriented normative economics, there is, of course, an impressive body of descriptive or "positive" theory which rivals in its mathematical beauty and elegance some of the finest theories in the physical sciences. As examples I need only remind you of Walrasian general equilibrium theories and their modern descendants in the works of Henry Schultz, Samuelson, Hicks, and others; or the subtle and impressive body of theory created by Arrow, Hurwicz, Debreu, Malinvaud, and their colleagues showing the equivalence, under certain conditions, of competitive equilibrium with Pareto optimality.

The relevance of some of the more refined parts of this work to the real world can be, and has been, questioned. Perhaps some of these intellectual mountains have been climbed simply because they were there—because of the sheer challenge and joy of scaling them. That is as it should be in any human scientific or artistic effort. But regardless of the motives of the climbers, regardless of real world veridicality, there is no question but that positive political economy has been strongly shaped by the demands of economic policy for advice on basic public issues.

This too is as it should be. It is a vulgar fallacy to suppose that scientific inquiry cannot be fundamental if it threatens to become useful, or if it arises in response to problems posed by the everyday world. The real world, in fact, is perhaps the most fertile of all sources of good research questions calling for basic scientific inquiry.

A. Decision Theory in the Service of Political Economy

There is, however, a converse fallacy that deserves equal condemnation: the fallacy of supposing that fundamental inquiry is worth pursuing only if its relevance to questions of policy is immediate and obvious. In the contemporary world, this fallacy is perhaps not widely accepted, at least as far as the natural sciences are concerned. We have now lived through three centuries or more of vigorous and highly successful inquiry into the laws of nature. Much of that inquiry has been driven by the simple urge to understand, to find the beauty of order hidden in complexity. Time and again, we have found the "idle" truths arrived at through the process of inquiry to be of the greatest moment for practical human affairs. I need not take time here to argue the point. Scientists know it, engineers and physicians know it, congressmen and members of parliaments know it, the man on the street knows it.

But I am not sure that this truth is as widely known in economics as it ought to be. I cannot otherwise explain the rather weak and backward development of the descriptive theory of decision making including the theory of the firm, the sparse and scattered settlement of its terrain, and the fact that many, if not most, of its investigators are drawn from outside economics—from sociolo-

gy, from psychology, and from political science. Respected and distinguished figures in economics—Edward Mason, Fritz Machlup, and Milton Friedman, for example—have placed it outside the Pale (more accurately, have placed economics outside *its* Pale), and have offered it full autonomy provided that it did not claim close kinship with genuine economic inquiry.

Thus, Mason, commenting on Papandreou's 1952 survey of research on the behavioral theory of the firm, mused aloud:

> . . . has the contribution of this literature to economic analysis really been a large one? . . . The writer of this critique must confess a lack of confidence in the marked superiority, *for purposes of economic analysis*, of this newer concept of the firm, over the older conception of the entrepreneur. [pp. 221–22]

And, in a similar vein, Friedman sums up his celebrated polemic against realism in theory:

> Complete "realism" is clearly unattainable, and the question whether a theory is realistic "enough" can be settled only by seeing whether it yields predictions that are good enough *for the purpose in hand* or that are better than predictions from alternative theories. [p. 41, emphasis added]

The "purpose in hand" that is implicit in both of these quotations is providing decision-theoretic foundations for positive, and then for normative, political economy. In the views of Mason and Friedman, fundamental inquiry into rational human behavior in the context of business organizations is simply not (by definition) economics—that is to say, political economy—unless it contributes in a major way to that purpose. This is sometimes even interpreted to mean that economic theories of decision making are not falsified in any interesting or relevant sense when their empirical predictions of *microphenomena* are found to be grossly incompatible with the observed data. Such theories, we are told, are still realistic "enough" provided that they do not contradict aggregate observations of concern to political economy. Thus economists who are zealous in insisting that economic actors maximize turn around and become satisficers when the evaluation of their own theories is concerned. They believe that businessmen maximize, but they know that economic theorists satisfice.

The application of the principle of satisficing to theories is sometimes defended as an application of Occam's Razor: accept the simplest theory that works.[1] But Occam's Razor has a double edge. Succinctness of statement is not the only measure of a theory's simplicity. Occam understood his rule as recommending theories that make no more assumptions than necessary to account for the phenomena (*Essentia non sunt multiplicanda praeter necessitatem*). A theory of profit or utility maximization can be stated more briefly than a satisficing theory of the sort I shall discuss later. But the former makes much stronger assumptions than the latter about the human cognitive system. Hence, in the case before us, the two edges of the razor cut in opposite directions.

In whichever way we interpret Occam's principle, parsimony can be only a secondary consideration in choosing between theories, unless those theories make identical predictions. Hence, we must come back to a consideration of the phenomena that positive decision theory is supposed to handle. These may include both phenomena at the microscopic level of the decision-making agents, or aggregative phenomena of concern to political economy.

---

[1]The phrase "that works" refutes, out of hand, Friedman's celebrated paean of praise for lack of realism in assumptions. Consider his example of falling bodies (pp. 16–19). His valid point is that it is advantageous to use the simple law, ignoring air resistance, when it gives a "good enough" approximation. But of course the conditions under which it gives a good approximation are not at all the conditions under which it is unrealistic or a "wildly inaccurate descriptive representation of reality." We can use it to predict the path of a body falling in a vacuum, but not the path of one falling through the Earth's atmosphere. I cannot in this brief space mention, much less discuss, all of the numerous logical fallacies that can be found in Friedman's 40-page essay. For additional criticism, see Simon (1963) and Samuelson (1963).

B. *Decision Theory Pursued for its Intrinsic Interest*

Of course the definition of the word "economics" is not important. Like Humpty Dumpty, we can make words mean anything we want them to mean. But the professional training and range of concern of economists does have importance. Acceptance of the narrow view that economics is concerned only with the aggregative phenomena of political economy defines away a whole rich domain of rational human behavior as inappropriate for economic research.

I do not wish to appear to be admitting that the behavioral theory of the firm *has been* irrelevant to the construction of political economy. I will have more to say about its relevance in a moment. My present argument is counterfactual in form: *even if* there were no present evidence of such relevance, human behavior in business firms constitutes a highly interesting body of empirical phenomena that calls out for explanation as do all bodies of phenomena. And if we may extrapolate from the history of the other sciences, there is every reason to expect that as explanations emerge, relevance for important areas of practical application will not be long delayed.

It has sometimes been implied (Friedman, p. 14) that the correctness of the assumptions of rational behavior underlying the classical theory of the firm is not merely irrelevant, but is not even empirically testable in any direct way, the only valid test being whether these assumptions lead to tolerably correct predictions at the macroscopic level. That would be true, of course, if we had no microscopes, so that the micro-level behavior was not directly observable. But we do have microscopes. There are many techniques for observing decision-making behavior, even at second-by-second intervals if that is wanted. In testing our economic theories, we do not have to depend on the rough aggregate time-series that are the main grist for the econometric mill, or even upon company financial statements.

The classical theories of economic decision making and of the business firm make very specific testable predictions about the concrete behavior of decision-making agents. Behavioral theories make quite different predictions. Since these predictions can be tested directly by observation, either theory (or both) may be falsified as readily when such predictions fail as when predictions about aggregate phenomena are in error.

C. *Aggregative Tests of Decision Theory: Marginalism*

If some economists have erroneously supposed that micro-economic theory can only be tested by its predictions of aggregate phenomena, we should avoid the converse error of supposing that aggregate phenomena are irrelevant to testing decision theory. In particular, are there important, *empirically verified,* aggregate predictions that follow from the theory of perfect rationality but that do not follow from behavioral theories of rationality?

The classical theory of omniscient rationality is strikingly simple and beautiful. Moreover, it allows us to predict (correctly or not) human behavior without stirring out of our armchairs to observe what such behavior is like. All the predictive power comes from characterizing the shape of the environment in which the behavior takes place. The environment, combined with the assumptions of perfect rationality, fully determines the behavior. Behavioral theories of rational choice—theories of bounded rationality—do not have this kind of simplicity. But, by way of compensation, their assumptions about human capabilities are far weaker than those of the classical theory. Thus, they make modest and realistic demands on the knowledge and computational abilities of the human agents, but they also fail to predict that those agents will equate costs and returns at the margin.

D. *Have the Marginalist Predictions Been Tested?*

A number of empirical phenomena have been cited as providing more or less conclusive support for the classical theory of the firm as against its behavioral competitors (see Dale Jorgensen and Calvin Siebert). But

there are no direct observations that individuals or firms do actually equate marginal costs and revenues. The empirically verified consequences of the classical theory are almost always weaker than this. Let us look at four of the most important of them: the fact that demand curves generally have negative slopes; the fact that fitted Cobb-Douglas functions are approximately homogeneous of the first degree; the fact of decreasing returns to scale; and the fact that executive salaries vary with the logarithm of company size. Are these indeed facts? And does the evidence support a maximizing theory against a satisficing theory?

Negatively Sloping Demand Curves. Evidence that consumers actually distribute their purchases in such a way as to maximize their utilities, and hence to equate marginal utilities, is nonexistent. What the empirical data do confirm is that demand curves generally have negative slopes. (Even this "obvious" fact is tricky to verify, as Henry Schultz showed long years ago.) But negatively sloping demand curves could result from a wide range of behaviors satisfying the assumptions of bounded rationality rather than those of utility maximization. Gary Becker, who can scarcely be regarded as a hostile witness for the classical theory, states the case very well:

> Economists have long been aware that some changes in the feasible or opportunity sets of households would lead to the same response *regardless of the decision rule used.* For example, a decrease in real income necessarily decreases the amount spent on at least one commodity. . . It has seldom been realized, however, that the change in opportunities resulting from a change in relative prices also tends to produce a systematic response, regardless of the decision rule. In particular, the fundamental theorem of traditional theory—that demand curves are negatively inclined—largely results from the change in opportunities alone and is largely independent of the decision rule. [p. 4]

Later, Becker is even more explicit, saying, "Not only utility maximization but also many other decision rules, incorporating a wide variety of irrational behavior, lead to negatively inclined demand curves because of the effect of a change in prices on opportunities" (p. 5).[2]

First-Degree Homogeneity of Production Functions. Another example of an observed phenomenon for which the classical assumptions provide sufficient, but not necessary, conditions is the equality between labor's share of product and the exponent of the labor factor in fitted Cobb-Douglas production functions (see Simon and Ferdinand Levy). Fitted Cobb-Douglas functions are homogeneous, generally of degree close to unity and with a labor exponent of about the right magnitude. These findings, however, cannot be taken as strong evidence for the classical theory, for the identical results can readily be produced by mistakenly fitting a Cobb-Douglas function to data that were in fact generated by a linear accounting identity (value of goods equals labor cost plus capital cost), (see E. H. Phelps-Brown). The same comment applies to the SMAC production function (see Richard Cyert and Simon). Hence, the empirical findings do not allow us to draw any particular conclusions about the relative plausibility of classical and behavioral theories, both of which are equally compatible with the data.

The Long-Run Cost Curve. Somewhat different is the case of the firm's long-run cost curve, which classical theory requires to be U shaped if competitive equilibrium is to be stable. Theories of bounded rationality do not predict this—fortunately, for the observed data make it exceedingly doubtful that the cost curves are in fact generally U shaped. The evidence for many industries shows costs at the high-scale ends of the curves to be essentially constant or even declining (see Alan Walters). This finding is compatible with stochastic models of business firm growth and size (see Y. Ijiri and Simon), but not with the static equilibrium model of classical theory.

Executive Salaries. Average salaries of

---

[2]In a footnote, Becker indicates that he denotes as irrational "[A]ny deviation from utility maximization." Thus, what I have called "bounded rationality" is "irrationality" in Becker's terminology.

top corporate executives grow with the logarithm of corporate size (see David Roberts). This finding has been derived from the assumptions of the classical theory of profit maximization only with the help of very particular *ad hoc* assumptions about the distribution of managerial ability (see Robert Lucas, 1978). The observed relation is implied by a simple behavioral theory that assumes only that there is a single, culturally determined, parameter which fixes the average ratio of the salaries of managers to the salaries of their immediate subordinates (see Simon, 1957). In the case of the executive salary data, the behavioral model that explains the observations is substantially more parsimonious (in terms of assumptions about exogenous variables) than the classical model that explains the same observations.

Summary: Phenomena that Fail to Discriminate. It would take a much more extensive review than is provided here to establish the point conclusively, but I believe it is the case that specific phenomena requiring a theory of utility or profit maximization for their explanation rather than a theory of bounded rationality simply have not been observed in aggregate data. In fact, as my last two examples indicate, it is the classical rather than the behavioral form of the theory that faces real difficulties in handling some of the empirical observations.

Failures of Classical Theory. It may well be that classical theory can be patched up sufficiently to handle a wide range of situations where uncertainty and outguessing phenomena do not play a central role—that is, to handle the behavior of economies that are relatively stable and not too distant from a competitive equilibrium. However, a strong positive case for replacing the classical theory by a model of bounded rationality begins to emerge when we examine situations involving decision making under uncertainty and imperfect competition. These situations the classical theory was never designed to handle, and has never handled satisfactorily. Statistical decision theory employing the idea of subjective expected utility, on the one hand, and game theory, on the other, have contributed enormous conceptual clarification to these kinds of situations without providing satisfactory descriptions of actual human behavior, or even, for most cases, normative theories that are actually usable in the face of the limited computational powers of men and computers.

I shall have more to say later about the positive case for a descriptive theory of bounded rationality, but I would like to turn first to another territory within economic science that has gained rapidly in population since World War II, the domain of normative decision theory.

E. *Normative Decision Theory*

Decision theory can be pursued not only for the purposes of building foundations for political economy, or of understanding and explaining phenomena that are in themselves intrinsically interesting, but also for the purpose of offering direct advice to business and governmental decision makers. For reasons not clear to me, this territory was very sparsely settled prior to World War II. Such inhabitants as it had were mainly industrial engineers, students of public administration, and specialists in business functions, none of whom especially identified themselves with the economic sciences. Prominent pioneers included the mathematician, Charles Babbage, inventor of the digital computer, the engineer, Frederick Taylor, and the administrator, Henri Fayol.

During World War II, this territory, almost abandoned, was rediscovered by scientists, mathematicians, and statisticians concerned with military management and logistics, and was renamed "operations research" or "operations analysis." So remote were the operations researchers from the social science community that economists wishing to enter the territory had to establish their own colony, which they called "management science." The two professional organizations thus engendered still retain their separate identities, though they are now amicably federated in a number of common endeavors.

Optimization techniques were transported into management science from economics, and new optimization techniques, notably linear programming, were invented and developed, the names of Dantzig, Kantorovich, and Koopmans being prominent in the early development of that tool.

Now the salient characteristic of the decision tools employed in management science is that they have to be capable of actually making or recommending decisions, taking as their inputs the kinds of empirical data that are available in the real world, and performing only such computations as can reasonably be performed by existing desk calculators or, a little later, electronic computers. For these domains, idealized models of optimizing entrepreneurs, equipped with complete certainty about the world—or, at worst, having full probability distributions for uncertain events—are of little use. Models have to be fashioned with an eye to practical computability, no matter how severe the approximations and simplifications that are thereby imposed on them.

Model construction under these stringent conditions has taken two directions. The first is to retain optimization, but to simplify sufficiently so that the optimum (in the simplified world!) is computable. The second is to construct satisficing models that provide good enough decisions with reasonable costs of computation. By giving up optimization, a richer set of properties of the real world can be retained in the models. Stated otherwise, decision makers can satisfice either by finding optimum solutions for a simplified world, or by finding satisfactory solutions for a more realistic world. Neither approach, in general, dominates the other, and both have continued to co-exist in the world of management science.

Thus, the body of theory that has developed in management science shares with the body of theory in descriptive decision theory a central concern with the *ways* in which decisions are made, and not just with the decision outcomes. As I have suggested elsewhere (1978b), these are theories of *how* to decide rather than theories of *what* to decide.

Let me cite one example, from work in which I participated, of how model building in normative economics is shaped by computational considerations (see Charles Holt, Franco Modigliani, John Muth, and Simon).

In face of uncertain and fluctuating production demands, a company can smooth and stabilize its production and employment levels at the cost of holding buffer inventories. What kind of decision rule will secure a reasonable balance of costs? Formally, we are faced with a dynamic programming problem, and these generally pose formidable and often intolerable computational burdens for their solution.

One way out of this difficulty is to seek a special case of the problem that will be computationally tractable. If we assume the cost functions facing the company all to be quadratic in form, the optimal decision rule will then be a linear function of the decision variables, which can readily be computed in terms of the cost parameters. Equally important, under uncertainty about future sales, only the expected values, and not the higher moments, of the probability distributions enter into the decision rule (Simon, 1956b). Hence the assumption of quadratic costs reduces the original problem to one that is readily solved. Of course the solution, though it provides optimal decisions for the simplified world of our assumptions, provides, at best, satisfactory solutions for the real-world decision problem that the quadratic function approximates. In-principle, unattainable optimization is sacrificed for in-practice, attainable satisfaction.

If human decision makers are as rational as their limited computational capabilities and their incomplete information permit them to be, then there will be a close relation between normative and descriptive decision theory. Both areas of inquiry are concerned primarily with procedural rather than substantive rationality (Simon, 1978a). As new mathematical tools for computing optimal and satisfactory decisions are discovered, and as computers become more and more powerful, the recommendations of normative decision theory will change. But as the new recommendations are diffused, the actual, observed, practice of decision making in business firms will change also. And these changes may have macro-economic consequences. For example, there is some agreement that average inventory holdings of American firms have been reduced significantly by the introduction of formal procedures for calculating reorder points and quantities.

II. Characterizing Bounded Rationality

The principal forerunner of a behavioral theory of the firm is the tradition usually called Institutionalism. It is not clear that all of the writings, European and American, usually lumped under this rubric have much in common, or that their authors would agree with each other's views. At best, they share a conviction that economic theory must be reformulated to take account of the social and legal structures amidst which market transactions are carried out. Today, we even find a vigorous development within economics that seeks to achieve institutionalist goals within the context of neoclassical price theory. I will have more to say about that a little later.

The name of John R. Commons is prominent—perhaps the most prominent—among American Institutionalists. Commons' difficult writings (for example, *Institutional Economics*) borrow their language heavily from the law, and seek to use the *transaction* as their basic unit of behavior. I will not undertake to review Commons' ideas here, but simply remark that they provided me with many insights in my initial studies of organizational decision making (see my *Administrative Behavior*, p. 136).

Commons also had a substantial influence on the thinking of Chester I. Barnard, an intellectually curious business executive who distilled from his experience as president of the New Jersey Bell Telephone Company, and as executive of other business, governmental, and nonprofit organizations, a profound book on decision making titled *The Functions of the Executive*. Barnard proposed original theories, which have stood up well under empirical scrutiny, of the nature of the authority mechanism in organizations, and of the motivational bases for employee acceptance of organizational goals (the so-called "inducements-contributions" theory); and he provided a realistic description of organizational decision making, which he characterized as "opportunistic." The numerous references to Barnard's work in *Adminis-trative Behavior* attest, though inadequately, to the impact he had on my own thinking about organizations.

A. *In Search of a Descriptive Theory*

In 1934–35, in the course of a field study of the administration of public recreational facilities in Milwaukee, which were managed jointly by the school board and the city public works department, I encountered a puzzling phenomenon. Although the heads of the two agencies appeared to agree as to the objectives of the recreation program, and did not appear to be competing for empire, there was continual disagreement and tension between them with respect to the allocation of funds between physical maintenance, on the one hand, and play supervision on the other. Why did they not, as my economics books suggested, simply balance off the marginal return of the one activity against that of the other?

Further exploration made it apparent that they didn't equate expenditures at the margin because, intellectually, they couldn't. There was no measurable production function from which quantitative inferences about marginal productivities could be drawn; and such qualitative notions of a production function as the two managers possessed were mutually incompatible. To the public works administrator, a playground was a physical facility, serving as a green oasis in the crowded gray city. To the recreation administrator, a playground was a social facility, where children could play together with adult help and guidance.

How can human beings make rational decisions in circumstances like these? How are they to apply the marginal calculus? Or, if it does not apply, what do they substitute for it?

The phenomenon observed in Milwaukee is ubiquitous in human decision making. In organization theory it is usually referred to as *subgoal identification*. When the goals of an organization cannot be connected operationally with actions (when the production function can't be formulated in concrete terms),

then decisions will be judged against subordinate goals that can be so connected. There is no unique determination of these subordinate goals. Their formulation will depend on the knowledge, experience, and organizational environment of the decision maker. In the face of this ambiguity, the formulation can also be influenced in subtle, and not so subtle, ways by his self-interest and power drives.

The phenomenon arises as frequently in individual as in social decision making and problem solving. Today, under the rubric of *problem representation*, it is a central research interest of cognitive psychology. Given a particular environment of stimuli, and a particular background of previous knowledge, how will a person organize this complex mass of information into a problem formulation that will facilitate his solution efforts? How did Newton's experience of the apple, if he had one, get represented as an instance of attraction of apple by Earth?

Phenomena like these provided the central theme for *Administrative Behavior*. That study represented "an attempt to construct tools useful in my own research in the field of public administration." The product was actually not so much a theory as prolegomena to a theory, stemming from the conviction "that decision making is the heart of administration, and that the vocabulary of administrative theory must be derived from the logic and psychology of human choice." It was, if you please, an exercise in problem representation.

On examination, the phenomenon of subgoal identification proved to be the visible tip of a very large iceberg. The shape of the iceberg is best appreciated by contrasting it with classical models of rational choice. The classical model calls for knowledge of all the alternatives that are open to choice. It calls for complete knowledge of, or ability to compute, the consequences that will follow on each of the alternatives. It calls for certainty in the decision maker's present and future evaluation of these consequences. It calls for the ability to compare consequences, no matter how diverse and heterogeneous, in terms of some consistent measure of utility. The task, then, was to replace the classical model with one that would describe how decisions could be (and probably actually were) made when the alternatives of search had to be sought out, the consequences of choosing particular alternatives were only very imperfectly known both because of limited computational power and because of uncertainty in the external world, and the decision maker did not possess a general and consistent utility function for comparing heterogeneous alternatives.

Several procedures of rather general applicability and wide use have been discovered that transform intractable decision problems into tractable ones. One procedure already mentioned is to look for satisfactory choices instead of optimal ones. Another is to replace abstract, global goals with tangible subgoals, whose achievement can be observed and measured. A third is to divide up the decision-making task among many specialists, coordinating their work by means of a structure of communications and authority relations. All of these, and others, fit the general rubric of "bounded rationality," and it is now clear that the elaborate organizations that human beings have constructed in the modern world to carry out the work of production and government can only be understood as machinery for coping with the limits of man's abilities to comprehend and compute in the face of complexity and uncertainty.

This rather vague and general initial formulation of the idea of bounded rationality called for elaboration in two directions: greater formalization of the theory, and empirical verification of its main claims. During the decade that followed the publication of *Administrative Behavior*, substantial progress was made in both directions, some of it through the efforts of my colleagues and myself, much of it by other research groups that shared the same Zeitgeist.

B. *Empirical Studies*

The principal source of empirical data about organizational decision making has been straightforward "anthropological" field study, eliciting descriptions of decision-making procedures and observing the course of specific decision-making episodes. Examples are my study, with Guetzkow, Kozmetsky, and Tyndall (1954), of the ways in which accounting data were used in decision making in large corporations; and a series of studies, with Richard Cyert, James March, and others, of specific nonprogrammed policy decisions in a number of different companies (see Cyert, Simon, and Donald Trow). The latter line of work was greatly developed and expanded by Cyert and March and its theoretical implications for economics explored in their important work, *A Behavioral Theory of the Firm*.

At about the same time, the fortuitous availability of some data on businessmen's perceptions of a problem situation described in a business policy casebook enabled DeWitt Dearborn and me to demonstrate empirically the cognitive basis for identification with subgoals, the phenomenon that had so impressed me in the Milwaukee recreation study. The businessmen's perceptions of the principal problems facing the company described in the case were mostly determined by their own business experiences—sales and accounting executives identified a sales problem, manufacturing executives, a problem of internal organization.

Of course there is vastly more to be learned and tested about organizational decision making than can be dealt with in a handful of studies. Although many subsequent studies have been carried out in Europe and the United States, this domain is still grossly undercultivated (for references, see March, 1965; E. Johnsen, 1968; G. Eliasson, 1976). Among the reasons for the relative neglect of such studies, as contrasted, say, with laboratory experiments in social psychology, is that they are extremely costly and time consuming, with a high grist-to-grain ratio, the methodology for carrying them out is primitive, and satisfactory access to decision-making behavior is hard to secure. This part of economics has not yet acquired the habits of patience and persistence in the pursuit of facts that is exemplified in other domains by the work, say, of Simon Kuznets or of the architects of the MIT-SSRC-Penn econometric models.

C. Theoretical Inquiries

On the theoretical side, three questions seemed especially to call for clarification: what are the circumstances under which an employment relation will be preferred to some other form of contract as the arrangement for securing the performance of work; what is the relation between the classical theory of the firm and theories of organizational equilibrium first proposed by Chester Barnard; and what are the main characteristics of human rational choice in situations where complexity precludes omniscience?

The Employment Relation. A fundamental characteristic of modern industrial society is that most work is performed, not by individuals who produce products for sale, nor by individual contractors, but by persons who have accepted employment in a business firm and the authority relation with the employer that employment entails. Acceptance of authority means willingness to permit one's behavior to be determined by the employer, at least within some zone of indifference or acceptance. What is the advantage of this arrangement over a contract for specified goods or services? Why is so much of the world's work performed in large, hierarchic organizations?

Analysis showed (Simon, 1951) that a combination of two factors could account for preference for the employment contract over other forms of contracts: uncertainty as to which future behaviors would be advantageous to the employer, and a greater indifference of the employee as compared with the employer (within the former's area of acceptance) as to which of these behaviors he carried out. When the secretary is hired, the employer does not know what letters he will want her to type, and the secretary has no great preference for typing one letter rather than another. The employment contract permits the choice to be postponed until the uncertainty is resolved, with little cost to the employee and great advantage to the employer. The explanation is closely analogous to one Jacob Marschak had proposed for liquidity preference. Under conditions of uncertainty it is advantageous to hold resources in liquid, flexible form.

Organizational Equilibrium. Barnard had described the survival of organizations in terms of the motivations that make their participants (employees, investors, customers, suppliers) willing to remain in the system. In *Administrative Behavior,* I had developed this notion further into a motivational theory of the balance between the inducements that were provided by organizations to their participants, and the contributions those participants made to the organizations' resources.

A formalization of this theory (Simon, 1952; 1953) showed its close affinity to the classical theory of the firm, but with an important and instructive difference. In comparing the two theories, each inducement-contribution relation became a supply schedule for the firm. The survival conditions became the conditions for positive profit. But while the classical theory of the firm assumes that all profits accrue to a particular set of participants, the owners, the organization theory treats the surplus more symmetrically, and does not predict how it will be distributed. Hence the latter theory leaves room, under conditions of monopoly and imperfect competition, for bargaining among the participants (for example, between labor and owners) for the surplus. The survival conditions—positive profits rather than maximum profits—also permit a departure from the assumptions of perfect rationality.

Mechanisms of Bounded Rationality. In *Administrative Behavior,* bounded rationality is largely characterized as a residual category—rationality is bounded when it falls short of omniscience. And the failures of omniscience are largely failures of knowing all the alternatives, uncertainty about relevant exogenous events, and inability to calculate consequences. There was needed a more positive and formal characterization of the mechanisms of choice under conditions of bounded rationality. Two papers (Simon, 1955; 1956a) undertook first steps in that direction.

Two concepts are central to the characterization: *search* and *satisficing.* If the alternatives for choice are not given initially to the decision maker, then he must search for them. Hence, a theory of bounded rationality must incorporate a theory of search. This idea was later developed independently by George Stigler in a very influential paper that took as its example of a decision situation the purchase of a second-hand automobile. Stigler poured the search theory back into the old bottle of classical utility maximization, the cost of search being equated with its marginal return. In my 1956 paper, I had demonstrated the same formal equivalence, using as my example a dynamic programming formulation of the process of selling a house.

But utility maximization, as I showed, was not essential to the search scheme—fortunately, for it would have required the decision maker to be able to estimate the marginal costs and returns of search in a decision situation that was already too complex for the exercise of global rationality. As an alternative, one could postulate that the decision maker had formed some *aspiration* as to how good an alternative he should find. As soon as he discovered an alternative for choice meeting his level of aspiration, he would terminate the search and choose that alternative. I called this mode of selection *satisficing*. It had its roots in the empirically based psychological theories, due to Lewin and others, of aspiration levels. As psychological inquiry had shown, aspiration levels are not static, but tend to rise and fall in consonance with changing experiences. In a benign environment that provides many good alternatives, aspirations rise; in a harsher enviornment, they fall.

In long-run equilibrium it might even be the case that choice with dynamically adapting aspiration levels would be equivalent to optimal choice, taking the costs of search into account. But the important thing about the search and satisficing theory is that it showed how choice could actually be made with reasonable amounts of calculation, and using very incomplete information, without the need of performing the impossible—of carrying out this optimizing procedure.

D. *Summary*

Thus, by the middle 1950's, a theory of bounded rationality had been proposed as an alternative to classical omniscient rationality,

a significant number of empirical studies had been carried out that showed actual business decision making to conform reasonably well with the assumptions of bounded rationality but not with the assumptions of perfect rationality, and key components of the the-ory—the nature of the authority and employment relations, organizational equilibrium, and the mechanisms of search and satisficing—had been elucidated formally. In the remaining parts of this paper, I should like to trace subsequent developments of decision-making theory, including developments competitive with the theory of bounded rationality, and then to comment on the implications (and potential implications) of the new descriptive theory of decision for political economy.

III. The Neoclassical Revival

Peering forward from the late 1950's, it would not have been unreasonable to predict that theories of bounded rationality would soon find a large place in the mainstream of economic thought. Substantial progress had been made in providing the theories with some formal structure, and an increasing body of empirical evidence showed them to provide a far more veridical picture of decision making in business organizations than did the classical concepts of perfect rationality.

History has not followed any such simple course, even though many aspects of the Zeitgeist were favorable to movement in this direction. During and after World War II, a large number of academic economists were exposed directly to business life, and had more or less extensive opportunities to observe how decisions were actually made in business organizations. Moreover, those who became active in the development of the new management science were faced with the necessity of developing decision-making procedures that could actually be applied in practical situations. Surely these trends would be conducive to moving the basic assumptions of economic rationality in the direction of greater realism.

But these were not the only things that were happening in economics in the postwar period. First, there was a vigorous reaction that sought to defend classical theory from behavioralism on methodological grounds. I have already commented on these methodological arguments in the first part of my talk. However deeply one may disagree with them, they were stated persuasively and are still influential among academic economists.

Second, the rapid spread of mathematical knowledge and competence in the economics profession permitted the classical theory, especially when combined with statistical decision theory and the theory of games due to von Neumann and Morgenstern, to develop to new heights of sophistication and elegance, and to expand to embrace, albeit in highly stylized form, some of the phenomena of uncertainty and imperfect information. The flowering of mathematical economics and econometrics has provided two generations of economic theorists with a vast garden of formal and technical problems that have absorbed their energies and postponed encounters with the inelegancies of the real world.

If I sound mildly critical of these developments, I should confess that I have also been a part of them, admire them, and would be decidedly unhappy to return to the premathematical world they have replaced. My concern is that the economics profession has exhibited some of the serial one-thing-at-a-time character of human rationality, and has seemed sometimes to be unable to distribute its attention in a balanced fashion among neoclassical theory, macroeconometrics, and descriptive decision theory. As a result, not as much professional effort has been devoted to the latter two, and especially the third, as one might have hoped and expected. The Heartland is more overpopulated than ever, while rich lands in other parts of the empire go untilled.

A. Search and Information Transfer

Let me allude to just three of the ways in which classical theory has sought to cope with some of its traditional limitations, and has even sought to make the development of a behavioral theory, incorporating psychological assumptions, unnecessary. The first was to introduce search and information transfer explicitly as economic activities, with associated costs and outputs, that could be inserted into the classical production function. I have already referred to Stigler's 1961 paper on the economics of information, and my own venture in the same direction in the 1956 essay cited earlier.

In theory of this genre, the decision maker is still an individual. A very important new direction, in which decisions are made by groups of individuals, in teams or organizations, is the economic theory of teams developed by Jacob Marschak and Roy Radner. Here we see genuine organizational phenomena—specialization of decision making as a consequence of the costs of transmitting information—emerge from the rational calculus. Because the mathematical difficulties are formidable, the theory remains largely illustrative and limited to very simple situations in miniature organizations. Nevertheless, it has greatly broadened our understanding of the economics of information.

In none of these theories—any more than in statistical decision theory or the theory of games—is the assumption of perfect maximization abandoned. Limits and costs of information are introduced, not as psychological characteristics of the decision maker, but as part of his technological environment. Hence, the new theories do nothing to alleviate the computational complexities facing the decision maker—do not see him coping with them by heroic approximation, simplifying and satisficing, but simply magnify and multiply them. Now he needs to compute not merely the shapes of his supply and demand curves, but, in addition, the costs and benefits of computing those shapes to greater accuracy as well. Hence, to some extent, the impression that these new theories deal with the hitherto ignored phenomena of uncertainty and information transmission is illusory. For many economists, however, the illusion has been persuasive.

B. Rational Expectations Theory

A second development in neoclassical theory on which I wish to comment is the so-called "rational expectations" theory.

There is a bit of historical irony surrounding its origins. I have already described the management science inquiry of Holt, Modigliani, Muth, and myself that developed a dynamic programming algorithm for the special (and easily computed) case of quadratic cost functions. In this case, the decision rules are linear, and the probability distributions of future events can be replaced by their expected values, which serve as certainty equivalents (see Simon, 1956; Henri Theil, 1957).

Muth imaginatively saw in this special case a paradigm for rational behavior under uncertainty. What to some of us in the HMMS research team was an approximating, satisficing simplification, served for him as a major line of defense for perfect rationality. He said in his seminal 1961 *Econometrica* article, "It is sometimes argued that the assumption of rationality in economics leads to theories inconsistent with, or inadequate to explain, observed phenomena, especially changes over time... Our hypothesis is based on exactly the opposite point of view: that dynamic economic models do not assume enough rationality" (p. 316).

The new increment of rationality that Muth proposed was that "expectations, since they are informed predictions of future events, are essentially the same as the predictions of the relevant economic theory" (p. 316). He would cut the Gordian knot. Instead of dealing with uncertainty by elaborating the model of the decision process, he would once and for all—if his hypothesis were correct—make process irrelevant. The subsequent vigorous development of rational expectations theory, in the hands of Sargent, Lucas, Prescott, and others, is well known to most readers (see, for example, Lucas, 1975).

It is too early to render a final verdict on the rational expectations theory. The issue will ultimately be decided, as all scientific debates should be, by a gradual winnowing of the empirical evidence, and that winnowing process has just begun. Meanwhile, certain grave theoretical difficulties have already been noticed. As Muth himself has pointed out, it is rational (i.e., profit maximizing) to use the "rational expectations" decision rule if the relevant cost equations are in fact quadratic. I have suggested elsewhere (1978a) that it might therefore be less misleading to call the rule a "consistent expectations" rule.

Perhaps even more important, Albert Ando and Benjamin Friedman (1978, 1979) have shown that the policy implications of the rational expectations rule are quite different under conditions where new information continually becomes available to the system, structural changes occur, and the decision maker learns, than they are under steady-state conditions. For example, under the more dynamic conditions, monetary neutrality—which in general holds for the static consistent expectations models—is no longer guaranteed for any finite time horizon.

In the recent "revisionist" versions of consistent expectations theory, moreover, where account is taken of a changing environment of information, various behavioral assumptions reappear to explain how expectations are formed—what information decision makers will consider, and what they will ignore. But unless these assumptions are to be made on a wholly *ad hoc* and arbitrary basis, they create again the need for an explicit and valid theory of the decision-making *process* (see Simon, 1958a; B. Friedman, 1979).

C. Statistical Decision Theory and Game Theory

Statistical decision theory and game theory are two other important components of the neoclassical revival. The former addresses itself to the question of incorporating uncertainty (or more properly, risk) into the decision-making models. It requires heroic assumptions about the information the decision maker has concerning the probability distributions of the relevant variables, and simply increases by orders of magnitude the computational problems he faces.

Game theory addresses itself to the "outguessing" problem that arises whenever an economic actor takes into account the possible reactions to his own decisions of the other actors. To my mind, the main product of the very elegant apparatus of game theory has been to demonstrate quite clearly that it is virtually impossible to define an unambiguous criterion of rationality for this class of situations (or, what amounts to the same thing, a definitive definition of the "solution" of a game). Hence, game theory has not brought to the theories of oligopoly and imperfect competition the relief from their contradictions and complexities that was originally hoped for it. Rather, it has shown that these difficulties are ineradicable. We may be able to reach consensus that a certain criterion of rationality is appropriate to a particular game, but if someone challenges the consensus, preferring a different criterion, we will have no logical basis for persuading him that he is wrong.

D. Conclusion

Perhaps I have said enough about the neoclassical revival to suggest why it has been a highly attractive commodity in competition with the behavioral theories. To some economists at least, it has held open the possibility and hope that important questions that had been troublesome for classical economics could now be addressed without sacrifice of the central assumption of perfect rationality, and hence also with a maximum of a priori inference and a minimum of tiresome grubbing with empirical data. I have perhaps said enough also with respect to the limitations of these new constructs to indicate why I do not believe that they solve the problems that motivated their development.

IV. Advances in the Behavioral Theory

Although they have played a muted role in the total economic research activity during the past two decades, theories of bounded rationality and the behavioral theory of the business firm have undergone steady development during that period. Since surveying the whole body of work would be a major undertaking, I shall have to be satisfied here with suggesting the flavor of the whole by citing a few samples of different kinds of important research falling in this domain. Where surveys on particular topics have been published, I will limit myself to references to them.

First, there has been work in the psychological laboratory and the field to test whether people in relatively simple choice situations behave as statistical decision theory (maximization of expected utilities) say they do. Second, there has been extensive psychological research, in which Allen Newell and I have been heavily involved, to discover the actual microprocesses of human decision making and problem solving. Third, there have been numerous empirical observations—most of them in the form of "case studies"—of the actual processes of decision making in organizational and business contexts. Fourth, there have been reformulations and extensions of the theory of the firm replacing classical maximization with behavioral decision postulates.

A. Utility Theory and Human Choice

The axiomatization of utility and probability after World War II and the revival of Bayesian statistics opened the way to testing empirically whether people behaved in choice situations so as to maximize subjective expected utility (SEU). In early studies, using extremely simple choice situations, it appeared that perhaps they did. When even small complications were introduced into the situations, wide departures of behavior from the predictions of SEU theory soon became evident. Some of the most dramatic and convincing empirical refutations of the theory have been reported by D. Kahneman and A. Tversky, who showed that under one set of circumstances, decision makers gave far too little weight to prior knowledge and based their choices almost entirely on new evidence, while in other circumstances new evidence had little influence on opinions already formed. Equally large and striking departures from the behavior predicted by the SEU theories were found by Howard Kunreuther and his colleagues in their studies of individual decisions to purchase or not to purchase flood insurance. On the basis of these and other pieces of evidence, the conclusion seems unavoidable that the SEU theory does not provide a good prediction—not even a good approximation—of actual behavior.

Notice that the refutation of the theory has to do with the *substance* of the decisions, and not just the process by which they are reached. It is not that people do not go through the calculations that would be required to reach the *SEU* decision—neoclassical thought has never claimed that they did. What has been shown is that they do not even behave *as if* they had carried out those calculations, and that result is a direct refutation of the neoclassical assumptions.

B. *Psychology of Problem Solving*

The evidence on rational decision making is largely negative evidence, evidence of what people do *not* do. In the past twenty years a large body of positive evidence has also accumulated about the processes that people use to make difficult decisions and solve complex problems. The body of theory that has been built up around this evidence is called information processing psychology, and is usually expressed formally in computer programming languages. Newell and I have summed up our own version of this theory in our book, *Human Problem Solving*, which is part of a large and rapidly growing literature that assumes an information processing framework and makes use of computer simulation as a central tool for expressing and testing theories.

Information processing theories envisage problem solving as involving very selective search through problem spaces that are often immense. Selectivity, based on rules of thumb or "heuristics," tends to guide the search into promising regions, so that solutions will generally be found after search of only a tiny part of the total space. Satisficing criteria terminate search when satisfactory problem solutions have been found. Thus, these theories of problem solving clearly fit within the framework of bounded rationality that I have been expounding here.

By now the empirical evidence for this general picture of the problem solving process is extensive. Most of the evidence pertains to relatively simple, puzzle-like situations of the sort that can be brought into the psychological laboratory for controlled study, but a

great deal has been learned, also, about professional level human tasks like making medical diagnoses, investing in portfolios of stocks and bonds, and playing chess. In tasks of these kinds, the general search mechanisms operate in a rich context of information stored in human long-term memory, but the general organization of the process is substantially the same as for the simpler, more specific tasks.

At the present time, research in information processing psychology is proceeding in several directions. Exploration of professional level skills continues. A good deal of effort is now being devoted also to determining how initial representations for new problems are acquired. Even in simple problem domains, the problem solver has much latitude in the way he formulates the problem space in which he will search, a finding that underlines again how far the actual process is from a search for a uniquely determined optimum (see J. R. Hayes and Simon).

The main import for economic theory of the research in information processing psychology is to provide rather conclusive empirical evidence that the decision-making process in problem situations conforms closely to the models of bounded rationality described earlier. This finding implies, in turn, that choice is not determined uniquely by the objective characteristics of the problem situation, but depends also on the particular heuristic process that is used to reach the decision. It would appear, therefore, that a model of process is an essential component in any positive theory of decision making that purports to describe the real world, and that the neoclassical ambition of avoiding the necessity for such a model is unrealizable (Simon, 1978a).

C. *Organizational Decision Making*

It would be desirable to have, in addition to the evidence from the psychological research just described, empirical studies of the process of decision making in organizational contexts. The studies of individual problem solving and decision making do not touch on the many social-psychological factors that enter into the decision process in organizations. A substantial number of investigations have been carried out in the past twenty years of the decision-making process in organizations, but they are not easily summarized. The difficulty is that most of these investigations have taken the form of case studies of specific decisions or particular classes of decisions in individual organizations. To the best of my knowledge, no good review of this literature has been published, so that it is difficult even to locate and identify the studies that have been carried out.[3] Nor have any systematic methods been developed and tested for distilling out from these individual case studies their implications for the general theory of the decision-making process.

The case studies of organizational decision making, therefore, represent the natural history stage of scientific inquiry. They provide us with a multitude of facts about the decision-making process—facts that are almost uniformly consistent with the kind of behavioral model that has been proposed here. But we do not yet know how to use these facts to test the model in any formal way. Nor do we quite know what to do with the observation that the specific decision-making procedures used by organizations differ from one organization to another, and within each organization, even from one situation to another. We must not expect from these data generalizations as neat and precise as those incorporated in neoclassical theory.

Perhaps the closest approach to a method for extracting theoretically relevant information from case studies is computer simulation. By converting empirical evidence about a decision-making process into a computer program, a path is opened both for testing the adequacy of the program mechanisms for explaining the data, and for discovering the key features of the program that account, qualitatively, for the interesting and important characteristics of its behavior. Examples

of the use of this technique are G.P.E. Clarkson's simulation of the decision making of an investment trust officer, Cyert, E. A. Feigenbaum, and March's simulation of the history of a duopoly, and C. P. Bonini's model of the effects of accounting information and supervisory pressures in altering employee motivations in a business firm. The simulation methodology is discussed from a variety of viewpoints in Dutton and Starbuck.[4]

D. Theories of the Business Firm

The general features of bounded rationality—selective search, satisficing, and so on—have been taken as the starting points for a number of attempts to build theories of the business firm incorporating behavioral assumptions. Examples of such theories would include the theory of Cyert and March, already mentioned; William Baumol's theory of sales maximization subject to minimum profit constraints; Robin Marris' models of firms whose goals are stated in terms of rates of growth; Harvey Leibenstein's theory of "X-inefficiency" that depresses production below the theoretically attainable; Janos Kornai's dichotomy between supply-driven and demand-driven management; Oliver Williamson's theory of transactional costs; the evolutionary models of Richard Nelson and Sidney Winter (1973); Cyert and Morris DeGroot's (1974) models incorporating adaptive learning; Radner's (1975a,b) explicit satisficing models; and others.

Characterized in this way, there seems to be little commonality among all of these theories and models, except that they depart in one way or another from the classical assumption of perfect rationality in firm decision making. A closer look, however, and a more abstract description of their assumptions, shows that they share several basic characteristics. Most of them depart from the assumption of profit maximization in the short run, and replace it with an assumption

---

[3]For leads into the literature, see March and Simon; March; Johnsen; J. M. Dutton and W. H. Starbuck. However, there are large numbers of specific case studies, some of them carried out as thesis projects, some concerned with particular fields of business application, which have never been recorded in these reference sources (for example, Eliasson, 1976).

[4]In addition to simulations of the firm, there are very interesting and potentially important efforts to use simulation to build bridges directly from decision theory to political economy. See G. Orcutt and R. Caldwell-Wertheimer, and Eliasson (1978).

of goals defined in terms of targets—that is, they are to greater or lesser degree satisficing theories. If they do retain maximizing assumptions, they contain some kind of mechanism that prevents the maximum from being attained, at least in the short run. In the Cyert-March theory, and that of Leibenstein, this mechanism can be viewed as producing "organizational slack," the magnitude of which may itself be a function of motivational and environmental variables.

Finally, a number of these theories assume that organizational learning takes place, so that if the environment were stationary for a sufficient length of time, the system equilibrium would approach closer and closer to the classical profit-maximizing equilibrium. Of course they generally also assume that the environmental disturbances will generally be large enough to prevent the classical solution from being an adequate approximation to the actual behavior.

The presence of something like organizational slack in a model of the business firm introduces complexity in the firm's behavior in the short run. Since the firm may operate very far from any optimum, the slack serves as a buffer between the environment and the firm's decisions. Responses to environmental events can no longer be predicted simply by analyzing the "requirements of the situation," but depend on the specific decision processes that the firm employs. However well this characteristic of a business firm model corresponds to reality, it reduces the attractiveness of the model for many economists, who are reluctant to give up the process-independent predictions of classical theory, and who do not feel at home with the kind of empirical investigation that is required for disclosing actual real world decision processes.

But there is another side to the matter. If, in the face of identical environmental conditions, different decision mechanisms can produce different firm behaviors, this sensitivity of outcomes to process can have important consequences for analysis at the level of markets and the economy. Political economy, whether descriptive or normative, cannot remain indifferent to this source of variability in response. At the very least it demands

that—before we draw policy conclusions from our theories, and particularly before we act on those policy conclusions—we carry out sensitivity analyses to test how far our conclusions would be changed if we made different assumptions about the decision mechanisms at the micro level.

If our conclusions are robust—if they are not changed materially by substituting one or another variant of the behavioral model for the classical model—we will gain confidence in our predictions and recommendations; if the conclusions are sensitive to such substitutions, we will use them warily until we can determine which micro theory is the correct one.

As reference to the literature cited earlier in this section will verify, our predictions of the operations of markets and of the economy *are* sensitive to our assumptions about mechanisms at the level of decision processes. Moreover, the assumptions of the behavioral theories are almost certainly closer to reality than those of the classical theory. These two facts, in combination, constitute a direct refutation of the argument that the unrealism of the assumptions of the classical theory is harmless. We cannot use the *in vacua* version of the law of falling bodies to predict the sinking of a heavy body in molasses. The predictions of the classical and neoclassical theories and the policy recommendations derived from them must be treated with the greatest caution.

V. Conclusion

There is a saying in politics that "you can't beat something with nothing." You can't defeat a measure or a candidate simply by pointing to defects and inadequacies. You must offer an alternative.

The same principle applies to scientific theory. Once a theory is well entrenched, it will survive many assaults of empirical evidence that purports to refute it unless an alternative theory, consistent with the evidence, stands ready to replace it. Such conservative protectiveness of established beliefs is, indeed, not unreasonable. In the first place, in empirical science we aspire only to approximate truths; we are under no illusion that we can find a single formula, or even a moderately complex one, that captures the whole truth and nothing else. We are committed to a strategy of successive approximations, and when we find discrepancies between theory and data, our first impulse is to patch rather than to rebuild from the foundations.

In the second place, when discrepancies appear, it is seldom immediately obvious where the trouble lies. It may be located in the fundamental assumptions of the theory, but it may as well be merely a defect in the auxiliary hypotheses and measurement postulates we have had to assume in order to connect theory with observations. Revisions in these latter parts of the structure may be sufficient to save the remainder.

What then is the present status of the classical theory of the firm? There can no longer be any doubt that the micro assumptions of the theory—the assumptions of perfect rationality—are contrary to fact. It is not a question of approximation; they do not even remotely describe the processes that human beings use for making decisions in complex situations.

Moreover, there is an alternative. If anything, there is an embarrassing richness of alternatives. Today, we have a large mass of descriptive data, from both laboratory and field, that show how human problem solving and decision making actually take place in a wide variety of situations. A number of theories have been constructed to account for these data, and while these theories certainly do not yet constitute a single coherent whole, there is much in common among them. In one way or another, they incorporate the notions of bounded rationality: the need to search for decision alternatives, the replacement of optimization by targets and satisficing goals, and mechanisms of learning and adaptation. If our interest lies in descriptive decision theory (or even normative decision theory), it is now entirely clear that the classical and neoclassical theories have been replaced by a superior alternative that provides us with a much closer approximation to what is actually going on.

But what if our interest lies primarily in normative political economy rather than in the more remote regions of the economic sciences? Is there then any reason why we should give up the familiar theories? Have the newer concepts of decision making and the firm shown their superiority "for purposes of economic analysis"?

If the classical and neoclassical theories were, as is sometimes argued, simply powerful tools for deriving aggregative consequences that held alike for both perfect and bounded rationality, we would have every reason to retain them for this purpose. But we have seen, on the contrary, that neoclassical theory does not always lead to the same conclusions at the level of aggregate phenomena and policy as are implied by the postulate of bounded rationality, in any of its variants. Hence, we cannot defend an uncritical use of these contrary-to-fact assumptions by the argument that their veridicality is unimportant. In many cases, in fact, this veridicality may be crucial to reaching correct conclusions about the central questions of political economy. Only a comparison of predictions can tell us whether a case before us is one of these.

The social sciences have been accustomed to look for models in the most spectacular successes of the natural sciences. There is no harm in that, provided that it is not done in a spirit of slavish imitation. In economics, it has been common enough to admire Newtonian mechanics (or, as we have seen, the Law of Falling Bodies), and to search for the economic equivalent of the laws of motion. But this is not the only model for a science, and it seems, indeed, not to be the right one for our purposes.

Human behavior, even rational human behavior, is not to be accounted for by a handful of invariants. It is certainly not to be accounted for by assuming perfect adaptation to the environment. Its basic mechanisms may be relatively simple, and I believe they are, but that simplicity operates in interaction with extremely complex boundary conditions imposed by the environment and by the very facts of human long-term memory and of the capacity of human beings, individually and collectively, to learn.

If we wish to be guided by a natural science metaphor, I suggest one drawn from biology rather than physics (see Newell and Simon, 1976). Obvious lessons are to be learned from evolutionary biology, and rather less obvious ones from molecular biology. From molecular biology, in particular, we can glimpse a picture of how a few basic mechanisms—the DNA of the Double Helix, for example, or the energy transfer mechanisms elucidated so elegantly by Peter Mitchell—can account for a wide range of complex phenomena. We can see the role in science of laws of qualitative structure, and the power of qualitative as well as quantitative explanation.

I am always reluctant to end a talk about the sciences of man in the future tense. It conveys too much the impression that these are potential sciences which may some day be actualized, but that do not really exist at the present time. Of course that is not the case at all. However much our knowledge of human behavior falls short of our need for such knowledge, still it is enormous. Sometimes we tend to discount it because so many of the phenomena are accessible to us in the very activity of living as human beings among human beings that it seems commonplace to us. Moreover, it does not always answer the questions for which we need answers. We cannot predict very well the course of the business cycle nor manage the employment rate. (We cannot, it might be added, predict very well the time of the next thunderstorm in Stockholm, or manage the earth's climates.)

With all these qualifications and reservations, we do understand today many of the mechanisms of human rational choice. We do know how the information processing system called Man, faced with complexity beyond his ken, uses his information processing capacities to seek out alternatives, to calculate consequences, to resolve uncertainties, and thereby—sometimes, not always—to find ways of action that are sufficient unto the day, that satisfice.

REFERENCES

A. A. Alchian, "Uncertainty, Evolution, and Economic Theory," *J. Polit. Econ.*, June 1950, *58*, 211-21.

A. Ando, "On a Theoretical and Empirical Basis of Macroeconometric Models," paper presented to the NSF-NBER Conference on Macroeconomic Modeling, Ann Arbor, Oct. 1978.

Chester I. Barnard, *The Functions of the Executive*, Cambridge, Mass. 1938.

William Baumol, *Business Behavior, Value and Growth*, New York 1959.

G. S. Becker, "Irrational Behavior and Economic Theory," *J. Polit. Econ.*, Feb. 1962, *70*, 1–13.

Charles P. Bonini, *Simulation of Information and Decision Systems in the Firm*, Englewood Cliffs 1963.

Alfred Chandler, *Strategy and Structure*, Cambridge, Mass. 1962.

N. C. Churchill, W. W. Cooper, and T. Sainsbury, "Laboratory and Field Studies of the Behavioral Effects of Audits," in C. P. Bonini et al., eds., *Management Controls*, New York 1964.

G. P. E. Clarkson, "A Model of the Trust Investment Process," in E. A. Feigenbaum and J. Feldman, eds., *Computers and Thought*, New York 1963.

John R. Commons, *Institutional Economics*, Madison 1934.

R. M. Cyert, E. A. Feigenbaum, and J. G. March, "Models in a Behavioral Theory of the Firm," *Behav. Sci.*, Apr. 1959, *4*, 81–95.

_____and M. H. DeGroot, "Rational Expectations and Bayesian Analysis," *J. Polit. Econ.*, May/June 1974, *82*, 521–36.

_____ and _____ "Adaptive Utility," in R. H. Day and T. Groves, eds., *Adaptive Economic Models*, New York 1975, 233–46.

_____and James G. March, *A Behavioral Theory of the Firm*, Englewood Cliffs 1963.

_____ and H. A. Simon, "Theory of the Firm: Behavioralism and Marginalism," unpublished work. paper, Carnegie-Mellon Univ. 1971.

_____, _____, and D. B. Trow, "Observation of a Business Decision," *J. Bus., Univ. Chicago*, Oct. 1956, *29*, 237–48.

D. C. Dearborn and H. A. Simon, "Selective Perception: The Identifications of Executives," *Sociometry*, 1958, *21*, 140–144; reprinted in *Administrative Behavior*, ch. 15, 3d ed., New York 1976.

J. M. Dutton and W. H. Starbuck, *Computer Simulation of Human Behavior*, New York 1971.

G. Eliasson, *Business Economic Planning*, New York 1976.

_____, *A Micro-to-Macro Model of the Swedish Economy*, Stockholm 1978.

B. M. Friedman, "Optimal Expectations and the Extreme Information Assumptions of 'Rational Expectations' Macromodels," *J. Monet. Econ.*, Jan. 1979 *5*, 23–41.

_____, "A Discussion of the Methodological Premises of Professors Lucas and Sargent," in *After the Phillips Curve: The Persistence of High Inflation and High Unemployment*, Boston 1978.

Milton Friedman, *Essays in Positive Economics*, Chicago 1953.

J. R. Hayes and H. A. Simon, "Understanding Written Problem Instructions," in W. Gregg, ed., *Knowledge and Cognition*, Potomac 1974, 167–200.

A. O. Hirschman, *Exit, Voice and Loyalty*, Cambridge, Mass. 1970.

Charles C. Holt, Franco Modigliani, John F. Muth, and Herbert A. Simon, *Planning Production, Inventories and Work Force*, Englewood Cliffs 1960.

Y. Ijiri and H. A. Simon, *Skew Distributions and the Sizes of Business Firms*, Amsterdam 1977.

E. Johnsen, *Studies in Multiobjective Decision Models*, Lund 1968.

D. W. Jorgenson and C. D. Siebert, "A Comparison of Alternative Theories of Corporate Investment Behavior," *Amer. Econ. Rev.*, Sept. 1968, *58*, 681–712.

D. Kahneman and A. Tversky, "On the Psychology of Prediction," *Psychol. Rev.*, July 1973, *80*, 237–51.

Janos Kornai, *Anti-Equilibrium*, Amsterdam 1971.

Howard Kunreuther et al., *Disaster Insurance Protection: Public Policy Lessons*, New York 1978.

Harvey Leibenstein, *Beyond Economic Man*, Cambridge, Mass. 1976.

J. Lesourne, *A Theory of the Individual for Economic Analysis*, Vol. 1, Amsterdam 1977.

R. E. Lucas, Jr., "An Equilibrium Model of the Business Cycle," *J. Polit. Econ.*, Dec. 1975, *83*, 1113–44.

_____, "On the Size Distribution of Business Firms," *Bell J. Econ.*, Autumn 1978, *9*, 508–23.

James G. March, *Handbook of Organizations*, Chicago 1965.

_____ and H. A. Simon, *Organizations*, New York 1958.

Robin Marris, *The Economic Theory of "Managerial" Capitalism*, London 1964.

Jacob Marschak, "Role of Liquidity under Complete and Incomplete Information," *Amer. Econ. Rev. Proc.*, May 1949, *39*, 182–95.

_____ and Roy Radner, *Economic Theory of Teams*, New Haven 1972.

Alfred Marshall, *Principles of Economics*, 8th ed., New York 1920.

E. S. Mason, "Comment," in Bernard T. Haley, ed., *A Survey of Contemporary Economics*, Vol. II, Homewood 1952, 221–22.

J. M. Montias, *The Structure of Economic Systems*, New Haven 1976.

J. F. Muth, "Rational Expectations and the Theory of Price Movements," *Econometrica*, July 1961, *29*, 315–53.

_____, "Optimal Properties of Exponentially Weighted Forecasts," *J. Amer. Statist. Assn.*, June 1960, *55*, 299–306.

R. R. Nelson, and S. Winter, "Toward an Evolutionary Theory of Economic Capabilities," *Amer. Econ. Rev. Proc.*, May 1973, *63*, 440–49.

_____ and _____, "Neoclassical vs. Evolutionary Theories of Economic Growth," *Econ. J.*, Dec. 1974, *84*, 886–905.

Allen Newell and Herbert A. Simon, *Human Problem Solving*, Englewood Cliffs, 1972.

_____ and _____, "Computer Science as Empirical Inquiry: Symbols and Search," *Communications of the ACM*, Mar. 1976, *19*,113–26.

G. Orcutt, and R. Caldwells-Wertheimer II, *Policy Exploration through Microanalytic Simulation*, Washington 1976.

A. Papandreou, "Some Basic Problems in the Theory of the Firm," in Bernard F. Haley, ed., *A Survey of Contemporary Economics*, Vol. II, Homewood 1952.

E. H. Phelps-Brown, "The Meaning of the Fitted Cobb-Douglas Function," *Quart. J. Econ.*, Nov. 1957, *71*, 546–60.

R. Radner, (1975a) "A Behavioral Model of Cost Reduction," *Bell J. Econ.*, Spring 1975, *6*, 196–215.

———, (1975b) "Satisficing," *J. Math. Econ.*, June–Sept. 1975, *2*, 253–62.

David R. Roberts, *Executive Compensation*, Glencoe 1959.

P. A. Samuelson, "Discussion: Problems of Methodology," *Amer. Econ. Rev. Proc.*, May 1963, *53*, 231–36.

Henry Schultz, *The Theory and Measurement of Demand*, Chicago 1938.

Herbert A. Simon, *Administrative Behavior*, New York 1947; 3d ed. 1976.

———, "A Formal Theory of the Employment Relation," *Econometrica*, July 1951, *19*, 293–305

———, "A Comparison of Organization Theories," *Rev. Econ. Stud.*, No. 1, 1952, *20*, 40–48.

———, "A Behavioral Model of Rational Choice," *Quart. J. Econ.*, Feb. 1955, *69*, 99–118.

———, "Rational Choice and the Structure of the Environment," *Psychol. Rev.*, Mar. 1956, *63*, 129–38.

———, "Dynamic Programming under Uncertainty with a Quadratic Criterion Function," *Econometrica*, Jan. 1956, *24*, 74–81.

———, *Models of Man*, New York 1957.

———, "The Compensation of Executives," *Sociometry*, 1957, *20*, 32–35.

———, "Theories of Decision Making in Economics and Behavioral Science," *Amer.*

Econ. Rev., June 1959, *49*, 223–83.

———, "Discussion: Problems of Methodology," *Amer. Econ. Rev. Proc.*, May 1963, *53*, 229–31.

———, "From Substantive to Procedural Rationality," in Spiro J. Latsis, ed., *Methodological Appraisal in Economics*, Cambridge 1976.

———, (1978a) "Rationality as Process and as Product of Thought," *Amer. Econ. Rev. Proc.*, May 1978, *68*, 1–16.

———, (1978b) "On How to Decide What to Do," *Bell J. Econ.*, Autumn 1978, *9*, 494–507.

———, G. Kozmetsky, H. Guetzkow, and G. Tyndall, *Centralization vs. Decentralization in Organizing the Controller's Department*, New York 1954; reprinted Houston 1978.

——— and F. K. Levy, "A Note on the Cobb-Douglas Function," *Rev. Econ. Stud.*, June 1963, *30*, 93–94.

G. J. Stigler, "The Economics of Information," *J. Polit. Econ.*, June 1961, *69*, 213–15.

H. Theil, "A Note on Certainty Equivalence in Dynamic Planning," *Econometrica*, Apr. 1957, *25*, 346–49.

John von Neumann and Oscar Morgenstern, *Theory of Games and Economic Behavior*, Princeton 1944.

A. A. Walters, "Production and Cost Functions: An Econometric Survey," *Econometrica*, Jan.–Apr. 1963, *31*, 1–66.

Oliver Williamson, *Markets and Hierarchies: Analysis and Antitrust Implications*, New York 1975.

S. Winter, "Satisficing, Selection, and the Innovating Remnant," *Quart. J. Econ.*, May 1971, *85*, 237–61.

Reprinted from

THE AMERICAN ECONOMIC REVIEW

INDEX

Neoclassical economics, 401. *See also* Economic theory, classical

Neoclassical revival, the, 484–487

Nerlove, M., 314

Newborn, N. M., 465, 473

Newcomb, T. M., 237, 354

Newell, Allen, 73, 75, 187, 189, 316, 354, 368, 431, 443, 463–464, 473, 487–488, 492–493

Neyman, Jerzy, 221, 293

Nilsson, Nils, 458, 465, 473

Nogee, P., 316

Non-linear systems, analysis of, 37–41

Nonprogrammed decision, 381–382, 393–398

O'Donnell, C., 50

Occam's Razor, 451, 476

One-period change analysis, 357

Operations research, 55, 58, 117–118, 288, 433–435, 460–462, 479, 484

bounded rationality in, 420–421

and productivity, 99–100

simulation in, 358–359

Opportunity cost, 227, 394

of participation, 26

Optimality, 25, 248, 266, 430

economic, 25

technological, 25

Optimization, 241, 388, 479

and survival, 220–221

Optimizing versus adapting, 219–221

Orcutt, G., 366, 489, 493

Ordeshook, Peter C., 448, 458

Ordinal variables, 34, 39–40

Organization, business firm as, 1–6

as system of memories, 166

Organizational equilibrium, 2, 483

Organizational survival, 26

Organization design, 171–185

information storage in, 146–170

Organization structure as index, 164

Organization theories, 25–27, 146

comparison of, 24–32

Organizational decision making, 204, 488–489. *See also* Decision making

Overproduction, 126–127

Ownership and control, separation of, 331, 337

Papandreou, A. G., 292, 296, 299, 316, 336, 354, 371, 475, 493

Pareto, Vilfredo, 291

Pareto optimality, 474

Parsons, T., 406

Partial reinforcement, 294

Participants, 25–32, 44

Participation hypothesis, 338

Patent and copyright laws, 137–138

Patton, A., 50

Pay-off, acceptable, 255–258

Pay-off function, 242. *See also* Utility function

partial ordering of, 248–250

simple, 244–246

Pearson, Egon, 221, 293

Peck, M. J., 316

Perception, distortion by, 342–343

Phase diagram, 38

Phelps-Brown, E. H., 478, 494

Pitts, G., 428

Planning, 419–420

city, and decision making, 51–55

social, 70

Planning horizons, 52–53, 59–60, 253, 261–262, 387, 392

Plans of business firms, 372–379

Pleasantness, zero-point for, 226–227

Political economy, 474–476

Pople, H. E., 464, 473

Population growth, 122, 124

Poverty, elimination of, 132

Powers, D. J., 464, 473

Predictability of social events, 390

Preference fields, 222

Preferences, probabilistic, 295–296

Premises of decision, 345–346

Price mechanism, 67, 69, 175

Pricing decisions, empirical study of, 64–65

Privacy, effect of computers on, 197–198

Probability, subjective, 324–325

Problem representation, 481, 488

Problem solving, psychology of, 488

Problem solving processes in decision making, 284–285

Processing capacity as resource limit, 167

Production functions, 136, 478

Production planning, 385–388

Samuelson, Paul A., 36–37, 236–237, 368–369, 434, 443, 450, 458, 476, 494
Satisfaction functions, 13–15
Satisficing, 3, 60, 70, 244–245, 250–251, 257, 259, 266, 275, 285–286, 299, 311, 331, 335, 348, 386–397, 414–415, 419, 433, 435, 444, 453, 455, 476, 479, 483–484, 489–491
versus maximizing, 296–298, 332–333, 417–418
Sauerlender, O., 372–378
Savage, L. J., 271, 292, 317, 383, 388–389
Saving and spending behavior, 327–328
Savings, lifetime pattern of, 328
Say's Law, 124–125
Schelling, T. C., 300, 317, 354
Schultz, Henry, 354, 357, 368, 477, 494
Scientific laws as redundancy, 168–169
Scientists, social responsibility of, 74
Search, 260, 275
allocation of resources to, 410
associative, 165–166
best-first, 465
costs of, 252
efficiency of, 418
optimal amount of, 417–418
search, 265–267
theory of, 453–456
time requirements for, 158–161
Search processes, 285, 382, 393–396, 483–485
Search strategies, 261–262, 264–267
Seltzer, Lawrence H., 135
Selznick, P., 380
Sensitivity analysis, 59–60, 387–388, 490
Sequential sampling theory, 60, 305
Serial systems, 174, 456
Servomechanisms, 220, 375–377
Shannon, Claude, 178, 185
Shaw, J. C., 354, 368, 463, 473
Shepard, L. J., 195
Sherif, M., 355
Shortliffe, E. H., 464, 472
Shubik, Martin, 57, 300, 366
Sidney, J. B., 466, 473
Siebert, C. D., 477, 493

Siegel, S., 317, 355
Significance, statistical, 371
Silberman, Charles, 134
Simmel, George, 446, 458
Simon, P. A., 419, 423
Simulation
of human thinking. *See* Computer simulation
microeconomic, 356
non-numerical, 360–361
varieties of, 358–360
Situational determinism, 424
Simulation research, directions of, 366–367
Simulation techniques, 62–63
Slutsky, E., 291
Smithburg, Donald W., 25, 236, 238
Social control, effect of computers on, 197–198
Social disintegration, modeling, 230
Social exchange theories, 3, 446
Social groups, interaction in, 33–41
Social science models. *See also* Homans model
methodology for constructing, 209–238
Social sciences, reintegration of, 210
Sociological models of organizational phenomena, 2–3
Socio-psychological theories, models for, 211–212
Soelberg, P., 431, 443
Software developments, financing the costs of, 137–138
Solow, R. M., 434, 443
Span of control, 47–50
Sprowls, R. C., 355
Stability of equilibrium. *See* Equilibrium
Starbuck, W. H., 353, 489, 493
Statistical decision theory, 269, 293, 304, 485–487
Stedry, A. C., 355
Stigler, George J., 59, 410, 423, 447, 453, 459, 461, 473, 484–485, 494
Stochastic learning models, 305
Storage capacity and survival, 261–262
Store versus recompute, economics of, 148–150
Structural change, 205
Subgoal identification, 481–482